https://cc.ivytech.edu

Programming Logic and Design, Comprehensive, Fifth Edition

Programming Logic and Design, Comprehensive, Fifth Edition

Joyce Farrell

THOMSON

COURSE TECHNOLOGY ™

Australia ▪ Canada ▪ Mexico ▪ Singapore ▪ Spain ▪ United Kingdom ▪ United States

THOMSON

COURSE TECHNOLOGY™

Programming Logic and Design, Comprehensive, Fifth Edition
by Joyce Farrell

Vice President, Technology and Trades:
Dave Garza

Director of Learning Solutions:
Sandy Clark

Acquisitions Editor:
Amy Jollymore

Managing Editor:
Tricia Coia

Development Editor:
Lisa Ruffolo

Product Marketing Manager:
Bryant Chrzan

Editorial Assistant:
Patrick Frank

Content Project Manager:
Aimee Poirier

Cover Designer:
Steve Deschene

Compositor:
International Typesetting and Composition

Manufacturing Coordinator:
Julio Esperas

BRIEF CONTENTS

TABLE OF CONTENTS

PREFACE

Programming Logic and Design, Comprehensive, Fifth Edition provides the beginning programmer with a guide to developing structured program logic. This textbook assumes no programming language experience. The writing is nontechnical and emphasizes good programming practices. The examples are business examples; they do not assume mathematical background beyond high school business math. Additionally, the examples illustrate one or two major points; they do not contain so many features that students become lost following irrelevant and extraneous details.

The examples in *Programming Logic and Design* have been created to provide students with a sound background in logic, no matter what programming languages they eventually use to write programs. This book can be used in a stand-alone logic course that students take as a prerequisite to a programming course, or as a companion book to an introductory programming text using any programming language.

ORGANIZATION AND COVERAGE

Programming Logic and Design, Comprehensive, Fifth Edition introduces students to programming concepts and enforces good style and logical thinking. General programming concepts are introduced in Chapter 1. Chapter 2 discusses the key concepts of structure, including what structure is, how to recognize it, and, most importantly, the advantages to writing structured programs. Chapter 3 extends the information on structured programming to include good programming practices. In particular, it discusses documentation, modularization, and sound design principles. Chapters 4, 5, and 6 explore the intricacies of decision making, looping, and array manipulation. Chapter 7 provides a thorough background in methods, particularly passing data to and returning data from them. Chapter 8 provides students with an opportunity to recap all that they have learned by describing control break programs that employ decision-making, looping, array-handling and parameter-passing. Chapter 9 explores advanced topics in array handling, and Chapter 10 describes the complexities of file handling.

Chapter 11 thoroughly covers the major concepts of object-oriented programming. Students learn about classes, objects, instance and static class members, constructors, destructors, inheritance, and the advantages object-oriented thinking provides. Chapter 12 explores additional object-oriented programming issues: event-driven GUI programming, animation, and exception handling. Chapter 13 discusses system design issues and details the features of the Unified Modeling Language. Chapter 14 is a thorough introduction to the most important database concepts business programmers should understand.

Five appendices allow students to gain extra experience with structuring large unstructured programs, creating print charts, using the binary numbering system, working with large decision tables, and testing software.

Programming Logic and Design combines text explanation with flowcharts and pseudocode examples to provide students with alternative means of expressing structured logic.

Numerous detailed, full-program exercises at the end of each chapter illustrate the concepts explained within the chapter, and reinforce understanding and retention of the material presented.

Programming Logic and Design distinguishes itself from other programming logic books in the following ways:

» It is written and designed to be non-language specific. The logic used in this book can be applied to any programming language.

» The examples are everyday business examples; no special knowledge of mathematics, accounting, or other disciplines is assumed.

» The concept of structure is covered earlier than in many other texts. Students are exposed to structure naturally, so they will automatically create properly designed programs.

» Text explanation is interspersed with both flowcharts and pseudocode so students can become comfortable with both logic development tools and understand their interrelationship. Screen shots of running programs also are included, providing students with a clear and concrete image of the programs' execution.

» Complex programs are built through the use of complete business examples. Students see how an application is constructed from start to finish instead of studying only segments of programs.

FEATURES OF THE TEXT

This edition of the text includes many features to help students become better programmers and understand the big picture in program development. Many new features have been added, and the popular features from the first four editions are still included.

Major changes from the fourth edition include:

NEW!

Increased emphasis on input and output as generic operations. Over the years, logic texts have varied in their approach to input—does it come from user input at the keyboard, from the click of a mouse, or from a file? This book introduces all three techniques, and, whenever possible, uses a generic approach to emphasize that whatever approach is taken, input is simply input. However, frequently when input is used in a concrete example, the interactive approach is emphasized. When instructors assign first programs in a programming language, they almost always assign interactive programs. Such programs are easier for a student to understand, provide more immediate feedback, and avoid the overhead of opening and closing files.

This book also continues to emphasize that output is output—identical in concept whether output is displayed on a screen, sent to a printed page, or stored in a database. As a result of this new emphasis, this edition contains a new appendix on creating print charts. The earliest editions of this book incorporated print charts in the first chapters so students could plan program output. Our feedback was that companies were no longer using print charts, so we virtually eliminated them in the fourth edition of *Programming Logic and Design*. However, some instructors using the book complained when the print charts were missing.

These instructors felt that using the charts was a valuable planning lesson even if charts in the exact format might not be used on the job. Therefore, they are included in an appendix with complete instructions on how to create them so that instructors can add them to their lessons as they deem appropriate.

The approach to methods has been completely revised. The use of methods is consistent with the languages in which the student is likely to have first programming experiences. In particular, this book emphasizes using methods as black boxes, declaring all variables and constants as local to methods, and passing arguments to and receiving returned values from methods as needed. **NEW!**

More figures. Screenshots of programs during execution are frequently included. Students see command-line and GUI sample screens to show just how input and output will look. **NEW!**

Increased emphasis on testing programs and selecting appropriate test data. A new appendix on data verification and software testing is included. **NEW!**

Earlier and more consistent use of named constants. Using named constants instills good programming practices and avoids "magic numbers". **NEW!**

Don't Do It icon. It is sometimes illustrative to show an example of how *not* to do something—for example, having a dead code path in a program. However, students do not always read carefully and sometimes use logic similar to that shown in what is intended to be a "bad" example. When the instructor is critical, the frustrated student says, "But that's how they did it in the book!" Therefore, although the text continues to describe bad examples, and the captions for the related figures mention that they are bad examples, the book also includes a Don't Do It icon near the offending section of logic. This icon provides a visual jolt to the student , emphasizing that particular figures are *not* to be emulated. **NEW!**

Two Truths and a Lie. A new quiz called Two Truths and a Lie appears after each chapter section, with answers provided. This quiz contains three statements from the preceding section of text—two true and one false. Over the years, students have requested answers to problems, but we have hesitated to distribute them in case instructors want to use problems as assignments or test questions. These true-false mini-quizzes provide students with immediate feedback as they read, without giving away answers to the existing multiple choice and programming problem questions. **NEW!**

Game Zone. A new section of exercises called Game Zone is included at the end of each chapter. This section provides one or more exercises in which the student can create a game as an additional entertaining way to understand key concepts presented in the chapter. **NEW!**

Data files. The Student Disk contains data files that can be used with the exercises in many of the later chapters in the book. Students might want to use these files in any of several ways: to look at the file contents to gain a better understanding of the types of data each program uses, to use as sample data to desk check the logic of flowcharts or pseudocode, to use as input files if the solutions are implemented in a programming language using data files as input, or as guides to appropriate values to enter if solutions are implemented as interactive programs. **NEW!**

FEATURES CONTINUED
FROM PREVIOUS EDITIONS...

» **Objectives:** Each chapter begins with a list of objectives so the student knows the topics that will be presented in the chapter. In addition to providing a quick reference to topics covered, this feature provides a useful study aid.

» **Flowcharts:** This book has plenty of figures and illustrations, including flowcharts, which provide the reader with a visual learning experience, rather than one that involves simply studying text. You can see an example of a flowchart in the sample page shown in this Preface.

» **Pseudocode:** This book also includes numerous examples of pseudocode, which illustrate correct usage of the programming logic and design concepts being taught. You can see an example of pseudocode in the sample page shown in this Preface.

» **Notes:** These tips provide additional information—for example, another location in the book that expands on a topic, or a common error to watch out for.

» **Chapter Summaries:** Following each chapter is a summary that recaps the programming concepts and techniques covered in the chapter. This feature provides a concise means for students to review and check their understanding of the main points in each chapter.

» **Key Terms:** Each chapter lists key terms and their definitions; the list appears in the order the terms are encountered in the chapter. Along with the chapter summary, the list of key terms provides a snapshot overview of a chapter's main ideas. A glossary at the end of the book lists all the key terms in alphabetical order, along with working definitions.

» **Debugging Exercises:** Because examining programs critically and closely is a crucial programming skill, each chapter includes a "Find the Bugs" section in which programming examples are presented that contain syntax errors and logical errors for the student to find and correct.

» **Review Questions:** Multiple-choice review questions appear at the end of every chapter to allow students to test their comprehension of the major ideas and techniques presented.

» **Exercises:** Multiple end-of-chapter flowcharting and pseudocoding exercises are included so students have more opportunities to practice concepts as they learn them. These exercises increase in difficulty and are designed to allow students to explore logical programming concepts. Each exercise can be completed using flowcharts, pseudocode, or both. In addition, instructors can choose to assign the exercises as programming problems to be coded and executed in a programming language.

» **Essay questions:** Each chapter contains a "Detective Work" section that presents programming-related topics for the student to research. Each chapter also contains a section called "Up For Discussion," in which questions present personal and ethical issues that programmers must consider. These questions can be used for written assignments or as a starting point for classroom discussions.

Accompanying Software:

» **Microsoft® Office Visio® Professional 2007, 60-day version.** Visio 2007 is a diagramming program that helps users create flowcharts and diagrams easily while working through the text, enabling them to visualize concepts and learn more effectively. A 60-day version of Visio 2007 comes with each new, unused copy of the text.

» **Visual Logic™, version 2.0.** Visual Logic™ is a simple but powerful tool for teaching programming logic and design without traditional high-level programming language syntax. Visual Logic uses flowcharts to explain essential programming concepts, including variables, input, assignment, output, conditions, loops, procedures, graphics, arrays, and files. It also has the ability to interpret and execute flowcharts, providing students with immediate and accurate feedback about their solutions. By executing student solutions, Visual Logic combines the power of a high-level language with the ease and simplicity of flowcharts. You may purchase Visual Logic along with your text. Please contact your Course Technology sales representative for more information.

TEACHING TOOLS AND SUPPLEMENTS

The following supplemental materials are available when this book is used in a classroom setting. All of the teaching tools available with this book are provided to the instructor on a single CD-ROM. *Programming Logic and Design* is a superior textbook because it includes the following features:

» **Electronic Instructor's Manual.** The Instructor's Manual that accompanies this textbook provides additional instructional material to assist in class preparation, including items such as Sample Syllabi, Chapter Outlines, Technical Notes, Lecture Notes, Quick Quizzes, Teaching Tips, Discussion Topics, and Key Terms.

» **ExamView®.** This textbook is accompanied by ExamView, a powerful testing software package that allows instructors to create and administer printed, computer (LAN-based), and Internet exams. ExamView includes hundreds of questions that correspond to the topics covered in this text, enabling students to generate detailed study guides that include page references for further review. The computer-based and Internet testing components allow students to take exams at their computers, and save the instructor time by grading each exam automatically.

» **PowerPoint Presentations.** This book comes with Microsoft PowerPoint slides for each chapter. These are included as a teaching aid for classroom presentation, to make available to students on your network for chapter review, or to be printed for classroom distribution. Instructors can add their own slides for additional topics they introduce to the class.

» **Solutions.** Suggested solutions to Review Questions and Exercises are provided on the Teaching Tools CD-ROM and may also be found on the Course Technology Web site at www.course.com. The solutions are password protected.

» **Distance Learning.** Course Technology offers online WebCT and Blackboard (versions 5.0 and 6.0) courses for this text to provide the most complete and dynamic learning experience possible. When you add online content to one of your courses, you're adding a lot: automated tests, topic reviews, quick quizzes, and additional case projects with solutions. For more information on how to bring distance learning to your course, contact your local Course Technology sales representative.

ACKNOWLEDGMENTS

I would like to thank all of the people who helped to make this book a reality, especially Lisa Ruffolo, Development Editor, whose hard work and attention to detail have made this a quality textbook. I have worked with Lisa for many years now, and she is indispensable in making me look good. Thanks also to Tricia Coia, Managing Editor; Amy Jollymore, Acquisitions Editor; Aimee Poirier, Content Project Manager; and Green Pen QA, Technical Editors. I am grateful to be able to work with so many fine people who are dedicated to producing quality instructional materials.

I am grateful to the many reviewers who provided helpful and insightful comments during the development of this book, including Betty Clay, Southeastern Oklahoma State University; Dave Courtaway, DeVry University – Pomona; and Judy Scholl, Austin Community College.

Thanks, too, to my husband, Geoff, who acts as friend and advisor in the book-writing process. This book is, as were its previous editions, dedicated to him and to my daughters, Andrea and Audrey.

—Joyce Farrell

AN OVERVIEW OF COMPUTERS AND LOGIC

In this chapter you will:

Understand computer components and operations

Learn about the steps involved in the programming process

Learn about interactive input

Learn about the data hierarchy and file input

Use flowchart symbols and pseudocode statements

Use and name variables

Use a sentinel, or dummy value, to end a program

Manage large flowcharts

Assign values to variables

Describe data types

Understand the evolution of programming techniques

UNDERSTANDING COMPUTER COMPONENTS AND OPERATIONS

Hardware and software are the two major components of any computer system. **Hardware** is the equipment, or the devices, associated with a computer. For a computer to be useful, however, it needs more than equipment; a computer needs to be given instructions. The instructions that tell the computer what to do are called **software**, or programs, and are written by programmers. This book focuses on the process of writing these instructions.

> **» NOTE** Software can be classified as application software or system software. Application software comprises all the programs you apply to a task—word-processing programs, spreadsheets, payroll and inventory programs, and even games. System software comprises the programs that you use to manage your computer—including operating systems, such as Windows, Linux, or UNIX. This book focuses on the logic used to write application software programs, although many of the concepts apply to both types of software.

Together, computer hardware and software accomplish four major operations:

1. Input
2. Processing
3. Output
4. Storage

Hardware devices that perform **input** include keyboards and mice. Through these devices, **data**, or facts, enter the computer system. **Processing** data items may involve organizing them, checking them for accuracy, or performing mathematical operations on them. The piece of hardware that performs these sorts of tasks is the **central processing unit**, or **CPU**. After data items have been processed, the resulting information is sent to a printer, monitor, or some other **output** device so people can view, interpret, and use the results. Often, you also want to store the output information on hardware, such as magnetic disks, tapes, compact discs, or flash media; these **storage devices** hold the information for later retrieval. Computer software consists of all the instructions that control how and when the data items are input, how they are processed, and the form in which they are output or stored.

> **» NOTE** Data includes all the text, numbers, and other information that are processed by a computer. However, many computer professionals reserve the term "information" for data that has been processed. For example, your name, Social Security number, and hourly pay rate are data items, but your paycheck holds information.

Computer hardware by itself is useless without a programmer's instructions, or software, just as your stereo equipment doesn't do much until you provide music on a CD or tape. You can buy prewritten software that is stored on a disk or that you download from the Web, or you can write your own software instructions. You can enter instructions into a computer system through any of the hardware devices you use for data; most often, you type your instructions using a keyboard and store them on a device such as a disk or CD.

You write computer instructions in a computer **programming language**, such as Visual Basic, C#, C++, Java, or COBOL. Just as some people speak English and others speak Japanese, programmers also write programs in different languages. Some programmers work exclusively in one language, whereas others know several and use the one that seems most appropriate for the task at hand.

No matter which programming language a computer programmer uses, the language has rules governing its word usage and punctuation. These rules are called the language's **syntax**. If you ask, "How the get to store do I?" in English, most people can figure out what you probably mean, even though you have not used proper English syntax. However, computers are not nearly as smart as most people; with a computer, you might as well have asked, "Xpu mxv ot dodnm cadf B?" Unless the syntax is perfect, the computer cannot interpret the programming language instruction at all.

Every computer operates on circuitry that consists of millions of on/off switches. Each programming language uses a piece of software to translate the specific programming language into the computer's on/off circuitry language, or **machine language**. Machine language is represented as a series of 0s and 1s, also called **binary** form. The language translation software that converts a programmer's statements to binary form is called a **compiler** or **interpreter**, and it tells you if you have used a programming language incorrectly. Therefore, syntax errors are relatively easy to locate and correct—the compiler or interpreter you use highlights every syntax error. If you write a computer program using a language such as C++ but spell one of its words incorrectly or reverse the proper order of two words, the translator lets you know that it found a mistake by displaying an error message as soon as you try to translate the program.

>> **NOTE** Although there are differences in how compilers and interpreters work, their basic function is the same—to translate your programming statements into code the computer can use. When you use a compiler, an entire program is translated before it can execute; when you use an interpreter, each instruction is translated just prior to execution. Usually, you do not choose which type of translation to use—it depends on the programming language. However, there are some languages for which both compilers and interpreters are available.

>> **NOTE** Besides the popular full-blown programming languages such as Java and C++, many programmers use **scripting languages** (also called **scripting programming languages** or **script languages**) such as Python, Lua, Perl, and PHP. Scripts written in these languages usually can be typed directly from a keyboard and are stored as text rather than as binary executable files. Scripting language programs are interpreted line by line each time the program executes instead of being stored in a compiled (binary) form.

A program without syntax errors can be executed on a computer, but it might not produce correct results. For a program to work properly, you must give the instructions to the computer in a specific sequence, you must not leave any instructions out, and you must not add extraneous instructions. By doing this, you are developing the **logic** of the computer program. Suppose you instruct someone to make a cake as follows:

```
Stir
Add two eggs
Add a gallon of gasoline
Bake at 350 degrees for 45 minutes
Add three cups of flour
```

>> **DON'T DO IT**
Don't bake a cake like this!

>> **NOTE**
The dangerous cake-baking instructions are shown with a Warning icon. You will see this icon when a table or figure contains an unrecommended programming practice that is being used as an example of what *not* to do.

Even though you have used the English language syntax correctly, the instructions are out of sequence, some instructions are missing, and some instructions belong to procedures other than baking a cake. If you follow these instructions, you are not going to end up with an edible cake, and you may end up with a disaster. Logical errors are much more difficult to locate than syntax errors; it is easier for you to determine whether "eggs" is spelled incorrectly in a recipe than it is for you to tell if there are too many eggs or if they are added too soon.

> **》NOTE** Programmers call some code errors semantic errors. For example, if you misspell a programming language word, you commit a syntax error, but if you use an otherwise correct word that does not make any sense in the current context, you commit a **semantic error**.

Just as baking directions can be given correctly in French, German, or Spanish, the same logic of a program can be expressed in any number of programming languages. This book is almost exclusively concerned with the logic development process. Because this book is not concerned with any specific language, the programming examples could have been written in Japanese, C++, or Java. The logic is the same in any language. For convenience, the book uses English!

Once instructions have been input to the computer and translated into machine language, a program can be **run**, or **executed**. You can write a program that takes a number (an input step), doubles it (processing), and tells you the answer (output) in a programming language such as Java or C++, but if you were to write it using English-like statements, it would look like this:

```
Get inputNumber.
Compute calculatedAnswer as inputNumber times 2.
Print calculatedAnswer.
```

> **》NOTE**
> You will learn about the odd elimination of the space between words like "input" and "Number" in the next few pages.

The instruction to `Get inputNumber` is an example of an input operation. When the computer interprets this instruction, it knows to look to an input device to obtain a number. Computers often have several input devices, perhaps a keyboard, a mouse, a CD drive, and two or more disk drives. When you learn a specific programming language, you learn how to tell the computer which of those input devices to access for input. Logically, however, it doesn't really matter which hardware device is used, as long as the computer knows to look for a number. The logic of the input operation—that the computer must obtain a number for input, and that the computer must obtain it before multiplying it by two—remains the same regardless of any specific input hardware device. The same is true in your daily life. If you follow the instruction "Get eggs from store," it does not really matter if you are following a handwritten instruction from a list or a voice-mail instruction left on your cell phone—the process of getting the eggs, and the result of doing so, are the same.

> **》NOTE**
> Many computer professionals categorize disk drives and CD drives as storage devices rather than input devices. Such devices actually can be used for input, storage, and output.

Processing is the step that occurs when the arithmetic is performed to double `inputNumber`; the statement `Compute calculatedAnswer as inputNumber times 2` represents processing. Mathematical operations are not the only kind of processing, but they are very typical. After you write a program, the program can be used on computers of different brand names, sizes, and speeds. Whether you use an IBM, Macintosh, Linux, or UNIX operating system, and whether you use a personal computer that sits on your desk or a mainframe that costs hundreds of thousands of dollars and resides in a special building in a university, multiplying by 2 is the same process. The hardware is not important; the processing will be the same.

In the number-doubling program, the `Print calculatedAnswer` statement represents output. Within a particular program, this statement could cause the output to appear on the monitor (which might be a flat panel screen or a cathode-ray tube), or the output could go to a printer (which could be laser or ink-jet), or the output could be written to a disk or CD. The logic of the process called "`Print`" is the same no matter what hardware device you use.

Besides input, processing, and output, the fourth operation in any computer system is storage. When computers produce output, it is for human consumption. For example, output might be displayed on a monitor or sent to a printer. Storage, on the other hand, is meant for future computer use (for example, when data items are saved on a disk).

Computer storage comes in two broad categories. All computers have **internal storage**, often referred to as **memory**, **main memory**, **primary memory**, or **random access memory (RAM)**. This storage is located inside the system unit of the machine. (For example, if you own a microcomputer, the system unit is the large case that holds your CD or other disk drives. On a laptop computer, the system unit is located beneath the keyboard.) Internal storage is the type of storage most often discussed in this book.

Computers also use **external storage**, which is persistent (relatively permanent) storage on a device such as a floppy disk, hard disk, or flash media. In other words, external storage is outside the main memory, not necessarily outside the computer. Both programs and data are sometimes stored on each of these kinds of media.

To use computer programs, you must first load them into memory. You might type a program into memory from the keyboard, or you might use a program that has already been written and stored on a disk. Either way, a copy of the instructions must be placed in memory before the program can be run.

A computer system needs both internal memory and external storage. Internal memory is needed to run the programs, but internal memory is **volatile**—that is, its contents are lost every time the computer loses power. Therefore, if you are going to use a program more than once, you must store it, or **save** it, on some nonvolatile medium. Otherwise, the program in main memory is lost forever when the computer is turned off. External storage (such as a disk) provides a nonvolatile (or persistent) medium.

> **≫NOTE** Even though a hard disk drive is located inside your computer, the hard disk is not main, internal memory. Internal memory is temporary and volatile; a hard drive is permanent, nonvolatile storage. After one or two "tragedies" of losing several pages of a typed computer program due to a power failure or other hardware problem, most programmers learn to periodically save the programs they are in the process of writing, using a nonvolatile medium such as a disk.

Once you have a copy of a program in main memory, you want to execute, or run, the program. To do so, you must place any data that the program requires into memory. For example, after you place the following program into memory and start to run it, you need to provide an actual inputNumber—for example, 8—that you also place in main memory.

```
Get inputNumber.
Compute calculatedAnswer as inputNumber times 2.
Print calculatedAnswer.
```

The value of inputNumber is placed in memory at a specific memory location that the program will call inputNumber. Then, and only then, can the calculatedAnswer, in this case 16, be calculated and printed.

> **≫NOTE** Computer memory consists of millions of numbered locations where data can be stored. The memory location of inputNumber has a specific numeric address, for example, 48604. Your program associates inputNumber with that address. Every time you refer to inputNumber within a program, the computer retrieves the value at the associated memory location. When you write programs, you seldom need to be concerned with the value of the memory address; instead, you simply use the easy-to-remember name you created.

>>**NOTE** Computer programmers often refer to memory addresses using hexadecimal notation, or base 16. Using this system, they might use a value like 42FF01A to refer to a memory address. Despite the use of letters, such an address is still a number. When you use the hexadecimal numbering system, the letters A through F stand for the values 10 through 15.

TWO TRUTHS AND A LIE:
UNDERSTANDING COMPUTER COMPONENTS AND OPERATIONS

Two of the following statements are true, and one is false. Identify the false statement and explain why it is false.

1. Application software comprises the programs that you use to manage your computer such as operating systems.

2. Data includes all the text, numbers, and other information that are processed by a computer.

3. Programming languages have rules governing word usage and punctuation; these rules are called the language's syntax.

The false statement is #1. Application software comprises the programs you apply to a task such as word processing.

UNDERSTANDING THE PROGRAMMING PROCESS

A programmer's job involves writing instructions (such as the three instructions in the doubling program in the preceding section), but a professional programmer usually does not just sit down at a computer keyboard and start typing. The programmer's job can be broken down into six programming steps:

1. Understanding the problem
2. Planning the logic
3. Coding the program
4. Using software to translate the program into machine language
5. Testing the program
6. Putting the program into production

UNDERSTANDING THE PROBLEM

Professional computer programmers write programs to satisfy the needs of others. Examples could include a Human Resources Department that needs a printed list of all employees, a Billing Department that wants a list of clients who are 30 or more days overdue on their payments, and an Order Department that needs a Web site to provide buyers with an on-line shopping cart in which to gather their orders. Because programmers are providing a service to these users, programmers must first understand what it is the users want.

Suppose the director of human resources says to a programmer, "Our department needs a list of all employees who have been here over five years, because we want to invite them to a special thank-you dinner." On the surface, this seems like a simple enough request. An experienced programmer, however, will know that he or she may not yet understand the whole problem. Does the director want a list of full-time employees only, or a list of full- and part-time employees together? Does she want people who have worked for the company on a month-to-month contractual basis over the past five years, or only regular, permanent employees? Do the listed employees need to have worked for the organization for five years as of today, as of the date of the dinner, or as of some other cutoff date? What about an employee who worked three years, took a two-year leave of absence, and has been back for three years? Does he or she qualify? The programmer cannot make any of these decisions; the user is the one who must address these questions.

More decisions still might be required. For example, what does the user want the report of five-year employees to look like? Should it contain both first and last names? Social Security numbers? Phone numbers? Addresses? Is all this data available? Several pieces of documentation are often provided to help the programmer understand the problem. This documentation might include items such as sample output and file specifications.

Really understanding the problem may be one of the most difficult aspects of programming. On any job, the description of what the user needs may be vague—worse yet, the user may not even really know what he or she wants, and users who think they know what they want frequently change their minds after seeing sample output. A good programmer is often part counselor, part detective!

PLANNING THE LOGIC

The heart of the programming process lies in planning the program's logic. During this phase of the programming process, the programmer plans the steps of the program, deciding what steps to include and how to order them. You can plan the solution to a problem in many ways. The two most common planning tools are flowcharts and pseudocode. Both tools involve writing the steps of the program in English, much as you would plan a trip on paper before getting into the car, or plan a party theme before going shopping for food and favors.

> **»NOTE** Besides flowcharts and pseudocode, programmers use a variety of other tools to help in the program development process. One such tool is an **IPO chart** which delineates input, processing, and output tasks. Some object-oriented programmers also use **TOE charts**, which list tasks, objects, and events.

> **»NOTE**
> You may hear programmers refer to planning a program as "developing an algorithm." An **algorithm** is the sequence of steps necessary to solve any problem. You will learn more about flowcharts and pseudocode later in this chapter.

The programmer doesn't worry about the syntax of any particular language at this point, just about figuring out what sequence of events will lead from the available input to the desired output. Planning the logic includes thinking carefully about all the possible data values a program might encounter and how you want the program to handle each scenario. The process of walking through a program's logic on paper before you actually write the program is called **desk-checking**. You will learn more about planning the logic later; in fact, this book focuses on this crucial step almost exclusively.

CODING THE PROGRAM

Once the programmer has developed the logic of a program, only then can he or she write the program in one of more than 400 programming languages. Programmers choose a particular language because some languages have built-in capabilities that make them more efficient than others at handling certain types of operations. Despite their differences, programming languages are quite alike—each can handle input operations, arithmetic processing, output operations, and other standard functions. The logic developed to solve a programming problem can be executed using any number of languages. It is only after a language is chosen that the programmer must worry about each command being spelled correctly and all of the punctuation getting into the right spots—in other words, using the correct *syntax*.

Some very experienced programmers can successfully combine the logic planning and the actual instruction writing, or **coding**, of the program in one step. This may work for planning and writing a very simple program, just as you can plan and write a postcard to a friend using one step. A good term paper or a Hollywood screenplay, however, needs planning before writing, and so do most programs.

Which step is harder: planning the logic or coding the program? Right now, it may seem to you that writing in a programming language is a very difficult task, considering all the spelling and grammar rules you must learn. However, the planning step is actually more difficult. Which is more difficult: thinking up the twists and turns to the plot of a best-selling mystery novel, or writing a translation of an already written novel from English to Spanish? And who do you think gets paid more, the writer who creates the plot or the translator? (Try asking friends to name any famous translator!)

USING SOFTWARE TO TRANSLATE THE PROGRAM INTO MACHINE LANGUAGE

Even though there are many programming languages, each computer knows only one language, its machine language, which consists of many 1s and 0s. Computers understand machine language because computers themselves are made up of thousands of tiny electrical switches, each of which can be set in either the on or off state, which is represented by a 1 or 0, respectively.

Languages like Java or Visual Basic are available for programmers to use because someone has written a translator program (a compiler or interpreter) that changes the English-like **high-level programming language** in which the programmer writes into the **low-level machine language** that the computer understands. If you write a programming language statement incorrectly (for example, by misspelling a word, using a word that doesn't exist in the language, or using "illegal" grammar), the translator program doesn't know what to do and issues an error message identifying a **syntax error**, or misuse of a language's grammar rules. You receive the same response when you speak nonsense to a human-language translator. Imagine trying to look up a list of words in a Spanish-English dictionary if some of the listed words are misspelled—you can't complete the task until the words are spelled correctly. Although making errors is never desirable, syntax errors are not a major concern to programmers because the compiler or interpreter catches every syntax error, and the computer will not execute a program that contains them.

A computer program must be free of syntax errors before you can execute it. Typically, a programmer develops a program's logic, writes the code, and then compiles the program, receiving a list of syntax errors. The programmer then corrects the syntax errors, and compiles the program again. Correcting the first set of errors frequently reveals new errors that originally were not apparent to the compiler. For example, if you could use an English compiler and submit the sentence The grl go to school, the compiler at first would point out only one syntax error to you. The second word, grl, is illegal because it is not part of the English language. Only after you corrected the word girl would the compiler find another syntax error on the third word, go, because it is the wrong verb form for the subject girl. This doesn't mean go is necessarily the wrong word. Maybe girl is wrong; perhaps the subject should be girls, in which case go is right. Compilers don't always know exactly what you mean, nor do they know what the proper correction should be, but they do know when something is wrong with your syntax.

When writing a program, a programmer might need to recompile the code several times. An executable program is created only when the code is free of syntax errors. When you run an executable program, it typically also might require input data. Figure 1-1 shows a diagram of this entire process.

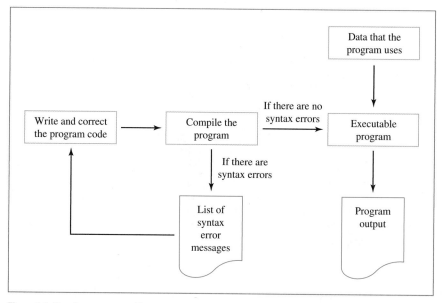

Figure 1-1 Creating an executable program

TESTING THE PROGRAM

A program that is free of syntax errors is not necessarily free of **logical errors**. For example, the sentence The girl goes to school, although syntactically perfect, is not logically correct if the girl is a baby or a dropout.

Once a program is free from syntax errors, the programmer can test it—that is, execute it with some sample data to see whether the results are logically correct. Recall the number-doubling program:

```
Get inputNumber.
Compute calculatedAnswer as inputNumber times 2.
Print calculatedAnswer.
```

If you provide the value 2 as input to the program and the answer 4 prints, you have executed one successful test run of the program.

However, if the answer 40 prints, maybe it's because the program contains a logical error. Maybe the second line of code was mistyped with an extra zero, so that the program reads:

```
Get inputNumber.
Compute calculatedAnswer as inputNumber times 20.
Print calculatedAnswer.
```

The error of placing 20 instead of 2 in the multiplication statement caused a logical error. Notice that nothing is syntactically wrong with this second program—it is just as reasonable to multiply a number by 20 as by 2—but if the programmer intends only to double inputNumber, then a logical error has occurred.

Programs should be tested with many sets of data. For example, if you write the program to double a number and enter 2 and get an output value of 4, that doesn't necessarily mean you have a correct program. Perhaps you have typed this program by mistake:

```
Get inputNumber.
Compute calculatedAnswer as inputNumber plus 2.
Print calculatedAnswer.
```

An input of 2 results in an answer of 4, but that doesn't mean your program doubles numbers—it actually only adds 2 to them. If you test your program with additional data and get the wrong answer—for example, if you use a 3 and get an answer of 5—you know there is a problem with your code.

Selecting test data is somewhat of an art in itself, and it should be done carefully. If the Human Resources Department wants a list of the names of five-year employees, it would be a mistake to test the program with a small sample file of only long-term employees. If no newer employees are part of the data being used for testing, you do not really know if the program would have eliminated them from the five-year list. Many companies do not know that their software has a problem until an unusual circumstance occurs—for example, the first time an employee has more than nine dependents, the first time a customer orders more than 999 items at a time, or when (in an example that was well-documented in the popular press) a new century begins.

》 NOTE
Appendix E contains more information on testing programs.

PUTTING THE PROGRAM INTO PRODUCTION

Once the program is tested adequately, it is ready for the organization to use. Putting the program into production might mean simply running the program once, if it was written to satisfy a user's request for a special list. However, the process might take months if the program will be run on a regular basis, or if it is one of a large system of programs being developed. Perhaps data-entry people must be trained to prepare the input for the new program, users must be trained to understand the output, or existing data in the company must be changed to an entirely new format to accommodate this program. **Conversion**, the entire set of actions an organization must take to switch over to using a new program or set of programs, can sometimes take months or years to accomplish.

》 NOTE You might consider maintaining programs as a seventh step in the programming process. After programs are put into production, making required changes is called maintenance. **Maintenance** is necessary for many reasons: for example, new tax rates are legislated, the format of an input file is altered, or the end user requires additional information not included in the original output specifications. Frequently, your first programming job will require maintaining previously written programs. When you maintain the programs others have written, you will appreciate the effort the original programmer put into writing clear code, using reasonable variable names, and documenting his or her work.

》 NOTE You might consider retiring the program as the eighth and final step in the programming process. A program is retired when it is no longer needed by an organization—usually when a new program is in the process of being put into production.

UNDERSTANDING INTERACTIVE USER INPUT

Some very simple programs require very simple data. For example, the number-doubling program requires just one value as input. In this type of program, data values are often entered from a keyboard. When a user must enter data, usually the user is shown a prompt. A **prompt** is a message that is displayed on a monitor, asking the user for a response. For example, the first screen shown in Figure 1-2 is one that might be displayed while a number-doubling program is running. The second screen shows the result after the user has entered a response to the prompt.

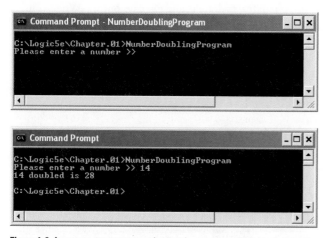

Figure 1-2 A prompt, a response, and output in a command line environment

The program in Figure 1-2 is being executed at the command prompt. The **command prompt** is the location on your computer screen at which you type entries to communicate with the computer's operating system using text. In this case, the user has asked the operating system to run a program named NumberDoublingProgram, and then the program has supplied the prompt to the user. Many programs are not run at the command prompt in a text environment, but are run using a **graphical user interface**, or **GUI** (pronounced "gooey"), which allows users to interact with a program in a graphical environment. Figure 1-3 shows a number-doubling program that performs exactly the same task as the one that appears in Figure 1-2, but this program uses a GUI. The user is presented with a prompt and an empty text box. When the user types a number in the text box, the result appears.

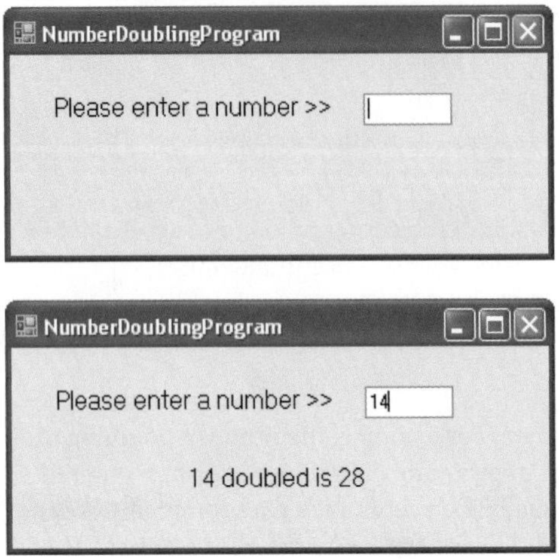

❱❱NOTE
You can learn more about creating GUI programs in Chapter 12 of the Comprehensive version of this book.

Figure 1-3 A prompt, a response, and output in a GUI environment

Although the programs in Figures 1-2 and 1-3 look different when they execute, their logic is the same. Each accepts a user's input, calculates its double, and displays output. When you learn to program in a programming language, you will create programs that look similar to the ones in Figures 1-2 and 1-3. In this book, however, you will not be concerned with the appearance of input and output as much as you will be concerned with the logic behind those processes.

TWO TRUTHS AND A LIE:

UNDERSTANDING INTERACTIVE USER INPUT

1. A prompt is a message that is displayed on a monitor, asking the user for a response.

2. The command prompt allows users to interact with a program in a graphical nontext environment.

3. The logic for a command line interactive program and a GUI interactive program is basically the same.

The false statement is #2. The command prompt is the location on your computer screen at which you type entries to communicate with the computer's operating system using text.

UNDERSTANDING THE DATA HIERARCHY AND FILE INPUT

Whatever format the interface takes, the number-doubling program requires just one value as input. Most business programs, however, use much more data—inventory files list thousands of items, while personnel and customer files list thousands of people. When data items are stored for use on computer systems, they are often stored in what is known as a **data hierarchy**, that describes the relationships between data components. In the data hierarchy, the smallest usable unit of data is the character. **Characters** are letters, numbers, and special symbols, such as "A", "7", and "$". Anything you can type from the keyboard in one keystroke (including a space or a tab) is a character. Characters are made up of smaller elements called bits. But just as most human beings can use a pencil without caring whether atoms are flying around inside it, most computer users can store characters without caring about these bits.

>> **NOTE**
> Computers also recognize characters you cannot enter from the keyboard, such as foreign alphabet characters like φ or Σ.

Characters are grouped together to form a field. A **field** is a single data item, such as `lastName`, `streetAddress`, or `annualSalary`. For most of us, an "S", an "m", an "i", a "t", and an "h" don't have much meaning individually, but if the combination of characters makes up your last name, "Smith", then as a group, the characters have useful meaning.

Related fields are often grouped together to form a record. **Records** are groups of fields that go together for some logical reason. A random name, address, and salary aren't very useful, but if they're your name, your address, and your salary, then that's your record. An inventory record might contain fields for item number, color, size, and price; a student record might contain ID number, grade point average, and major.

>> **NOTE**
> Chapter 14 of the Comprehensive version of this text covers database creation.

Related records, in turn, are grouped together to form a file. **Files** are groups of records that go together for some logical reason. The individual records of each student in your class might go together in a file called STUDENTS. Records of each person at your company might be in a file called PERSONNEL. Items you sell might be in an INVENTORY file.

Some files can have just a few records; others, such as the file of credit-card holders for a major department-store chain or policyholders of an insurance company, can contain thousands or even millions of records.

>> **NOTE**
> When records are stored in a file that is not part of a database, programmers often refer to the file as a **flat file**.

Finally, many organizations use database software to organize many files. A **database** holds groups of files, often called tables, that together serve the information needs of an organization. Database software establishes and maintains relationships between fields in these tables, so that users can write questions called queries. **Queries** pull related data items together in a format that allows businesspeople to make managerial decisions efficiently.

In summary, you can picture the data hierarchy, as shown in Figure 1-4.

A database contains many files. A file contains many records. Each record in a file has the same fields. Each record's fields contain different data items that consist of one or more stored characters in each field.

```
Database
    File
        Record
            Field
                Character
```

Figure 1-4 The data hierarchy

As an example, you can picture a file as a set of index cards, as shown in Figure 1-5. The stack of cards is the EMPLOYEE file, in which each card represents one employee record. On each card, each line holds one field—name, address, or salary. Almost all the program examples in this book use files that are organized in this way.

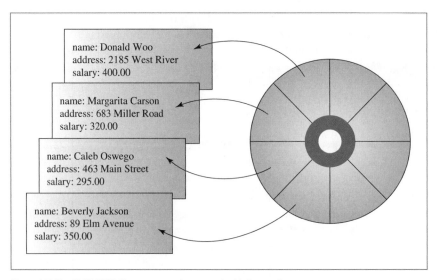

Figure 1-5 The EMPLOYEE file represented as a stack of index cards

Whether the data has been stored in a flat file or a database, when a program needs all the fields in a record, you can write programming statements to get or input each field in one of several ways. For example, if a program needs an employee's name, address, and salary, most programming languages allow you to write separate statements such as the following:

```
Get name
Get address
Get salary
```

Most languages also allow you to write a single statement in the following format:

```
Get name, address, salary
```

Additionally, most programming languages provide a way for you to use a group name for record data, as in the following statement:

```
Get EmployeeRecord
```

When this format is used, you need to define the separate fields that compose an EmployeeRecord elsewhere in the program. When programs in this book need the fields in a record, this simplified "group" approach will be used. However, keep in mind that the logic is the same no matter from where data items are retrieved.

TWO TRUTHS AND A LIE:
UNDERSTANDING THE DATA HIERARCHY AND FILE INPUT

1. In the data hierarchy, a field is a single data item, such as lastName, streetAddress, or annualSalary.

2. In the data hierarchy, fields are grouped together to form a record; records are groups of fields that go together for some logical reason.

3. In the data hierarchy, related records are grouped together to form a field.

The false statement is #3. Related records form a file.

USING FLOWCHART SYMBOLS AND PSEUDOCODE STATEMENTS

When programmers plan the logic for a solution to a programming problem, they often use one of two tools, flowcharts or pseudocode (pronounced "sue-doe-code"). A **flowchart** is a pictorial representation of the logical steps it takes to solve a problem. **Pseudocode** is an English-like representation of the same thing. *Pseudo* is a prefix that means "false," and to *code* a program means to put it in a programming language; therefore, *pseudocode* simply means "false code," or sentences that appear to have been written in a computer programming language but do not necessarily follow all the syntax rules of any specific language.

You have already seen examples of statements that represent pseudocode earlier in this chapter, and there is nothing mysterious about them. The following five statements constitute a pseudocode representation of a number-doubling problem:

```
start
   get inputNumber
   compute calculatedAnswer as inputNumber times 2
   print calculatedAnswer
stop
```

Using pseudocode involves writing down all the steps you will use in a program. Usually, programmers preface their pseudocode statements with a beginning statement like "start" and end them with a terminating statement like "stop". The statements between "start" and "stop" look like English and are indented slightly so that "start" and "stop" stand out. Most programmers do not bother with punctuation such as periods at the end of pseudocode statements, although it would not be wrong to use them if you prefer that style. Similarly, there is no need to capitalize the first word in a sentence, although you might choose to do so. This book follows the conventions of using lowercase letters for verbs that begin pseudocode statements and omitting periods at the end of statements.

Some professional programmers prefer writing pseudocode to drawing flowcharts, because using pseudocode is more similar to writing the final statements in the programming language. Others prefer drawing flowcharts to represent the logical flow, because flowcharts allow programmers to visualize more easily how the program statements will connect. Especially for beginning programmers, flowcharts are an excellent tool to help visualize how the statements in a program are interrelated.

Almost every program involves the steps of input, processing, and output. Therefore, most flowcharts need some graphical way to separate these three steps. When you create a flowchart, you draw geometric shapes around the individual statements and connect them with arrows.

> **» NOTE** You can draw a flowchart by hand or you can use software that contains flowcharting tools such as Microsoft Word and Microsoft PowerPoint. There are also several software programs you can buy specifically for creating flowcharts, such as Visio and Visual Logic.

When you draw a flowchart, you use a parallelogram to represent an **input symbol**, which indicates an input operation. You write an input statement, in English, inside the parallelogram, as shown in Figure 1-6.

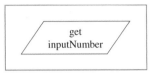

Figure 1-6 Input symbol

Arithmetic operation statements are examples of processing. In a flowchart, you use a rectangle as the **processing symbol** that contains a processing statement, as shown in Figure 1-7.

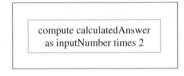

Figure 1-7 Processing symbol

To represent an output statement, you use the same symbol as for input statements—the **output symbol** is a parallelogram, as shown in Figure 1-8.

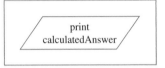

Figure 1-8 Output symbol

> **NOTE** Some software programs that use flowcharts (such as Visual Logic) use a left-slanting parallelogram to represent output. As long as the flowchart creator and the flowchart reader are communicating, the actual shape used is irrelevant. This book will follow the most standard convention of always using the right-slanting parallelogram for both input and output.

> **NOTE** As with input, output statements can be organized in whatever way seems most reasonable. A program that prints the length and width of a room might use two statements:
>
> ```
> print length
> print width
> ```
>
> Most languages allow you to print several values in a single statement as in the following:
>
> ```
> print length, width
> ```
>
> In some programming languages, using two print statements places the output values on two separate lines on the monitor or printer, whereas using a single print statement places the values next to each other on the same line. Many languages provide two types of output statements—one that produces output on a line and then advances the insertion point to the next line, and another that produces output on a line and does not advance the insertion point, so that subsequent output appears on the same line. As you learn a programming language, you will understand the different types of output statements available in that language. This book follows the convention of using one print statement per line of output.

To show the correct sequence of these statements, you use arrows, or **flowlines**, to connect the steps. Whenever possible, most of a flowchart should read from top to bottom or from left to right on a page. That's the way we read English, so when flowcharts follow this convention, they are easier for us to understand.

To be complete, a flowchart should include two more elements: **terminal symbols**, or start/stop symbols, at each end. Often, you place a word like "start" or "begin" in the first terminal symbol and a word like "end" or "stop" in the other. The standard terminal symbol is shaped like a racetrack; many programmers refer to this shape as a lozenge, because it resembles the shape of a medicated candy lozenge you might use to soothe a sore throat. Figure 1-9 shows a complete flowchart for the program that doubles a number, and the pseudocode for the same problem.

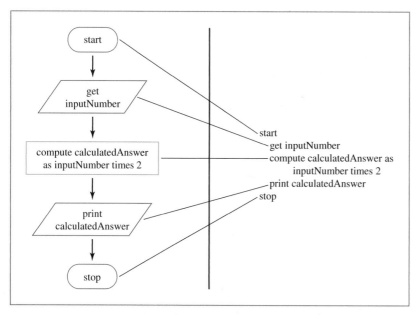

Figure 1-9 Flowchart and pseudocode of program that doubles a number

The logic for the program represented by the flowchart and pseudocode in Figure 1-9 is correct no matter what programming language the programmer eventually uses to write the corresponding code. Just as the same statements could be translated into Italian or Chinese without losing their meaning, they also can be coded in C#, Java, or any other programming language.

After the flowchart or pseudocode has been developed, the programmer only needs to: (1) buy a computer, (2) buy a language compiler, (3) learn a programming language, (4) code the program, (5) attempt to compile it, (6) fix the syntax errors, (7) compile it again, (8) test it with several sets of data, and (9) put it into production.

"Whoa!" you are probably saying to yourself. "This is simply not worth it! All that work to create a flowchart or pseudocode, and *then* all those other steps? For five dollars, I can buy a pocket calculator that will double any number for me instantly!" You are absolutely right. If this were a real computer program, and all it did was double the value of a number, it simply would not be worth all the effort. Writing a computer program would be worth the effort only if you had many—let's say 10,000—numbers to double in a limited amount of time—let's say the next two minutes. Then, it would be worth your while to create a computer program.

Unfortunately, the number-doubling program represented in Figure 1-9 does not double 10,000 numbers; it doubles only one. You could execute the program 10,000 times, of course, but that would require you to sit at the computer telling it to run the program over and over again. You would be better off with a program that could process 10,000 numbers, one after the other.

One solution is to write the program as shown in Figure 1-10 and execute the same steps 10,000 times. Of course, writing this program would be very time consuming; you might as well buy the calculator.

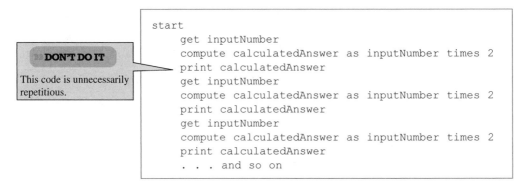

DON'T DO IT

This code is unnecessarily repetitious.

```
start
    get inputNumber
    compute calculatedAnswer as inputNumber times 2
    print calculatedAnswer
    get inputNumber
    compute calculatedAnswer as inputNumber times 2
    print calculatedAnswer
    get inputNumber
    compute calculatedAnswer as inputNumber times 2
    print calculatedAnswer
    . . . and so on
```

Figure 1-10 Inefficient pseudocode for program that doubles 10,000 numbers

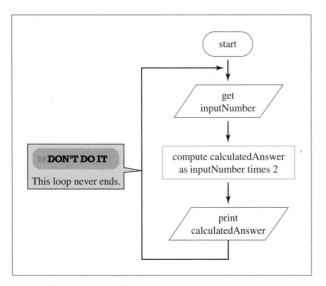

DON'T DO IT

This loop never ends.

Figure 1-11 Flowchart of infinite number-doubling program

A better solution is to have the computer execute the same set of three instructions over and over again, as shown in Figure 1-11. With this approach, the computer gets a number, doubles it, prints the answer, and then starts over again with the first instruction. The same spot in memory, called inputNumber, is reused for the second number and for any subsequent numbers. The spot in memory named calculatedAnswer is reused each time to store the result of the multiplication operation. The logic illustrated in the flowchart shown in Figure 1-11 contains a major problem—the sequence of instructions never ends. You will learn to handle this problem later in this chapter.

TWO TRUTHS AND A LIE:
USING FLOWCHART SYMBOLS AND PSEUDOCODE STATEMENTS

1. When you draw a flowchart, you use a parallelogram to represent an input operation.

2. When you draw a flowchart, you use a parallelogram to represent a processing operation.

3. When you draw a flowchart, you use a parallelogram to represent an output operation.

The false statement is #2. When you draw a flowchart, you use a rectangle to represent a processing operation.

USING AND NAMING VARIABLES

Programmers commonly refer to the locations in memory called inputNumber and calculatedAnswer as variables. **Variables** are named memory locations, whose contents can vary or differ over time. At any moment in time, a variable holds just one value. Sometimes, inputNumber holds 2 and calculatedAnswer holds 4; at other times, inputNumber holds 6 and calculatedAnswer holds 12. It is the ability of memory variables to change in value that makes computers and programming worthwhile. Because one memory location can be used over and over again with different values, you can write program instructions once and then use them for thousands of separate calculations. *One* set of payroll instructions at your company produces each individual's paycheck, and *one* set of instructions at your electric company produces each household's bill.

The number-doubling example requires two variables, inputNumber and calculatedAnswer. These can just as well be named userEntry and programSolution, or inputValue and twiceTheValue. As a programmer, you choose reasonable names for your variables. The language interpreter then associates the names you choose with specific memory addresses.

A variable name is also called an **identifier**. Every computer programming language has its own set of rules for creating identifiers. Most languages allow both letters and digits within variable names. Some languages allow hyphens in variable names—for example, hourly-wage. Others allow underscores, as in hourly_wage. Still others allow neither. Some languages allow dollar signs or other special characters in variable names (for example, hourly$); others allow foreign alphabet characters, such as π or Ω.

>> **NOTE** Every variable has a data type and a name. You will learn more about both of these features later in this chapter.

>> **NOTE** You can also refer to a variable name as a **mnemonic**. In everyday language, a mnemonic is a memory device, like the sentence "Every good boy does fine," which makes it easier to remember the notes that occupy the lines on the staff in sheet music. In programming, a variable name is a device that makes it easier to reference a memory address.

Different languages put different limits on the length of variable names, although in general, newer languages allow longer names. For example, in some very old versions of BASIC, a variable name could consist of only one or two letters and one or two digits. You could have some cryptic variable names like hw or a3. Fortunately, most modern languages allow variable names to be much longer; in the newest versions of C++, C#, and Java, the length of identifiers is virtually unlimited. Variable names in these languages usually consist of lower-case letters, don't allow hyphens, but do allow underscores, so you can use a name like price_of_item. These languages are case sensitive, so HOURLYWAGE, hourlywage, and hourlyWage are considered three separate variable names, although the last example, in which the new word begins with an uppercase letter, is easiest to read. Most programmers who use the more modern languages employ the format in which multiple-word variable names begin with a lowercase letter, are run together, and each new word within the variable name begins with an uppercase letter. This format is called **camel casing**, because such variable names, like `hourlyWage`, have a "hump" in the middle. The variable names in this text are shown using camel casing.

Even though every language has its own rules for naming variables, when designing the logic of a computer program, you should not concern yourself with the specific syntax of any particular computer language. The logic, after all, works with any language. The variable names used throughout this book follow only two rules:

1. *Variable names must be one word*. The name can contain letters, digits, hyphens, underscores, or any other characters you choose, with the exception of *spaces*. Therefore, r is a legal variable name, as is `rate`, as is `interestRate`. The variable name `interest rate` is not allowed because of the space. No programming language allows spaces within a variable name. If you see a name such as interest rate in a flowchart or pseudocode, you should assume that the programmer is discussing two variables, `interest` and `rate`, each of which individually would be a fine variable name.

» NOTE As a convention, this book begins variable names with a lowercase letter. You might find programming texts in languages such as Visual Basic and C++ in which the author has chosen to begin variable names with an uppercase letter. As long as you adopt a convention and use it consistently, your programs will be easier to read and understand.

» NOTE When you write a program using an editor that is packaged with a compiler, the compiler may display variable names in a different color from the rest of the program. This visual aid helps your variable names stand out from words that are part of the programming language.

2. *Variable names should have some appropriate meaning*. This is not a rule of any programming language. When computing an interest rate in a program, the computer does not care if you call the variable g, u84, or `fred`. As long as the correct numeric result is placed in the variable, its actual name doesn't really matter. However, it's much easier to follow the logic of a program with a statement in it like `compute finalBalance as equal to initialInvestment times interestRate` than one with a statement in it like `compute someBanana as equal to j89 times myFriendLinda`. You might think you will remember how you intended to use a cryptic variable name within a program, but several months or years later when a program requires changes, you, and other programmers working with you, will appreciate clear, descriptive variable names.

Notice that the flowchart in Figure 1-11 follows these two rules for variables: both variable names, `inputNumber` and `calculatedAnswer`, are one word without embedded spaces, and they both have appropriate meanings. Some programmers have fun with their variable names by naming them after friends or creating puns with them, but such behavior is unprofessional and marks those programmers as amateurs. Table 1-1 lists some possible variable names that might be used to hold an employee's last name and provides a rationale for the appropriateness of each one.

» NOTE Another general rule in all programming languages is that variable names may not begin with a digit, although usually they may contain digits. Thus, in most languages `budget2013` is a legal variable name, but `2013Budget` is not.

Suggested Variable Names for Employee's Last Name	Comments
Best suggestions	
employeeLastName	Good—descriptive identifier
employeeLast	Good—most people would interpret Last as meaning Last Name
empLast	Good—emp is short for employee
Inferior and illegal suggestions	
emlstnam	Legal—but cryptic
lastNameOfTheEmployeeInQuestion	Legal—but awkward
last name	Not legal—embedded space
employeelastname	Legal—but hard to read without camel casing

DON'T DO IT

The four suggestions below this point are *not* recommended.

Table 1-1 Suitability of suggested variable names for an employee's last name

TWO TRUTHS AND A LIE:
USING AND NAMING VARIABLES

1. As a programmer, you choose specific memory addresses for your variables.

2. A variable name is also called an identifier.

3. Variable names must be one word, without spaces.

The false statement is #1. As a programmer, you choose reasonable names for your variables. The language interpreter then associates the names you choose with specific memory addresses.

ENDING A PROGRAM BY USING SENTINEL VALUES

Recall that the logic in the flowchart for doubling numbers, shown in Figure 1-11, has a major flaw—the program never ends. This programming situation is known as an **infinite loop**—a repeating flow of logic with no end. If, for example, the input numbers are being entered at the keyboard, the program will keep accepting numbers and printing doubles forever. Of course, the user could refuse to type in any more numbers. But the computer is very patient, and if you refuse to give it any more numbers, it will sit and wait forever. When you finally type in a number, the program will double it, print the result, and wait for another. The program cannot progress any further while it is waiting for input; meanwhile, the program is occupying computer memory and tying up operating system resources. Refusing to enter any more numbers is not a practical solution. Another way to end the program is simply to turn off the computer. But again, that's neither the best nor an elegant way to bring the program to an end.

A better way to end the program is to set a predetermined value for inputNumber that means "Stop the program!" For example, the programmer and the user could agree that the user will never need to know the double of 0 (zero), so the user could enter a 0 when he or she wants to stop. The program could then test any incoming value contained in `inputNumber` and, if it is a 0, stop the program. Testing a value is also called **making a decision**.

You represent a decision in a flowchart by drawing a **decision symbol**, which is shaped like a diamond. The diamond usually contains a question, the answer to which is one of two mutually exclusive options—often yes or no. All good computer questions have only two mutually exclusive answers, such as yes and no or true and false. For example, "What day of the year is your birthday?" is not a good computer question because there are 366 possible answers. But "Is your birthday June 24?" is a good computer question because, for everyone in the world, the answer is either yes or no.

The question to stop the doubling program should be "Is the value of `inputNumber` just entered equal to 0?" or "`inputNumber = 0?`" for short. The complete flowchart will now look like the one shown in Figure 1-12.

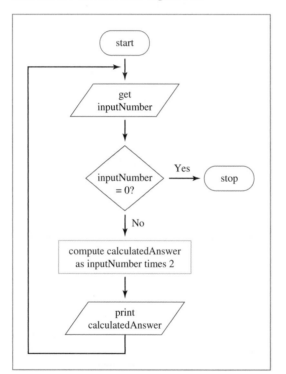

Figure 1-12 Flowchart of number-doubling program with sentinel value of 0

One drawback to using 0 to stop a program, of course, is that it won't work if the user does need to find the double of 0. In that case, some other data-entry value that the user will never need, such as 999 or –1, could be selected to signal that the program should end. A preselected value that stops the execution of a program is often called a **dummy value** because it does not represent real data, but just a signal to stop. Sometimes, such a value is called a **sentinel value** because it represents an entry or exit point, like a sentinel who guards a fortress.

Not all programs rely on user data entry from a keyboard; many read data from an input device, such as a disk. When organizations store data on a disk or other storage device, they do not commonly use a dummy value to signal the end of the file. For one thing, an input record might have hundreds of fields, and if you store a dummy record in every file, you are wasting a large quantity of storage on "non-data." Additionally, it is often difficult to choose sentinel values for fields in a company's data files. Any `balanceDue`, even a zero or a negative number, can be a legitimate value, and any `customerName`, even "ZZ", could be someone's name. Fortunately, programming languages can recognize the end of data in a file automatically, through a code that is stored at the end of the data. Many programming languages use the term **eof** (for "end of file") to talk about this marker that automatically acts as a sentinel. This book, therefore, uses `eof` to indicate the end of data, regardless of whether the code is a special disk marker or a dummy value such as 0 that comes from the keyboard. Therefore, the flowchart can look like the example shown in Figure 1-13.

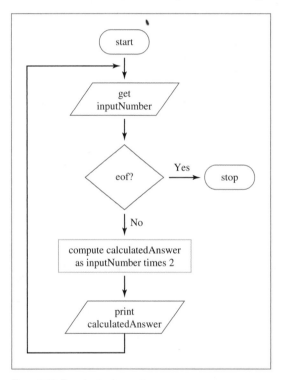

Figure 1-13 Flowchart using `eof`

TWO TRUTHS AND A LIE:

ENDING A PROGRAM BY USING SENTINEL VALUES

1. A program that contains an infinite loop is one that never ends.

2. A preselected value that stops the execution of a program is often called a dummy value or a sentinel value.

3. Many programming languages use the term `fe` (for "file end") to talk about a marker that automatically acts as a sentinel.

The false statement is #3. The term `eof` (for "end of file") is the common term for a file sentinel.

MANAGING LARGE FLOWCHARTS

By using just the input, processing, output, decision, and terminal symbols, you can represent the flowcharting logic for many diverse applications. When drawing a large flowchart segment, you might use another symbol, the connector. You can use a connector when limited page size forces you to continue a flowchart in an unconnected location or on another page. If a flowchart has six processing steps and a page provides room for only three, you might represent the logic as shown in Figure 1-14.

By convention, programmers use a circle as an on-page **connector symbol**, and a symbol that looks like a square with a pointed bottom as an off-page connector symbol. The on-page connector at the bottom of the left column in Figure 1-14 tells someone reading the flowchart that there is more to the flowchart. The circle should contain a number or letter that can then be matched to another number or letter somewhere else, in this case on the right. If a large flowchart needed more connectors, new numbers or letters would be assigned in sequence

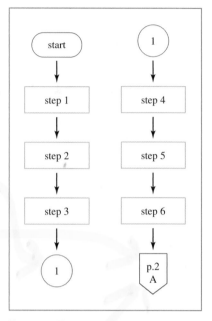

Figure 1-14 Flowchart using the connector

(1, 2, 3 . . . or A, B, C . . .) to each successive pair of connectors. The off-page connector at the bottom of the right column in Figure 1-14 tells the reader that there is more to the flowchart on another page.

When you are creating your own flowcharts, you should avoid using any connectors, if at all possible; flowcharts are more difficult to follow when their segments do not fit together on a page. Some programmers would even say that if a flowchart must connect to another page, it is a sign of poor design. Your instructor or future programming supervisor may require that long flowcharts be redrawn so you don't need to use the connector symbol. However, when continuing to a new location or page is unavoidable, the connector provides the means.

TWO TRUTHS AND A LIE:
MANAGING LARGE FLOWCHARTS

1. You can use a connector when limited page size forces you to continue a flowchart in an unconnected location or on another page.

2. By convention, programmers use a parallelogram as an on-page connector symbol.

3. By convention, programmers use a symbol that looks like a square with a pointed bottom as an off-page connector symbol.

The false statement is #2. By convention, programmers use a circle as an on-page connector symbol.

ASSIGNING VALUES TO VARIABLES

When you create a flowchart or pseudocode for a program that doubles numbers, you can include the statement compute calculatedAnswer as inputNumber times 2. This statement incorporates two actions. First, the computer calculates the arithmetic value of inputNumber times 2. Second, the computed value is stored in the calculatedAnswer memory location. Most programming languages allow a shorthand expression for **assignment statements** such as compute calculatedAnswer as inputNumber times 2. The shorthand takes the form calculatedAnswer = inputNumber * 2. The equal sign is the **assignment operator**; it always requires the name of a memory location on its left side—the name of the location where the result will be stored.

> **NOTE** When they write pseudocode or draw a flowchart, most programmers use the asterisk (*) to represent multiplication. When you write pseudocode, you can use an X or a dot for multiplication (as most mathematicians do), but you will be using an unconventional format. This book will always use an asterisk to represent multiplication.

According to the rules of algebra, a statement like calculatedAnswer = inputNumber * 2 should be exactly equivalent to the statement inputNumber * 2 = calculatedAnswer. That's because in algebra, the equal sign always represents equivalency. In most programming languages, however, the equal sign represents assignment, and calculatedAnswer = inputNumber * 2 means "multiply inputNumber by 2 and store the result in the variable called calculatedAnswer". Whatever operation is performed to the right of the equal sign results in a value that is placed in the memory location to the left of the equal sign. Therefore, the incorrect statement inputNumber * 2 = calculatedAnswer means to attempt to take the value of calculatedAnswer and store it in a location called inputNumber * 2, but there can't be a location called inputNumber * 2. For one thing, you should recognize that the expression inputNumber * 2 can't be a variable because it has spaces in it. For another, a location can't be multiplied. Its contents can be multiplied, but the location itself cannot. The backward statement inputNumber * 2 = calculatedAnswer contains a syntax error, no matter what programming language you use; a program with such a statement will not execute.

> **NOTE** When you create an assignment statement, it may help to imagine the word "let" in front of the statement. Thus, you can read the statement calculatedAnswer = inputNumber * 2 as "Let calculatedAnswer equal inputNumber times two." The BASIC programming language allows you to use the word "let" in such statements. You might also imagine the word "gets" or "receives" in place of the assignment operator. In other words, calculatedAnswer = inputNumber * 2 means both calculatedAnswer gets inputNumber * 2 and calculatedAnswer receives inputNumber * 2.

> **NOTE** Computer memory is made up of millions of distinct locations, each of which has an address. Fifty or sixty years ago, programmers had to deal with these addresses and had to remember, for instance, that they had stored a salary in location 6428 of their computer. Today, we are very fortunate that high-level computer languages allow us to pick a reasonable "English" name for a memory address and let the computer keep track of where it is located. Just as it is easier for you to remember that the president lives in the White House than at 1600 Pennsylvania Avenue, Washington, D.C., it is also easier for you to remember that your salary is in a variable called mySalary than at memory location 6428104.

Similarly, it does not usually make sense to perform mathematical operations on names given to memory addresses, but it does make sense to perform mathematical operations on the *contents* of memory addresses. If you live in blueSplitLevelOnTheCorner, adding 1 to that would be meaningless, but you certainly can add 1 person to the number of people already in that house. For our purposes, then, the statement calculatedAnswer = inputNumber * 2 means exactly the same thing as the statement calculate inputNumber * 2 (that is, double the contents in the memory location named inputNumber) and store the result in the memory location named calculatedAnswer.

> **NOTE** Many programming languages allow you to create named constants. A **named constant** is a named memory location, similar to a variable, except its value never changes during the execution of a program. If you are working with a programming language that allows it, you might create a constant for a value such as PI = 3.14 or COUNTY_SALES_TAX_RATE = 0.06. Many programmers follow the convention of using camel casing for variable identifiers but all capital letters for constant identifiers.

In programming languages, every operator follows **rules of precedence** that dictate the order in which the operations in the same statement are carried out. For example, multiplication and division always take precedence over addition and subtraction, so in an expression such as a + b *c, b and c are multiplied producing a temporary result before a is added to it. The assignment operator has a very low precedence meaning in a statement such as d = e + f + g, the operations on the right of the assignment operator are always performed before the final assignment to the variable on the left is made.

> **NOTE** In arithmetic statements, the rules of precedence can be overridden using parentheses. For example, in the expression h = (j + k) * m, j and k are summed before the temporary result is multiplied by m. However, in most programming languages (C and C++ are notable exceptions), you cannot override the precedence of the equal sign using a statement such as (d = e) + f + g.

TWO TRUTHS AND A LIE:
ASSIGNING VALUES TO VARIABLES

1. The equal assignment operator always requires the name of a memory location on its right side.

2. Variable names are easier to remember than memory addresses.

3. A named constant is a named memory location, similar to a variable, except its value never changes during the execution of a program.

The false statement is #1. The equal assignment operator always requires the name of a memory location on its left side.

UNDERSTANDING DATA TYPES

Computers deal with two basic types of data—text and numeric. When you use a specific numeric value, such as 43, within a program, you write it using the digits and no quotation marks. A specific numeric value is often called a **numeric constant** (or **literal numeric constant**), because it does not change—a 43 always has the value 43. When you use a specific text value, or string of characters, such as "Amanda", you enclose the literal **string constant**, or **text constant**, within quotation marks.

> **NOTE** Some languages require single quotation marks surrounding character constants, whereas others require double quotation marks. Many languages, including C++, C#, and Java, reserve single quotes for a single character such as 'A', and double quotes for a character string such as "Amanda".

Similarly, most computer languages allow at least two distinct types of variables. A variable's **data type** describes the kind of values the variable can hold and the types of operations that can be performed with it. One type of variable can hold a number, and is called a numeric variable. A **numeric variable** is one that can have mathematical operations performed on it; it can hold digits, and usually can hold a decimal point and a sign indicating positive or negative if you want. In the statement calculatedAnswer = inputNumber * 2, both calculatedAnswer and inputNumber are numeric variables; that is, their intended contents are numeric values, such as 6 and 3, 150 and 75, or –18 and –9.

NOTE
In many languages, the term character variable is reserved for a single character, such as *A*, and string refers to data that is made up of one or more characters, such as *Andrea*.

Most programming languages have a separate type of variable that can hold letters of the alphabet and other special characters, such as punctuation marks. Depending on the language, these variables are called character, **text**, or **string variables**. If a working program contains the statement lastName = "Lincoln", then lastName is a text or string variable.

Programmers must distinguish between numeric and string variables, because computers handle the two types of data differently. Therefore, means are provided within the syntax rules of computer programming languages to tell the computer which type of data to expect. How this is done is different in every language; some languages have different rules for naming the variables, but with others you must include a simple statement (called a **declaration**) telling the computer which type of data to expect.

Some languages allow for several types of numeric data. Languages such as C++, C#, Visual Basic, and Java distinguish between **integer** (whole number) numeric variables and **floating-point** (fractional) numeric variables that contain a decimal point. Thus, in some languages, the values 4 and 4.3 would be stored in different types of numeric variables.

Some programming languages allow even more specific variable types, but the text versus numeric distinction is universal. For the programs you develop in this book, assume that each variable is one of the two broad types. If a variable called taxRate is supposed to hold a value of 2.5, assume that it is a numeric variable. If a variable called inventoryItem is supposed to hold a value of "monitor", assume that it is a string variable.

> **NOTE** Values such as "monitor" and 2.5 are called constants or literal constants because they never change. A variable value *can* change. Thus, inventoryItem can hold "monitor" at one moment during the execution of a program, and later you can change its value to "modem".

> **NOTE** Object-oriented programming languages allow you to create new data types called classes. Classes are covered in all object-oriented programming language textbooks as well as in Chapter 11 of the Comprehensive version of this book.

By convention, this book encloses string data like "monitor" within quotation marks to distinguish the string of characters from yet another variable name. Also by convention, numeric data values are not enclosed within quotation marks. According to these conventions, then, if you declare taxRate as a numeric variable and inventoryItem as a string, then taxRate = 2.5 and inventoryItem = "monitor" are both valid statements. The statement inventoryItem = monitor is a valid statement only if monitor is also a string variable. In other words, if monitor = "Model 86", and subsequently inventoryItem = monitor, then the end result is that the memory address named inventoryItem contains the string of characters "Model 86". Data can only be assigned from one variable to another if the variables are the same data type.

NOTE
The process of naming program variables and assigning a type to them is called **making declarations**, or **declaring variables**. You will learn how to declare variables in Chapter 3.

Every computer handles text or string data differently from the way it handles numeric data. You may have experienced these differences if you have used application software such as spreadsheets or database programs. For example, in a spreadsheet, you cannot sum a column of words. Similarly, every programming language requires that you distinguish variables as to their correct type, and that you use each type of variable appropriately. Identifying your variables correctly as numeric or string is one of the first steps you have to take when writing programs in any programming language. Table 1-2 provides you with a few examples of legal and illegal variable assignment statements.

Assume `lastName` *and* `firstName` *are string variables.*

Assume `quizScore` *and* `homeworkScore` *are numeric variables.*

Examples of valid assignments	**DON'T DO IT** Each of these assignments is invalid. Examples of invalid assignments	Explanation of invalid examples
`lastName = "Parker"`	`lastName = Parker`	If `Parker` is the last name, it requires quotation marks. If `Parker` is a named string variable, this assignment would be allowed.
`firstName = "Laura"`	`"Parker" = lastName`	Value on left must be a variable name, not a constant.
`lastName = firstName`	`lastName = quizScore`	The data types do not match.
`quizScore = 86`	`homeworkScore = firstName`	The data types do not match.
`homeworkScore = quizScore`	`homeworkScore = "92"`	The data types do not match.
`homeworkScore = 92`	`quizScore = "zero"`	The data types do not match.
`quizScore = homeworkScore + 25`	`firstName = 23`	The data types do not match.
`homeworkScore = 3 * 10`	`100 = homeworkScore`	Value on left must be a variable name, not a constant.

Table 1-2 Some examples of legal and illegal assignments

TWO TRUTHS AND A LIE:
UNDERSTANDING DATA TYPES

1. A variable's data type describes the kind of values the variable can hold and the types of operations that can be performed with it.

2. If `name` is a string variable, then the statement `name = "Ed"` is valid.

3. If `salary` is a numeric variable, then the statement `salary = "12.50"` is valid.

The false statement is #3. If `salary` is a numeric variable, then the statement `salary = 12.50` (with no quotation marks) is valid. If `salary` is a string variable, then the statement `salary = "12.50"` is valid.

UNDERSTANDING THE EVOLUTION OF PROGRAMMING TECHNIQUES

People have been writing modern computer programs since the 1940s. The oldest programming languages required programmers to work with memory addresses and to memorize awkward codes associated with machine languages. Newer programming languages look much more like natural language and are easier for programmers to use. Part of the reason it is easier to use newer programming languages is that they allow programmers to name variables instead of using awkward memory addresses. Another reason is that newer programming languages provide programmers with the means to create self-contained modules or program segments that can be pieced together in a variety of ways. The oldest computer programs were written in one piece, from start to finish; modern programs are rarely written that way—they are created by teams of programmers, each developing his or her own reusable and connectable program procedures. Writing several small modules is easier than writing one large program, and most large tasks are easier when you break the work into units and get other workers to help with some of the units.

Currently, there are two major techniques used to develop programs and their procedures. One technique, **procedural programming**, focuses on the procedures that programmers create. In other words, procedural programmers focus on the actions that are carried out—for example, getting input data for an employee and writing the calculations needed to produce a paycheck from the data. Procedural programmers would approach the job of producing a paycheck by breaking down the paycheck-producing process into manageable subtasks.

The other popular programming technique, **object-oriented programming**, focuses on objects, or "things," and describes their features, or attributes, and their behaviors. For example, object-oriented programmers might design a payroll application by thinking about employees and paychecks, and describing their attributes (such as last name or check amount) and behaviors (such as the calculations that result in the check amount).

With either approach, procedural or object-oriented, you can produce a correct paycheck, and both techniques employ reusable program modules. The major difference lies in the focus the programmer takes during the earliest planning stages of a project. For now, this book focuses on procedural programming techniques. The skills you gain in programming procedurally—declaring variables, accepting input, making decisions, producing output, and so on—will serve you well whether you eventually write programs in either procedural or object-oriented fashion, or in both.

> **》NOTE**
> Ada Byron Lovelace predicted the development of software in 1843; she is often regarded as the first programmer. The basis for most modern software was proposed by Alan Turing in 1935.

> **》NOTE**
> You will learn to create program modules in Chapter 3 and learn more about them in Chapter 7.

> **》NOTE**
> Object-oriented programming employs a large vocabulary; you can learn this terminology in Chapter 11 of the Comprehensive version of this book.

TWO TRUTHS AND A LIE:
UNDERSTANDING THE EVOLUTION OF PROGRAMMING TECHNIQUES

1. The oldest computer programs were written in many separate pieces.

2. Procedural programmers focus on actions that are carried out by a program.

3. Object-oriented programmers focus on a program's objects and their attributes and behaviors.

The false statement is #1. The oldest programs were written in a single piece; newer programs are divided into modules.

CHAPTER SUMMARY

» Together, computer hardware (equipment) and software (instructions) accomplish four major operations: input, processing, output, and storage. You write computer instructions in a computer programming language that requires specific syntax; the instructions are translated into machine language by a compiler or interpreter. When both the syntax and logic of a program are correct, you can run, or execute, the program to produce the desired results.

» A programmer's job involves understanding the problem, planning the logic, coding the program, translating the program into machine language, testing the program, and putting the program into production.

» When a program's data values are entered from a keyboard, they can be entered in response to a prompt in a text environment or in a GUI one. Either way, the logic is similar.

» When data items are stored for use on computer systems, they are stored in a data hierarchy of character, field, record, file, and database.

» When programmers plan the logic for a solution to a programming problem, they often use flowcharts or pseudocode. When you draw a flowchart, you use parallelograms to represent input and output operations, and rectangles to represent processing.

» Variables are named memory locations, the contents of which can vary. As a programmer, you choose reasonable names for your variables. Every computer programming language has its own set of rules for naming variables; however, all variable names must be written as one word without embedded spaces, and should have appropriate meaning.

» Testing a value involves making a decision. You represent a decision in a flowchart by drawing a diamond-shaped decision symbol containing a question, the answer to which is either yes or no. You can stop a program's execution by using a decision to test for a sentinel value.

» A connector symbol is used to continue a flowchart that does not fit together on a page, or must continue on an additional page.

» Most programming languages use the equal sign to assign values to variables. Assignment always takes place from right to left.

» Programmers must distinguish between numeric and text variables, because computers handle the two types of data differently. A variable declaration tells the computer which type of data to expect. By convention, text data values are included within quotation marks.

» Procedural and object-oriented programmers approach program problems differently. Procedural programmers concentrate on the actions performed with data. Object-oriented programmers focus on objects and their behaviors and attributes.

KEY TERMS

Hardware is the equipment of a computer system.

Software consists of the programs that tell the computer what to do.

Input devices include keyboards and mice; through these devices, data items enter the computer system. Data can also enter a system from storage devices such as magnetic disks and CDs.

Data includes all the text, numbers, and other information that are processed by a computer.

Processing data items may involve organizing them, checking them for accuracy, or performing mathematical operations on them.

The **central processing unit**, or **CPU**, is the piece of hardware that processes data.

Information is sent to a printer, monitor, or some other **output** device so people can view, interpret, and work with the results.

Storage devices are the hardware apparatuses that hold information for later retrieval.

Programming languages, such as Visual Basic, C#, C++, Java, or COBOL, are used to write programs.

The **syntax** of a language consists of its rules.

Machine language is a computer's on/off circuitry language.

Binary is a numbering system that uses two values, 0s and 1s.

A **compiler** or **interpreter** translates a high-level language into machine language and tells you if you have used a programming language incorrectly.

Scripting languages (also called **scripting programming languages** or **script languages**) such as Python, Lua, Perl, and PHP are used to write programs that are typed directly from a keyboard and are stored as text rather than as binary executable files.

You develop the **logic** of the computer program when you give instructions to the computer in a specific sequence, without leaving any instructions out or adding extraneous instructions.

A **semantic error** occurs when a correct word is used in an incorrect context.

The **running**, or **executing**, of a program occurs when the computer actually uses the written and translated program.

Internal storage is called **memory**, **main memory**, **primary memory**, or **random access memory (RAM)**.

External storage is persistent (relatively permanent) storage outside the main memory of the machine, on a device such as a floppy disk, hard disk, or flash media.

Internal memory is **volatile**; that is, its contents are lost every time the computer loses power.

You **save** a program on some nonvolatile medium.

An **algorithm** is the sequence of steps necessary to solve any problem.

An **IPO chart** is a program development tool that delineates input, processing, and output tasks.

A **TOE chart** is a program development tool that lists tasks, objects, and events.

Desk-checking is the process of walking through a program solution on paper.

Coding a program means writing the statements in a programming language.

High-level programming languages are English-like.

Machine language is the **low-level language** made up of 1s and 0s that the computer understands.

A **syntax error** is an error in language or grammar.

Logical errors occur when incorrect instructions are performed, or when instructions are performed in the wrong order.

Conversion is the entire set of actions an organization must take to switch over to using a new program or set of programs.

Maintenance consists of all the improvements and corrections made to a program after it is in production.

A **prompt** is a message that is displayed on a monitor, asking the user for a response.

The **command prompt** is the location on your computer screen at which you type entries to communicate with the computer's operating system using text.

A **graphical user interface**, or **GUI** (pronounced "gooey"), allows users to interact with a program in a graphical environment.

The **data hierarchy** represents the relationship of databases, files, records, fields, and characters.

Characters are letters, numbers, and special symbols, such as "A", "7", and "$".

A **field** is a single data item, such as lastName, streetAddress, or annualSalary.

Records are groups of fields that go together for some logical reason.

Files are groups of records that go together for some logical reason.

A **database** holds groups of files, often called tables, that together serve the information needs of an organization.

Queries are questions that pull related data items together from a database in a format that enhances efficient management decision making.

A **flat file** contains records in a file that is not part of a database.

A **flowchart** is a pictorial representation of the logical steps it takes to solve a problem.

Pseudocode is an English-like representation of the logical steps it takes to solve a problem.

Input symbols, which indicate input operations, are represented as parallelograms in flowcharts.

Processing symbols are represented as rectangles in flowcharts.

Output symbols, which indicate output operations, are represented as parallelograms in flowcharts.

Flowlines, or arrows, connect the steps in a flowchart.

A **terminal symbol**, or start/stop symbol, is used at each end of a flowchart. Its shape is a lozenge.

Variables are named memory locations of a specific data type, whose contents can vary or differ over time.

A variable name is also called an **identifier**.

A **mnemonic** is a memory device; variable identifiers act as mnemonics for hard-to-remember memory addresses.

Camel casing is the format for naming variables in which the initial letter is lowercase, multiple-word variable names are run together, and each new word within the variable name begins with an uppercase letter.

Pascal casing is the format for naming variables in which the initial letter is uppercase, multiple-word variable names are run together, and each new word within the variable name begins with an uppercase letter.

An **infinite loop** is a repeating flow of logic without an ending.

Testing a value is also called **making a decision**.

You represent a decision in a flowchart by drawing a **decision symbol**, which is shaped like a diamond.

A yes-or-no decision is called a **binary decision**, because there are two possible outcomes.

A **dummy value** is a preselected value that stops the execution of a program. Such a value is sometimes called a **sentinel value** because it represents an entry or exit point, like a sentinel who guards a fortress.

Many programming languages use the term **eof** (for "end of file") to talk about an end-of-data file marker.

A **connector symbol** is a flowchart symbol used when limited page size forces you to continue the flowchart elsewhere on the same page or on the following page.

An **assignment statement** stores the result of any calculation performed on its right side to the named location on its left side.

The equal sign is the **assignment operator**; it always requires the name of a memory location on its left side.

A **named constant** is a named memory location, similar to a variable, except its value never changes during the execution of a program. Conventionally, constants are named using all capital letters.

Rules of precedence dictate the order the operations in the same statement are carried out.

A **numeric constant** (or **literal numeric constant**) is a specific numeric value.

A **literal string constant**, or **text constant**, is enclosed within quotation marks.

A variable's **data type** describes the kind of values the variable can hold and the types of operations that can be performed with it.

Numeric variables hold numeric values.

Text variables, or **string variables**, hold character values.

A **declaration** is a statement that names a variable and tells the computer which type of data to expect.

Integer values are whole-number, numeric variables.

Floating-point values are fractional, numeric variables that contain a decimal point.

The process of naming program variables and assigning a type to them is called **making declarations**, or **declaring variables**.

The technique known as **procedural programming** focuses on the procedures that programmers create.

The technique known as **object-oriented programming** focuses on objects, or "things," and describes their features, or attributes, and their behaviors.

REVIEW QUESTIONS

1. **The two major components of any computer system are its _____ .**

   a. input and output

   b. data and programs

   c. hardware and software

   d. memory and disk drives

2. **The major computer operations include _____ .**

   a. hardware and software

   b. input, processing, output, and storage

   c. sequence and looping

   d. spreadsheets, word processing, and data communications

3. **Another term meaning "computer instructions" is _____ .**

   a. hardware   c. queries

   b. software   d. data

4. **Visual Basic, C++, and Java are all examples of computer _____ .**

   a. operating systems

   b. hardware

   c. machine languages

   d. programming languages

5. **A programming language's rules are its _____ .**

   a. syntax   c. format

   b. logic   d. options

6. **The most important task of a compiler or interpreter is to _____ .**

   a. create the rules for a programming language

   b. translate English statements into a language such as Java

   c. translate programming language statements into machine language

   d. execute machine language programs to perform useful tasks

7. **Which of the following is a typical input instruction?**

   a. `get accountNumber`

   b. `calculate balanceDue`

   c. `print customerIdentificationNumber`

   d. `total = janPurchase + febPurchase`

8. **Which of the following is a typical processing instruction?**

    a. `print answer`

    b. `get userName`

    c. `pctCorrect = rightAnswers / allAnswers`

    d. `print calculatedPercentage`

9. **Which of the following is *not* associated with internal storage?**

    a. main memory   c. primary memory

    b. hard disk   d. volatile storage

10. **Which of the following pairs of steps in the programming process is in the correct order?**

    a. code the program, plan the logic

    b. test the program, translate it into machine language

    c. put the program into production, understand the problem

    d. code the program, translate it into machine language

11. **The two most commonly used tools for planning a program's logic are _____ .**

    a. flowcharts and pseudocode   c. Java and Visual Basic

    b. ASCII and EBCDIC   d. word processors and spreadsheets

12. **The most important task a programmer must do before planning the logic to a program is _____ .**

    a. decide which programming language to use

    b. code the problem

    c. train the users of the program

    d. understand the problem

13. **Writing a program in a language such as C++ or Java is known as _____ the program.**

    a. translating   c. interpreting

    b. coding   d. compiling

14. **A compiler would find all of the following programming errors *except* _____ .**

    a. the misspelled word "prrint" in a language that includes the word "print"

    b. the use of an "X" for multiplication in a language that requires an asterisk

    c. `newBalanceDue` calculated by adding `customerPayment` to `oldBalanceDue` instead of subtracting it

    d. an arithmetic statement written as `regularSales + discountedSales = totalSales`

15. **Which of the following is true regarding the data hierarchy?**

   a. files contain records   c. fields contain files

   b. characters contain fields   d. fields contain records

16. **The parallelogram is the flowchart symbol representing _____ .**

   a. input   c. both a and b

   b. output   d. none of the above

17. **Which of the following is not a legal variable name in any programming language?**

   a. `semester grade`

   b. `fall2009_grade`

   c. `GradeInCIS100`

   d. `MY_GRADE`

18. **In flowcharts, the decision symbol is a _____ .**

   a. parallelogram   c. lozenge

   b. rectangle   d. diamond

19. **The term "eof" represents _____ .**

   a. a standard input device

   b. a generic sentinel value

   c. a condition in which no more memory is available for storage

   d. the logical flow in a program

20. **The two broadest types of data are _____ .**

   a. internal and external

   b. volatile and constant

   c. text and numeric

   d. permanent and temporary

FIND THE BUGS

Since the early days of computer programming, program errors have been called "bugs." The term is often said to have originated from an actual moth that was discovered trapped in the circuitry of a computer at Harvard University in 1945. Actually, the term "bug" was in use prior to 1945 to mean trouble with any electrical apparatus; even during Thomas Edison's life, it meant an "industrial defect." However, the process of finding and correcting program errors has come to be known as debugging.

Each of the following pseudocode segments contains one or more bugs that you must find and correct.

1. **This pseudocode segment is intended to describe computing your average score of two classroom tests.**

```
input midtermGrade
input finalGrade
average = (inputGrade + final) / 3
print average
```

2. **This pseudocode segment is intended to describe computing the number of miles per gallon you get with your automobile.**

```
input milesTraveled
input gallonsOfGasUsed
gallonsOfGasUsed / milesTravelled = milesPerGallon
print milesPerGal
```

3. **This pseudocode segment is intended to describe computing the cost per day and the cost per week for a vacation.**

```
input totalDollarsSpent
input daysOnTrip
costPerDay = totalMoneySpent * daysOnTrip
weeks = daysOnTrip / 7
costPerWeek = daysOnTrip / numberOfWeeks
print costPerDay, week
```

EXERCISES

1. **Match the definition with the appropriate term.**

   1. Computer system equipment   a. compiler

   2. Another word for programs   b. syntax

   3. Language rules   c. logic

   4. Order of instructions   d. hardware

   5. Language translator   e. software

2. **In your own words, describe the steps to writing a computer program.**

3. Consider a student file that contains the following data:

Last Name	First Name	Major	Grade Point Average
Andrews	David	Psychology	3.4
Broederdorf	Melissa	Computer Science	4.0
Brogan	Lindsey	Biology	3.8
Carson	Joshua	Computer Science	2.8
Eisfelder	Katie	Mathematics	3.5
Faris	Natalie	Biology	2.8
Fredricks	Zachary	Psychology	2.0
Gonzales	Eduardo	Biology	3.1

Would this set of data be suitable and sufficient to use to test each of the following programs? Explain why or why not.

   a. a program that prints a list of Psychology majors

   b. a program that prints a list of Art majors

   c. a program that prints a list of students on academic probation—those with a grade point average under 2.0

   d. a program that prints a list of students on the dean's list

   e. a program that prints a list of students from Wisconsin

   f. a program that prints a list of female students

4. Suggest a good set of test data to use for a program that gives an employee a $50 bonus check if the employee has produced more than 1,000 items in a week.

5. Suggest a good set of test data for a program that computes gross paychecks (that is, before any taxes or other deductions) based on hours worked and rate of pay. The program computes gross as hours times rate, unless hours are over 40. If so, the program computes gross as regular rate of pay for 40 hours, plus one and a half times the rate of pay for the hours over 40.

6. Suggest a good set of test data for a program that is intended to output a student's grade point average based on letter grades (A, B, C, D, or F) in five courses.

7. Suggest a good set of test data for a program for an automobile insurance company that wants to increase its premiums by $50 per month for every ticket a driver receives in a three-year period.

8. Assume that a grocery store keeps a file for inventory, where each grocery item has its own record. Two fields within each record are the name of the manufacturer and the weight of the item. Name at least six more fields that might be stored for each record. Provide an example of the data for one record. For example, for one product the manufacturer is DelMonte, and the weight is 12 ounces.

9. Assume that a library keeps a file with data about its collection, one record for each item the library lends out. Name at least eight fields that might be stored for each record. Provide an example of the data for one record.

10. Match the term with the appropriate shape.

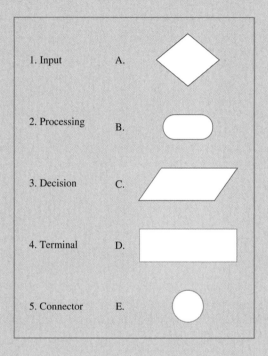

1. Input   A.

2. Processing   B.

3. Decision   C.

4. Terminal   D.

5. Connector   E.

11. Which of the following names seem like good variable names to you? If a name doesn't seem like a good variable name, explain why not.

    a. c

    b. cost

    c. costAmount

    d. cost amount

    e. cstofdngbsns

    f. costOfDoingBusinessThisFiscalYear

    g. cost2004

12. If `myAge` and `yourRate` are numeric variables, and `departmentName` is a string variable, which of the following statements are valid assignments? If a statement is not valid, explain why not.

  a. `myAge = 23`

  b. `myAge = yourRate`

  c. `myAge = departmentName`

  d. `myAge = "departmentName"`

  e. `42 = myAge`

  f. `yourRate = 3.5`

  g. `yourRate = myAge`

  h. `yourRate = departmentName`

  i. `6.91 = yourRate`

  j. `departmentName = Personnel`

  k. `departmentName = "Personnel"`

  l. `departmentName = 413`

  m. `departmentName = "413"`

  n. `departmentName = myAge`

  o. `departmentName = yourRate`

  p. `413 = departmentName`

  q. `"413" = departmentName`

13. Draw a flowchart or write pseudocode to represent the logic of a program that allows the user to enter a value. The program multiplies the value by 10 and prints the result.

14. Draw a flowchart or write pseudocode to represent the logic of a program that allows the user to enter a value that represents the radius of a circle. The program calculates the diameter (by multiplying the radius by 2), and then calculates the circumference (by multiplying the diameter by 3.14). The program prints both the diameter and the circumference.

15. Draw a flowchart or write pseudocode to represent the logic of a program that allows the user to enter two values. The program prints the sum of the two values.

16. Draw a flowchart or write pseudocode to represent the logic of a program that allows the user to enter three values. The first value represents hourly pay rate, the second represents the number of hours worked this pay period, and the third represents the percentage of gross salary that is withheld. The program multiplies the hourly pay rate by the number of hours worked, giving the gross pay; then, it multiplies the gross pay by the withholding percentage, giving the withholding amount. Finally, it subtracts the withholding amount from the gross pay, giving the net pay after taxes. The program prints the net pay.

GAME ZONE

1. In 1952, A. S. Douglas wrote his University of Cambridge Ph.D. dissertation on human-computer interaction, and created the first graphical computer game—a version of Tic-Tac-Toe. The game was programmed on an EDSAC vacuum-tube mainframe computer. The first computer game is generally assumed to be "Spacewar!", developed in 1962 at MIT; the first commercially available video game was "Pong," introduced by Atari in 1973. In 1980, Atari's "Asteroids" and "Lunar Lander" became the first video games to be registered with the U. S. Copyright Office. Throughout the 1980s, players spent hours with games that now seem very simple and unglamorous; do you recall playing "Adventure," "Oregon Trail," "Where in the World Is Carmen Sandiego?," or "Myst"?

   Today, commercial computer games are much more complex; they require many programmers, graphic artists, and testers to develop them, and large management and marketing staffs are needed to promote them. A game might cost many millions of dollars to develop and market, but a successful game might earn hundreds of millions of dollars. Obviously, with the brief introduction to programming you have had in this chapter, you cannot create a very sophisticated game. However, you can get started.

   Mad Libs is a children's game in which players provide a few words that are then incorporated into a silly story. The game helps children understand different parts of speech because they are asked to provide specific types of words. For example, you might ask a child for a noun, another noun, an adjective, and a past-tense verb. The child might reply with such answers as "table," "book," "silly," and "studied." The newly created Mad Lib might be:

   Mary had a little *table*

   Its *book* was *silly* as snow

   And everywhere that Mary *studied*

   The *table* was sure to go.

   Create the logic for a Mad Lib program that prints a message asking the user to provide five words, and then accept those words and create and display a short story or nursery rhyme that uses them.

DETECTIVE WORK

1. Even Shakespeare referred to a "bug" as a negative occurrence. Name the work in which he wrote, "Warwick was a bug that fear'd us all."

2. What are the distinguishing features of the programming language called Short Code? When was it invented?

3. What is the difference between a compiler and an interpreter? Under what conditions would you prefer to use one over the other?

UP FOR DISCUSSION

1. Which is the better tool for learning programming—flowcharts or pseudocode? Cite any educational research you can find.

2. What advantages are there to requiring variables to have a data type?

3. In this chapter, you learned the term *mnemonic*, which is a memory device like the sentence "Every good boy does fine." Another popular mnemonic is "May I have a large container of coffee?" What is its meaning? Have you learned other mnemonics as you have studied various subjects? Describe at least five other mnemonics that people use for remembering lists of items.

4. What is the image of the computer programmer in popular culture? Is the image different in books than in TV shows and movies? Would you like that image for yourself?

UNDERSTANDING STRUCTURE

In this chapter you will:

Learn about the features of unstructured spaghetti code

Understand the three basic structures—sequence, selection, and loop

Use a priming read

Appreciate the need for structure

Recognize structure

Learn about three special structures—case, do-while, and do-until

UNDERSTANDING UNSTRUCTURED SPAGHETTI CODE

Professional computer programs usually get far more complicated than the number-doubling program from Chapter 1, shown in Figure 2-1.

```
get inputNumber
calculatedAnswer = inputNumber * 2
print calculatedAnswer
```

Figure 2-1 Number-doubling program

Imagine the number of instructions in the computer program that NASA uses to calculate the launch angle of a space shuttle, or in the program the IRS uses to audit your income tax return. Even the program that produces your paycheck on your job contains many, many instructions. Designing the logic for such a program can be a time-consuming task. When you add several thousand instructions to a program, including several hundred decisions, it is easy to create a complicated mess. The popular name for logically snarled program statements is **spaghetti code**. The reason for the name should be obvious—the code is as confusing to read as following one noodle through a plate of spaghetti.

For example, suppose you are in charge of admissions at a college and you have decided you will admit prospective students based on the following criteria:

» You will admit students who score 90 or better on the admissions test your college gives, as long as they are in the upper 75 percent of their high-school graduating class. (These are smart students who score well on the admissions test. Maybe they didn't do so well in high school because it was a tough school, or maybe they have matured.)

» You will admit students who score at least 80 on the admissions test if they are in the upper 50 percent of their high-school graduating class. (These students score fairly well on the test, and do fairly well in school.)

» You will admit students who score as low as 70 on your test if they are in the top 25 percent of their class. (Maybe these students don't take tests well, but obviously they are achievers.)

Table 2-1 summarizes the admission requirements.

Test score	High-school rank
90–100	Upper 75 percent (from 25th to 100th percentile)
80–89	Upper half (from 50th to 100th percentile)
70–79	Upper 25 percent (from 75th to 100th percentile)

Table 2-1 Admission requirements

The flowchart for this program could look like the one in Figure 2-2. This kind of flowchart is an example of spaghetti code. Many computer programs (especially older computer programs) bear a striking resemblance to the flowchart in Figure 2-2. Such programs might "work"—that is, they might produce correct results—but they are very difficult to read and maintain, and their logic is difficult to follow.

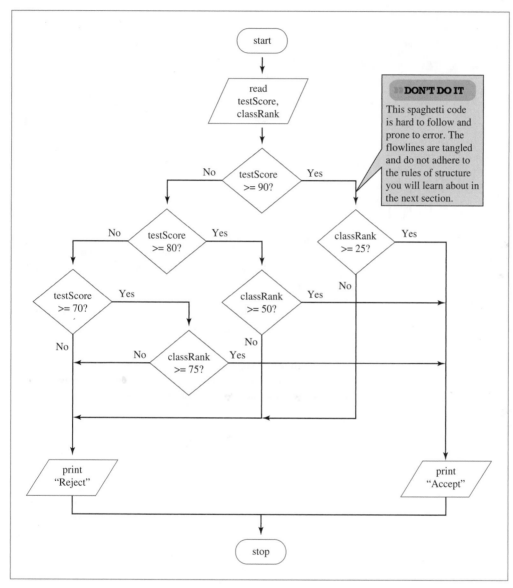

Figure 2-2 Spaghetti code example

UNDERSTANDING THE THREE BASIC STRUCTURES: SEQUENCE, SELECTION, AND LOOP

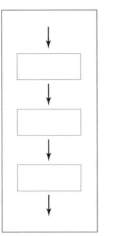

In the mid-1960s, mathematicians proved that any program, no matter how complicated, can be constructed using one or more of only three structures. A **structure** is a basic unit of programming logic; each structure is a sequence, selection, or loop. With these three structures alone, you can diagram any task, from doubling a number to performing brain surgery. You can diagram each structure with a specific configuration of flowchart symbols.

The first of these structures is a sequence, as shown in Figure 2-3. With a **sequence structure**, you perform an action or task, and then you perform the next action, in order. A sequence can contain any number of tasks, but there is no chance to branch off and skip any of the tasks. Once you start a series of actions in a sequence, you must continue step by step until the sequence ends.

Figure 2-3 Sequence structure

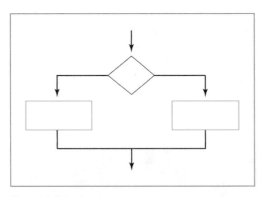

The second structure is called a **selection structure** or **decision structure**, as shown in Figure 2-4. With this structure, you ask a question, and, depending on the answer, you take one of two courses of action. Then, no matter which path you follow, you continue with the next task.

Figure 2-4 Selection structure

Some people call the selection structure an **if-then-else** because it fits the following statement:

```
if someCondition is true then
    do oneProcess
else
    do theOtherProcess
```

For example, while cooking you may decide the following:

```
if we have brownSugar then
    use brownSugar
else
    use whiteSugar
```

Similarly, a payroll program might include a statement such as:

```
if hoursWorked is more than 40 then
    calculate regularPay and overtimePay
else
    calculate regularPay
```

The previous examples can also be called **dual-alternative ifs** (or **dual-alternative selections**), because they contain two alternatives—the action taken when the tested condition is true and the action taken when it is false. Note that it is perfectly correct for one branch of the selection to be a "do nothing" branch. For example:

```
if it is raining then
    take anUmbrella
```

or

```
if employee belongs to dentalPlan then
    deduct $40 from employeeGrossPay
```

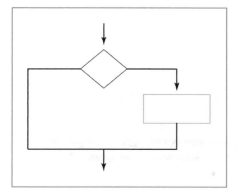

The previous examples are **single-alternative ifs** (or **single-alternative selections**), and a diagram of their structure is shown in Figure 2-5. In these cases, you don't take any special action if it is not raining or if the employee does not belong to the dental plan. The case where nothing is done is often called the **null case**.

Figure 2-5 Single-alternative selection structure

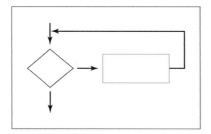

Figure 2-6 Loop structure

The third structure, shown in Figure 2-6, is a loop. In a **loop structure**, you continue to repeat actions based on the answer to a question. In the most common type of loop, you first ask a question; if the answer requires an action, you perform the action and ask the original question again. If the answer requires that the action be taken again, you take the action and then ask the original question again. This continues until the answer to the question is such that the action is no longer required; then you exit the structure. You may hear programmers refer to looping as **repetition** or **iteration**.

Some programmers call this structure a `while...do`, or more simply, a `while` **loop**, because it fits the following statement:

```
while testCondition continues to be true
    do someProcess
```

You encounter examples of looping every day, as in:

```
while you continue to beHungry
    take anotherBiteOfFood
```

or

```
while unreadPages remain in the readingAssignment
    read another unreadPage
```

In a business program, you might write:

```
while quantityInInventory remains low
    continue to orderItems
```

or

```
while there are more retailPrices to be discounted
    calculate a discount
```

All logic problems can be solved using only these three structures—sequence, selection, and loop. The three structures, of course, can be combined in an infinite number of ways. For example, you can have a sequence of tasks followed by a selection, or a loop followed by a sequence. Attaching structures end-to-end is called **stacking** structures. For example, Figure 2-7 shows a structured flowchart achieved by stacking structures, and shows pseudocode that might follow that flowchart logic.

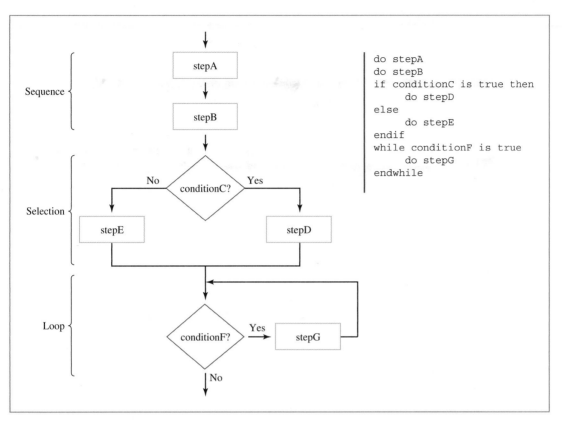

Figure 2-7 Structured flowchart and pseudocode

The pseudocode in Figure 2-7 shows two end-structure statements—endif and endwhile. You can use an endif statement to clearly show where the actions that depend on a decision end. The instruction that follows if occurs when its tested condition is true, the instruction that follows else occurs when the tested condition is false, and the instruction that follows endif occurs in either case—it is not dependent on the if statement at all. In other words, statements beyond the endif statement are "outside" the decision structure. Similarly, you use an endwhile statement to show where a loop structure ends. In Figure 2-7, while conditionF continues to be true, stepG continues to execute. If any statements followed the endwhile statement, they would be outside of, and not a part of, the loop.

> **▶▶ NOTE** Whether you are drawing a flowchart or writing pseudocode, you can use either of the following pairs to represent decision outcomes: yes and no or true and false. This book follows the convention of using yes and no in flow-chart diagrams and true and false in pseudocode.

Besides stacking structures, you can replace any individual tasks or steps in a structured flow-chart diagram or pseudocode segment with additional structures. In other words, any sequence, selection, or loop can contain other sequences, selections, or loops. For example, you can have a sequence of three tasks on one side of a selection, as shown in Figure 2-8. Placing a structure within another structure is called **nesting** the structures.

When you write the pseudocode for the logic shown in Figure 2-8, the convention is to indent all statements that depend on one branch of the decision, as shown in the pseudocode. The indentation and the `endif` statement both show that all three statements (`do stepB`, `do stepC`, and `do stepD`) must execute if `conditionA` is not true. The three statements constitute a **block**, or a group of statements that executes as a single unit.

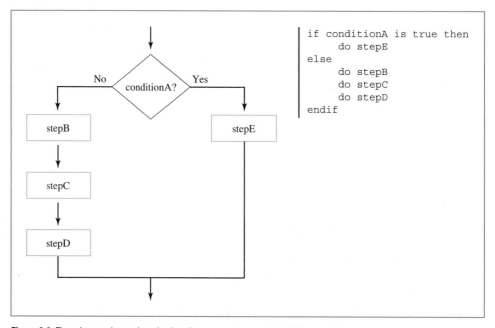

```
if conditionA is true then
      do stepE
else
      do stepB
      do stepC
      do stepD
endif
```

Figure 2-8 Flowchart and pseudocode showing a sequence nested within a selection

In place of one of the steps in the sequence in Figure 2-8, you can insert a selection. In Figure 2-9, the process named `stepC` has been replaced with a selection structure that begins with a test of the condition named `conditionF`.

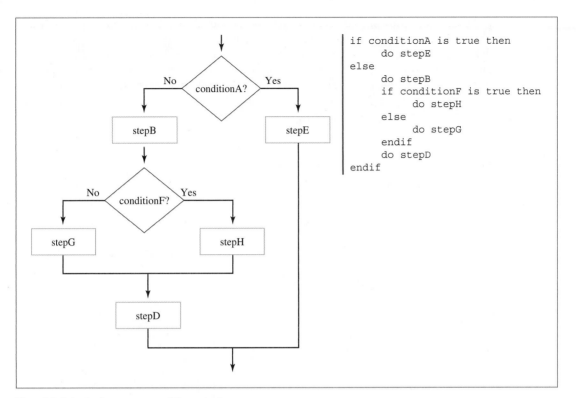

```
if conditionA is true then
      do stepE
else
      do stepB
      if conditionF is true then
            do stepH
      else
            do stepG
      endif
      do stepD
endif
```

Figure 2-9 Selection in a sequence within a selection

In the pseudocode shown in Figure 2-9, notice that the following all align vertically with each other:

```
do stepB
if conditionF is true then
else
endif
do stepD
```

This shows that they are all "on the same level." If you look at the same problem flowcharted in Figure 2-9, you see that you could draw a vertical line through the symbols containing stepB, conditionF, and stepD. The flowchart and the pseudocode represent exactly the same logic. The stepH and stepG processes, on the other hand, are one level "down"; they are dependent on the answer to the conditionF question. Therefore, the do stepH and do stepG statements are indented one additional level in the pseudocode.

Also notice that the pseudocode in Figure 2-9 has two endif statements. Each is aligned to correspond to an if. An endif always partners with the most recent if that does not already have an endif partner, and an endif should always align vertically with its if partner.

In place of do stepH on one side of the new selection in Figure 2-9, you can insert a loop. This loop, based on conditionI, appears inside the selection that is within the sequence that constitutes the "No" side of the original conditionA selection. In the pseudocode in Figure 2-10, notice that the while aligns with the endwhile, and that the entire while structure is indented within the true ("Yes") half of the if structure that begins with the decision based on conditionF. The indentation used in the pseudocode reflects the logic you can see laid out graphically in the flowchart.

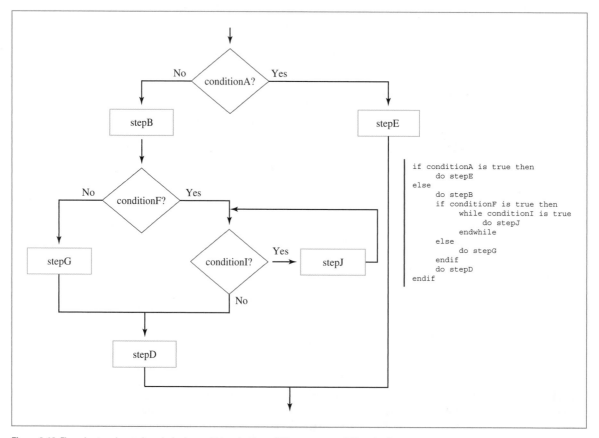

```
if conditionA is true then
        do stepE
else
        do stepB
        if conditionF is true then
                while conditionI is true
                        do stepJ
                endwhile
        else
                do stepG
        endif
        do stepD
endif
```

Figure 2-10 Flowchart and pseudocode for loop within selection within sequence within selection

The combinations are endless, but each of a structured program's segments is a sequence, a selection, or a loop. The three structures are shown together in Figure 2-11. Notice that each structure has one entry and one exit point. One structure can attach to another only at one of these points.

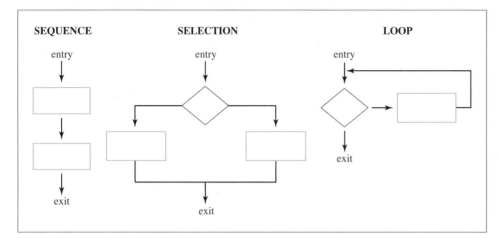

Figure 2-11 The three structures

>> **NOTE** Try to imagine physically picking up any of the three structures using the "handles" marked entry and exit. These are the spots at which you could connect a structure to any of the others. Similarly, any complete structure, from its entry point to its exit point, can be inserted within the process symbol of any other structure.

In summary, a structured program has the following characteristics:

» A structured program includes only combinations of the three basic structures—sequence, selection, and loop. Any structured program might contain one, two, or all three types of structures.

» Structures can be stacked or connected to one another only at their entry or exit points.

» Any structure can be nested within another structure.

>> **NOTE** A structured program is never required to contain examples of all three structures; a structured program might contain only one or two of them. For example, many simple programs contain only a sequence of several tasks that execute from start to finish without any needed selections or loops. As another example, a program might display a series of numbers, looping to do so, but never making any decisions about the numbers.

TWO TRUTHS AND A LIE:
UNDERSTANDING THE THREE BASIC STRUCTURES

1. Each structure in structured programming is a sequence, selection, or loop.

2. All logic problems can be solved using only these three structures—sequence, selection, and loop.

3. The three structures cannot be combined in a single program.

The false statement is #3. The three structures can be stacked or nested in an infinite number of ways.

USING THE PRIMING READ

For a program to be structured and work the way you want it to, sometimes you need to add extra steps. The priming read is one kind of added step. A **priming read** or **priming input** is the statement that reads the first input (whether it is a single data item or a complete data record). For example, if a program will read 100 data records, you read the first data record in a statement that is separate from the other 99. You must do this to keep the program structured.

At the end of Chapter 1, you read about a program like the one in Figure 2-12. The program gets a number and checks for the end-of-file condition. If it is not the end of file, then the number is doubled, the answer is printed, and the next number is input.

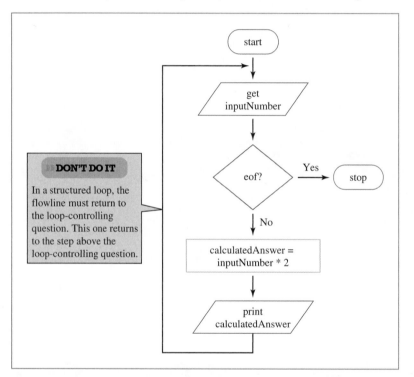

Figure 2-12 Unstructured flowchart of a number-doubling program

Is the program represented by Figure 2-12 structured? At first, it might be hard to tell. The three allowed structures were illustrated in Figure 2-11.

The flowchart in Figure 2-12 does not look exactly like any of the three shapes shown in Figure 2-11. However, because you may stack and nest structures while retaining overall structure, it might be difficult to determine whether a flowchart as a whole is structured. It's easiest to analyze the flowchart in Figure 2-12 one step at a time. The beginning of the flowchart looks like Figure 2-13.

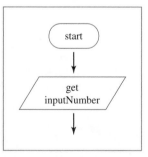

Figure 2-13 Beginning of a number-doubling flowchart

Is this portion of the flowchart structured? Yes, it's a sequence. (Even a single task can be a sequence—it's just a brief sequence.) Adding the next piece of the flowchart looks like Figure 2-14.

The sequence is finished; either a selection or a loop is starting. You might not know which one, but you do know the sequence is not continuing, because sequences can't contain questions. With a sequence, each task or step must follow without any opportunity to branch off. Therefore, which type of structure starts with the question in Figure 2-14? Is it a selection or a loop?

With a selection structure, the logic goes in one of two directions after the question, and then the flow comes back together; the question is not asked a second time. However, in a loop, if the

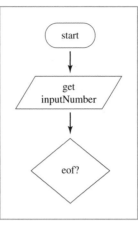

Figure 2-14 Number-doubling flowchart continued

answer to the question results in the loop being entered and the loop statements executing, then the logic returns to the question that started the loop; when the body of a loop executes, the question that controls the loop is always asked again.

In the number-doubling problem in the original Figure 2-12, if it is not eof (that is, if the end-of-file condition is not met), then some math is done, an answer is printed, a new number is obtained, and the eof question is asked again. In other words, while the answer to the eof question continues to be *no*, eventually the logic will return to the eof question. (Another way to phrase this is that while it continues to be true that eof has not yet been reached, the logic keeps returning to the same question.) Therefore, the number-doubling problem contains a structure beginning with the eof question that is more like the beginning of a loop than it is like a selection.

The number-doubling problem *does* contain a loop, but it's not a structured loop. In a structured loop, the rules are:

1. You ask a question.

2. If the answer indicates you should take some action or perform a procedure, then you do so.

3. If you perform the procedure, then you must go right back to repeat the question.

The flowchart in Figure 2-12 asks a question; if the answer is *no* (that is, while it is true that the eof condition has not been met), then the program performs two tasks: it does the arithmetic and it prints the results. Doing two things is acceptable because two tasks with no possible branching constitute a sequence, and it is fine to nest a structure within another structure. However, when the sequence ends, the logic doesn't flow right back to the question. Instead, it goes *above* the question to get another number. For the loop in Figure 2-12 to be a structured loop, the logic must return to the eof question when the embedded sequence ends.

The flowchart in Figure 2-15 shows the flow of logic returning to the eof question immediately after the sequence. Figure 2-15 shows a structured flowchart, but the flowchart has one major flaw—it doesn't do the job of continuously doubling different numbers.

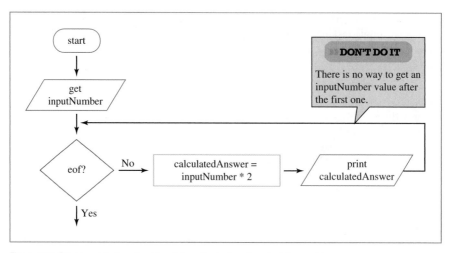

Figure 2-15 Structured, but nonfunctional, flowchart of number-doubling problem

Follow the flowchart in Figure 2-15 through a typical program run. Suppose when the program starts, the user enters a 9 for the value of `inputNumber`. That's not `eof`, so the number is multiplied by 2 and 18 prints out as the value of `calculatedAnswer`. Then the question `eof?` is asked again. It can't be `eof` because a new value representing the sentinel (ending) value can't be entered. The logic never returns to the `get inputNumber` task, so the value of `inputNumber` never changes. Therefore, 9 doubles again and the answer 18 prints again. It's still not `eof`, so the same steps are repeated. This goes on *forever*, with the answer 18 printing repeatedly. The program logic shown in Figure 2-15 is structured, but it doesn't work as intended; the program in Figure 2-16 works, but it isn't structured!

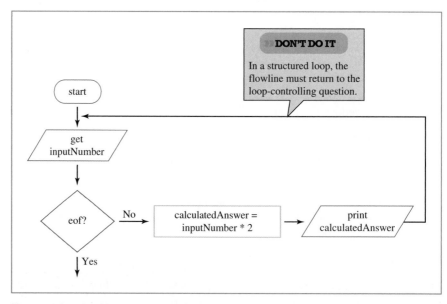

Figure 2-16 Functional, but nonstructured, flowchart

> **NOTE** The loop in Figure 2-16 is not structured because in a structured loop, after the tasks execute within the loop, the flow of logic must return directly to the loop-controlling question. In Figure 2-16, the logic does not return to the loop-controlling question; instead, it goes "too high" outside the loop to repeat the `get inputNumber` task.

How can the number-doubling problem be both structured and work as intended? Often, for a program to be structured, you must add something extra. In this case, it's an extra `get inputNumber` step. Consider the solution in Figure 2-17; it's structured *and* it does what it's supposed to do. The program logic illustrated in Figure 2-17 contains a sequence and a loop. The loop contains another sequence.

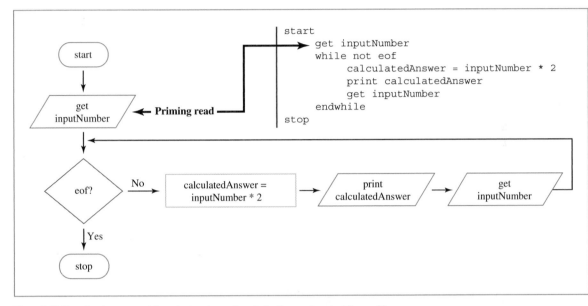

Figure 2-17 Functional, structured flowchart and pseudocode for the number-doubling problem

The additional `get inputNumber` step is typical in structured programs. The first of the two input steps is the priming input, or priming read. The term *priming* comes from the fact that the read is first, or *primary* (what gets the process going, as in "priming the pump"). The purpose of the priming read step is to control the upcoming loop that begins with the eof question. The last element within the structured loop gets the next, and all subsequent, input values. This is also typical in structured loops—the last step executed within the loop alters the condition tested in the question that begins the loop, which in this case is the eof question.

> **NOTE** In Chapter 3 you will learn that the group of preliminary tasks that sets the stage for the main work of a program is called the housekeeping section of the program. The priming read is an example of a housekeeping task.

> **NOTE** In interactive programs, the priming read most often requires two statements—one that displays a prompt such as "Input first number" and another that actually retrieves the number from the user through an input device. Then, the read operation within the repeating loop also requires two statements—its own prompt, such as "Enter next number" or "Enter next number or 0 to quit", and another that retrieves the user's number.

As an additional way to determine whether a flowchart segment is structured, you can try to write pseudocode for it. Examine the unstructured flowchart in Figure 2-12 again. To write pseudocode for it, you would begin with the following:

```
start
    get inputNumber
```

When you encounter the eof question in the flowchart, you know that either a selection or loop structure should begin. Because you return to a location higher in the flowchart when the answer to the eof question is *no* (that is, while the not eof condition continues to be *true*), you know that a loop is beginning. So you continue to write the pseudocode as follows:

```
start
    get inputNumber
    while not eof
        calculatedAnswer = inputNumber * 2
        print calculatedAnswer
```

Continuing, the step after print calculatedAnswer is get inputNumber. This ends the while loop that began with the eof question. So the pseudocode becomes:

```
start
    get inputNumber
    while not eof
        calculatedAnswer = inputNumber * 2
        print calculatedAnswer
        get inputNumber
    endwhile
stop
```

This pseudocode is identical to the pseudocode in Figure 2-17 and now matches the flowchart in the same figure. It does not match the flowchart in Figure 2-12, because that flowchart contains only one get inputNumber step. Creating the pseudocode correctly using the while statement requires you to repeat the get inputNumber statement. The structured pseudocode makes use of a priming read and forces the logic to become structured—a sequence followed by a loop that contains a sequence of three statements.

> **▶▶ NOTE** Years ago, programmers could avoid using structure by inserting a "go to" statement into their pseudocode. A "go to" statement would say something like "after print answer, go to the first get number box", and would be the equivalent of drawing an arrow starting after "print answer" and pointing directly to the first "get number" box in the flowchart. Because "go to" statements cause spaghetti code, they are not allowed in structured programming. Some programmers call structured programming "goto-less" programming.

Figure 2-18 shows another way you might attempt to draw the logic for the number-doubling program. At first glance, the figure might seem to show an acceptable solution to the problem—it is structured, contains a single loop with a sequence of three steps within it, and appears to eliminate the need for the priming input statement. When the program starts, the eof question is asked. The answer is *no*, so the program gets an input number, doubles it, and prints it.

Then, if it is still not eof, the program gets another number, doubles it, and prints it. The program continues until eof is encountered when getting input. The last time the get inputNumber statement executes, it encounters eof, but the program does not stop—instead, it calculates and prints one last time. This last output is extraneous—the eof value should not be doubled and printed. As a general rule, an eof question should always come immediately after an input statement because it is at input that the end-of-file condition will be detected. Therefore, the best solution to the number-doubling problem remains the one shown in Figure 2-17—the solution containing the priming input statement.

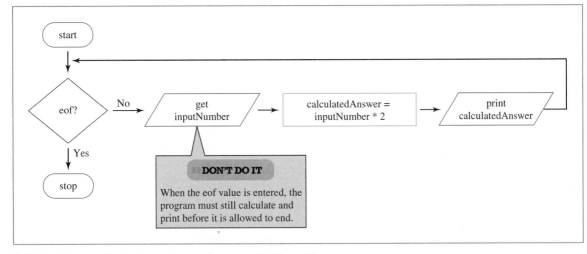

Figure 2-18 Structured but incorrect solution to the number-doubling problem

>> **NOTE** A few languages do not require the priming read. For example, programs written using the Visual Basic programming language can "look ahead" to determine whether the end of file will be reached on the next input record. However, most programming languages cannot predict the end of file until an actual read operation is performed, and they require a priming read to handle file data properly.

TWO TRUTHS AND A LIE:
USING THE PRIMING READ

1. A priming read is the statement that repeatedly reads all the input records in a program.

2. A structured program is sometimes longer than an unstructured one.

3. Some programmers call structured programming "goto-less" programming.

The false statement is # 1. A priming read reads the first input (whether it is a single data item or a complete data record).

UNDERSTANDING THE REASONS FOR STRUCTURE

At this point, you may very well be saying, "I liked the original number-doubling program back in Figure 2-12 just fine. I could follow it. Also, the first program had one less step in it, so it was less work. Who cares if a program is structured?"

Until you have some programming experience, it is difficult to appreciate the reasons for using only the three structures—sequence, selection, and loop. However, staying with these three structures is better for the following reasons:

» *Clarity*—The number-doubling program is a small program. As programs get bigger, they get more confusing if they're not structured.

» *Professionalism*—All other programmers (and programming teachers you might encounter) expect your programs to be structured. It's the way things are done professionally.

» *Efficiency*—Most newer computer languages are structured languages with syntax that lets you deal efficiently with sequence, selection, and looping. Older languages, such as assembly languages, COBOL, and RPG, were developed before the principles of structured programming were discovered. However, even programs that use those older languages can be written in a structured form, and structured programming is expected on the job today. Newer languages such as C#, C++, and Java enforce structure by their syntax.

» *Maintenance*—You, as well as other programmers, will find it easier to modify and maintain structured programs as changes are required in the future.

» *Modularity*—Structured programs can be easily broken down into routines or modules that can be assigned to any number of programmers. The routines are then pieced back together like modular furniture at each routine's single entry or exit point. Additionally, often a module can be used in multiple programs, saving development time in the new project.

Most programs that you purchase are huge, consisting of thousands or millions of statements. If you've worked with a word-processing program or spreadsheet, think of the number of menu options and keystroke combinations available to the user. Such programs are not the work of one programmer. The modular nature of structured programs means that work can be divided among many programmers; then the modules can be connected, and a large program can be developed much more quickly. Money is often a motivating factor—the faster you write a program and make it available for use, the sooner it begins making money for the developer.

Consider the college admissions program from the beginning of this chapter. It has been rewritten in structured form in Figure 2-19 and is easier to follow now. Figure 2-19 also shows structured pseudocode for the same problem.

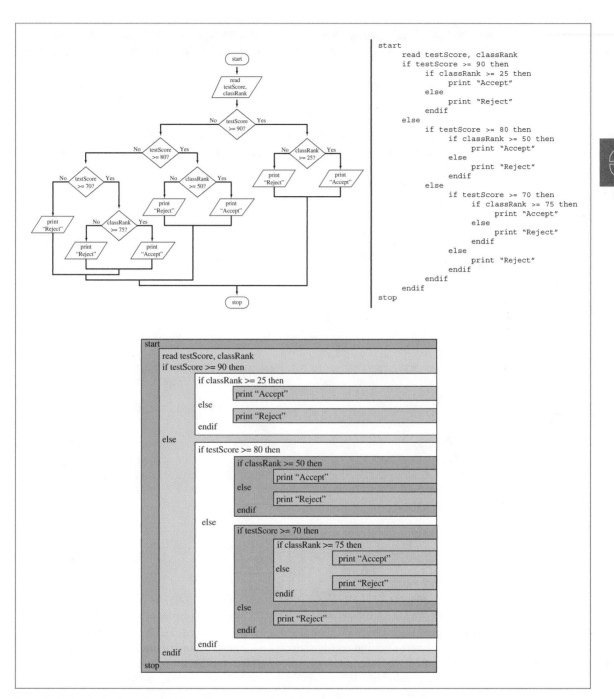

Figure 2-19 Flowchart and pseudocode of structured college admission program

>> **NOTE** Don't be alarmed if it is difficult for you to follow the many nested ifs within the pseudocode in Figure 2-19. After you study the selection process in more detail, reading this type of pseudocode will become much easier for you.

>> **NOTE** In the lower portion of Figure 2-19, the pseudocode is repeated using colored backgrounds to help you identify the indentations that match, distinguishing the different levels of the nested structures.

>> **NOTE** As you examine Figure 2-19, notice that the bottoms of the three testScore decision structures join at the bottom of the diagram. These three joinings correspond to the last three endif statements in the pseudocode.

TWO TRUTHS AND A LIE:
UNDERSTANDING THE REASONS FOR STRUCTURE

1. Structured programs are clearer than those that are not.

2. You, as well as other programmers, will find it easier to modify and maintain structured programs as changes are required in the future.

3. Structured programs are not easily divided into parts, making them less prone to error.

The false statement is #3. Structured programs can be easily broken down into routines or modules that can be assigned to any number of programmers.

RECOGNIZING STRUCTURE

Any set of instructions can be expressed in a structured format. If you can teach someone how to perform any ordinary activity, then you can express it in a structured way. For example, suppose you wanted to teach a child how to play Rock, Paper, Scissors. In this game, two players simultaneously show each other one hand in one of three positions—clenched in a fist, representing a rock; opened flat, representing a piece of paper; or with two fingers extended in a V, representing scissors. The goal is to guess which hand position your opponent might show, so that you can show the one that beats it. The rules are that a flat hand beats a fist (because a piece of paper can cover a rock), a fist beats a hand with two extended fingers (because a rock can smash a pair of scissors), and a hand with two extended fingers beats a flat hand (because scissors can cut paper). Figure 2-20 shows the pseudocode for the game.

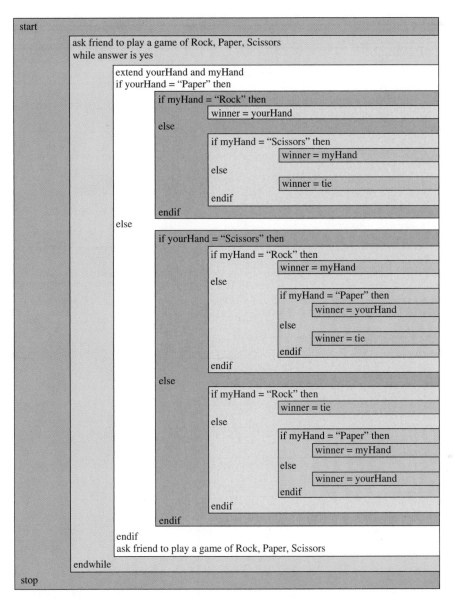

```
start
    ask friend to play a game of Rock, Paper, Scissors
    while answer is yes
        extend yourHand and myHand
        if yourHand = "Paper" then
            if myHand = "Rock" then
                winner = yourHand
            else
                if myHand = "Scissors" then
                    winner = myHand
                else
                    winner = tie
                endif
            endif
        else
            if yourHand = "Scissors" then
                if myHand = "Rock" then
                    winner = myHand
                else
                    if myHand = "Paper" then
                        winner = yourHand
                    else
                        winner = tie
                    endif
                endif
            else
                if myHand = "Rock" then
                    winner = tie
                else
                    if myHand = "Paper" then
                        winner = myHand
                    else
                        winner = yourHand
                    endif
                endif
            endif
        endif
        ask friend to play a game of Rock, Paper, Scissors
    endwhile
stop
```

Figure 2-20 Pseudocode for the Rock, Paper, Scissors game

Figure 2-20 also shows a fairly complicated set of statements. Its purpose is not to teach you how to play a game (although you could learn how to play by following the logic), but rather to convince you that any task to which you can apply rules can be expressed logically using only combinations of sequence, selection, and looping. In this example, a game continues while a friend agrees to play, and within that loop, several decisions must be made in order to determine the winner.

When you are just learning about structured program design, it is difficult to detect whether a flowchart of a program's logic is structured. For example, is the flowchart segment in Figure 2-21 structured?

Yes, it is. It has a sequence and a selection structure.

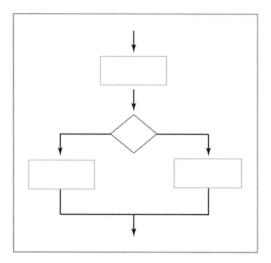

Figure 2-21 Example 1

Is the flowchart segment in Figure 2-22 structured?

Yes, it is. It has a loop, and within the loop is a selection.

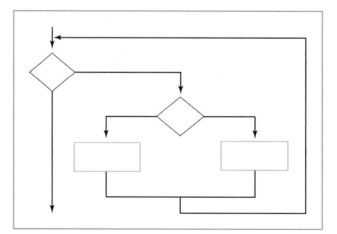

Figure 2-22 Example 2

Is the flowchart segment in Figure 2-23 structured? (The symbols are lettered so you can better follow the discussion.)

No, it isn't; it is not constructed from the three basic structures. One way to straighten out a flowchart segment that isn't structured is to use what you can call the "spaghetti bowl" method; that is, picture the flowchart as a bowl of spaghetti that you must untangle. Imagine you can grab one piece of pasta at the top of the bowl, and start pulling. As you "pull" each symbol out of the tangled mess, you can untangle the separate paths until the entire segment is structured.

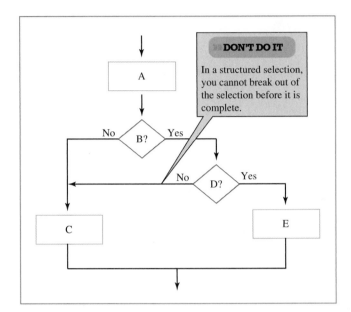

Figure 2-23 Example 3

For example, with the diagram in Figure 2-23, if you start pulling at the top, you encounter a procedure box, labeled A. (See Figure 2-24.)

A single process like A is part of an acceptable structure—it constitutes at least the beginning of a sequence structure. Imagine you continue pulling symbols from the tangled segment.

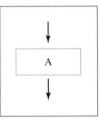

Figure 2-24 Untangling Example 3, first step

The next item in the flowchart is a question that tests a condition labeled B, as you can see in Figure 2-25.

At this point, you know the sequence that started with A has ended. Sequences never have decisions in them, so the sequence is finished; either a selection or a loop is beginning. A loop must return to the question at some later point. You can see from the original logic in Figure 2-23 that whether the answer to B is yes or no, the logic never returns to B. Therefore, B begins a selection structure, not a loop structure.

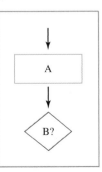

Figure 2-25 Untangling Example 3, second step

To continue detangling the logic, you (imaginarily) pull up on the flowline that emerges from the left side (the "No" side) of Question B. You encounter C, as shown in Figure 2-26. When you continue beyond C, you reach the end of the flowchart.

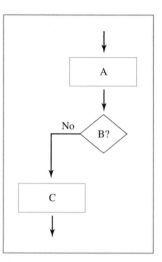

Figure 2-26 Untangling Example 3, third step

Now you can turn your attention to the "Yes" side (the right side) of the condition tested in B. When you pull up on the right side, you encounter Question D. (See Figure 2-27.)

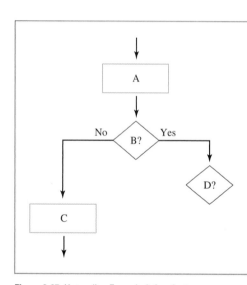

Figure 2-27 Untangling Example 3, fourth step

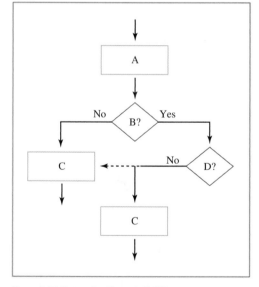

Figure 2-28 Untangling Example 3, fifth step

In the original version in Figure 2-23, follow the line on the left side of Question D. The line extending from the selection is attached to a task outside the selection. The line emerging from the left side of selection D is attached to Step C. You might say the D selection is becoming entangled with the B selection, so you must untangle the structures by repeating the step that is causing the tangle. (In this example, you repeat Step C to untangle it from the other usage of C.) Continue pulling on the flowline that emerges from Step C until you reach the end of the program segment, as shown in Figure 2-28.

Now pull on the right side of Question D. Process E pops up, as shown in Figure 2-29; then you reach the end.

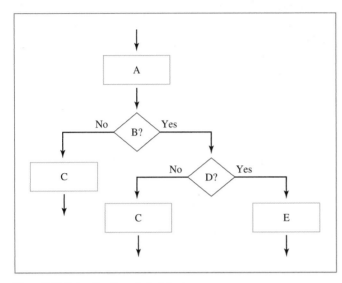

Figure 2-29 Untangling Example 3, sixth step

At this point, the untangled flowchart has three loose ends. The loose ends of Question D can be brought together to form a selection structure; then the loose ends of Question B can be brought together to form another selection structure. The result is the flowchart shown in Figure 2-30. The entire flowchart segment is structured—it has a sequence (A) followed by a selection inside a selection.

» NOTE
If you want to try structuring a very difficult example of an unstructured program, see Appendix A.

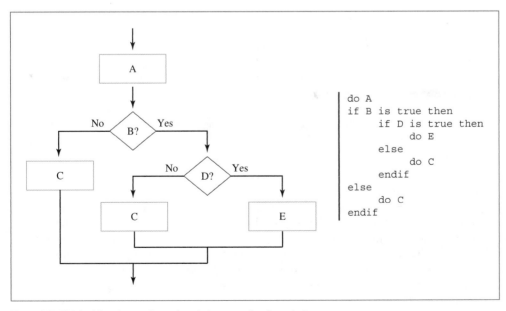

```
do A
if B is true then
        if D is true then
              do E
        else
              do C
        endif
else
        do C
endif
```

Figure 2-30 Finished flowchart and pseudocode for untangling Example 3

TWO TRUTHS AND A LIE:
RECOGNIZING STRUCTURE

1. Most, but not all, sets of instructions can be expressed in a structured format.

2. When you are first learning about structured program design, it can be difficult to detect whether a flowchart of a program's logic is structured.

3. Any unstructured flowchart can be "detangled" to become structured.

The false statement is #1. Any set of instructions can be expressed in a structured format.

THREE SPECIAL STRUCTURES—CASE, DO-WHILE, AND DO-UNTIL

NOTE You can skip this section for now without any loss in continuity. Your instructor may prefer to discuss the case structure with the Decision chapter (Chapter 4) and the do-while and do-until loops with the Looping chapter (Chapter 5).

You can solve any logic problem you might encounter using only the three structures: sequence, selection, and loop. However, many programming languages allow three more structures: the case structure and the do-while and do-until loops. These structures are never *needed* to solve any problem—you can always use a series of selections instead of the case structure, and you can always use a sequence plus a while loop in place of the do-while or do-until loops. However, sometimes these additional structures are convenient. Programmers consider them all to be acceptable, legal structures.

THE CASE STRUCTURE

You can use the **case structure** when there are several distinct possible values for a single variable you are testing, and each value requires a different course of action. Suppose you administer a school at which tuition is $75, $50, $30, or $10 per credit hour, depending on whether a student is a freshman, sophomore, junior, or senior. The structured flowchart and pseudocode in Figure 2-31 show a series of decisions that assigns the correct tuition to a student.

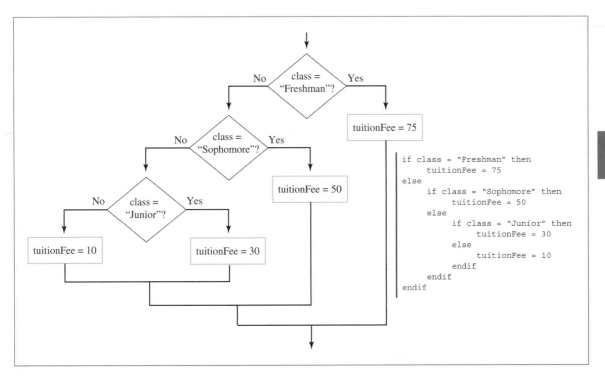

```
if class = "Freshman" then
    tuitionFee = 75
else
    if class = "Sophomore" then
        tuitionFee = 50
    else
        if class = "Junior" then
            tuitionFee = 30
        else
            tuitionFee = 10
        endif
    endif
endif
```

Figure 2-31 Flowchart and pseudocode of tuition decisions

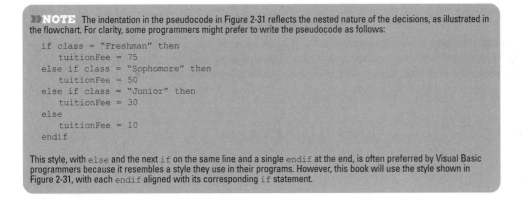

>> **NOTE** The indentation in the pseudocode in Figure 2-31 reflects the nested nature of the decisions, as illustrated in the flowchart. For clarity, some programmers might prefer to write the pseudocode as follows:

```
if class = "Freshman" then
    tuitionFee = 75
else if class = "Sophomore" then
    tuitionFee = 50
else if class = "Junior" then
    tuitionFee = 30
else
    tuitionFee = 10
endif
```

This style, with `else` and the next `if` on the same line and a single `endif` at the end, is often preferred by Visual Basic programmers because it resembles a style they use in their programs. However, this book will use the style shown in Figure 2-31, with each `endif` aligned with its corresponding `if` statement.

The logic shown in Figure 2-31 is absolutely correct and completely structured. The `class = "Junior"` selection structure is contained within the `class = "Sophomore"` structure, which is contained within the `class = "Freshman"` structure. Note that there is no need to ask if a student is a senior, because if a student is not a freshman, sophomore, or junior, it is assumed the student is a senior.

Even though the program segments in Figure 2-31 are correct and structured, many programming languages permit using a case structure, as shown in Figure 2-32. When using the case structure, you test a variable against a series of values, taking appropriate action based on the variable's value. To many, such programs seem easier to read, and the case structure is allowed because the same results *could* be achieved with a series of structured selections (thus making the program structured). That is, if the first program is structured and the second one reflects the first one point by point, then the second one must also be structured.

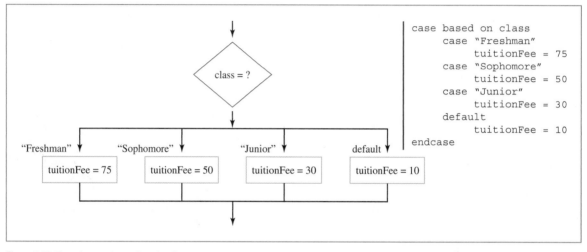

Figure 2-32 Flowchart and pseudocode of case structure

»NOTE
The term "default" used in Figure 2-32 means "if none of the other cases were true." Each programming language you learn may use a different syntax for the default case.

Even though a programming language permits you to use the case structure, you should understand that the case structure is just a convenience that might make a flowchart, pseudocode, or actual program code easier to understand at first glance. When you write a series of decisions using the case structure, the computer still makes a series of individual decisions, just as though you had used many if-then-else combinations. In other words, you might prefer looking at the diagram in Figure 2-32 to understand the tuition fees charged by a school, but a computer actually makes the decisions as shown in Figure 2-31—one at a time. When you write your own programs, it is always acceptable to express a complicated decision-making process as a series of individual selections.

»NOTE You use the case structure only when a series of decisions is based on different values stored in a single variable. If multiple variables are tested, then you must use a series of decisions.

THE DO-WHILE AND DO-UNTIL LOOPS

Recall that a structured loop (often called a while loop) looks like Figure 2-33. A special-case loop called a do-while or do-until loop looks like Figure 2-34.

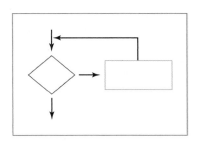

Figure 2-33 The while loop, which is a pretest loop

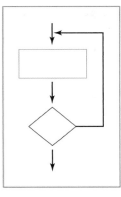

Figure 2-34 Structure of a do-while or do-until loop, which are posttest loops

An important difference exists between these two structures. In a while loop, you ask a question and, depending on the answer, you might or might not enter the loop to execute the loop's procedure. Conversely, in **do-while** and **do-until loops**, you ensure that the procedure executes at least once; then, depending on the answer to the controlling question, the loop may or may not execute additional times. In a do-while loop, the loop body continues to execute as long as the answer to the controlling question is yes, or true. In a do-until loop, the loop body continues to execute as long as the answer to the controlling question is no, or false; that is, the body executes *until* the controlling question is yes or true.

In a while loop, the question that controls a loop comes at the beginning, or "top," of the loop body. A while loop is also called a **pretest loop** because a condition is tested before entering the loop even once. In a do-while or do-until loop, the question that controls the loop comes at the end, or "bottom," of the loop body. Do-while and do-until loops are also called **posttest loops** because a condition is tested after the loop body has executed.

You encounter examples of do-until looping every day. For example:

```
do
    pay a bill
until all bills are paid
```

and

```
do
    wash a dish
until all dishes are washed
```

Similarly, you encounter examples of do-while looping every day. For example:

```
do
    pay a bill
while more bills remain to be paid
```

and

```
do
    wash a dish
while more dishes remain to be washed
```

In these examples, the activity (paying bills or washing dishes) must occur at least one time. With both a do-while and a do-until loop, you ask the question that determines whether

<table>
<tr><td>

» NOTE

Notice that the word "do" begins the names of both the do-while and do-until loops. This should remind you that the action you "do" precedes testing the condition.

</td></tr>
</table>

you continue only after the activity has been executed at least once. The only difference between these two structures is whether the answer to the bottom loop-controlling question must be false for the loop to continue (as in all bills are paid), which is a `do-until` loop, or true for the loop to continue (as in more bills remain to be paid), which is a `do-while` loop.

You are never required to use a posttest loop. You can duplicate the same series of actions generated by any posttest loop by creating a sequence followed by a standard, pretest while loop. For example, the following code performs the bill-paying task once, then asks the loop-controlling question at the top of a `while` loop, in which the action might be performed again:

```
pay a bill
while there are more bills to pay
    pay a bill
endwhile
```

Consider the flowcharts and pseudocode in Figures 2-35 and 2-36.

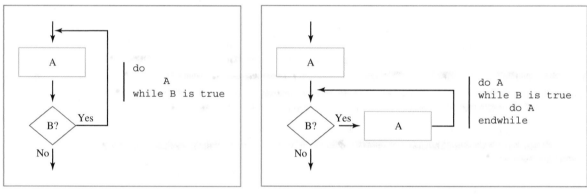

Figure 2-35 Flowchart and pseudocode for `do-while` loop   **Figure 2-36** Flowchart and pseudocode for sequence followed by `while` loop

In Figure 2-35, A is done, and then B is asked. If B is yes, then A is done and B is asked again. In Figure 2-36, A is done, and then B is asked. If B is yes, then A is done and B is asked again. In other words, both flowcharts and pseudocode segments do exactly the same thing.

Because programmers understand that any posttest loop (`do-while` or `do-until`) can be expressed with a sequence followed by a `while` loop, most languages allow at least one of the versions of the posttest loop. (Frequently, languages allow one type of posttest loop or the other.) Again, you are never required to use a posttest loop; you can always accomplish the same tasks with a sequence followed by a pretest `while` loop.

Figure 2-37 shows an unstructured loop. It is neither a `while` loop (which begins with a decision and, after an action, returns to the decision) nor a `do-while` or `do-until` loop (which begins with an action and ends with a decision that might repeat the action). Instead, it begins like a posttest loop (a `do-while` or a `do-until` loop), with a process followed by a decision, but one branch of the decision does not repeat the initial process; instead, it performs an additional new action before repeating the initial process. If you need to use the logic shown in Figure 2-37—performing a task, asking a question, and perhaps performing an additional task before looping back to the first process—then the way to make the logic structured is to repeat the initial process within the loop, at the end of the loop. Figure 2-38 shows the same logic as Figure 2-37, but now it is structured logic, with a sequence of two actions occurring within the loop. Does this diagram look familiar to you? It uses the same technique of repeating a needed step that you saw earlier in this chapter, when you learned the rationale for the priming read.

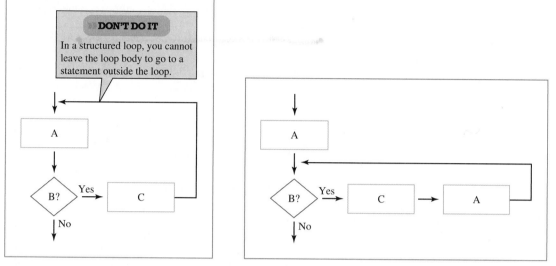

Figure 2-37 Unstructured loop

Figure 2-38 Sequence and structured loop that accomplish the same tasks as Figure 2-37

It is difficult for beginning programmers to distinguish among while, do-while, and do-until loops. A while loop asks the question first—for example, while you are hungry, eat. The answer to the question might never be true and the loop body might never execute. A while loop is the only type of loop you ever need to solve a problem. You can think of a do-while loop as one that continues to execute while a condition remains true—for example, process records while not end of file is true, or eat food while hungry is true. On the other hand, a do-until loop continues while a condition is false, or, in other words, until the condition becomes true—for example, address envelopes until there are no more envelopes, or eat food until you are full. When you use a do-while or a do-until loop, at least one performance of the action always occurs.

NOTE Especially when you are first mastering structured logic, you might prefer to only use the three basic structures—sequence, selection, and while loop. Every logical problem can be solved using only these three structures, and you can understand all of the examples in the rest of this book using only these three.

TWO TRUTHS AND A LIE:

THREE SPECIAL STRUCTURES—CASE, DO-WHILE, **AND** DO-UNTIL

1. You can use the case structure when there are several distinct possible values for a single variable you are testing, and each value requires a different course of action.

2. In do-while and do-until loops, a procedure executes at least once; then, depending on the answer to the controlling question, the loop may or may not execute additional times.

3. A while loop is also called a posttest loop because a condition is tested after the loop body has executed.

The false statement is #3. A while loop is also called a pretest loop because a condition is tested before entering the loop even once. Do-while and do-until loops are also called posttest loops because a condition is tested after the loop body has executed.

CHAPTER SUMMARY

» The popular name for snarled program statements is spaghetti code.

» Clearer programs can be constructed using only three basic structures: sequence, selection, and loop. These three structures can be combined in an infinite number of ways by stacking and nesting them. Each structure has one entry and one exit point; one structure can attach to another only at one of these points.

» A priming read or priming input is the statement that reads the first input data record prior to starting a structured loop. The last step within the loop gets the next, and all subsequent, input values.

» You use structured techniques to promote clarity, professionalism, efficiency, and modularity.

» One way to straighten a flowchart segment that isn't structured is to imagine the flowchart as a bowl of spaghetti that you must untangle.

» You can use a `case` structure when there are several distinct possible values for a variable you are testing. When you write a series of decisions using the `case` structure, the computer still makes a series of individual decisions.

» In a pretest `while` loop, you ask a question and, depending on the answer, you might never enter the loop to execute the loop's body. In a posttest `do-while` loop (which executes as long as the answer to the controlling question is true) or a posttest `do-until` loop (which executes as long as the answer to the controlling question is false), you ensure that the loop body executes at least once. You can duplicate the same series of actions generated by any posttest loop by creating a sequence followed by a `while` loop.

KEY TERMS

Spaghetti code is snarled, unstructured program logic.

A **structure** is a basic unit of programming logic; each structure is a sequence, selection, or loop.

With a **sequence structure**, you perform an action or task, and then you perform the next action, in order. A sequence can contain any number of tasks, but there is no chance to branch off and skip any of the tasks.

With a **selection**, or **decision**, **structure**, you ask a question, and, depending on the answer, you take one of two courses of action. Then, no matter which path you follow, you continue with the next task.

An **if-then-else** is another name for a selection structure.

Dual-alternative ifs (or **dual-alternative selections**) define one action to be taken when the tested condition is true, and another action to be taken when it is false.

Single-alternative ifs (or **single-alternative selections**) take action on just one branch of the decision.

The **null case** is the branch of a decision in which no action is taken.

With a **loop structure**, you continue to repeat actions based on the answer to a question.

Repetition and **iteration** are alternate names for a loop structure.

A **while...do**, or more simply, a **while loop**, is a loop in which a process continues while some condition continues to be true.

Attaching structures end-to-end is called **stacking** structures.

Placing a structure within another structure is called **nesting** the structures.

A **block** is a group of statements that execute as a single unit.

A **priming read** or **priming input** is the statement that reads the first input data record prior to starting a structured loop.

You can use the **case structure** when there are several distinct possible values for a single variable you are testing, and each requires a different course of action.

In **do-while** and **do-until loops**, you ensure that a procedure executes at least once; then, depending on the answer to the controlling question, the loop may or may not execute additional times.

A while loop is also called a **pretest loop** because a condition is tested before entering the loop even once.

Do-while and do-until loops are also called **posttest loops** because a condition is tested after the loop body has executed.

REVIEW QUESTIONS

1. **Snarled program logic is called _____ code.**
   a. snake
   b. spaghetti
   c. string
   d. gnarly

2. **A sequence structure can contain _____ .**
   a. any number of tasks
   b. exactly three tasks
   c. no more than three tasks
   d. only one of task

3. **Which of the following is not another term for a selection structure?**
   a. decision structure
   b. if-then-else structure
   c. dual-alternative if structure
   d. loop structure

4. **The structure in which you ask a question, and, depending on the answer, take some action and then ask the question again, can be called all of the following except _____ .**
   a. iteration
   b. loop
   c. repetition
   d. if-then-else

5. **Placing a structure within another structure is called _____ the structures.**
   a. stacking
   b. untangling
   c. building
   d. nesting

6. **Attaching structures end-to-end is called _____.**
   a. stacking
   b. untangling
   c. building
   d. nesting

7. **The statement `if age >= 65 then seniorDiscount = "yes"` is an example of a _____.**
   a. sequence
   b. loop
   c. dual-alternative selection
   d. single-alternative selection

8. **The statement `while temperature remains below 60, leave the furnace on` is an example of a _____.**
   a. sequence
   b. loop
   c. dual-alternative selection
   d. single-alternative selection

9. **The statement `if age < 13 then movieTicket = 4.00 else movieTicket = 8.50` is an example of a _____.**
   a. sequence
   b. loop
   c. dual-alternative selection
   d. single-alternative selection

10. **Which of the following attributes do all three basic structures share?**
    a. Their flowcharts all contain exactly three processing symbols.
    b. They all contain a decision.
    c. They all have one entry and one exit point.
    d. They all begin with a process.

11. **When you read input data in a loop within a program, the input statement that precedes the loop _____.**
    a. is the only part of a program allowed to be unstructured
    b. cannot result in `eof`
    c. is called a priming input
    d. executes hundreds or even thousands of times in most business programs

12. **A group of statements that execute as a unit is a _____.**
    a. block
    b. family
    c. chunk
    d. cohort

13. **Which of the following is acceptable in a structured program?**
    a. placing a sequence within the true half of a dual-alternative decision
    b. placing a decision within a loop
    c. placing a loop within one of the steps in a sequence
    d. All of these are acceptable.

14. **Which of the following is not a reason for enforcing structure rules in computer programs?**

    a. Structured programs are clearer to understand than unstructured ones.

    b. Other professional programmers will expect programs to be structured.

    c. Structured programs usually are shorter than unstructured ones.

    d. Structured programs can be broken down into modules easily.

15. **Which of the following is not a benefit of modularizing programs?**

    a. Modular programs are easier to read and understand than nonmodular ones.

    b. If you use modules, you can ignore the rules of structure.

    c. Modular components are reusable in other programs.

    d. Multiple programmers can work on different modules at the same time.

16. **Which of the following is true of structured logic?**

    a. You can use structured logic with newer programming languages, such as Java and C#, but not with older ones.

    b. Any task can be described using some combination of the three structures.

    c. Structured programs require that you break the code into easy-to-handle modules that each contain no more than five actions.

    d. All of these are true.

17. **The structure that you can use when you must make a decision with several possible outcomes, depending on the value of a single variable, is the _____ .**

    a. multiple-alternative `if` structure

    b. `do-until` structure

    c. `do-while` structure

    d. `case` structure

18. **Of the following loops, which type ensures that an action will take place at least one time?**

    a. a `do-over` loop

    b. a `while` loop

    c. a `do-until` loop

    d. any structured loop

19. **A `do-until` loop can always be converted to _____ .**

    a. a sequence followed by a `while`

    b. a `while` followed by a sequence

    c. a `case` structure

    d. a selection followed by a `while`

20. **Which of the following structures is never required by any program?**

    a. a `while`

    b. a selection

    c. a `do-until`

    d. a sequence

FIND THE BUGS

Each of the following pseudocode segments contains one or more bugs that you must find and correct.

1. **This pseudocode segment is intended to describe determining whether you have passed or failed a course based on the average score of two classroom tests.**

```
input midtermGrade
input finalGrade
average = (midGrade + finalGrade) / 2
print avg
if average >= 60 then
    print "Pass"
endif
else
    print "Fail"
```

2. **This pseudocode segment is intended to describe computing the number of miles per gallon you get with your automobile. The program segment should continue as long as the user enters a positive value for miles traveled.**

```
input gallonsOfGasUsed
input milesTraveled
while milesTraveled > 0
    milesPerGallon = gallonsOfGasUsed / milesTraveled
    print milesPerGal
endwhile
```

3. **This pseudocode segment is intended to describe computing the cost per day for a vacation. The user enters a value for total dollars available to spend and can continue to enter new dollar amounts while the amount entered is not 0. For each new amount entered, if the amount of money available to spend per day is below $100, a message displays.**

```
input totalDollarsAvailable
while totalDollarsAvailable not = 0
    dollarsPerDay = totalMoneyAvailable / 7
    print dollarsPerDay
endwhile
input totalDollarsAvailable
if dollarsPerDay > 100 then
    print "You better search for a bargain vacation"
endwhile
```

EXERCISES

1. **Match each term with one of the three structure diagrams. (Because the diagrammed structures go by more than one name, there are more terms than diagrams.)**

   C 1. sequence → 5. decision b

   b 2. selection → 6. if-then-else b

   a 3. loop → 7. iteration a

   a 4. do-while

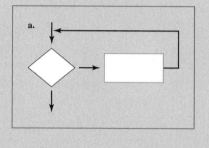
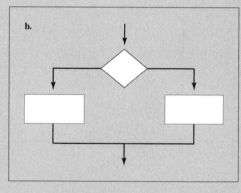
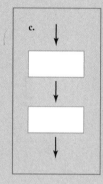

2. **Match the term with the pseudocode segment. (Because the structures go by more than one name, there are more terms than pseudocode segments.)**

1. sequence	4. decision
2. selection	5. if-then-else
3. loop	6. iteration

   a. ```
      while not eof
          print theAnswer
      endwhile
      ```

   Ivy

   b. ```
      if inventoryQuantity  >  0 then
          do fillOrderProcess
      else
          do backOrderNotification
      endif
      ```

   c. ```
      do localTaxCalculation
      do stateTaxCalculation
      do federalTaxCalculation
      ```
      ```

3. **Is each of the following segments structured or unstructured? If unstructured, redraw it so that it does the same thing but is structured.**

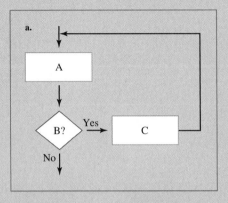

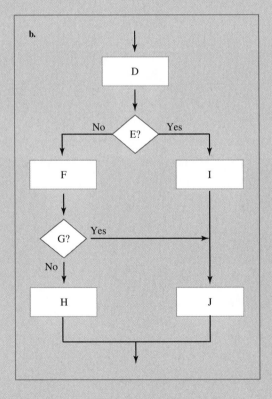

c.

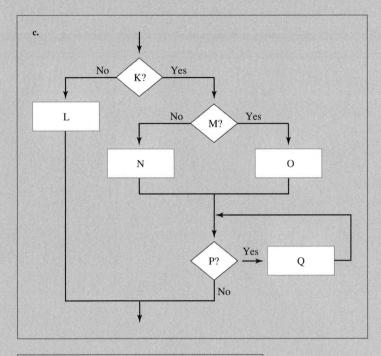

d.

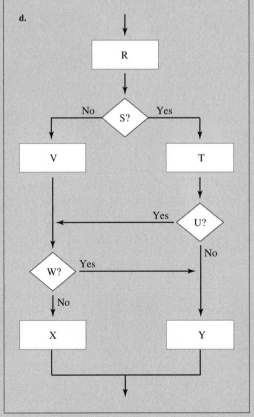

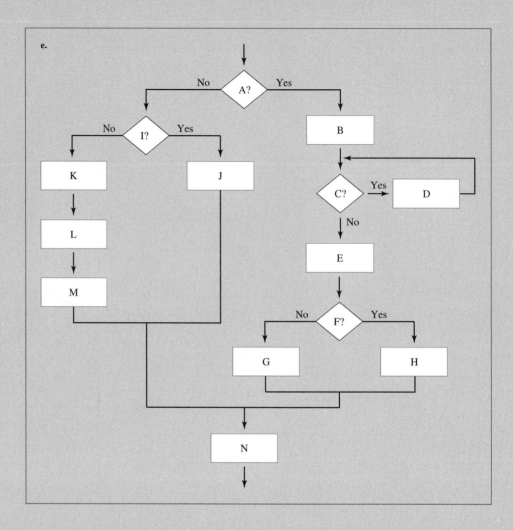

4. **Write pseudocode for each example (a through e) in Exercise 3 making sure your pseudocode is structured but accomplishes the same tasks as the flowchart segment.**

5. **Assume you have created a mechanical arm that can hold a pen. The arm can perform the following tasks:**

   » Lower the pen to a piece of paper.

   » Raise the pen from the paper.

   » Move the pen 1 inch along a straight line. (If the pen is lowered, this action draws a 1-inch line from left to right; if the pen is raised, this action just repositions the pen 1 inch to the right.)

   » Turn 90 degrees to the right.

   » Draw a circle that is 1 inch in diameter.

Draw a structured flowchart or write structured pseudocode describing the logic that would cause the arm to draw the following:

a. a 1-inch square

b. a 2-inch by 1-inch rectangle

c. a string of three beads

d. Write a short word (for example, "cat"). Do not reveal the word to your mechanical arm partner before the partner attempts to carry out your instructions.

Have a fellow student act as the mechanical arm and carry out your instructions.

6. **Assume you have created a mechanical robot that can perform the following tasks:**

» Stand up.

» Sit down.

» Turn left 90 degrees.

» Turn right 90 degrees.

» Take a step.

Additionally, the robot can determine the answer to one test condition:

» Am I touching something?

Place two chairs 20 feet apart, directly facing each other. Draw a structured flowchart or write pseudocode describing the logic that would allow the robot to start from a sitting position in one chair, cross the room, and end up sitting in the other chair.

Have a fellow student act as the robot and carry out your instructions.

7. **Looking up a word in a dictionary can be a complicated process. For example, assume you want to look up "logic." You might proceed by opening the dictionary to a random page and see "juice." You know that word comes alphabetically before "logic," so you flip forward and see "lamb." That is still not far enough, so you flip forward and see "monkey." That means you have gone too far, so now you flip back, and so on. Draw a structured flowchart or write pseudocode that describes the process of looking up a word in a dictionary. Pick a word at random and have a fellow student attempt to carry out your instructions.**

8. **Draw a structured flowchart or write structured pseudocode describing your preparation to go to work or school in the morning. Include at least two decisions and two loops.**

9. **Draw a structured flowchart or write structured pseudocode describing your preparation to go to bed at night. Include at least two decisions and two loops.**

10. **Draw a structured flowchart or write structured pseudocode describing how your paycheck is calculated. Include at least two decisions.**

11. Draw a structured flowchart or write structured pseudocode describing the steps a retail store employee should follow to process a customer purchase. Include at least two decisions.

GAME ZONE

1. Choose a very simple children's game and describe its logic, using a structured flowchart or pseudocode. For example, you might try to explain Musical Chairs; Duck, Duck, Goose; the card game War; or the elimination game Eenie, Meenie, Minie, Moe.

2. Choose a television game show such as *Deal or No Deal* or *Jeopardy*! and describe its rules using a structured flowchart or pseudocode.

3. Choose a professional sport such as baseball or football and describe the actions in one play period using a structured flowchart or pseudocode.

DETECTIVE WORK

1. In this chapter, you learned what spaghetti code is. What is "ravioli code"?

2. Who was Edsger Dijkstra? What programming statement did he want to eliminate?

3. Who were Bohm and Jacopini? What contribution did they make to programming?

4. Who was Grace Hopper? What term did she claim to coin?

UP FOR DISCUSSION

1. Just because every logical program can be solved using only three structures (sequence, selection, and loop) does not mean there cannot be other useful structures. For example, the case, do-while, and do-until structures are never required, but they exist in many programming languages and can be quite useful. Try to design a new structure of your own and explain situations in which it would be useful.

2. Computer programs can contain structures within structures and stacked structures, creating very large programs. Computers can also perform millions of arithmetic calculations in an hour. How can we possibly know the results are correct?

3. Develop a checklist of rules you can use to help you determine whether a flowchart or pseudocode segment is structured.

THE PROGRAM PLANNING PROCESS: DOCUMENTATION AND DESIGN

In this chapter you will:

Learn about documentation

Learn about the advantages of modularization

Learn how to modularize a program

Declare local and global variables and constants

Understand the mainline logic for many procedural
    programs

Create hierarchy charts

Understand the features of good program design

UNDERSTANDING DOCUMENTATION

Documentation refers to all of the supporting material that goes with a program. Two broad categories of documentation are the documentation intended for users and the documentation intended for programmers. People who use completed computer programs are called **end users**, or **users** for short. Most likely, you have been the end user of an application such as a word-processing program or a game. When you purchase software that other programmers have written, you appreciate clearly written instructions on how to install and use the software. These instructions constitute user documentation. In a small organization, programmers may write user documentation, but in most organizations, systems analysts or technical writers produce end-user instructions. These instructions may take the form of a printed manual, or may be presented online through a Web site or on a compact disc.

When programmers begin to plan the logic of a computer program, they require instructions known as **program documentation**. End users never see program documentation; rather, programmers use it when planning or modifying programs.

Program documentation falls into two categories: internal and external. **Internal program documentation** consists of **program comments,** which are nonexecuting statements that programmers place within their code to explain program statements in English. Comments serve only to clarify code; they do not affect the running of a program. Because methods for inserting comments vary, you will learn how to insert comments when you learn a specific programming language.

>> **NOTE**   In Visual Basic, program comments begin with the letters REM (for REMark) or with a single apostrophe. In C++, C#, and Java, comments can begin with two forward slashes (//). Some newer programming languages, such as C# and Java, provide a tool that automatically converts the programmer's internal comments to external documentation.

External program documentation includes all the supporting paperwork that programmers develop before they write a program. Because most programs have input, processing, and output, usually there is documentation for each of these functions.

OUTPUT DOCUMENTATION

Output documentation describes the results the user can see when a program is complete. Output documentation is usually the first type of documentation to be written. This may seem backwards, but if you're planning a trip, which do you decide first: how to get to your destination or where you're going?

Most requests for programs arise because a user needs particular information to be output, so the planning of program output is usually done in consultation with the person or persons who will be using it. Often the programmer does not design the output. Instead, the user who requests the output presents the programmer (or programming team) with an example or sketch of the desired result. Then the programmer might work with the user to refine the request, suggest improvements in the design, or clarify the user's needs.

Only after the desired output is known can the programmer hope to plan the processes needed to produce the output. If you don't determine precisely what the user wants or needs at this point, you will write a program that the user soon wants redesigned and rewritten. The two most common types of output are:

» printed reports

» screen output

DESIGNING PRINTED REPORTS

A very common type of output is a printed report. You can design a printed report on a **printer spacing chart**, which is also referred to as a **print chart** or a **print layout**. Appendix B contains complete details on creating a print chart. Besides using handwritten print charts, you can also design report layouts on a computer using a word-processing program or design software. For example, Figure 3-1 shows the plan for output for an inventory report created using a word processor. In the plan in Figure 3-1, the programmer has used Xs to represent inventory item names and all 9s to represent numeric values. This is a commonly used technique as opposed to making up names and numbers. Additionally, the designer has created only three sample data lines. If a report contains many more data items, it is assumed they will all follow the same format.

```
        INVENTORY REPORT        PRINTED ON 99/99/9999

    ITEM NAME          PRICE     QUANTITY IN STOCK

    XXXXXXXXXXXXXX     999.99          999
    XXXXXXXXXXXXXX     999.99          999
    XXXXXXXXXXXXXX     999.99          999

                       TOTAL:        9999
```

Figure 3-1 Sample inventory report planned using a simple word-processing program

»NOTE In Figure 3-1, each line containing Xs and 9s representing data is a **detail line**, or a line that displays the data details. Detail lines typically appear many times per page, as opposed to **heading lines**, which contain the title and any column headings and usually appear only once per page, and **total** or **summary lines**, which typically appear at the end of a report after all details lines have been printed.

»NOTE
A printed report is also called a **hard copy**, whereas screen output is referred to as a **soft copy**.

Instead of typing sample report lines, more sophisticated report-designing software might allow you to choose data fields from lists that appear on the screen and to drag columns to change their order or appearance. No matter what tool you use, it makes sense to have a plan of how output should appear before deciding how the program should operate.

»NOTE
Achieving good screen design is an art that requires much study and thought to master. Besides being visually pleasing, good screen design also requires ease of use and accessibility.

DESIGNING SCREEN OUTPUT

Not all program output takes the form of printed reports. If your program's output will appear on a monitor screen, particularly if you are working in a GUI (graphical user interface) environment like Windows, your design issues will differ. In a GUI program, the user sees a screen and can typically make selections using a mouse or other pointing device. Instead of a printed report, your output design might resemble a sketch of a screen. Figure 3-2 shows a hand-drawn sketch of a window that displays inventory records in a graphical environment. On a monitor, you might choose to allow the user to see only one or a few records at a time, so one concern is providing a means for users to scroll through displayed records.

»NOTE
You first learned the acronym GUI in Chapter 1.

In Figure 3-2, records are accessed using a single button that the user can click to read the next record; in a more sophisticated design, the user might be able to "jump" to the first or last record, or look up a specific record. Figure 3-3 shows how the design in Figure 3-2 would look after it is incorporated into a running program.

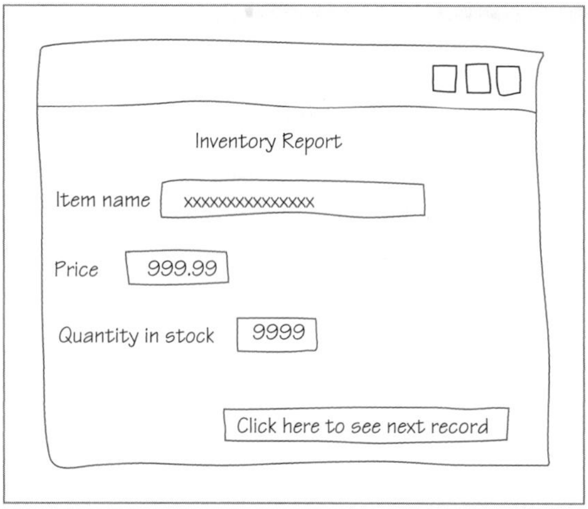

Figure 3-2 Inventory records displayed in a GUI environment

Figure 3-3 Inventory records displayed in a running program

>> **NOTE** GUI programs often include several screen formats that a user sees while running a program. In such cases, you would design several screens.

>> **NOTE** Instead of planning screen output by hand, the tools that are packaged with some programming language compilers allow you to design your output on screen by dragging components onto a form where you can adjust their sizes and positions. In addition, you usually can alter aesthetic features of the GUI components, such as the font used for their text or their color.

>> **NOTE** Some programs do not produce a printed report or screen display, but instead produce an output file that is stored directly on a storage device, such as a disk. If your program produces file output, you will create a file description for your output. Other programs then may use your output file description as an input description. You learn about file descriptions in the next section.

INPUT DOCUMENTATION

Once you have planned the design of the output, you need to know what input is available to produce this output. If you are writing an interactive program that will execute in a GUI environment, you might sketch the screen design. Figure 3-4 shows a sketch for a form that accepts inventory data from the user. Figure 3-5 shows how the screen would look in a running program.

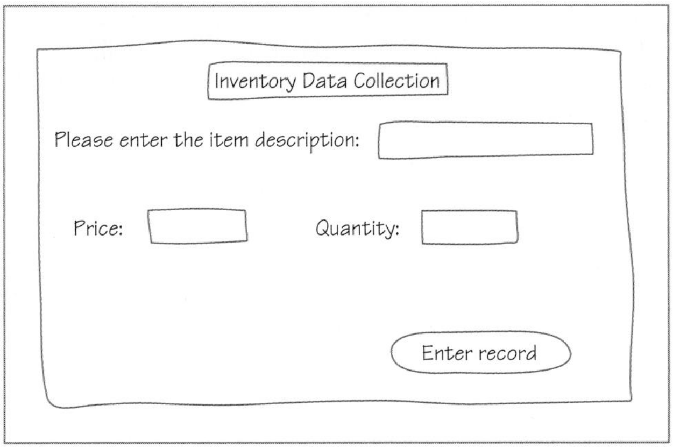

Figure 3-4 Sketch of input screen for inventory data

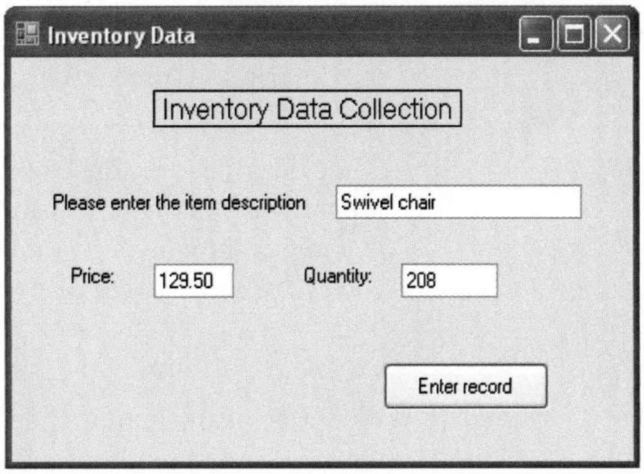

Figure 3-5 Input screen for inventory data during program execution

If you are producing output from data that is not entered interactively, but has already been stored, you frequently will be provided with a **file description** that describes the data contained in a file. You usually find a file's description as part of an organization's information systems documentation; physically, the description might be on paper in a binder in the Information Systems department, or it might be stored on a disk. If the file you will use comes from an outside source, the person requesting the report will have to provide you with a description of the data stored on the file. Figure 3-6 shows an example of an inventory file description.

```
INVENTORY FILE DESCRIPTION
File name: INVENTORY
FIELD DESCRIPTION        DATA TYPE      COMMENTS
Name of item             String         15 characters maximum
Price of item            Numeric        2 decimal places
Quantity in stock        Numeric        0 decimal places
```

Figure 3-6 Inventory file description

>> **NOTE**
Whether input comes from a file or interactively from a user, the logic and the process are very similar.

The inventory file description in Figure 3-6 shows that each item's name is string data that is no longer than 15 characters. Not all file descriptions will identify such a limitation.

Input files can be organized in different ways. For example, in some systems, a field like an item name might occupy exactly 15 characters for each record in a file. Some item names may require all 15 positions allowed for the name in the input file—for example, "12 by 16 carpet", which contains exactly 15 characters, including spaces. Other item names require fewer than the allotted 15 positions—for example, "door mat". In such cases, the remaining allotted positions might remain blank, or the short description might be followed by a string-terminating character. (For example, in some systems, a string is followed by a special character in which all the bits are 0s.) When you add extra characters, such as spaces, to the end of a data field to force it to be a specific size, you are **padding the field**. On the other hand, when only 15 storage positions are allowed for a name, some names might be too long and have to be truncated

» NOTE
Appendix C contains information on how data is coded when it is stored in computer files.

or abbreviated. For example, "hand woven carpet" might be stored as "hand woven carp". Whether the item name requires all 15 positions or not, you can see from the input file description in Figure 3-6 that the price for each item begins after the description name, and if the descriptions are all the same size, then the price begins in position 16 of each input record.

Some data files are constructed so that each field is not the same size. Instead, each field is separated from the next using a predetermined character called a **delimiter**. For example, you might store inventory data using a comma as a delimiter character between each field. If you are using a system that recognizes this format, then you might choose not to pad fields. In other words, an item description is defined to end after any comma, instead of after exactly 15 character positions.

The price of any item in the inventory file in Figure 3-6 is numeric. In different storage systems, a number might occupy a different number of physical file positions, measured in **bytes**. Additionally, numbers with decimal places frequently are stored using more bytes than integer numbers, even when the integer number is a "bigger" number. For example, in many systems, 5678 might be stored in a 4-byte numeric integer field, while 2.2 might be stored in an 8-byte floating-point numeric field. When thinking logically about numeric fields, you do not care how many bytes of storage they occupy; what's important is that they hold numbers. For convenience, this book will simply designate numeric values as such, and let you know whether decimal places are included.

> **» NOTE** Repeated characters whose position is assumed frequently are not stored in data files. For example, dashes in Social Security numbers or telephone numbers, dollar signs on money amounts, or a period after a middle initial are seldom stored in data files. These symbols are used on printed reports, where it is important for the reader to be able to easily interpret these values.

Typically, programmers create one program variable for each field that is part of the input file. In addition to the field descriptions contained in the input documentation, the programmer might be given specific variable names to use for each field, particularly if such variable names must agree with the ones that other programmers working on the project are using. In many cases, however, programmers are allowed to choose their own variable names. Therefore, you can choose `itemName`, `nameOfItem`, `itemDescription`, or any other reasonable one-word identifier when you refer to the inventory item name within your program. The variable names you use within your program need not match constants, such as column headings, that might be printed on a hard copy report. Thus, the variable `itemName` might hold the characters that will print under the column heading "NAME OF ITEM".

For example, examine the input file description in Figure 3-6. When this file is used for a project in which the programmer can choose variable names, he or she might choose the following variable declaration list:

```
string itemName
num itemPrice
num itemQuantity
```

Each data field in the list is declared using the data type that corresponds to the data type indicated in the file description, and has an appropriate, easy-to-read, single-word variable name.

> **NOTE** Some programmers argue that starting each field with a **prefix** indicating the file name (for example, "item" in `itemName` and `itemPrice`) helps to identify those variables as "belonging together." Others argue that repeating the "item" prefix is redundant and requires unnecessary typing by the programmer; these programmers would argue that `name`, `price`, and `quantity` are descriptive enough.

> **NOTE** When a programmer uses an identifier like `itemName`, that variable identifier exists in computer memory only for the duration of the program in which the variable is declared. Another program can use the same input file and refer to the same field as `nameOfItem`. Variable names exist in memory during the run of a program—they are not stored in the data file. Variable names simply represent memory addresses at which pieces of data are stored while a program executes.

Recall the data hierarchy relationship introduced in Chapter 1:

» Database
» File
» Record
» Field
» Character

Whether the inventory file is part of a database or not, it will contain many records; each record will contain an item name, price, and quantity, which are fields. In turn, the field that holds the name of an item might contain up to 15 characters—for example, "12 by 16 carpet", "blue miniblinds", or "plastic CD case".

Organizations may use different forms to relay the information about records and fields, but the very least the programmer needs to know is:

» What is the name of the file?
» What data fields does it contain, and in what order?
» What type of data can be stored in each field—text or numeric?

Notice that a data field's position on the input file never has to correspond with the same item's position in an output file, on a screen, or in a printed report. For example, you can use the data file described in Figure 3-6 to produce a report in which each line contains the three field values in any order. In other words, you might display the quantity first, followed by the description and price. Alternately, you might choose to not display some fields. For example, you might design a report that displays only item descriptions and quantities, omitting prices.

> **NOTE** You are never required to output all the available characters that exist in a field in an input record. For example, even though the item name in the input file description in Figure 3-6 shows that each item contains up to 15 stored characters, you might decide to display only 10 of them on output, especially if your output report contained many columns and you were "crunched" for space.

The inventory file description in Figure 3-6 contains all the data the programmer needs to create the output requested in Figure 3-1 or 3-2—the output lists each item's name, price, and quantity, and the input records clearly contain that data. Often, however, a file description contains more data than any one program requires. For example, your credit card company stores historical data about your past purchases, but these are not included on every bill. Similarly, your school records contain more data than are printed on each report card or tuition bill.

Each value that is output does not need to come from input. For example, assume that a user requests a report in the format shown in the example in Figure 3-7, which includes a column labeled "Discounted Price", and that the input file description is the one in Figure 3-4. Also assume the discounted price is 75 percent of the original price. In this case, the data in the "Discounted Price" column is calculated within the program.

```
DISCOUNTED PRICES REPORT        PRINTED ON 99/99/9999

ITEM NAME           PRICE     DISCOUNTED PRICE

XXXXXXXXXXXXXX      999.99         999.99
XXXXXXXXXXXXXX      999.99         999.99
XXXXXXXXXXXXXX      999.99         999.99
```

Figure 3-7 Plan for discounted prices report

COMPLETING THE DOCUMENTATION

When you have designed the output and confirmed that it is possible to produce it from the input, then you can plan the logic of the program, code the program, and test the program. The original output design, input description, flowchart or pseudocode, and program code all become part of the program documentation. These pieces of documentation are typically stored together in a binder within the programming department of an organization, where they can be studied later when program changes become necessary.

In addition to this program documentation, you typically must create user documentation. **User documentation** includes all the manuals or other instructional materials that nontechnical people use, as well as the operating instructions that computer operators and data-entry personnel need. It needs to be written clearly, in plain language, with reasonable expectations of the users' expertise. Within a small organization, the programmer may prepare the user documentation. In a large organization, user documentation is usually prepared by technical writers or systems analysts, who oversee programmers' work and coordinate programmers' efforts. These professionals consult with the programmers to ensure that the user documentation is complete and accurate.

The areas addressed in user documentation may include:

- » How to prepare input for the program
- » To whom the output should be distributed
- » How to interpret the normal output
- » How to interpret and react to any error message generated by the program
- » How frequently the program needs to run

»NOTE Complete documentation might also include operations support documentation. This type of documentation provides backup and recovery information, run-time instructions, and security considerations for computer center personnel who run large applications within data centers.

All these issues must be addressed before a program can be fully functional in an organization. When users throughout an organization can supply input data to computer programs and obtain the information they need to do their jobs well, then a skilled programmer has provided a complete piece of work.

UNDERSTANDING THE ADVANTAGES OF MODULARIZATION

Programmers seldom write programs as one long series of steps. Instead, they break down the programming problem into reasonable units, and tackle one small task at a time. These reasonable units are called **modules**. Programmers also refer to them as **subroutines**, **procedures**, **functions**, or **methods**.

> **NOTE** The name that programmers use for their modules usually reflects the programming language they use. For example, Visual Basic programmers use "procedure" (or "subprocedure"). C and C++ programmers call their modules "functions," whereas C#, Java, and other object-oriented language programmers are more likely to use "method." Programmers in COBOL, RPG, and BASIC (all older languages) are most likely to use "subroutine."

To execute a method, you **invoke** it or **call** it from another program or method; the **calling method** invokes the **called method**. Any program can contain an unlimited number of methods, and each method can be called an unlimited number of times. Within a program, the simplest methods you can invoke don't require any data items to be sent to them, nor do they send any data back to you. You will learn about methods that receive and return data in Chapter 7.

The process of breaking down a large program into modules is called **modularization**. You are never required to break down a large program into modules in order to make it run on a computer, but there are at least three reasons for doing so:

» Modularization provides abstraction.

» Modularization allows multiple programmers to work on a problem.

» Modularization allows you to reuse your work.

MODULARIZATION PROVIDES ABSTRACTION

One reason modularized programs are easier to understand is that they enable a programmer to see the big picture. **Abstraction** is the process of paying attention to important properties

Aburrido

while ignoring nonessential details. Abstraction is selective ignorance. Life would be <u>tedious</u> without abstraction. For example, you can create a list of things to accomplish today:

```
Do laundry
Call Aunt Nan
Start term paper
```

Without abstraction, the list of chores would begin:

```
Pick up laundry basket
Put laundry basket in car
Drive to laundromat
Get out of car with basket
Walk into laundromat
Set basket down
Find quarters for washing machine
. . . and so on.
```

You might list a dozen more steps before you finish the laundry and move on to the second chore on your original list. If you had to consider every small, **low-level detail** of every task in your day, you would probably never make it out of bed in the morning. Using a higher-level, more abstract list makes your day manageable. Abstraction makes complex tasks look simple.

Likewise, some level of abstraction occurs in every computer program. Fifty years ago, a programmer had to understand the low-level circuitry instructions the computer used. But now, newer **high-level programming languages** allow you to use English-like vocabulary in which one broad statement corresponds to dozens of machine instructions. No matter which high-level programming language you use, if you display a message on the monitor, you are never required to understand how a monitor works to create each pixel on the screen. You write an instruction like `print message` and the details of the hardware operations are handled for you.

Modules or subroutines provide another way to achieve abstraction. For example, a payroll program can call a module named `computeFederalWithholdingTax()`. You can write the mathematical details of the function later, someone else can write them, or you can purchase them from an outside source. When you plan your main payroll program, your only concern is that a federal withholding tax will have to be calculated; you save the details for later.

MODULARIZATION ALLOWS MULTIPLE PROGRAMMERS TO WORK ON A PROBLEM

examiner

When you dissect any large task into modules, you gain the ability to divide the task among various people. Rarely does a single programmer write a commercial program that you buy. Consider any word-processing, spreadsheet, or database program you have used. Each program has so many options, and responds to user selections in so many possible ways, that it would take years for a single programmer to write all the instructions. Professional software developers can write new programs in weeks or months, instead of years, by dividing large programs into modules and assigning each module to an individual programmer or programming team.

MODULARIZATION ALLOWS YOU TO REUSE YOUR WORK

If a subroutine or function is useful and well written, you may want to use it more than once within a program or in other programs. For example, a routine that checks the current date to make sure it is valid (the month is not lower than 1 or higher than 12, the day is not lower than 1 or higher than 31 if the month is 1, and so on) is useful in many programs written for a business. A program that uses a personnel file containing each employee's birth date, hire date, last promotion date, and termination date can use the date-validation module four times with each employee record. Other programs in an organization can also use the module; these include programs that ship customer orders, plan employees' birthday parties, and calculate when loan payments should be made. If you write the date-checking instructions so they are entangled with other statements in a program, they are difficult to extract and reuse. On the other hand, if you place the instructions in their own module, the unit is easy to use and portable to other applications. The feature of modular programs that allows individual modules to be used in a variety of applications is known as **reusability**.

You can find many real-world examples of reusability. When you build a house, you don't invent plumbing and heating systems; you incorporate systems with proven designs. This certainly reduces the time and effort it takes to build a house. Assuming the plumbing and electrical systems you choose are in service in other houses, they also improve the reliability of your house's systems—they have been tested under a variety of circumstances and have been proven to function correctly. Similarly, software that is reusable is more reliable. **Reliability** is the feature of programs that assures you a module has been tested and proven to function correctly. Reliable software saves time and money. If you create the functional components of your programs as stand-alone modules and test them in your current programs, much of the work will already be done when you use the modules in future applications.

> **》NOTE** Modularization also makes it easier to identify structures because the program units are manageable in size. A professional programmer will never modularize simply to *identify* whether a program is structured—he or she modularizes for reasons of abstraction, ease of dividing the work, and reusability. However, for a beginning programmer, being able to see and identify structure is important.

> **》NOTE** Reducing a large program into more manageable modules is sometimes called **functional decomposition**.

> ### TWO TRUTHS AND A LIE:
> #### UNDERSTANDING THE ADVANTAGES OF MODULARIZATION
>
> 1. Modularization eliminates abstraction, a feature that makes programs more confusing.
> 2. Modularization allows multiple programmers to work on a problem.
> 3. Modularization allows you to more easily reuse your work.
>
> The false statement is #1. Modularization enables abstraction, which allows you to more easily see the big picture.

MODULARIZING A PROGRAM

Most programs consist of a **main program** (or **main program method**) which contains the mainline logic; this module then accesses other modules or subroutines. When you create a module or subroutine, you give it an identifying name. The rules for naming modules are different in every programming language, but they are often similar to the language's rules for variable names. In this text, module names follow the same two rules used for variable identifiers:

» Module names must be one word.
» Module names should have some meaning.

Additionally, in this text, module names are followed by a set of parentheses. This will help you distinguish module names from variable names. This style corresponds to the way modules are named in many programming languages, such as Java, C++, and C#.

Table 3-1 lists some possible module names for a module that calculates an employee's gross pay, and provides a rationale for the appropriateness of each one.

Suggested Module Names	Comments
Superior identifiers	
calculateGrossPay()	Good
calculateGross()	Good—most people would interpret "Gross" to be short for "Gross pay"
Inferior or illegal identifiers	
calGrPy()	Legal, but cryptic
calculateGrossPayForOneEmployee()	Legal, but awkward
calculate gross()	Not legal—embedded space
calculategrosspay()	Legal, but hard to read without camel casing

DON'T DO IT

These identifiers are not recommended.

Table 3-1 Suggested identifiers for a module that calculates an employee's gross pay

>>**NOTE** As you learn more about modules in specific programming languages, you will find that you sometimes place variable names within the parentheses of module names. Any variables enclosed in the parentheses contain information you want to send to the module. For now, the parentheses we use at the end of module names will be empty.

>>**NOTE** Most programming languages require that module names begin with an alphabetic character. This text follows that convention.

>>**NOTE** Although it is not a requirement of any programming language, it frequently makes sense to use a verb as all or part of a module's name, because modules perform some action. Typical module names begin with words such as get, calculate, and print. When you program in visual languages that use screen components such as buttons and text boxes, the module names frequently contain verbs representing user actions, such as "click and drag."

When a program or module uses another module, you refer to the main program as the calling program (or calling module), because it "calls" the module's name when it wants to use the module. The flowchart symbol used to call a module is a rectangle with a bar across the top. You place the name of the module you are calling inside the rectangle.

>> **NOTE** When one module calls another, the called module is a **submodule**.

>> **NOTE** Instead of placing only the name of the module they are calling in the flowchart, many programmers insert an appropriate verb, such as "perform" or "do," before the module name. These verbs help clarify that the module represents an action to be carried out.

>> **NOTE** A module can call another module, and the called module can call another. The number of chained calls is limited only by the amount of memory available on your computer.

In a flowchart, you draw each module separately with its own sentinel symbols. The symbol that is the equivalent of the `start` symbol in a program contains the name of the module. This name must be identical to the name used in the calling program. The symbol that is the equivalent of the `stop` symbol in a program does not contain "stop"; after all, the program is not ending. Instead, the module ends with a "gentler," less final term, such as `exit` or `return`. These words correctly indicate that when the module ends, the logical progression of statements will exit the module and return to the calling program. Similarly, in pseudocode, you start each module with its name, and end with a `return` or `exit` statement; the module name and return statements are vertically aligned and all the module statements are indented between them.

>> **NOTE** When you call a module, the action is similar to putting a DVD player on pause. You abandon your first action (watching a video), take care of some other task (for example, making a sandwich), and when the secondary task is complete, you return to the main task exactly where you left off.

For example, consider the logic in Figure 3-8. Its generic steps might represent any actions, but you should be able to tell the steps are structured. The sequence A is followed by a selection, represented by B. The condition B starts a selection structure with a sequence followed by a selection when B is true, and a sequence when B is false. The second selection, represented by G is nested within the B selection, and it contains a sequence.

If you examine the steps in Figure 3-8, you can see that the sequence represented by H, I, and J occurs in two locations. It is perfectly acceptable to have the same tasks performed in different program locations under different conditions, but when the same tasks are repeated in different places, it can be convenient to create a method that is called at each location where it should execute.

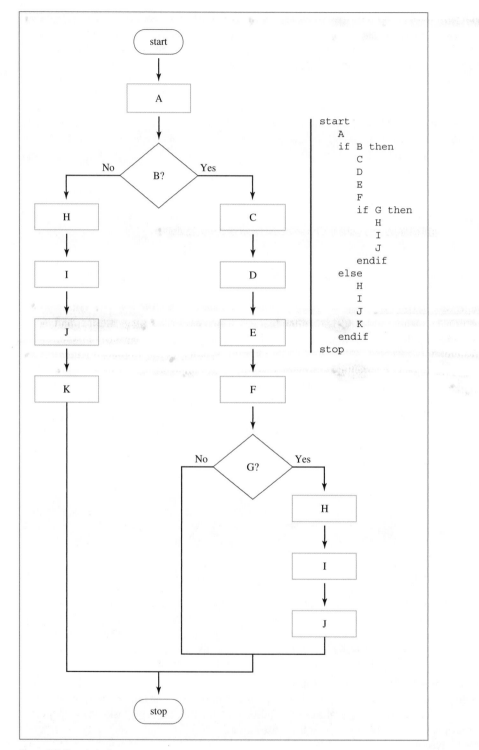

Figure 3-8 Sample logic

Figure 3-9 shows the same logic as Figure 3-8, but the three statements, H, I, and J, have been contained, or **encapsulated**, into a method named methodHtoJ(). The method has its own terminals (see shading), and it contains a sequence composed of the three actions. When the logic in the original segment is ready to execute the three statements, it calls the method. (See the two shaded calls in the figure.) In the flowchart, the method calls are represented by process symbols that contain a stripe across the top. When you see the stripe you understand that the symbol represents a module that might contain many steps. In the pseudocode, the method call is indicated by using the method's name when you want to call it. (Remember, you can tell it is a method because it is followed by parentheses.) In the program in Figure 3-9, the individual steps H, I, and J need only be written once and they can be called as a unit from multiple program locations.

>> **NOTE** Some programmers use a rectangle with stripes down each side to represent a module in a flowchart. This book uses the convention that if a module is external to a program, then a rectangle with side stripes is used, but if the module is part of the program, as is the case in all examples in this chapter, then a rectangle with a single stripe across the top is used. Many programming languages come with built-in methods that you do not write. For example, a language might come with a method that generates a random number or computes a trigonometric function. Such methods are external to your programs. If you create the Game Zone guessing game at the end of this chapter, you should use the external module symbol to represent the statement that generates a random number.

>> **NOTE** Whenever a main program calls a module, the logic transfers to the called module. When the called module ends, the logical flow transfers back to the main calling program and resumes where it left off. The computer keeps track of the correct memory address to which it should return after executing a module by recording the memory address in a location known as the **stack**.

In Figure 3-10, the same logic has been modularized even further. The steps C, D, E, and F have been placed into their own method, not to save repeating them (because they are not repeated anywhere in the program), but just to group them. Just as it is more convenient for you to say, "Bake a cake," than it is for you to say, "Get out a mixing bowl, get a cup of sugar, get 3 eggs" and so on, it can be clearer and more convenient to be able to call a method name and have the specific directions listed elsewhere. Creating submethods makes the calling method's logic more concise, easier to read, and somewhat easier to identify as structured. You would not want to place steps C through F into their own method without a good reason or if they were unrelated, but you would do so if they represent four closely related steps, and especially if they represent steps to a process that might be needed by another program at some future point in time.

Deciding which steps to place in their own methods is an art, and two programmers certainly might disagree on which steps to modularize in any given program. However, creating methods makes large programs easier to manage, and in very large programs, allows the work to be split up among multiple programmers more easily. No matter how many methods a program contains, however, each one must be structured, containing only some combination of sequence, selection, and loop structures, and each must be called as part of a larger program that is also structured.

>> **NOTE** Methods are crucial to modern programming. You will learn much more about their construction later in this book. For now, as you work through the sample programs in the next few chapters, try to envision how they might logically be divided in smaller, more concise modules.

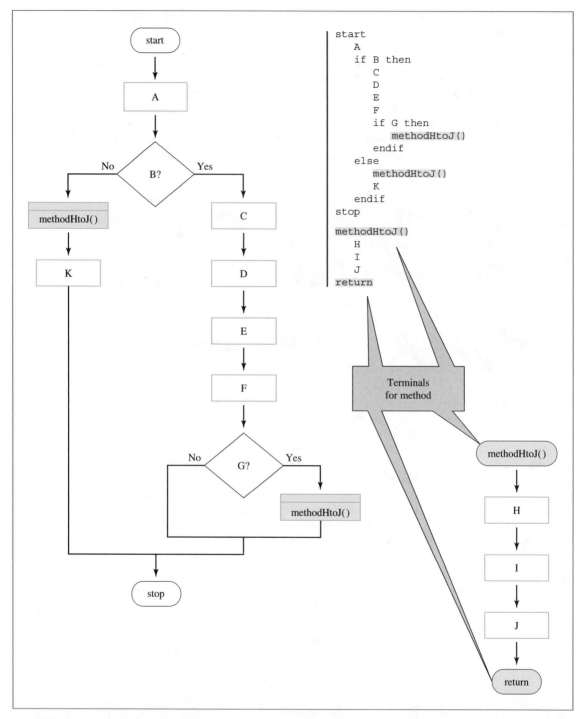

Figure 3-9 Logic from Figure 3-8 using a method

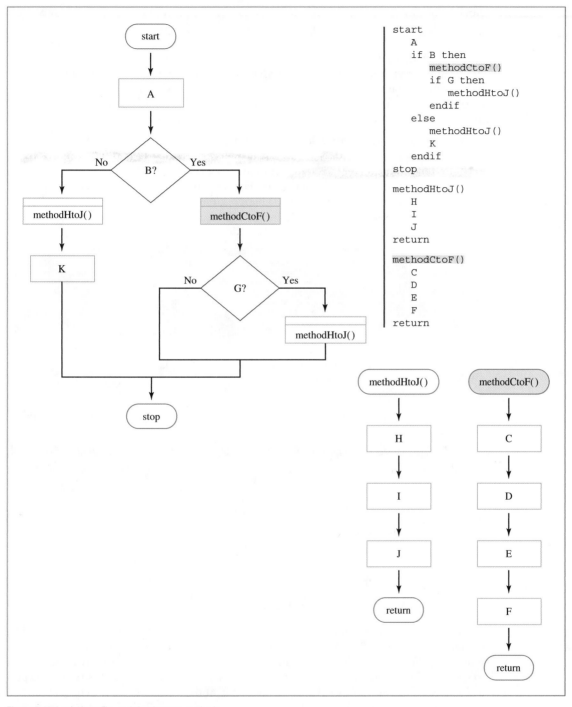

Figure 3-10 Logic from Figure 3-9 using two methods

None of the program segments shown in Figures 3-8, 3-9, and 3-10 is superior to the others in terms of functionality, but you may prefer to modularize to help you divide or reuse the work. Determining when to break down any particular module into its own subroutines or submodules does not depend on any fixed set of rules; it requires experience and insight. Programmers do follow some guidelines when deciding how far to break down subroutines, or how much to put in each of them. Some companies may have arbitrary rules, such as "a subroutine should never take more than a page," or "a module should never have more than 30 statements in it," or "never have a method or function with only one statement in it."

Rather than use such arbitrary rules, a better policy is to place together statements that contribute to one specific task. The more the statements contribute to the same job, the greater the **functional cohesion** of the module. A routine that checks the validity of a date variable's value, or one that prompts a user and allows the user to type in a value, is considered cohesive. A routine that checks date validity, deducts insurance premiums, and computes federal withholding tax for an employee would be less cohesive.

>>**NOTE** Date-checking is an example of a commonly used module in business programs, and one that is quite functionally cohesive. In business programs, many dates are represented using six or eight digits in month-day-year format. For example, January 21, 2009 might be stored as 012109 or 01212009. However, you might also see day-month-year format, as in 21012009. The current International Organization for Standardization (ISO) standard for representing dates is to use eight digits, with the year first, followed by the month and day. For example, January 21, 2009 is 20090121 and would be displayed as 2009-01-21. The ISO creates standards for businesses that make products more reliable and trade between countries easier and fairer.

TWO TRUTHS AND A LIE:
MODULARIZING A PROGRAM

1. Most programs contain a main program, which contains the mainline logic; this program then accesses other modules or subroutines.

2. A calling program (or calling module) calls a module's name when it wants to use the module.

3. Whenever a main program calls a module, the logic transfers to the module, and when the module ends, the program ends.

The false statement is #3. When a module ends, the logical flow transfers back to the main calling program and resumes where it left off.

DECLARING LOCAL AND GLOBAL VARIABLES AND CONSTANTS

Any program can contain an unlimited number of methods, and each method can be called an unlimited number of times. Within a program, the simplest methods you can invoke don't require any data items (called **arguments**) to be sent to them, nor do they send any data back to you (called **returning a value**). Consider the simple application in Figure 3-11 that accepts a customer's name and balance due and prints a bill. At the top of the bill, the company's name and address are displayed on three lines. You can simply include three `print` statements in the mainline logic of a program as shown in Figure 3-11, or you can create both the mainline logic and a `nameAndAddress()` method, as shown in Figure 3-12.

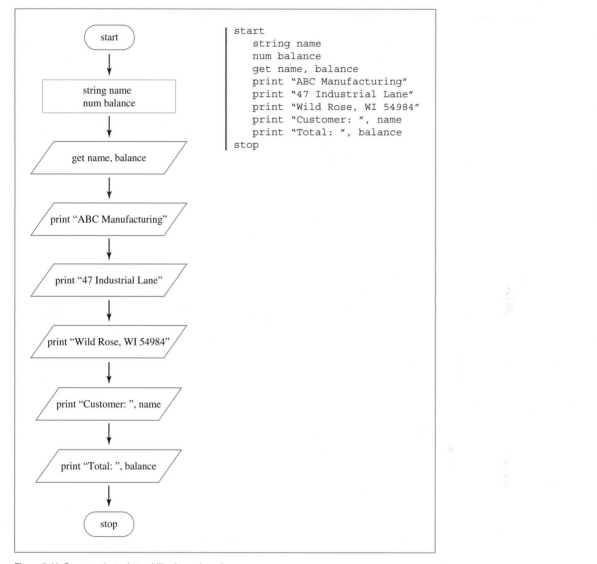

```
start
    string name
    num balance
    get name, balance
    print "ABC Manufacturing"
    print "47 Industrial Lane"
    print "Wild Rose, WI 54984"
    print "Customer: ", name
    print "Total: ", balance
stop
```

Figure 3-11 Program that prints a bill using only main program

>> **NOTE** In Figure 3-11, the instruction `get name, balance` is expressed in its simplest form so this example remains uncomplicated. If this program is intended to be an interactive one that will be executed from the command line, the instructions would include displaying prompts and would look something like this:

```
print "Please enter a name "
get name
print "Enter balance due "
get balance
```

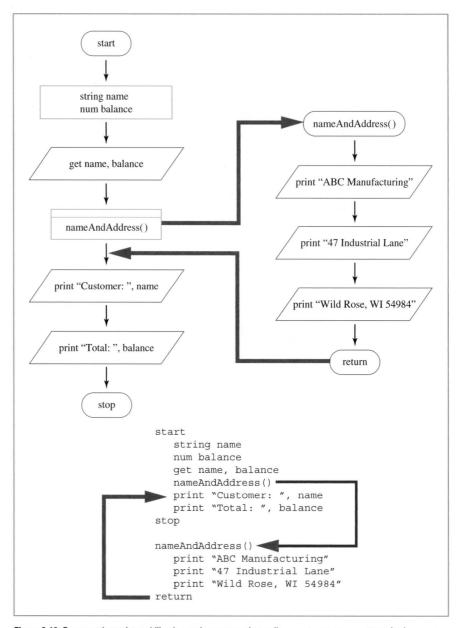

Figure 3-12 Program that prints a bill using main program that calls `nameAndAddress()` method

In Figure 3-12, when the `nameAndAddress()` method is called, logic transfers from the main program to the `nameAndAddress()` method, as shown by the large arrow. There, each method statement executes in turn, before logical control is transferred back to the main program where it continues with the statement that follows the method call. There are two major reasons to create a separate method to display the three address lines. First, the main program remains short and easy to follow because it contains just one statement to call the method, rather than three separate `print` statements to perform the work of the method. What is more important is that a method is easily reusable. After you create the name and address method, you can use it in any application that needs the company's name and address. In other words, you do the work once, and then you can use the method many times.

A method must include the following:

» A header (also called the declaration or definition). A **method's header** includes the method identifier and possibly other necessary identifying information.

» A body. A **method's body** contains all the statements in the method.

» A return statement. A method's **return statement** marks the end of the method and identifies the point at which control returns to the calling method.

>> **NOTE** In most programming languages, if you do not include a `return` statement at the end of a method, the method will still return. This book follows the convention of explicitly including a `return` statement with every method.

>> **NOTE** Each of two different programs can have its own method named `nameAndAddress()`. Such a method in the second program would be entirely distinct from the identically named method in the first program. Two methods in an application cannot have the same name if they both have empty parentheses. In Chapter 7, you will learn how methods can have the same name if different items are placed within their parentheses.

The program in Figure 3-12 contains many print statements that print literal constants. Your programs will be easier to maintain and modify if, in general, you use named constants to hold fixed values. You might decide to modify the program in Figure 3-12 so it looks like the one in Figure 3-13. You would declare string constants to hold the three company address lines, and then when you need to print the address, you would print these constants. (See the shaded portions of Figure 3-13.) However, this program will not work.

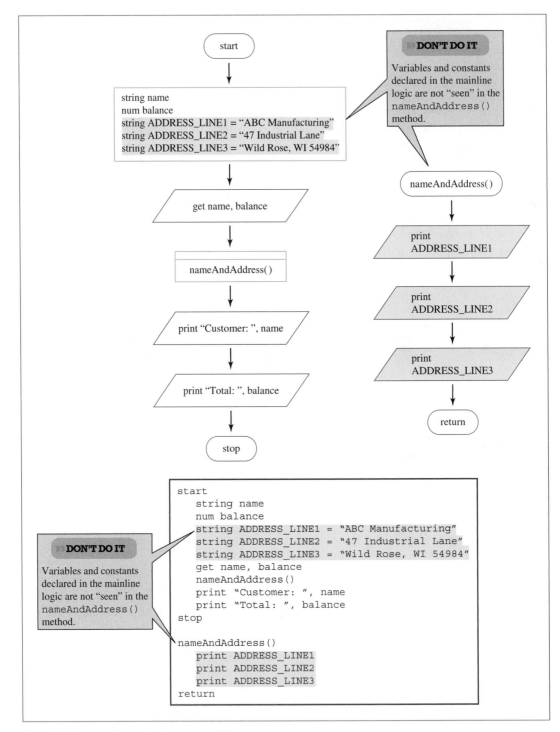

Figure 3-13 Incorrect declarations for customer billing program

In most modern programming languages, the variables and constants declared in the main-line logic are usable only there, and any variables and constants declared within a method are useable only within that method. Programmers say the data items are "**visible**" or "can be seen" only within the method in which they are declared. Programmers also say that variables and constants declared within a method are **in scope** only within that method. Programmers also say that variables and constants are **local** to the method in which they are declared. All this means that when the strings ADDRESS_LINE1, ADDRESS_LINE2, and ADDRESS_LINE3 are declared in the main program in Figure 3-13, they are not recognized and cannot be used by the nameAndAddress() method.

One of the motivations for creating methods is that separate methods are easily reusable in multiple programs. If the nameAndAddress() method is going to be used by several programs within the organization, it makes sense that the definitions for the variables and constants it uses must come with it. Therefore, the superior solution for the customer billing program is to create it, as shown in Figure 3-14. In this version, the data items that are needed by the main program are defined in the main program, and the ones needed by the nameAndAddress() method are defined within that method. Each method contains its own data and does not "know about" the data in any other methods.

Besides local variables and constants, you can create global variables and constants. **Global** variables and constants are those that are known to the entire program. Figure 3-15 shows how the three address line constants might be declared globally in code a program that prints customer bills. Variables and constants that are declared outside any method are declared at the **program level**. In general, and in this case, this is not a recommended practice.

There are a few occasions in which you might consider declaring variables and constants globally:

» Some programmers approve of declaring global variables for constants that will be needed in many methods throughout a program. For example, if a mathematical program contains many methods that require a constant for a value such as pi, or a business program contains many methods that require a standard tax or discount rate, many programmers would allow these to be declared globally.

» When you learn about object-oriented programming and create a class from which you will derive objects, you can declare the class's data fields at the class level. Chapter 11 of the Comprehensive version of this text discusses this topic more thoroughly.

In most other circumstances, however, you should not declare global variables and constants. When you do, you violate the programming principle of encapsulation, which states that a task's instructions and its data should be contained in the same method. If you declare variables and constants within the methods that use them, the methods are more **portable**; that is, they can more easily be reused in multiple programs. Sometimes, however, two or more methods in a program require access to the same data; when this is the case, you do not declare global data items. Instead, you **pass the data** from one method to another. You will learn to do this in Chapter 7.

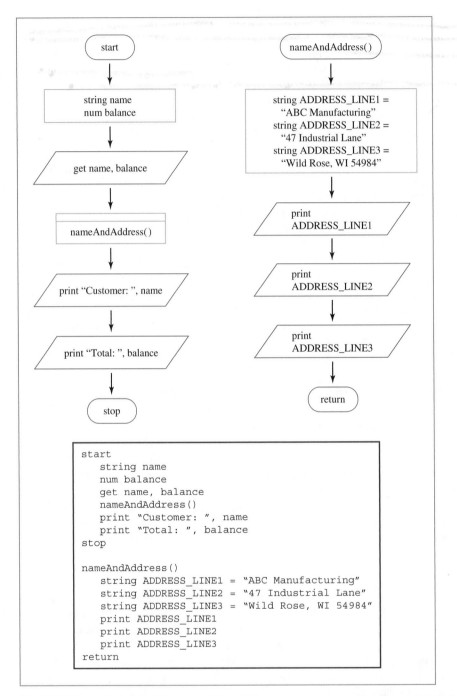

```
start
    string name
    num balance
    get name, balance
    nameAndAddress()
    print "Customer: ", name
    print "Total: ", balance
stop

nameAndAddress()
    string ADDRESS_LINE1 = "ABC Manufacturing"
    string ADDRESS_LINE2 = "47 Industrial Lane"
    string ADDRESS_LINE3 = "Wild Rose, WI 54984"
    print ADDRESS_LINE1
    print ADDRESS_LINE2
    print ADDRESS_LINE3
return
```

Figure 3-14 Program that prints a bill program with variables and constants declared locally in each method

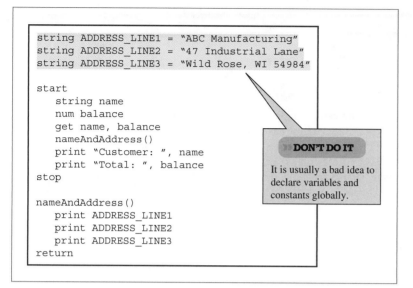

```
string ADDRESS_LINE1 = "ABC Manufacturing"
string ADDRESS_LINE2 = "47 Industrial Lane"
string ADDRESS_LINE3 = "Wild Rose, WI 54984"

start
    string name
    num balance
    get name, balance
    nameAndAddress()
    print "Customer: ", name
    print "Total: ", balance
stop

nameAndAddress()
    print ADDRESS_LINE1
    print ADDRESS_LINE2
    print ADDRESS_LINE3
return
```

DON'T DO IT

It is usually a bad idea to declare variables and constants globally.

Figure 3-15 Program that prints a bill with some constants declared globally

TWO TRUTHS AND A LIE:
DECLARING LOCAL AND GLOBAL VARIABLES AND CONSTANTS

1. In most modern programming languages, data items are visible in all program modules.

2. In most modern programming languages, constants and variables declared within a method are in scope only within that method.

3. In most modern programming languages, variables and constants are local to the method in which they are declared.

The false statement is #1. In most languages, data items are visible only within the method in which they are declared.

UNDERSTANDING THE MAINLINE LOGIC FOR MANY PROCEDURAL PROGRAMS

In Chapter 1, you learned that a procedural program is one in which one procedure follows another from the beginning until the end. The overall logic, or **mainline logic**, of almost every procedural computer program can follow a general structure that consists of three distinct parts:

1. Housekeeping, or initialization tasks. **Housekeeping tasks** include any steps you must perform at the beginning of a program to get ready for the rest of the program.

2. Main loop tasks that repeatedly execute within the program. **Main loop tasks** include the instructions that are executed for every record until you reach the end of the input of records, or eof.

3. End-of-job tasks. **End-of-job tasks** are the steps you take at the end of the program to finish the application.

» NOTE Not all programs are procedural; some are object-oriented. A distinguishing feature of many (but not all) object-oriented programs is that they are event-driven; often the user determines the timing of events in the main loop of the program by using an input device such as a mouse. As you advance in your knowledge of programming, you will learn more about object-oriented techniques.

For example, a main program can be viewed as shown in the flowchart and pseudocode in Figure 3-16. Many everyday tasks follow the format of this mainline logic. For example, consider a candy factory. In the morning, the factory is opened for the day and the machines are started and filled with ingredients. These tasks occur just once at the start of the day; they are the housekeeping tasks. Then, repeatedly during the day, candy is manufactured. This process might take many steps, each of which occurs hundreds or thousands of times. These are the steps in the main loop. Then, at the end of the day, the machines are cleaned and shut down. These are the end-of-job tasks.

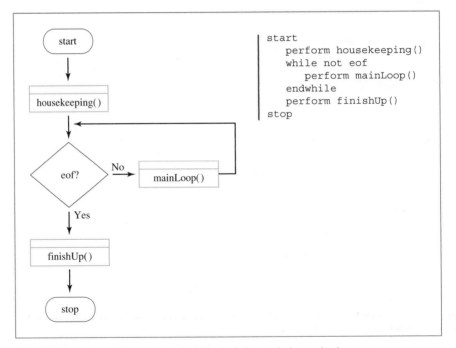

Figure 3-16 Flowchart and pseudocode of mainline logic for a typical procedural program

In many business programs:

» Housekeeping tasks include all the steps that must take place at the beginning of a program. Very often, this includes declaring variables and constants, opening any data files that will be used, performing any one-time-only tasks that should occur at the beginning of the program, such as printing headings at the beginning of a report, and reading the first input record.

> **NOTE** **Opening a data file** is the process of locating it on a storage device, physically preparing it for reading, and associating it with an identifier inside a program. In most languages, no files need to be opened if a program uses only the **standard input device** (usually the keyboard) and the **standard output device** (usually the monitor).

» Main loop tasks include the process that must occur for every data record. For example, in a payroll program, all the computations for a check are carried out and a paycheck is printed. In a business program, there might be hundreds or thousands of records to process. The main loop of a program, typically controlled by the `eof` decision, is the program's "workhorse." Each data record will pass once through the main loop, where it is processed. Whether the main loop calculates a paycheck, produces a customer's bill, prepares a client's income tax return, diagnoses a patient's condition from a list of symptoms, or performs any other logical task, the main loop activities execute one time for each input record.

» Within any program, the end-of-job tasks are the steps you must take just before the end of the program after all input records are processed. Some programs require summaries or grand totals to be printed at the end of a report. Others might print a message such as "End of Report", so readers can be confident that they have received all the information that should be included. Such end-of-job message lines often are called **footer lines**, or **footers** for short. Very often, an end-of-job task is to close any open files.

Not all programs take the format of the logic shown in Figure 3-16, but many do. Keep this general "shape" in mind as you think about how you might organize many programs. For example, Figure 3-17 shows a sample payroll report for a small company. Examine the logic in Figure 3-18 to identify the components that comprise the housekeeping, main loop, and end-of-job tasks.

```
PAYROLL REPORT

ID Number    Hours    Rate     Gross Pay

XXXXX           99    99.99     9999.99
XXXXX           99    99.99     9999.99
XXXXX           99    99.99     9999.99

End of Payroll Report
```

Figure 3-17 Sample payroll report

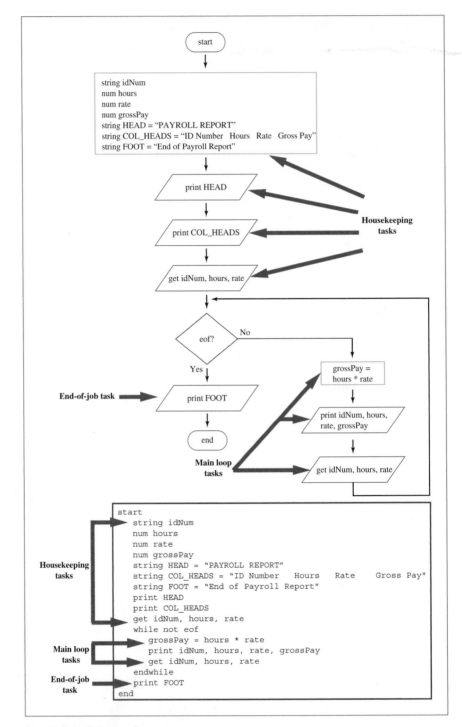

Figure 3-18 Logic for payroll report

CREATING HIERARCHY CHARTS

Besides describing program logic with a flowchart or pseudocode, when a program has several modules calling other modules, programmers often use a tool to show the overall picture of how these modules are related to one another. You can use a **hierarchy chart** to illustrate modules' relationships. A hierarchy chart does not tell you what tasks are to be performed within a module; it doesn't tell you *when* or *how* a module executes. It tells you only which routines exist within a program and which routines call which other routines.

The hierarchy chart for the program in Figure 3-16 looks like Figure 3-19. It shows which modules call which others. You don't know *when* the modules are called or *why* they are called; that information is in the flowchart or pseudocode. A hierarchy chart just tells you *which* modules are called by other modules.

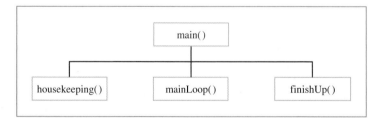

Figure 3-19 Hierarchy chart program in Figure 3-16

You may have seen hierarchy charts for organizations, such as the one in Figure 3-20. The chart shows who reports to whom, not when or how often they report. Program hierarchy charts operate in an identical manner.

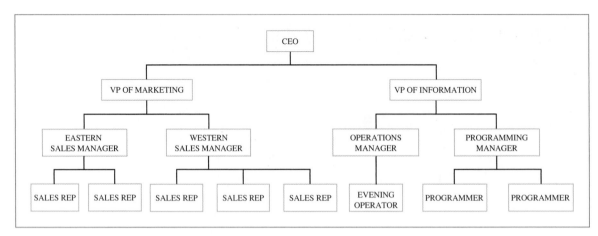

Figure 3-20 An organizational hierarchy chart

Figure 3-21 shows an example of a hierarchy chart for the billing program of a mail-order company. The hierarchy chart is for a more complicated program, but like the chart in Figure 3-19, it supplies module names and a general overview of the tasks to be performed, without specifying any details.

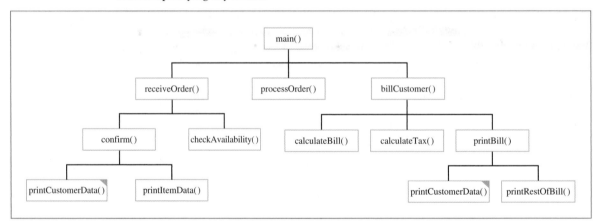

Figure 3-21 Billing program hierarchy chart

Because program modules are reusable, a specific module may be called from several locations within a program. For example, in the billing program hierarchy chart in Figure 3-21, you can see that the printCustomerData() module is used twice. By convention, you blacken a corner of each box representing a module used more than once. This action alerts readers that any change to this module will affect more than one location.

The hierarchy chart can be a useful tool when a program must be modified months or years after the original writing. For example, if a tax law changes, a programmer might be asked to rewrite the calculateTax() module in the billing program diagrammed in Figure 3-21. As the programmer changes the calculateTax() routine, the hierarchy chart shows what other dependent routines might be affected. If a change is made to printCustomerData(), the programmer is alerted that changes will occur in multiple locations. A hierarchy chart is useful for "getting the big picture" in a complex program.

TWO TRUTHS AND A LIE:
CREATING HIERARCHY CHARTS

1. You can use a hierarchy chart to illustrate modules' relationships.

2. A hierarchy chart tells you what tasks are to be performed within a module.

3. A hierarchy chart tells you only which routines call other routines.

The false statement is #2. A hierarchy chart tells you nothing about tasks performed within a module; it only tells you how modules are related to each other.

FEATURES OF GOOD PROGRAM DESIGN

As your programs become larger and more complicated, the need for good planning and design increases. Think of an application you use, such as a word processor or a spreadsheet. The number and variety of user options are staggering. Not only would it be impossible for a single programmer to write such an application, but without thorough planning and design, the components would never work together properly. Ideally, each program module you design needs to work well as a stand-alone module and as an element of larger systems. Just as a house with poor plumbing or a car with bad brakes is fatally flawed, a computer-based application can be great only if each component is designed well. Some, but not all, of the aspects of design you should consider include the following:

» You should follow expected and clear naming conventions.

» You should consider storing program components in separate files.

» You should strive to design clear statements within your programs and modules.

» You should continue to maintain good programming habits as you progress in your programming skills.

FOLLOWING NAMING CONVENTIONS

You learned in Chapter 1 that different programming languages provide different variable types, but that all allow at least the distinction between text and numeric data. The rest of this book uses just two data types: num, which holds number values, and string, which holds all other values, including those that contain letters and combinations of letters and numbers. Remember, you also learned in Chapter 1 that variable names must not contain spaces, so this book uses statements such as string lastName and num weeklySalary to declare two variables of different types.

Although it is not a requirement of any programming language, it usually makes sense to give a variable a name that is a noun (or a combination of an adjective and a noun), because it represents a thing.

>> **NOTE** Some programming languages, such as Visual Basic and BASIC, do not require you to name any variable until the first time you use it. However, other languages, including C++, C#, and Java, require that you declare variables with a name and a data type before you can use them. Some languages require that you declare all variables at the beginning of a module, before you write any executable statements; others allow you to declare variables at any point. This book follows the convention of declaring any variable that a module uses at the beginning of the module.

>> **NOTE** Organizations sometimes enforce different rules for programmers to follow when naming variables. Some use a variable-naming convention called **Hungarian notation**, in which a variable's data type or other information is stored as part of the name. For example, a numeric field might always start with the prefix num as in numAge or numSalary.

>> **NOTE** Programmers sometimes create a **data dictionary**, which is a list of every variable name used in a program, along with its type, size, and description. When a data dictionary is created, it becomes part of the program documentation.

After you name a variable, you must use that exact name every time you refer to the variable within your program. In many programming languages, even the case matters, so a variable name like firstNumber represents a different memory location than firstnumber or FirstNumber.

An often-overlooked element in program design is the selection of good data and module names (sometimes generically called identifiers). Some general guidelines include the following:

» Use meaningful names. Creating a data field named someData or a module named firstModule() makes a program cryptic. Not only will others find it hard to read your programs, but you will forget the purpose of these identifiers even within your own programs. All programmers occasionally use short, nondescriptive names such as x or temp in a quick program written to test a procedure; however, in most cases, data and module names should be meaningful. Programmers refer to programs that contain meaningful names as **self-documenting**. This means that even without further documentation, the program code explains itself to readers.

>> **NOTE**
Don't forget that not all programmers share your culture. An abbreviation whose meaning seems obvious to you might be cryptic to someone in a different part of the world.

» Usually, you should use pronounceable names. A variable name like pzf is neither pronounceable nor meaningful. A name that looks meaningful when you write it might not be as meaningful when someone else reads it; for instance, preparead() might mean "Prepare ad" to you, but "Prep a read" to others. Look at your names critically to make sure they are pronounceable. Very standard abbreviations do not have to be pronounceable. For example, most business people would interpret ssn as Social Security number.

» Be judicious in your use of abbreviations. You can save a few keystrokes when creating a module called getStat(), but is its purpose to find the state in which a city is located, output some statistics, or determine the status of some variables? Similarly, is a variable named fn meant to hold a first name, file number, or something else?

>> **NOTE** To save typing time when you develop a program, you can use a short name like efn. After the program operates correctly, you can use an editor's Search and Replace feature to replace your coded name with a more meaningful name such as employeeFirstName.

» Usually, avoid digits in a name. Zeroes get confused with the letter "O", and lowercase "l"s are misread as the numeral 1. Of course, use your judgment: `budgetFor2010` is probably not going to be misinterpreted.

» Use the system your language allows to separate words in long, multiword variable names. For example, if the programming language you use allows dashes or underscores, then use a method name like `initialize-data()` or `initialize_data()`, which is easier to read than `initializedata()`. Another option is to use camel casing, creating an identifier such as `initializeData()`. If you use a language that is case sensitive, it is legal but confusing to use variable names that differ only in case—for example, `empName`, `EmpName`, and `Empname`.

» Consider including a form of the verb *to be*, such as *is* or *are*, in names for variables that are intended to hold a status. For example, use `isFinished` as a flag variable that holds a "Y" or "N" to indicate whether a file is exhausted. The shorter name `finished` is more likely to be confused with a module that executes when a program is done.

» Many programmers follow the convention of naming constants using all uppercase letters, inserting underscores between words for readability. In this chapter you saw examples such as `ADDRESS_LINE1`.

When you begin to write programs, the process of determining what data variables, constants, and modules you will need and what to name them all might seem overwhelming. The design process is crucial, however. When you acquire your first professional programming assignment, the design process might very well be completed already. Most likely, your first assignment will be to write or make modifications to one small member module of a much larger application. The more the original programmers stuck to these guidelines, the better the original design was, and the easier your job of modification will be.

STORING PROGRAM COMPONENTS IN SEPARATE FILES

When you start to work on professional programs, you will see that many of them are quite lengthy, with some containing hundreds of variables and thousands of lines of code. Earlier in this chapter, you learned you can manage lengthy procedural programs by breaking them down into modules. Although modularization helps you to organize your programs, sometimes it is still difficult to manage all of a program's components.

Most modern programming languages allow you to store program components in separate files. If you write a module and store it in the same file as the program that uses it, your program files become large and hard to work with, whether you are trying to read them on a screen or on multiple printed pages. In addition, when you define a useful module, you might want to use it in many programs. Of course, you can copy module definitions from one file to another, but this method is time-consuming as well as prone to error. A better solution (if you are using a language that allows it) is to store your modules in individual files and use an instruction to include them in any program that uses them. The statement needed to access modules from separate files varies from language to language, but it usually involves using a verb such as *include*, *import*, or *copy*, followed by the name of the file that contains the module.

For example, suppose your company has a standard employee record definition, part of which is shown in Figure 3-22. Files with the same format are used in many applications within the organization—personnel reports, production reports, payroll, and so on. It would be a tremendous waste of resources if every programmer rewrote this file definition in multiple applications. Instead, once a programmer writes the statements that constitute the file definition, those statements should be imported in their entirety into any program that uses a record with the same structure. For example, Figure 3-23 shows how the data fields in Figure 3-22 would be defined in the C++ programming language. If the statements in Figure 3-23 are saved in a file named EMPLOYEES, then any C++ program can contain a statement that directs the program to include all the data fields in the employee group.

```
EMPLOYEES FILE DESCRIPTION
File name: EMPLOYEES
FIELD DESCRIPTION        DATA TYPE      COMMENTS
Employee ID              String
Last name                String
First name               String
Hire date                Numeric        8 digits - yyyymmdd
Hourly wage              Numeric        2 decimal places
Birth date               Numeric        8 digits - yyyymmdd
Termination date         Numeric        8 digits - yyyymmdd
```

Figure 3-22 Partial EMPLOYEES file description

```
class Employee
{
    string employeeId;
    string lastName;
    string firstName;
    long hireDate;
    double hourlyWage;
    long birthDate;
    long terminationDate;
};
```

Figure 3-23 Data fields in Figure 3-22 defined in the C++ language

>> **NOTE** Don't be concerned with the syntax used in the file description in Figure 3-23. The words *class, string, long,* and *double* are all part of the C++ programming language and are not important to you now. Similarly, the curly braces and semicolons are parts of the language that serve to separate program elements. Additionally, an Employee class defined in C++ would always contain more features than shown here. For now, simply concentrate on how the variable names in Figure 3-23 reflect the field descriptions in Figure 3-22.

As another example of when it can be useful to store program components in separate files, suppose you write a useful module that checks dates to guarantee their validity. For example, the two digits that represent a month can be neither less than 01 nor greater than 12, and the two digits that represent the day can contain different possible values, depending on the month. Any program that uses the employee file description shown in Figure 3-22 might want to call the date-validating module several times in order to validate any employee's hire date, birth date, and termination date. Not only do you want to call this module from several locations within any one program, you want to call it from many programs. For example, programs used for company ordering and billing would each contain several dates. If the date-validating module is useful and well-written, you might even want to market it to other companies. By storing the module in its own file, you enable its use to be flexible. When you write a program of any length, you should consider storing each of its components in its own file.

Storing components in separate files can provide an advantage beyond ease of reuse. When you let others use your programs or modules, you often provide them with only the compiled (that is, machine-language) version of your code, not the **source code**, which is composed of readable statements. Storing your program statements in a separate, nonreadable, compiled file is an example of **implementation hiding**, or hiding the details of how the program or module works. Other programmers can use your code, but cannot see the statements you used to create it. A programmer who cannot see your well-designed modules is more likely to use them simply as they were intended; the programmer also will not be able to attempt to make adjustments to your code, thereby introducing error. Of course, in order to work with your modules or data definitions, a programmer must know the names and types of data you are using. Typically, you provide programmers who use your definitions with written documentation of the data names and purposes.

> **» NOTE**
> Recall from Chapter 1 that when you write a program in a programming language, you must compile or interpret it into machine language before the computer can actually carry out your instructions.

DESIGNING CLEAR STATEMENTS

In addition to selecting good identifiers, you can use the following tactics to contribute to the clarity of the statements within your programs:

» Avoid confusing line breaks.

» Use temporary variables to clarify long statements.

» Use constants where appropriate.

AVOIDING CONFUSING LINE BREAKS

Some older programming languages require that program statements be placed in specific columns. Most modern programming languages are free-form; you can arrange your lines of code any way you see fit. As in real life, with freedom comes responsibility; when you have flexibility in arranging your lines of code, you must take care to make sure your meaning is clear. With free-form code, programmers often do not provide enough line breaks, or they provide inappropriate ones.

Figure 3-24 shows an example of code that does not provide enough line breaks for clarity. If you have been following the examples used throughout this book, the code in Figure 3-25 looks clearer to you; it will also look clearer to most other programmers.

```
open files print mainHeading print columnHead1
   print columnHead2 read invRecord
```

DON'T DO IT

Insufficient line breaks make this code hard to read.

Figure 3-24 Code segment with insufficient line breaks

```
open files
print mainHeading
print columnHead1
print columnHead2
read invRecord
```

Figure 3-25 Code segment with appropriate line breaks

Figure 3-25 shows that more, but shorter, lines usually improve your ability to understand a program's logic; appropriately breaking lines will become even more important as you introduce decisions and loops into your programs in the next chapters.

USING TEMPORARY VARIABLES TO CLARIFY LONG STATEMENTS

When you need several mathematical operations to determine a result, consider using a series of temporary variables to hold intermediate results. A **temporary variable** (or a **work variable**) is one that is not used for input or output, but instead is just a working variable that you use during a program's execution. For example, Figure 3-26 shows two ways to calculate a value for a real estate salespersonCommission variable. Each method achieves the same result—the salesperson's commission is based on the square feet multiplied by the price per square foot, plus any premium for a lot with special features, such as a wooded or waterfront lot. However, the second example uses two temporary variables, sqFootPrice and totalPrice. When the computation is broken down into less complicated, individual steps, it is easier to see how the total price is calculated. In calculations with even more computation steps, performing the arithmetic in stages would become increasingly helpful.

```
salespersonCommission = (sqFeet * pricePerSquareFoot + lotPremium) * commissionRate
sqFootPrice = sqFeet * pricePerSquareFoot
totalprice = sqFootPrice + lotPremium
salespersonCommission = totalPrice * commissionRate
```

Figure 3-26 Two ways of achieving the same salespersonCommission result

>> **NOTE** A statement, or part of a statement, that performs arithmetic and has a resulting value is called an **arithmetic expression**. For example, 2 + 3 is an arithmetic expression with the value 5.

>> **NOTE** Programmers might say using temporary variables, like the example in Figure 3-26, is *cheap*. When executing a lengthy arithmetic statement, even if you don't explicitly name temporary variables, the programming language compiler creates them behind the scenes (although without descriptive names), so declaring them yourself does not cost much in terms of program execution time.

USING CONSTANTS WHERE APPROPRIATE

Whenever possible, use named values in your programs. If your program contains a statement like salesTax = price * TAX_RATE instead of salesTax = price * 0.06, you gain several benefits:

» It is easier for readers to know that the price is being multiplied by a tax rate instead of a discount, commission, or some other rate represented by 0.06.

» When the tax rate changes, you make one change to the value where TAX_RATE is defined, rather than searching through a program for every instance of 0.06.

» Using named constants helps prevent typographical errors. When a program is written in a programming language and compiled, the translation software will issue an error statement if TAX_RATE is misspelled in the program. However, if the programmer uses a constant numeric value instead, and mistakenly types say, 0.60 instead of 0.06, the compiler would not recognize an error, and incorrect taxes would be calculated.

For example, the program shown in Figure 3-27 uses the constants `TUITION_PER_CREDIT_HOUR` and `ATHLETIC_FEE` in the shaded statements. Because this book follows the convention that identifiers that appear in all uppercase letters are constants, you know that the values of these fields will not change during the execution of the program. If the values of either of these should need to be changed in the future, then a programmer would assign new values to the constants and recompile the program code; the actual program statements that perform the arithmetic with the values do not have to be disturbed.

>> **NOTE** Some programmers refer to unnamed numeric constants as **"magic numbers."** Just as a trick by a magician is beyond explanation, such numbers are not explained. Using magic numbers is considered a poor programming practice, and you should almost always provide descriptive named constants instead. Because named constants describe the purpose of numbers, they provide a form of internal documentation.

MAINTAINING GOOD PROGRAMMING HABITS

When you learn a programming language and begin to write lines of program code, it is easy to forget the principles you have learned in this text. Having some programming knowledge and a keyboard at your fingertips can lure you into typing lines of code before you think things through. But every program you write will be better if you plan before you code. If you maintain the habits of first drawing flowcharts or writing pseudocode, as you have learned here, your future programming projects will go more smoothly. If you walk through your program logic on paper (called **desk-checking**) before starting to type statements in C++, Visual Basic, Java, or any other programming language, your programs will run correctly sooner. If you think carefully about the variable and module names you use, and design your program statements so they are easy for others to read, you will be rewarded with programs that are easier to get up and running, and are easier to maintain as well.

TWO TRUTHS AND A LIE:
FEATURES OF GOOD PROGRAM DESIGN

1. After you name a variable, you must use that exact name every time you refer to the variable within your program.

2. Most modern programming languages allow you to store program components in separate files.

3. Most modern programming languages require that lines of code begin in the left-most column of your code editor.

The false statement is #3. Most newer languages are free form, allowing you to arrange code lines any way you see fit.

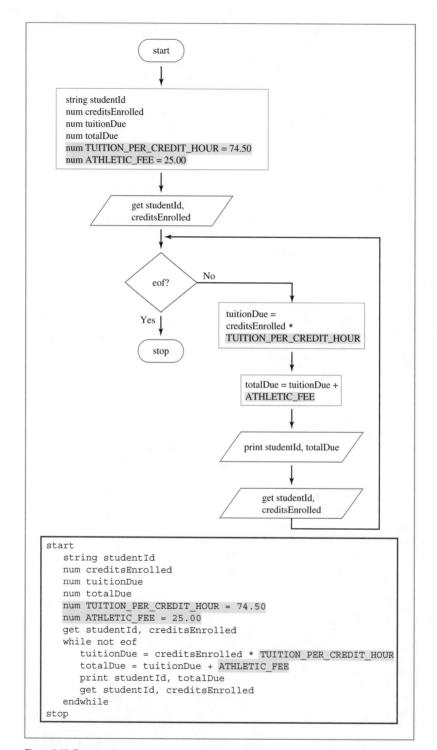

Figure 3-27 Program that uses named constants

CHAPTER SUMMARY

» Documentation refers to all of the supporting material that goes with a program. Output documentation is usually written first to describe the appearance of screens or printed reports. File descriptions list the data contained in files and include field descriptions, data types, and any other necessary information. User documentation includes the manuals or other instructional materials that nontechnical people use, as well as the operating instructions that computer operators and data-entry personnel may need.

» Programmers break down programming problems into smaller, reasonable units called modules, subroutines, procedures, functions, or methods. Modularization provides abstraction, allows multiple programmers to work on a problem, makes it easy to reuse your work, and allows you to identify structures more easily.

» When you create a module or subroutine, you give the module a name that a calling program uses when the module is about to execute. The flowchart symbol used to call a subroutine is a rectangle with a bar across the top; the name of the module that you are calling is inside the rectangle. You draw a flowchart for each module separately, with its own sentinel symbols.

» Declaring a variable involves providing a name for the memory location where the computer will store the variable value, and notifying the computer of what type of data to expect. In most modern programming languages, the variables and constants declared in a method are local to that method.

» Many procedural programs perform housekeeping, main loop, and end-of-job tasks. Housekeeping tasks typically include declaring variables, opening files, performing any one-time-only tasks (such as printing headings at the beginning of a report), and reading the first input record. The main loop of a program is controlled by the eof decision. Each data record passes once through the main loop, where calculations are performed with the data and results are printed. Within any program, the end-of-job tasks include the steps you must take at the end of the program, after all the input records have been processed. Typical tasks include printing summaries, grand totals, or final messages at the end of a report, and closing all open files.

» You can use a hierarchy chart to illustrate modules' relationships.

» As your programs become larger and more complicated, the need for good planning and design increases. Storing program components in separate files can provide the advantages of easy reuse and implementation hiding. When selecting data and module names, use meaningful, pronounceable names. Be judicious in your use of abbreviations, avoid digits in a name, and visually separate words in multiword names. Consider including a form of the verb *to be*, such as *is* or *are*, in names for variables that are intended to hold a status. The naming convention for constants is to use all uppercase letters. When writing program statements, you should avoid confusing line breaks, use temporary variables to clarify long statements, and use constants where appropriate. Every program you write will be better if you plan before you code.

KEY TERMS

Documentation refers to all of the supporting material that goes with a program.

End users, or **users**, are people who use completed computer programs.

Program documentation is the set of instructions that programmers use when they begin to plan the logic of a program.

Internal program documentation is documentation within a program.

Program comments are nonexecuting statements that programmers place within their code to explain program statements in English.

External program documentation includes all the supporting paperwork that programmers develop before they write a program.

Output documentation describes the results the user will be able to see when a program is complete.

A **printer spacing chart**, which is also referred to as a **print chart** or a **print layout**, is a tool for planning program output.

A **detail line** on a report is a line that contains data details. Most reports contain many detail lines.

Heading lines on a report contain the title and any column headings, and usually appear only once per page.

Total lines or **summary lines** contain end-of-report information.

A **hard copy** is a printed output.

Soft copy is screen output.

A **file description** is a document that describes the data contained in a file.

Padding a field is the process of adding extra characters, such as spaces, to the end of a data field to force it to be a specific size.

A **delimiter** is a character used to separate fields in a file.

A **byte** is a unit of computer storage. It can contain any of 256 combinations of 0s and 1s that often represent a character.

A **prefix** is a set of characters used at the beginning of related variable names.

User documentation includes all the manuals or other instructional materials that nontechnical people use, as well as the operating instructions that computer operators and data-entry personnel need.

Modules are small program units that you can use together to make a program. Programmers also refer to modules as **subroutines**, **procedures**, **functions**, or **methods**.

To execute a method, you **invoke** it or **call** it from another method.

A **calling program** or **calling method** is one that calls a module.

A **called method** is one that is invoked by a program or another module.

Modularization is the process of breaking down a program into modules.

Abstraction is the process of paying attention to important properties while ignoring nonessential details.

Low-level details are small, nonabstract steps.

High-level programming languages allow you to use English-like vocabulary in which one broad statement corresponds to dozens of machine instructions.

Reusability is the feature of modular programs that allows individual modules to be used in a variety of applications.

Reliability is the feature of modular programs that assures you that a module has been tested and proven to function correctly.

Functional decomposition is the act of reducing a large program into more manageable modules.

A **main program** (or **main program method**) runs from start to stop and calls other modules.

A **submodule** is one that is called by another module.

Encapsulation is the act of containing a task's instructions and data in the same method.

A **stack** is a memory location in which the computer keeps track of the correct memory address to which it should return after executing a module.

The **functional cohesion** of a module is a measure of the degree to which all the module statements contribute to the same task.

Arguments are data items that are sent to methods.

Returning a value is the process whereby a called module sends a value to its calling module.

A **method's header** includes the method identifier and possibly other necessary identifying information.

A **method's body** contains all the statements in the method.

A method's **return statement** marks the end of the method and identifies the point at which control returns to the calling method.

Data items are "**visible**" or "can be seen" only within the method in which they are declared.

Variables and constants declared within a method are **in scope** only within that method.

Local variables are declared within each module that uses them.

Global variables are declared outside any modules, and then can be used in all modules of the program.

Global variables are declared at the **program level**.

A **portable method** is one that can more easily be reused in multiple programs.

Passing data from one method to another is the way local data is exchanged between modules.

The **mainline logic** of a program is the overall logic of the main program from beginning to end.

Housekeeping tasks include steps you must perform at the beginning of a program to get ready for the rest of the program.

Main loop tasks of a program include the steps that are repeated for every record.

End-of-job tasks hold the steps you take at the end of the program to finish the application.

Opening a data file is the process of locating it on a storage device, physically preparing it for reading, and associating it with an identifier inside a program.

The **standard input device** is the default device from which input comes, most often the keyboard.

The **standard output device** is the default device to which output is sent, usually the monitor.

Footer lines, or **footers**, are end-of-report message lines.

A **hierarchy chart** is a diagram that illustrates modules' relationships to each other.

Hungarian notation is a variable-naming convention in which a variable's data type or other information is stored as part of its name.

A **data dictionary** is a list of every variable name used in a program, along with its type, size, and description.

Self-documenting programs are those that contain meaningful data and module names that describe the programs' purpose.

Source code is the readable statements of a program written in a programming language.

Implementation hiding is hiding the details of the way a program or module works.

A **temporary variable** (or a **work variable**) is a working variable that you use to hold intermediate results during a program's execution.

An **arithmetic expression** is a statement, or part of a statement, that performs arithmetic and has a value.

Magic numbers are unnamed numeric constants.

Desk-checking is the process of walking through a program's logic on paper.

REVIEW QUESTIONS

1. **Two broad categories of documentation are the documentation intended for _____ .**

   a. management and workers

   b. end users and programmers

   c. people and the computer

   d. defining variables and defining actions

2. **Nonexecuting statements that programmers place within their code to explain program statements in English are called _____ .**

   a. comments   c. trivia

   b. pseudocode   d. user documentation

3. **The first type of documentation usually created when writing a program pertains to _____ .**

   a. end users   c. output

   b. input   d. data

4. Which of the following is *not* a term used as a synonym for "module" in any programming language?

    a. structure

    b. procedure

    c. method

    d. function

5. Which of the following is *not* a reason to use modularization?

    a. Modularization provides abstraction.

    b. Modularization allows multiple programmers to work on a problem.

    c. Modularization allows you to reuse your work.

    d. Modularization eliminates the need for structure.

6. What is the name for the process of paying attention to important properties while ignoring nonessential details?

    a. structure

    b. iteration

    c. abstraction

    d. modularization

7. All modern programming languages that use English-like vocabulary to create statements that correspond to dozens of machine instructions are referred to as _____ .

    a. high-level

    b. object-oriented

    c. modular

    d. obtuse

8. Programmers say that one module can _____ another, meaning that the first module causes the second module to execute.

    a. declare

    b. define

    c. enact

    d. call

9. The more that a module's statements contribute to the same job, the greater the _____ of the module.

    a. structure

    b. modularity

    c. functional cohesion

    d. size

10. A method must include all of the following except _____ .

    a. a header

    b. an argument

    c. a body

    d. a return statement

11. In most modern programming languages, when a variable or constant is declared in a method, the variable or constant is _____ in that method.

    a. global

    b. invisible

    c. in scope

    d. undefined

12. A hierarchy chart tells you _____ .

    a. what tasks are to be performed within each program module

    b. when a module executes

    c. which routines call which other routines

    d. All of the above

13. A program in which one operation follows another from the beginning until the end is a _____ program.

    a. modular   c. procedural

    b. functional   d. object-oriented

14. In most modern programming languages, the variables and constants declared in the mainline logic are _____ .

    a. local to the main program

    b. unnamed

    c. never assigned a value

    d. global

15. Which of the following is *not* a typical housekeeping task?

    a. declaring variables

    b. printing summaries

    c. opening files

    d. performing a priming read

16. When a programmer uses a data file and names the first field stored in each record `idNumber`, then other programmers who use the same file _____ in their programs.

    a. must also name the field `idNumber`

    b. might name the field `idNumber`

    c. cannot name the field `idNumber`

    d. cannot name the field

17. A computer system's standard input device is most often a _____ .

    a. mouse   c. keyboard

    b. floppy disk   d. compact disc

18. Most procedural programs contain a _____ that executes as many times as there are records in the program's input file.

    a. housekeeping module   c. finish routine

    b. main loop   d. terminal symbol

19. Common end-of-job tasks in programs include all of the following except _____ .

    a. opening files   c. printing end-of-job messages

    b. printing totals   d. closing files

20. Which of the following is least likely to be performed as an end-of-job task?

    a. closing files

    b. checking for `eof`

    c. printing the message "End of report"

    d. adding two values

FIND THE BUGS

Each of the following pseudocode segments contains one or more bugs that you must find and correct.

1. This pseudocode is intended to describe a program that computes the number of miles per gallon you get with your automobile as well as the cost of gasoline per mile. The main program calls a module that displays useful information.

```
start
    num gallonsOfGasUsed
    num milesTraveled
    num pricePerGallon
    num milesPerGallon
    num costPerMile
    get gallonsOfGasUsed
    get milesTravelled
    get pricePerGallonOfGas
    milesPerGallon = gallonsOfGasUsed / milesTraveled
    costPerMile = pricePerGallon - milesPerGallon
    print milesPerGal
    print costPerMile
    displayInformation()
stop

displayInfo()
    string MSG1 = " The higher the value,"
    string MSG2 = "the more economical a vehicle is. "
    string MSG3 = "The average mid-size car gets"
    string MSG4 = "27 miles per gallon"
    print MSG1
    print MSG2
    print MSG3
    print MSG4
return
```

2. **This pseudocode should create a report containing rental agents' commissions at an apartment complex. Input records contain each salesperson's ID number and name, as well as number of three-bedroom, two-bedroom, one-bedroom, and studio apartments rented during the month. The commission for each apartment rented is $50 times the number of bedrooms, except for studio apartments, for which the commission is $35.**

```
start
    num salesPersonID
    string name
    num numThreeBedroomAptsRented
    num numTwoBedroomAptsRented
    num numOneBedroomAptsRented
    num numStudioAptsRented
    string MAIN_HEADER = "Commission Report"
    string COLUMN_HEADERS
        = "Salesperson ID        Name        Commission Earned"
    num commissionEarned
    num REGULAR_RATE = 50.00
    num STUDIO_RATE = 35.00
    print MAIN_HEADER
    print COLUMN_HEADERS
    get salespersonId, name, numThreeBedroomAptsRented,
        numTwoBedroomAptsRented, numOneBedroomAptsRented,
        numStudioAptsRented
    while eof
        commissionEarned = (numThreeBedroomAptsRented * 3 +
            numTwoBedroomAptsRented +
            numOneBedroomAptsRented) * REGULAR_RATE +
            (numStudioAptsRented * STUDIO_RATE)
        print ID, salesPersonName,
            commissionEarned
        get salespersonId, name, numThreeBedroomAptsRented,
            numTwoBedroomAptsRented, numOneBedroomAptsRented,
            numStudioAptsRented
    endif
stop
```

EXERCISES

1. **Draw a typical hierarchy chart for a paycheck-producing program. Try to think of at least 10 separate modules that might be included. For example, one module might calculate an employee's dental insurance premium.**

2. Design the output and draw a flowchart or write pseudocode for a program that calculates the gown size that students need for a graduation ceremony. The program accepts as input a student's height in feet and inches and weight in pounds, and does so continuously until the user enters 0 for the height. It converts each student's height to centimeters and weight to grams. Then, it calculates the graduation gown size needed by adding $\frac{1}{3}$ of the weight in grams to the value of the height in centimeters. The program prints the result for each student. There are 2.54 centimeters in an inch and 453.59 grams in a pound. Use named constants wherever you think they are appropriate.

3. Design the output and draw a flowchart or write pseudocode for a program that calculates the service charge a customer owes for writing a bad check. The program accepts a customer's name, the date the check was written (year, month, and day), the current date (year, month, and day), and the amount of the check in dollars and cents. The program continues until an eof value is encountered. The service charge is $20 plus 2 percent of the amount of the check, plus $5 for every month that has passed since the check was written. A check is one month late as soon as a new month starts—so a bad check written on September 30 is one month overdue on October 1.

4. The owner of the Fuzzy Logic Pet Store needs the following programs:

   a. The owner has agreed to make a donation to the local animal shelter for every pet sale. The user enters an animal type and sale price. Output is the donation amount, calculated as 10 percent of the sale price. Design the interactive screen, then draw the flowchart or write the pseudocode for this program.

   b. The pet store owner needs a weekly sales report. The user continuously inputs records containing an animal type and the price, ending with "XXX" as a sentinel animal type. The output consists of a printed report titled PET SALES, with column headings Type of Animal and Price. After all records print, a footer line "END OF REPORT" prints. Design the report, then draw the flowchart or write the pseudocode for this program.

5. The owner of Bits and Pieces Manufacturing Company needs the following programs:

   a. The human resources manager wants a program that calculates the result if she gives an employee a raise in salary. The output is the projected salary with the raise. The input is the current salary and the percentage increase expressed as a decimal (for example, 0.04 for a 4 percent raise). Design the interactive screen, then draw a flowchart or write pseudocode for a program that accepts the input and produces the report.

   b. The human resources manager wants to produce a personnel report that shows the end result if she gives everyone a 10 percent raise in salary. The output consists of a printed report titled Projected Raises. Fields printed on output are: last name of employee, first name of employee, and current weekly salary. Include appropriate column headings and a footer. Design the report, then draw a flowchart or write pseudocode for a program that accepts the input fields continuously and produces the report.

6. **The sales manager of The Couch Potato Furniture Company needs the following programs:**

   a. The sales manager wants to quickly see the profit on any item sold. Input includes the wholesale price and retail price for an item. The output is the item's profit, which is the retail price minus the wholesale price. Design the interactive screen for this program, then draw the flowchart or write the pseudocode.

   b. The sales manager maintains an inventory file that includes data about every item it sells. The manager wants a report that lists each stock number, description, and profit, which is the retail price minus the wholesale price. Input fields include a stock number, description, wholesale price, and retail price. Design the report, then draw the flowchart or write the pseudocode for this program.

7. **The head counselor at Roughing It Summer Camp needs the following programs:**

   a. The counselor wants to compute a camper's skill scores so each camper can be assigned to a group with similar skills. She needs an interactive program that can be used as each camper arrives at the campgrounds and reports his or her estimated skill levels. The user enters a score in each of four areas. Scores range from 1 to 10. The four areas are: swimming, tennis, horsemanship, and crafts. Output is a total score that is the sum of the camper's four skill scores. Design the interactive screen for this program, then draw the flowchart or write the pseudocode.

   b. The camp keeps a record for every camper, including first name, last name, birth date, and skill scores that range from 1 to 10 in four areas: swimming, tennis, horsemanship, and crafts. (The birth date is stored in the format YYYYMMDD without any punctuation. For example, January 21, 1997 is 19970121.) The camp wants a printed report listing each camper's data, plus a total score that is the sum of the camper's four skill scores. The input file description is shown below. Design the output for this program, then draw the flow-chart or write the pseudocode.

```
File name: CAMPERS
FIELD DESCRIPTION      DATA TYPE    COMMENTS
First Name             String       15 characters maximum
Last Name              String       15 characters maximum
Birth Date             Numeric      8 digits in the format YYYYMMDD
Swimming Skill         Numeric      0 decimals
Tennis Skill           Numeric      0 decimals
Horsemanship Skill     Numeric      0 decimals
Crafts Skill           Numeric      0 decimals
```

8. **All in a Day's Work is a temporary employment agency. The manager needs to determine how much tax to withhold for each employee. This withholding amount computes as 20 percent of each employee's weekly pay. The weekly pay is the hourly pay times 40.**

   a. Design an interactive screen that displays an employee's weekly pay and withholding amount. The user inputs the hourly pay rate for an employee. Draw the flowchart or write the pseudocode for this program.

   b. Design a printed report titled WITHHOLDING FOR EACH EMPLOYEE. Input fields include the first and last names of each employee and hourly pay rate. Fields printed on output are: last name of employee, first name of employee, hourly pay, weekly pay, and withholding amount per week. Draw the flowchart or write the pseudocode for this program.

9. **The manager of the Jeter County Softball team wants the following computer programs that compute batting averages. A batting average is computed as hits divided by at-bats, and is usually expressed to three decimal positions (for example, .235).**

   a. The manager wants an interactive program that produces a report showing a player's batting average. The user is prompted for a player's number of hits and at-bats. Design the interactive screen, then draw the flowchart or write the pseudocode for this program.

   b. The team manager wants a report showing her players' batting statistics. The output consists of a printed report titled TEAM STATISTICS. Input data include a player's number, first name, last name, hits, and at-bats. Fields printed on output are: player number, first name, last name, and batting average. Design the report, then draw the flowchart or write the pseudocode for this program.

10. **The manager of Endeavor Car Rental company wants programs that compute the amount earned per mile for cars rented. An automobile's miles traveled are computed by subtracting the odometer reading when the car is rented from the odometer reading when the car is returned. The amount earned per mile is computed by dividing the rental fee by the miles traveled.**

   a. Design an interactive program that calculates the revenue earned per mile on a vehicle. The user inputs both odometer readings and the rental fee charged. The output includes miles traveled, rental fee, and amount earned per mile. Design the interactive screen, then draw the flowchart or write the pseudocode for this program.

   b. Design a program that produces a report showing the revenue earned per mile on vehicles rented each week. Input fields include the vehicle identification number, both odometer readings, and the rental fee charged. The output consists of a printed report titled CAR RENTAL REVENUE STATISTICS. Fields printed on output are: vehicle identification number, odometer reading out, odometer reading in, miles traveled, rental fee, and amount earned per mile. Design the report, then draw the flowchart or write the pseudocode for this program.

GAME ZONE

For games to hold your interest, they almost always include some random, unpredictable behavior. For example, a game in which you shoot asteroids loses some of its fun if the asteroids follow the same, predictable path each time you play the game. Therefore, generating random values is a key component in creating most interesting computer games. Many programming languages come with a built-in method you can use to generate random numbers. The syntax varies in each language, but it is usually something like the following:

```
myRandomNumber = random(10)
```

In this statement, `myRandomNumber` is a numeric variable you have declared and the expression `random(10)` means "get a random number between 1 and 10." By convention, in a flowchart, you would place a statement like this is in a processing symbol with two vertical stripes at the edges as shown below.

Create a flowchart or pseudocode that shows the logic for a program that generates a random number, then asks the user to think of a number between 1 and 10. Then display the randomly generated number so the user can see whether his or her guess was accurate. (In future chapters you will improve this game so that the user can enter a guess and the program can determine whether the user was correct.)

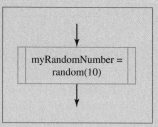

DETECTIVE WORK

1. **Explore the job opportunities in technical writing. What are the job responsibilities? What is the average starting salary? What is the outlook for growth?**

2. **Explore the job opportunities in programming. What are the job responsibilities? What is the average starting salary? What is the outlook for growth?**

3. **Many programming style guides are published on the Web. These guides suggest good identifiers, standard indentation rules, and similar issues in specific programming languages. Find style guides for at least two languages (for example, C++, Java, Visual Basic, C#, COBOL, RPG, or Pascal) and list any differences you notice.**

UP FOR DISCUSSION

1. **Would you prefer to be a programmer, write documentation, or both? Why?**

2. **Would you prefer to write a large program by yourself, or work on a team in which each programmer produces one or more modules? Why?**

3. **Can you think of any disadvantages to providing program documentation for other programmers or for the user?**

4. **Extreme programming is a system for rapidly developing software. One of its tenets is that all production code is written by two programmers sitting at one machine. Is this a good idea? Does working this way as a programmer appeal to you? Why or why not?**

MAKING DECISIONS

In this chapter you will:

Evaluate Boolean expressions to make comparisons
Use the relational comparison operators
Learn about AND logic
Learn about OR logic
Make selections within ranges
Learn about precedence when combining AND and OR
  selections
Learn more about the case structure
Use a decision table

EVALUATING BOOLEAN EXPRESSIONS TO MAKE COMPARISONS

The reason people frequently think computers are smart lies in the computer program's ability to make decisions. A medical diagnosis program that can decide if your symptoms fit various disease profiles seems quite intelligent, as does a program that can offer different potential vacation routes based on your destination.

The selection structure (sometimes called a decision structure) involved in such programs is not new to you—it's one of the basic structures you learned about in Chapter 2. See Figures 4-1 and 4-2.

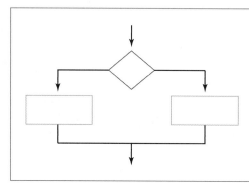

Figure 4-1 The dual-alternative selection structure

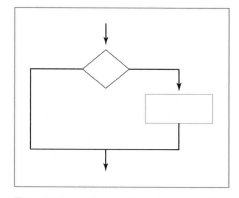

Figure 4-2 The single-alternative selection structure

In Chapter 2 you learned that you can refer to the structure in Figure 4-1 as a dual-alternative, or binary, selection because an action is associated with each of two possible outcomes: depending on the answer to the question represented by the diamond, the logical flow proceeds either to the left branch of the structure or to the right. The choices are mutually exclusive; that is, the logic can flow only to one of the two alternatives, never to both. This selection structure is also called an if-then-else structure.

> **»NOTE** This book follows the convention that the two logical paths emerging from a decision are drawn to the right and left in a flowchart. Some programmers draw one flowline emerging from the side of the diamond shape that represents a selection, and then draw the other emerging from the bottom. The exact format of the diagram is not as important as the idea that one logical path flows into a selection, and two possible outcomes emerge.

> **»NOTE**
> You can call a single-alternative decision (or selection) a *single-sided decision*. Similarly, a dual-alternative decision is a *double-sided decision* (or selection).

The flowchart segment in Figure 4-2 represents a single-alternative selection where action is required for only one outcome of the question. You call this form of the if-then-else structure an **if-then**, because no alternative or "else" action is necessary.

Figure 4-3 shows the flowchart and pseudocode for a program that contains a typical if-then-else decision in a business program. Many organizations pay employees time and a half (one and one-half times their usual hourly rate) for hours worked in excess of 40 per week.

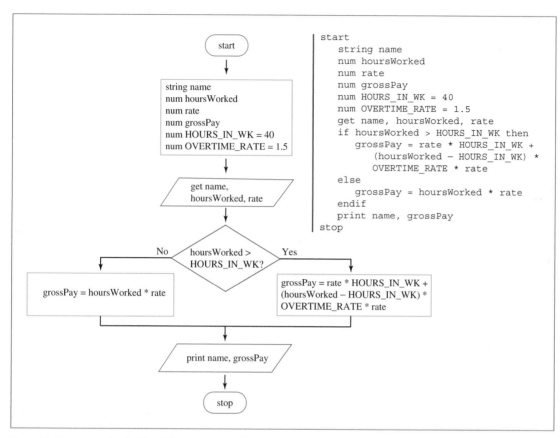

Figure 4-3 Flowchart and pseudocode for overtime payroll program

>> **NOTE** Throughout this book, you will see many examples presented in both flowchart and pseudocode form. When you first analyze a solution, you might find it easier if you concentrate on just one of the two design tools at first. When you understand how the program works using one tool (for example, the flowchart), you can proceed to confirm that the solution is identical using the other tool (for example, the pseudocode).

In the program in Figure 4-3, several variables and constants are declared. The variables include those that will be retrieved from input (name, which is a string, and hoursWorked and rate, which are numbers) and one that will be calculated from the input values (grossPay, which is a number). The program in Figure 4-3 also uses two named constants: HOURS_IN_WK, which represents the number of hours in a standard workweek, and OVERTIME_RATE, which represents a multiplication factor for the premium rate at which an employee is paid after working the standard number of hours in a week.

After the input data is retrieved in the program in Figure 4-3, a decision is made about the value of hoursWorked. The longer calculation that adds a time-and-a-half factor to an employee's gross pay executes only when the expression hoursWorked > HOURS_IN_WK is true. The long calculation exists in the **if clause** of the decision—the part of the decision that holds the action or actions that execute when the tested condition in the decision is true. The shorter calculation, which produces grossPay by multiplying hoursWorked by rate, constitutes the **else clause** of the decision—the part that executes only when the tested condition in the decision is false.

>> **NOTE**
The statement get name, hoursWorked, rate is intended to represent any type of input whether interactive or from a file. With interactive input, you would want to add a prompt before each data item was retrieved.

>> **NOTE**
In Chapter 3 you learned that named constants conventionally are created using all uppercase letters.

Suppose an employee's paycheck should be reduced if the employee participates in the company dental plan and that no action is taken if the employee is not a dental plan participant. Figure 4-4 shows how this decision might be added to the payroll program. The additions from Figure 4-3 are shaded.

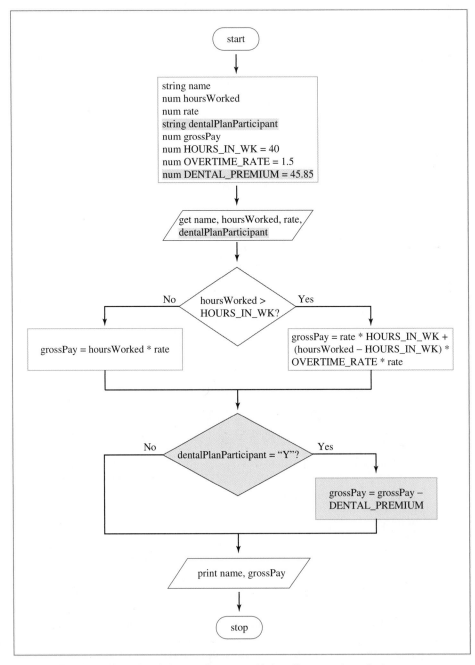

Figure 4-4 Flowchart and pseudocode for payroll program with dental insurance determination

```
start
   string name
   num hoursWorked
   num rate
   string dentalPlanParticipant
   num grossPay
   num HOURS_IN_WK = 40
   num OVERTIME_RATE = 1.5
   num DENTAL_PREMIUM = 45.85
   get name, hoursWorked, rate, dentalPlanParticipant
   if hoursWorked > HOURS_IN_WK then
      grossPay = rate * HOURS_IN_WK +
         (hoursWorked - HOURS_IN_WK) *
         OVERTIME_RATE * rate
   else
      grossPay = hoursWorked * rate
   endif
   if dentalPlanParticipant = "Y" then
      grossPay = grossPay - DENTAL_PREMIUM
   endif
   print name, grossPay
stop
```

Figure 4-4 Flowchart and pseudocode for payroll program with dental insurance determination (*continued*)

The expressions hoursWorked > HOURS_IN_WK and dentalPlanParticipant = "Y" in Figures 4-3 and 4-4 are Boolean expressions. A **Boolean expression** is one that represents only one of two states, usually expressed as true or false. Every decision you make in a computer program involves evaluating a Boolean expression. True/false evaluation is "natural" from a computer's standpoint, because computer circuitry consists of two-state on-off switches, often represented by 1 or 0. Every computer decision yields a true-or-false, yes-or-no, 1-or-0 result.

» NOTE Mathematician George Boole (1815–1864) approached logic more simply than his predecessors did, by expressing logical selections with common algebraic symbols. He is considered the founder of mathematical logic, and Boolean (true/false) expressions are named for him.

TWO TRUTHS AND A LIE:
EVALUATING BOOLEAN EXPRESSIONS TO MAKE COMPARISONS

1. The if clause is the part of a decision that executes when a tested condition in a decision is true.

2. The else clause is the part of a decision that executes only when the tested condition in a decision is false.

3. A case expression is one that represents only one of two states, usually expressed as true or false.

The false statement is #3. A Boolean expression is one that represents only one of two states, usually expressed as true or false.

USING THE RELATIONAL COMPARISON OPERATORS

Usually, you can compare only values that are of the same type; that is, you can compare numeric values to other numeric values, and text strings to other strings. You can ask every programming question by using one of only three types of comparison operators in a Boolean expression. For any two values that are the same type, you can decide whether:

» The two values are equal.

» The first value is greater than the second value.

» The first value is less than the second value.

>>**NOTE** Usually, string variables are not considered to be equal unless they are identical, including the spacing and whether they appear in uppercase or lowercase. For example, "black pen" is *not* equal to "blackpen", "BLACK PEN", or "Black Pen".

>>**NOTE** Some programming languages allow you to compare a character to a number. If you do, then a single character's numeric code value is used in the comparison. For example, many computers use the American Standard Code for Information Interchange (ASCII) system or the Unicode system. In both coding schemes, an uppercase "A" is represented numerically as a 65, an uppercase "B" is a 66, and so on.

In any Boolean expression, the two values compared can be either variables or constants. For example, the expression currentTotal = 100? compares a variable, currentTotal, to a numeric constant, 100. Depending on the currentTotal value, the expression is true or false. In the expression currentTotal = previousTotal?, both values are variables, and the result is also true or false depending on the values stored in each of the two variables. Although it's legal to do so, you would never use expressions in which you compare two constants—for example 20 = 20? or 30 = 40?. Such expressions are considered **trivial** because each will always evaluate to the same result: true for 20 = 20? and false for 30 = 40?.

Each programming language supports its own set of **relational comparison operators**, or comparison symbols, that express these Boolean tests. For example, many languages such as Visual Basic and Pascal use the equal sign (=) to express testing for equivalency, so balanceDue = 0 compares balanceDue to zero. COBOL programmers can use the equal sign, but they can also spell out the expression, as in balanceDue equal to 0?. Report Program Generator (RPG) programmers use the two-letter operator EQ in place of a symbol. C#, C++, and Java programmers use two equal signs to test for equivalency, so they write balanceDue == 0 to compare the two values. Although each programming language supports its own syntax for comparing values' equivalency, all languages provide for the same logical concept of equivalency.

>>**NOTE**
The term "relational comparison operators" is somewhat redundant. You can also call these operators **relational operators** or **comparison operators**.

>>**NOTE** The reason some languages use two equal signs for comparisons is to avoid confusion with assignment statements such as balanceDue = 0. In C++, C#, or Java, this statement only assigns the value 0 to balanceDue; it does not compare balanceDue to zero.

Most languages allow you to use the algebraic signs for greater than (>) and less than (<) to make the corresponding comparisons. In addition to the three basic comparisons of equal to, greater than, and less than, most programming languages provide three others. For any two values that are the same type, you can decide whether:

» The first is greater than or equal to the second.

» The first is less than or equal to the second.

» The two are not equal.

» **NOTE**
Whenever you use a comparison operator, you must provide a value on each side of the operator. Comparison operators are sometimes called *binary operators* because of this requirement.

Most programming languages allow you to express "greater than or equal to" by typing a greater-than sign immediately followed by an equal sign (>=). When you are drawing a flow-chart or writing pseudocode, you might prefer a greater-than sign with a line under it ($\geq$) because mathematicians use that symbol to mean "greater than or equal to." However, when you write a program, you type >= as two separate characters, because no single key on the keyboard expresses this concept and no programming language has been designed to understand it. Similarly, "less than or equal to" is written with two symbols, < immediately followed by =.

> » **NOTE** The operators >= and <= are always treated as a single unit; no spaces separate the two parts of the operator. Also, the equal sign always appears second. No programming language allows => or =< as a comparison operator.

Any relational situation can be expressed using just three types of comparisons: equal, greater than, and less than. You never need the three additional comparisons (greater than or equal, less than or equal, or not equal), but using them often makes decisions more convenient. For example, assume you need to issue a 10 percent discount to any customer whose age is 65 or greater, and charge full price to other customers. You can use the greater-than-or-equal-to symbol to write the logic as follows:

```
if customerAge >= 65 then
    discount = 0.10
else
    discount = 0
endif
```

As an alternative, if you want to avoid using the >= operator, you can express the same logic by writing:

```
if customerAge < 65 then
    discount = 0
else
    discount = 0.10
endif
```

In any decision for which a >= b is true, then a < b is false. Conversely, if a >= b is false, then a < b is true. By rephrasing the question and swapping the actions taken based on the outcome, you can make the same decision in multiple ways. The clearest route is often to ask a question so the positive or true outcome results in the action that was your motivation for making the test. When your company policy is to "provide a discount for those who are 65 and older," the phrase "greater than or equal to" comes to mind, so it is the most natural to use. Conversely, if your policy is to "provide no discount for those under 65," then it is more natural to use the "less than" syntax. Either way, the same people receive a discount.

Comparing two amounts to decide if they are *not* equal to each other is the most confusing of all the comparisons. Using "not equal to" in decisions involves thinking in double negatives, which makes you prone to include logical errors in your programs. For example, consider the flowchart segment in Figure 4-5.

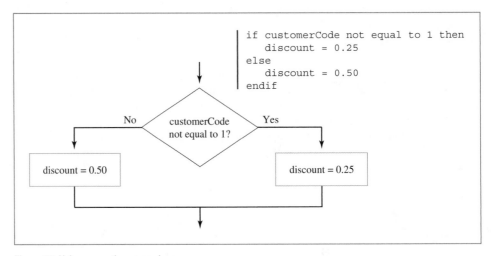

```
if customerCode not equal to 1 then
    discount = 0.25
else
    discount = 0.50
endif
```

Figure 4-5 Using a negative comparison

In Figure 4-5, if the value of customerCode *is* equal to 1, the logical flow follows the false branch of the selection. If customerCode not equal to 1 is true, the discount is 0.25; if customerCode not equal to 1 is not true, it means the customerCode *is* 1, and the discount is 0.50. Even using the phrase "customerCode not equal to 1 is not true" is awkward.

Figure 4-6 shows the same decision, this time asked in the positive. Making the decision if customerCode *is* 1 then discount = 0.50 is clearer than trying to determine what customerCode is *not*.

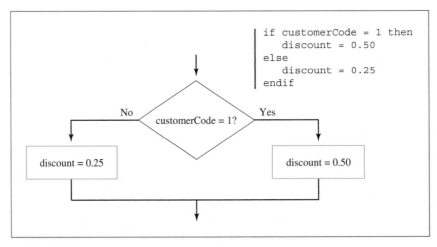

```
if customerCode = 1 then
    discount = 0.50
else
    discount = 0.25
endif
```

Figure 4-6 Using the positive equivalent of the negative comparison in Figure 4-5

Besides being awkward to use, the "not equal to" comparison operator is the one most likely to be different in various programming languages. Visual Basic and Pascal use a less-than sign followed immediately by a greater-than sign (<>); C#, C++, C, and Java use an exclamation point followed by an equal sign (!=). In a flowchart or in pseudocode, you can use the symbol that mathematicians use to mean "not equal," an equal sign with a slash through it (≠). When you program, you will not be able to use this symbol, because no single key on the keyboard produces it. When drawing a flowchart or writing pseudocode in which you must use a negative decision, writing "not" is also quite acceptable.

>> **NOTE** Although NOT comparisons can be awkward to use, your meaning is sometimes clearest if you use one. Frequently, this occurs when you use an `if` without an `else`, taking action only when some comparison is false. An example would be: `if customerZipCode is not equal to LOCAL_ZIP_CODE then add deliveryCharge to total`.

Table 4-1 summarizes the six comparison operators and contrasts trivial (both true and false) examples with typical examples of their use.

Comparison	Trivial True Example	Trivial False Example	Typical Example
Equal to	7 = 7?	7 = 4?	amtOrdered = 12?
Greater than	12 > 3?	4 > 9?	hoursWorked > 40?
Less than	1 < 8?	13 < 10?	hourlyWage < 5.65?
Greater than or equal to	5 >= 5?	3 >= 9?	customerAge >= 65?
Less than or equal to	4 <= 4?	8 <= 2?	daysOverdue <= 60?
Not equal to	16 <> 3?	18 <> 18?	customerBalance <> 0?

Table 4-1 Relational comparisons

TWO TRUTHS AND A LIE:
USING THE RELATIONAL COMPARISON OPERATORS

1. Usually, you can compare only values that are of the same data type.

2. A Boolean expression is defined as one that decides whether two values are equal.

3. In any Boolean expression, the two values compared can be either variables or constants.

The false statement is #2. Although deciding whether two values are equal is a Boolean expression, so is deciding whether one is greater than or less than another. A Boolean expression is one that results in a true or false value.

UNDERSTANDING AND LOGIC

Often, you need more than one selection structure to determine whether an action should take place. When you need to ask multiple questions before an outcome is determined, you must create a **compound condition**. One type of compound condition is needed when the results of at least two decisions must be true for some action to take place.

For example, suppose you have salespeople for whom you calculate bonus payments based on sales performance. A salesperson receives a $50 bonus only if the salesperson sells more than three items that total at least $1,000 in value. This type of situation is known as an **AND decision** because the salesperson's data must pass two tests—a minimum number of items sold *and* a minimum value—before the salesperson receives the bonus. An AND decision can be constructed using a **nested decision**, or a **nested if**—that is, a decision "inside of" another decision. The flowchart and pseudocode for the program are shown in Figure 4-7.

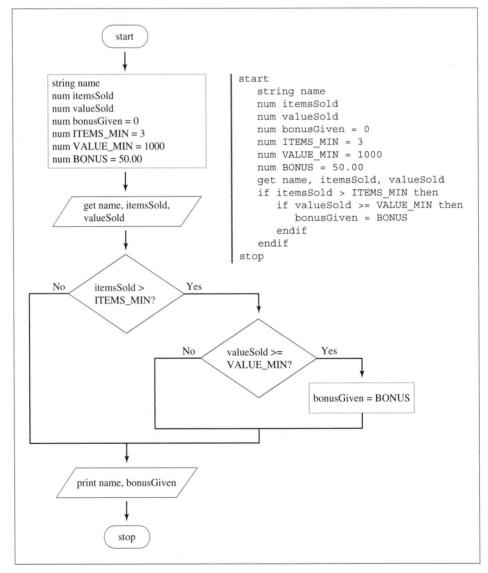

```
start
    string name
    num itemsSold
    num valueSold
    num bonusGiven = 0
    num ITEMS_MIN = 3
    num VALUE_MIN = 1000
    num BONUS = 50.00
    get name, itemsSold, valueSold
    if itemsSold > ITEMS_MIN then
        if valueSold >= VALUE_MIN then
            bonusGiven = BONUS
        endif
    endif
stop
```

Figure 4-7 Flowchart and pseudocode for salesperson bonus-determining program in which salesperson must meet two criteria to get a bonus

>> **NOTE** You first learned about nesting structures in Chapter 2. You can always stack and nest any of the basic structures.

>> **NOTE** A series of nested if statements is also called a **cascading if statement**.

In Figure 4-7, variables are declared to hold a salesperson's name, the number of items the salesperson has sold, and the value of the items sold. Constants are declared to hold the minimums needed to receive a bonus and for the value of the bonus itself. In the nested if structure in Figure 4-7, the expression itemsSold > ITEMS_MIN is evaluated first. If this expression is true, then, and only then, is the second Boolean expression (valueSold >= VALUE_MIN) evaluated. If that expression is also true, then the bonus assignment executes and the nested if structure ends.

>> **NOTE** In Figure 4-7, notice that bonusGiven is initialized to 0. That way, if the result of either decision is false and no new value is assigned to bonusGiven, it still will have a usable value. If you chose not to initialize bonusGiven, you could add statements to assign 0 to it if either decision's result was false.

When you use nested if statements, you must pay careful attention to the placement of any else clauses and the endif statements in your pseudocode. For example, suppose you want to distribute bonuses on a revised schedule, as follows:

» If the salesperson does not sell at least three items, you want to give a $10 bonus.
» If the salesperson sells at least three items, the bonus is $25 if the value of the items is under $1,000, or $50 if the value is $1,000 or more.

Figure 4-8 shows the section of logic that assigns the bonuses. In the flowchart, you can see that the shaded, second selection structure is contained entirely within one side of the first structure. When one if statement follows another in the pseudocode, the first else clause encountered is paired with the last if encountered. The complete nested if-else structure that is shaded fits entirely within the if portion of the outer if-else statement. No matter how many levels of if-else statements are needed to produce a solution, the else statements always are associated with their ifs on a "first in-last out" basis.

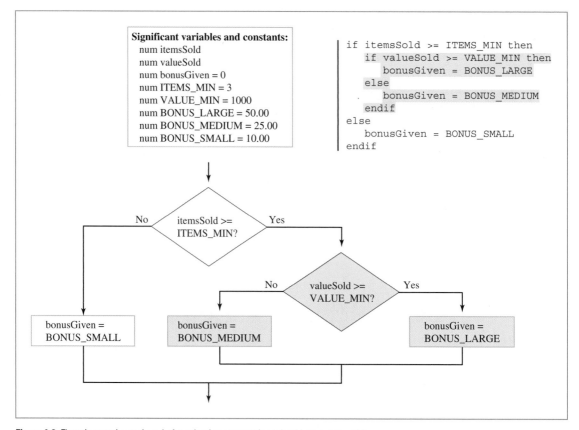

Figure 4-8 Flowchart and pseudocode for selection process in revised bonus-determining program

NESTING AND DECISIONS FOR EFFICIENCY

When you nest decisions because the resulting action requires that two conditions be true, you must decide which of the two decisions to make first. Logically, either selection in an AND decision can come first. However, when there are two selections, you can often improve your program's performance by correctly choosing which selection to make first.

For example, Figure 4-9 shows two ways to design the nested decision structure that assigns a $50 bonus to salespeople who sell more than three items valued at $1,000 or more. If you want to assign this bonus, you can ask about the items sold first, eliminate those salespeople who do not qualify, and ask about the value of the items sold only for those salespeople who "pass" the number of items test. Or, you could ask about the value of the items first, eliminate those who do not qualify, and ask about the number of items only for those salespeople who "pass" the value test. Either way, only salespeople who pass both tests receive the $50 bonus. Does it make a difference which question is asked first? As far as the result goes, no. Either way, the same salespeople receive the bonus—those who qualify on the basis of both criteria. As far as program efficiency goes, however, it *might* make a difference which question is asked first.

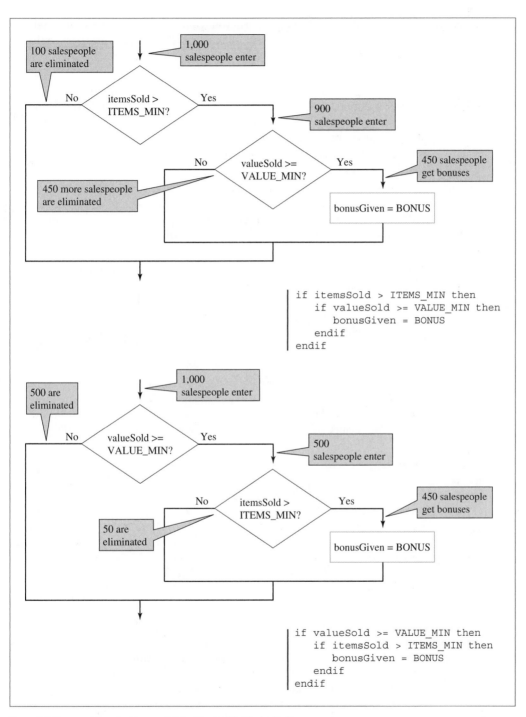

100 salespeople are eliminated

1,000 salespeople enter

itemsSold > ITEMS_MIN?

No   Yes

900 salespeople enter

valueSold >= VALUE_MIN?

No   Yes

450 salespeople get bonuses

450 more salespeople are eliminated

bonusGiven = BONUS

```
if itemsSold > ITEMS_MIN then
    if valueSold >= VALUE_MIN then
        bonusGiven = BONUS
    endif
endif
```

500 are eliminated

1,000 salespeople enter

valueSold >= VALUE_MIN?

No   Yes

500 salespeople enter

itemsSold > ITEMS_MIN?

No   Yes

450 salespeople get bonuses

50 are eliminated

bonusGiven = BONUS

```
if valueSold >= VALUE_MIN then
    if itemsSold > ITEMS_MIN then
        bonusGiven = BONUS
    endif
endif
```

Figure 4-9 Two ways to select bonus recipients using identical criteria

Assume you know that out of 1,000 salespeople in your company, about 90 percent, or 900, sell more than three items in a pay period. Assume you also know that because many of the items are relatively low-priced, only about half the 1,000 salespeople, or 500, sell items valued at $1,000 or more.

If you use the logic shown first in Figure 4-9, and you need to determine bonuses for 1,000 salespeople, the first question, `itemsSold > ITEMS_MIN?`, will execute 1,000 times. For approximately 90 percent of the salespeople, or 900 of them, the answer is `true`, so 100 salespeople are eliminated from the bonus assignment, and 900 proceed to the next question about the value of the items sold. Only about half the salespeople sell at least $1,000 worth of merchandise, so 450 of the 900 receive the bonus.

Using the alternate logic in Figure 4-9, the first question `valueSold >= VALUE_MIN?` will also be asked 1,000 times—once for each salesperson. Because only about half the company's salespeople sell at this higher dollar level, only 500 will "pass" this test and proceed to the question for number of items sold. Then about 90 percent of the 500, or 450 salespeople, will pass this second test and receive the bonus.

Whether you use the first or second decision order in Figure 4-9, the same 450 employees who surpass both sales criteria receive the bonus. The difference is that when you ask about the items sold first, the program must ask 1,900 questions to assign the correct bonuses—the first question tests the data for all 1,000 salespeople, and 900 continue to the second question. If you use the alternate logic, asking about `valueSold` first, the program asks only 1,500 questions—all 1,000 records are tested with the first question, but only 500 proceed to the second question. By asking about the dollar value of the goods first, you "save" 400 decisions.

The 400-question difference between the first and second set of decisions doesn't take much time on most computers. But it does take *some* time, and if a corporation has hundreds of thousands of salespeople instead of only 1,000, or if many such decisions have to be made within a program, performance time can be significantly improved by asking questions in the proper order.

In many AND decisions, you have no idea which of two events is more likely to occur; in that case, you can legitimately ask either question first. In addition, even though you know the probability of each of two conditions, the two events might not be mutually exclusive; that is, one might depend on the other. For example, salespeople who sell more items are also likely to have surpassed a requisite dollar value. Depending on the relationship between these questions, the order in which you ask them might matter less or not matter at all. However, if you do know the probabilities of the conditions, or can make a reasonable guess, the general rule is: *In an AND decision, first ask the question that is less likely to be true*. This eliminates as many instances of the second decision as possible, which speeds up processing time.

COMBINING DECISIONS IN AN AND SELECTION

Most programming languages allow you to ask two or more questions in a single comparison by using a **conditional AND operator**, or more simply, an **AND operator**. For example, if you want to provide a bonus for salespeople who sell more than ITEMS_MIN items and at least VALUE_MIN in value, you can use nested ifs, or you can include both decisions in a single statement by writing `itemsSold > ITEMS_MIN AND valueSold >= VALUE_MIN?`. When you use one or more AND operators to combine two or more Boolean expressions, each Boolean expression must be true for the entire expression to be evaluated as true. For example, if you ask, "Are you at least 18, and are you a registered voter, and did you vote in the last election?", the answer to all three parts of the question must be "yes" before the response can be a single, summarizing "yes". If any part of the expression is false, then the entire expression is false.

One tool that can help you understand the AND operator is a truth table. **Truth tables** are diagrams used in mathematics and logic to help describe the truth of an entire expression based on the truth of its parts. Table 4-2 shows a truth table that lists all the possibilities with an AND decision. As the table shows, for any two expressions x and y, the expression x AND y is true only if both x and y are individually true. If either x or y alone is false, or if both are false, then the expression x AND y is false.

x	y	x AND y
True	True	True
True	False	False
False	True	False
False	False	False

Table 4-2 Truth table for the AND operator

If the programming language you use allows an AND operator, you must realize that the question you place first is the one that will be asked first, and cases that are eliminated based on the first question will not proceed to the second question. In other words, each part of an expression that uses an AND operator is evaluated only as far as necessary to determine whether the entire expression is true or false. This feature is called **short-circuit evaluation**. The computer can ask only one question at a time; even when your pseudocode looks like the first example in Figure 4-10, the computer will execute the logic shown in the second example.

```
if itemsSold > ITEMS_MIN AND valueSold >= VALUE_MIN then
    bonusGiven = BONUS
endif
```

Even when you write *this*

```
if itemsSold > ITEMS_MIN then
    if valueSold >= VALUE_MIN then
        bonusGiven = BONUS
    endif
endif
```

the logic executes as *this*

Figure 4-10 Using an AND operator and the logic behind it

>> **NOTE** The conditional AND operator in Java, C++, and C# consists of two ampersands, with no spaces between them (&&). In Visual Basic, you use the word And.

>> **NOTE** Using an AND operator in a decision that involves multiple conditions does not eliminate your responsibility for determining which condition to test first. Even when you use an AND operator, the computer makes decisions one at a time, and makes them in the order you ask them. If the first question in an AND expression evaluates to false, then the entire expression is false, and the second question is not even tested.

>> **NOTE** Some languages provide an additional type of AND statement that does not employ short circuitry.

>> **NOTE** You never are required to use the AND operator because using nested if statements can always achieve the same result, but using the AND operator often makes your code more concise, less error-prone, and easier to understand.

AVOIDING COMMON ERRORS IN AN AND SELECTION

When you must satisfy two or more criteria to initiate an event in a program, you must make sure that the second decision is made entirely within the first decision. For example, if a program's objective is to assign a $50 bonus to salespeople who sell more than ITEMS_MIN items with a value of at least VALUE_MIN, then the program segment shown in Figure 4-11 contains three different types of logic errors.

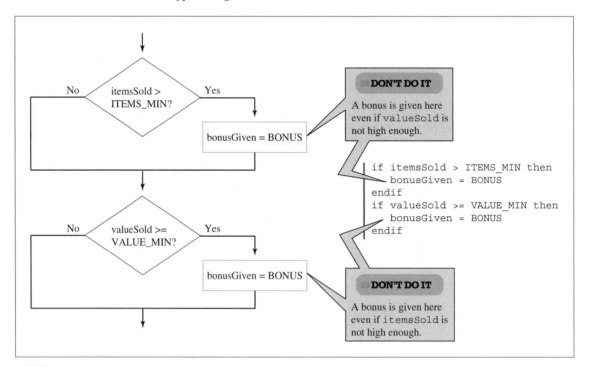

Figure 4-11 Incorrect logic to assign bonuses to salespeople who meet two criteria

The logic in Figure 4-11 shows that a salesperson who sells more than the minimum required items receives a $50 bonus. This salesperson should not necessarily receive the bonus—the dollar value might not be high enough, and it has not yet been tested. In addition, a salesperson who has not sold the minimum number of items is not eliminated from the second question. Instead, all salespeople endure the dollar value question, and some are assigned the bonus even though they might not have passed the criterion for number of items sold. Additionally, any salesperson who passes both tests has a bonus assigned twice. This does not result in an error, because the second $50 assignment replaces the first one, but processing time is wasted. For many reasons, the logic shown in Figure 4-11 is *not* correct for this problem.

Beginning programmers often make another type of error when they must make two comparisons on the same variable while using a logical AND operator. For example, suppose you want to assign a $75 bonus to those who have sold between 5 and 10 items inclusive. When you make this type of decision, you are basing it on a **range of values**—every value between low and high limits. For example, you want to select salespeople whose itemsSold value is greater than or equal to 5 AND whose itemsSold value is less than or equal to 10; therefore, you need to make two comparisons on the same variable. Without the logical AND operator, the comparison is:

```
num itemsSold
num bonusGiven
num MIN_FOR_BONUS = 5
num MAX_FOR_BONUS = 10
num BONUS = 75
if itemsSold >= MIN_FOR_BONUS then
    if itemsSold <= MAX_FOR_BONUS then
        bonusGiven = BONUS
    endif
endif
```

The correct way to make this comparison with the AND operator is as follows:

```
if itemsSold >= MIN_FOR_BONUS AND itemsSold <= MAX_FOR_BONUS then
    bonusGiven = BONUS
endif
```

You substitute the AND operator for the phrase then if. However, some programmers might try to make the comparison as follows:

```
if itemsSold >= MIN_FOR_BONUS AND <= MAX_FOR_BONUS then
    bonusGiven = BONUS
endif
```

DON'T DO IT

This Boolean expression is missing an operand.

In most programming languages, the phrase itemsSold >= MIN_FOR_BONUS AND <= MAX_FOR_BONUS is incorrect. The logical AND is usually a binary operator that requires a complete Boolean expression on each side. The expression to the right of the AND operator is <= MAX_FOR_BONUS which is not a complete Boolean expression; you must indicate *what* is being compared to MAX_FOR_BONUS.

> **TIP** In some programming languages, such as COBOL and RPG, you can write the equivalent of itemsSold >= MIN_FOR_BONUS AND <= MAX_FOR_BONUS? and the itemsSold variable is implied for both comparisons. Still, it is clearer, and therefore preferable, to use the two full Boolean expressions.

> **TIP** For clarity, many programmers prefer to surround each Boolean expression in a compound Boolean expression with its own set of parentheses. For example:
>
> ```
> if((itemsSold >= MIN_FOR_BONUS) && (itemsSold <= MAX_FOR_BONUS))
>     bonusGiven = BONUS;
> endif
> ```
>
> Use this format if it is clear to you.

TWO TRUTHS AND A LIE:
UNDERSTANDING AND LOGIC

1. When you nest decisions because the resulting action requires that two conditions be true, logically, either selection in an AND decision can come first.

2. When two selections are required, you can often improve your program's performance by making an appropriate choice as to which selection to make first.

3. For efficiency, in a nested selection, you should first ask the question that is more likely to be true.

The false statement is # 3. For efficiency, in a nested selection, you should first ask the question that is less likely to be true.

UNDERSTANDING OR LOGIC

Sometimes you want to take action when one *or* the other of two conditions is true. This is called an **OR decision** because either one condition must be met *or* some other condition must be met in order for an event to take place. If someone asks, "Are you free Friday or Saturday?", only one of the two conditions has to be true for the answer to the whole question to be "yes"; only if the answers to both halves of the question are false is the value of the entire expression false.

For example, suppose you want to assign a $300 bonus to salespeople when they have achieved one of two goals—selling at least five items, or selling at least $2,000 worth of merchandise. Figure 4-12 shows a program that accomplishes this objective.

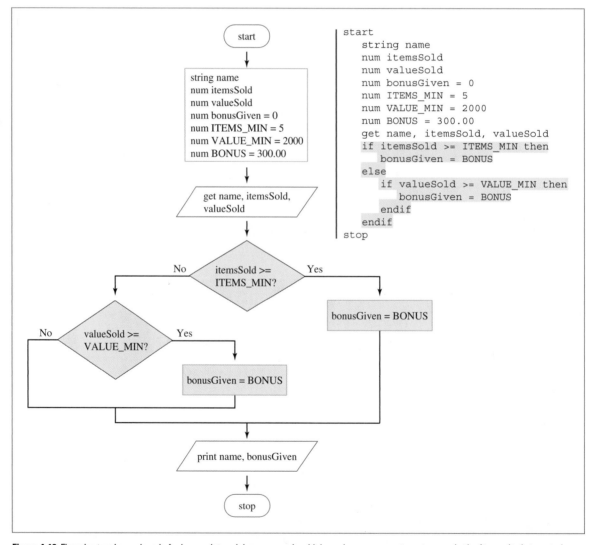

Figure 4-12 Flowchart and pseudocode for bonus-determining program in which a salesperson must meet one or both of two criteria to get a bonus

After a salesperson's data is input in the program in Figure 4-12, you ask the question `itemsSold >= ITEMS_MIN?`, and if the result is true, you assign the $300 bonus. Because selling `ITEMS_MIN` items is enough to qualify for the bonus, there is no need for further questioning. If the salesperson has not sold enough items, only then do you need to ask `if valueSold >= VALUE_MIN?`. If the employee did not sell `ITEMS_MIN` items, but did sell a high dollar value nonetheless, the salesperson receives the bonus.

WRITING OR DECISIONS FOR EFFICIENCY

As with an AND selection, when you use an OR selection, you can choose to ask either question first. For example, you can assign a bonus to salespeople who meet one or the other of two criteria using the logic in either part of Figure 4-13.

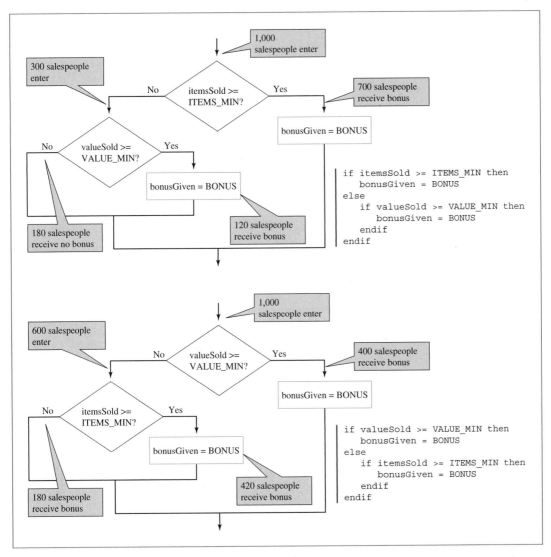

Figure 4-13 Two ways to select bonus recipients using identical criteria

You might have guessed that one of these selections is superior to the other when you have some background information about the relative likelihood of each condition you are testing. For example, assume you know that out of 1,000 employees in your company, about 70 percent, or 700, sell at least ITEMS_MIN items during a given period of time, and that only 40 percent, or 400, sell VALUE_MIN worth of goods or more.

When you use the logic shown in the first half of Figure 4-13 to assign bonuses, you first ask about the number of items sold. For 700 salespeople the answer is true and you assign the bonus. Only about 300 records continue to the next question regarding the dollar amount sold, where about 40 percent of the 300, or 120, fulfill the bonus requirement. In the end, you have made 1,300 decisions to correctly assign bonuses to 820 employees (700 plus 120).

If you use the OR logic in the second half of Figure 4-13, you ask about the dollar value sold first—1,000 times, once each for 1,000 salespeople. The result is true for 40 percent, or 400 employees, who receive a bonus. For 600 salespeople, you ask whether itemsSold is at least the minimum required. For 70 percent of the 600, the result is true, so bonuses are assigned to 420 additional people. In the end, the same 820 salespeople (400 plus 420) receive a bonus, but after executing 1,600 decisions—300 more decisions than when using the first decision logic.

The general rule is: *In an* OR *decision, first ask the question that is more likely to be true.* In the preceding example, a salesperson qualifies for a bonus as soon as the person's data passes one test. Asking the question that is more likely true first eliminates as many repetitions as possible of the second decision, and the time it takes to process all the salespeople is decreased. As with the AND situation, you might not always know which question is more likely to be true, but when you can make a reasonable guess, it is more efficient to eliminate as many extra decisions as possible.

COMBINING DECISIONS IN AN OR SELECTION

When you need to take action when either one or the other of two conditions is met, you can use two separate, nested selection structures, as in the previous examples. However, most programming languages allow you to ask two or more questions in a single comparison by using a **conditional OR operator** (or simply the OR **operator**)—for example, valueSold >= VALUE_MIN OR itemsSold >= ITEMS_MIN. When you use the logical OR operator, only one of the listed conditions must be met for the resulting action to take place. Table 4-3 shows the truth table for the OR operator. As you can see in the table, the entire expression x OR y is false only when x and y each are false individually.

x	y	x OR y
True	True	True
True	False	True
False	True	True
False	False	False

Table 4-3 Truth table for the OR operator

If the programming language you use supports the OR operator, you must still realize that the question you place first is the question that will be asked first, and cases that pass the test of the first question will not proceed to the second question. As with the AND operator, this feature is called short-circuiting. The computer can ask only one question at a time; even when you write code as shown at the top of Figure 4-14, the computer will execute the logic shown at the bottom.

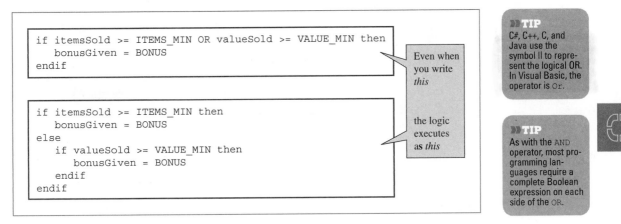

TIP
C#, C++, C, and Java use the symbol || to represent the logical OR. In Visual Basic, the operator is Or.

TIP
As with the AND operator, most programming languages require a complete Boolean expression on each side of the OR.

Figure 4-14 Using an OR operator and the logic behind it

> **TIP** A common use of the OR operator is to decide to take action whether a character variable is uppercase or lowercase. For example, assume that selection has been declared as a string variable, and that the user has entered a value for selection. Using the following decision, any subsequent action occurs whether the selection variable holds an uppercase or lowercase "A":
>
> ```
> if selection == "A" OR selection == "a" then…
> ```

AVOIDING COMMON ERRORS IN AN OR SELECTION

You might have noticed that the assignment statement bonusGiven = BONUS appears twice in the decision-making processes in Figures 4-12 and 4-13. When you create a flowchart, the temptation is to draw the logic to look like Figure 4-15. Logically, you can argue that the flowchart in Figure 4-15 is correct because the correct salespeople receive bonuses. However, this flowchart is not allowed because it is not structured. The second question is not a self-contained structure with one entry and exit point; instead, the flowline "breaks out" of the inner selection structure to join the true side of the outer selection structure.

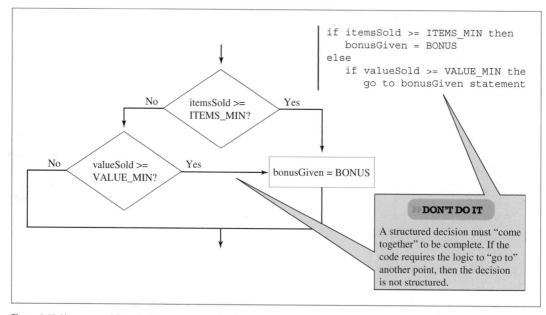

```
if itemsSold >= ITEMS_MIN then
    bonusGiven = BONUS
else
    if valueSold >= VALUE_MIN the
        go to bonusGiven statement
```

DON'T DO IT

A structured decision must "come together" to be complete. If the code requires the logic to "go to" another point, then the decision is not structured.

Figure 4-15 Unstructured flowchart for determining bonuses

>> **NOTE** If you are having trouble understanding why the flowchart segment in Figure 4-15 is unstructured, go back and review Chapter 2.

An additional source of error that is specific to the OR selection stems from a problem with language and the way people use it more casually than computers do. When a sales manager wants to assign bonuses to salespeople who have sold three or more items or who have achieved $2,000 in sales, she is likely to say, "Give a bonus to anyone who has sold at least three items and to anyone who has achieved $2,000 in sales." Her request contains the word "and" between two types of people—those who sold three items and those who sold $2,000 worth—placing the emphasis on the people. However, each decision you make is about a bonus for a single salesperson who has surpassed one goal *or* the other *or* both. The logical situation requires an OR decision. Instead of the manager's previous statement, it would be clearer if she said, "Give a bonus to anyone who has sold at least three items or has achieved $2,000 in sales." In other words, because you are making each decision about a single salesperson, it is more correct to put the "or" conjunction between the achieved sales goals than between types of people, but bosses and other human beings often do not speak like computers. As a programmer, you have the job of clarifying what really is being requested. Often, a request for A *and* B means a request for A *or* B.

The way we casually use English can cause another type of error when you are required to find whether a value falls between two other values. For example, a movie theater manager might say, "Provide a discount to patrons who are under 13 years old and those who are over 64 years old; otherwise, charge the full price." Because the manager has used the word "and" in the request, you might be tempted to create the decision shown in Figure 4-16; however, this logic will not provide a discounted price for any movie patron. You must remember that every time the decision is made in Figure 4-16, it is made for a single movie patron. If patronAge contains a value lower than 13, then it cannot possibly contain a value over 64. Similarly, if it contains a value over 64, there is no way it can contain a lesser value. Therefore, no value could be stored in patronAge for which both parts of the AND question could be true—and the price will never be set to the discounted price for any patron. Figure 4-17 shows the correct logic.

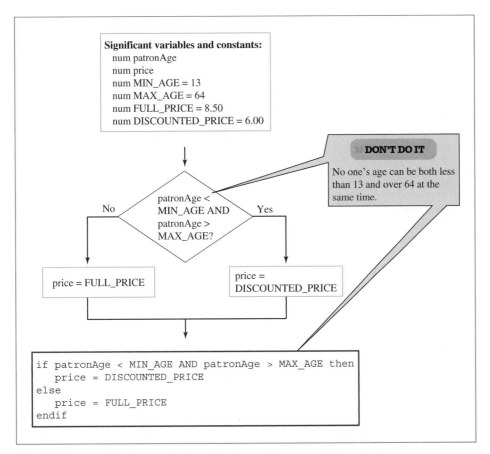

Figure 4-16 Incorrect logic that attempts to provide a discount for young and old movie patrons

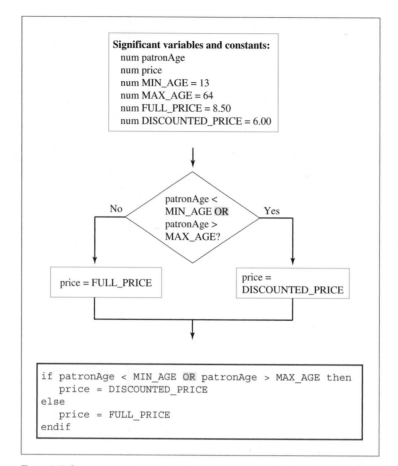

Figure 4-17 Correct logic that provides a discount for young and old movie patrons

A similar error can occur in your logic if the theater manager says something like, "Don't give a discount—that is, charge full price—if a patron is over 12 or under 65." Because the word "or" appears in the request, you might plan your logic to resemble Figure 4-18. As in Figure 4-16, no patron ever receives a discount, because every patron is either over 12 or under 65. Remember, in an OR decision, only one of the conditions needs to be true for the entire expression to be evaluated as true. So, for example, because a patron who is 10 is under 65, the full price is charged, and because a patron who is 70 is over 12, the full price also is charged. Figure 4-19 shows the correct logic for this decision.

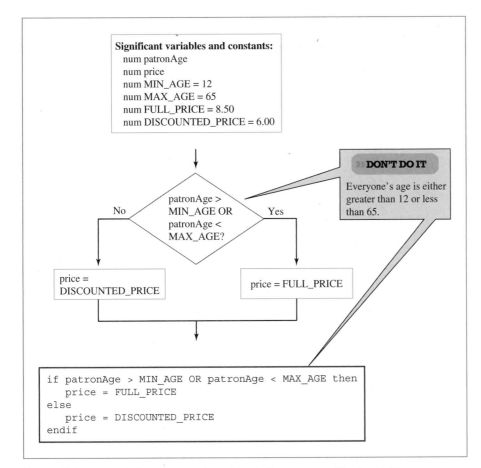

Significant variables and constants:
num patronAge
num price
num MIN_AGE = 12
num MAX_AGE = 65
num FULL_PRICE = 8.50
num DISCOUNTED_PRICE = 6.00

DON'T DO IT
Everyone's age is either greater than 12 or less than 65.

patronAge > MIN_AGE OR patronAge < MAX_AGE?

No

Yes

price = DISCOUNTED_PRICE

price = FULL_PRICE

```
if patronAge > MIN_AGE OR patronAge < MAX_AGE then
   price = FULL_PRICE
else
   price = DISCOUNTED_PRICE
endif
```

Figure 4-18 Incorrect logic that attempts to charge full price for patrons over 12 and under 65

» NOTE Using an OR operator in a decision that involves multiple conditions does not eliminate your responsibility for determining which condition to test first. Even when you use an OR operator, the computer makes decisions one at a time, and makes them in the order you ask them. If the first question in an OR expression evaluates to true, then the entire expression is true, and the second question is not even tested.

» NOTE Besides AND and OR, most languages support a NOT operator. You use the **logical NOT operator** to reverse the meaning of a Boolean expression. For example, the statement if NOT (age < 21) print "OK" prints "OK" when age is greater than or equal to 21. The NOT operator is unary instead of binary—that is, you do not use it between two expressions, but you use it in front of a single expression. In C++, Java, and C#, the exclamation point is the symbol used for the NOT operator. In Visual Basic, the operator is Not.

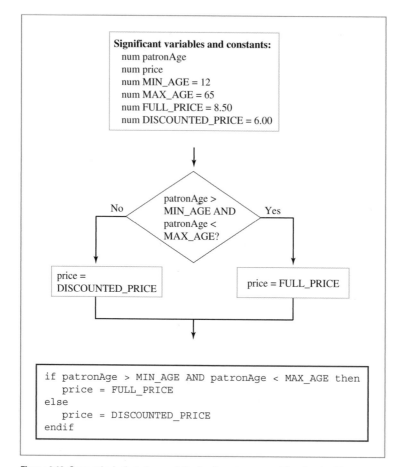

Figure 4-19 Correct logic that charges full price for patrons over 12 and under 65

TWO TRUTHS AND A LIE:
UNDERSTANDING OR **LOGIC**

1. In an OR selection two or more conditions must be met in order for an event to take place.

2. When you use an OR selection, you can choose to ask either question first and still achieve a useable program.

3. The general rule is: In an OR decision, first ask the question that is more likely to be true.

The false statement is #1. In an OR selection only one of two conditions must be met in order for an event to take place.

MAKING SELECTIONS WITHIN RANGES

You often need to make selections based on a variable falling within a range of values. For example, suppose a company president wants to meet with every department next week to discuss an impending merger, and wants to print a series of memos to notify employees of their department's meeting day and time. Figure 4-20 shows the meeting schedule, which has been arranged by department numbers so that each meeting group is a manageable size. Figure 4-21 shows a typical memo—the shaded portions will change for each employee.

Meeting Day and Time	Departments
Monday at 9 a.m.	1 through 4
Monday at 1 p.m.	5 through 9
Tuesday at 1 p.m.	10 through 17
Wednesday at 9 a.m.	18 through 20

Figure 4-20 Proposed meeting schedule

```
To: Allison Darnell
From: Walter Braxton
Re: Pending merger


Your department will meet with me on Monday at 9 a.m.
in the Blue Conference Room where we will address
questions about the upcoming merger.
```

Figure 4-21 Typical meeting memo

When you write the program that reads an employee's name and department number, you could make 20 decisions before printing each employee's memo, such as department = 1?, department = 2?, and so on. However, it is more convenient to find the meeting day and time by using a range check.

When you use a **range check**, you compare a variable to a series of values that mark the limiting ends of ranges. To perform a range check, make comparisons using either the lowest or highest value in each range of values. For example, to find each employee's meeting day and time as listed in Figure 4-20, either use the values 1, 5, 10, and 18, which represent the low ends of each meeting's department range, or use the values 4, 9, 17, and 20, which represent the high ends.

Figure 4-22 shows the flowchart and pseudocode that represent the logic for a program that chooses a meeting time for every employee by using the high end of each range of values for department numbers. The housekeeping tasks in this program include declaring the variables and reading the first employee's name and department number into memory. While the end-of-file condition is not met, the main loop of the program executes. In this loop, the employee's department value is compared to the high end of the lowest range group (RANGE1). If the department is less than or equal to that value, then you know the meeting time (TIME1), and can store it in the time variable; if not, you continue checking. If department is less than or equal to the high end of the next range (RANGE2), then the time is TIME2; if not you continue checking, and time eventually is set to TIME3 or TIME4.

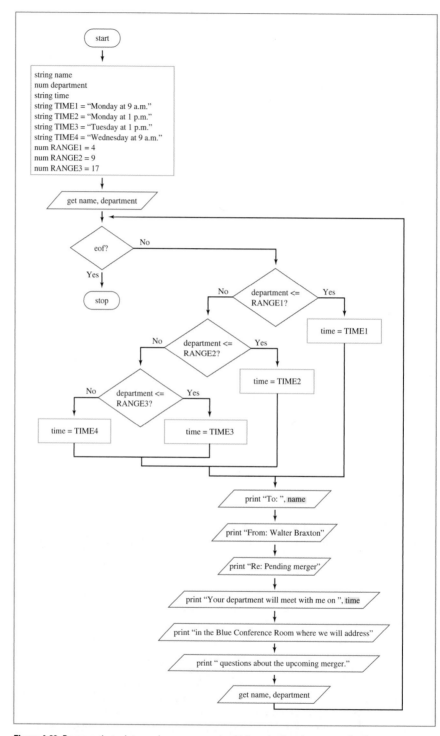

start

string name
num department
string time
string TIME1 = "Monday at 9 a.m."
string TIME2 = "Monday at 1 p.m."
string TIME3 = "Tuesday at 1 p.m."
string TIME4 = "Wednesday at 9 a.m."
num RANGE1 = 4
num RANGE2 = 9
num RANGE3 = 17

get name, department

eof?

No

Yes

stop

department <= RANGE1?

No

Yes

time = TIME1

department <= RANGE2?

No

Yes

time = TIME2

department <= RANGE3?

No

Yes

time = TIME4

time = TIME3

print "To: ", name

print "From: Walter Braxton"

print "Re: Pending merger"

print "Your department will meet with me on ", time

print "in the Blue Conference Room where we will address"

print " questions about the upcoming merger."

get name, department

Figure 4-22 Program that prints employee memo using high-end values in a range check

```
start
   string name
   num department
   string time
   string TIME1 = "Monday at 9 a.m."
   string TIME2 = "Monday at 1 p.m."
   string TIME3 = "Tuesday at 1 p.m."
   string TIME4 = "Wednesday at 9 a.m."
   num RANGE1 = 4
   num RANGE2 = 9
   num RANGE3 = 17
   get name, department
   while not eof
      if department <= RANGE1 then
         time = TIME1
      else
         if department <= RANGE2 then
            time = TIME2
         else
            if department <= RANGE3 then
               time = TIME3
            else
               time = TIME4
            endif
         endif
      endif
      print "To: ", name
      print "From: Walter Braxton"
      print "Re: Pending merger"
      print "Your department will meet with me on ", time
      print "in the Blue Conference Room where we will address"
      print "questions about the upcoming merger."
      get name, department
   endwhile
stop
```

Figure 4-22 Program that prints employee memo using high-end values in a range check (*continued*)

> **»NOTE**
> In the pseudocode in Figure 4-22, notice how each `if`, `else`, and `endif` group aligns vertically.

> **»NOTE** This book assumes that one print statement prints one line of output. In most programming languages you can print many lines with a single statement; you can also use several statements to print one line. The exact process varies among languages.

After the decision-making process is complete, the memo is printed one line at a time, with the employee's name and time (see shaded variables) inserted into the text of the memo. Then the next values for `name` and `department` are read into memory, and if it is not `eof`, the process starts all over again.

For example, consider four employees who work in different departments, and compare how they would be handled by the set of decisions in Figure 4-22.

» First, assume that the value of `department` for an employee is 2. Using the logic in Figure 4-22, the value of the Boolean expression `department <= RANGE1` is true, `time` is set to TIME1, "Monday at 9 a.m.", and the selection structure ends. In this case, the second and third decisions, checking RANGE2 and RANGE3, are never made, because the `else` half of `department <= RANGE1` never executes.

» Next, assume that the value of department is 7 for another employee. Then, department <= RANGE1 evaluates as false, so the else clause of the decision executes. There, department <= RANGE2 is evaluated and found to be true, so time becomes TIME2, which is "Monday at 1 p.m.".

» Next, assume department is 17. The expression department <= RANGE1 evaluates as false, so the else clause of the decision executes. There, department <= RANGE2 also evaluates to false, so its else clause executes. The expression department <= RANGE3 is true, so time becomes TIME3, "Tuesday at 1 p.m.".

» Finally, assume that the value of department is 19. The first expression, department <= RANGE1, is false, department <= RANGE2 is false, and department <= RANGE3 is false so the else clause of this last decision executes, and time becomes TIME4, "Wednesday at 9 a.m.". In this example, the 9 a.m. Wednesday meeting represents a default value, because if none of the decision expressions is true, the last meeting time is selected by default. A **default value** is the value assigned after a series of selections all are false.

>> **NOTE** Using the logic in Figure 4-22, the 9 a.m. Wednesday meeting time is set even if the department is a high invalid value like 21, 22, or even 300. The example is intended to be simple, using only three decisions. However, in a business application, you might consider amending the logic so an additional, fourth decision is made that compares department to 20. Then, you could assign the Wednesday meeting time when department is less than or equal to 20, and issue an error message otherwise. You might also want to insert a similar decision at the beginning of the selection process to make sure department is not less than 1.

You could just as easily choose a meeting time using the reverse of this method, by comparing the employee department to the low end of the range values that represent each meeting. For example, you could first compare department to the low end (18) of the highest range (18 to 20). If an employee's department falls in the range, the meeting day and time are known (TIME4); otherwise, you check the next lower group. If department is greater than or equal to 10, you use the next meeting time (TIME3). If department does not fall in that range but is greater than or equal to 5, then the time is TIME2. In this example, "Monday at 9 a.m." becomes the default value. That is, if the department number is not greater than or equal to 18, and it is also not greater than or equal to 10 and it also is not greater than or equal to 5, then the meeting is on Monday morning by default.

UNDERSTANDING COMMON ERRORS USING RANGE CHECKS

Two common errors that occur when programmers perform range checks both entail more work than is necessary. Figure 4-23 shows a program segment that contains a range check in which the programmer has asked one question too many. If you know that all department values are positive numbers (perhaps because they have been verified previously in the program), then if department is not greater than or equal to RANGE4 (18), and it is also not greater than or equal to RANGE3 (10), and it is also not greater than or equal to RANGE2 (5), by default it must be greater than or equal to 1. Asking whether department is greater than or equal to RANGE1 (1), the shaded question in Figure 4-23, is a waste of time; no employee record can ever travel the logical path on the far left. You might say that the path that can never be traveled is a **dead** or **unreachable path**, and that the statements written there constitute dead or unreachable code. Although a program that contains such logic will execute and assign the correct meeting times to employees, providing such a path is always a logical error.

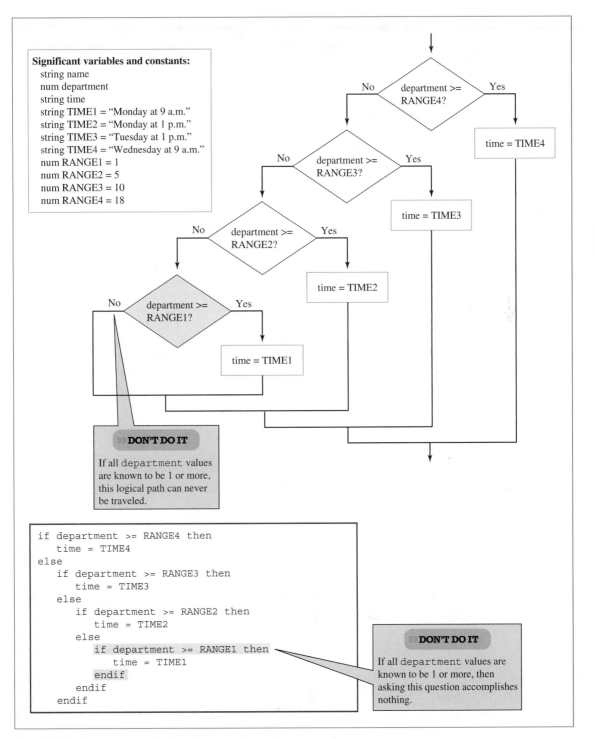

Significant variables and constants:
string name
num department
string time
string TIME1 = "Monday at 9 a.m."
string TIME2 = "Monday at 1 p.m."
string TIME3 = "Tuesday at 1 p.m."
string TIME4 = "Wednesday at 9 a.m."
num RANGE1 = 1
num RANGE2 = 5
num RANGE3 = 10
num RANGE4 = 18

department >= RANGE4? No / Yes

time = TIME4

department >= RANGE3? No / Yes

time = TIME3

department >= RANGE2? No / Yes

time = TIME2

department >= RANGE1? No / Yes

time = TIME1

DON'T DO IT
If all department values
are known to be 1 or more,
this logical path can never
be traveled.

```
if department >= RANGE4 then
   time = TIME4
else
   if department >= RANGE3 then
      time = TIME3
   else
      if department >= RANGE2 then
         time = TIME2
      else
         if department >= RANGE1 then
            time = TIME1
         endif
      endif
   endif
endif
```

DON'T DO IT
If all department values are
known to be 1 or more, then
asking this question accomplishes
nothing.

Figure 4-23 Inefficient range selection including unreachable path

>>**NOTE** In Figure 4-23, it is easier to see the useless path in the flowchart than in the pseudocode representation of the same logic. However, anytime you use an `if` without an `else` you are doing nothing when the question's answer is false.

>>**NOTE** When you ask questions of human beings, you sometimes ask a question to which you already know the answer. For example, a good trial lawyer seldom asks a question in court if the answer will be a surprise. With computer logic, however, such questions are an inefficient waste of time.

Another error that programmers make when writing the logic to perform a range check also involves asking unnecessary questions. You should never ask a question if there is only one possible answer or outcome. Figure 4-24 shows an inefficient range selection that asks two unneeded questions. In the figure, if `department` is greater than or equal to RANGE3, "Wednesday at 9 a.m." is the scheduled meeting. If department is not greater than or equal to RANGE3, then it must be less than RANGE3, so the next question (shaded in the figure) does not have to check for less than RANGE3. The computer logic will never execute the shaded decision unless `department` is already less than RANGE3—that is, unless it follows the `false` branch of the first selection. If you use the logic in Figure 4-24, you are wasting computer time asking a question that has previously been answered. Similarly, if `department` is not greater than or equal to RANGE3 and it is also not greater than or equal to RANGE2, then it must be less than RANGE2. Therefore, there is no reason to compare `department` to RANGE2 in the last decision.

>>**NOTE** Beginning programmers sometimes justify their use of unnecessary questions as "just making really sure." Such caution is unnecessary when writing computer logic.

TWO TRUTHS AND A LIE:
MAKING SELECTIONS WITHIN RANGES

1. When you perform a range check, you compare a variable to every value in a series of ranges.

2. You can perform a range check by making comparisons using the lowest value in each range of values you are using.

3. You can perform a range check by making comparisons using the highest value in each range of values you are using.

The false statement is #1. When you use a range check, you compare a variable to a series of values that marks the ends of ranges of values.

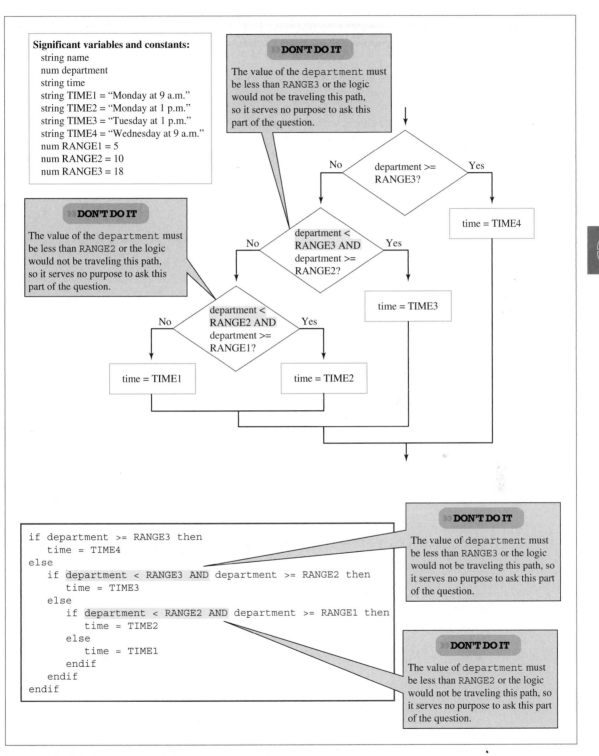

Figure 4-24 Inefficient range selection including unnecessary questions

UNDERSTANDING PRECEDENCE WHEN COMBINING AND AND OR SELECTIONS

Most programming languages allow you to combine as many AND and OR operators in an expression as you need. For example, assume you need to achieve a score of at least 75 on each of three tests to pass a course. You can declare a constant MIN_SCORE equal to 75 and test the multiple conditions with a statement like the following:

```
if score1 >= MIN_SCORE AND score2 >= MIN_SCORE AND score3 >=
MIN_SCORE then
    classGrade = "Pass"
else
    classGrade = "Fail"
endif
```

On the other hand, if you are enrolled in a course in which you need to pass only one of three tests to pass the course, then the logic is as follows:

```
if score1 >= MIN_SCORE OR score2 >= MIN_SCORE OR score3 >= MIN_SCORE
then
    classGrade = "Pass"
else
    classGrade = "Fail"
endif
```

The logic becomes more complicated when you combine AND and OR operators within the same statement. When you combine AND and OR operators, the AND operators take **precedence**, meaning their Boolean values are evaluated first.

For example, consider a program that determines whether a movie theater patron can purchase a discounted ticket. Assume discounts are allowed for children (age 12 and under) and senior citizens (age 65 and older) who attend "G"-rated movies. The following code looks reasonable, but produces incorrect results, because the AND operator evaluates before the OR.

```
if age <= 12 OR age >= 65 AND rating = "G" then
    print "Discount applies"
endif
```

> **DON'T DO IT**
> The AND evaluates first, which is not the intention.

For example, assume a movie patron is 10 years old and the movie rating is "R". The patron should not receive a discount (or be allowed to see the movie!). However, within the if statement, the part of the expression that contains the AND, age >= 65 AND rating = "G", is evaluated first. For a 10-year-old and an "R"-rated movie, the question is false (on both counts), so the entire if statement becomes the equivalent of the following:

```
if age <= 12 OR aFalseExpression then
    print "Discount applies"
endif
```

Because the patron is 10, age <= 12 is true, so the original if statement becomes the equivalent of:

```
if aTrueExpression OR aFalseExpression then
    print "Discount applies"
endif
```

The combination `true OR false` evaluates as `true`. Therefore, the string "Discount applies" prints when it should not.

Many programming languages allow you to use parentheses to correct the logic and force the OR expression to be evaluated first, as shown in the following pseudocode.

```
if (age <= 12 OR age >= 65) AND rating = "G" then
    print "Discount applies"
endif
```

With the added parentheses, if the patron's `age` is 12 or under OR the `age` is 65 or over, the expression is evaluated as:

```
if aTrueExpression AND rating = "G" then
    print "Discount applies"
endif
```

When the age value qualifies a patron for a discount, then the rating value must also be acceptable before the discount applies. This was the original intention of the statement.

You can always avoid the confusion of mixing AND and OR decisions by nesting `if` statements instead. With the flowchart and pseudocode shown in Figure 4-25, it is clear which movie patrons receive the discount. In the flowchart, you can see that the OR is nested entirely within the Yes branch of the `rating = "G"?` selection. Similarly, in the pseudocode in Figure 4-25, you can see by the alignment that if the rating is not "G", the logic proceeds directly to the last `endif` statement, bypassing any checking of `age` at all.

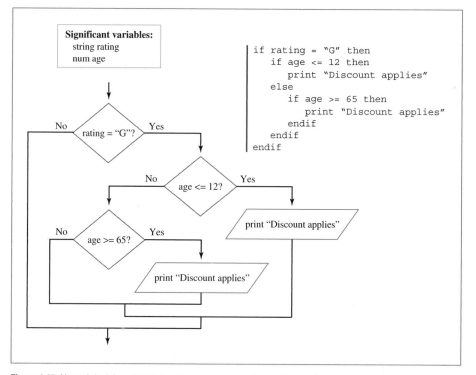

Figure 4-25 Nested decisions that determine movie patron discount

TWO TRUTHS AND A LIE:

UNDERSTANDING PRECEDENCE WHEN COMBINING AND **AND** OR **SELECTIONS**

1. Most programming languages allow you to combine as many AND and OR operators in an expression as you need.

2. When you combine AND and OR operators, the OR operators take precedence, meaning their Boolean values are evaluated first.

3. You can always avoid the confusion of mixing AND and OR decisions by nesting if statements instead of using ANDS and ORS.

The false statement is #2. When you combine AND and OR operators, the AND operators take precedence, meaning their Boolean values are evaluated first.

THE CASE STRUCTURE

When you have a series of decisions based on the value stored in the same variable, most languages allow you to use a case structure. You first learned about the case structure in Chapter 2. There you learned that you can solve any programming problem using only the three basic structures—sequence, selection, and loop. You are never required to use a case structure—you can always substitute a series of selections. The **case structure** simply provides a convenient alternative to using a series of decisions when you must make choices based on the value stored in a single variable.

»NOTE The syntax used to implement the case structure varies among languages. For example, Visual Basic uses select case, and C#, C++, and Java use switch.

For example, suppose you work for a real estate developer who is selling houses that have one of three different model numbers, each with a unique price. The logic segment of a program that determines the base price of the house might look like the logic shown in Figure 4-26.

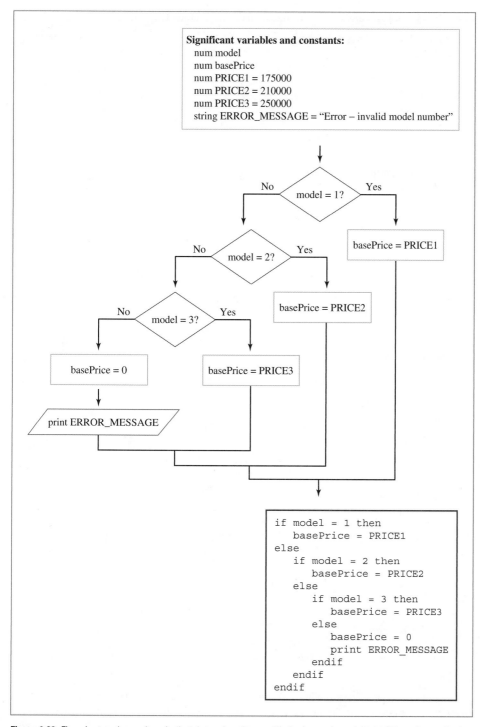

Figure 4-26 Flowchart and pseudocode that determines base price for house based on model number and using nested decision structures

The logic shown in Figure 4-26 is completely structured. However, rewriting the logic using a case structure, as shown in Figure 4-27, might make it easier to understand. When using the case structure, you test a variable against a series of values, taking appropriate action based on the variable's value.

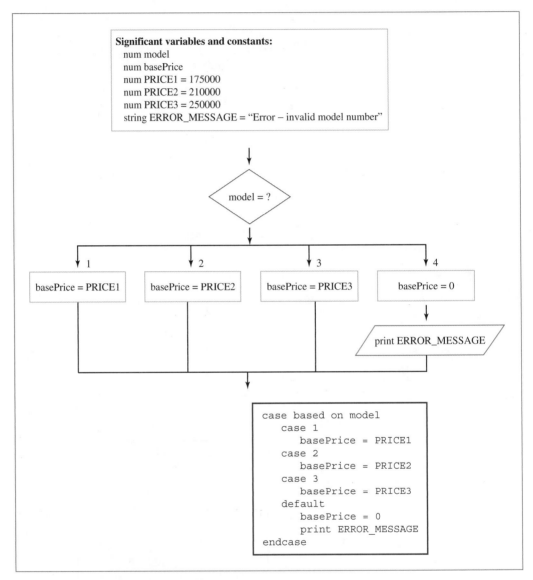

Figure 4-27 Flowchart and pseudocode that determines base price for house based on model number and using the case structure

In Figure 4-27, the model variable is compared in turn with 1, 2, and 3, and an appropriate basePrice value is set. The default case is the case that executes in the event no other cases execute. The logic shown in Figure 4-27 is identical to that shown in Figure 4-26; your choice of method to set the housing model base prices is entirely a matter of preference.

>> **NOTE** When a nested `if-else` structure contains an outer and inner selection, and the inner nested selection structure is within the `if` portion of the outer selection structure, the program segment is a candidate for AND logic. On the other hand, if the inner `if` is within the `else` portion of the outer `if`, the program segment might be a candidate for the `case` structure.

>> **NOTE**
In Visual Basic, the default indicator is `Case Else`. C++, C#, and Java all use `default`.

>> **NOTE** Some languages require a `break` statement at the end of each case selection segment. In those languages, once a case is true, all the following cases execute until a `break` statement is encountered. When you study a specific programming language, you will learn how to use `break` statements if they are required in that language.

TWO TRUTHS AND A LIE:
UNDERSTANDING THE CASE STRUCTURE

1. You are required to use a case structure when three or more decisions are based on a single variable's value.

2. The case structure frequently provides a convenient alternative to using a series of decisions.

3. You use the case structure when you must make choices based on the value stored in a single variable.

The false statement is #1. You are never required to use a case structure—you can always substitute a series of selections.

USING DECISION TABLES

Some applications require multiple decisions to produce useful results. Managing all the possible outcomes of multiple decisions can be a difficult task, so programmers sometimes use a tool called a decision table to help organize the possible combinations of decision outcomes.

A **decision table** is a problem-analysis tool that consists of four parts:

>> Conditions
>> Possible combinations of Boolean values for the conditions
>> Possible actions based on the outcomes
>> The specific action that corresponds to each Boolean value of each condition

For example, suppose a college collects input data from students including an ID number, first and last names, age, and a variable that indicates whether the student has requested a residence hall that enforces quiet study hours. The `quietRequest` variable holds either a "Y" or an "N" for each student indicating whether the student has requested a residence hall with quiet hours. Assume the Director of Student Housing makes residence hall assignments based on the following rules:

>> Students who are under 21 years old and request a residence hall with quiet study hours are assigned to Addams Hall.

>> Students who are under 21 years old and do not request a residence hall with quiet study hours are assigned to Grant Hall.

» Students who are 21 years old or older and request a residence hall with quiet study hours are assigned to Lincoln Hall.

» Students who are 21 years old and over who do not request a residence hall with quiet study hours are also assigned to Lincoln Hall, because it is the only residence hall for students who are at least 21.

You want to write an application that accepts student data and assigns each student to the appropriate residence hall, displaying the results in a report similar to Figure 4-28.

```
Residence Hall Assignments

ID      First Name    Last Name    Age Quiet   Hall

2134    Jennifer      Olson        18   Y       Addams
2671    Henry         VanMarks     21   N       Lincoln
3167    Paul          Thompson     18   N       Grant
3652    Monica        Marcos       19   N       Grant
4182    Francine      Jensen       22   Y       Lincoln
5622    Lee           Ricardo      20   Y       Addams
```

Figure 4-28 Sample residence hall assignments report

Before you draw the flowchart or write the pseudocode, you can create a decision table to help you manage the decisions. You can begin the decision table by listing all the possible conditions that affect the outcome:

» Student's age is under 21, or not

» Student's quietRequest is "Y", or not

Next, you determine all the possible Boolean value combinations that exist for the conditions. In this case, there are four possible combinations, as shown in Table 4-4.

Condition	Outcome			
age < 21	T	T	F	F
quietRequest = "Y"	T	F	T	F

Table 4-4 Conditions and possible values for residence hall determination

Next, add rows to the decision table to list the possible outcome actions. A student might be assigned to Addams, Grant, or Lincoln Hall. There are no other possibilities, so three possible action or outcome rows are added to the decision table. Table 4-5 shows the expanded table that includes the possible outcomes.

Condition	Outcome			
age < 21	T	T	F	F
quietRequest = "Y"	T	F	T	F
assignedHall = "Addams"				
assignedHall = "Grant"				
assignedHall = "Lincoln"				

Table 4-5 Conditions, possible values, and possible actions for residence hall determination

To complete the decision table, you choose one outcome for each possible combination of conditions. As shown in Table 4-6, you place an "X" (or any other symbol you prefer) in the Addams Hall row when a student's age is less than 21 and the student has requested quiet study hours. You place an "X" in the Grant Hall row when the student is under 21 and has not requested study hours. Finally, you place an "X" in the Lincoln Hall row whenever a student is not under 21 years old. In this case, the request for quiet study hours is irrelevant because all students who are 21 and older are assigned to Lincoln Hall.

Condition	Outcome			
age < 21	T	T	F	F
quietRequest = "Y"	T	F	T	F
assignedHall = "Addams"	X			
assignedHall = "Grant"		X		
assignedHall = "Lincoln"			X	X

Table 4-6 Completed decision table for residence hall selection

In Table 4-6, the decision table is complete. There are four possible outcomes, and there is one "X" for each. Now you can begin to design the logic that achieves the correct results. You can begin to write pseudocode for the decision-making process by writing a selection statement for the first condition as follows:

```
if age < 21 then
```

Whether this expression is true or false, you do not know the final residence hall assignment—in the decision table, two columns are affected when the expression is true, and results are marked with an "X" in two different rows. Therefore, you need to insert another question, and the code becomes:

```
if age < 21 then
    if quietRequest = "Y" then
        assignedHall = "Addams"
```

At this point, you have written pseudocode that describes the first column of the decision table. The second column of the table describes the situation when the first decision is `true`, but the second decision is `false`. To include the information in the second column, the code becomes:

```
if age < 21 then
    if quietRequest = "Y" then
        assignedHall = "Addams"
    else
        assignedHall = "Grant"
    endif
```

If the student's age is not less than 21, then a second set of decisions applies as follows:

```
if age < 21 then
    if quietRequest = "Y" then
        assignedHall = "Addams"
    else
        assignedHall = "Grant"
    endif
else
    if quietRequest = "Y" then
        assignedHall = "Lincoln"
    else
        assignedHall = "Lincoln"
    endif
endif
```

Now the code matches the decision table exactly. However, you might notice that if the student's age is not under 21, the `quietRequest` really does not matter—the student is assigned to Lincoln Hall no matter what the study request was. Whenever both the `true` and `false` outcomes of a Boolean selection result in the same action, there is no need to ask the question to make the selection. Figure 4-29 shows a completed program that continuously gets student data and makes residence hall selections. Appropriate constants have been assigned in this completed application. After the housekeeping tasks of declaring variables and constants and printing headings are completed, the first record is read into memory. While it is not `eof`, decisions are made that result in the correct residence hall assignment for the student. The student's data is printed, and the next record is read into memory.

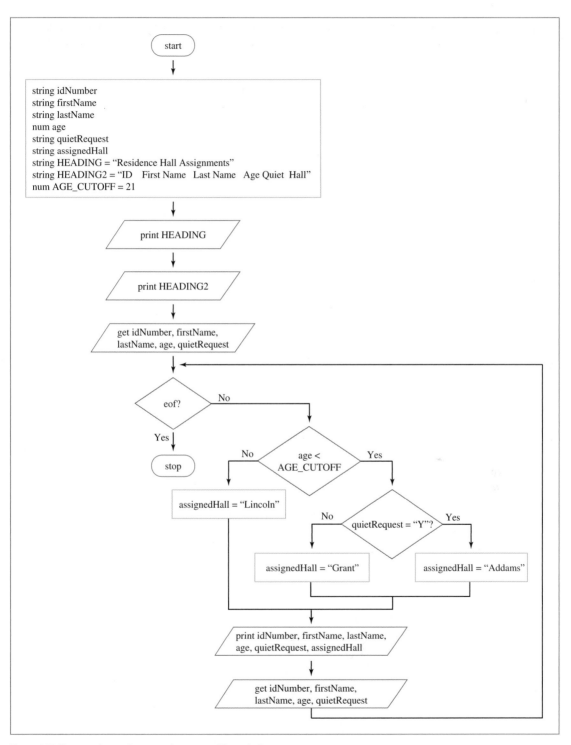

Figure 4-29 Program that assigns a student to a residence hall

```
start
   string idNumber
   string firstName
   string lastName
   num age
   string quietRequest
   string assignedHall
   string HEADING = "Residence Hall Assignments"
   string HEADING2 = "ID    First Name   Last Name   Age Quiet   Hall"
   num AGE_CUTOFF = 21
   print HEADING
   print HEADING2
   get idNumber, firstName, lastName, age, quietRequest
   while not eof
      if age < AGE_CUTOFF then
         if quietRequest = "Y" then
            assignedHall = "Addams"
         else
            assignedHall = "Grant"
         endif
      else
         assignedHall = "Lincoln"
      endif
      print idNumber, firstName, lastName, age, quietRequest, assignedHall
      get idNumber, firstName, lastName, age, quietRequest
   endwhile
stop
```

Figure 4-29 Program that assigns a student to a residence hall (*continued*)

Perhaps you could have created the decisions of the final version of the residence hall assignment program without creating the decision table first. If so, you need not use the decision table. Decision tables are more useful to the programmer when the decision-making process becomes more complicated. Additionally, they frequently serve as a useful graphic tool when you want to explain a program's decision-making process to a user who is not familiar with flowcharting symbols or the format of pseudocode statements.

TWO TRUTHS AND A LIE:
USING DECISION TABLES

1. A decision table is a problem-analysis tool that contains conditions and possible combinations of Boolean values for the conditions.

2. A decision table is a problem-analysis tool that contains possible actions based on conditions.

3. A decision table is a requirement when program logic requires more than just a few decisions.

The false statement is #3. Although decision tables are more useful to the programmer when the decision-making process becomes more complicated, they are never required.

CHAPTER SUMMARY

» Every decision you make in a computer program involves evaluating a Boolean expression. You can use `if-then-else` or `if-then` structures to choose between two possible outcomes. You use `if-then-else` structures when action is required whether the selection is true or false, and `if-then` structures when there is only one outcome for the question for which action is required.

» For any two values that are the same type, you can use relational comparison operators to decide whether the two values are equal, the first value is greater than the second value, or the first value is less than the second value. The two values used in a Boolean expression can be either variables or constants.

» An `AND` decision occurs when two conditions must be true in order for a resulting action to take place. An `AND` decision requires a nested decision or a nested `if`. In an `AND` decision, first ask the question that is less likely to be true. This eliminates as many records as possible from the number that have to go through the second decision, which speeds up processing time. Most programming languages allow you to ask two or more questions in a single comparison by using a logical `AND` operator. When you must satisfy two or more criteria to initiate an event in a program, you must make sure that the second decision is made entirely within the first decision, and that you use a complete Boolean expression on both sides of the `AND`.

» An `OR` decision occurs when you want to take action when one or the other of two conditions is true. Errors occur in `OR` decisions when programmers do not maintain structure. An additional source of errors that are particular to the `OR` selection stems from people using the word `AND` to express `OR` requirements. In an `OR` decision, first ask the question that is more likely to be true. Most programming languages allow you to ask two or more questions in a single comparison by using a logical OR operator.

» To perform a range check, make comparisons with either the lowest or highest value in each range of values you are using. Common errors that occur when programmers perform range checks include asking unnecessary and previously answered questions.

» When you combine `AND` and `OR` operators, the `AND` operators take precedence, meaning their Boolean values are evaluated first.

» The case structure provides a convenient alternative to using a series of decisions when you must make choices based on the value stored in a single variable.

» A decision table is a problem-analysis tool that lists conditions and Boolean combinations of outcomes when those conditions are tested. It helps you identify the conditions under which each possible outcome occurs.

KEY TERMS

An **if-then** structure is similar to an if-then-else, but no alternative or "else" action is necessary.

An **if clause** of a decision holds the action that results when a Boolean expression in a decision is true.

The **else clause** of a decision holds the action or actions that execute only when the Boolean expression in the decision is false.

A **Boolean expression** is one that represents only one of two states, usually expressed as true or false.

A **trivial** Boolean expression is one that always evaluates to the same result.

Relational comparison operators are the symbols that express Boolean comparisons. Examples include =, >, <, >=, <=, and <>. These operators are also called **relational operators** or **comparison operators**.

A **compound condition** is constructed when you need to ask multiple questions before determining an outcome.

With an **AND decision**, two conditions must both be true for an action to take place.

A **nested decision**, or a **nested if** is a decision "inside of" another decision.

A series of nested if statements can also be called a **cascading if statement**.

A **conditional AND operator** (or, more simply, an **AND operator**) is a symbol that you use to combine decisions so that two (or more) conditions must be true for an action to occur.

Truth tables are diagrams used in mathematics and logic to help describe the truth of an entire expression based on the truth of its parts.

Short-circuit evaluation is a logical feature in which expressions in each part of a larger expression are evaluated only as far as necessary to determine the final outcome.

A **range of values** encompasses every value between a high and low limit.

An **OR decision** contains two (or more) decisions; if at least one condition is met, the resulting action takes place.

A **conditional OR operator** (or, more simply, an **OR** operator) is a symbol that you use to combine decisions when any one condition can be true for an action to occur.

The **logical NOT operator** is a symbol that reverses the meaning of a Boolean expression.

When you use a **range check**, you compare a variable to a series of values that mark the limiting ends of ranges.

A **default value** is one that is assigned after all test conditions are found to be false.

A **dead** or **unreachable path** is a logical path that can never be traveled.

When an operator has **precedence**, it is evaluated before others.

The **case structure** provides a convenient alternative to using a series of decisions when you must make choices based on the value stored in a single variable.

A **decision table** is a problem-analysis tool that lists conditions, Boolean combinations of outcomes when those conditions are tested, and possible actions based on the outcomes.

REVIEW QUESTIONS

1. The selection statement `if quantity > 100 then discountRate = RATE` is an example of a _____ .

   a. dual-alternative selection   c. structured loop

   b. single-alternative selection   d. all of these

2. **The selection statement** `if dayOfWeek = "Sunday" then price = LOWER_PRICE else price = HIGHER_PRICE` **is an example of a** _____.

   a. dual-alternative selection

   b. single-alternative selection

   c. unary selection

   d. all of the above

3. **All selection statements must have** _____.

   a. an `if` clause

   b. an `else` clause

   c. both of these

   d. none of these

4. **An expression like** `amount < 10` **is a(n)** _____ **expression.**

   a. Gregorian

   b. Edwardian

   c. Machiavellian

   d. Boolean

5. **Usually, you compare only variables that have the same** _____.

   a. type

   b. size

   c. name

   d. value

6. **Symbols such as > and < are known as** _____ **operators.**

   a. arithmetic

   b. sequential

   c. relational comparison

   d. scripting accuracy

7. **If you could use only three relational comparison operators, you could get by with** _____.

   a. greater than, less than, and greater than or equal to

   b. equal to, less than, and greater than

   c. less than, less than or equal to, and not equal to

   d. equal to, not equal to, and less than

8. **If** `a > b` **is false, then which of the following is always true?**

   a. `a <= b`

   b. `a < b`

   c. `a = b`

   d. `a >= b`

9. **Usually, the most difficult comparison operator to work with is** _____.

   a. equal to

   b. greater than

   c. less than

   d. not equal to

10. **Which of the lettered choices is equivalent to the following decision?**

```
if x > 10 then
    if y > 10 then
        print "X"
    endif
endif
```
a. if x > 10 OR y > 10 then print "X"

b. if x > 10 AND x > y then print "X"

c. if y > x then print "X"

d. if x > 10 AND y > 10 then print "X"

11. **The Acme Computer Company operates in all 50 states of the United States. The Midwest Sales region consists of five states—Illinois, Indiana, Iowa, Missouri, and Wisconsin. Suppose you have input records containing Acme customer data, including state of residence. To most efficiently select and display all customers who live in the Midwest Sales region, you would use _____.**

a. five completely separate unnested `if` statements

b. nested `if` statements using AND logic

c. nested `if` statements using OR logic

d. Not enough information is given.

12. **The Midwest Sales region of Acme Computer Company consists of five states— Illinois, Indiana, Iowa, Missouri, and Wisconsin. About 50 percent of the regional customers reside in Illinois, 20 percent in Indiana, and 10 percent in each of the other three states. Suppose you have input records containing Acme customer data, including state of residence. To most efficiently select and display all customers who live in the Midwest Sales region, you would ask first about residency in _____.**

a. Illinois

b. Indiana

c. Either Iowa, Missouri, or Wisconsin—it does not matter which one of these three is first.

d. Any of the five states—it does not matter which one is first.

13. **The Boffo Balloon Company makes helium balloons. Large balloons cost $13.00 a dozen, medium-sized balloons cost $11.00 a dozen, and small balloons cost $8.60 a dozen. About 60 percent of the company's sales are the smallest balloons, 30 percent are the medium, and large balloons constitute only 10 percent of sales. Customer order records include customer information, quantity ordered, and size. When you write a program to determine price based on size, for the most efficient decision, you should ask first whether the size is _____.**

a. large

b. medium

c. small

d. It does not matter.

14. **The Boffo Balloon Company makes helium balloons in three sizes, 12 colors, and with a choice of 40 imprinted sayings. As a promotion, the company is offering a 25 percent discount on orders of large, red "Happy Valentine's Day" balloons. To most efficiently select the orders to which a discount applies, you would use _____ .**

    a. nested `if` statements using OR logic

    b. nested `if` statements using AND logic

    c. three completely separate unnested `if` statements

    d. Not enough information is given.

15. **Radio station FM 99 keeps a record of every song played on the air in a week. Each record contains the day, hour, and minute the song started, and the title and artist of the song. The station manager wants a list of every title played during the important 8 a.m. commute hour on the two busiest traffic days, Monday and Friday. Which logic would select the correct titles?**

```
a. if day = "Monday" OR day = "Friday" OR hour = 8 then
        print title
   endif
b. if day = "Monday" then
       if hour = 8 then
           print title
       else
           if day = "Friday" then
               print title
           endif
       endif
   endif
c. if hour = 8 AND day = "Monday" OR day = "Friday" then
       print title endif
d. if hour = 8 then
       if day = "Monday" OR day = "Friday" then
           print title
       endif
   endif
```

16. **In the following pseudocode, what percentage raise will an employee in Department 5 receive?**

```
if department < 3 then
    raise = SMALL_RAISE
else
    if department < 5 then
        raise = MEDIUM_RAISE
    else
        raise = BIG_RAISE
    endif
endif
```

a. SMALL_RAISE   c. BIG_RAISE

b. MEDIUM_RAISE   d. impossible to tell

17. **In the following pseudocode, what percentage raise will an employee in Department 8 receive?**

```
if department < 5 then
    raise = SMALL_RAISE
else
    if department < 14 then
        raise = MEDIUM_RAISE
    else
        if department < 9
            raise = BIG_RAISE
        endif
    endif
endif
```

a. SMALL_RAISE   c. BIG_RAISE

b. MEDIUM_RAISE   d. impossible to tell

18. **In the following pseudocode, what percentage raise will an employee in Department 10 receive?**

```
if department < 2 then
    raise = SMALL_RAISE
else
    if department < 6 then
        raise = MEDIUM_RAISE
    else
        if department < 10
            raise = BIG_RAISE
        endif
    endif
endif
```

a. SMALL_RAISE   c. BIG_RAISE

b. MEDIUM_RAISE   d. impossible to tell

19. When you use a range check, you compare a variable to the _____ value in the range.

a. lowest   c. highest

b. middle   d. lowest or highest

pg 179

20. Which of the following can be used as an alternative to a series of `if` statements based on the same variable?

a. a sequence structure   c. an action structure

b. a loop structure   d. a case structure

pg 170

FIND THE BUGS

Each of the following pseudocode segments contains one or more bugs that you must find and correct.

1. **This pseudocode should create a report containing a rental agent's commission at an apartment complex. The program accepts the ID number and name of the agent who rented the apartment, and the number of bedrooms in the apartment. The commission is $100 for renting a three-bedroom apartment, $75 for renting a two-bedroom apartment, $55 for renting a one-bedroom apartment, and $30 for renting a studio (zero-bedroom) apartment. Output is the salesperson's name and ID number and the commission earned on the rental.**

```
start
    num salesPersonID
    string salesPersonName
    num numBedrooms
    num COMM_3 = 100.00
    num COMM_2 = 75.00
    num COMM_1 = 55.00
    num COMM_STUDIO = 30.00
    get salesPersonID, salesPersonName, numBedrooms
    if numBedrooms = 3 then
        commissionEarned = COMM_3
    else
        if numBedrooms = 3 then
            commissionEarned = COMM_3
        else
            if numBedrooms = 1 then
                commission = COMM_1
            else
                commission = COMM_STUDIO
            endif
        endif
    endif
    print salesPersonID, salesPersonName, commissionEarned
stop
```

2. **This pseudocode should create a report containing annual profit statistics for a retail store. Input records contain a department name (for example, "Cosmetics") and profits for each quarter for the last two years. The program should determine whether the profit is higher, lower, or the same for this entire year compared to the last entire year.**

```
start
    string department
    num salesQuarter1ThisYear
    num salesQuarter2ThisYear
    num salesQuarter3ThisYear
    num salesQuarter4ThisYear
    num salesQuarter1LastYear
    num salesQuarter2LastYear
    num salesQuarter3ThisYear
    num salesQuarter4LastYear
    string MAIN_HEAD = "Profit Report"
    string COL_HEAD = "Department      Status"
    num totalThisYear
    num totalLastYear
    string status
    print MAIN_HEAD
    print COL_HEAD
    get department, salesQuarter1ThisYear, salesQuarter2ThisYear,
        salesQuarter3ThisYear, salesQuarter4ThisYear,
        salesQuarter1LastYear, salesQuarter2LastYear,
        salesQuarter3LastYear, salesQuarter4LastYear
    while not eof
        totalThisYear = salesQuarter1ThisYear - salesQuarter2ThisYear +
            salesQuarter3LastYear * salesQuarter4ThisYear
        totalLastYear = salesQuarter1LastYear + salesQuarter1LastYear +
            salesQuarter3LastYear + salesQuarter1LastYear
        if totalThisYear > totalLastYear then
            status = "Higher"
        else
            if totalThisYear > totalLastYear then
                status = "Lower"
            else
                status = "Same"
          endif
        endif
        print department, status
        get department, salesQuarter1ThisYear, salesQuarter2ThisYear,
            salesQuarter3ThisYear, salesQuarter4ThisYear,
            salesQuarter1LastYear, salesQuarter2LastYear,
            salesQuarter3LastYear, salesQuarter4LastYear
    endwhile
stop
```

EXERCISES

Use Page 140-141

1. **Assume the following variables contain the values shown:**

numberRed = 100   numberBlue = 200   numberGreen = 300
wordRed = "Wagon"   wordBlue = "Sky"   wordGreen = "Grass"

For each of the following Boolean expressions, decide whether the statement is true, false, or illegal.

a. numberRed = numberBlue?
b. numberBlue > numberGreen?
c. numberGreen < numberRed?
d. numberBlue = wordBlue?
e. numberGreen = "Green"?
f. wordRed = "Red"?
g. wordBlue = "Blue"?
h. numberRed <= numberGreen?
i. numberBlue >= 200?
j. numberGreen >= numberRed + numberBlue?

2. **Chocolate Delights Candy Company manufactures several types of candy. Design a flowchart or pseudocode for the following:**

a. A program that accepts a candy name (for example, "chocolate-covered blueberries"), price per pound, and number of pounds sold in the average month, and displays the item's data only if it is a best-selling item. Best-selling items are those that sell more than 2,000 pounds per month.

b. A program that accepts candy data continuously until eof and produces a report that lists high-priced, best-selling items. Best-selling items are those that sell more than 2,000 pounds per month. High-priced items are those that sell for $10 per pound or more.

3. **Pastoral College is a small college in the Midwest. Design a flowchart or pseudocode for following:**

a. A program that accepts a student's data: an ID number, first and last name, major field of study, and grade point average. Display a student's data if the student's grade point average is below 2.0.

b. A program that continuously accepts students' data until eof and produces a report that lists all students whose grade point averages are below 2.0.

c. A program for the Literary Honor Society that continuously reads student data and displays every student who is an English major with a grade point average of 3.5 or higher.

4. **The Summerville Telephone Company charges 10 cents per minute for all calls outside the customer's area code that last over 20 minutes. All other calls are 13 cents per minute. Design a flowchart or pseudocode for following:**

a. A program that accepts data about one phone call: customer area code (three digits), customer phone number (seven digits), called area code (three digits), called number (seven digits), and call time in minutes (four digits). Display the calling number, called number, and price for the call.

b. A program that accepts data about a phone call and displays all the details about only a call that costs over $10.

c. A program that continuously accepts data about phone calls until `eof` is reached and displays details about only calls placed from the 212 area code to the 704 area code that last over 20 minutes.

d. A program that prompts the user for a three-digit area code. Then the program continuously accepts phone call data until `eof` is reached, and displays data for any phone call to or from the specified area code.

5. **Equinox Nursery maintains records about all the plants it has in stock. Design a flowchart or pseudocode for following:**

a. A program that accepts a plant's name, price, and the plant's light and soil preferences. (The light variable might contain a description such as "sunny", "partial sun", or "shady". The soil variable might contain a description such as "clay" or "sandy".) Display the details for a plant if it is appropriate for a shady, sandy yard.

b. A program that accepts a plant's data and displays the results for a plant if it is appropriate for a shady or partially sunny yard with clay soil.

c. A program that prompts the user for yard conditions (light and soil preferences) and then continuously accepts plant data until `eof` and displays plants that meet the requested criteria.

6. **The Drive-Rite Insurance Company provides automobile insurance policies for drivers. Design a flowchart or pseudocode for following:**

a. A program that accepts insurance policy holder data including a policy number, customer last name, customer first name, age, premium due month, day and year, and the number of accidents in which the driver has been involved in the last three years. If a policy number entered is not between 1000 and 9999 inclusive, then set the policy number to 0. If the month is not between 1 and 12 inclusive, or the day is not correct for the month (that is, between 1 and 31 for January, 1 and 29 for February, and so on), then set the month, day, and year all to 0. Display the policy holder data after any revisions have been made.

b. A program that accepts a policy holder's data and displays the data for any policy holder over 35 years old.

c. A program that accepts a policy holder's data and displays the data for any policy holder who is at least 21 years old.

d. A program that accepts a policy holder's data and displays the data for any policy holder no more than 30 years old.

e. A program that accepts a policy holder's data and displays the data for any policy holder whose premium is due no later than March 15 any year.

f. A program that accepts a policy holder's data and displays the data for any policy holder whose premium is due up to and including January 1, 2010.

g. A program that accepts a policy holder's data and displays the data for any policy holder whose premium is due by April 27, 2009.

h. A program that accepts a policy holder's data and displays the data for any policy holder who has a policy number between 1000 and 4000 inclusive, whose policy comes due in April or May of any year, and has had fewer than three accidents.

7. **The Barking Lot is a dog day care center. Design a flowchart or pseudocode for following:**

a. A program that accepts data for an ID number of a dog's owner, and the name, breed, age, and weight of the dog. Display a bill containing all the input data as well as the weekly day care fee which is $55 for dogs under 15 pounds, $75 for dogs at least 15 pounds but no more than 30 pounds, $105 for dogs over 30 pounds but no more than 80 pounds, and $125 for dogs over 80 pounds.

b. A program that continuously accepts dogs' data until eof is reached and displays a bill for each dog.

c. A program that continuously accepts dogs' data until eof is reached and displays bills for dog owners who owe more than $100.

8. **Rick Hammer is a carpenter who wants an application to compute the price of any desk a customer orders, based on the following: desk length and width in inches, type of wood, and number of drawers. The price is computed as follows:**

» The minimum charge for all desks is $200.

» If the surface (length * width) is over 750 square inches, add $50.

» If the wood is "mahogany" add $150; for "oak" add $125. No charge is added for "pine."

» For every drawer in the desk, there is an additional $30 charge.

Design a flowchart or pseudocode for following:

a. A program that accepts data for an order number, customer name, length and width of the desk ordered, type of wood, and number of drawers. Display all the entered data and the final price for the desk.

b. A program that continuously accepts desk order data and displays all the relevant information for oak desks that are over 36 inches long and have at least one drawer.

9. **Black Dot Printing is attempting to organize carpools to save energy. Each input record contains an employee's name and town of residence. Ten percent of the company's employees live in Wonder Lake; 30 percent live in Woodstock. Because these towns are both north of the company, Black Dot wants to encourage employees who live in either town, to drive to work together. Design a flowchart or pseudocode for following:**

a. A program that accepts an employee's data and displays it with a message that indicates whether the employee is a candidate for the carpool.

b. A program that continuously accepts employee data until eof is reached and displays a list of all employees who are carpool candidates.

10. **Diana Lee, a supervisor in a manufacturing company, wants to know which employees have increased their production this year over last year, so that she can issue them certificates of commendation and bonuses. Design a flowchart or pseudocode for following:**

   a. A program that continuously accepts each worker's first and last names, this year's number of units produced, and last year's number of units produced. Display each employee with a message indicating whether the employee's production has increased over last year's production.

   b. A program that accepts each worker's data and displays the name and a bonus amount. The bonuses will be distributed as follows:

   If this year's production is greater than last year's production and this year's production is:

   » 1,000 units or fewer, the bonus is $25

   » 1,001 to 3,000 units, the bonus is $50

   » 3,001 to 6,000 units, the bonus is $100

   » 6,001 units and up, the bonus is $200

   c. Modify Exercise 10b to reflect the following new facts, and have the program execute as efficiently as possible:

   » Thirty percent of employees have greater production this year than last year.

   » Sixty percent of employees produce over 6,000 units per year; 20 percent produce 3,001 to 6,000; 15 percent produce 1,001 to 3,000 units; and only 5 percent produce fewer than 1,001.

11. **The Richmond Riding Club wants to assign the title of Master or Novice to each of its members. A member earns the title of Master by accomplishing two or more of the following:**

   » Participating in at least eight horse shows

   » Winning a first- or second-place ribbon in at least two horse shows, no matter how many shows the member has participated in

   » Winning a first-, second-, third-, or fourth-place ribbon in at least four horse shows, no matter how many shows the member has participated in

   Design a flowchart or pseudocode for following:

   A program that accepts a rider's last name, first name, number of shows in which the rider has participated, and number of first-, second-, third-, and fourth-place ribbons the rider has received. If the sum of the first-, second-, third-, and fourth-place ribbons exceeds the number of shows, then set all the ribbon values to 0 and display the rider's name and an error message. Otherwise, display the rider's name and either "Master" or "Novice".

12. **The Dorian Gray Portrait Studio charges its customers for portrait sittings based on the number of subjects posing for the portrait. The fee schedule is as follows:**

Subjects in Portrait	Base Price
1	$100
2	$130
3	$150
4	$165
5	$175
6	$180
7 or more	$185

Portrait sittings on Saturday or Sunday cost an extra 20 percent more than the base price.

Design a flowchart or pseudocode for following:

a. A program that accepts the following data: the last name of the family sitting for the portrait, the number of subjects in the portrait, the scheduled day of the week, and the scheduled time of day. Display all the input data as well as the calculated sitting fee.

b. A program that accepts customer data continuously until eof and displays data only for a sitting scheduled on Thursday after 1 p.m. or Friday before noon.

GAME ZONE

1. In Chapter 3, you learned that in many programming languages you can generate a random number between 1 and a limiting value named LIMIT by using a statement similar to randomNumber = random(LIMIT). Create the logic for a guessing game in which the application generates a random number and the player tries to guess it. Display a message indicating whether the player's guess was correct, too high, or too low. (After you finish Chapter 5, you will be able to modify the application so that the user can continue to guess until the correct answer is entered.)

2. Create a lottery game application. Generate three random numbers, each between 0 and 9. Allow the user to guess three numbers. Compare each of the user's guesses to the three random numbers and display a message that includes the user's guess, the randomly determined three-digit number, and the amount of money the user has won as follows:

Matching Numbers	Award ($)
Any one matching	10
Two matching	100
Three matching, not in order	1000
Three matching in exact order	1,000,000
No matches	0

Make certain that your application accommodates repeating digits. For example, if a user guesses 1, 2, and 3, and the randomly generated digits are 1, 1, and 1, do not give the user credit for three correct guesses—just one.

DETECTIVE WORK

1. Computers are expert chess players because they can make many good decisions very rapidly. Explore the history of computer chess playing.

2. George Boole is considered the father of symbolic logic. Find out about his life.

UP FOR DISCUSSION

1. Computer programs can be used to make decisions about your insurability as well as the rates you will be charged for health and life insurance policies. For example, certain preexisting conditions may raise your insurance premiums considerably. Is it ethical for insurance companies to access your health records and then make insurance decisions about you? Explain your answer.

2. Job applications are sometimes screened by software that makes decisions about a candidate's suitability based on keywords in the applications. Is such screening fair to applicants? Explain your answer.

3. Medical facilities often have more patients waiting for organ transplants than there are available organs. Suppose you have been asked to write a computer program that selects which of several candidates should receive an available organ. What data would you want on file to be able to use in your program, and what decisions would you make based on the data? What data do you think others might use that you would choose not to use?

LOOPING

In this chapter you will:

Learn about the advantages of looping
Control loops with counters and sentinel values
Nest loops
Learn to avoid common loop mistakes
Use a `for` loop
Use posttest loops
Recognize the characteristics shared by all loops
Learn about common loop applications

UNDERSTANDING THE ADVANTAGES OF LOOPING

While making decisions is what makes computers seem intelligent, it's looping that makes computer programming both efficient and worthwhile. When you use a loop within a computer program, you can write one set of instructions that operates on multiple, separate sets of data. Consider the following set of tasks required for each employee in a typical payroll program:

» Determine regular pay.
» Determine overtime pay, if any.
» Determine federal withholding tax based on gross wages and number of dependents.
» Determine state withholding tax based on gross wages, number of dependents, and state of residence.
» Determine insurance deduction based on insurance code.
» Determine Social Security deduction based on gross pay.
» Subtract federal tax, state tax, Social Security, and insurance from gross pay.

In reality, this list is too short—companies deduct stock option plans, charitable contributions, union dues, and other items from checks in addition to the items mentioned in this list. Also, they might pay bonuses and commissions and provide sick days and vacation days that must be taken into account and handled appropriately. As you can see, payroll programs are complicated.

The advantage of having a computer perform payroll calculations is that all of the deduction instructions need to be written only once and can be repeated over and over again for each paycheck using a **loop**, the structure that repeats actions while some condition continues.

TWO TRUTHS AND A LIE:
UNDERSTANDING THE ADVANTAGES OF LOOPING

1. When you use a loop within a computer program, you can write one set of instructions that operates on multiple, separate sets of data.

2. A major advantage of having a computer perform complicated tasks is the ability to repeat them.

3. A loop is a structure that branches in two logical paths before continuing.

The false statement is #3. A loop is a structure that repeats actions while some condition continues.

CONTROLLING LOOPS WITH COUNTERS AND SENTINEL VALUES

Recall the loop, or `while` structure, that you learned about in Chapter 2. There you learned about loops that look like Figure 5-1. As long as a Boolean expression remains true, a `while` loop's body executes. When you write a loop, you must control the number of repetitions it performs; if you do not, you run the risk of creating an infinite loop. Commonly, you control a loop's repetitions by using either a counter or a sentinel value.

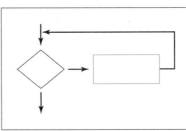

>> NOTE
You first learned about infinite loops in Chapter 2.

Figure 5-1 The `while` loop

USING A DEFINITE `while` LOOP WITH A COUNTER

You can use a `while` loop to execute a body of statements continuously as long as some condition continues to be true. To make a `while` loop end correctly, three separate actions should occur:

» A variable, the **loop control variable**, is initialized (before entering the loop).

» The loop control variable is tested, and, if the result is true, the loop body is entered.

» The body of the loop must take some action that alters the value of the loop control variable (so that the `while` expression eventually evaluates as false).

> **>> NOTE** The decision that controls every loop is always based on a Boolean comparison. In Chapter 4 you learned about six comparison operators that you can use in a selection. You can use any of the same six to control a loop. They are equal to, greater than, less than, greater than or equal to, less than or equal to, and not equal to.

For example, the code in Figure 5-2 shows a loop that displays "Hello" four times. The variable `count` is the loop control variable, and it is initialized to 0. Then the shaded `while` expression compares `count` to 4, finds it is less than 4, and so the loop body executes. The loop body shown in Figure 5-2 consists of two statements. The first statement prints "Hello" and the second statement adds 1 to `count`. The next time `count` is evaluated, its value is 1, which is still less than 4, so the loop body executes again. "Hello" prints a second time and `count` becomes 2, "Hello" prints a third time and `count` becomes 3, then "Hello" prints a fourth time and `count` becomes 4. Now when the expression `count < 4` evaluates, it is `false`, so the loop ends.

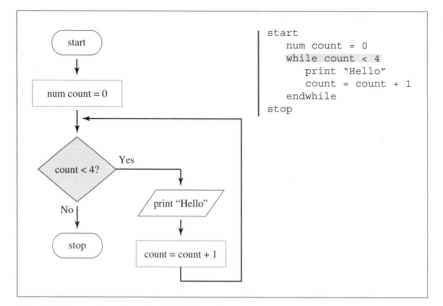

Figure 5-2 A `while` loop that prints "Hello" four times

Within a correctly functioning loop's body, you can change the value of the loop control variable in a number of ways. Many loop control variable values are altered by **incrementing**, or adding to them, as in Figure 5-2. Other loops are controlled by reducing, or **decrementing**, a variable and testing whether the value remains greater than some benchmark value. For example, the loop in Figure 5-2 could be rewritten so that `count` is initialized to 4, and reduced by 1 on each pass through the loop. The loop should then continue while `count` remains greater than 0.

A loop such as the one in Figure 5-2, for which the number of iterations is predetermined, is called a **definite loop** or **counted loop**. The looping logic shown in Figure 5-2 uses a counter. A **counter** is any numeric variable you use to count the number of times an event has occurred. In everyday life, people usually count things starting with 1. Many programmers prefer starting their counted loops with a variable containing a 0 value for two reasons. First, in many computer applications, numbering starts with 0 because of the 0-and-1 nature of computer circuitry. Second, when you learn about arrays in Chapter 6, you will discover that array manipulation naturally lends itself to 0-based loops. However, you are not required to start counting using 0. You could achieve exactly the same results in a program as the one in Figure 5-2 by initializing count to 1 and continuing the loop while it remains less than 5. You could even initialize count to some arbitrary value such as 23 and continue while it remains less than 27 (which is 4 greater than 23). This last choice is not recommended, because it is confusing; however, the program would work just as well.

Often, the value of a loop control variable is not altered by arithmetic, but instead is altered by user input. For example, perhaps you want to continue performing some task while the user indicates a desire to continue. In that case, you do not know when you write the program whether the loop will be executed two times, 200 times, or not at all. This type of loop is an **indefinite loop**.

USING AN INDEFINITE while LOOP WITH A SENTINEL VALUE

Consider a program that displays a bank balance and asks if the user wants to see what the balance will be after one year of interest has accumulated. Each time the user indicates she wants to continue, an increased balance appears. When the user finally indicates she has seen enough, the program ends. The loop is indefinite because each time the program executes, the loop might be performed a different number of times. The program appears in Figure 5-3. Figure 5-4 shows how this program might be executed when written as a command-line interactive program.

>> **NOTE** The first get response statement in the program in Figure 5-3 is a priming input statement. You learned about the priming input statement in Chapter 2.

>> **NOTE** The program shown in Figure 5-3 continues to display bank balances while response is Y. It could also be written to display while response is not N. In Chapter 2, you learned that a value such as "Y" or "N" that a user must supply to stop a loop is called a sentinel value.

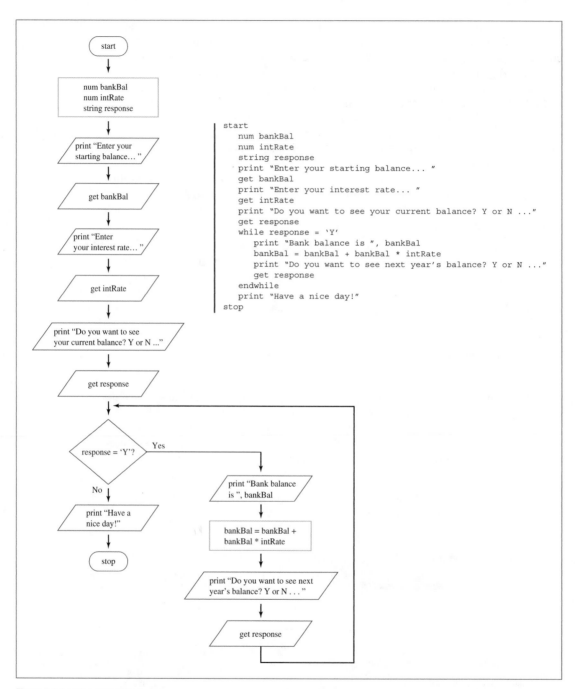

Figure 5-3 Looping bank balance program

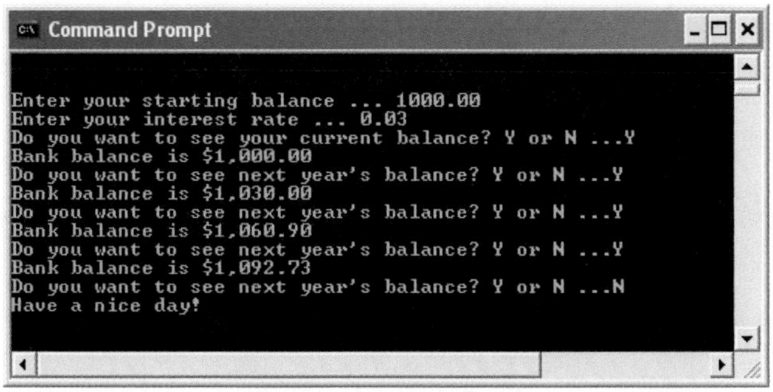

Figure 5-4 Typical execution of the looping bank balance program

The program shown in Figure 5-3 contains three variables that are involved in the looping process: a bank balance, an interest rate, and a response. The variable named `response` is the loop control variable. It is initialized when the program asks the user, "Do you want to see your current balance?" and reads the response. The loop control variable is tested with `response = "Y"?`. If the user has entered any response other than *Y*, then the test expression is false, and the loop body never executes; instead, the next statement to execute is to display "Have a nice day!". However, if the user enters *Y*, then the test expression is true and all four statements within the loop body execute. Within the loop body, the current balance is displayed, and the program increases the balance by the interest rate percentage; this value will not be displayed unless the user requests another loop repetition. Within the loop, the program prompts the user and reads in a new value for `response`. This is the statement that potentially alters the loop control variable. The loop body ends when program control returns to the top of the loop where the Boolean expression in the `while` statement is tested again. If the user typed *Y* at the last prompt, then the loop is entered and the increased `bankBal` value that was calculated during the last loop cycle is finally displayed.

>> **NOTE** In most programming languages, character data is case sensitive. If a program tests `response = "Y"`, a user response of *y* will result in a `false` evaluation.

The flowchart and pseudocode segments in Figure 5-3 contain three steps that must occur in every loop, and these crucial steps are shaded in Figure 5-5.

1. You must provide a starting value that will control the loop. In this case, the starting value is provided by the first request for a user's response.

2. You must make a comparison using the value that controls whether the loop continues or stops. In this case, you compare the user's response with the character 'Y'.

3. Within the loop, you must alter the value that controls the loop. In this case, you alter the loop control variable by asking the user for a new response.

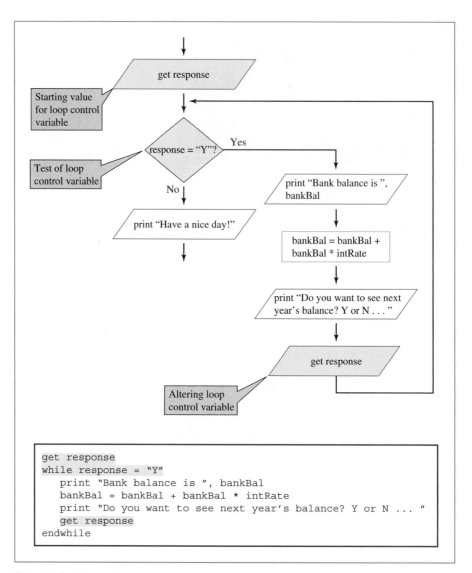

Figure 5-5 Crucial steps that must occur in every loop

On each pass through the loop, the value in the response variable determines whether the loop will continue. Therefore variables like response are known as **loop control variables**. Any variable that determines whether a loop will continue is a loop control variable.

> **» NOTE** The body of a loop might contain any number of statements, including method calls, decisions, and other loops. Once your logic enters the body of a structured loop, the entire loop body must execute. Your program can leave a structured loop only at the comparison that tests the loop control variable.

NESTED LOOPS

Program logic gets more complicated when you must use loops within loops, or **nested loops**. When one loop appears inside another, the loop that contains the other loop is called the **outer loop**, and the loop that is contained is called the **inner loop**. You need to create nested loops when the values of two (or more) variables repeat to produce every combination of values.

For example, suppose you want to write a program that produces a quiz answer sheet like the one shown in Figure 5-6. The quiz has five parts with three questions in each part, and you want a fill-in-the-blank line for each question. You could write a program that uses 21 separate print statements to produce the sheet, but it is more efficient to use nested loops.

Figure 5-7 shows the logic of the program that produces the answer sheet. Two variables, named `partCounter` and `questionCounter`, are declared to keep track of the answer sheet parts and questions, respectively. Four named constants are also declared to hold the number of parts and questions in each, and to hold the text that will be printed—

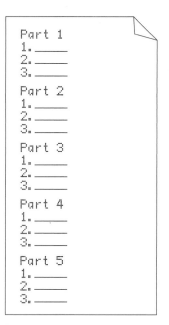

Figure 5-6 A quiz answer sheet

the word "Part" with each part number, and a period, space, and underscores to form a fill-in line for each question. When the program starts, `partCounter` is initialized to 1. The `partCounter` variable is the loop control variable for the outer loop in this program. The outer loop continues while `partCounter` is less than or equal to `PARTS`. The last statement in the outer loop adds 1 to `partCounter`. In other words, the outer loop will execute when `partCounter` is 1, 2, 3, 4, and 5.

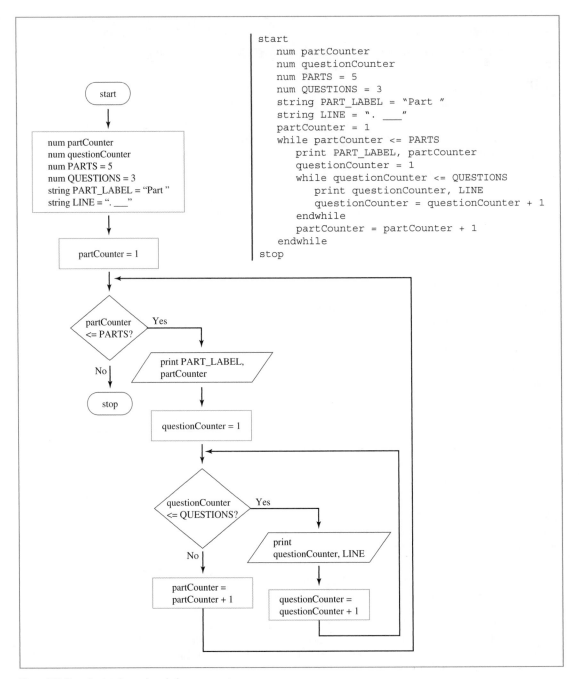

```
start
   num partCounter
   num questionCounter
   num PARTS = 5
   num QUESTIONS = 3
   string PART_LABEL = "Part "
   string LINE = ". ___"
   partCounter = 1
   while partCounter <= PARTS
      print PART_LABEL, partCounter
      questionCounter = 1
      while questionCounter <= QUESTIONS
         print questionCounter, LINE
         questionCounter = questionCounter + 1
      endwhile
      partCounter = partCounter + 1
   endwhile
stop
```

Figure 5-7 Flowchart and pseudocode for `AnswerSheet` program

In the outer loop in Figure 5-7, the word "Part" and the current partCounter value are printed. Then questionCounter is set to 1. The variable questionCounter is the loop control variable for the inner loop in the nested loop pair. The loop-controlling question compares questionCounter to QUESTIONS, and while it does not exceed QUESTIONS, questionCounter is printed, followed by a period and a fill-in-the-blank line. Then 1 is added to questionCounter and the questionCounter comparison is made again. In other words, when partCounter is 1, lines print for questions 1, 2, and 3. Then partCounter becomes 2, the part heading prints, and lines print for new questions 1, 2, and 3.

MIXING CONSTANT AND VARIABLE SENTINEL VALUES

The number of times a loop executes can depend on a constant or a value that varies. Suppose you own a factory and have decided to place a label on every product you manufacture. The label contains the words "Made for you personally by" followed by the first name of one of your employees. Assume that for one week's production, you need 100 personalized labels for each employee.

Figure 5-8 shows the program that creates 100 labels for each employee entered. In the main-line logic, the user is prompted for an employee's name, and while the user does not type the QUIT value ("ZZZ"), the program continues. The loopCounter variable is set to 0 and a label that contains the employee's name is printed. Then the loop control variable labelCounter is incremented. Its value is tested again, and if it is not equal to LABELS (100), another label is printed. When the value of labelCounter reaches 100, the user is prompted for a new employee name.

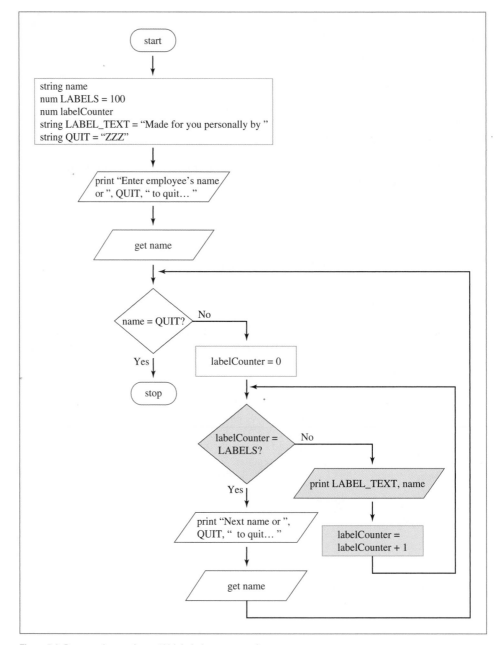

Figure 5-8 Program that produces 100 labels for every employee

```
start
   string name
   numeric LABELS = 100
   numeric labelCounter
   string LABEL_TEXT = "Made for you personally by "
   string QUIT = "ZZZ"
   print "Enter employee's name or ", QUIT, " to quit... "
   get name
      while name not equal to QUIT
      labelCounter = 0
      while labelCounter not equal to LABELS
         print LABEL_TEXT, name
         labelCounter = labelCounter + 1
      endwhile
      print "Next name or ", QUIT, " to quit..."
      get name
   endwhile
stop
```

Figure 5-8 Program that produces 100 labels for every employee (*continued*)

Figure 5-8 contains an indefinite outer loop that is controlled by the value of the name that the user enters, and a definite inner loop that executes exactly 100 times. In the inner loop (shaded in Figure 5-8), while the counter, named `labelCounter`, continues to be less than 100, a label is printed and `labelCounter` is increased. When 100 labels have printed, control returns to the outer loop, where the next employee `name` is retrieved.

> **NOTE** Setting `labelCounter` to 0 within the outer loop is important. After `labelCounter` reaches 100 for the first employee entered, a second employee is entered and you need to start counting from 0 again. If `labelCounter` is never reset after the first employee, no labels will print for any subsequent employees. Although some languages initialize a newly declared variable to 0 for you, some do not, and either way, your intentions are clearer if you explicitly assign 0 to `labelCounter`.

Sometimes you don't want to be forced to repeat every pass through a loop the same number of times. For example, instead of printing 100 labels for each employee, you might want to vary the number of labels based on how many items a worker actually produces. That way, high-achieving workers won't run out of labels, and less productive workers won't have too many. Instead of printing the same, constant number of labels for every employee, a more sophisticated program prints a different number of labels for each employee, depending on that employee's usual production level.

Figure 5-9 shows a slightly modified version of the label-producing program. The changes from Figure 5-8 are shaded. In this version, after the user enters a valid name for an employee, the user is prompted for a production level. The Boolean expression used in the `while` statement in the inner loop compares `labelCounter` to `production`, instead of to a constant, fixed value. Some employees might get 100 labels, but some might get more or fewer.

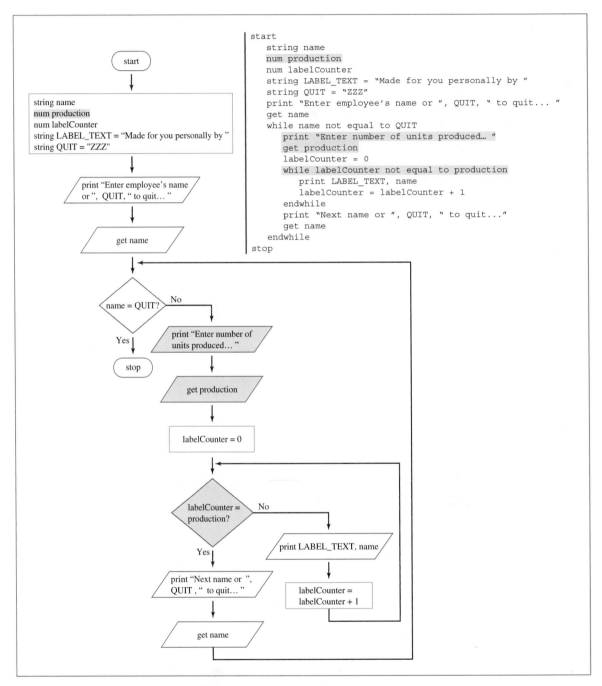

Figure 5-9 Program that produces a variable number of labels for every employee

AVOIDING COMMON LOOP MISTAKES

The mistakes programmers make most often with loops are:

» Neglecting to initialize the loop control variable
» Neglecting to alter the loop control variable
» Using the wrong comparison with the loop control variable
» Including statements inside the loop that belong outside the loop

MISTAKE: NEGLECTING TO INITIALIZE THE LOOP CONTROL VARIABLE

It is always a mistake to fail to initialize a loop's control variable. For example, assume you remove either or both of the loop initialization statements that appeared in the label production program in Figure 5-8; Figure 5-10 shows the results.

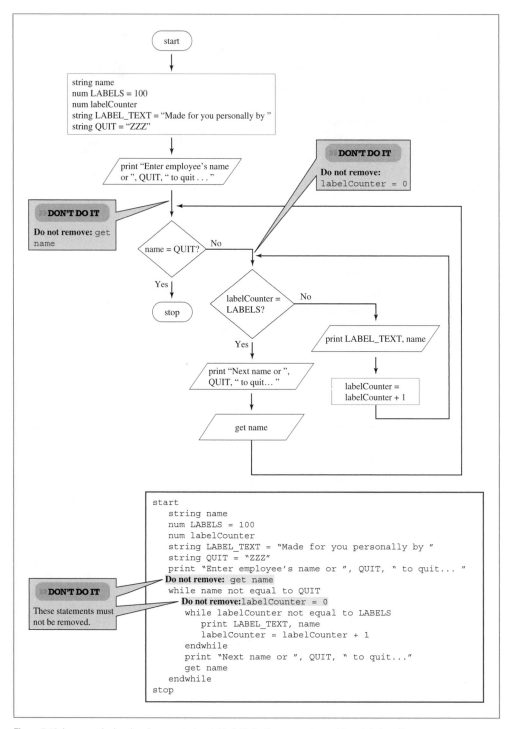

Figure 5-10 Incorrect logic when loop control variable initializations are removed from label-making program

If the get name statement is removed, as shown in the first shaded statement in Figure 5-10, then when name is tested at the start of the outer loop, its value is unknown, or garbage. Is name equal to the value of QUIT? Maybe it is, by accident, or, more likely, it is not. If it is, the program ends before any labels can be printed. If it is not, the inner loop is entered, and 100 labels are printed with an invalid name (QUIT).

If the labelCounter = 0 statement is removed, as shown in the second shaded statement in Figure 5-10, then in many languages, the value of labelCounter is unpredictable. It might or might not be equal to LABELS, and the loop might or might not execute. In a language in which numeric variables are automatically initialized to 0, the first employee's labels will print correctly, but no labels will print for subsequent employees because labelCounter will never be altered and will remain equal to LABELS for the rest of the program's execution. Either way, a logical error has occurred.

MISTAKE: NEGLECTING TO ALTER THE LOOP CONTROL VARIABLE

Different sorts of errors will occur if you fail to alter a loop control variable within the loop. You create such an error if you remove either of the statements that alter the loop control variables from the original label-making program in Figure 5-8. Figure 5-11 shows the resulting logic.

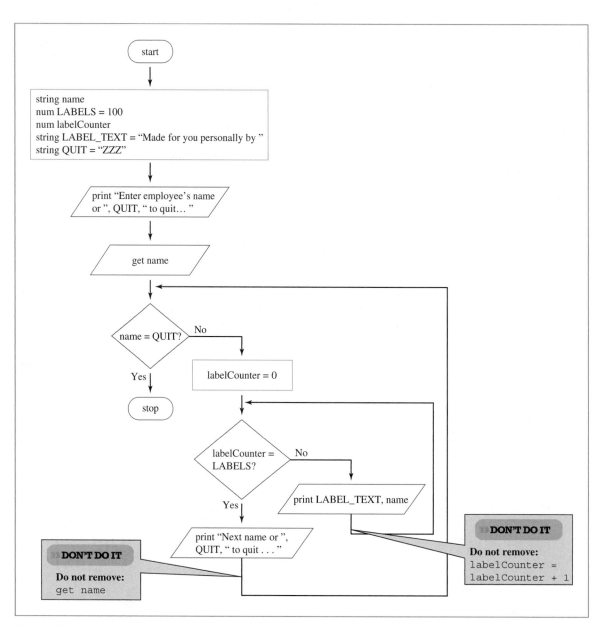

Figure 5-11 Incorrect logic when loop control variable altering statements are removed from label-making program

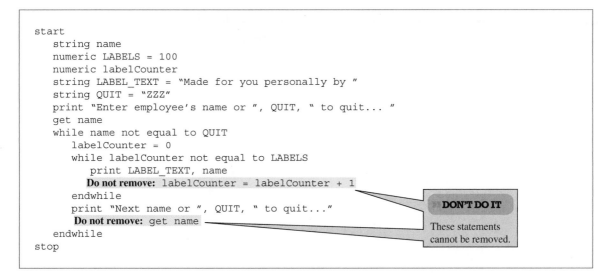

```
start
   string name
   numeric LABELS = 100
   numeric labelCounter
   string LABEL_TEXT = "Made for you personally by "
   string QUIT = "ZZZ"
   print "Enter employee's name or ", QUIT, " to quit... "
   get name
   while name not equal to QUIT
      labelCounter = 0
      while labelCounter not equal to LABELS
         print LABEL_TEXT, name
         Do not remove: labelCounter = labelCounter + 1
      endwhile
      print "Next name or ", QUIT, " to quit..."
      Do not remove: get name
   endwhile
stop
```

DON'T DO IT

These statements cannot be removed.

Figure 5-11 Incorrect logic when loop control variable altering statements are removed from label-making program (*continued*)

If you remove the get name instruction from the outer loop in the program, the user never has the opportunity to enter a name after the first one. For example, assume when the program starts, the user enters "Fred". The name will be compared to the QUIT value, and the inner loop will be entered. After labels print for Fred, no new name is entered, so when the logic returns to the name = QUIT? question, the answer will still be No. So, labels containing "Made for you personally by" and the same worker's name will continue to print infinitely. Similarly, if you remove the statement that increments labelCounter from the inner loop in the program, then labelCounter never can equal LABELS and the inner loop executes infinitely. It is always incorrect to create a loop that cannot terminate.

MISTAKE: USING THE WRONG COMPARISON WITH THE LOOP CONTROL VARIABLE

Programmers must be careful to use the correct comparison in the statement that controls a loop. Although there is only a one-keystroke difference between the following two code segments, one performs the loop 10 times and the other performs the loop 11 times.

```
counter = 0
while counter < 10
      print "Hello"
      counter = counter + 1
endwhile

counter = 0
while counter <= 10
      print "Hello"
      counter = counter + 1
endwhile
```

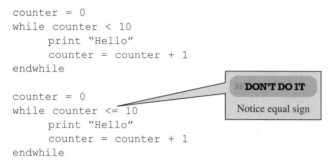

DON'T DO IT

Notice equal sign

The seriousness of the error of using <= or >= when only < or > is needed depends on the actions performed within the loop. For example, if such an error occurred in a loan company application, each customer might be charged a month's additional interest; if the error occurred in an airline's application, it might overbook a flight; and if it occurred in a pharmacy's drug-dispensing application, each patient might receive one extra (and possibly harmful and expensive) unit of medication.

MISTAKE: INCLUDING STATEMENTS INSIDE THE LOOP THAT BELONG OUTSIDE THE LOOP

Consider a program like the one in Figure 5-12. It calculates a user's projected weekly pay raise based on different raise rates from half a percent to 10 percent. The user enters an hourly pay rate and the number of hours he works per week. Then the rate of the raise is set to a starting value of 0.005 (half a percent). While the raise rate is not greater than the maximum the program allows, the user's weekly pay is calculated, and then the raise as a percentage of the weekly amount. The results are displayed, and before the loop ends, the loop control variable, percent, is increased by half a percent. Figure 5-13 shows a typical execution of the program in a command-line environment.

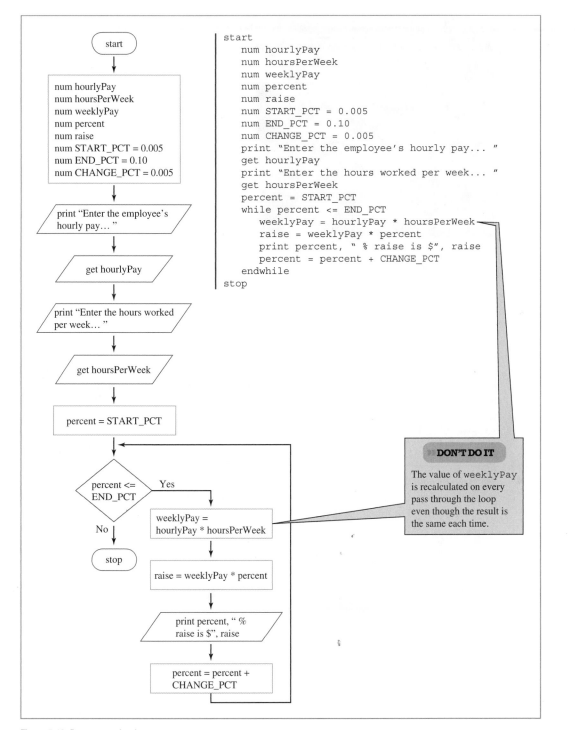

```
start
    num hourlyPay
    num hoursPerWeek
    num weeklyPay
    num percent
    num raise
    num START_PCT = 0.005
    num END_PCT = 0.10
    num CHANGE_PCT = 0.005
    print "Enter the employee's hourly pay... "
    get hourlyPay
    print "Enter the hours worked per week... "
    get hoursPerWeek
    percent = START_PCT
    while percent <= END_PCT
        weeklyPay = hourlyPay * hoursPerWeek
        raise = weeklyPay * percent
        print percent, " % raise is $", raise
        percent = percent + CHANGE_PCT
    endwhile
stop
```

DON'T DO IT

The value of weeklyPay is recalculated on every pass through the loop even though the result is the same each time.

Figure 5-12 Pay rate projection program

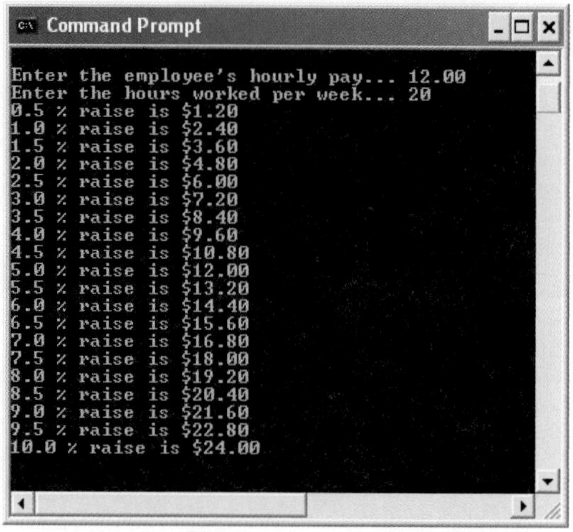

Figure 5-13 Typical execution of pay rate projection program

The program in Figure 5-12 works correctly. However, it is a little inefficient. The user enters his pay rate and hours worked once at the beginning of the program, and at that point the weekly pay could be calculated. However, the weekly pay calculation does not occur until the loop is entered, so in this program, the same calculation is made 20 times. Of course, it does not take a computer very long to perform 20 multiplication calculations, but if the calculation were more complicated and performed for thousands of employees, the program performance would suffer.

Figure 5-14 shows the same program in which the weekly pay rate calculation has been moved to a better place (see the shaded statement). The programs in Figures 5-12 and 5-14 do the same thing. However, one does it more efficiently. As you become more proficient at programming, you will recognize many opportunities to perform the same tasks in alternate, more elegant, and more efficient ways.

>> **NOTE** When you describe people or events as "elegant," you mean they possess a refined gracefulness. Similarly, programmers use the term "elegant" to describe programs that are well designed and easy to understand and maintain.

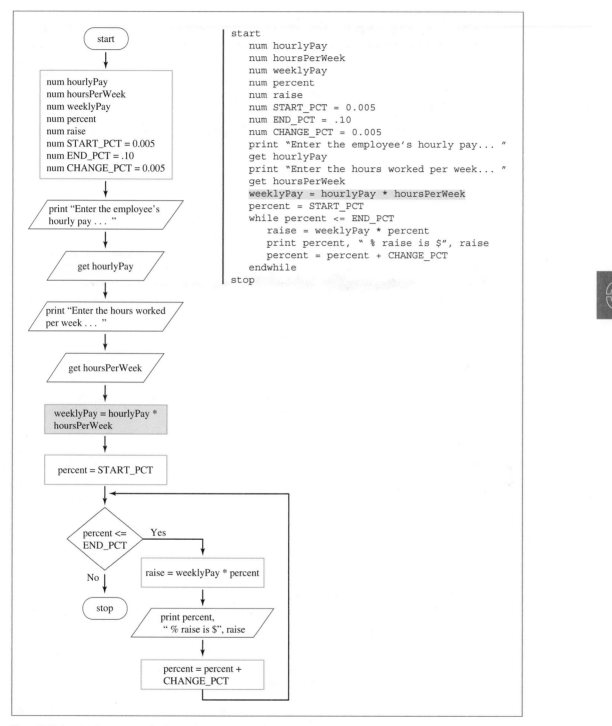

Figure 5-14 Improved pay rate projection program

```
start
    num hourlyPay
    num hoursPerWeek
    num weeklyPay
    num percent
    num raise
    num START_PCT = 0.005
    num END_PCT = .10
    num CHANGE_PCT = 0.005
    print "Enter the employee's hourly pay... "
    get hourlyPay
    print "Enter the hours worked per week... "
    get hoursPerWeek
    weeklyPay = hourlyPay * hoursPerWeek
    percent = START_PCT
    while percent <= END_PCT
        raise = weeklyPay * percent
        print percent, " % raise is $", raise
        percent = percent + CHANGE_PCT
    endwhile
stop
```

USING A for LOOP

Every high-level computer programming language contains a while statement that you can use to code any loop, including both indefinite and definite loops. In addition to the while statement, most computer languages also support a for statement. You can use the **for statement**, or **for loop**, with definite loops—those that will loop a specific number of times—frequently when you know exactly how many times the loop will repeat. The for statement provides you with three actions in one compact statement. The for statement uses a loop control variable that it automatically:

» Initializes

» Evaluates

» Increments

The for statement takes the form:

```
for initialValue to finalValue
    do something
endfor
```

For example, to print 100 labels you can write:

```
for count = 0 to 99
    print LABEL_TEXT, name
endfor
```

This for statement accomplishes several tasks at once in a compact form:

» The for statement initializes count to 0.

» The for statement checks count against the limit value 99 and makes sure that count is less than or equal to that value.

» If the evaluation is true, the for statement body that prints the label executes.

» After the for statement body executes, the value of count increases by 1, and the comparison to the limit value is made again.

As an alternative to using the loop for count = 0 to 99, you can use for count = 1 to 100. To achieve the same results, you can use any combination of values, as long as there are 100 whole number values between (and including) the two limits. Of course, the superior option would be to avoid the "magic number" and use a constant defined as numeric LIMIT = 99 and write the following:

```
for count = 0 to LIMIT
    print LABEL_TEXT, name
endfor
```

> **NOTE** You first learned about magic numbers in Chapter 3. It is common practice to use 0 and 1 as unnamed constants, but most other constant numeric values in your programs should be named.

You never are required to use a for statement; the label loop executes correctly using a while statement. However, when a loop's execution is based on a loop control variable progressing from a known starting value to a known ending value in equal increments, the for loop provides you with a convenient shorthand. It is easy for others to read, and because the loop control variable initialization, testing, and alteration are all performed in one location, you are less likely to leave out one of these crucial elements.

> **NOTE** The programmer doesn't need to know the starting or the ending value for the loop control variable; only the application must know those values. For example, instead of being a constant, the value compared to count might be entered by the user.

> **NOTE**
> The for loop is particularly useful when processing arrays. You will learn about arrays in Chapter 6.

In most programming languages, you can provide a for loop with a step value other than 1. A **step value** is a number you use to increase a loop control variable on each pass through a loop. In some programming languages, you must always provide a statement that indicates the for loop step value. In others, the default loop step value is 1. You specify a step value when you want each pass through the loop to change the loop control variable by a value other than 1.

> **TWO TRUTHS AND A LIE:**
> **USING A FOR LOOP**
>
> 1. The for statement provides you with three actions in one compact statement: initializing, evaluating, and incrementing.
> 2. A for statement body always executes at least one time.
> 3. In most programming languages, you can provide a for loop with any step value.
>
> The false statement is #2. A for statement body might not execute depending on the initial value of loop control variable.

USING POSTTEST LOOPS

When you use either a while (also called a while-do) or a for loop, the body of the loop may never execute. For example, in the following pseudocode segment, it's possible that the loop never executes because initialValue and finalValue might be equal at the start.

```
for initialValue to finalValue
    do something
endfor
```

When you want to ensure that a loop's body executes at least one time, you can use a posttest loop. In Chapter 2 you learned there are two types of posttest loops—the do-until loop, which executes until a condition becomes true, and a do-while loop, which executes while a condition remains true; that is, until it becomes false. In either type of posttest loop, the loop body always executes at least one time.

> **»NOTE** Sometimes a do-until loop is called a repeat until loop, and a do-while loop is called a repeat while loop.

For example, suppose you want to create a program that produces employee "Made for you personally by . . ." labels like the one discussed earlier in this chapter (see Figure 5-9). The way the program was originally written, the inner loop was a while loop, shown in Figure 5-15. For each employee, labelCounter was initialized to 0, and then while labelCounter was not equal to the employee's production figure, a label was printed. With this version of the program, if an employee's production was 0 (perhaps for a new employee), then no labels were printed.

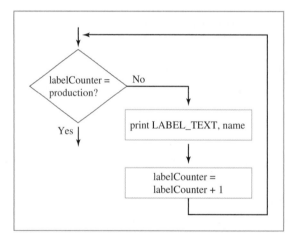

Figure 5-15 Inner loop from label production program in Figure 5-9

Suppose you wanted to guarantee that at least one label is printed for every employee, even if the employee's production value is 0. You could simply add one label-printing statement as soon as you entered the while loop, before checking production, or you could use a posttest loop that would require the loop body to execute at least one time. Figure 5-16 shows this approach using a do-until loop. In this program, labelCounter starts at -1 for each employee. Then, in the shaded inner loop, a label is printed and counted. Then, and only then, is labelCounter tested, and if it is now equal to production, the inner loop ends.

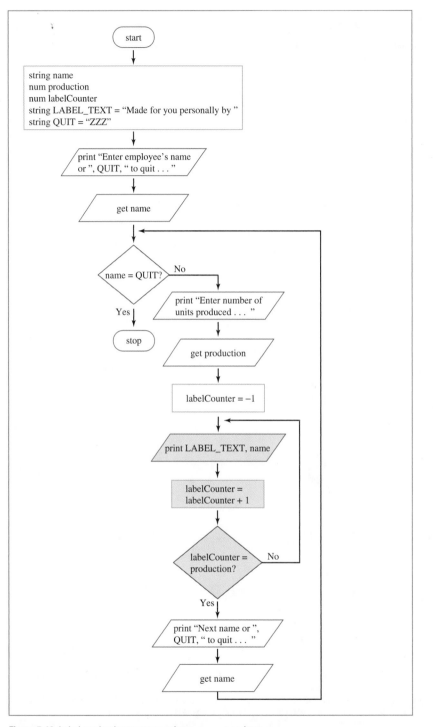

Figure 5-16 Label production program using a `do-until` loop

```
start
    string name
    num production
    num labelCounter
    string LABEL_TEXT = "Made for you personally by "
    string QUIT = "ZZZ"
    print "Enter employee's name or ", QUIT, " to quit... "
    get name
    while name not = QUIT
        print "Enter number of units produced... "
        get production
        labelCounter = -1
        do
            print LABEL_TEXT, name
            labelCounter = labelCounter + 1
        until labelCounter = production
        print "Next name or ", QUIT, " to quit... "
        get name
    endwhile
stop
```

Figure 5-16 Label production program using a `do-until` loop (*continued*)

The `do-until` loop in Figure 5-16 could be replaced with a one-time label-printing statement followed by a `do-while` loop. There is almost always more than one way to solve the same programming problem. As you learned in Chapter 2, a posttest loop can always be replaced by pairing a sequence followed by a while loop. Which method you choose depends on your (or your instructor's or supervisor's) preferences.

TWO TRUTHS AND A LIE:
USING POSTTEST LOOPS

1. When you want to ensure that a loop's body executes at least one time, you use a pretest loop.

2. The `do-until` loop executes until a condition becomes true.

3. The `do-while` loop executes until a condition becomes false.

The false statement is #1. When you want to ensure that a loop's body executes at least one time, you use a posttest loop.

RECOGNIZING THE CHARACTERISTICS SHARED BY ALL LOOPS

In this chapter you have seen both pretest and posttest loops. You have learned the differences between `while`, `for`, `do-until`, and `do-while` loops. You could solve every logical problem using only the `while` loop—the other forms are conveniences for special situations.

>> **NOTE** If you can express the logic you want to perform by saying "while a is true, keep doing b," you probably want to use a `while` loop. If what you want to accomplish seems to fit the statement "do a until b is true," you can probably use a do-until loop.

As you examine Figures 5-15 and 5-16, notice that with the `while` loop, the loop-controlling question is placed at the beginning of the steps that repeat, and with the `do-until` loop, the loop-controlling question is placed at the end of the sequence of the steps that repeat.

All structured loops, both pretest and posttest, share these two characteristics:

» The loop-controlling question must provide either entry to or exit from the repeating structure.

» The loop-controlling question provides the *only* entry to or exit from the repeating structure.

In other words, there is exactly one loop-controlling value and it provides either the only entrance to or the only exit from the loop. You should also notice the difference between unstructured loops and the structured do-until and while loops. Figure 5-17 diagrams the outline of two unstructured loops. In each case, the decision labeled X breaks out of the loop prematurely. The loop control variable (labeled LC) does not provide the only entry to or exit from either loop.

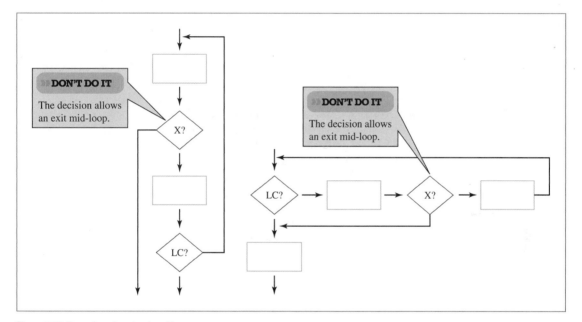

Figure 5-17 Examples of unstructured loops

COMMON LOOP APPLICATIONS

Although every computer program is different, many techniques are common to a variety of applications. Loops, for example, are frequently used to accumulate totals and to validate data.

USING A LOOP TO ACCUMULATE TOTALS

Business reports often include totals. The supervisor requesting a list of employees who participate in the company dental plan is often as interested in the number of participating employees as in who they are. When you receive your telephone bill at the end of the month, you are usually more interested in the total than in the charges for the individual calls.

For example, a real estate broker might want to see a list of all properties sold in the last month, as well as the total value for all the properties. A program might read sales data including the street address of the property sold and its selling price. The data records might be entered by a clerk as each sale is made, and stored in a file until the end of the month; then they can be used in the month-end report. Figure 5-18 shows an example of such a report.

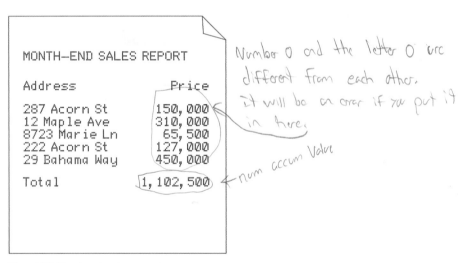

Figure 5-18 Month-end real estate sales report

To calculate the total value of all properties, when you read a real estate listing record, besides printing it you must add its value to an accumulator. An **accumulator** is a variable that you use to gather or accumulate values. An accumulator is very similar to a counter that you use to count loop iterations. The difference lies in the value that you add to the variable; usually you add just one to a counter, whereas you add some other value to an accumulator. If the real estate broker wants to know how many listings the company holds, you count them. When she wants to know total real estate value, you accumulate it.

To accumulate total real estate prices, you declare a numeric variable at the beginning of the application, as shown in Figure 5-19. You must initialize the accumulator, accumValue, to 0. As you read each real estate transaction's data record, you print it and add its value to the accumulator accumValue, as shown in shaded statement. Then you can read the next record.

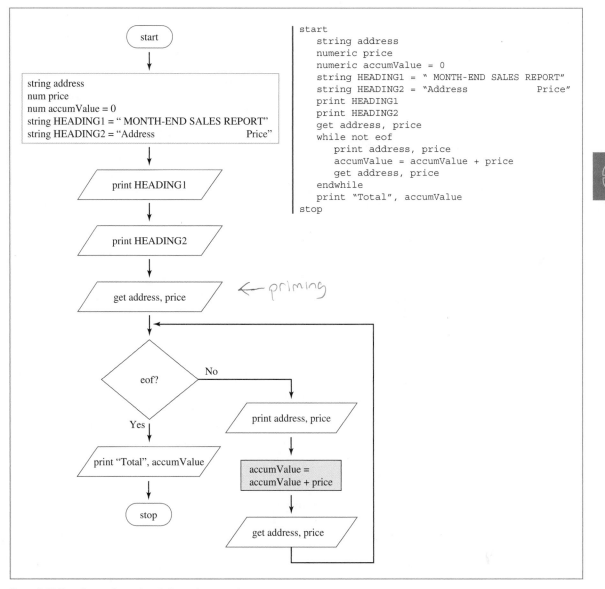

```
start
    string address
    numeric price
    numeric accumValue = 0
    string HEADING1 = " MONTH-END SALES REPORT"
    string HEADING2 = "Address            Price"
    print HEADING1
    print HEADING2
    get address, price
    while not eof
        print address, price
        accumValue = accumValue + price
        get address, price
    endwhile
    print "Total", accumValue
stop
```

Figure 5-19 Flowchart and pseudocode for real estate sales report program

> **▶▶NOTE** Some programming languages assign 0 to a variable you fail to initialize explicitly. Some programming languages issue an error message if you don't initialize a variable but then use it for accumulating. Other languages let you accumulate using an uninitialized variable, but the results are worthless because you start with garbage. The safest and clearest course of action is to assign the value 0 to accumulators before using them.

After the last record is read in the program in Figure 5-19, the `eof` indicator is reached, and loop execution is done. At that point, the accumulator will hold the grand total of all the real estate values. The program prints the word "Total" and the accumulated value, accumValue. Then the program ends.

New programmers often want to reset accumValue to 0 after printing it. Although you can take this step without harming the execution of the program, it does not serve any useful purpose. You cannot set accumValue to 0 in anticipation of having it ready for the next program, or even for the next time you execute this program. Variables exist only for the life of the application, and even if a future application happens to contain a variable named accumValue, the variable will not necessarily occupy the same memory location as this one. Even if you run the same application a second time, the variables might occupy physical memory locations different from those they occupied during the first run. At the beginning of any method, it is the programmer's responsibility to initialize all variables that must start with a specific value. There is no benefit to changing a variable's value when it will never be used again during the current execution.

> **▶▶NOTE** You could revise the program in Figure 5-19 to become a program that creates only a summary report that contains the total of the sale prices but no individual transaction details simply by removing the first statement in the loop—the one that prints each address and price.

USING A LOOP TO VALIDATE DATA

When you ask a user to enter data into a computer program, you have no assurance that the data the user enters will be accurate. Loops are frequently used to **validate data**; that is, to make sure it falls within an acceptable range. For example, suppose part of a program you are writing asks a user to enter a number that represents his or her birth month. If the user types a number lower than 1 or greater than 12, you must take some sort of action. For example:

» You could display an error message and stop the program.

» You could choose to assign a default value for the month, for example 1, before proceeding.

» You could reprompt the user for valid input.

If you choose this last course of action, there are at least two approaches you could take. You could use a selection, and if the month is invalid, you can ask the user to reenter a number, as shown in Figure 5-20.

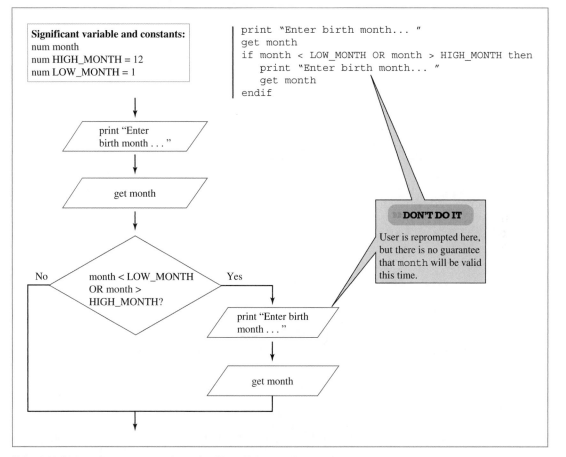

Figure 5-20 Reprompting a user once after an invalid month is entered

The problem with the logic in Figure 5-20 is that it is possible that on the second attempt to enter a month, the user still does not enter valid data. So, you could add a third decision. Of course, you can't control what the user enters that time either.

The superior solution is to use a loop to continuously prompt a user for a month until the user enters it correctly. Figure 5-21 shows this approach.

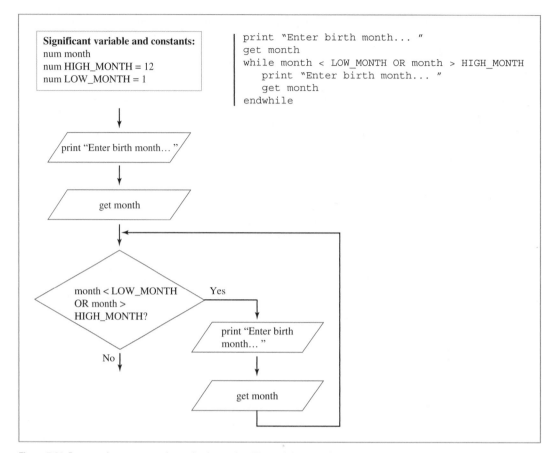

```
print "Enter birth month... "
get month
while month < LOW_MONTH OR month > HIGH_MONTH
    print "Enter birth month... "
    get month
endwhile
```

Significant variable and constants:
num month
num HIGH_MONTH = 12
num LOW_MONTH = 1

print "Enter birth month… "

get month

month < LOW_MONTH OR month > HIGH_MONTH?

Yes

No

print "Enter birth month… "

get month

Figure 5-21 Reprompting a user continuously after an invalid month is entered

» **NOTE** Most languages provide a built-in way to check whether data that is entered is numeric or not. When you rely on user input, you frequently accept each piece of input data as a string and then attempt to convert it to a number. The procedure for accomplishing numeric checks is slightly different in different programming languages.

» **NOTE** Just because a data item is valid does not mean that it is correct. For example, a program can determine that 5 is a valid birth month, but not if your birthday actually falls in month 5.

TWO TRUTHS AND A LIE:
COMMON LOOP APPLICATIONS

1. An accumulator is a variable that you use to gather or accumulate values.

2. An accumulator typically is initialized to 0.

3. An accumulator is typically reset to 0 after it is printed or displayed.

The false statement is #3. There is typically no need to reset an accumulator after it is displayed or printed.

CHAPTER SUMMARY

» When you use a loop within a computer program, you can write one set of instructions that operates on multiple, separate sets of data.

» Three steps must occur in every loop: You must initialize a loop control variable, compare the variable to some value that controls whether the loop continues or stops, and alter the variable that controls the loop.

» When you must use loops within loops, you use nested loops. When nesting loops, you must maintain two individual loop control variables and alter each at the appropriate time.

» Common mistakes that programmers make when writing loops include neglecting to initialize the loop control variable, neglecting to alter the loop control variable, using the wrong comparison with the loop control variable, and including statements inside the loop that belong outside the loop.

» Most computer languages support a for statement or for loop that you can use with definite loops when you know how many times a loop will repeat. The for statement uses a loop control variable that it automatically initializes, evaluates, and increments.

» When you want to ensure that a loop's body executes at least one time, you can use a posttest loop in which the loop control variable is evaluated after the loop body executes.

» All structured loops share these characteristics: The loop-controlling question provides either entry to or exit from the repeating structure, and the loop-controlling question provides the *only* entry to or exit from the repeating structure.

» Loops are used in many applications. For example, business reports often include totals. Summary reports list no detail records—only totals. An accumulator is a variable that you use to gather or accumulate values. Loops are also used to ensure user data is valid by continuously reprompting the user.

KEY TERMS

A **loop** is a structure that repeats actions while a condition continues.

A **loop control variable** is a variable that determines whether a loop will continue.

Incrementing a variable is adding a constant value to it, frequently 1.

Decrementing a variable is decreasing it by a constant value, frequently 1.

A **definite loop**, or **counted loop**, is one for which the number of repetitions is a predetermined value.

A **counter** is any numeric variable you use to count the number of times an event has occurred.

An **indefinite loop** is one for which you cannot predetermine the number of executions.

Nested loops occur when a loop structure exists within another loop structure; nesting loops are loops within loops.

When loops are nested, the loop that contains the other loop is the **outer loop**.

When loops are nested, the loop that is contained within the other is the **inner loop**.

A **for statement**, or **for loop**, can be used to code definite loops. It contains a loop control variable that it automatically initializes, evaluates, and increments.

A **step value** is a number you use to increase a loop control variable on each pass through a loop.

A **summary report** lists only totals, without individual detail records.

An **accumulator** is a variable that you use to gather or accumulate values.

When you **validate data**, you make sure it falls within an acceptable range.

REVIEW QUESTIONS

1. **The structure that allows you to write one set of instructions that operates on multiple, separate sets of data is the _____ .**

   a. sequence

   b. selection

   c. loop

   d. case

2. **Which of the following is not a step that must occur in every loop?**

   a. Initialize a loop control variable.

   b. Set the loop control value equal to a sentinel.

   c. Compare the loop control value to a sentinel.

   d. Alter the loop control variable.

3. **The statements executed within a loop are known collectively as the _____ .**

   a. loop body

   b. loop controls

   c. sequences

   d. sentinels

4. **A counter keeps track of _____ .**

   a. the number of times an event has occurred

   b. the number of machine cycles required by a segment of a program

   c. the number of loop structures within a program

   d. the number of times software has been revised

5. **Adding 1 to a variable is also called _____ it.**

   a. digesting

   b. resetting

   c. decrementing

   d. incrementing

6. In the following pseudocode, what is printed?

```
a = 1
b = 2
c = 5
while a < c
Loop    a = a + 1
        b = b + c
endwhile
print a, b, c
```

a. 1 2 5   c. 5 6 5

b. 5 22 5   d. 6 22 9

7. In the following pseudocode, what is printed?

```
d = 4
e = 6
f = 7
while d > f
    d = d + 1
    e = e - 1
endwhile
print d, e, f
```

a. 4 6 7   c. 7 3 7

b. 8 2 8   d. 5 5 7

8. When you decrement a variable, you _____ .

a. set it to 0   c. subtract 1 from it

b. reduce it by one-tenth d. remove it from a program

9. In the following pseudocode, what is printed?

```
g = 4
h = 6
while g < h
    g = g + 1
endwhile
print g, h
```

a. nothing   c. 5 6

b. 4 6   d. 6 6

10. Most programmers use a `for` loop _____ .

a. for every loop they write

b. when a loop will not repeat

c. when they do not know the exact number of times a loop will repeat

d. when they know the exact number of times a loop will repeat

11. Unlike a pretest loop, you use a posttest loop when _____ .

    a. you can predict the exact number of loop repetitions

    b. the loop body might never execute

    c. the loop body must execute exactly one time

    d. the loop body must execute at least one time

12. Which of the following is a characteristic shared by `while` loops and do-until loops?

    a. Both have one entry and one exit.

    b. Both have a body that executes at least once.

    c. Both compare a loop control variable at the top of the loop.

    d. All of the above

13. A comparison with a loop control variable provides _____ .

    a. the only entry to a while loop

    b. the only exit from a do-until loop

    c. Both of the above

    d. None of the above

14. When two loops are nested, the loop that is contained by the other is the _____ loop.

    a. captive   c. inner

    b. unstructured   d. outer

15. In the following pseudocode, how many times is "Hello" printed?

```
j = 2
k = 5
m = 6
n = 9
while j < k
    while m < n
        print "Hello"
        m = m + 1
    endwhile
    j = j + 1
endwhile
```

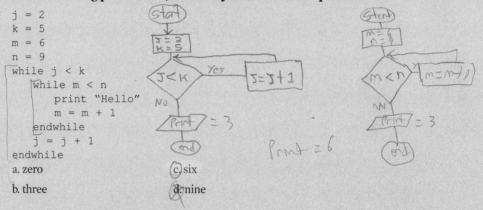

    a. zero   c. six

    b. three   d. nine

16. In the following pseudocode, how many times is "Goodbye" printed?

```
j = 2
k = 5
n = 9
while j < k
    m = 6
    while m < n
        print "Goodbye"
        m = m + 1
    endwhile
    j = j + 1
endwhile
```

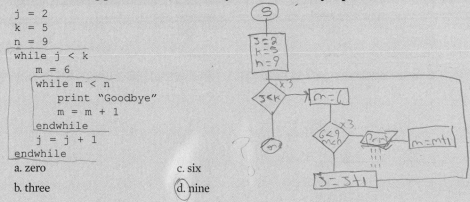

a. zero   c. six

b. three   d. nine

17. In the following pseudocode, how many times is "Adios" printed?

```
p = 2
q = 4
while p < q
    print "Adios"
    r = 1
    while r < q
        print "Adios"
        r = r + 1
    endwhile
    p = p + 1
endwhile
```

a. zero   c. six

b. four   d. eight

18. A report that lists no details about individual records, but only totals, is a(n) _____ report.

a. accumulator   c. summary

b. final   d. detailless

19. Typically, the value added to a counter variable is _____ .

a. 0   c. 10

b. 1   d. 100

20. Typically, the value added to an accumulator variable is _____ .

a. 0

b. 1

c. smaller than a value added to a counter variable

d. larger than a value added to a counter variable

FIND THE BUGS

Each of the following pseudocode segments contains one or more bugs that you must find and correct.

1. **This program is supposed to print every fifth year starting with 2010; that is, 2010, 2015, 2020, and so on, for 30 years.**

```
start
    num START_YEAR = 2010
    num FACTOR = 5
    num END_YEAR = 2040
    year = START_YEAR
    while year > END_YEAR
        print year
        year = year + 1
    endwhile
stop
```

2. **A standard mortgage is paid monthly over 30 years. This program is intended to print 360 payment coupons for a new borrower. Each coupon lists the month number, year number, and a friendly mailing reminder.**

```
start
    num MONTHS = 12
    num YEARS = 30
    string MSG = "Remember to allow 5 days for mailing"
    num monthCounter = 1
    num yearCounter = 1
    while yearCounter <= YEARS
        while monthCounter <= MONTHS
            print monthCounter, yearCounter, MSG
            monthCounter = monthCounter + 1
        endwhile
    endwhile
stop
```

EXERCISES

1. Design the logic for a program that prints every number from 1 through 10.

2. Design the logic for a program that prints every number from 1 through 10 along with its square and cube.

3. Design the logic for a program that prints every even number from 2 through 30.

4. Design the logic for a program that prints numbers in reverse order from 10 down to 1.

5. The No Interest Credit Company provides zero-interest loans to customers. (They make a profit by selling advertising space in their monthly statements and selling their customer lists.) Design an application that gets customer account data that includes an account number, customer name, and balance due. For each customer, print the account number and name; then print the customer's projected balance each month for the next 10 months. Assume that there is no finance charge on this account, that the customer makes no new purchases, and that the customer pays off the balance with equal monthly payments, which are 10 percent of the original bill.

6. The Some Interest Credit Company provides loans to customers at 1.5 percent interest per month. Design an application that gets customer account data that includes an account number, customer name, and balance due. For each customer, print the account number and name; then print the customer's projected balance each month for the next 10 months. Assume that when the balance reaches $10 or less, the customer can pay off the account. At the beginning of every month, 1.5 percent interest is added to the balance, and then the customer makes a payment equal to 5 percent of the current balance. Assume the customer makes no new purchases.

7. The Howell Bank provides savings accounts that compound interest on a yearly basis. In other words, if you deposit $100 for two years at 4 percent interest, at the end of one year you will have $104. At the end of two years, you will have the $104 plus 4 percent of that, or $108.16. Design a program that accepts an account number, the account owner's first and last names, and a balance. Print the projected running total balance for each year for the next 20 years.

8. Henry Clay Community College wants to print name tags for each student and teacher to wear at the first meeting of each class this semester. The tags look like the following:

Hello!

My name is _____

Class: XXXXXX Section: 999

The name tag border is preprinted, but you must design the program to print all the text you see on the sticker. Design a program that reads course information, including the class code (for example, CIS111), the three-digit section number (for example, 101), the teacher's last name (for example, "Zaplatynsky"), the number of students enrolled in the section (for example, 25), and the room in which the class meets (for example, "A213"). Print as many name tags as a section needs to provide one for each enrolled student, plus one for the teacher. Each name tag leaves a blank for the student's (or teacher's) name—each recipient writes his or her name in with a pen because the individual student names are not part of the input.

9. **The Vernon Hills Mail-Order Company often sends multiple packages per order. For each customer order, print enough mailing labels to use on each of the separate boxes that will be mailed. The mailing labels contain the customer's complete name and address, along with a box number in the form "Box 9 of 9". For example, an order that requires three boxes produces three labels: "Box 1 of 3", "Box 2 of 3", and "Box 3 of 3". Design an application that continuously accepts a customer's title (for example "Mrs."), a first name, last name, street address, city, state, zip code, and number of boxes in the order until an appropriate sentinel value is entered. Produce enough mailing labels for each order.**

10. **Secondhand Rose Resale Shop is having a seven-day sale during which the price of any unsold item drops 10 percent each day. The inventory file includes an item number, description, and original price on day one. For example, an item that costs $10.00 on the first day costs 10 percent less, or $9.00, on the second day. On the third day, the same item is 10 percent less than $9.00, or $8.10. Design an application that reads inventory records and produces a report that shows the price of every item on each day, one through seven.**

11. **The state of Florida maintains a census file in which each record contains the name of a county, the current population, and a number representing the rate at which the population is increasing per year. For example, one record might contain Miami-Dade County, 2,253,000, and 2 percent. The governor wants a report listing each county and the number of years it will take for the population of the county to double, assuming the present rate of growth remains constant. Design an application that reads records from an input file and prints the county's name and the number of years it will take for the population to double. If a county's record contains a negative growth rate, then instead of printing the number of years it takes for the population to double, print a message indicating that the population is never expected to double.**

12. **The Human Resources Department of Apex Manufacturing Company wants a report that shows its employees the benefits of saving for retirement. Produce a report that shows 12 predicted retirement account values for each employee—the values if the employee saves 5, 10, or 15 percent of his or her annual salary for 10, 20, 30, or 40 years. Design an application that gets employee's names and salaries and prints a report for each employee, including using the employee's name in a heading line. Assume that savings grow at a rate of 8 percent per year.**

13. Mr. Roper owns 20 apartment buildings. Each building contains 15 units that he rents for $800 per month each. Design the application that would print 12 payment coupons for each of the 15 apartments in each of the 20 buildings. Each coupon should contain the building number (1 through 20), the apartment number (1 through 15), the month (1 through 12), and the amount of rent due.

14. Mr. Furly owns 20 apartment buildings. Each building contains 15 units that he rents. The usual monthly rent for apartments numbered 1 through 9 in each building is $700; the monthly rent is $850 for apartments numbered 10 through 15. The usual rent is due every month except July and December; in those months Mr. Furly gives his renters a 50 percent credit, so they owe only half the usual amount. Design the application that would print 12 payment coupons for each of the 15 apartments in each of the 20 buildings. Each coupon should contain the building number (1 through 20), the apartment number (1 through 15), the month (1 through 12), and the amount of rent due.

15. Oliver Wendell Holmes College assigns students to an academic advisor based on declared major and grade point average as follows:

Major	Grade Point Average	Advisor
Business	3.0–4.0	Donna Trump
Business	0.0–2.9	Edgar Skilling
Computer Information Systems	3.0–4.0	Wilma Gates
Computer Information Systems	0.0–2.9	Carl Careers
Liberal Arts	0.0–4.0	Andrea Worhol

Design the application that allows a user to enter a student's major and grade point average continuously until a sentinel value is entered. If the major is not one of the three offered by the college or the grade point average is not within range, consider the student unassigned. Display the assigned advisor for each student or a message indicating the student is unassigned. At the end of the program's execution, display a count to the number of students who have been assigned to each advisor and the number who are unassigned.

GAME ZONE

1. In Chapter 3, you learned that in many programming languages you can generate a random number between 1 and a limiting value named LIMIT by using a statement similar to randomNumber = random(LIMIT). In Chapter 4, you created the logic for a guessing game in which the application generates a random number and the player tries to guess it. Now, create a guessing game in which the application generates a random number and the player tries to guess it. After each guess display a message indicating whether the player's guess was correct, too high, or too low. When the player eventually guesses the correct number, display a count of the number of guesses that were required.

2. Design the logic for an application that creates a quiz. The quiz contains at least five questions about a hobby, popular music, astronomy, or any other personal interest. Each question should be a multiple-choice question with at least four options. When the user answers the question correctly, display a congratulatory message. If the user responds to a question incorrectly, display an appropriate message and ask the question repeatedly, until the user is correct.

3. Create the logic for a game that simulates rolling two dice by generating two numbers between 1 and 6 inclusive. The player chooses a number between 2 (the lowest total possible from two dice) and 12 (the highest total possible). The player then "rolls" two dice up to three times. If the number chosen by the user comes up, the user wins and the game ends. If the number does not come up within three rolls, the computer wins.

4. Create the logic for the dice game Pig in which a player can compete with the computer. The object of the game is to be the first to score 100 points. The user and computer take turns rolling a pair of dice following these rules:

   » On a turn, each player "rolls" two dice. If no 1 appears, the dice values are added to a running total, and the player can choose whether to roll again or pass the turn to the other player.

   » If a 1 appears on one of the dice, nothing more is added to the player's total and it becomes the other player's turn.

   » If a 1 appears on both of the dice, not only is the player's turn over, but the player's entire accumulated score is reset to 0.

   » In this version of the game, when the computer does not roll a 1 and can choose whether to roll again, generate a random value from 1 to 2, having the computer decide to continue when the value is 1 and decide to quit and pass the turn to the player when the value is not 1.

DETECTIVE WORK

1. What company's address is at One Infinite Loop, Cupertino, California?

2. What are fractals? How do they use loops? Find some examples of fractal art on the Web.

UP FOR DISCUSSION

1. **If programs could only make decisions or loops, but not both, which structure would you prefer to retain? Why?**

2. **Suppose you wrote a program that you suspect is in an infinite loop because it just keeps running for several minutes with no output and without ending. What would you add to your program to help you discover the origin of the problem?**

3. **Suppose you know that every employee in your organization has a seven-digit ID number used for logging on to the computer system to retrieve sensitive information about their own customers. A loop would be useful to guess every combination of seven digits in an ID. Are there any circumstances in which you should try to guess another employee's ID number?**

ARRAYS

In this chapter you will:

Understand arrays and how they occupy computer memory

Manipulate an array to replace nested decisions

Use a named constant to refer to an array's size

Declare and initialize an array

Understand the difference between variable and constant arrays

Search an array for an exact match

Use parallel arrays

Search an array for a range match

Learn about remaining within array bounds

Use a `for` loop to process arrays

UNDERSTANDING ARRAYS AND HOW THEY OCCUPY COMPUTER MEMORY

An **array** is a series or list of variables in computer memory, all of which have the same name and data type but are differentiated with special numbers called subscripts. Usually, all the values in an array have something in common; for example, they might represent a list of employee ID numbers or a list of prices for items a store sells. A **subscript**, also called an **index**, is a number that indicates the position of a particular item within an array. Whenever you require multiple storage locations for objects, you are using a real-life counterpart of a programming array. For example, if you store important papers in a series of file folders and label each folder with a consecutive letter of the alphabet, then you are using the equivalent of an array. If you store mementos in a series of stacked shoeboxes, each labeled with a year, or if you sort mail into slots, each labeled with a name, then you are also using a real-life equivalent of a programming array.

When you look down the left side of a tax table to find your income level before looking to the right to find your income tax obligation, you are using an array. Similarly, if you look down the left side of a train schedule to find your station before looking to the right to find the train's arrival time, you are also using an array.

Each of these real-life arrays helps you organize real-life objects. You *could* store all your papers or mementos in one huge cardboard box, or find your tax rate or train's arrival time if both were printed randomly in one large book. However, using an organized storage and display system makes your life easier in each case. Using a programming array will accomplish the same results for your data.

HOW ARRAYS OCCUPY COMPUTER MEMORY

When you declare an array, you declare a structure that contains multiple variables. Each variable within an array has the same name and the same data type; each separate array variable is one **element** of the array. Each array element occupies an area in memory next to, or contiguous to, the others, as shown in Figure 6-1. You can indicate the number of elements an array will hold—the **size of the array**—when you declare the array along with your other variables.

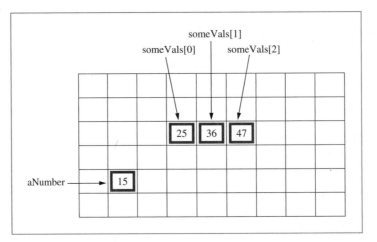

Figure 6-1 Appearance of a three-element array and a single variable in computer memory

All array elements have the same group name, but each individual element also has a unique subscript indicating how far away it is from the first element. Therefore, any array's subscripts are always a sequence of integers such as 0 through 4 or 0 through 9.

Depending on the syntax rules of the programming language you use, you place the subscript within parentheses or square brackets following the group name; this text will use square brackets to hold array element subscripts so that you don't mistake array names for method names, and because many newer programming languages such as C++, Java, and C# use the bracket notation. For example, Figure 6-1 shows how a single variable and an array are stored in computer memory. The single variable named aNumber holds the value 15. The array named someVals contains three elements, so the elements are someVals[0], someVals[1], and someVals[2]. The value stored in someVals[0] is 25; someVals[1] holds 36, and someVals[2] holds 47. The element someVals[0] is zero numbers away from the beginning of the array—in other words, it is located at the same memory address as the array. The element someVals[1] is one number away from the beginning of the array and someVals[2] is two numbers away.

> **》》NOTE** An error commonly made by beginning programmers is to forget that array subscripts start with 0. If you assume an array's first subscript is 1, you will always be "off by one" in your array manipulation.

> **》》NOTE** In all languages, subscript values must be nonnegative integers (whole numbers) and sequential.

> **》》NOTE** You can picture the memory address of someVals[0] as the address of the someVals array plus 0 more numbers. Similarly, you can picture the memory address of someVals[1] as the memory address of the someVals array plus one more number.

> **》》NOTE** You are never required to use arrays within your programs, but learning to use arrays correctly can make many programming tasks far more efficient and professional. When you understand how to use arrays, you will be able to provide elegant solutions to problems that otherwise would require tedious programming steps.

TWO TRUTHS AND A LIE:

UNDERSTANDING ARRAYS AND HOW THEY OCCUPY COMPUTER MEMORY

1. In an array, each element has the same data type.

2. Each array element is accessed using a subscript which can be a number or a string.

3. Array elements always occupy adjacent memory locations.

The false statement is #2. An array subscript must be a number. It can be a constant or a variable.

MANIPULATING AN ARRAY TO REPLACE NESTED DECISIONS

Consider an application requested by a Human Resources Department to produce statistics on employees' claimed dependents. The department wants a report that lists the number of employees who have claimed 0, 1, 2, 3, 4, or 5 dependents. (Assume you know that no employees have more than five dependents.) For example, Figure 6-2 shows a typical report.

```
Dependents Report

Dependents        Count

    0              34
    1              62
    2              71
    3              42
    4              28
    5               7
```

Figure 6-2 The Dependents report

Without using an array, you could write the application that produces counts for the six categories of dependents (for each number of dependents, 0 through 5) by using a series of decisions. Figure 6-3 shows the pseudocode and flowchart for the decision-making part of an application that counts dependents in each of six different categories. Although this program works, its length and complexity are unnecessary once you understand how to use an array.

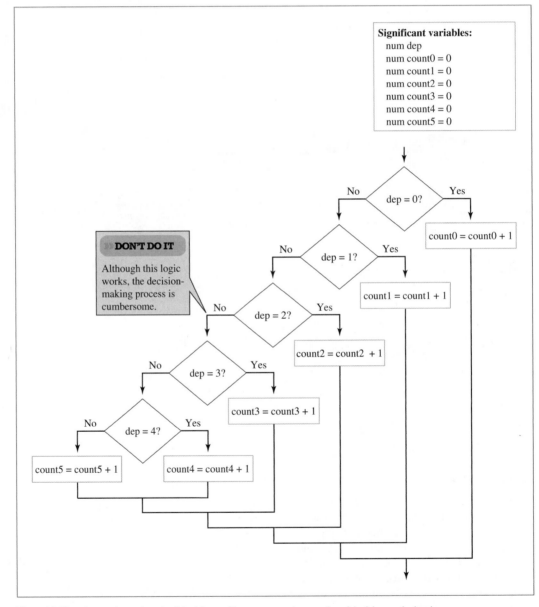

Figure 6-3 Flowchart and pseudocode of decision-making process using a series of decisions—the hard way

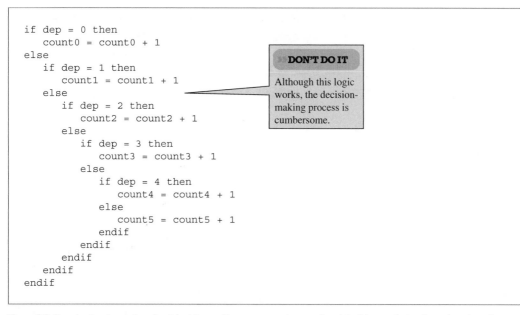

```
if dep = 0 then
    count0 = count0 + 1
else
    if dep = 1 then
        count1 = count1 + 1
    else
        if dep = 2 then
            count2 = count2 + 1
        else
            if dep = 3 then
                count3 = count3 + 1
            else
                if dep = 4 then
                    count4 = count4 + 1
                else
                    count5 = count5 + 1
                endif
            endif
        endif
    endif
endif
```

» DON'T DO IT

Although this logic works, the decision-making process is cumbersome.

Figure 6-3 Flowchart and pseudocode of decision-making process using a series of decisions—the hard way (*continued*)

In Figure 6-3, the variable dep is compared to 0. If it is 0, 1 is added to count0. If it is not 0, then dep is compared to 1. It is either added to count1, or compared to 2, and so on. Each time the application executes this decision-making process, 1 is added to one of the five variables that acts as a counter for one of the possible numbers of dependents. The dependent-counting application in Figure 6-3 works, but even with only six categories of dependents, the decision-making process is unwieldy. What if the number of dependents might be any value from 0 to 10, or 0 to 20? With either of these scenarios, the basic logic of the program would remain the same; however, you would need to declare many additional accumulator variables and you would need many additional decisions.

Using an array provides an alternate approach to this programming problem, which greatly reduces the number of statements you need. When you declare an array, you provide a group name for a number of associated variables in memory. For example, the six dependent count accumulators can be redefined as a single array named count. The individual elements become count[0], count[1], count[2], count[3], count[4], and count[5], as shown in the revised decision-making process in Figure 6-4.

The shaded statement in Figure 6-4 shows that when dep is 0, 1 is added to count[0]. You can see similar statements for the rest of the count elements; when dep is 1, 1 is added to count[1], when dep is 2, 1 is added to count[2], and so on. When the dep value is 5, it means it was not 1, 2, 3, or 4, so 1 is added to count[5]. In other words, 1 is added to one of the elements of the count array instead of to an individual variable named count0, count1, count2, count3, count4, or count5. Is this version a big improvement over the original in Figure 6-3? Of course, it isn't. You still have not taken advantage of the benefits of using the array in this application.

» NOTE
The decision-making process in Figure 6-3 accomplishes its purpose, and nothing is wrong with its logic, though it is cumbersome. Follow its logic here so that you understand how the application works.

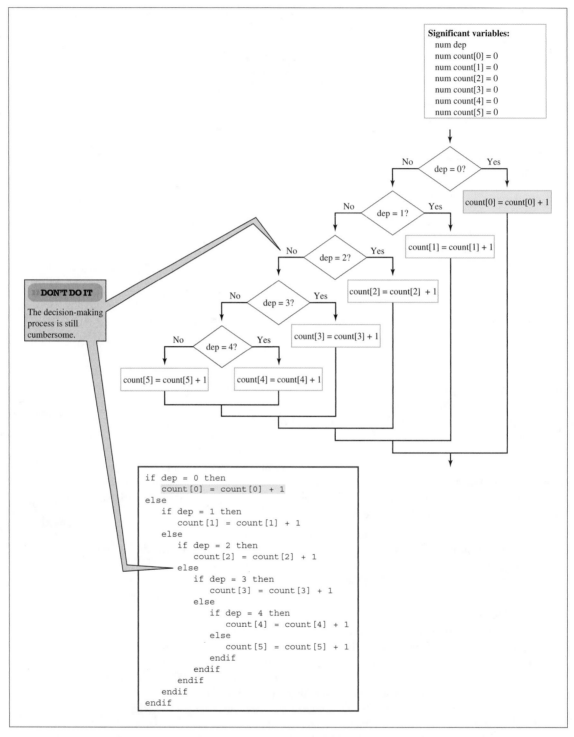

Figure 6-4 Flowchart and pseudocode of decision-making process—but still the hard way

The true benefit of using an array lies in your ability to use a variable as a subscript to the array, instead of using a constant such as 0 or 5. Notice in the logic in Figure 6-4 that within each decision, the value you are comparing to dep and the constant you are using as a subscript in the resulting "Yes" process are always identical. That is, when dep is 0, the subscript used to add 1 to the count array is 0; when dep is 1, the subscript used for the count array is 1, and so on. Therefore, you can just use dep as a subscript to the array. You can rewrite the decision-making process as shown in Figure 6-5.

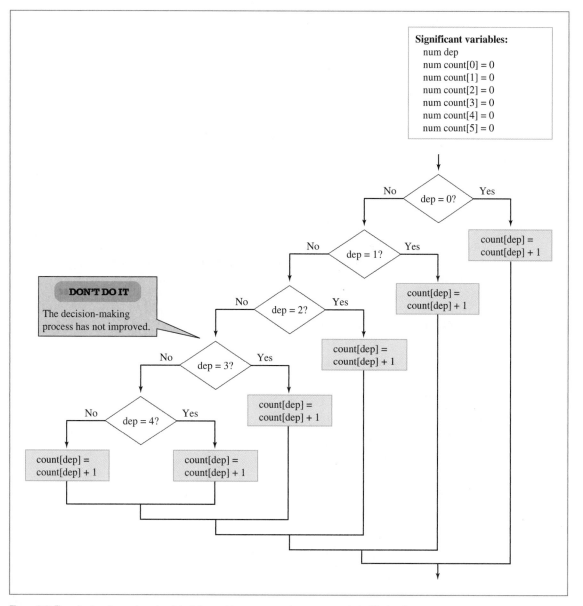

Figure 6-5 Flowchart and pseudocode of decision-making process using an array—but still a hard way

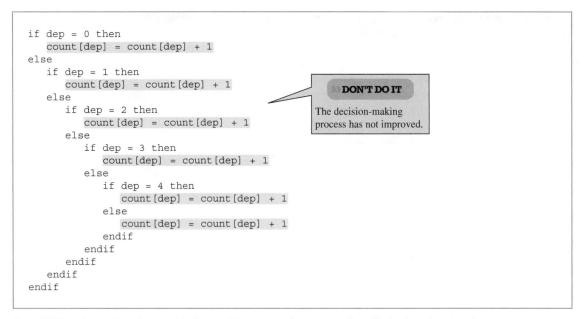

```
if dep = 0 then
    count[dep] = count[dep] + 1
else
    if dep = 1 then
        count[dep] = count[dep] + 1
    else
        if dep = 2 then
            count[dep] = count[dep] + 1
        else
            if dep = 3 then
                count[dep] = count[dep] + 1
            else
                if dep = 4 then
                    count[dep] = count[dep] + 1
                else
                    count[dep] = count[dep] + 1
                endif
            endif
        endif
    endif
endif
```

DON'T DO IT

The decision-making process has not improved.

Figure 6-5 Flowchart and pseudocode of decision-making process using an array—but still a hard way (*continued*)

Of course, the code segment in Figure 6-5 looks no more efficient than the one in Figure 6-4. However, notice that in Figure 6-5 the shaded statements are all the same—in other words, the process that occurs after each decision is exactly the same. In each case, no matter what the value of dep is, you always add 1 to count[dep]. If you are always going to take the same action no matter what the answer to a question is, why ask the question? Instead, you can rewrite the decision-making process as shown in Figure 6-6.

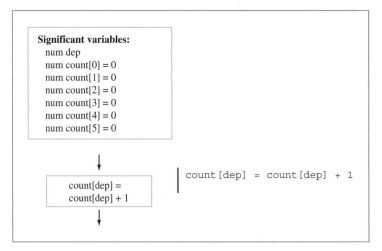

Significant variables:
num dep
num count[0] = 0
num count[1] = 0
num count[2] = 0
num count[3] = 0
num count[4] = 0
num count[5] = 0

count[dep] =
count[dep] + 1

count[dep] = count[dep] + 1

Figure 6-6 Flowchart and pseudocode of efficient decision-making process using an array

The single statement in Figure 6-6 eliminates the *entire* decision-making process that was the original highlighted section in Figure 6-5! When dep is 2, 1 is added to count[2]; when dep is 4, 1 is added to count[4], and so on. *Now* you have a big improvement to the original process. What's more, this process does not change whether there are 20, 30, or any other number of possible categories. To use more than five accumulators, you would declare additional count elements in the array, but the categorizing logic would remain the same as it is in Figure 6-6. Figure 6-7 shows an entire program that takes advantage of the array to produce the report that shows counts for dependent categories.

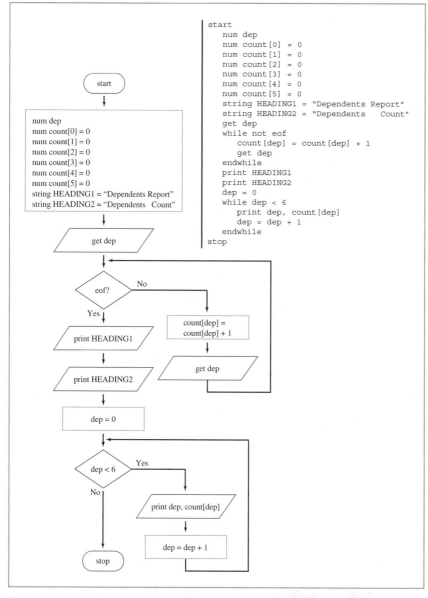

```
start
    num dep
    num count[0]  = 0
    num count[1]  = 0
    num count[2]  = 0
    num count[3]  = 0
    num count[4]  = 0
    num count[5]  = 0
    string HEADING1 = "Dependents Report"
    string HEADING2 = "Dependents    Count"
    get dep
    while not eof
        count[dep]  = count[dep] + 1
        get dep
    endwhile
    print HEADING1
    print HEADING2
    dep = 0
    while dep < 6
        print dep, count[dep]
        dep = dep + 1
    endwhile
stop
```

Figure 6-7 Flowchart and pseudocode for Dependents Report program

In the program in Figure 6-7, variables and constants are declared and a first value for dep is read into the program. If it is not the end of the file, then 1 is added to the appropriate element of the count array and the next record is read. When data entry is complete and the end of the file is reached, the report finally can be printed. After printing the report headers, you can set dep to 0, then print dep and count[dep]. The first line that prints contains 0 (as the number of dependents) and the value stored in count[0]. Then, add 1 to dep and use the same set of instructions again. You can use dep as a loop control variable to print the six individual count array values.

When you print the final count values at the end of the program, naming the loop control variable dep makes sense because it represents a number of dependents. However, this variable could be named dependents, sub, index, or any other legal identifier, and used as a subscript to the array as long as it is:

» Numeric with no decimal places
» Initialized to 0
» Incremented by 1 each time the logic passes through the loop

In other words, nothing is linking the identifier dep to the count array per se; when you cycle through the array to print the report, you are welcome to use a different variable name than you use when accumulating counts earlier in the program.

The dependent-counting program *worked* when it contained a long series of decisions and print statements, but the program is easier to write when you employ arrays. Additionally, the program is more efficient, easier for other programmers to understand, and easier to maintain. Arrays are never mandatory, but often they can drastically cut down on your programming time and make your logic easier to understand.

TWO TRUTHS AND A LIE:
MANIPULATING AN ARRAY TO REPLACE NESTED DECISIONS

1. You can manipulate an array to replace a long series of decisions.

2. You realize a major benefit to using arrays when you use a numeric constant as a subscript as opposed to using a variable.

3. The process of displaying every element in a 10-element array is basically no different from displaying every element in a 100-element array.

The false statement is #2. You realize a major benefit to using arrays when you use a variable as a subscript as opposed to using a constant.

USING A NAMED CONSTANT TO REFER TO AN ARRAY'S SIZE

The program in Figure 6-7 still contains one minor flaw. Throughout this book you have learned to avoid "magic numbers"; that is, unnamed constants. When the report-printing part of the program in Figure 6-7 executes, the array subscript is compared to the constant 6.

The program can be improved if you use a named constant instead. In most programming languages you can take one of two approaches.

You can declare a named numeric constant such as ARRAY_SIZE = 6. Then you can use this constant every time you access the array, always making sure any subscript you use remains less than the constant value.

In many languages, when you declare an array, a constant that represents the array size is automatically created for you. For example, in Java, after you declare an array named count, its size is stored in a field named count.length, and in both C# and Visual Basic, the array size is count.Length. (The difference is in the "L" in Length.)

> **»NOTE** Besides making your code easier to modify, using a named constant makes the code easier to understand.

TWO TRUTHS AND A LIE:
USING A NAMED CONSTANT TO REFER TO AN ARRAY'S SIZE

1. If you create a named constant equal to an array size, you can use it as a subscript to the array.

2. If you create a named constant equal to an array size, you can use it best by making sure any subscript you use remains less than the constant value.

3. In Java, C#, and Visual Basic, when you declare an array, a constant that represents the array size is automatically created for you.

The false statement is #1. If the constant is equal to the array size, then it is larger than any valid array subscript.

ARRAY DECLARATION AND INITIALIZATION

In the completed dependent-counting program in Figure 6-7, the six count array elements were declared and initialized to 0s at the start of the class. They need to be initialized to 0 so you can add to them during the course of the program. In Figure 6-7, the initialization is provided using six separate statements:

```
num count[0] = 0
num count[1] = 0
num count[2] = 0
num count[3] = 0
num count[4] = 0
num count[5] = 0
```

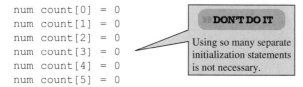

»DON'T DO IT

Using so many separate initialization statements is not necessary.

Separately declaring and initializing each count element is acceptable only if there are a small number of counts. If the dependent-counting program were updated to keep track of employees with up to 20 dependents, you would have to initialize 20 separate fields; it would be tedious to write 20 separate declaration statements.

Programming languages do not require the programmer to name each count element count[0], count[1], and so on. Instead, you can make a declaration such as one of those in Table 6-1.

Programming Language	Declaration of a 20-element Array
Visual Basic	Dim Count[20] As Integer
C#, C++	int count[20]
Java	int[] count = new int[20]

Table 6-1 Declaring a 20-element array named count in several common languages

> **NOTE** C, C#, C++, and Java programmers typically create variable names that start with a lowercase letter. Visual Basic programmers are likely to begin variable names with an uppercase letter. (All these languages typically use an uppercase letter for second and subsequent words in an identifier.) In Chapter 1, you learned these styles are called camel casing and Pascal casing, respectively. Table 6-1 uses these conventions.

> **NOTE** The terms int and Integer in the code samples in Table 6-1 both indicate that the count array will hold whole-number values. These terms are more specific than the num data type this book uses to declare all numeric variables.

All the declarations in Table 6-1 have two things in common: They name the count array and indicate that there will be 20 separate numeric elements. For flowcharting or pseudocode purposes, a statement such as numeric count[20] indicates the same thing.

Declaring a numeric array does not necessarily set its individual elements to 0 (although it does in some programming languages, such as Visual Basic and Java). Most programming languages allow a statement similar to the following:

```
num count[20] = 0
```

You should use a statement like this when you want to initialize an array in your flowcharts or pseudocode.

When you want to set all the elements in an array to different values after it is declared, you can always make individual assignments, as in the following:

```
count[0] = 5
count[1] = 12
count[2] = 24
```

As an alternative to defining the values of count[0], count[1], and so on separately, most programming languages allow a more concise version to initialize an array. It takes the general form:

```
num count[3] = 5, 12, 24
```

When you use this form of array initialization, the first value you list is assigned to the first array element, and the subsequent values are assigned in order. Most programming languages allow you to assign fewer values than there are array elements declared, but no language allows you to assign more values.

Alternately, to start all array elements with the same initial value, you can use an initialization loop. An **initialization loop** is a loop structure that provides initial values for every element in any array. To create an initialization loop, you must use a numeric field as a subscript. For example, if you declare a field named sub, and initialize sub to 0, then you can use a loop like the one shown in Figure 6-8 to set all the array elements to 0.

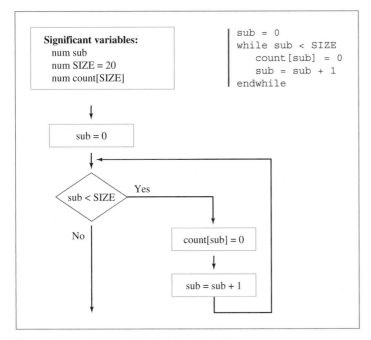

Figure 6-8 A loop that sets values for every element in an array

TWO TRUTHS AND A LIE:
ARRAY DECLARATION AND INITIALIZATION

1. An array defined as `num scores[15]` contains 15 elements.
2. In some, but not all, programming languages, declaring a numeric array sets its individual elements to 0.
3. You cannot set array elements to new values after the array is declared.

The false statement is #3. You can set all the elements in an array to different values after it is declared; you can always make individual assignments.

VARIABLE AND CONSTANT ARRAYS

The array that you used to accumulate dependent counts in the application that produces the Dependents Report is a **variable array** because the values in it change during program execution. The values that you want to use—the final dependent counts—are created during an actual run, or execution, of the application. In other words, if there will be 200 employees with 0 dependents, you don't know that fact at the beginning of the program. Instead, that value is accumulated during the execution of the application and not known until the end.

Sometimes you can use an array that is a **constant array**; when an array is constant, it can be assigned its permanent and final values when you write the program code. For example, let's say you own an apartment building with apartments in the basement as well as three other floors. The floors are numbered 0 (for the basement), or 1, 2, or 3. Every month you print a rent bill for each tenant. Your rent charges are based on the floor of the building, as shown in Figure 6-9.

Floor	Rent in $
0 (basement)	350
1	400
2	600
3 (penthouse)	1000

Figure 6-9 Rents by floor

Suppose you want to create an application that accepts each tenant's name and floor number and prints a letter to each tenant showing the amount of rent due, similar to the letter shown in Figure 6-10. To determine the correct rent for each tenant, you could use a series of decisions concerning the floor number. However, it is more efficient to use an array to hold the four rent figures. The array is initialized with values that are **hard-coded** into the array; that is, they are explicitly assigned to the array elements.

NOTE
Remember that another name for an array is a *table*. If you can use paper and pencil to list items like tenants' rent values in a table format, then using an array is an appropriate programming option.

```
Dear Rosa Martinez,
   Reminder - the rent for your apartment on floor 2
is due on the first of the month. The rent is $600.

Sincerely,
The Management
```

Figure 6-10 Typical letter to a tenant

The program in Figure 6-11 assigns the correct rent to every tenant. When you declare variables at the start of the program, you also create a constant array for the four rent figures and assign the correct rent to each.

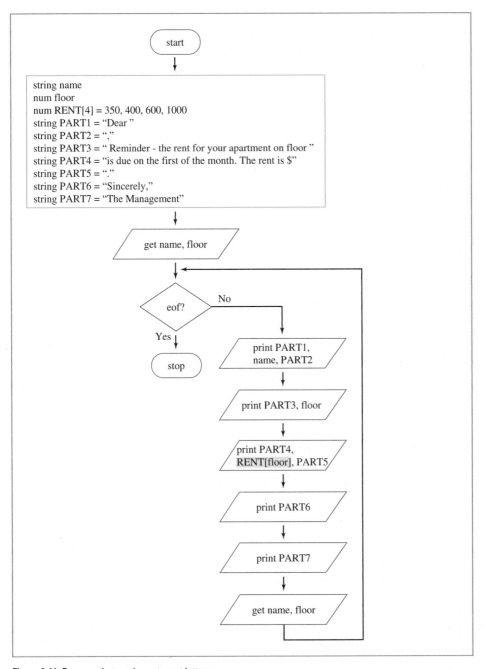

Figure 6-11 Program that produces tenant letters

```
start
   string name
   num floor
   num RENT[4] = 350, 400, 600, 1000
   string PART1 = "Dear "
   string PART2 = ","
   string PART3 = " Reminder - the rent for your apartment on floor "
   string PART4 = "is due on the first of the month. The rent is $"
   string PART5 = "."
   string PART6 = "Sincerely,"
   string PART7 = "The Management"
   get name, floor
   while not eof
      print PART1, name, PART2
      print PART3, floor
      print PART4, RENT[floor], PART5
      print PART6
      print PART7
      get name, floor
   endwhile
stop
```

Figure 6-11 Program that produces tenant letters (*continued*)

After you get the first tenant's name and floor number in the program in Figure 6-11, and as long as the end-of-file (eof) condition is not met, you print 10 separate items spread over five lines:

» The string "Dear "

» The tenant's name, retrieved from input

» A string containing a comma to follow the name

» A string that contains "Reminder - the rent for your apartment on floor "

» The floor number, from input

» A string that contains "is due on the first of the month. The rent is $"

» The rent amount, retrieved from the array with RENT[floor]

» A string that contains the period that follows the rent amount

» A string that contains "Sincerely,"

» A string that contains "The Management"

Instead of making a series of selections such as if floor = 0 then print RENT[0] and if floor = 1 then print RENT[1], you take advantage of the RENT array by using floor as a subscript to access the correct RENT array element. (See the shaded statement in Figure 6-11.) When deciding what variable to use as a subscript with an array, ask yourself, "Of all the values available in the array, what does the correct selection depend on?" When printing a RENT value, the rent you use depends on the floor on which the tenant lives, so the correct action is print RENT[floor].

Without a RENT array, the program that prints the tenant's letters would have to contain three decisions and four different resulting actions. With the RENT array, there are no decisions. Each tenant's rent is simply based on the RENT element that corresponds to the tenant's floor number. In other words, the floor number indicates the positional value of the corresponding rent. Arrays can really lighten the work load required to write a program.

> **» NOTE** A common scenario is for rent values to be stored in a file and read into the array at the beginning of the program. That way, a data entry operator can update the file as often as needed without having to modify the program. Chapter 10 of the Comprehensive version of this book covers file handling.

TWO TRUTHS AND A LIE:
VARIABLE AND CONSTANT ARRAYS

1. Arrays can contain variables or constants.

2. When array values are hard-coded, they are explicitly assigned to the array elements.

3. Arrays cause more work for the programmer, but they are worth it because programs that use them run faster.

The false statement is #3. Arrays often make the programmer's job easier.

SEARCHING AN ARRAY FOR AN EXACT MATCH

In both the dependent-counting application and the rent-determining application that you've seen in this chapter, the fields that the arrays depend on conveniently hold small whole numbers. The number of dependents allowed in the first application was 0 through 5, and the number of a tenant's floor in the second application was 0 through 3. Unfortunately, real life doesn't always happen in small integers. Sometimes you don't have a variable that conveniently holds an array position; sometimes you have to search through an array to find a value you need.

Consider a mail-order business in which orders come in with a customer name, address, item number ordered, and quantity ordered. Assume the item numbers from which a customer can choose are three-digit numbers, but perhaps they are not consecutive 001 through 999. Instead, over the years, items have been deleted and new items have been added to the inventory. For example, there might no longer be an item with number 105 or 129. Sometimes there might be a hundred-number gap or more between items. For example, let's say that this season you are down to offering the six items shown in Figure 6-12.

```
ITEM PRICE      ITEM NUMBER
     106            0.59
     108            0.99
     307            4.50
     405           15.99
     457           17.50
     688           39.00
```

Figure 6-12 Available items in mail-order company

When a customer orders an item, you want to determine whether the item number is valid. You could use a series of six decisions to determine whether the ordered item is valid by comparing, in turn, each customer order's item number to each of the six allowed values. However, a superior approach is to create an array that holds the list of valid item numbers. Then you can search through the array for an exact match to the ordered item. If you search through the entire array without finding a match for the item the customer ordered, you can print an error message—for example: "Item not found."

Suppose you create an array named VALID_ITEM that contains six elements, and that you set each to a valid item number. In an office without a computer, if a customer orders item 307, a clerical worker can tell whether it is valid by looking down the list and verifying that 307 is a member of the list. In a similar fashion, in a computer program, you can use a loop to test each VALID_ITEM against the ordered item number.

The technique for verifying that an item number exists involves setting a subscript to 0 and setting a flag variable to indicate that you have not yet determined whether the customer's order is valid. A **flag** is a variable that you set to indicate whether some event has occurred; frequently it holds a true or false value. For example, you can set a string variable named foundIt to "N", indicating "No". (See the first shaded statement in Figure 6-13.) Then you compare the customer's ordered item number to the first item in the array. If the customer-ordered item matches the first item in the array, you can set the flag variable to "Y", or any other value that is not "N". (See the second shaded statement in Figure 6-13.) If the items do not match, you increase the subscript and continue to look down the list of numbers stored in the array. If you check all six valid item numbers and the customer item matches none of them, then the flag variable foundIt still holds the value "N". If the flag variable is "N" after you have looked through the entire list, you can issue an error message indicating that no match was ever found. Figure 6-13 shows a program that accepts customer order data and accomplishes the item verification.

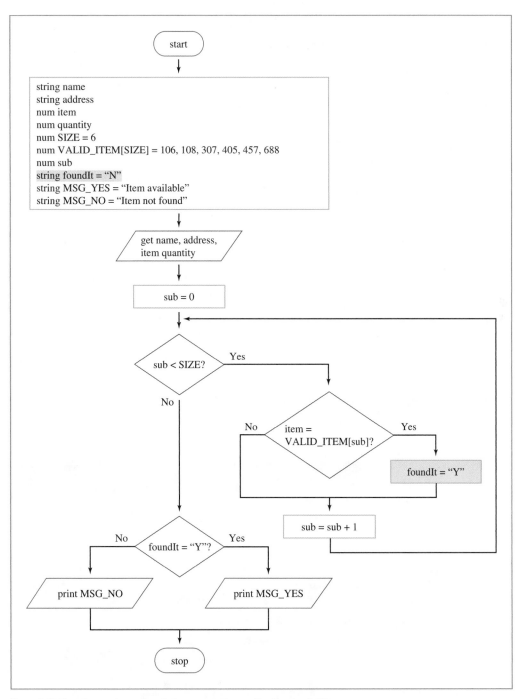

Figure 6-13 Flowchart and pseudocode for program that verifies item availability

```
start
   string name
   string name
   string address
   num item
   num quantity
   num SIZE = 6
   num VALID_ITEM[SIZE] = 106, 108, 307, 405, 457, 688
   num sub
   string foundIt = "N"
   string MSG_YES = "Item available"
   string MSG_NO = "Item not found"
   get name, address, item, quantity
   sub = 0
   while sub < SIZE
      foundIt = "N"
      if item = VALID_ITEM[sub] then
         foundIt = "Y"
      endif
      sub = sub + 1
   endwhile
   if foundIt = "Y"
      print MSG_YES
   else
      print MSG_NO
   endif
stop
```

Figure 6-13 Flowchart and pseudocode for program that verifies item availability (*continued*)

▶▶ NOTE Instead of the string `foundIt` variable in the method in Figure 6-13, you might prefer to use a numeric variable that you set to 1 or 0. Most programming languages also support a Boolean data type that you can use for `foundIt`; when you declare a variable to be Boolean, you can set its value to true or false.

TWO TRUTHS AND A LIE:
SEARCHING AN ARRAY FOR AN EXACT MATCH

1. Only whole numbers can be stored in arrays.

2. Only whole numbers can be used as array subscripts.

3. A flag is a variable that you set to indicate whether some event has occurred.

The false statement is #1. Whole numbers can be stored in arrays, but so can many other objects including strings and numbers with decimal places.

USING PARALLEL ARRAYS

When you read a customer's order in a mail-order company program, you usually want to accomplish more than simply verifying the item's existence. For example, you might want to determine the price of the ordered item, multiply that price by quantity ordered, and print a bill. Using the prices listed in Figure 6-12, you *could* write a program in which you read in a customer order record and then use the order's item number as a subscript to pull a price from an array. To use this method, you would need an array with at least 688 elements. Then, if a customer ordered item 405, the price would be found at PRICE[item], which is PRICE[405], or the 405th element of the array. Such an array would need 688 elements (because the highest item number is 688), but because you sell only six items, you would waste 682 of the reserved memory positions. Instead of reserving a large quantity of memory that remains unused, you can set up this program to use two much smaller arrays.

Consider the program in Figure 6-14. Two arrays are set up—one contains six elements named VALID_ITEM; all six elements are valid item numbers. The other array, highlighted in the figure, also has six elements. The array is named VALID_ITEM_PRICE ; all six elements are prices. Each price in this VALID_ITEM_PRICE array is conveniently and purposely in the same position as the corresponding item number in the other VALID_ITEM array. Two corresponding arrays such as these are **parallel arrays** because each element in one array is associated with the element in the same relative position in the other array.

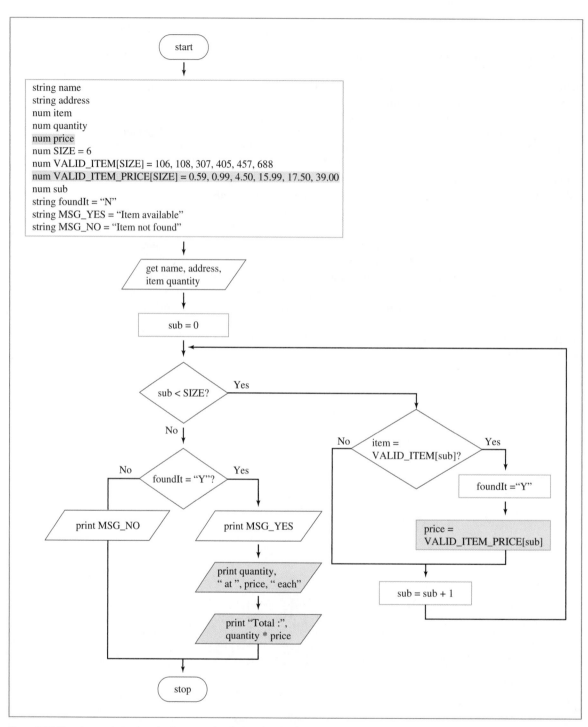

Figure 6-14 Flowchart and pseudocode of program that finds an item's price

```
start
   string name
   string address
   num item
   num quantity
   num price
   num SIZE = 6
   num VALID_ITEM[SIZE] = 106, 108, 307, 405, 457, 688
   num VALID_ITEM_PRICE[SIZE] = 0.59, 0.99, 4.50, 15.99, 17.50, 39.00
   num sub
   string foundIt = "N"
   string MSG_YES = "Item available"
   string MSG_NO = "Item not found"
   get name, address, item, quantity
   sub = 0
   while sub < SIZE
      if item = VALID_ITEM[sub] then
         foundIt = "Y"
         price = VALID_ITEM_PRICE[sub]
      endif
      sub = sub + 1
   endwhile
   if foundIt = "Y" then
      print MSG_YES
      print quantity, " at ", price, " each"
      print "Total ", quantity * price
   else
      print MSG_NO
   endif
stop
```

Figure 6-14 Flowchart and pseudocode of program that finds an item's price (*continued*)

As the program in Figure 6-14 receives each customer's order data, you look through each of the VALID_ITEM values separately by varying the subscript sub from 0 to the number of items available. When a match for the item number is found, you pull the corresponding parallel price out of the list of VALID_ITEM_PRICE values and store it in the price variable. (See shaded statements in Figure 6-14.)

> **»NOTE** Some programmers object to using a cryptic variable name for a subscript, such as sub or x, because such names are not descriptive. These programmers would prefer a name like priceIndex. Others approve of short names when the variable is used only in a limited area of a program, as it is used here, to step through an array. Programmers disagree on many style issues like this one. As a programmer, it is your responsibility to find out what conventions are used among your peers in your organization.

Once you find a match for the ordered item number in the VALID_ITEM array, you know that the price of that item is in the same position in the other array, VALID_ITEM_PRICE. When VALID_ITEM[sub] is the correct item, VALID_ITEM_PRICE[sub] must be the correct price. You can then print the price, and multiply it by the quantity ordered to produce a total, as shown in the last shaded statements in Figure 6-14.

Suppose that a customer orders item 457. If the program is written in a GUI environment, the results might look like Figure 6-15. Walk through the logic yourself to see if you come up with the correct price per item, $17.50.

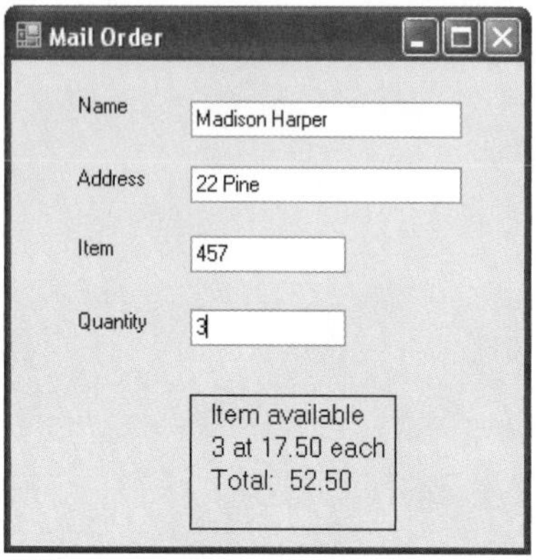

Figure 6-15 Typical execution of program that finds item's price

IMPROVING SEARCH EFFICIENCY USING AN EARLY EXIT

The mail-order program in Figure 6-14 is still a little inefficient. The problem is that if lots of customers order item 106 or 108, their price is found on the first or second pass through the loop. The program continues searching through the item array, however, until sub reaches the value SIZE. One way to stop the search when the item has been found and foundIt is set to "Y" is to force (that is, explicitly assign) sub to the value of SIZE immediately. Then, when the program loops back to check whether sub is still less than SIZE, the loop will be exited and the program won't bother checking any of the higher item numbers. Leaving a loop as soon as a match is found is called an **early exit**; it improves the program's efficiency. The larger the array, the more beneficial it becomes to exit the searching loop as soon as you find what you're looking for.

Figure 6-16 shows the improved version of the loop that finds an item's price. Notice the shaded improvement. You search the VALID_ITEM array, element by element. If an item number is not matched in a given location, the subscript is increased and the next location is checked. As soon as an item number is located in the array, you store the price, turn on the flag, and force the subscript to a high number (6) so the program will not check the item number array any further.

> **» NOTE** Instead of forcing sub to SIZE when an item number is found, you could change the comparison that controls the while loop to continue while sub < SIZE AND foundIt = "N". If you use this approach, the loop is exited as soon as an item is found and foundIt becomes "Y", even though sub is still less than SIZE. Many programmers prefer this approach to the one shown in Figure 6-16.

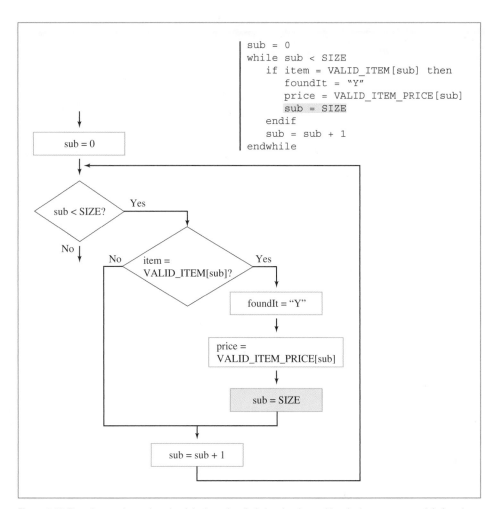

```
sub = 0
while sub < SIZE
    if item = VALID_ITEM[sub] then
        foundIt = "Y"
        price = VALID_ITEM_PRICE[sub]
        sub = SIZE
    endif
    sub = sub + 1
endwhile
```

Figure 6-16 Flowchart and pseudocode of the loop that finds item's price, exiting the loop as soon as it is found

»NOTE In the shaded portion of the logic in Figure 6-16, `sub` could be set to any value of 5 or over. At the end of the loop ,1 is added to `sub`; as long as the result is 6 or more, the loop will not continue. It is convenient to use the named constant `SIZE` because it makes your intentions clear. Also, if the program is modified at some future point when a different number of items is needed, you can change the value of `SIZE` just once where it is declared, and the rest of the program will automatically work correctly.

»NOTE Notice that the price-finding program is most efficient when the most frequently ordered items are stored at the beginning of the array. When you use this technique, only the seldom-ordered items require many cycles through the searching loop before finding a match.

TWO TRUTHS AND A LIE:
USING PARALLEL ARRAYS

1. Parallel arrays must be the same data type.
2. Parallel arrays usually contain the same number of elements.
3. You can improve the efficiency of searching through parallel arrays by using an early exit.

The false statement is #1. Parallel arrays do not need to be the same data type. For example, you might look up a name in a string array to find each person's age in a parallel numeric array.

SEARCHING AN ARRAY FOR A RANGE MATCH

Customer order item numbers need to match available item numbers exactly to determine the correct price of an item. Sometimes, however, programmers want to work with ranges of values in arrays. In Chapter 4, you learned that a range of values is any series of values—for example 1 through 5, or 20 through 30. Consider the mail order item-pricing program discussed in the previous section. Suppose the company decides to offer quantity discounts, as shown in Figure 6-17.

Quantity	Discount %
0–8	0
9–12	10
13–25	15
26 or more	20

Figure 6-17 Discounts on orders by quantity

You want to be able to read in customer order data and determine a discount percentage based on the value in the `quantity` field. For example, if a customer has ordered 20 items, you want to be able to print "Your discount is 15 percent". One ill-advised approach might be to set up an array with as many elements as any customer might ever order, and store the appropriate discount for each possible number, as shown in Figure 6-18. This array is set up to contain the discount for 0 item, 1 item, 2 items, and so on. This approach has at least three drawbacks:

- It requires a very large array that uses a lot of memory.
- You must store the same value repeatedly. For example, each of the first nine elements receives the same value, 0, and each of the next four elements receives the same value, 10.
- How do you know you have enough array elements? Is a customer order quantity of 75 items enough? What if a customer orders 100 or 1,000 items? No matter how many elements you place in the array, there's always a chance that a customer will order more.

```
numeric DISCOUNT[76]
  = 0, 0, 0, 0, 0, 0, 0, 0, 0,
    0.10, 0.10, 0.10, 0.10,
    0.15, 0.15, 0.15, 0.15, 0.15,
    0.15, 0.15, 0.15, 0.15, 0.15,
    0.15, 0.15, 0.15,
    0.20, 0.20, 0.20, 0.20, 0.20,
    0.20, 0.20, 0.20, 0.20, 0.20,
    0.20, 0.20, 0.20, 0.20, 0.20,
    0.20, 0.20, 0.20, 0.20, 0.20,
    0.20, 0.20, 0.20, 0.20, 0.20,
    0.20, 0.20, 0.20, 0.20, 0.20,
    0.20, 0.20, 0.20, 0.20, 0.20,
    0.20, 0.20, 0.20, 0.20, 0.20,
    0.20, 0.20, 0.20, 0.20, 0.20,
    0.20, 0.20, 0.20, 0.20, 0.20
```

DON'T DO IT

Although this array is usable, it is repetitious, prone to error, and difficult to use.

Figure 6-18 Usable—but inefficient—discount array

A better approach is to create just four discount array elements, one for each of the possible discount rates, as shown in Figure 6-19. The four-element array holds each possible discount, with no repetition.

```
num DISCOUNT [4]
  = 0, 0.10, 0.15, 0.20
```

Figure 6-19 Superior discount array

With the new four-element DISCOUNT array, you need a parallel array to search for the appropriate discount level. At first, beginning programmers might consider creating an array of constants named DISCOUNT_RANGE, similar to the following, and then testing whether the quantity ordered equals one of the four stored values.

```
num DISCOUNT_RANGE[4] = 0 through 8, 9 through 12,
    13 through 25, 26 and higher
```

DON'T DO IT

Each array element can hold only one value.

However, you cannot create an array like this one. Each element in any array is simply a single variable. A simple variable like age or payRate can hold 6 or 12, but it can't hold every value 6 *through* 12. Similarly, the DISCOUNT_RANGE[0] variable can hold a 0, 1, 8, or any other single value, but it can't hold 0 *through* 8; there is no such numeric value.

One solution to create a usable array holds only the low-end value of each range, as Figure 6-20 shows.

```
num DISCOUNT_RANGE [4]
  = 0, 9, 13, 26
```

Figure 6-20 The DISCOUNT_RANGE array using the low end of each range

To find the correct discount for any customer's ordered quantity, you can start with the *last* range limit (DISCOUNT_RANGE[3]). If the quantity ordered is at least that value, 26, the loop is never entered and the customer gets the highest discount rate (DISCOUNT[3], or 20 percent). If the quantity ordered is not at least DISCOUNT_RANGE[3]—that is, if it is less than 26—then you reduce the subscript and check to see if the quantity is at least DISCOUNT_RANGE[2], or 13. If so, the customer receives DISCOUNT[2], or 15 percent, and so on. Figure 6-21 shows a program that accepts a customer's quantity ordered and determines the appropriate discount rate.

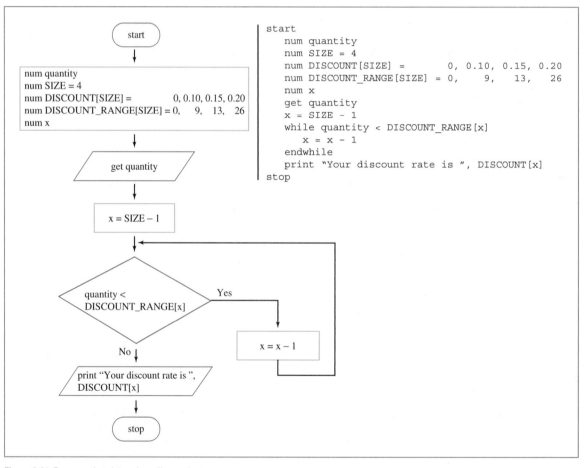

Figure 6-21 Program that determines discount rate

> **NOTE** A full-blown order program would also accept data such as a customer's name and address as well as which item was being ordered. These details are left out of the program in Figure 6-21 so you can concentrate on the method that determines the discount based on quantity ordered.

NOTE An alternate approach to the one taken in Figure 6-21 is to store the high end of every range in an array. Then you start with the *lowest* element and check for values *less than or equal to* each array element value.

When using an array to store range limits, you use a loop to make a series of comparisons that would otherwise require many separate decisions. The program that determines customer discount rates is written using fewer instructions than would be required if you did not use an array, and modifications to your method will be easier to make in the future.

TWO TRUTHS AND A LIE:

SEARCHING AN ARRAY FOR A RANGE MATCH

1. To locate a target value's range, you can store the highest value in each range in an array and compare the target with each array element.

2. To locate a target value's range, you can store the lowest value in each range in an array and compare the target with each array element.

3. When using an array to store range limits, you use a series of comparisons that would otherwise require many separate loop structures.

The false statement is #3. When using an array to store range limits, you use a loop to make a series of comparisons that would otherwise require many separate decisions.

REMAINING WITHIN ARRAY BOUNDS

Every array has a finite size. You can think of an array's size in one of two ways—either by the number of elements in the array or by the number of bytes in the array. Arrays are always composed of elements of the same data type, and elements of the same data type always occupy the same number of bytes of memory, so the number of bytes in an array is always a multiple of the number of elements in an array. For example, in Java, integers occupy 4 bytes of memory, so an array of 10 integers occupies exactly 40 bytes.

In every programming language, when you access data stored in an array, it is important to use a subscript containing a value that accesses memory occupied by the array. For example, examine the `PrintMonthName` program in Figure 6-22. The method accepts a numeric `month` and displays the name associated with that month.

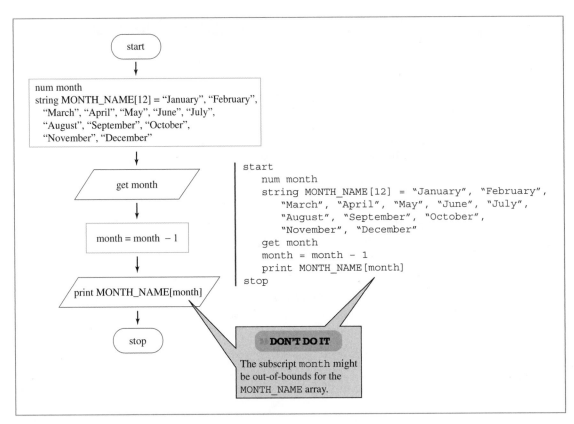

Figure 6-22 Determining the month string from user's numeric entry

» NOTE
In the program in Figure 6-22, notice that 1 is subtracted from month when it is used as a subscript. That's because although most people think of January as month 1, its name occupies the location in the array with the 0 subscript.

The logic makes a dangerous assumption: that every number entered by the user is a valid month number. If the user enters a number that is too small or too large, one of two things will happen depending on the programming language you use. When you use a subscript value that is negative or higher than the number of elements in an array:

» Some programming languages will stop execution of the program and issue an error message.

» Other programming languages will not issue an error message but will access a value in a memory location that is outside the area occupied by the array. That area might contain garbage, or worse, it accidentally might contain the name of an incorrect month.

» NOTE
Besides entering an invalid number, a user might not enter a number at all. You will handle this type of error when you write programs in a specific language.

Either way, a logical error occurs. When you use a subscript that is not within the range of acceptable subscripts, your subscript is said to be **out of bounds**. Users enter incorrect data frequently; a good program should be able to handle the mistake and not allow the subscript to be out of bounds.

You can improve the program in Figure 6-22 by adding a test that ensures the subscript used to access the array is within the array bounds. Figure 6-23 shows one method that ensures that the subscript used with the array is appropriate; it tests the subscript and displays an error message if the subscript is not valid. Figure 6-24 shows another approach. This program repeatedly prompts the user for a month until a valid value is entered. Which technique you use depends on the requirements of your program.

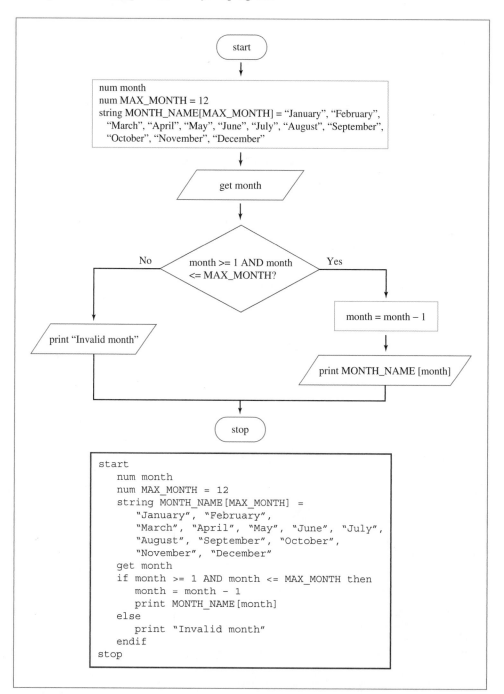

```
start
    num month
    num MAX_MONTH = 12
    string MONTH_NAME[MAX_MONTH] =
        "January", "February",
        "March", "April", "May", "June", "July",
        "August", "September", "October",
        "November", "December"
    get month
    if month >= 1 AND month <= MAX_MONTH then
        month = month - 1
        print MONTH_NAME[month]
    else
        print "Invalid month"
    endif
stop
```

Figure 6-23 Program that uses a selection to ensure a valid subscript

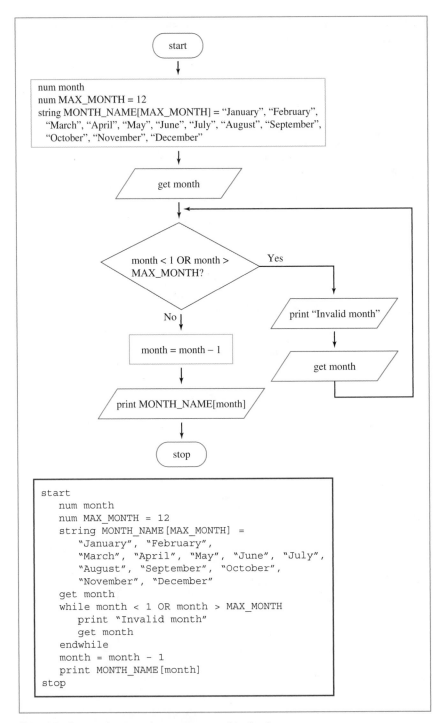

Figure 6-24 Program that uses a loop to ensure a valid subscript

```
start
   num month
   num MAX_MONTH = 12
   string MONTH_NAME[MAX_MONTH] =
       "January", "February",
       "March", "April", "May", "June", "July",
       "August", "September", "October",
       "November", "December"
   get month
   while month < 1 OR month > MAX_MONTH
       print "Invalid month"
       get month
   endwhile
   month = month - 1
   print MONTH_NAME[month]
stop
```

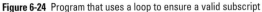

Every time you use an array, you should keep its size and boundaries in mind. For example, when a user's input value is used to access an array, you should always test the size of the value to make sure it is within bounds before using the value. If the value of the variable used as a subscript is too low (below 0) or too high (the size of the array or larger), you should either not access the array or force the value to a usable value with an assignment statement.

TWO TRUTHS AND A LIE:

REMAINING WITHIN ARRAY BOUNDS

1. Elements in an array are frequently different data types, so calculating the amount of memory the array occupies is difficult.

2. If you attempt to access an array with a subscript that is too small, some programming languages will stop execution of the program and issue an error message.

3. If you attempt to access an array with a subscript that is too large, some programming languages access an incorrect memory location outside the array bounds.

The false statement is #1. Array elements are always the same data type, and elements of the same data type always occupy the same number of bytes of memory, so the number of bytes in an array is always a multiple of the number of elements in an array.

USING A FOR LOOP TO PROCESS ARRAYS

In Chapter 4, you learned about the `for` loop—a loop that, in a single statement, initializes a loop control variable, compares it to a limit, and alters it. The `for` loop is a particularly convenient tool when working with arrays because you frequently need to process every element of an array from beginning to end. As with a `while` loop, when you use a `for` loop, you must be careful to stay within array bounds, remembering that the highest usable array subscript is one less than the size of the array. Figure 6-25 shows a `for` loop that correctly prints all the month names in the MONTH_NAME array. Notice that `month` is incremented through 1 less than the number of months because with a 12-item array, the subscripts you can use are 0 through 11.

```
start
    num month
    num MAX_MONTH = 12
    string MONTH_NAME[MAX_MONTH] =
        "January", "February",
        "March", "April", "May", "June", "July",
        "August", "September", "October",
        "November", "December"
    for month = 0 to MAX_MONTH - 1
        print MONTH_NAME[month]
    endfor
stop
```

Figure 6-25 Pseudocode that uses a `for` loop to print month names

The loop in Figure 6-25 is slightly inefficient because, as it executes 12 times, the subtraction operation that deducts 1 from MAX_MONTH occurs each time. Twelve subtraction operations do not consume much computer power or time, but in a loop that processes thousands or millions of array elements, the program's efficiency would be compromised. Figure 6-26 shows a superior solution. A new constant, ARRAY_LIMIT is calculated once, then used repeatedly in the comparison operation to determine when to stop cycling through the array.

```
start
    num month
    num MAX_MONTH = 12
    num ARRAY_LIMIT = MAX_MONTH - 1
    string MONTH_NAME[MAX_MONTH] =
        "January", "February",
        "March", "April", "May", "June", "July",
        "August", "September", "October",
        "November", "December"
    for month = 0 to ARRAY_LIMIT
        print MONTH_NAME[month]
    endfor
stop
```

Figure 6-26 Pseudocode that uses a more efficient for loop to print month names

>> **NOTE** In Java, C++, and C#, the for loop looks the same. To control a loop in which month varies from 0 to one less than MAX_MONTH, you can write the following:

```
for(month = 0; month < MAX_MONTH; month++)
```

The keyword for is followed by parentheses. The parentheses contain three sections, separated with semicolons. The first section sets month to a starting value. The middle section makes a comparison; the for loop continues to execute while this expression is true. The last section executes when the body of the loop is complete; usually it alters the loop control variable. In Java, C++, and C#, month++ means "add one to month".

>> **NOTE** Chapter 9 of the Comprehensive version of this book covers advanced array concepts.

TWO TRUTHS AND A LIE:
USING A for LOOP TO PROCESS ARRAYS

1. The for loop is a particularly convenient tool when working with arrays.

2. You frequently need to process every element of an array from beginning to end.

3. An advantage to using a for loop to process array elements is that you are relieved from worrying about array bounds.

The false answer is #3. As with a while loop, when you use a for loop, you must be careful to stay within array bounds.

CHAPTER SUMMARY

» An array is a series or list of variables in computer memory, all of which have the same name and data type but are differentiated with special numbers called subscripts.

» You can often use a variable as a subscript to an array, which allows you to replace multiple nested decisions with many fewer statements.

» Using a named constant for an array's size makes the code easier to understand and less likely to contain an error.

» You can declare and initialize all of the elements in an array using a single statement that provides a type, a name, and a quantity of elements for the array. You can also initialize array values within an initialization loop.

» Some arrays contain values that are determined during the execution of a program; other arrays are more useful when their final desired values are hard-coded when you write the program.

» Searching through an array to find a value you need involves initializing a subscript, using a loop to test each array element, and setting a flag when a match is found.

» With parallel arrays, each element in one array is associated with the element in the same relative position in the other array.

» When you need to compare a value to a range of values in an array, you can store either the low- or high-end value of each range for comparison.

» When you access data stored in an array, it is important to use a subscript containing a value that accesses memory occupied by the array. When you use a subscript that is not within the defined range of acceptable subscripts, your subscript is said to be out of bounds.

» The `for` loop is a particularly convenient tool when working with arrays because you frequently need to process every element of an array from beginning to end.

KEY TERMS

An **array** is a series or list of variables in computer memory, all of which have the same name but are differentiated with special numbers called subscripts.

A **subscript**, also called an **index**, is a number that indicates the position of a particular item within an array.

Each separate array variable is one **element** of the array.

The **size of the array** is the number of elements it can hold.

An **implicitly sized** array is one that is automatically given a size based on a list of provided values.

Arrays whose size can be altered are **dynamic arrays**, or **dynamically allocated** arrays.

An **initialization loop** is a loop structure that provides initial values for every element in any array.

Populating an array is the act of assigning values to the array elements.

A **variable array** is one whose values change during program execution.

A **constant array** is one whose values are assigned permanently when you write the program code.

Hard-coded values are explicitly assigned.

A **flag** is a variable that you set to indicate whether some event has occurred.

Parallel arrays are two or more arrays in which each element in one array is associated with the element in the same relative position in the other array or arrays.

Leaving a loop as soon as a match is found is called an **early exit**.

An array subscript is **out of bounds** when it is not within the range of acceptable subscripts.

REVIEW QUESTIONS

1. **A subscript is a(n) _____ .**

   a. element in an array

   b. alternate name for an array

   c. number that represents the highest value stored within an array

   d. number that indicates the position of a particular item in an array

2. **Each variable in an array must have the same _____ as the others.**

   a. data type   c. value

   b. subscript   d. memory location

3. **Each variable in an array is called a(n) _____ .**

   a. data type   c. component

   b. subscript   d. element

4. **The subscripts of any array are always _____ .**

   a. integers   c. characters

   b. fractions   d. strings of characters

5. **Suppose you have an array named `number`, and two of its elements are `number[1]` and `number[4]`. You know that _____ .**

   a. the two elements hold the same value

   b. the array holds exactly four elements

   c. there are exactly two elements between those two elements

   d. the two elements are at the same memory location

6. Suppose you want to write a program that reads customer records and prints a summary of the number of customers who owe more than $1,000 each, in each of 12 sales regions. Customer fields include `name`, `zipCode`, `balanceDue`, and `regionNumber`. At some point during record processing, you would add 1 to an array element whose subscript would be represented by _____ .

    a. `name`

    b. `zipCode`

    c. `balanceDue`

    d. `regionNumber`

7. Arrays are most useful when you use a _____ as a subscript when accessing their values.

    a. numeric constant

    b. variable

    c. character

    d. filename

8. Suppose you create a program containing a seven-element array that contains the names of the days of the week. At the start of the program, you display the day names using a subscript named `dayNum`. You display the same array values again at the end of the program where you _____ as a subscript to the array.

    a. must use `dayNum`

    b. can use `dayNum` but can also use another variable

    c. must not use `dayNum`

    d. must use a numeric constant instead of a variable

9. Declaring a numeric array sets its individual elements' values to _____ .

    a. 0 in every programming language

    b. 0 in some programming languages

    c. consecutive digits in every programming language

    d. consecutive digits in some programming languages

10. Filling an array with values during a program's execution is known as _____ the array.

    a. executing

    b. colonizing

    c. populating

    d. declaring

11. A hard-coded array is one whose final desired values are set _____ .

    a. to variable values during the execution of the program

    b. to constant values at the beginning of the program

    c. to values by the end of the program

    d. to 0

12. A _____ is a variable that you set to indicate whether some event has occurred.

a. subscript

c. counter

b. banner

d. flag

13. What do you call two arrays in which each element in one array is associated with the element in the same relative position in the other array?

a. cohesive arrays

c. hidden arrays

b. parallel arrays

d. perpendicular arrays

14. In most modern programming languages, the highest subscript you should use with a 10-element array is _____ .

a. 8

c. 10

b. 9

d. 11

15. When you perform an early exit from a loop while searching through an array for a match, you _____ .

a. quit searching before you find a match

b. quit searching as soon as you find a match

c. set a flag as soon as you find a match, but keep searching for additional matches

d. repeat a search only if the first search was unsuccessful

16. Each element in a five-element array can hold _____ value(s).

a. one

c. at least five

b. five

d. an unlimited number of

17. After the annual dog show in which the Barkley Dog Training Academy awards points to each participant, the academy assigns a status to each dog based on the following criteria:

Points Earned	Level of Achievement
0–5	Good
6–7	Excellent
8–9	Superior
10	Unbelievable

The academy needs a program that compares a dog's points earned with the grading scale, so that each dog can receive a certificate acknowledging the appropriate level of achievement. Of the following, which set of values would be most useful for the contents of an array used in the program?

a. 0, 6, 9, 10

c. 5, 7, 9, 10

b. 5, 7, 8, 10

d. any of these

18. **When you use a subscript value that is negative or higher than the number of elements in an array, _____ .**

    a. execution of the program stops and an error message is issued

    b. a value in a memory location that is outside the area occupied by the array will be accessed

    c. a value in a memory location that is outside the area occupied by the array will be accessed, but only if the value is the correct data type

    d. the resulting action depends on the programming language used

19. **In every array, a subscript is out of bounds when it is _____ .**

    a. negative   c. 1

    b. 0   d. 999

20. **You can access every element of an array using a _____ .**

    a. `while` loop   c. posttest loop

    b. `for` loop   d. any of the above

FIND THE BUGS

Each of the following pseudocode segments contains one or more bugs that you must find and correct.

1. **This application prints a summary report for an aluminum can recycling drive at a high school. When a student brings in cans, a user enters the student's year in school (1, 2, 3, or 4) and the number of cans submitted. After all the data has been entered, a report lists each of the four grades and the total number of cans recycled for each grade.**

```
start
   num year
   num cans
   num SIZE = 4
   num collected[SIZE] = 0, 0, 0, 0
   string HEAD1 = "Can Recycling Report"
   string HEAD2 = "Year     Cans Collected"
   get year, cans
   while not eof
      collected[year] = collected[year] + cans
   endwhile
   print HEAD1
   print HEAD2
   while year <= SIZE
      print year, collected[year]
      year = year + 1
   endwhile
stop
```

2. **This application prints a report that lists students and their course grades. A user enters each student's name, and four test scores. The program calculates a numeric average from the scores and prints a report that contains each student's name and a letter grade based on the following scale:**

90–100 A

80–89 B

70–79 C

60–69 D

59 and below F

```
start
    string name
    num score
    num NUM_TESTS = 4
    num NUM_RANGES = 5
    num RANGES[NUM_RANGES] = 90, 80, 70, 60, 0
    string GRADES[NUM_RANGES] = "A", "B", "C", "D", "F"
    num total = 0
    num average
    num sub
    get name
    while not eof
        sub = 0
        while sub < NUM_TESTS
            get score
            total = total + score
            sub = sub + 1
        endwhile
        average = total / NUM_RANGES
        sub = 0
        while average < RANGES[NUM_RANGES]
            sub = sub + 1
        endwhile
        letterGrade = GRADES[NUM_RANGES]
        print name, letterGrade
        get name
    endwhile
stop
```

EXERCISES

1. **Design the logic for a program that allows a user to enter 10 numbers, then displays them in the reverse order of their entered order.**

2. **Design the logic for a program that allows a user to enter 10 numbers, then displays each and its difference from the numeric average of the numbers.**

3a. **The city of Cary is holding a special census. The census takers collect one record for each resident. Each record contains a resident's age, gender, marital status, and** voting district. The voting district field contains a number from 1 through 22. Design a program that accepts data for each resident until all have been entered and then produces a list of all 22 districts and the number of residents in each.

3b. Design a program that accepts resident data and produces a count of the number of residents in each of the following age groups: under 18, 18 through 30, 31 through 45, 46 through 64, and 65 and older.

4a. The Midville Park District maintains records containing information about players on its soccer teams. Each record contains a player's first name, last name, and team number. The teams are:

Team Number	Team Name
1	Goal Getters
2	The Force
3	Top Guns
4	Shooting Stars
5	Midfield Monsters

Design a program that accepts player data and creates a report that lists each player along with his or her team number and team name.

4b. Design an application that produces a count of the number of players registered for each team listed in Exercise 4a.

5a. Watson Elementary School contains 30 classrooms numbered 1 through 30. Each classroom can contain any number of students up to 35. Each student takes an achievement test at the end of the school year and receives a score from 0 through 100. Write a program that accepts data for each student in the school—student ID, classroom number, and score on the achievement test.

Design a program that lists the total points scored for each of the 30 classrooms.

5b. Modify Exercise 5a so that each classroom's average of the test scores prints, rather than each classroom's total.

5c. Watson Elementary School maintains a file containing the teacher's name for each classroom. Each record in this file contains a room numbered 1 through 30, and the last name of the teacher. Modify the program in Exercise 5b so that the correct teacher's name appears on the list with his or her class's average.

6. **The Billy Goat Fast-Food restaurant sells the following products:**

Product	Price ($)
Cheeseburger	2.49
Pepsi	1.00
Chips	0.59

Design the logic for an application that reads in a customer's item ordered and prints either the correct price or the message "Sorry, we do not carry that" as output.

7a. **Design the logic for an application for a company that wants a report containing a breakdown of payroll by department. Input includes each employee's last name, first name, department number, hourly salary, and number of hours worked. The output is a list of the seven departments in the company (numbered 1 through 7) and the total gross payroll (rate times hours) for each department.**

7b. **Modify Exercise 7a so that the report lists department names as well as numbers. The department names are:**

Department Number	Department Name
1	Personnel
2	Marketing
3	Manufacturing
4	Computer Services
5	Sales
6	Accounting
7	Shipping

7c. **Modify the report created in Exercise 7b so that it prints a line of information for each employee before printing the department summary at the end of the report. Each detail line must contain the employee's name, department number, department name, hourly wage, hours worked, gross pay, and withholding tax.**

Withholding taxes are based on the following percentages of gross pay:

Weekly Gross Pay ($)	Withholding Percent (%)
0.00–200.00	10
200.01–350.00	14
350.01–500.00	18
500.01–up	22

8. The Perfect Party Catering Company hosts events for clients. Create an application
    that accepts an event number, the event host's last name, and numeric month, day,
    and year values representing the event date. The applications should also accept the
    number of guests that will attend the event and a numeric meal code that repre-
    sents the entrée that the event hosts will serve. As each client's data is entered,
    verify that the month, day, year, and meal code are valid; if any of these is not valid,
    continue to prompt the user until it is. The valid meal codes are as follows:

Code	Entrée	Price per Person ($)
1	Roast beef	24.50
2	Salmon	19.00
3	Linguine	16.50
4	Chicken	18.00

Design the logic for an application that produces a report that lists each event number,
host name, validated date, meal code, entrée name, number of guests, gross total price for
the party, and price for the party after discount. The gross total price for the party is the
price per guest for the meal times the number of guests. The final price includes a discount based on the following table:

Number of Guests	Discount ($)
1–25	0
26–50	75
51–100	125
101–250	200
251 and over	300

9a. *Daily Life Magazine* wants an analysis of the demographic characteristics of its
     readers. The Marketing Department has collected reader survey records contain-
     ing the age, gender, marital status, and annual income of readers. Design an appli-
     cation that accepts reader data and produces a count of readers by age groups as
     follows: under 20, 20–29, 30–39, 40–49, and 50 and older.

9b. Create the logic for a program that would produce a count of readers by gender
     within age group—that is, under 20 females, under 20 males, and so on.

9c. Create the logic for a program that would produce a count of readers by annual
     income groups as follows: under $20,000, $20,000–$29,999, $30,000–$49,999,
     $50,000–$69,999, and $70,000 and up.

10. Glen Ross Vacation Property Sales employs seven salespeople as follows:

ID Number	Salesperson Name
103	Darwin
104	Kratz
201	Shulstad
319	Fortune
367	Wickert
388	Miller
435	Vick

When a salesperson makes a sale, a record is created including the date, time, and dollar amount of the sale. The time is expressed in hours and minutes, based on a 24-hour clock. The sale amount is expressed in whole dollars. Salespeople earn a commission that differs for each sale, based on the following rate schedule:

Sale Amount ($)	Commission Rate (%)
0–50,999	4
51,000–125,999	5
126,000–200,999	6
201,000 and up	7

Design an application that produces each of the following reports:

a. A report listing each salesperson number, name, total sales, and total commissions

b. A report listing each month of the year as both a number and a word (for example, "01 January"), and the total sales for the month for all salespeople

c. A report listing total sales as well as total commissions earned by all salespeople for each of the following time frames, based on hour of the day: 00–05, 06–12, 13–18, and 19–23

GAME ZONE

1. Create the logic for an application that contains an array of 10 multiple-choice questions related to your favorite hobby. Each question contains three answer choices. Also create a parallel array that holds the correct answer to each question—A, B, or C. Display each question and verify that the user enters only A, B, or C as the answer—if not, keep prompting the user until a valid response is entered. If the user responds to a question correctly, display "Correct!"; otherwise, display "The correct answer is" and the letter of the correct answer. After the user answers all the questions, display the number of correct and incorrect answers.

2a. Create the logic for a dice game. The application randomly "throws" five dice for the computer and five dice for the player. As each random "throw" is made, store it in an array. The application displays all the values, which can be from 1 to 6 inclusive for each die. Decide the winner based on the following hierarchy of die values. Any higher combination beats a lower one; for example, five of a kind beats four of a kind.

» Five of a kind

» Four of a kind

» Three of a kind

» A pair

For this game, the numeric dice values do not count. For example, if both players have three of a kind, it's a tie, no matter what the values of the three dice are. Additionally, the game does not recognize a full house (three of a kind plus two of a kind). Figure 6-27 shows how the game might be played in a command-line environment.

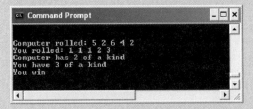

Figure 6-27 Typical execution of the dice game

2b. Improve the dice game so that when both players have the same combination of dice, the higher value wins. For example, two 6s beats two 5s.

3. Design the logic for the game Hangman, in which the user guesses letters in a hidden word. Store the letters of a word in an array of characters. Display a dash for each missing letter. Allow the user to continuously guess a letter until all the letters in the word are correctly guessed. As the user enters each guess, display the word again, filling in the guess if it was correct. For example, if the hidden word is "computer", first display --------. After the user guesses "p", the display becomes ---p----. Make sure that when a user makes a correct guess, all the matching letters are filled in. For example, if the word is "banana" then when the user guesses "a", all three "a" characters are filled in.

4. Create two parallel arrays that represent a standard deck of 52 playing cards. One array is numeric and holds the values 1 through 13 (representing Ace, 2 through 10, Jack, Queen, and King). The other array is a string array and holds suits ("Clubs", "Diamonds", "Hearts", and "Spades"). Create the arrays so that all 52 card combinations are represented. Create a War card game that randomly selects two cards (one for the player and one for the computer) and declares a winner (or a tie) based on the numeric value of the two cards. The game should play for 26 rounds of War, dealing a full deck with no repeated cards. For this game, assume the cards' values are based on their numbers—that is, the lowest card is the Ace. Display the values of the player's and computer's cards, compare their values, and determine the winner. When all the cards in the deck are exhausted, display a count of the number of times the player wins, the number of times the computer wins, and the number of ties.

Some hints:

» Start by creating an array of all 52 playing cards.

» Select a random number for the deck position of the player's first card and assign the card at that array position to the player.

» Move every higher-positioned card in the deck "down" one to fill in the gap. In other words, if the player's first random number is 49, select the card at position 49 (both the numeric value and the string), move the card that was in position 50 to position 49, and move the card that was in position 51 to position 50. Only 51 cards remain in the deck after the player's first card is dealt, so the available-card array is smaller by one.

» In the same way, randomly select a card for the computer and "remove" the card from the deck.

5. Create the logic for a guessing game called "Does It Have Legs?", in which you think of an animal and the computer tries to guess what it is. The game continually becomes "smarter" as you play because you teach it how to become more specific with its questions. For example, a typical game session might proceed as follows:

Computer: Does the animal you are thinking of have legs?
Player: Yes.
Computer: Is it a dog?
Player: Yes.
Computer: Yay! I win. Do you want to play again?
Player: Yes.
Computer: Does the animal you are thinking of have legs?
Player: Yes.
Computer: Is it a dog?
Player: No.
Computer: I give up. What was your animal?
Player: horse.
Computer: Type a question for which the answer is Yes for dog but No for horse.
Player: Does it live in the house?
Computer: Do you want to play again?
Player: Yes.
Computer: Does the animal you are thinking of have legs?
Player: Yes.
Computer: Does it live in the house?
Player: No.
Computer: Is it a horse?
Player: No.
Computer: I give up. What was your animal?
Player: cow.
Computer: Type a question for which the answer is Yes for horse but No for cow.
Player: Do people ride it?
Computer: Do you want to play again?
Player: Yes.
Computer: Does the animal you are thinking of have legs?
Player: Yes.

Computer: Does it live in the house?
Player: No.
Computer: Do people ride it?
Player: No.
Computer: Is it a cow?
Player: Yes.
Computer: Yay! I win. Do you want to play again?
Player: No.

(*Hint:* You might want to look up "binary trees" on the Web as a method to organize this application.)

DETECTIVE WORK

1. **Find at least five definitions of an array.**

2. **Using Help in Microsoft Excel or another spreadsheet program, discover how to use the `vlookup()` function. How is this function used?**

3. **What is a Fibonacci sequence? How do Fibonacci sequences apply to natural phenomena? Why do programmers use an array when working with this mathematical concept?**

UP FOR DISCUSSION

1. **A train schedule is an everyday, real-life example of an array. Think of at least four more.**

2. **Every element in an array always has the same data type. Why is this necessary?**

USING METHODS

In this chapter you will:

Review how to use a simple method with local variables
and constants
Create a method that requires a single parameter
Create a method that requires multiple parameters
Create a method that returns a value
Pass an array to a method
Overload methods
Learn how to avoid ambiguous methods
Use prewritten, built-in methods
Learn about IPO charts
Learn to reduce coupling and increase cohesion

REVIEW OF SIMPLE METHODS

In Chapter 3, you learned about many features of program modules, or methods. You also learned a lot of the vocabulary associated with methods. For example, you learned the following:

» A **method** is a program module that contains a series of statements that carry out a task; you can invoke or call a method from another program or method.

» Any program can contain an unlimited number of methods, and each method can be called an unlimited number of times.

» The rules for naming modules are different in every programming language, but they often are similar to the language's rules for variable names. In this text, module names are followed by a set of parentheses.

» A method must include a **header** (also called the declaration or definition), a **body**, and a **return statement**.

» Within a program, the simplest methods you can invoke don't require any data items (called **arguments**) to be sent to them, nor do they send any data back to you (called **returning a value**).

» Variables and constants are **in scope** within or **local** to only the method in which they are declared.

Figure 7-1 shows a program that allows a user to enter his or her weight. The program then calculates the user's weight on the moon as 16.6 percent of the weight on earth. The main program contains two variables and a constant, all of which are local to the main program. The program calls the `printInstructions()` method, which prompts the user for a language indicator and displays a prompt in the selected language. The `printInstructions()` method contains its own local variable and constants, which are invisible to the main program. Figure 7-2 shows a typical program execution in a command-line environment.

> **»» NOTE** In Chapter 3 you learned that this book uses a rectangle with a horizontal stripe across the top to represent a module call statement in a flowchart. Some programmers prefer to use a rectangle with two vertical stripes at the sides; a popular flowcharting program called Visual Logic also uses this other convention.

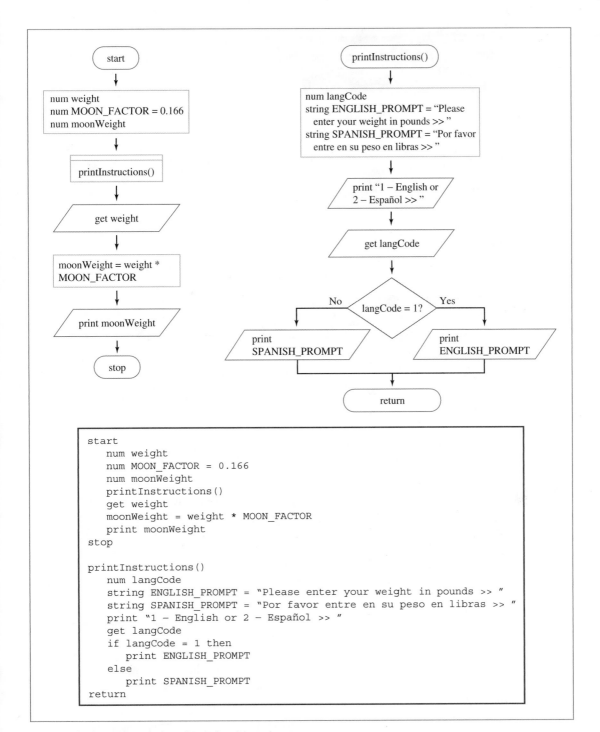

Figure 7-1 A program that calculates the user's weight on the moon

Figure 7-2 Output of moon weight calculator program in Figure 7-1

> **»NOTE** The output shown in Figure 7-2 is just a number without explanation. Usually, this is a poor practice. In a superior program, the language code would be passed back from the `printInstructions()` method so that the output could be displayed with an explanation in the user's chosen language. (For example, typical output might be "At 150 earth pounds, you would weigh 24.9 pounds on the moon.") You learn how to make this improvement in the next section.

In the program in Figure 7-1, each method contains only what it needs. However, sometimes two or more methods in a program require access to the same data. When methods must share data, you must pass the data from one method to another.

> **TWO TRUTHS AND A LIE:**
> **REVIEW OF SIMPLE METHODS**
>
> 1. Any program can contain an unlimited number of methods, but each method can be called once.
>
> 2. A method must include a header, a body, and a return statement.
>
> 3. Variables and constants are in scope within or local to only the method in which they are declared.
>
> The false statement is #1. Each method can be called an unlimited number of times.

CREATING METHODS THAT REQUIRE A SINGLE PARAMETER

Some methods require information to be sent in from the outside. If a method could not receive your communications, called **parameters**, then you would have to write an infinite number of methods to cover every possible situation. As a real-life example, when you make a restaurant reservation, you do not need to employ a different method for every date of the year at every possible time of day. Rather, you can supply the date and time as information to the person who carries out the method. The method, recording the reservation, is then carried out in the same manner, no matter what date and time are involved. In a program, if you design a method to square numeric values, it makes sense to design a `square()` method that you can supply with a parameter that represents the value to be squared, rather than having to develop a `square1()` method (that squares the value 1), a `square2()` method (that squares the value 2), and so on. To call a `square()` method that accepts a parameter, you might write a statement like `square(17)` or `square(86)` and let the method use whatever value you send. When you call a method with a value within its parentheses, the value is an argument to the method.

> **»NOTE** *Parameter* and *argument* are closely related terms. A calling method sends an argument to a called method. A called method accepts the value as its parameter.

An important principle of modularization is the notion of **implementation hiding**, the encapsulation of method details. That is, when you make a request to a method, you don't know the details of how the method is executed. For example, when you make a real-life restaurant reservation, you do not need to know how the reservation is actually recorded at the restaurant—perhaps it is written in a book, marked on a large chalkboard, or entered into a computerized database. The implementation details don't concern you as a patron, and if the restaurant changes its methods from one year to the next, the change does not affect your use of the reservation method—you still call and provide your name, a date, and a time. With well-written methods, using implementation hiding means that a method that calls another must know the name of the called method, what type of information to send it, and what type of return data to expect, but the program does not need to know how the method works internally. The calling method needs to understand only the **interface to the method** that is called. In other words, the interface is the only part of a method with which the method's **client** (or method's caller) sees or interacts. Additionally, if you substitute a new, improved method implementation, as long as the interface to the method does not change, you won't need to make changes in any methods that call the altered method.

> **» NOTE** Programmers refer to hidden implementation details as existing in a **black box**. This means that you can examine what goes in and what comes out, but not the details of how it works inside.

When you write the method declaration for a method that can receive a parameter, you must include the following items within the method declaration parentheses:

» The type of the parameter
» A local name for the parameter

For example, suppose you decide to improve the moon weight program in Figure 7-1 by making the output more user-friendly and adding explanatory text to the value that is displayed. It makes sense that if the user can request a prompt in a specific language, then the user would also want to see the output explanation in the same language. However, in Figure 7-1, the `langCode` variable is local to the `printInstructions()` method and therefore cannot be used in the main program. You could rewrite the program taking several approaches:

» You could rewrite the program without including any methods. That way, you could prompt the user for a language preference, and display the prompt and the result in the appropriate language. This approach would work, but you would not be taking advantage of the benefits provided by modularization, including making the main program more streamlined and abstract.

» You could retain the `printInstructions()` method as is and add a section to the main program that asks the user for a preferred language for displaying output. The disadvantage to this approach is that during one execution of the program, the user must answer the same basic question twice.

» You could store the variable that holds the language code in the main program so that it could be used to determine output. You could also retain the `printInstructions()` method, but pass the language code to it so the prompt would appear in the appropriate language. This is the best choice of the three, and is illustrated in Figure 7-3.

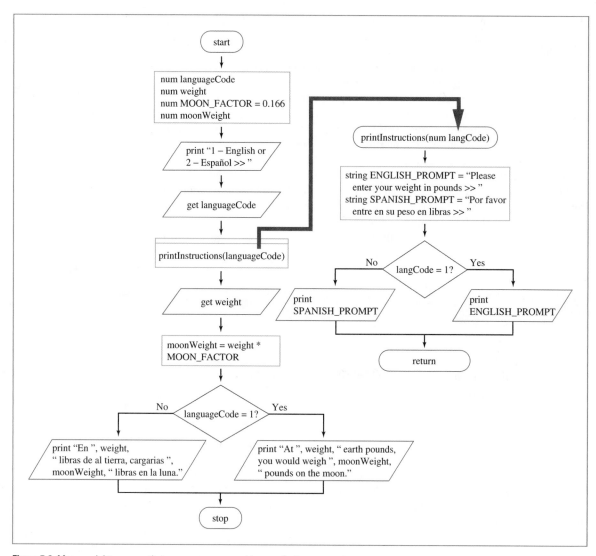

Figure 7-3 Moon weight program that passes an argument to a method

```
start
   num languageCode
   num weight
   num MOON_FACTOR = 0.166
   num moonWeight
   print "1 - English or 2 - Español >> "
   get languageCode
   printInstructions(languageCode)
   get weight
   moonWeight = weight * MOON_FACTOR
   if languageCode = 1 then
      print "At ", weight,
         " earth pounds, you would weigh ", moonWeight,
         " pounds on the moon."
   else
      print "En ", weight,
         " libras de al tierra, cargarias ", moonWeight,
         " libras en la luna."
   endif
stop

printInstructions(num langCode)
   string ENGLISH_PROMPT = "Please enter your weight in pounds >> "
   string SPANISH_PROMPT = "Por favor entre en su peso en libras >> "
   if langCode = 1 then
      print ENGLISH_PROMPT
   else
      print SPANISH_PROMPT
return
```

Figure 7-3 Moon weight program that passes an argument to a method (*continued*)

Figure 7-4 Typical execution of moon weight program in Figure 7-3

In the main program in Figure 7-3, a numeric variable named languageCode is declared and the user is prompted for a value. The value then is passed to the printInstructions() method. The method call is printInstructions(languageCode) and the method declaration or header is printInstructions(num langCode). You can think of the parentheses in a method declaration as a funnel into the method—parameters listed there hold values that are "dropped in" to the method.

In the program in Figure 7-3, the numeric variable languageCode is sent as an argument to the method. The parameter defined within the parentheses in the method header (num langCode) indicates that the method will receive a value of type num, and that within the method, the passed value representing a code will be known as langCode. Within the method, it is used to make the decision about which prompt to display.

The printInstructions() method could be called from the main program any number of times, if needed. It could be called using any numeric variable. For example, if you declare a numeric variable named usersCode, you can call printInstructions(usersCode). The method could also be called using a literal constant, for example printInstructions(1). The only requirement is that each time the printInstructions() method is called, it must be called using a numeric argument. Within the printInstructions() method, each of these arguments, whether variable or constant, would become known as langCode. The identifier langCode represents a variable that holds any numeric value passed into the method.

If the value used as an argument in the method call to printInstructions() is a variable, it might possess the same identifier as langCode, or a different one. Figure 7-5 shows a new version of the moon weight program in which the programmer has chosen to use the same identifier for the main program variable and the method parameter. (The identifier is shaded in all six places where it is used in the figure.) Within the printInstructions() method, the identifier langCode is simply a temporary placeholder; it does not make any difference what name it "goes by" in the calling program. The variable langCode is declared in the method header and is a local variable to the printInstructions() method; that is, it is known only within the boundaries of the method and goes out of scope when the method ends. It is newly declared within the method header; if it was not, it would not need a declared data type.

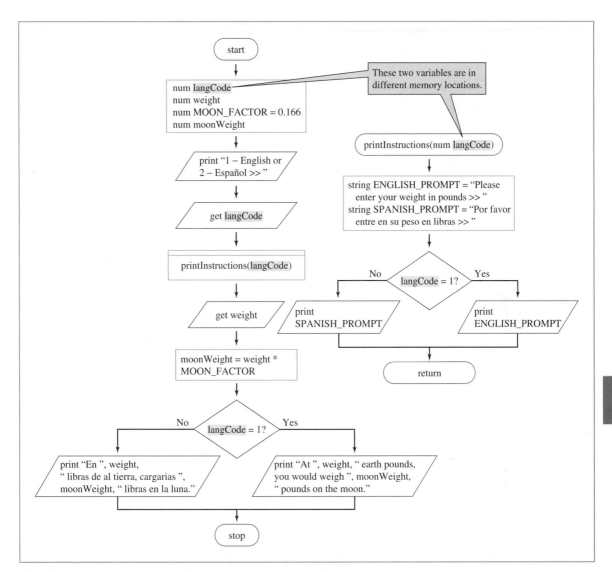

Figure 7-5 Alternate version of the moon weight program in which the programmer uses the same identifier for two variables

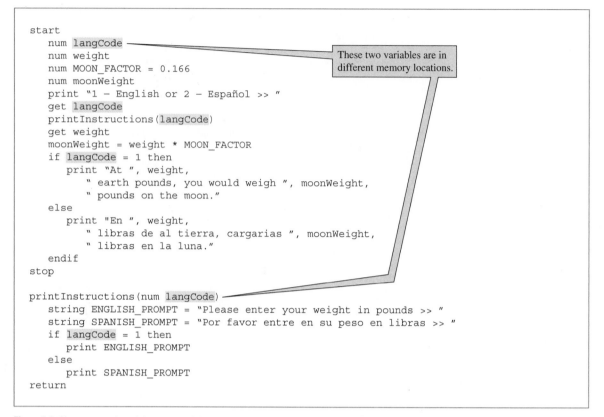

```
start
    num langCode
    num weight
    num MOON_FACTOR = 0.166
    num moonWeight
    print "1 - English or 2 - Español >> "
    get langCode
    printInstructions(langCode)
    get weight
    moonWeight = weight * MOON_FACTOR
    if langCode = 1 then
        print "At ", weight,
            " earth pounds, you would weigh ", moonWeight,
            " pounds on the moon."
    else
        print "En ", weight,
            " libras de al tierra, cargarias ", moonWeight,
            " libras en la luna."
    endif
stop

printInstructions(num langCode)
    string ENGLISH_PROMPT = "Please enter your weight in pounds >> "
    string SPANISH_PROMPT = "Por favor entre en su peso en libras >> "
    if langCode = 1 then
        print ENGLISH_PROMPT
    else
        print SPANISH_PROMPT
return
```

These two variables are in different memory locations.

Figure 7-5 Alternate version of the moon weight program in which the programmer uses the same identifier for two variables (*continued*)

Each time the printInstructions() method in Figure 7-3 or 7-5 executes, a langCode variable is redeclared—that is, a new memory location large enough to hold a numeric value is set up and named langCode. Within the printInstructions() method, langCode holds whatever value is passed into the method by the main program. When the printInstructions() method ends at the return statement, the local langCode variable ceases to exist. After the correct prompt is chosen in the method, assigning a new value to langCode would make no difference. That is, if you change the value of langCode after you have used it to select a prompt within `printInstructions()`, it affects nothing else. A variable passed into a method is **passed by value**; that is, a copy of its value is sent to the method and stored in a new memory location accessible to the method. The memory location that holds `langCode` is released at the end of the method, and if you change its value, it does not affect any variable in the calling method. In particular, don't think there would be any change in the variable named `langCode` in the main program in Figure 7-5; that variable is a different variable with its own memory address and is totally different from the one in the `printInstructions()` method.

TWO TRUTHS AND A LIE:
CREATING METHODS THAT REQUIRE A SINGLE PARAMETER

1. A method needs to know the interface of a method that calls it.

2. When you write the method declaration for a method that can receive a parameter, you must include the type and local name in the method declaration parentheses.

3. When a variable is used as an argument in a method call, it can have the same identifier as the parameter in the method header.

The false statement is #1. A calling method needs to know the called method's interface.

CREATING METHODS THAT REQUIRE MULTIPLE PARAMETERS

A method can require more than one parameter. You indicate that a method requires multiple parameters by listing their data types and local identifiers within the method header's parentheses and separating them by commas. You can pass multiple arguments from a calling method to a called method by listing the arguments within the method call and separating them with commas. For example, suppose you want to create a `computeTax()` method that calculates a tax on any value passed into it. You can create a method to which you pass two values—the amount to be taxed, as well as a percentage figure by which to tax it. Figure 7-6 shows a method that uses two such arguments.

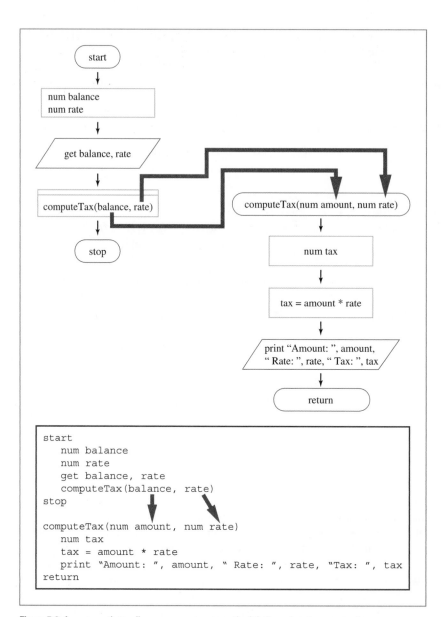

```
start
   num balance
   num rate
   get balance, rate
   computeTax(balance, rate)
stop

computeTax(num amount, num rate)
   num tax
   tax = amount * rate
   print "Amount: ", amount, " Rate: ", rate, "Tax: ", tax
return
```

Figure 7-6 A program that calls a `computeTax()` method that requires two parameters

>> **NOTE** A declaration for a method that receives two or more arguments must list the type for each parameter separately, even if the parameters have the same type.

>> **NOTE** In Figure 7-6, notice that one of the arguments to the method has the same name as the corresponding method parameter, and the other has a different name from its corresponding parameter. Each could have the same identifier as its counterpart, or all could be different. Each identifier is local to its own method.

In Figure 7-6, two parameters (`num amount` and `num rate`) appear within the parentheses in the method header. A comma separates each parameter, and each requires its own declared type (in this case, both are numeric) as well as its own identifier. When values are passed to the method in a statement such as `computeTax(balance, rate)`, the first value passed will be referenced as `amount` within the method, and the second value passed will be referenced as `rate`. Therefore, arguments passed to the method must be passed in the correct order. A call `computeTax(rate, balance)` instead of `computeTax(balance, rate)` would result in incorrect values being displayed in the print statement.

> **NOTE** When multiple parameters appear in a method header, they comprise a **parameter list**. If method arguments are the same type—for example, two numeric arguments—passing them to a method in the wrong order results in a logical error; that is, the program will compile and execute, but produce incorrect results. If a method expects arguments of diverse types, then passing arguments in the wrong order constitutes a syntax error, and the program will not compile.

You can write a method so that it takes any number of parameters in any order. However, when you call a method, the arguments you send to a method must match in order—both in number and in type—the parameters listed in the method declaration. Thus, a method to compute an automobile salesperson's commission amount might require arguments such as a string for the salesperson's name, a number for the value of a car sold, and a number for the commission rate. The method will execute correctly only when three arguments of the correct types are sent in the correct order.

> **NOTE** The arguments sent to a method in a method call are often referred to as **actual parameters**. The variables in the method declaration that accept the values from the actual parameters are the **formal parameters**.

> **NOTE** A method's name and parameter list constitute the method's **signature**.

TWO TRUTHS AND A LIE:
CREATING METHODS THAT REQUIRE MULTIPLE PARAMETERS

1. You indicate that a method requires multiple parameters by listing their data types and local identifiers within the method header's parentheses and separating them by commas.

2. You pass multiple arguments to a method by listing the arguments within the method call and separating them with commas.

3. When you call a method, you must include no more than the number of parameters listed in the method declaration.

The false statement is #3. When you call a method, the arguments you send to a method must match in order—both in number and in type—the arguments listed in the method declaration.

CREATING METHODS THAT RETURN VALUES

When a variable is declared within a method, it ceases to exist when the method ends—it goes out of scope. When you want to retain a value that exists in a method, then you can return the value from the method. That is, you can send the value back to the calling method. When a method returns a value, the method must have a return type. The **return type** for a method can be any type, which includes numeric, character, and string, as well as other more specific types that exist in the programming language with which you are working. Of course, a method can also return nothing, in which case the return type is usually indicated as void, and the method is a **void method**. (The term *void* means "nothing" or "empty".) A method's return type is known more succinctly as a **method's type**. A method's type is indicated in front of the method name when the method is defined.

> **NOTE** Along with an identifier and parameter list, a return type is part of a method's declaration. Some programmers claim a method's return type is part of its signature, but this is not the case. Only the method name and parameter list constitute the signature.

> **NOTE** Up to this point, this book has not included return types for methods because all the methods have been void methods. From this point forward, a return type is included with every method.

For example, a method that returns the number of hours an employee has worked might have the header num getHoursWorked(). This method returns a numeric value, so its type is num.

When a method returns a value, you usually want to use the returned value in the calling method (although using it is not required). For example, Figure 7-7 shows how a program might use the value returned by the getHoursWorked() method. In Figure 7-7, a variable named hours is declared in the main program. The getHoursWorked() method call is part of an assignment statement. When the method is called, the logic transfers to the getHoursWorked() method which contains a variable named workHours. A value is obtained for this variable, and is returned to the main program where it is assigned to hours. After the logic returns to the main program from the getHoursWorked() method, the method's local variable workHours no longer exists. However, its value has been stored in the main program where, as hours, it can be displayed and used in a calculation.

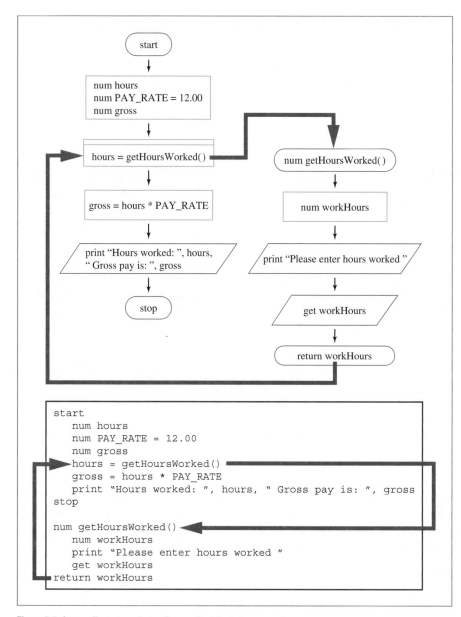

```
start
   num hours
   num PAY_RATE = 12.00
   num gross
   hours = getHoursWorked()
   gross = hours * PAY_RATE
   print "Hours worked: ", hours, " Gross pay is: ", gross
stop

num getHoursWorked()
   num workHours
   print "Please enter hours worked "
   get workHours
return workHours
```

Figure 7-7 A payroll program that calls a method that returns a value

Notice the return type num that precedes the method name in the getHoursWorked()
method header. A numeric value is included in the return statement that is the last statement within the getHoursWorked() method. When you place a value in a return statement, the value is sent from the called method back to the calling method. A method's
declared return type must match the type of the value used in the return statement; if it
does not, the program will not compile.

>> **NOTE** A method's return statement can return, at most, one value. The value can be a simple data type or it can
be a more complex type, for example a structure or an object. Chapter 11 of the Comprehensive version of this text discusses objects in more depth.

>> **NOTE** The value returned from a method is not required to be a variable. Instead, you might return a constant as in
return 0.

You are not required to assign a method's return value to a variable in order to use the
value. Instead, you can choose to use a method's returned value directly, without storing
it. When you use a method's value, you use it the same way you would use any variable
of the same type. For example, you can print a return value in a statement such as the
following:

```
print "Hours worked is ", getHoursWorked()
```

Because getHoursWorked() returns a numeric value, you can use the method call
getHoursWorked() in the same way that you would use any simple numeric value.
Figure 7-8 shows an example of a program that uses a method's return value directly
without storing it. The shaded workHours returned from the method is used directly
in the calculation of gross in the main program.

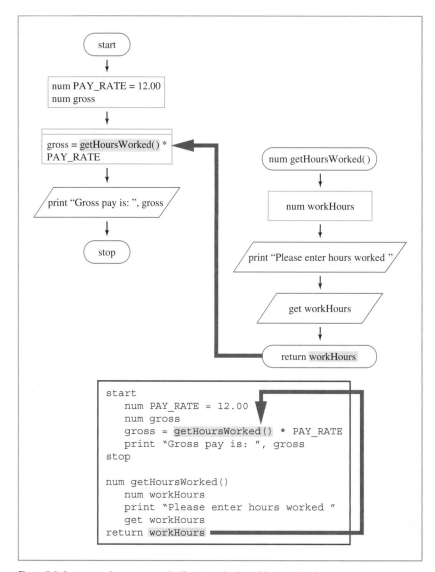

Figure 7-8 A program that uses a method's returned value without storing it

> **» NOTE** When a program needs to use a method's returned value in more than one place, it makes sense to store the returned value in a variable instead of calling the method multiple times. A program statement that calls a method requires more computer time and resources than a statement that does not call any outside methods. Programmers use the term **overhead** to describe any extra time and resources required by an operation.

In most programming languages, you are allowed to include multiple return statements in a method. For example, consider the findLargest() method in Figure 7-9. The method accepts three arguments and returns the largest of the values. Although this method works correctly (and you might see this technique used in programs written by others), it is not the recommended way to write the method. In Chapter 2, you learned that structured logic requires that each structure contains one entry point and one exit point. The return statements in Figure 7-9 violate this convention by leaving the decision structure before it is complete. Figure 7-10 shows the superior and recommended way to handle the problem. In Figure 7-10 the largest value is stored in a variable. Then, when the decision structure is complete, the stored value is returned.

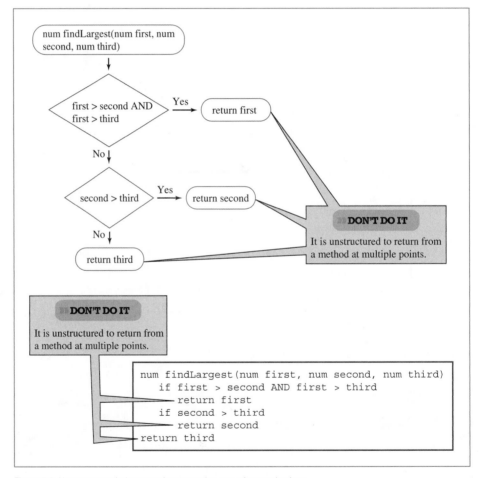

Figure 7-9 Unrecommended approach to returning one of several values

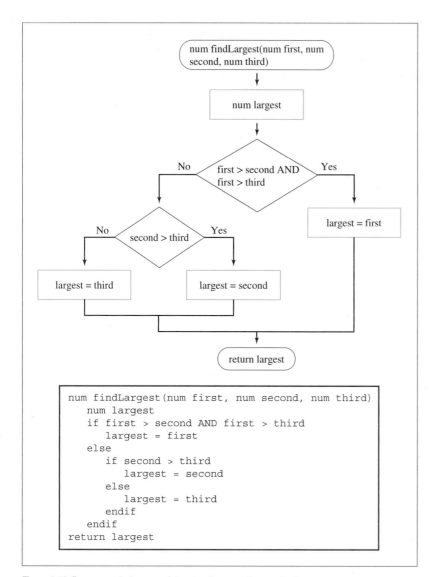

```
num findLargest(num first, num second, num third)
   num largest
   if first > second AND first > third
      largest = first
   else
      if second > third
         largest = second
      else
         largest = third
      endif
   endif
return largest
```

Figure 7-10 Recommended approach to returning one of several values

TWO TRUTHS AND A LIE:
CREATING METHODS THAT RETURN VALUES

1. The return type for a method can be any type, which includes numeric, character, and string, as well as other more specific types that exist in the programming language with which you are working.

2. A method's return type is known more succinctly as a method's type.

3. When a method returns a value, you must use the returned value in the same statement.

The false statement is #3. When a method returns a value, you usually want to use the returned value in the calling method, but it is not required.

PASSING AN ARRAY TO A METHOD

In Chapter 6, you learned that you can declare an array to create a list of elements, and that you can use any individual array element in the same manner as you would use any single variable of the same type. That is, suppose you declare a numeric array as follows:

```
num someNums[12]
```

You can subsequently print someNums[0] or perform arithmetic with someNums[11], just as you would for any simple variable that is not part of an array. Similarly, you can pass a single array element to a method in exactly the same manner as you would pass a variable or constant.

Consider the program shown in Figure 7-11. This program creates an array of four numeric values, and then prints them. Next, the program calls a method named tripleTheValue() four

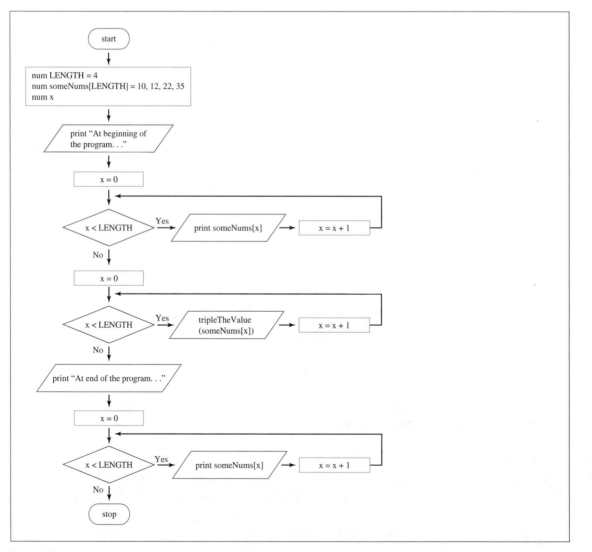

Figure 7-11 PassArrayElement program

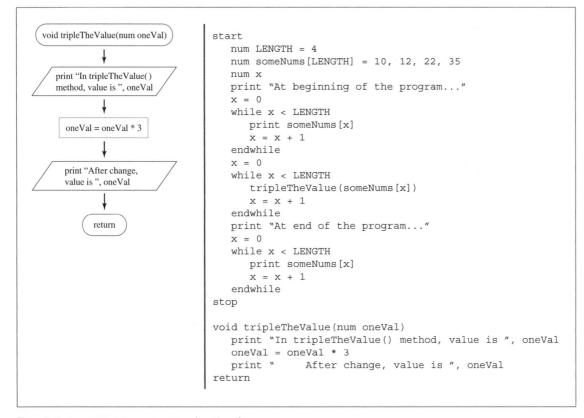

Figure 7-11 `PassArrayElement` program (*continued*)

times, passing each of the array elements in turn. The method prints the passed value, multiplies it by 3, and prints it again. Finally, back in the calling program, the four numbers are printed again. Figure 7-12 shows an execution of this program in a command-line environment.

```
Command Prompt                                        _ □ ×

At beginning of the program...    10    12    22    35
In tripleTheValue() method, value is 10
      After change, value is 30
In tripleTheValue() method, value is 12
      After change, value is 36
In tripleTheValue() method, value is 22
      After change, value is 66
In tripleTheValue() method, value is 35
      After change, value is 105
At end of the program..........   10    12    22    35
```

Figure 7-12 Output of `PassArrayElement` program

As you can see in Figure 7-12, the program displays the four original values, then passes each to the `tripleTheValue()` method, where it is displayed, multiplied by 3, and displayed again. After the method executes four times, the logic returns to the main program where the four values are displayed again, showing that they are unchanged by the new assignments within `tripleTheValue()`. The `oneVal` variable is local to the `tripleTheValue()` method; therefore, any changes to it are not permanent and are not reflected in the array declared in the main program. Each `oneVal` variable in the `tripleTheValue()` method holds only a copy of the array element passed into the method, and the `oneVal` variable that holds each newly assigned, larger value exists only while the `tripleTheValue()` method is executing.

Instead of passing a single array element to a method, you can pass an entire array as an argument. You can indicate that a method parameter must be an array by placing square brackets after the data type in the method's parameter list. When you pass an array to a method, changes you make to array elements within the method are permanent; that is, they are reflected in the original array that was sent to the method. Arrays, unlike simple built-in types, are **passed by reference**; that is, the method receives the actual memory address of the array and has access to the actual values in the array elements.

> **» NOTE** The name of an array represents a memory address, and the subscript used with an array name represents an offset from that address.

> **» NOTE** Simple nonarray variables usually are passed to methods by value. Many programming languages provide the means to pass variables by reference as well as by value. The syntax to accomplish this differs among the languages that allow it; you will learn this technique when you study a specific language.

The program shown in Figure 7-13 creates an array of four numeric values. After the numbers are printed, the entire array is passed to a method named `quadrupleTheValues()`. Within the method header, the parameter is declared as an array by using square brackets after the parameter type. Within the method the numbers are printed, which shows that they retain their values from the main program upon entering the method; then the array values are multiplied by 4. Even though `quadrupleTheValues()` returns nothing to the calling program, when the program prints the array for the second time within the mainline logic, all of the values have been changed to their new quadruples values. Figure 7-14 shows an execution of the program. Because arrays are passed by reference, the `quadrupleTheValues()` method "knows" the address of the array declared in the calling program and makes its changes directly to the original array that was declared in the calling program.

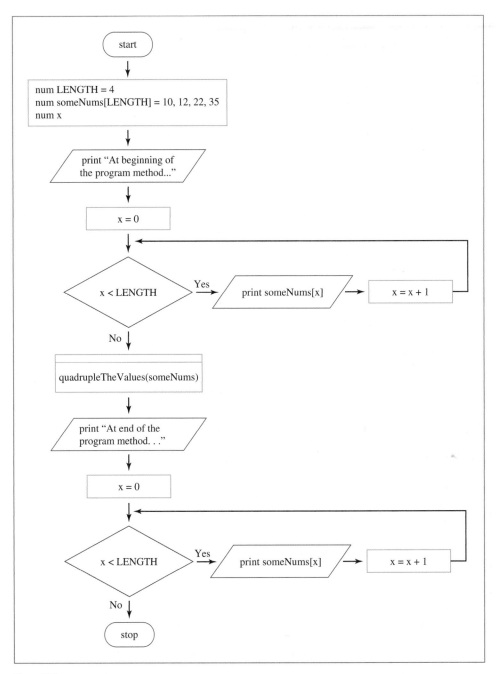

Figure 7-13 `PassEntireArray` program

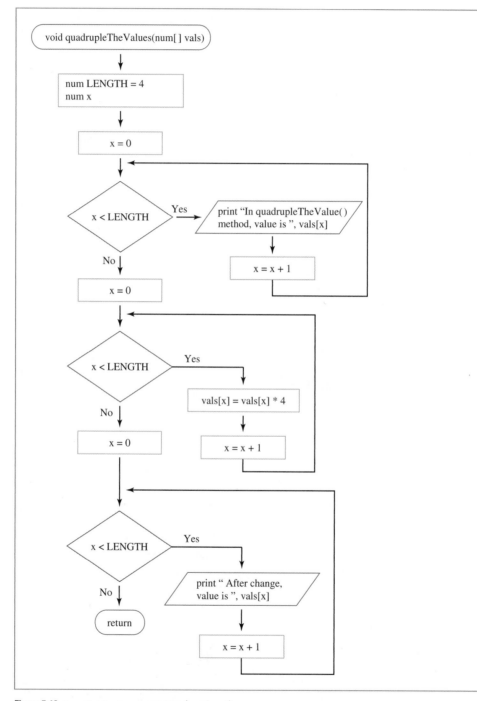

Figure 7-13 `PassEntireArray` program (*continued*)

```
start
   num LENGTH = 4
   num someNums[LENGTH] = 10, 12, 22, 35
   num x
   print "At beginning of main() method..."
   x = 0
   while x < LENGTH
      print someNums[x]
      x = x + 1
   endwhile
   quadrupleTheValues(someNums)
   print "At end of main() method..."
   x = 0
   while x < LENGTH
      print someNums[x]
      x = x + 1
   endwhile
stop

void quadrupleTheValues(num[] vals)
   num LENGTH = 4
   num x
   x = 0
   while x < LENGTH
      print "In quadrupleTheValues() method, value is ", vals[x]
      x = x + 1
   endwhile
   x = 0
   while x < LENGTH
      vals[x] = vals[x] * 4
      x = x + 1
   endwhile
   x = 0
   while x < LENGTH
      print "   After change, value is ", vals[x]
      x = x + 1
   endwhile
return
```

Figure 7-13 `PassEntireArray` program (*continued*)

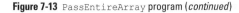

Figure 7-14 Output of the `PassEntireArray` program

>>**NOTE** In the `quadrupleTheValues()` method in Figure 7-13, if the language you are using supports it, you could use the built-in constant that holds an array's size instead of declaring and using LENGTH. For example, in Java, you could use `vals.length`. You learned about these built-in array constants in Chapter 6.

>>**NOTE** When an array is a method parameter, the square brackets in the method header remain empty and do not hold a size. The array name that is passed is a memory address that indicates the start of the array. Depending on the language you are using, you can control the values you use for a subscript to the array in different ways. In some languages, you might also want to pass a constant that indicates the array size to the method. In other languages, you can access the automatically created length field for the array. Either way, the array size itself is never implied in the array name. The array name only indicates the starting point from which subscripts will be used.

TWO TRUTHS AND A LIE:
PASSING AN ARRAY TO A METHOD

1. You can pass an entire array as a method's argument.

2. You can indicate that a method parameter must be an array by placing square brackets after the data type in the method's parameter list.

3. Arrays, unlike simple built-in types, are passed by value; that is, the method receives a copy of the original array.

The false statement is #3. Arrays, unlike simple built-in types, are passed by reference; that is, the method receives the actual memory address of the array and has access to the actual values in the array elements.

OVERLOADING METHODS

In programming, **overloading** involves supplying diverse meanings for a single identifier. When you use the English language, you frequently overload words. When you say, "break a window," "break bread," "break the bank," and "take a break," you describe four very different actions that use different methods and produce different results. However, anyone who speaks English fluently has no trouble comprehending your meaning because the "break" is understood in the context of the words that accompany it. In most programming languages, some operators are overloaded. For example, a + between two values indicates addition, but a single + to the left of a value means the value is positive. The + sign has different meanings based on the arguments used with it.

>>**NOTE** Overloading is used in modern, object-oriented programming languages such as C++, C#, Java, and Visual Basic. Overloading was not possible in older languages. Chapter 11 of the Comprehensive version of this book covers other object-oriented programming concepts.

>>**NOTE** Overloading a method is an example of **polymorphism**—the ability of a method to act appropriately depending on the context. Literally, *polymorphism* means "many forms."

When you **overload a method**, you write multiple methods with a shared name but different parameter lists. The language translator understands your meaning based on the arguments you use when you call the method. For example, suppose you create a method to print a message and the amount due on a customer's bill. The method receives a numeric parameter that represents the customer's balance and prints two lines of output. Figure 7-15 shows the method.

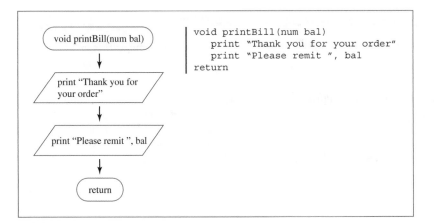

```
void printBill(num bal)
    print "Thank you for your order"
    print "Please remit ", bal
return
```

Figure 7-15 The `printBill()` method with a numeric parameter

Assume you need a method that is similar to `printBill()`, except the new method applies a discount to the customer's bill. One solution to this problem would be to write a new method with a different name, for example `printBillWithDiscount()`. A downside to this approach is that a programmer who uses your methods must remember the different names you gave to each slightly different version. It is more natural for your methods' clients to be able to use a single well-designed method name for the task of printing bills, but to be able to provide different arguments as appropriate. In this case, you can overload the `printBill()` method so that besides the version that takes a single numeric argument, you can create a version that takes two numeric arguments—one that represents the balance and the other that represents the discount rate. Figure 7-16 shows this version of the method.

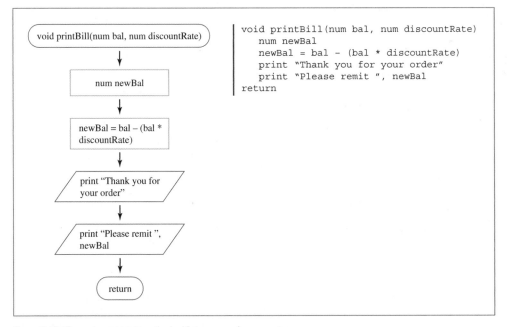

```
void printBill(num bal, num discountRate)
    num newBal
    newBal = bal - (bal * discountRate)
    print "Thank you for your order"
    print "Please remit ", newBal
return
```

Figure 7-16 The `printBill()` method with two numeric parameters

If both versions of `printBill()` are included in a program and you call the method using a single numeric argument, as in `printBill(custBalance)`, then the first version of the method (Figure 7-15) executes. If you use two numeric arguments in the call, as in `printBill(custBalance, rate)`, then the second version of the method (Figure 7-16) executes.

If it suited your needs, you could provide more versions of the `printBill()` method, as shown in Figures 7-17 and 7-18. The version in Figure 7-17 accepts a numeric parameter that holds the customer's balance, and a string parameter that holds an additional message that can be customized for the bill recipient and displayed on the bill. For example, if a program makes a method call such as the following, then the `printBill()` version in Figure 7-17 will execute: `printBill(custBal, "Due in 10 days")`.

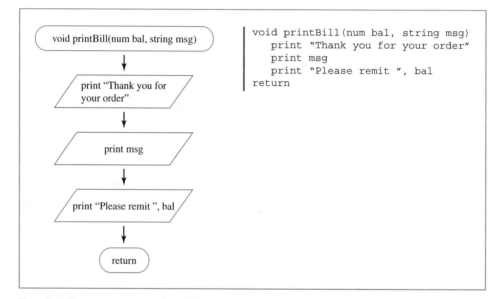

Figure 7-17 The `printBill()` method with a numeric parameter and a string parameter

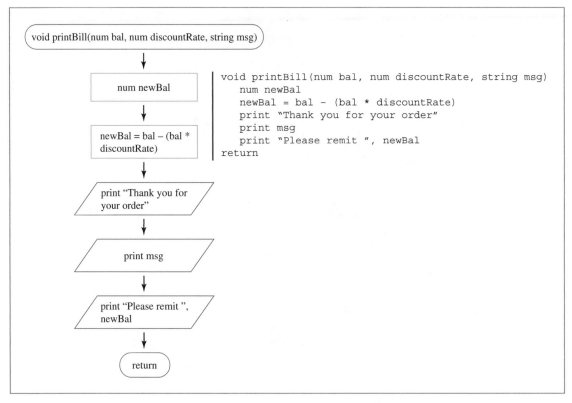

```
void printBill(num bal, num discountRate, string msg)
   num newBal
   newBal = bal - (bal * discountRate)
   print "Thank you for your order"
   print msg
   print "Please remit ", newBal
return
```

Figure 7-18 The `printBill()` method with two numeric parameters and a string parameter

In the version in Figure 7-18, `printBill()` accepts three parameters, providing a balance, discount rate, and customized message. For example, the following method call would use this version of the method:

```
printBill(balanceDue, discountRate, specialMessage)
```

Overloading methods is never required in a program. Instead, you could create multiple methods with unique identifiers such as `printBill()` and `printBillWithDiscountAndMessage()`. Overloading methods does not reduce the work you do when creating a program; you need to write each method individually. The advantage is provided to your method's clients; those that use your methods need to remember just one appropriate name for all related tasks.

>> **NOTE** Even though you have written two or more overloaded versions of a method, many program clients will use just one version. For example, suppose you create a bill-creating program that contains all four versions of the `printBill()` method just discussed, and then sell it to different companies. Any one organization that adopts your program and its methods might only want to use one or two versions of the method. You probably own many devices where only some of the features are meaningful to you; for example, many people who own microwave ovens only use the Popcorn button or never use Defrost.

>> **NOTE** In many programming languages, the `print` statement is actually an overloaded method that you call. It is convenient that you use a single name, such as `print`, whether you want to print a number, a `string`, or any combination of the two.

TWO TRUTHS AND A LIE:
OVERLOADING METHODS

1. In programming, overloading involves supplying diverse meanings for a single identifier.

2. When you overload a method, you write multiple methods with different names but identical parameter lists.

3. A method can be overloaded as many times as you want.

The false statement is #2. When you overload a method, you write methods with a shared name but different parameter lists.

AVOIDING AMBIGUOUS METHODS

When you overload a method, you run the risk of creating **ambiguous methods**—a situation in which the compiler cannot determine which method to use. Every time you call a method, the compiler decides whether a suitable method exists; if so, the method executes, and if not, you receive an error message. For example, suppose you write two versions of a `printBill()` method, as in the program in Figure 7-19. One version of the method is intended to accept a customer balance and a discount rate, and the other is intended to accept a customer balance and a discount amount expressed in dollars.

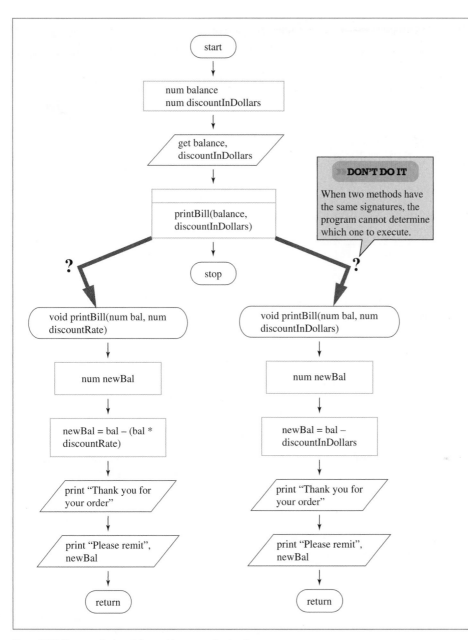

Figure 7-19 Program that contains ambiguous method call

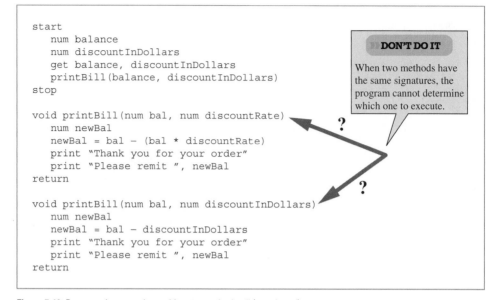

```
start
    num balance
    num discountInDollars
    get balance, discountInDollars
    printBill(balance, discountInDollars)
stop

void printBill(num bal, num discountRate)
    num newBal
    newBal = bal - (bal * discountRate)
    print "Thank you for your order"
    print "Please remit ", newBal
return

void printBill(num bal, num discountInDollars)
    num newBal
    newBal = bal - discountInDollars
    print "Thank you for your order"
    print "Please remit ", newBal
return
```

> **DON'T DO IT**
>
> When two methods have the same signatures, the program cannot determine which one to execute.

Figure 7-19 Program that contains ambiguous method call (*continued*)

> **» NOTE**
> An overloaded method is not ambiguous on its own—it becomes ambiguous only if you create an ambiguous situation. A program with potentially ambiguous methods will run without problems if you make no ambiguous method calls.

Each of the two versions of `printBill()` in Figure 7-19 is a valid method on its own. However, when the two versions exist in the same program, a problem arises. When the main program calls `printBill()` using two numeric arguments, the compiler cannot determine which version to call. Even though you could argue that the argument name `discountInDollars` in the main program implies that the second version of the method that uses the same parameter name should be called, the compiler makes no such assumptions. The compiler determines which version of a method to call based on argument data types only, not their identifiers. Because both versions of the method accept two numeric parameters, an error occurs and program execution stops.

Methods can be overloaded correctly by providing different parameter lists for methods with the same name. Methods with identical names that have identical parameter lists but different return types are not overloaded—they are illegal. For example, the following two methods cannot coexist within a program.

```
string aMethod(num x)
numeric aMethod(num y)
```

The compiler determines which of several versions of a method to call based on parameter lists. When the method call `aMethod(17)` is made, the compiler will not know which of the two methods to execute because both possibilities take a numeric argument.

> **» NOTE** All the popular object-oriented programming languages support multiple numeric data types. For example, Java, C#, C++, and Visual Basic all support integer (whole number) data types that are different from floating-point (decimal place) data types. Many languages have even more specialized numeric types, such as signed and unsigned. Methods that accept different specific types are correctly overloaded.

USING PREWRITTEN BUILT-IN METHODS

All modern programming languages contain many methods that have already been written for you. Methods are built into a language to save you time and effort. For example, in most languages, printing a message on the screen involves using a built-in method. When you want to display "Hello" on the command prompt screen in C#, you write the following:

```
Console.WriteLine("Hello");
```

In Java, you write:

```
System.out.println("Hello");
```

In these statements, you can recognize `WriteLine()` and `println()` as method names because they are followed by parentheses; the parentheses hold an argument that represents the message that is displayed. If these methods were not written for you, you would have to worry about the low-level details of how to manipulate pixels on a display screen to get the characters to print. Instead, by using the prewritten methods, you can concentrate on the higher level task of displaying a useful and appropriate message.

> **» NOTE** In C#, the convention is to begin method names with an uppercase letter, and in Java, the convention is to begin them with a lowercase letter. The `WriteLine()` and `println()` methods follow their respective language's convention.

> **» NOTE** The `WriteLine()` and `println()` methods are both overloaded methods. For example, if you pass a string to either method, the version of the method that can display it correctly is called, and if you pass a number, another version that can display it correctly is called. Several versions of each method exist.

Most programming languages also contain a variety of mathematical methods such as those that compute a square root or the absolute value of a number. Other methods perform tasks, such as retrieving the current date and time from the operating system or selecting a random number for you to use in a game application. These methods were written as a convenience for you—computing a square root and generating random numbers are complicated tasks, so it is convenient to have methods already written and tested and available to you when you need them. The names of the methods that perform these functions differ among programming languages, so you need to research the language's documentation to use them. For example, many of a language's methods are described in introductory programming language textbooks, and you can also find language documentation online.

When you want to use a prewritten, built-in method, you should know these four things:

» What the method does in general—for example, compute a square root

» The method's name—for example, it might be `sqrt()`

» The method's required parameters—for example, a square root method might require a single numeric parameter. There might be multiple overloaded versions of the method from which you can choose.

» The method's return type—for example, a square root method most likely returns a numeric value that is the square root of the argument that was passed to the method.

What you do not need to know is how the method is implemented; that is, how the instruction statements are written within it. Built-in methods are usually black boxes to you. You can use built-in methods without worrying about their low-level implementation details.

TWO TRUTHS AND A LIE:
USING PREWRITTEN BUILT-IN METHODS

1. The name of a method that performs a specific function (such as generating a random number) is likely to be different in various programming languages.

2. When you want to use a prewritten, built-in method, you should know what the method does in general, its name, required parameters, and return type.

3. When you want to use a prewritten, built-in method, you should know how the method is implemented.

The false answer is #3. You do not need to know a method's low-level implementation details to be able to use it effectively.

USING AN IPO CHART

When designing modules to use within larger programs, some programmers find it helpful to use an **IPO chart**, a tool that identifies and categorizes each item needed within the module as pertaining to input, processing, or output. For example, consider a module that finds the smallest of three numeric values. When you start to think about designing this module, you can start by placing each of the module's components in one of the three processing categories, as shown in Figure 7-20.

Input	Processing	Output
First value	If the first value is smaller than each of the other	Smallest value
Second value	two, save it as the smallest value; otherwise if the	
Third value	second value is smaller than the third, save it as	
	the smallest value; otherwise save the third value	
	as the smallest value	

Figure 7-20 IPO chart for the module that finds the smallest of three numeric values

The IPO chart in Figure 7-20 provides you with an overview of the processing steps involved in the module. Like a flowchart or pseudocode, an IPO chart is just another tool to help you plan the logic of your programs. Many programmers create an IPO chart only for specific modules in their programs and as an alternative to flowcharting or writing pseudocode. IPO charts provide an overview of input to the module, the processing steps that must occur, and the result. Figure 7-21 shows the flowchart and pseudocode of the resulting module.

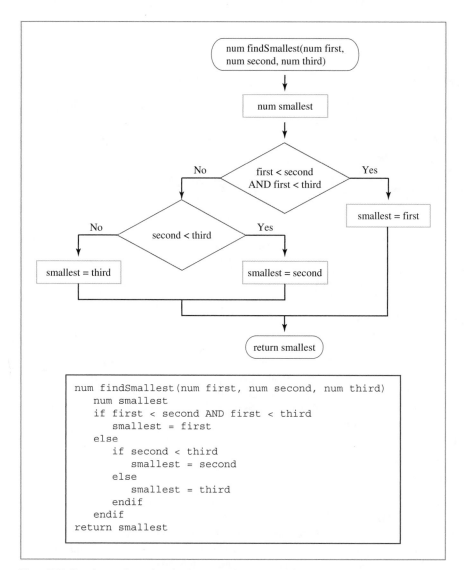

```
num findSmallest(num first, num second, num third)
   num smallest
   if first < second AND first < third
      smallest = first
   else
      if second < third
         smallest = second
      else
         smallest = third
      endif
   endif
return smallest
```

Figure 7-21 Flowchart and pseudocode of findSmallest() module

>>**NOTE** The `findSmallest()` module is similar to the `findLargest()` module described earlier in this chapter. Compare the two so you understand how they differ.

>>**NOTE** This book emphasizes creating flowcharts and pseudocode. You can find many more examples of IPO charts on the Web.

TWO TRUTHS AND A LIE:
USING AN IPO CHART

1. An IPO chart is a tool that identifies and categorizes each item needed within a module as pertaining to interest, printing, or organization.

2. An IPO chart provides you with an overview of the processing steps involved in a module.

3. An IPO chart is a tool to help you plan the logic of your programs, like a flowchart or pseudocode.

The false statement is #1. An IPO chart is a tool that identifies and categorizes each item needed within the module as pertaining to input, processing, or output.

REDUCING COUPLING AND INCREASING COHESION

When you begin to design computer programs, it is difficult to decide how much to put into a module. For example, a process that requires 40 instructions can be contained in a single module, two 20-instruction modules, 20 two-instruction modules, or any other combination. In most programming languages, any of these combinations is allowed. That is, you can write a program that will execute and produce correct results no matter how you divide the individual steps into modules. However, placing either too many or too few instructions in a single module makes a program harder to follow and reduces flexibility. When deciding how to organize your program steps into modules, you should adhere to two general rules:

» Reduce coupling.
» Increase cohesion.

REDUCING COUPLING

Coupling is a measure of the strength of the connection between two program modules; it is used to express the extent to which information is exchanged by subroutines. Coupling is either tight or loose, depending on how much one module depends on information from another. **Tight coupling**, which occurs when modules excessively depend on each other, makes programs more prone to errors. With tight coupling there are many data paths to keep track of, many chances for bad data to pass from one module to another, and many chances for one module to alter information needed by another module. **Loose coupling** occurs when modules do not depend on others. In general, you want to reduce coupling as much as possible because connections between modules make them more difficult to write, maintain, and reuse.

Imagine four cooks wandering in and out of the kitchen while preparing a stew. If each is allowed to add seasonings at will without the knowledge of the other cooks, you could end up with a culinary disaster. Similarly, if four payroll program modules are allowed to alter your gross pay figure "at will" without the "knowledge" of the other modules, you could end up with a financial disaster. A program in which several modules have access to your gross pay figure has modules that are tightly coupled. A superior program would control access to the payroll figure by limiting its passage to modules that need it.

You can evaluate whether coupling between modules is loose or tight by looking at the intimacy between modules and the number of parameters that are passed between them.

» Tight coupling—The least intimate situation is one in which modules have access to the same globally defined variables; these modules have tight coupling. When one module changes the value stored in a variable, other modules are affected. Because you should avoid tight coupling, all the examples in this book avoid using global variables. However, be aware that you might see them used in programs written by others.

» Loose coupling—The most intimate way to share data is to pass a copy of needed variables from one module to another. That way, the sharing of data is always purposeful— variables must be explicitly passed to and from modules that use them. The loosest (best) subroutines and methods pass single arguments rather than many variables or entire records, if possible.

INCREASING COHESION

Analyzing coupling lets you see how modules connect externally with other modules and programs. You also want to analyze a module's **cohesion**, which refers to how the internal statements of a module or subroutine serve to accomplish the module's purposes. In highly cohesive modules, all the operations are related, or "go together." Such modules are usually more reliable than those that have low cohesion; they are considered stronger, and they make programs easier to write, read, and maintain.

Functional cohesion occurs when all operations in a module contribute to the performance of only one task. Functional cohesion is the highest level of cohesion; you should strive for it in all methods you write. For example, a module that calculates gross pay appears in Figure 7-22. The module receives two parameters, `hours` and `rate`, and computes gross pay, including time-and-a-half for overtime. The functional cohesion of this module is high because each of its instructions contributes to one task—computing gross pay. If you can write a sentence describing what a module does, using only two words—for example, "Compute gross," "Cube value," or "Print record"—the module is probably functionally cohesive.

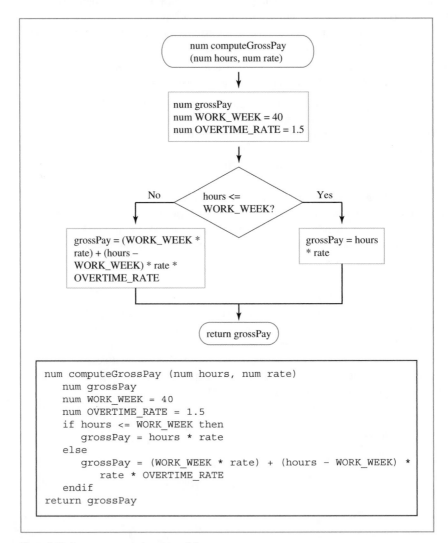

```
num computeGrossPay (num hours, num rate)
   num grossPay
   num WORK_WEEK = 40
   num OVERTIME_RATE = 1.5
   if hours <= WORK_WEEK then
      grossPay = hours * rate
   else
      grossPay = (WORK_WEEK * rate) + (hours - WORK_WEEK) *
         rate * OVERTIME_RATE
   endif
return grossPay
```

Figure 7-22 A `computeGrossPay()` module

You might work in a programming environment that has a rule such as "No module will be longer than can be printed on one page" or "No module will have more than 30 lines of code." The rule maker is trying to achieve more cohesion, but this is an arbitrary way of going about it. It's possible for a two-line module to have low cohesion and—although less likely—for a 40-line module to have high cohesion. Because good, functionally cohesive modules perform only one task, they tend to be short. However, the issue is not size. If it takes 20 statements to perform one task within a module, then the module is still cohesive.

If you sense that a module you have written has only procedural cohesion (that is, it consists of a series of steps that use unrelated data), you probably want to turn it into a **dispatcher module**. You accomplish this by changing the module so that, instead of performing many different types of tasks, it calls other modules in which the diverse tasks take place. Each of the new modules can be functionally, sequentially, or communicatively cohesive. **Logical cohesion** takes place when a member module performs one or more tasks depending on a decision, whether the decision is in the form of a `case` structure or a series of `if` statements. The actions performed might go together logically (that is, perform the same type of action), but they don't work on the same data. Like a module that has procedural cohesion, a module that has only logical cohesion should probably be turned into a dispatcher.

Most programmers do not think about cohesion on a day-to-day basis. In other words, they do not tend to say, "My, this program is cohesive." Rather, they develop a "feel" for what types of tasks rightfully belong together, and for which subsets of tasks should be diverted to their own modules.

Additionally, there is a time and a place for shortcuts. If you need a result from spreadsheet data in a hurry, you can type two values and take a sum rather than creating a formula with proper cell references. If a memo must go out in five minutes, you don't have to change fonts or add clip art with your word processor. Similarly, if you need a quick programming result, you might very well use cryptic variable names, tight coupling, and minimal cohesion. When you create a professional application, however, you should keep professional guidelines in mind.

TWO TRUTHS AND A LIE:
REDUCING COUPLING AND INCREASING COHESION

1. You should try to avoid tight coupling, which occurs when modules excessively depend on each other.

2. You should try to avoid loose coupling, which occurs when modules do not depend on others.

3. Functional cohesion occurs when all operations in a module contribute to the performance of only one task.

The false statement is #2. You should aim for loose coupling so that modules are independent.

CHAPTER SUMMARY

» A method is a program module that contains a series of statements that carry out a task. Any program can contain an unlimited number of methods, and each method can be called an unlimited number of times. The simplest methods you can invoke don't require any data items (called arguments or parameters) to be sent to them, nor do they send any data back to you (called returning a value). When you create methods, the calling method is easier to follow because it is more abstract. Additionally, methods are easily reusable. A method must include a declaration (or header or definition), a body, and a return statement that marks the end of the method.

» The variables and constants declared in any method are useable only within that method. That is, data items are local to, visible, or in scope only within the method in which they are declared. Besides local variables and constants, you can create global variables and constants that are known to multiple methods, but, in general, this is not a recommended practice because it violates the programming principle of encapsulation, which states that a method's instructions and its data should be contained in the same method.

» Some methods require information to be passed in. A calling method sends an argument to a called method. A called method accepts the value as its parameter. Passing arguments supports implementation hiding, which is the encapsulation of method details. When you write the method declaration for a method that can receive a parameter, you must declare the parameter type and a local identifier for the parameter within the method declaration parentheses. A variable passed into a method is passed by value; that is, a copy of its value is sent to the method and stored in a new memory location accessible to the method.

» You indicate that a method requires multiple arguments by listing their data types and local identifiers within the method header's parentheses. You can pass multiple arguments to a called method by listing the arguments within the method call and separating them with commas. When you call a method, the arguments you send to a method must match in order—both in number and in type—the arguments listed in the method declaration.

» When a method returns a value, the method must have a return type. A method's return type is known more succinctly as a method's type and is indicated in front of the method name when the method is defined. When a method returns a value, you usually want to use it in the calling method (although using it is not required).

» You can pass a single array element to a method in exactly the same manner as you would pass a variable or constant. Additionally, you can pass an entire array as a method. You can indicate that a method parameter must be an array by placing square brackets after the data type in the method's parameter list. When you pass an array to a method, it is passed by reference; that is, the method receives the actual memory address of the array and has access to the actual values in the array elements.

» When you overload a method, you write multiple methods with a shared name but different parameter lists. The compiler understands your meaning based on the arguments you use when you call the method.

» Overloading a method introduces the risk of creating ambiguous methods—a situation in which the compiler cannot determine which method to use. Every time you call a method, the compiler decides whether a suitable method exists; if so, the method executes, and if not, you receive an error message. Methods can be overloaded correctly by providing different parameter lists for methods with the same name.

» All modern programming languages contain many methods that have already been written for you. Methods are built into a language to save you time and effort.

» Some programmers design an IPO chart for some of the modules they create. An IPO chart is a tool that identifies and categorizes each item needed within the module as pertaining to input, processing, or output.

» When writing modules, you should strive to achieve loose coupling and high cohesion.

KEY TERMS

A **method** is a program module that contains a series of statements that carry out a task.

A method's **header** includes the method identifier and possibly other necessary identifying information.

A method's **body** contains all the statements in the method.

A method's **return statement** marks the end of the method and identifies the point at which control returns to the calling method.

Arguments are data items that are sent to methods.

Returning a value is the process whereby a called module sends a value to its calling module.

Variables and constants declared within a method are **in scope** only within that method.

Local variables are declared within each module that uses them.

Parameters are the data items received by methods.

Implementation hiding is a programming principle that describes the encapsulation of method details.

The **interface to a method** includes the method's return type, name, and arguments. It is the part that a client sees and uses.

A method's **client** is a program or other method that uses the method.

Programmers refer to hidden implementation details as existing in a **black box**.

A variable passed into a method is **passed by value**; that is, a copy of its value is sent to the method and stored in a new memory location accessible to the method.

A **parameter list** is all the data types and parameter names that appear in a method header.

Actual parameters are the arguments in a method call.

Formal parameters are the variables in the method declaration that accept the values from the actual parameters.

A method's **signature** includes its name and argument list.

A method's **return type** is the data type for any value it returns.

A **void method** returns no value.

A method's return type is known more succinctly as a **method's type**.

Overhead refers to all the resources and times required by an operation.

When an item is **passed by reference to a method**, the method receives the actual memory address item. Arrays are passed by reference.

Overloading involves supplying diverse meanings for a single identifier.

Polymorphism is the ability of a method to act appropriately depending on the context.

When you **overload a method**, you create multiple versions with the same name but different parameter lists.

Ambiguous methods are those that the compiler cannot distinguish because they have the same name and parameter types.

An **IPO chart** is a tool that identifies and categorizes each item needed within the module as pertaining to input, processing, or output.

Coupling is a measure of the strength of the connection between two program modules.

Tight coupling occurs when modules excessively depend on each other; it makes programs more prone to errors.

Loose coupling occurs when modules do not depend on others.

Cohesion is a measure of how the internal statements of a module or subroutine serve to accomplish the module's purposes.

Functional cohesion occurs when all operations in a module contribute to the performance of only one task. Functional cohesion is the highest level of cohesion; you should strive for it in all methods you write.

A **dispatcher module** is one that calls other modules in which diverse tasks take place.

Logical cohesion takes place when a member module performs one or more tasks depending on a decision.

REVIEW QUESTIONS

1. **Which of the following is true?**

   a. A program can call, at most, one method.

   b. A program can contain a method that calls another method.

   c. A method can contain one or more other methods.

   d. All of these are true.

2. **Which of the following must every method have?**

   a. a header

   b. a parameter list

   c. a return value

   d. All of these

3. **Which of the following is most closely related to the concept of "local"?**

   a. abstract

   b. object-oriented

   c. in scope

   d. program level

4. **Although the terms parameter and arguments are closely related, the difference between them is that "argument" refers to _____ .**

   a. a passed constant

   b. a value in a method call

   c. a formal parameter

   d. a variable that is local to a method

5. **The notion of _____ most closely describes the way a calling method is not aware of the statements within a called method.**

   a. abstraction

   b. object-oriented

   c. implementation hiding

   d. encapsulation

6. **A method's interface is its _____ .**

   a. signature

   b. return type

   c. identifier

   d. parameter list

7. **When you write the method declaration for a method that can receive a parameter, which of the following must be included in the method declaration?**

   a. the name of the argument that will be used to call the method

   b. a local name for the parameter

   c. the return value for the method

   d. All of these

8. **When you use a variable name in a method call, it _____ the same name as the variable in the method header.**

   a. can have

   b. cannot have

   c. must have

   d. must not have

9. **Assume you have written a method with the header `void myMethod(num a, string b)`. Which of the following is a correct method call?**

   a. `myMethod(12)`

   b. `myMethod(12, "Hello")`

   c. `myMethod("Goodbye")`

   d. It is impossible to tell.

10. Assume you have written a method with the header `num yourMethod(string name, num code)`. The method's type is _____.

   a. `num`

   b. `string`

   c. `num and string`

   d. `void`

11. Assume you have written a method with the header `string myMethod(num score, string grade)`. Also assume you have declared a numeric variable named `test`. Which of the following is a correct method call?

   a. `myMethod()`

   b. `myMethod(test)`

   c. `myMethod(test, test)`

   d. `myMethod(test, "A")`

12. The value used in a method's `return` statement must _____.

   a. be numeric

   b. be a variable

   c. match the data type used before the method name in the header

   d. Two of the above

13. When a method receives a copy of the value stored in an argument used in the method call, it means the variable was _____.

   a. unnamed

   b. passed by value

   c. passed by reference

   d. assigned its original value when it was declared

14. A `void` method _____.

   a. contains no statements

   b. requires no parameters

   c. returns nothing

   d. has no name

15. When an array is passed to a method, it is _____.

   a. passed by reference

   b. passed by value

   c. unnamed in the method

   d. unalterable in the method

16. **When you overload a method, you write multiple methods with the same _____.**

    a. name

    b. parameter list

    c. number of parameters

    d. return type

17. **A program contains a method with the header** `numeric calculateTaxes(num amount, string name)`. **Which of the following methods can coexist in the same program with no possible ambiguity?**

    a. `num calculateTaxes(string name, num amount)`

    b. `string calculateTaxes(num money, string taxpayer)`

    c. `num calculateTaxes(num annualPay, string taxpayerId)`

    d. All of these can coexist without ambiguity.

18. **Methods in the same program with identical names and identical parameter lists are _____.**

    a. overloaded

    b. overworked

    c. overwhelmed

    d. illegal

19. **Methods in different programs with identical names and identical parameter lists are _____.**

    a. overloaded

    b. illegal

    c. both of these

    d. none of these

20. **Programmers should strive to _____.**

    a. increase coupling

    b. increase cohesion

    c. both of the above

    d. neither a nor b

FIND THE BUGS

The following pseudocode contains one or more bugs that you must find and correct.

1. **The main program calls a method that prompts the user for a name and returns it.**

```
start
    string usersName
    user = askUserForName()
    print "Your name is ", user
stop

string askUserForNames()
    num name
    print "Please type your name "
    read name
return name
```

2. **The main program passes a user's entry to a method that displays a multiplication table using the entered value. The table includes the value multiplied by every value from 2 through 10.**

```
start
    num usersChoice
    print "Enter a number"
    read usersChoice
    multiplicationTable(choice)
stop

void multiplicationTable(value)
    num LOW = 2
    num HIGH = 10
    num x
    x = LOW
    while x = HIGH
        answer = value * x
        print value, " times ", x, " is ", answer
        x = 1
    endwhile
return
```

3. **The main program prompts a user for a Social Security number, name, and income, and then computes tax. The tax calculation and the printing of the taxpayer's report are in separate modules. Tax rates are based on the following table:**

Income ($)	Tax rate (%)
0–14,999	0
15,000–21,999	15
22,000–39,999	18
40,000–69,999	22
70,000–99,999	28
100,000 and up	30

```
start
    string socSecNum
    string name
    num income
    num taxDue
    print "Enter Social Security number "
    read socSec
    while socSecNum not = 0
        print "Enter name "
        read name
        print "Enter annual income "
        read name
        taxCalculations()
        print taxReport(socSecNum, taxDue)
        print "Enter Social Security number or 0 to quit "
        read socSecNum
    endwhile
stop

void taxCalculations(num income)
    num tax
    const num NUMBRKTS = 5
    num brackets[NUMBRAKTS] = 15000, 22000, 40000,
        70000, 100000
    num rates[NUMBRKTS] = 0, 0.15, 0.18, 0.22, 0.28, 0.30
    while count < NUMBRKTS AND income > brackets[count]
        count = count + 1
    endwhile
    tax = income * rates
return tax

void taxReport(string socSecNum, string name, num taxDue)
    print socSecNum, name, tax
return tax
```

EXERCISES

1. **Create an IPO chart for each of the following modules:**

   a. The module that produces your paycheck

   b. The module that calculates your semester tuition bill

   c. The module that calculates your monthly car payment

2. **Create the logic for a program that calculates and displays the amount of money you would have if you invested $1,000 at 5 percent interest for one year. Create a separate method to do the calculation and return the result to be displayed.**

3a. **Create the logic for a program that calculates the due date for a bill as follows:**

   Prompt the user for the month, day, and year a bill is received. Calculate the day the bill is due to be paid as one month later. Print each date by, in turn, passing its month, day, and year to a method that displays them with slashes between the parts of the date—for example, 6/24/2009.

3b. **Modify the date displaying method so it displays each date using a string for the month—for example, June 24, 2009.**

4a. **Create the logic for a program that performs arithmetic functions.**

   Design the program to contain two numeric variables. Prompt the user for values for the variables. Pass both variables to methods named sum() and difference(). Create the logic for the methods sum() and difference(); they compute the sum of and difference between the values of two arguments, respectively. Each method should perform the appropriate computation and display the results.

4b. **Add a method named product() to the program in Exercise 4a. The product() method should compute the result when multiplying two numbers, but not display the answer. Instead, it should return the answer to the calling program, which displays the answer.**

5. **Create the logic for a program that continuously prompts the user for a numeric number of dollars until the user enters 0. Pass each entered amount to a conversion method that displays breakdown of the passed amount into the fewest bills; in other words, it calculates the number of 20s, 10s, 5s, and 1s needed.**

6. **Create the logic for a program that continuously prompts a user for a numeric value until the user enters 0. The application passes the value in turn to a method that squares the number and to a method that cubes the number. The program prints the results before reprompting the user. Create the two methods that respectively square and cube a number that is passed to them, returning the calculated value.**

7. Create the logic for a program that calls a method that computes the final price for a sales transaction. The program contains variables that hold the price of an item, the salesperson's commission expressed as a percentage, and the customer discount, expressed as a percentage. Create a `calculatePrice()` method that determines the final price and returns the value to the calling method. The `calculatePrice()` method requires three arguments: product price, salesperson commission rate, and customer discount rate. A product's final price is the original price plus the commission amount minus the discount amount; the customer discount is taken as a percentage of the total price after the salesperson commission has been added to the original price.

8. Create the logic for a program that prompts the user for two numeric values that represent the sides of a rectangle. Include two overloaded methods that compute a rectangle's area. One method takes two numeric parameters and calculates the area by multiplying the parameters. The other takes a single numeric parameter, which is squared to calculate area. Each method displays its calculated result. If the user enters two positive nonzero numbers, call the method version that accepts two parameters. If the user enters only one value that is positive and nonzero, call the version of the method that accepts just one parameter. If the user enters two values that both are zero or negative, display an error message.

9a. Plan the logic for an insurance company's premium-determining program.

The program calls a method that prompts the user for the type of policy needed—health or auto. Pass the user's response to a second method, where the premium is set—$250 for a health policy or $175 for an auto policy. Pass the premium amount to a third module for printing.

9b. Modify Exercise 9a so that the second method calls one of two additional methods— one that determines the health premium or one that determines the auto premium. The health insurance method asks users whether they smoke; the premium is $250 for smokers and $190 for nonsmokers. The auto insurance method asks users to enter the number of traffic tickets they have received in the last three years. The premium is $175 for those with three or more tickets, $140 for those with one or two tickets, and $95 for those with no tickets. Each of these two methods returns the premium amount to the second method, which sends the premium amount to the printing module.

10. **Plan the logic for a program that prompts a user for a customer number, stock number of item being ordered, and quantity ordered.**

If the customer number is not between 1000 and 7999, inclusive, continue to prompt until a valid customer number is entered. If the stock number of the item is not between 201 and 850, inclusive, continue to prompt for the stock number. Pass the stock number to a method that a colleague at your organization has written; the module's signature is `num getPrice(num stockNumber)`. The `getPrice()` module accepts a stock number and returns the price of the item. Multiply the price by the quantity ordered, giving the total due. Pass the customer number and the calculated price to an already written method whose signature is `printBill(num custNum, num price)`. This method determines the customer's name and address by using the customer ID number, and calculates the final bill, including tax, using the price. Organize your program using as many modules as you feel are appropriate. You do not need to write the `getPrice()` and `printBill()` modules—assume they have already been written.

11. **Create the logic for a program that computes weekly salary.**

Include two overloaded methods named `computeWeeklySalary()`. One version accepts an annual salary as a number and calculates weekly salary as 1/52 of the annual amount. The other accepts a number of hours worked per week and an hourly pay rate and calculates weekly salary as a product of the two. Each returns the weekly salary to the calling program. The main program prompts the user for the type of calculation to perform, and based on the user's response, prompts for appropriate data, calls the correct method, and displays the result.

12. **Create the logic for a program that prompts a user for three numbers and stores them in an array. Pass the array to a method that reverses the order of the numbers. Display the reversed numbers in the main program.**

13. **Create the logic for a program that prompts a user for 10 numbers and stores them in an array. Pass the array to a method that calculates the arithmetic average of the numbers and returns the value to the calling program. Display each number and how far it is from the arithmetic average. Continue to prompt the user for additional sets of 10 numbers until the user indicates a desire to quit.**

14. **The Information Services Department at the Springfield Library has created modules with the following signatures:**

Signature	Description
`num getNumber(num high, num low)`	Prompts the user for a number. Continues to prompt until the number falls between designated high and low limits. Returns a valid number.
`string getCharacter()`	Prompts the user for a character string and returns the entered string.
`num lookUpISBN(string title)`	Accepts the title of a book and returns the ISBN. Returns a 0 if the book cannot be found.
`string lookUpTitle(num isbn)`	Accepts the ISBN of a book and returns a title. Returns a space character if the book cannot be found.
`string isBookAvailable(num isbn)`	Accepts an ISBN, searches the library database, and returns a "Y" or "N" indicating whether the book is currently available.

a. Design an interactive program that does the following, using the prewritten modules wherever they are appropriate.

» Prompt the user for and read a library card number, which must be between 1000 and 9999.

» Prompt the user for and read a search option—1 to search for a book by ISBN, 2 to search for a book by title, and 3 to quit. Allow no other values to be entered.

» While the user does not enter 3, prompt for an ISBN or title based on the user's previous selection. If the user enters an ISBN, get and display the book's title and ask for confirmation—a "Y" or "N" as to whether the title is correct.

» If the user has entered a valid ISBN, or a title that matches a valid ISBN, check whether the book is available, and display an appropriate message for the user.

» The user can continue to search for books until he or she enters 3 as the search option.

b. Develop the logic that implements each of the modules in Exercise 14a.

GAME ZONE

1. Create the logic for an application that contains an array of five multiple-choice quiz questions related to the topic of your choice. Each question contains four answer choices. Also create a parallel array that holds the correct answer to each question—A, B, C, or D. In turn, pass each question to a method that displays the question, and accepts the player's answer. If the player does not enter a valid answer choice, force the player to reenter the answer. Return the valid answer to the main program. After the answer is returned to the main program, pass it and the correct answer to a method that determines whether they are equal and displays an appropriate message. After the user answers all the questions, display the number of correct and incorrect answers.

2. In the Game Zone section of Chapter 6, you designed the logic for the game Hangman, in which the user guesses letters in a hidden word. Improve the game to store an array of 10 words. One at a time, pass each to a method that allows the user to continuously guess a letter until all the letters in the word are correctly guessed. The method returns the number of guesses it took to complete the word. Store the number in an array before returning to the method for the next word. After all 10 words have been guessed, display a summary of the number of guesses it took for each word as well as the average number of guesses per word.

DETECTIVE WORK

1. **What is beta testing?**

2. **Who is credited with inventing the subroutine?**

3. **In programming jargon, what is a method side effect?**

UP FOR DISCUSSION

1. One of the advantages to writing a program that is subdivided into methods is that such a structure allows different programmers to write separate methods, thus dividing the work. Would you prefer to write a large program by yourself, or to work on a team in which each programmer produces one or more modules? Why?

2. In this chapter, you learned that hidden implementations are often said to exist in a black box. What are the advantages and disadvantages to this approach in both programming and real life?

3. As a professional programmer, you might never write an entire program. Instead, you might be asked to write only specific modules that are destined to become part of a larger system. Explain why or why not this is appealing to you.

CONTROL BREAKS

In this chapter you will:

Learn about control break logic
Perform single-level control breaks
Use control data within a heading
Use control data within a footer
Perform control breaks with totals
Perform multiple-level control breaks

UNDERSTANDING CONTROL BREAK LOGIC

A **control break** is a temporary detour in the logic of a program. In particular, programmers refer to a program as a **control break program** when a change in the value of a variable initiates special actions or causes special or unusual processing to occur. You usually write control break programs to organize output for programs that handle data records that are organized logically in groups based on the value in a field. As you read records, you examine the same field in each record, and when you encounter a record that contains a different value from the ones that preceded it, you perform a special action. If you have ever read a report that lists items in groups, with each group followed by a subtotal, then you have read a type of **control break report**. For example, you might generate a report that lists all company clients in order by state of residence, with a count of clients after each state's client list. See Figure 8-1 for an example of a report that breaks after each change in state.

Company Clients by State of Residence			
Name	City	State	
Albertson	Birmingham	Alabama	
Davis	Birmingham	Alabama	
Lawrence	Montgomery	Alabama	
		Count for Alabama	3
Smith	Anchorage	Alaska	
Young	Anchorage	Alaska	
Davis	Fairbanks	Alaska	
Mitchell	Juneau	Alaska	
Zimmer	Juneau	Alaska	
		Count for Alaska	5
Edwards	Phoenix	Arizona	
		Count for Arizona	1

Figure 8-1 A control break report with totals after each state

Other examples of control break reports produced by control break programs include:

» All employees listed in order by department number, with a new page started for each department

» All books for sale in a bookstore in order by category (such as reference or self-help), with a count following each category of book

» All items sold in order by date of sale, with a different ink color for each new month

Each of these reports shares two traits:

» The records used in each report are listed in order by a specific variable: department, state, category, or date.

» When that variable changes, the program takes special action: starts a new page, prints a count or total, or switches ink color.

To generate a control break report, your input records must be organized in sequential order based on the field that will cause the breaks. In other words, if you are going to write a program that produces a report that lists customers by state, like the one in Figure 8-1, then the records must be grouped by state before you begin processing. Frequently, grouping by state will mean placing the records in alphabetical order by state, although they could just as easily be placed in order by population, governor's name, or any other factor as long as all of one state's records are together. As you grow more proficient in programming logic, you will learn techniques for writing programs that sort records before using control break logic. Programs that **sort** records take records that are not in order and rearrange them to be in order according to the data in some field. For now, assume that a sorting program already has been used to presort your records before you begin the part of a program that determines control breaks. For example, if you are writing a program that uses a data file as input, this means that the records are stored on a device from which they can be accessed in order. As another example, if you are entering customer orders interactively from a stack of paper invoices, this means you have manually sorted the pieces of paper before starting data entry.

>> **NOTE** Chapter 9 of the Comprehensive version of this book describes sorting in detail. It is easier to work with sorted records than unsorted ones, so you are learning the easier technique of control break processing first.

>> **NOTE** In this chapter you will get to use many of the skills you gained from all the previous chapters. You will be creating useful reports while taking advantage of declaring variables and constants, using loops and nested decisions, passing arguments to and returning values from methods, and working with arrays. With some newer languages, such as SQL, the details of control breaks are handled automatically. Still, understanding how control break programs work improves your competence as a programmer.

TWO TRUTHS AND A LIE:
UNDERSTANDING CONTROL BREAK LOGIC

1. A control break program is one in which a change in the value of a variable initiates special actions or causes special or unusual processing to occur.

2. When a control break variable changes, the program takes special action.

3. To generate a control break report, your input records must be organized in sequential order based on the first field in the record.

The false statement is #3. Your input records must be organized in sequential order based on the field that will cause the breaks.

PERFORMING A SINGLE-LEVEL CONTROL BREAK

Employees by Department

Amy Abbott
Bernard Garza
Donald Travis

Mary Billings
Kendall Worthington

Michael Anderson
Zachary Darnell
May Ann Denton
Francis Nichols

Figure 8-2 Employees by department

> **NOTE**
> In the report in Figure 8-2, each section contains employees from a new department. Later in this chapter, department numbers will be added to each section, making the division clearer to those who read the report.

Suppose you want to print a list of employees with a line between each department. Figure 8-2 shows a sample report with the desired output—a simple list of employee names, with a separator between each department.

The basic logic of the program works like this: Each time you read an employee's name and department number from the input file, or enter them from the keyboard, you will determine whether the employee belongs to the same department as the previous employee. If so, you simply print the employee's name and read another record, without any special processing. If there are 20 employees in a department, these steps are repeated 20 times in a row—read an employee's data and print the employee's name. However, eventually you will read an employee's name that does not belong to the same department. At that point, before you print the employee's name from the new department, you must print a separating line. Then, you can proceed to read and print employee names that belong to the new department, and you continue to do so until the next time you encounter an employee in a different department. This type of program contains a **single-level control break**, a break in the logic of the program (pausing or detouring to print a separator) that is based on the value of a single variable (the department number).

> **NOTE**
> In many programming languages, before you can print a report you have to open a print file. Chapter 10 of the Comprehensive version of this text discusses file handling.

However, you must solve a slight problem before you can determine whether a new department has the same number as the previous department. When you read input data, you copy the data from an input device to temporary computer memory locations called variables. After they are input, the data items that represent name and department occupy specific physical locations in computer memory. For each new record that is read from an input device, new data must occupy the same positions in memory as the previous data occupied, and the previous set of data is lost. For example, if you read a record containing data for Donald Travis in Department 1, when you read the next record for Mary Billings in Department 2, "Mary Billings" replaces "Donald Travis" in a string variable, and 2 replaces 1 in a numeric variable. After you read a new record into memory, there is no way to look back at the previous record to determine whether that record had a different department number. The previous record's data has been replaced in memory by the new record's data.

The technique you must use to "remember" the old department number is to create a special variable, called a **control break field**, to hold the previous department number. With a control break field, every time you read a record and print it, you can also save the crucial part of the record that will signal the change or control the program break. In this case, you want to store the department number in this specially created variable. Comparing the new and old department-number values will determine when it is time to print the department-separating line.

Figure 8-3 shows the logic for the main program. Variables are declared for `name` and `department`. An additional variable that is named `oldDepartment` will serve as the control break field. The report title is stored in a named constant.

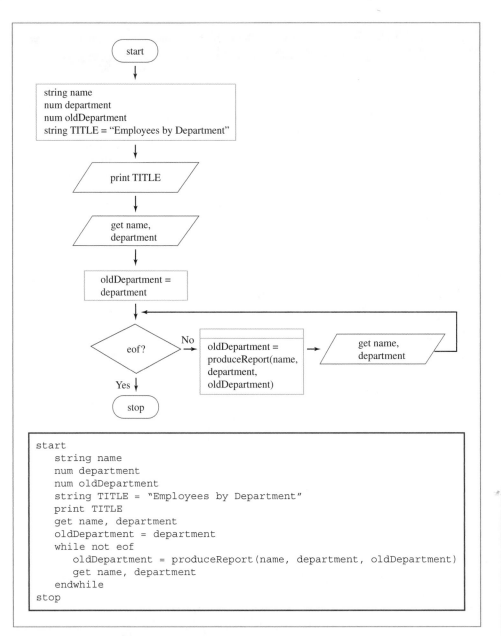

Figure 8-3 Main program logic for program that prints employees by department

NOTE
If the control break program in Figure 8-3 is interactive, then the step that gets the name and department would most likely be four steps—a prompt for the name, a statement to get the name, a prompt for the department, and a step to get the department.

In the logic in Figure 8-3, the report title is printed and then the first employee's name and department number are read into memory. Then, the department is copied to the oldDepartment variable. Note that it would be incorrect to initialize oldDepartment when it is declared. When you declare the variables at the beginning of the main program, you have not yet read the first record; therefore you don't know what the value of the first department will be. You might assume it is 1, and you might be right, but perhaps the first department is 2 or 10. You are assured of storing the correct first department number if you copy it from the first record.

The loop in the main program in Figure 8-3 performs just two tasks: it calls a method named produceReport() and it reads the next input record. You can tell from how the method is called in Figure 8-3 that the method must accept a string and two numeric variables, in that order. You can also tell that it must return a numeric value because the method's value is assigned to the numeric variable oldDepartment. The real "work" of the program is performed in the produceReport() module, which appears in Figure 8-4.

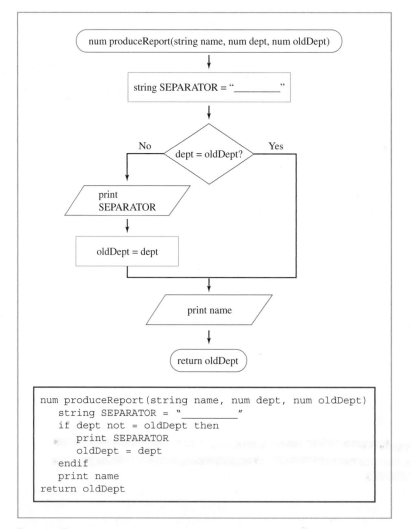

```
num produceReport(string name, num dept, num oldDept)
   string SEPARATOR = "_____"
   if dept not = oldDept then
      print SEPARATOR
      oldDept = dept
   endif
   print name
return oldDept
```

Figure 8-4 The produceReport() module

Within the produceReport() module, a string constant is declared to hold the separator that will appear between department groups. Then, the first task within the module is to check whether dept holds the same value as oldDept. For the first record, on the first pass through this method, the values are equal (because you set them to be equal right after getting the first input record). Therefore, you proceed without printing the separator or altering oldDept. Instead, you print the first employee's name and exit the method, returning the unaltered oldDept value.

At the end of the method, the logical flow returns to the main program in Figure 8-3. The next record is read, and if it is not eof, the logic travels back into the produceReport() module. There, you compare the second record's dept to oldDept. If the second record holds an employee from the same department as the first employee, then you simply print that second employee's name, return to the main program, and read a third record into memory. As long as each new record holds the same department value, you continue reading and printing, never pausing to print the SEPARATOR constant.

> **NOTE** In the flowchart in Figure 8-4, you could change the decision from dept = oldDept? to dept not = oldDept?. Then, the Yes branch of the decision structure would print the SEPARATOR, and the No branch would be null. This format would more closely resemble the pseudocode, but the logic would be identical.

Eventually, you will read in an employee whose department is different from the previous one. That's when the control break occurs. Whenever a new department differs from the old one, two tasks must be performed:

» The department-separating line must be printed.
» The control break field must be updated.

When the produceReport() method receives an employee record for which dept is not the same as oldDept, you cause a break in the normal flow of the program. The new employee record must "wait" while the separator is printed and the control break field oldDept acquires a new value. After the oldDept variable has been updated, and before produceReport() ends, the waiting employee's name is printed. The updated oldDept is returned to the main program and stored in the main program's oldDepartment variable. When you read the *next* employee record (and it is not eof), the produceReport() module is reentered and the next employee's dept value is compared to the updated oldDept field. If the new employee works in the same department as the one just preceding, then no separator is printed and normal processing continues—the employee's name is printed, the logic returns to the main program, and the next record is read.

The actions that take place when a new department is encountered are examples of two tasks required for all control breaks:

» Any necessary processing after the old group ends and before the new group starts. In this case, it means printing a separator.

» The control break field is updated. In this case, the `oldDept` variable is changed to hold the new department.

> **» NOTE** As an alternative to updating the control break field only when the separator is printed, you could set `oldDept` equal to `dept` for every record that passes through the `produceReport()` method. However, if you use this approach and there are 200 employees in Department 55, then you would set `oldDept` to the same value 200 times. It's more efficient to set `oldDept` to a different value only when there is a change in the value of the department.

Notice that in the control break program described in Figures 8-3 and 8-4, the department numbers of employees in the input file does not have to follow each other incrementally. That is, the departments might be 1, 2, 3, and so on, but they also might be 1, 4, 12, 35, and so on. A control break occurs when there is a change in the control break field; the change does not necessarily have to be a numeric change of 1.

> **TWO TRUTHS AND A LIE:**
> **PERFORMING A SINGLE-LEVEL CONTROL BREAK**
>
> 1. In a single-level control break program, there is a break in the logic of the program based on the value of a single variable.
>
> 2. In a control break program after the old group finishes, you print a line before the new group starts.
>
> 3. During a control break, it is critical that the control break field be updated.
>
> The false statement is #2. In a control break program, you perform any necessary processing before the new group starts, but that might be any task, not just printing a line.

USING CONTROL DATA WITHIN A HEADING

In the Employees by Department report program example in the last section, a line separated the names in each department. A more useful program might display the department number in a heading prior to starting each new department group. This feature would be useful if the departments were numbered sequentially, but would be even more useful if the department numbers skipped some values or were strings representing department names instead of numbers. In other words, it would be helpful to use the control data within a heading. For example, consider the sample report shown in Figure 8-5.

Employees by Department

Department 1

Amy Abbott
Bernard Garza
Donald Travis
_____

Department 4

Mary Billings
Kendall Worthington
_____

Department 7

Michael Anderson
Zachary Darnell
May Ann Denton
Francis Nichols

Figure 8-5 Employees by department with the department designated before each group

The difference between Figure 8-2 and Figure 8-5 is the headings that appear before each employee group in the later figure. To create a program that prints headings like these, you must make two changes in the existing program:

» First, you modify the `produceReport()` module, as shown in the shaded portion of Figure 8-6. After you print a separator to end a department group, you print a heading for the new group. In the shaded statement in Figure 8-6, notice that you use the department number that belongs to the employee record waiting to be printed while the separator is being printed.

» Additionally, you must modify the main program to ensure that the heading for the first department prints correctly. As Figure 8-7 shows, you must print the heading for the first department before entering the main loop of the program for the first time.

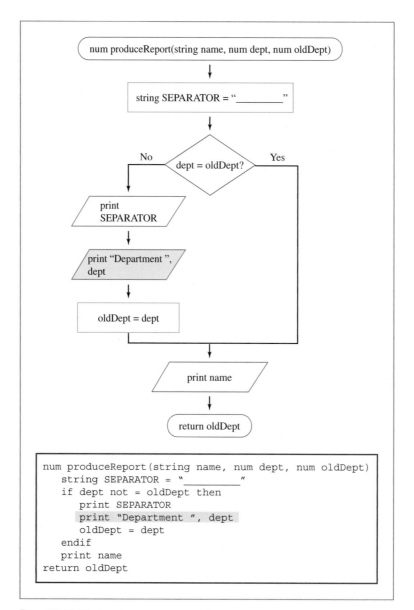

Figure 8-6 Modified produceReport() module

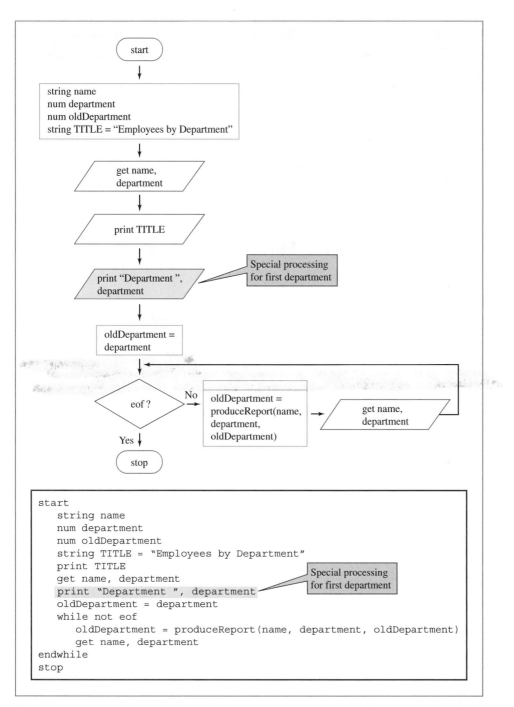

Figure 8-7 Main program that prints heading for the first department before entering the `produceReport()` method

>>**NOTE** As an alternative to the logic used to display the first group heading in Figure 8-7, you could initialize the `oldDepartment` variable to an impossible department value (for example, a negative number, or one known to be higher than any department in the organization). Then when the first record enters the `produceReport()` method, `dept` and `oldDept` would be unequal. The first headings would be printed and `oldDept` would be set to the value of the first department. As you have learned, in programming there are almost always multiple ways to produce the same result.

TWO TRUTHS AND A LIE:

USING CONTROL DATA WITHIN A HEADING

1. Displaying control data within a heading is particularly useful when the data is not sequential numbers.

2. To display control data in a group heading, you usually want to use the value of the control break field in the previous record.

3. To display control data in a group heading, you typically must use special processing for the first group.

The false statement is #2. To display control data in a group heading, you usually want to use the value of the control break field in the next record.

USING CONTROL DATA WITHIN A FOOTER

In the previous section, you learned how to use control break data in a heading. Figure 8-8 shows a different report format. For this report, the department number prints *following* the employee list for the department. In Chapter 3 you learned that a message that prints at the end of a page or other section of a report is called a footer. Headings usually require information about the *next* record; footers usually require information about the *previous* record.

```
Employees by Department

Department 1

Amy Abbott
Bernard Garza
Donald Travis
********** End of Department 1
_____

Department 4

Mary Billings
Kendall Worthington
********** End of Department 4
_____

Department 7

Michael Anderson
Zachary Darnell
May Ann Denton
Francis Nichols
Wendy Patterson
Barbara Proctor
********** End of Department 7
```

Figure 8-8 Employees by Department including a footer after each department

Figure 8-9 shows a program that prints a list of employees by department, including a footer that displays the department number at the end of each department's list. When you write a program that produces the report like the one shown in Figure 8-8, you continuously read input records, and each time an employee's department does not equal the previous one, you have reached a department break and you should perform the following control break tasks:

» You must finish any necessary processing for the previous department. In this case, you must print the footer for the previous department at the bottom of the employee list.

» You must perform any necessary processing for the new department. In this case, you must print the heading for the new department.

» You must update the control break field.

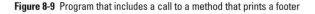

Figure 8-9 Program that includes a call to a method that prints a footer

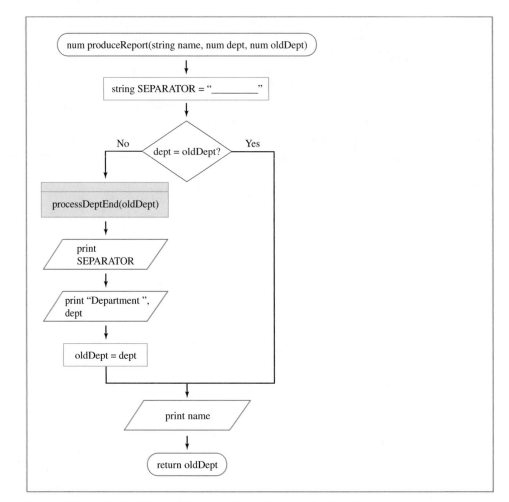

Figure 8-9 Program that includes a call to a method that prints a footer (*continued*)

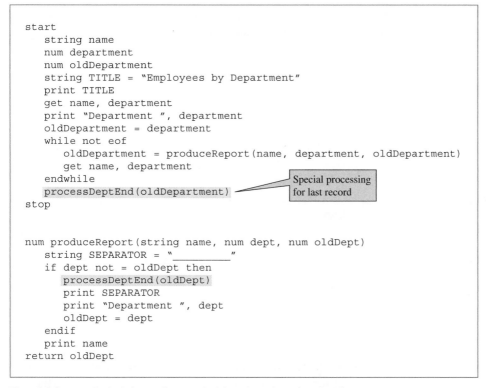

```
start
    string name
    num department
    num oldDepartment
    string TITLE = "Employees by Department"
    print TITLE
    get name, department
    print "Department ", department
    oldDepartment = department
    while not eof
        oldDepartment = produceReport(name, department, oldDepartment)
        get name, department
    endwhile
    processDeptEnd(oldDepartment)
stop


num produceReport(string name, num dept, num oldDept)
    string SEPARATOR = "_____"
    if dept not = oldDept then
        processDeptEnd(oldDept)
        print SEPARATOR
        print "Department ", dept
        oldDept = dept
    endif
    print name
return oldDept
```

Special processing for last record

Figure 8-9 Program that includes a call to a method that prints a footer (*continued*)

In Figure 8-9, when a record for a new department is encountered, the program calls a new method named processDeptEnd(). As shown in Figure 8-10, when a new department is encountered, you must print a footer at the bottom of the old group using the old department number. Additionally, in the main program, just before the end of the program, you must print a final footer for the last department.

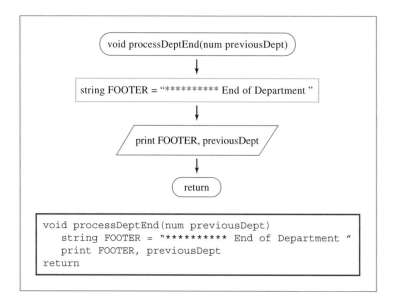

Figure 8-10 The `processDeptEnd()` method

For example, assume you have printed several employees from Department 12. When you read a record with an employee from Department 13 (or any other department), you pass the name, the department (13) and the old department (12) from the main program to the `produceReport()` method. There, you compare the new department and the old one and discover they are not equal, so the first thing you must do is print the footer for Department 12. You call the `processDeptEnd()` method, passing it the old department number. The method prints the footer and returns. Then, back in the `produceReport()` method, you can print the separation line and the header for the new department. Finally, you update `oldDept` to the current department, which in this example is 13. Then, and only then, the name of the first employee in the new department is printed.

The `produceReport()` module in Figure 8-9 performs three tasks required in all control break routines: it processes the previous group's finishing tasks, processes the new group's starting tasks, and updates the control break field.

When you first printed the department number in the header in the example in the previous section, you needed a special step at the beginning of the program, in the housekeeping section, to accommodate the first department's starting tasks before any records were processed. When you print the department number in the footer, the end of the program requires an extra step. Imagine that the last five records in the input file include two employees from Department 78, Ann and Bill, and three employees from Department 85, Carol, Don, and Ellen. The logical flow proceeds as follows:

1. After the first Department 78 employee (Ann) prints, you return to the main program and read the second Department 78 employee (Bill). It is not the end of the file, so the `produceReport()` method is entered.

2. At the top of the `produceReport()` module, Bill's department is compared to `oldDept`. The departments are the same, so no special processing occurs, and the second Department 78 employee (Bill) is printed. Then, you return to the main program and read the first Department 85 employee (Carol).

3. At the top of `produceReport()`, Carol's `dept` (85) and `oldDept` (78) are different, so you perform the `processDeptEnd()` method while Carol's record waits in memory.

4. In the `processDeptEnd()` module, you print "********** End of Department 78". Then, control returns to `produceReport()` where you print the separator and the heading for Department 85. Finally, you set `oldDept` to 85. You print Carol's name, and then return the `oldDept` value to the main program.

5. Back in the main program, you read the record for the second Department 85 employee (Don).

6. Back in the `produceReport()` method, you compare Don's department number to `oldDept`. The numbers are the same, so you print Don's name and return from the method to read in the last Department 85 employee (Ellen).

7. At the top of `produceReport()`, you determine that Ellen has the same department number as the previous record, so you print Ellen's name and return to the main program. There, you attempt to read from the input file, where you encounter `eof`.

8. The `eof` decision in the main program ends the loop.

You have printed the last Department 85 employee (Ellen), but the department footer for Department 85 has not printed. That's because every time you attempt to read an input record, you don't know whether there will be more records. The mainline logic checks for the `eof` condition, but if it determines that it is `eof`, the logic does not flow back into the `produceReport()` module, where the `processDeptEnd()` module can execute.

To print the footer for the last department, you must print a footer one last time at the end of the main program. The shaded statement at the end of the logic in Figure 8-9 illustrates this point. Printing the last footer at the end of the program corresponds to printing the first heading at the beginning. The very first heading prints separately from all the others at the beginning; the very last footer must print separately from all the others at the end.

TWO TRUTHS AND A LIE:
USING CONTROL DATA WITHIN A FOOTER

1. Headings and footers are alike in that they both usually require information about the next group to be processed.

2. When you display control data in a footer, you typically do so before performing any processing for the new group.

3. When you produce a footer, you need special processing after the last input record.

The false statement is #1. Headings usually require information about the next group, but footers usually require information about the previous group.

PERFORMING CONTROL BREAKS WITH TOTALS

Suppose you run a bookstore, and one of the files you maintain contains one record for every book title that you carry. Each record has fields that hold a book's title, author, category (fiction, reference, self-help, and so on), and price, as shown in the file description in Figure 8-11.

```
BOOK FILE DESCRIPTION
File name: BOOKS
FIELD DESCRIPTION        DATA TYPE      COMMENTS
Title                    String         45 characters maximum
Author                   String         30 characters maximum
Category                 String         15 characters maximum
Price                    Numeric        2 decimal places
```

Figure 8-11 Book file description

»NOTE You do not have to understand file processing to understand this bookstore example. Instead of reading from a file, the program could continuously prompt a user for each of the fields needed. The logic is the same.

Suppose you want to print a list of all the books that your store carries, with a total number of books at the bottom of the list, as shown in the sample report in Figure 8-12. You can use the logic shown in Figure 8-13. The program prints the heading, and then continuously reads records. For each record, the book title is printed and 1 is added to a grand total. At the end of the program, you print the grand total. You can't print grandTotal any earlier in the program because the grandTotal value isn't complete until the last record has been read.

BOOK LIST

A Brief History of Time
The Scarlet Letter
Math Magic
She's Come Undone
The Joy of Cooking
Walden
A Bridge Too Far
The Time Traveler's Wife
The DaVinci Code

Programming Logic and Design
Forever Amber

Total number of book titles 512

Figure 8-12 Sample Book List report

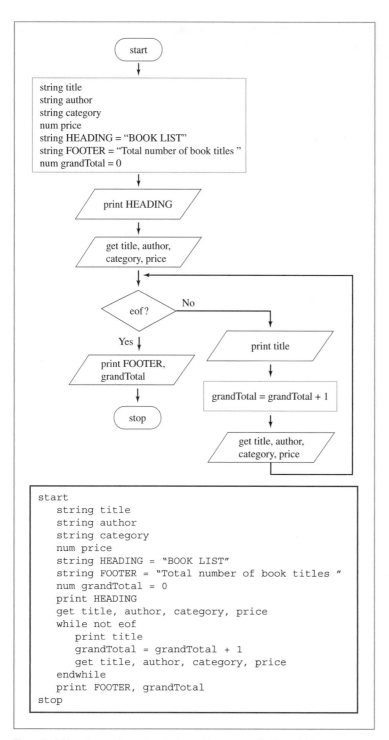

Figure 8-13 Flowchart and pseudocode that produces report in Figure 8-12

> **» NOTE** In Figure 8-13, you read in more data than is used in the program. When organizations store data, their records frequently contain more than specific programs need. For example, although your employer probably stores data such as your phone number and birth date in personnel records, neither of those items is used when your weekly paycheck is printed.

The logic of the book list report program is pretty straightforward. Suppose, however, that you decide you want a count for each category of book rather than just one grand total. For example, if all the book records contain a category that is either fiction, reference, or self-help, then the book records might be sorted in alphabetical order by category, and the output would consist of a list of all fiction books first, followed by a count; then all reference books, followed by a count; and finally all self-help books, followed by a count. The report is a control break report, because program control pauses when a change in category is encountered. The control break field is category. See Figure 8-14 for a sample report.

```
BOOK LIST

The Scarlet Letter
She's Come Undone
A Bridge Too Far
The Time Traveler's Wife
The DaVinci Code
Forever Amber

     Category Count 6

A Brief History of Time
Math Magic
```

Figure 8-14 Sample report that lists books by category with category counts

To produce the report with subtotals by category, you must declare two new variables: prevCategory and categoryTotal. You can also declare a constant for the text of the category footer. Every time you read a book record, you compare category to prevCategory; when there is a category change, you print the count of books for the previous category. The categoryTotal variable holds that count. See Figure 8-15.

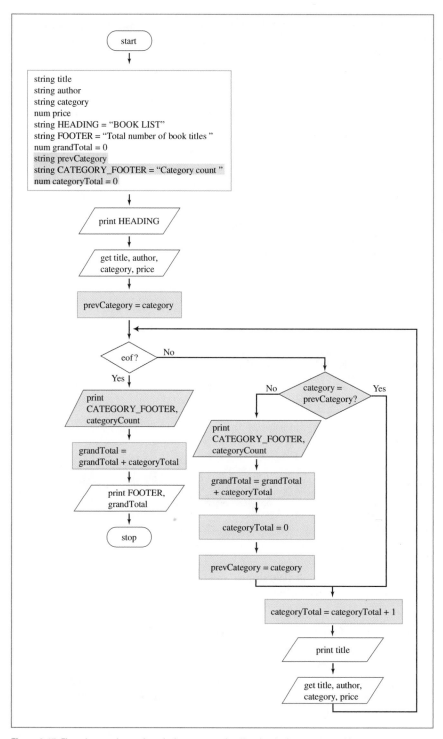

Figure 8-15 Flowchart and pseudocode for program that lists books by category with category counts

```
start
    string title
    string author
    string category
    num price
    string HEADING = "BOOK LIST"
    string FOOTER = "Total number of book titles "
    num grandTotal = 0
    string prevCategory
    string CATEGORY_FOOTER = "Category count "
    num categoryTotal = 0
    print HEADING
    get title, author, category, price
    prevCategory = category
    while not eof
        if category not = prevCategory then
            print CATEGORY_FOOTER, categoryCount
            grandTotal = grandTotal + categoryTotal
            categoryTotal = 0
            prevCategory = category
        endif
        categoryTotal = categoryTotal + 1
        print title
        get title, author, category, price
    endwhile
    print CATEGORY_FOOTER, categoryCount
    grandTotal = grandTotal + categoryTotal
    print FOOTER, grandTotal
stop
```

Figure 8-15 Flowchart and pseudocode for program that lists books by category with category counts (*continued*)

> **» NOTE** When you draw a flowchart, it usually is clearer to ask questions positively, as in "`category = prevCategory?`", and draw appropriate actions on the Yes or No side of the decision. In pseudocode, when action occurs only on the No side of a decision, it is usually clearer to ask negatively, as in "`category not equal to prevCategory?`" That way, you avoid an `if` statement in which all the actions are in the `else` part. Figure 8-15 uses these tactics.

The difference between the programs diagrammed in Figure 8-13 and Figure 8-15 are listed as follows:

» The new variables and constant are declared.

» The value of category for the first book is stored in the prevCategory variable.

» Every time a record enters the main loop of the program, the program checks to see if the current record represents a new category of work by comparing category to prevCategory. When you process the first record, the categories match (because prevCategory was just set to hold the category of the first book), so the book title prints, the categoryTotal increases by 1, and you read the next record.

» If the next record's `category` value matches the `prevCategory` value, processing continues as usual: printing a line and adding 1 to `categoryTotal`.

» At some point, the `category` for an input record does not match `prevCategory`. At that point, you print the category count, add the count for the category to the grand total, reset the category counter to 0 so it is ready to start counting the new category, and update the control break field. Adding a total to a higher-level total is called **rolling up the totals**.

» After all the records have been processed, the category total for the last group is printed, that category's total is added to the grand total, and the final grand total is printed.

You could write this program so that as you process each book, you add 1 to `categoryTotal` and add 1 to `grandTotal`. Then, there would be no need to roll totals up when the category changes. If there are 120 fiction books, using this technique would cause you to add 1 to `categoryTotal` 120 times; you would also add 1 to `grandTotal` 120 times. This technique would yield correct results, but you can eliminate executing 119 additional instructions by waiting until you have accumulated all 120 category counts before adding the total figure to `grandTotal`.

This control break report containing totals performs the five tasks required in all control breaks that print totals:

» It performs any necessary processing for the previous group—in this case, it prints `categoryTotal`.

» It rolls up the current-level totals to the next higher level—in this case, it adds `categoryTotal` to `grandTotal`.

» It resets the current level's totals to 0—in this case, `categoryTotal` is set to 0.

» It performs any necessary processing for the new group—in this case, there is none.

» It updates the control break field—in this case, `prevCategory`.

The end of the program in Figure 8-15 is more complicated than you might guess at first. It might seem as though you only need to print `grandTotal`. However, when you read after the last record, and encounter the `eof` decision, you have not printed the last `categoryTotal`, nor have you added the count for the last category to `grandTotal`. You must take care of both these tasks before printing `grandTotal`.

In Figure 8-15, notice that the first two steps that occur after a category changes, and the first two steps that occur after `eof` are identical. Encountering the end of the file is really just another form of break; it signals that the last category has finally completed.

Whenever a series of steps in a program is identical to another series of steps, you might consider placing those steps in a method that you write once but call from multiple locations. In this case, the repeated steps use `categoryCount` and alter `categoryTotal`. Therefore, you should write a method that accepts two parameters (the category count and the total) and returns a numeric value (the altered total). Figure 8-16 shows the new version of the program with a method that handles the repeated tasks.

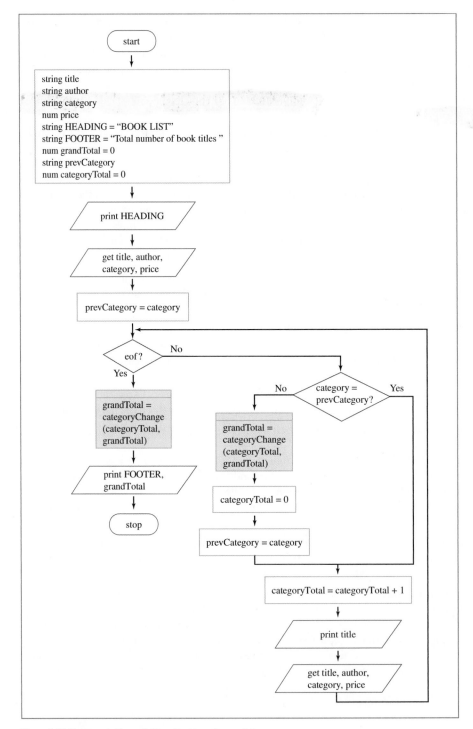

Figure 8-16 Program in Figure 8-15 revised to call a module

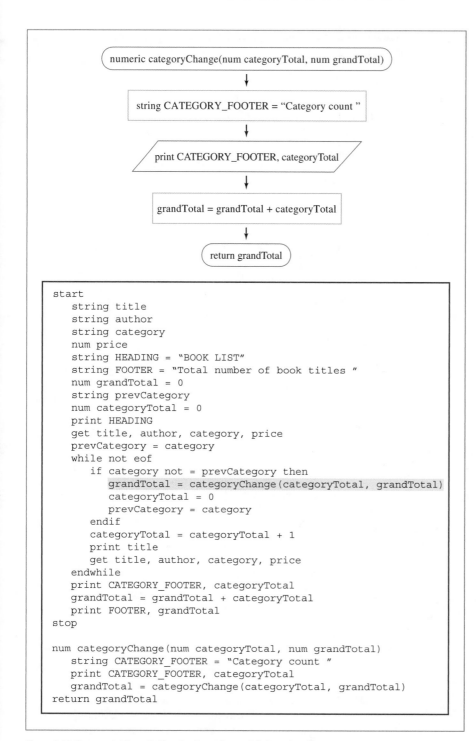

```
start
   string title
   string author
   string category
   num price
   string HEADING = "BOOK LIST"
   string FOOTER = "Total number of book titles "
   num grandTotal = 0
   string prevCategory
   num categoryTotal = 0
   print HEADING
   get title, author, category, price
   prevCategory = category
   while not eof
      if category not = prevCategory then
         grandTotal = categoryChange(categoryTotal, grandTotal)
         categoryTotal = 0
         prevCategory = category
      endif
      categoryTotal = categoryTotal + 1
      print title
      get title, author, category, price
   endwhile
   print CATEGORY_FOOTER, categoryTotal
   grandTotal = grandTotal + categoryTotal
   print FOOTER, grandTotal
stop

num categoryChange(num categoryTotal, num grandTotal)
   string CATEGORY_FOOTER = "Category count "
   print CATEGORY_FOOTER, categoryTotal
   grandTotal = categoryChange(categoryTotal, grandTotal)
return grandTotal
```

Figure 8-16 Program in Figure 8-15 revised to call a module (*continued*)

In the revised version of the program in Figure 8-16, the repeated tasks are placed in their own module. The declaration of CATEGORY_FOOTER is moved to the module because the main program no longer needs it. Each time the module is called, the current categoryTotal and grandTotal are passed in, and the categoryTotal value is printed and rolled up to the grandTotal level. The updated grandTotal is then returned to the calling program.

It is very important to understand that this control break program works whether there are three categories of books or 300. Note further that it does not matter what the categories of books are. For example, the program never asks a question like category = "fiction"?. Instead, the control of the program breaks when the category field *changes*, and it is in no way dependent on *what* that change is.

TWO TRUTHS AND A LIE:
PERFORMING CONTROL BREAKS WITH TOTALS

1. When you create a control break report with subtotals that appear after each of 10 groups, you typically create 10 variables to hold the 10 subtotals.

2. When a control break report prints a count after each group, the count is typically incremented by 1 with each new record.

3. Rolling up the totals is the process of adding a total to a higher-level total.

The false statement is #1. When you create a control break report with subtotals that appear after each of 10 groups, you typically create one variable that holds a subtotal and zero it out for each new group.

PERFORMING MULTIPLE-LEVEL CONTROL BREAKS

Let's say your bookstore from the last example is so successful that you have a chain of them across the country. Every time a sale is made, you create a record that stores the book's title and price and the city and state where the book was sold. You want a report that prints a summary of books sold in each city and each state, similar to the one shown in Figure 8-17. A report such as this one, which does not include any information about individual records, but instead includes only group totals, is a **summary report**.

BOOK SALES BY CITY AND STATE	
Ames	200
Des Moines	814
Iowa City	291
Total for IA	1305
Chicago	1093
Crystal Lake	564
McHenry	213
Springfield	365
Total for IL	2235
Springfield	289
Worcester	100
Total for MA	389
Grand Total	3929

Figure 8-17 Report of book sales by city and state

This program contains a **multiple-level control break**—that is, the normal flow of control (reading records and counting book sales) breaks away for special processing (in this case, to print totals) in response to more than just one change in condition. In this report, a control break occurs in response to either (or both) of two conditions: when the value of the city variable changes, as well as when the value of the state variable changes.

Just as the file you use to create a single-level control break report must be presorted, so must the input file you use to create a multiple-level control break report. The input file that you use for the book sales report must be sorted by city *within* state. That is, all of one state's records—for example, all records from IA—come first; then all of the records from another state, such as IL, follow. Within any one state, all of one city's records come first; then all of the next city's records follow. For example, the input file that produces the report shown in Figure 8-17 contains 200 records for book sales in Ames, IA, followed by 814 records for book sales in Des Moines, IA. The basic processing entails reading a book sale record, adding 1 to a counter, and reading the next book sale record. At the end of any city's records, you print a total for that city; at the end of a state's records, you print a total for that state.

As you would suspect, a typical multiple-level control break program is larger than one that contains only a single-level break. As programs get larger, it makes increasing sense to modularize them. Therefore, the Book Sales by City and State report program will contain separate modules for the city-break processing and the state-break processing. However, at each break level, totals and control break fields that store the city and state names must be updated. Unfortunately, as you learned in Chapter 6, a method can return, at most, one value. Fortunately, as you learned in Chapter 7, when you pass an array to a module, the array values can be altered in the calling program without returning any values. That's because arrays are passed by reference. Therefore, the Book Sales by City and State report program will use arrays to store the book counts as well as the control break fields.

The program will need three levels of totals (city, state, and grand), and two levels of previous-level control break value holders (city and state), so two arrays will be defined as follows:

```
num total[3] = 0, 0, 0
string prev[2]
```

Instead of using unnamed constants to access the arrays, your program will be much more clear if you use named constants. Therefore, three named constants will be defined as:

```
num GRAND = 2
num STATE = 1
num CITY = 0
```

In other words, `total[CITY]` will hold a count of books for a city, `total[STATE]` will hold a count of books for a state, and `total[GRAND]` will hold the grand total of all books. Additionally, `prev[CITY]` will hold the name of the previous city and `prev[STATE]` will hold the name of the previous state. Because all these values are stored in arrays, you will be able to pass the arrays to methods and update their values without requiring return values.

> **»NOTE** Notice how using well-named constants makes the use of arrays easier to understand. For example, there is little doubt that `total[CITY]` holds the total for a city.

Figure 8-18 shows the main program logic for the Book Sales by City and State report program. Shading appears wherever the arrays are used. After the first input record is read, the first state name is stored in `prev[STATE]`, which is `prev[1]`, and the first city name is stored in `prev[CITY]`, which is `prev[0]`. When the logic enters the main loop, the state and city questions are both true, so 1 is added to the city total (`total[CITY]` or `total[0]`) and the next record is read. As long as records continue to hold the same city and state name, 1 continues to be added to the city counter.

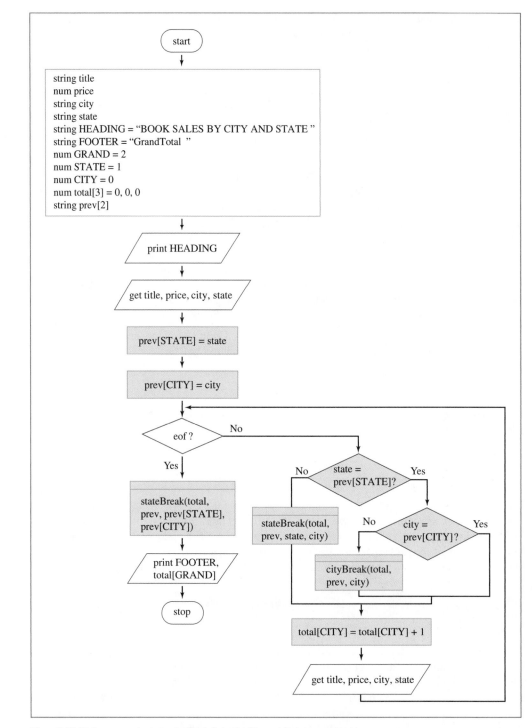

Figure 8-18 Main program logic for the Book Sales by City and State report program

```
start
   string title
   string author
   string category
   num price
   string HEADING = "BOOK LIST"
   string FOOTER = "Total number of book titles "
   num GRAND = 2
   num STATE = 1
   num CITY = 0
   num total[3] = 0, 0, 0
   string prev[2]

   print HEADING
   get title, price, city state
   prev[STATE] = state
   prev[CITY] = city
   while not eof
      if state not = prev[STATE] then
         stateBreak(total, prev, state, city)
      else
         if city not = prev[CITY] then
            cityBreak(total, prev, city)
         endif
      endif
      total[CITY] = total[CITY] + 1
      get title, price, city, state
   endwhile
   stateBreak(total, prev, state, city)
   print FOOTER, total[GRAND]
stop
```

Figure 8-18 Main program logic for the Book Sales by City and State report program (*continued*)

At some point, a record from a new city is read; assume this city is still in the first state. When the logic enters the main loop, the answer to state = prev[STATE]? is Yes, but the answer to city = prev[CITY]? is No. Therefore, the cityBreak() method executes. The two arrays (total and prev) are sent to the module, as is the name of the new city. The cityBreak() routine performs these standard control break tasks:

» It performs any necessary processing for the previous group—in this case, it prints the name and count for the previous city.

» It rolls up the current-level totals to the next higher level—in this case, it adds the city count to the state count.

» It resets the current level's totals to 0—in this case, it sets the city count to 0.

» It performs any necessary processing for the new group—in this case, there is none.

» It updates the control break field—in this case, it sets the previous city to the current city.

Figure 8-19 shows this method.

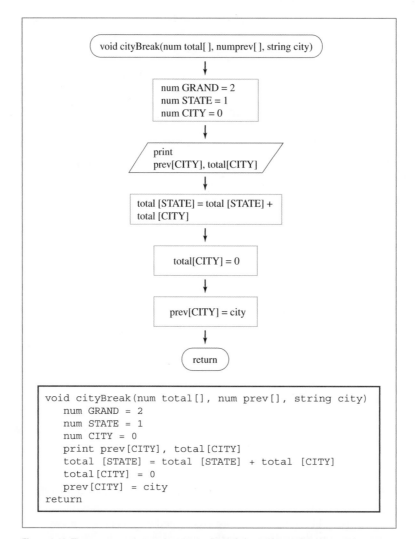

Figure 8-19 The `cityBreak()` method for the Book Sales by City and State report program

> **» NOTE** The declarations for the three constants (`GRAND`, `CITY`, and `STATE`) from the main program in Figure 8-18, are repeated in the method in Figure 8-19. You might prefer to take one of two alternate approaches. If the language you are working with allows it, some programmers would declare these three constants to be global. That is, they would be known to all methods within the program. Although some programmers object to making any data global, others agree that often it is an appropriate designation for constants. Another approach would be to pass the constants from the main program to the modules that need them. This approach was not taken here just so that the list of method parameters on which you need to concentrate could be kept short.

At some point, a record that contains a new state is read. For example, suppose the last record for Iowa City, IA is followed by the first one for Chicago, IL. When this record enters the program's main loop, the answer to `state = prev[STATE]?` is No, so you call the `stateBreak()` method. Within the `stateBreak()` module, shown in Figure 8-20, you must perform one new type of task, as well as the control break tasks with which you are familiar. The new task is the first task: Within the `stateBreak()` module, you must first perform cityBreak() because if there is a change in the state, there must also be a change in the city. The stateBreak() module does the following:

» It processes the lower-level break—in this case, cityBreak().

» It performs any necessary processing for the previous group—in this case, it prints the name and count for the previous state.

» It rolls up the current-level totals to the next higher level—in this case, it adds the state count to the grand total.

» It resets the current level's totals to 0—in this case, it sets the state count to 0.

» It performs any necessary processing for the new group—in this case, there is none.

» It updates the control break field—in this case, it sets the previous state to the current state.

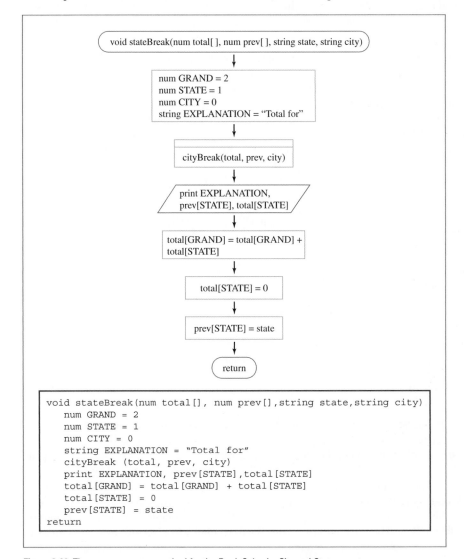

```
void stateBreak(num total[], num prev[],string state,string city)
    num GRAND = 2
    num STATE = 1
    num CITY = 0
    string EXPLANATION = "Total for"
    cityBreak (total, prev, city)
    print EXPLANATION, prev[STATE],total[STATE]
    total[GRAND] = total[GRAND] + total[STATE]
    total[STATE] = 0
    prev[STATE] = state
return
```

Figure 8-20 The stateBreak() method for the Book Sales by City and State report program

>> NOTE As you examine Figures 8-19 and 8-20, you should notice that the two modules are very similar; the `stateBreak()` routine contains just one extra type of task. When there is a change in state, you perform `cityBreak()` automatically before you perform any of the other necessary steps to change states.

The main program of this multiple-level control break program checks for any change in two different variables: `city` and `state`. When `city` changes, a city's name and its total are printed, and when `state` changes, "Total for", the state name, and its total are printed. As you can see from the sample report in Figure 8-17, all city totals within a state print before the state total for the same state, so, at first, it might seem logical to check for a change in `city` before checking for a change in `state`. However, the opposite is true. For the totals to be correct, you must check for any `state` change first. You do so because when `city` changes, `state` *might* also be changing, but when `state` changes, it means `city` *must* be changing.

Consider the sample input records shown in Figure 8-21, which are sorted by `city` within `state`. When you get to the point in the program where you read the first Illinois record (*The Scarlet Letter*), "Iowa City" is the value stored in the field `prev[CITY]`, and "IA" is the value stored in `prev[STATE]`. Because the values in the `city` and `state` variables in the new record are both different from the `prev[CITY]` and `prev[STATE]` fields, both a city and state total will print. However, consider the problem when you read the first record for Springfield, MA (*Walden*). At this point in the program, `prev[STATE]` is IL, but `prev[CITY]` is the same as the current `city`; both contain Springfield. If you check for a change in `city`, you won't find one, and no city total will print. Even though Springfield, MA, is definitely a different city from Springfield, IL, the computer recognizes no difference in them.

Title	Price	City	State
A Brief History of Time	20.00	Iowa City	IA
The Scarlet Letter	15.99	Chicago	IL
Math Magic	4.95	Chicago	IL
She's Come Undone	12.00	Springfield	IL
The Joy of Cooking	2.50	Springfield	IL
Walden	9.95	Springfield	MA
A Bridge Too Far	3.50	Springfield	MA

Figure 8-21 Sample data for Book Sales report

>> NOTE
If you need totals to print by city within county within state, you could say you have minor-, intermediate-, and major-level breaks.

Cities in different states can have the same name; if two cities with the same name follow each other in your control break program and you have written it to check for a change in city name first, the program will not recognize that you are working with a new city. Instead, you should always check for the **major-level break** first. If the records are sorted by `city` within `state`, then a change in `state` causes a major-level break, and a change in `city` causes a **minor-level break**. When the `state` value "MA" is not equal to the `prev[STATE]` value "IL", you force the `cityBreak()` method to execute, printing a city total for Springfield, IL, before a state total for IL and before continuing with the Springfield, MA, record. In other words, if there is a change in `state`, there is an implied change in `city`, even if the cities happen to have the same name.

The sample report containing book sales by city and state shows that you print the grand total for all book sales, so at the end of the program, you must print the total[GRAND] value. Before you can do so, however, you must perform both the cityBreak() and the stateBreak() modules one last time. You can accomplish this by performing stateBreak(), because the first step within stateBreak() is to perform cityBreak().

Again, consider the sample data shown in Figure 8-21. While you continue to read records for books sold in Springfield, MA, you continue to add to the total[CITY] for that city. At the moment you attempt to read one more record past the end of the file, you do not know whether there will be more records; therefore, you have not yet printed either the city total for Springfield or the state total for MA. After eof, you perform stateBreak(), which immediately performs cityBreak(). Within cityBreak(), the count for Springfield prints and rolls up to the state counter. Then, after the logic transfers back to the stateBreak() module, the total for MA prints and rolls up to total[GRAND]. Finally, you can print the grand total and end the program.

> **» NOTE** At the end of the program, four arguments are passed to stateBreak(). The stateBreak() module will need the total and prev arrays to display the correct information for the last city and state. The values of prev[STATE] and prev[CITY] are passed because the stateBreak() module requires two array and two string parameters.

Every time you write a program where you need control break routines, you should check whether you need to complete each of the following tasks within every module:

» Perform the lower-level break, if any
» Perform any control break processing for the previous group
» Roll up the current-level totals to the next higher level
» Reset the current level's totals to 0
» Perform any control break processing for the new group
» Update the control break field

TWO TRUTHS AND A LIE:
PERFORMING MULTIPLE-LEVEL CONTROL BREAKS

1. A summary report is one which does not include any information about individual records, but instead includes only group totals.

2. In a multiple-level control break, the normal flow of control breaks away for special processing in response to more than just one change in condition.

3. The advantage to creating a multiple-level control break report is that the input data need not be pre-sorted.

The false statement is #3. Just as the file you use to create a single-level control break report must be presorted, so must the input file you use to create a multiple-level control break report.

CHAPTER SUMMARY

» A control break is a temporary detour in the logic of a program. Programmers refer to a program as a control break program when a change in the value of a variable initiates special actions or causes special or unusual processing to occur. To generate a control break report, your input records must be organized in sorted order based on the field that will cause the breaks.

» You use a control break field to hold data from a previous record. You decide when to perform a control break routine by comparing the value in the control break field to the corresponding value in the current record. At minimum, the simplest control break tasks require processing for the new group and updating the control break field.

» Sometimes, you need to use control data during a control break, such as in a heading that requires information about the next record, or in a footer that requires information about the previous record. Frequently, the very first heading prints separately from all the others at the beginning of the program; the very last footer must print separately from all the others at the end.

» A complete single-level control break program contains and prints totals for the previous group, rolls up the current-level totals to the next higher level, resets the current level's totals to 0, performs any other needed control break processing, and updates the control break field.

» In a program containing a multiple-level control break, the normal flow of control breaks away for special processing in response to a change in more than one field. You should always test for a major-level break before a minor-level break, and include a call to the minor break module within the major break module.

» Every time you write a program in which you need control break processing, you should check whether you need to perform each of the following tasks within the routines: any lower-level break, any control break processing for the previous group, rolling up the current-level totals to the next higher level, resetting the current level's totals to 0, any control break processing for the new group, and updating the control break field.

KEY TERMS

A **control break** is a temporary detour in the logic of a program.

A **control break program** is one in which a change in the value of a variable initiates special actions or causes special or unusual processing to occur.

A **control break report** lists items in groups. Frequently, each group is followed by a subtotal.

Programs that **sort** records take records that are not in order and rearrange them to be in order based on some field.

A **single-level control break** is a break in the logic of a program based on the value of a single variable.

A **control break field** is a variable that holds the value that signals a break in a program.

Rolling up the totals is the process of adding a total to a higher-level total.

A **summary report** is one that does not include any information about individual records, but instead includes only group totals.

A **multiple-level control break** is one in which the normal flow of control breaks away for special processing in response to a change in more than one field.

A **major-level break** is a break in the flow of logic that is caused by a change in the value of a higher-level field.

A **minor-level break** is a break in the flow of logic that is caused by a change in the value of a lower-level field.

REVIEW QUESTIONS

1. **A control break occurs when a program _____.**

    a. takes one of two alternate courses of action for every record

    b. ends prematurely, before all records have been processed

    c. pauses to perform special processing based on the value of a field

    d. passes logical control to a module contained within another program

2. **Which of the following is an example of a control break report?**

    a. a list of all customers of a business in zip code order, with a count of the number of customers who reside in each zip code

    b. a list of all students in a school, arranged in alphabetical order, with a total count at the end of the report

    c. a list of all employees in a company, with a message "Retain" or "Dismiss" following each employee record

    d. a list of some of the patients of a medical clinic—those who have not seen a doctor for at least two years

3. **Placing records in sequential order based on the value in one of the fields is called _____.**

    a. collating

    b. sorting

    c. merging

    d. categorizing

4. **In a program with a single-level control break, _____.**

    a. the input file must contain a variable that contains a single digit

    b. the hierarchy chart must contain a single level below the main level

    c. the control break module must not contain any submodules

    d. special processing occurs based on the value in a single field

5. **A control break field _____ .**

    a. always prints prior to any group of records on a control break report

    b. always prints after any group of records on a control break report

    c. never prints on a report

    d. causes special processing to occur

6. **The value stored in a control break field _____ .**

    a. can be printed at the end of each group of records

    b. can be printed with each record

    c. both of these

    d. neither a nor b

7. **Whenever a control break occurs during record processing in any control break program, you must _____ .**

    a. declare a control break field

    b. set the control break field to 0

    c. update the value in the control break field

    d. print the control break field

8. **An insurance agency employs 10 agents and wants to print a report of claims based on the insurance agent who sold each policy. The agent's name should appear in a heading prior to the list of each agent's claims. At the start of this program, you should _____ .**

    a. read the first record before printing the first group heading

    b. print the first group heading before reading the first record

    c. read all the records that represent clients of the first agent before printing the group heading

    d. print the first group heading, but do not read the first record until within the program's main loop

9. **An insurance agency employs 30 agents and wants to print a report of claims based on the insurance agent who sold each policy. The agent's name should appear in a footer after a list of each agent's claims. At the end of this program, after the last data record is read, the first thing you should do is _____ .**

    a. end the program

    b. print the name of the last agent and that agent's total

    c. set the last agent's total to 0

    d. save the last agent's total in a control break field

10. **In contrast to using control break data in a heading, when you use control break data in a footer, you usually need data from the _____ record in the input data file.**

    a. previous

    b. next

    c. first

    d. priming

11. **An automobile dealer wants a list of cars sold, grouped by model, with a total dollar amount sold at the end of each group. The program contains a module named `modelBreak()` that prints a model name and the count for that model, sets the count to 0, and updates the control break field. The total for the last car model group should be printed _____ .**

    a. in the main program, after the last time the `modelBreak()` module is called

    b. in the main program, just before the last time the `modelBreak()` module is called

    c. in the `modelBreak()` module when it is called from the main program

    d. The total for the last car model group should not be printed.

12. **The Hampton City Zoo has a file that contains information about each of the animals it houses. Each animal record contains such information as the animal's ID number, date acquired by the zoo, and species. The zoo wants to print a list of animals, grouped by species, with a count after each group. As an example, a typical summary line might be "Species: Giraffe   Count: 7". Which of the following happens within the control break module that prints the count?**

    a. The previous species count prints, and then the previous species field is updated.

    b. The previous species field is updated, and then the previous species count prints.

    c. Either of these will produce the desired results.

    d. Neither a nor b will produce the desired results.

13. **Adding a total to a higher-level total is called _____ the totals.**

    a. sliding

    b. advancing

    c. rolling up

    d. replacing

14. **The Academic Dean of Creighton College wants a count of the number of students who have declared a major, in each of the college's 45 major courses of study, as well as a grand total count of students enrolled in the college. Individual student records contain each student's name, ID number, major, and other data, and are sorted in alphabetical order by major. A control break module executes when the program encounters a change in student major. Within this module, what must occur?**

a. The total count for the previous major prints.

b. The total count for the previous major prints, and the total count is added to the grand total.

c. The total count for the previous major prints, the total count for the major is added to the grand total, and the total count for the major is reset to 0.

d. The total count for the previous major prints, the total count for the major is added to the grand total, the total count for the major is reset to 0, and the grand total is reset to 0.

15. **In a control break program containing printed group totals and a grand total, after eof and before the end of the program, you must _____ .**

a. print the group total for the last group

b. roll up the total for the last group

c. both of these

d. neither a nor b

16. **A summary report _____ .**

a. contains detail lines

b. contains total lines   *group totals*

c. both of these

d. neither a nor b

17. **The Cityscape Real Estate Agency wants a list of all housing units sold last year, including a subtotal of sales that occurred each month. Within each month group, there are also subtotals of each type of property—single-family homes, condominiums, commercial properties, and so on. This report is a _____ control break report.**

a. single-level

b. multiple-level

c. semilevel

d. trilevel

18. **The Packerville Parks Commission has a file that contains picnic permit information for the coming season. The commission needs a report that lists each day's picnic permit information, including permit number and name of permit holder, starting on a separate page each day of the picnic season. (Figure 8-22 shows a sample page of output for the Packerville Parks report.) Within each day's permits, the commission wants subtotals that count permits in each of the city's 30 parks. The permit records have been sorted by park name within date. In the main loop of the report program, the first decision should check for a change in _____ .**

    a. park name

    b. date

    c. permit number

    d. any of these

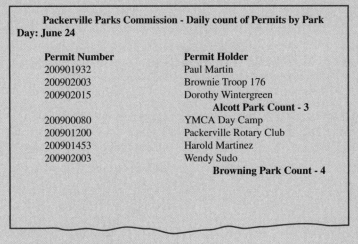

    Packerville Parks Commission - Daily count of Permits by Park
    Day: June 24

Permit Number	Permit Holder
200901932	Paul Martin
200902003	Brownie Troop 176
200902015	Dorothy Wintergreen
	Alcott Park Count - 3
200900080	YMCA Day Camp
200901200	Packerville Rotary Club
200901453	Harold Martinez
200902003	Wendy Sudo
	Browning Park Count - 4

Figure 8-22 Sample Parks Report

19. **Which of the following is *not* a task you need to complete in any control break module that has multiple levels and totals at each level?**

    a. Perform lower-level breaks.

    b. Roll up the totals.

    c. Update the control break field.

    d. Reset the current-level totals to the previous-level totals.

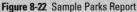

20. **The election commission for the state of Illinois maintains a file that contains the name of each registered voter, the voter's county, and the voter's precinct within the county. The commission wants to produce a report that counts the voters in each precinct and county. The file should be sorted in _____ .**

    Distrito

    a. county order within precinct

    b. last name order within precinct

    c. last name order within county

    d. precinct order within county

FIND THE BUGS

Each of the following pseudocode segments contains one or more bugs that you must find and correct.

1. **This application prints a list of students in an elementary school. Students have been sorted by grade level. A new section is started for each grade level, and the numeric grade level prints as part of the heading.**

```
start
    string studentName
    num gradeLevel
    string HEADING = "Students by Grade"
    num saveGrade
    print HEADING
    get studentName, gradeLevel
    print "Grade ", gradeLevel
    gradeLevel = saveGrade
    while not eof
        if grade = saveGrade then
            print "Grade ", gradeLevel
        endif
        print studentName
        get studentName, gradeLevel
    endwhile
stop
```

2. **The Friendly Insurance Company phones a birthday greeting to each of its clients on his or her birthday. The following program is intended to produce a report that lists the clients a salesperson should call each day for the coming year. Input records include the client's name and phone number as well as a numeric month and day. The records have been sorted by day within month. (It is very likely that some days of the year do not have a client birthday.) At the end of each daily section is a count of the number of calls that should be made that day. Part of a sample report is shown in Figure 8-23.**

```
Calls to make on day 1
of month 1

Enrique Nova          920-555-1929
Barbara Nuance        920-555-8291
Allison Sellers       414-555-6532
                          Calls to make today: 3

Calls to make on day 2
of month 1

Martin Richards       414-555-4551
Amanda Smith          715-555-6822
David Thompson        414-555-0900
Chris Urban           715-555-2331
                          Calls to make today: 4
```

Figure 8-23 Sample birthday report

```
start
    string name
    string phone
    num month
    num day
    string HEAD_DAY = "Calls to make on day "
    string HEAD_MONTH = "of month "
    string FOOT = "           Calls to make today: "
    num count = 0
    num prevDay
    num prevMonth
    get name, phone, month, day
    prevDay = day
    prevMonth = month
    print HEAD_DAY, day
    print HEAD_MONTH, month
    while not eof
        if month not = prevMonth AND day not = prevDay then
            print FOOT, count
            print HEAD_DAY, day
            print HEAD_MONTH, month
        endif
        count = 1
        get name, phone, month, day
    endwhile
stop
```

EXERCISES

1. **What fields might you want to use as the control break fields to produce a report that lists all inventory items in a grocery store? (For example, you might choose to group items by grocery store department.) Design a sample report.**

2. **What fields might you want to use as the control break fields to produce a report that lists all the people you know? (For example, you might choose to group friends by city of residence.) Design a sample report.**

> **》》 NOTE** Your Student Disk contains a comma-delimited sample data file for Exercises 3 through 10. You might want to use these files in any of several ways:
>
> 》 You can look at the files' contents to gain a better understanding of the types of data each program uses.
> 》 You can use the files' contents as sample data when you desk check the logic of your flowcharts or pseudocode.
> 》 You can use the files as input files if you implement the solutions in a programming language and write programs that accept file input.
> 》 You can use the data as guides to appropriate values to enter if you implement the solutions in a programming language and write interactive programs.

3. Cool's Department Store keeps a record of every sale including a transaction number, the dollar amount of the sale, and the department number in which the sale was made (values are 1 through 20). Design the logic for a program that reads the sales, sorted by department, and prints the transaction number and amount for each sale, with a total dollar amount at the end of each department.

4. Simon's Used Cars keeps records of car sales including the make and model of the car sold, the price, and a salesperson's ID number, which is a two-digit number. The records are sorted by salesperson ID. By the end of the week, a salesperson may have sold no cars (in which case the salesperson does not appear on the report), one car, or many cars. Create the logic for a program that prints one line for each salesperson, with that salesperson's total number of sales for the week, their total dollar value, and the salesperson's commission earned, which is 4 percent of the total sales.

5. Heartland Community College has a file of student records sorted by the hour of the student's first class on Mondays this semester. The hour of the first class is a two-digit number based on a 24-hour clock (for example, a 1 p.m. class is recorded as 13). Besides the hour, each record contains the student's name and town of residence. Create the logic to produce a report that students can use to organize carpools. The report lists the names and phone numbers of students from the city of Huntley. (Note that some students come from cities other than Huntley; these students should not be listed on the report.) Start a new group for each hour of the day, including the hour in a header that precedes the group.

6. The Stanton Insurance Agency needs a report summarizing the counts of life, health, and other types of insurance policies it sells. Input records contain a policy number, the name of the insured, the policy value, and the type of policy, and have been sorted in alphabetical order by type of policy. Create the logic for the program that produces a report that lists the policy numbers, names, and values of each type of policy holder. Include a heading before each group that indicates the policy type. Include a count of the number of policies as well as their total value after each group. At the end of the report, display a count of all the policies and their total value.

7. Riceland University is organized into colleges (such as Liberal Arts), divisions within the colleges (such as Languages), and departments within the divisions (such as French). Design the logic that produces a report that reads records that contain the department chairperson's name, the department, division, and college. Assume the input records have been sorted. Print each department chair's name and include a count after each department, division, and college group.

8. Allentown Zoo keeps track of the expense of feeding the animals it houses. Each record holds one animal's ID number, name, species (elephant, rhinoceros, tiger, lion, and so on), zoo residence (pachyderm house, large-cat house, and so on), and weekly food budget. The records are sorted by species within residence. Design the logic that produces a report that lists each animal's ID, name, and budgeted food amount. At the end of each species group, print a total budget for the species. At the end of each house (for example, the species lion, tiger, and leopard are all in the large-cat house), print the house total. At the end of the report, print the grand total.

9. The Sunshine Soft-drink Company produces several flavors of drink—for example, cola, orange, and lemon. Additionally, each flavor has several versions, such as regular, diet, and caffeine-free. The manufacturer operates factories in several states. Assume you have input records that list version, flavor, yearly production in gallons, and state (for example, Regular, Cola, 5000, Kansas). The records have been sorted in alphabetical order by version within flavor within state. Design the logic for the program that produces a report that lists each version and flavor, with minor total production figures for each flavor, and major total production figures for each state.

10. The Finley Fine Art Shop maintains records for each item in the shop, including the title of the work, the artist who made the item, the medium (for example, watercolor, oil, or clay), and the monetary value. The records are sorted by artist within medium. Design the logic that produces a report that lists all items in the store, with a minor total value following each artist's work, and a major total value following each medium.

GAME ZONE

1. The International FreeCell Championship was held last week. The championship sponsors want to produce a report summarizing the results. Each competitor completed as many games as possible in a one-hour period. After each game was played, a record was created that includes the time to complete the game and the player's first and last names. Records have been stored sorted in alphabetical order by the player's last name. When last names are the same, records are sorted by first name. Produce a report that lists each competitor, then lists the time for each game the player completed. At the end of each player's list of times, display a count of the number of games completed, and the average time for each game.

2. Design a game based on the television show *The Price Is Right*. Create parallel arrays that hold 20 prizes of your choice and an estimated retail value (for example, "big screen tv" and $4500). In turn, show the player each prize and allow him to guess the retail value. If the user guesses within 10 percent of the retail value without going over, he wins the prize; otherwise he does not. After each group of five prizes that are guessed, pause to display the player's statistics to that point—the number of prizes won and lost to that point and total retail value of each group. At the end of the game, list all the prizes won and their total value.

DETECTIVE WORK

Control break reports are just one type of frequently printed business report. Has paper consumption increased or decreased since computers became common office tools? How soon do experts predict we will have the "paperless office"?

UP FOR DISCUSSION

1. Suppose your employer asks you to write a control break program that lists all the company's employees, their salaries, and their ages, with breaks at each department to list a count of employees in that department. You are provided with the personnel file to use as input. You decide to take the file home with you so you can work on creating the report over the weekend. Is this acceptable? What if the file contained only employees' names and departments, and not more sensitive data such as salaries and ages?

2. Suppose your supervisor asks you to create a report that lists all employees by department and includes a break after each department to display the highest-paid employee in that department. Suppose you also know that your employer will use this report to lay off the highest-paid employee in each department. Would you agree to write the program? Instead, what if the report's purpose was to list the worst performer in each department in terms of sales? What if the report grouped employees by gender? What if the report grouped employees by race?

3. Suppose your supervisor asks you to write a control break report that lists employees in groups by the dollar value of medical insurance claims they have in a year. You fear the employer will use the report to eliminate workers who are driving up the organization's medical insurance policy costs. Do you agree to write the report? What if you know for certain that the purpose of the report is to eliminate workers?

ADVANCED ARRAY MANIPULATION

In this chapter you will:

Learn about the need for sorting data
Swap two values in computer memory
Understand the bubble sort
Understand the insertion sort
Understand the selection sort
Use multidimensional array
Use a built-in `Array` class
Use indexed files
Use a linked list

UNDERSTANDING THE NEED FOR SORTING RECORDS

When you store data records, they exist in some sort of order; that is, one record is first, another second, and so on. When records are in **sequential order**, they are arranged one after another on the basis of the value in some field. Examples of records in sequential order include employee records stored in numeric order by Social Security number or department number, or in alphabetic order by last name or department name. Even if the records are stored in a random order—for example, the order in which a data-entry clerk felt like entering them—they still are in *some* order, although probably not the order desired for processing or viewing. When this is the case, the data records need to be **sorted**, or placed in order, based on the contents of one or more fields. When you sort data, you can sort either in **ascending order**, arranging records from lowest to highest value within a field, or **descending order**, arranging records from highest to lowest value. Here are some examples of occasions when you would need to sort records:

» A college stores students' records in ascending order by student ID number, but the registrar wants to view the data in descending order by credit hours earned so he can contact students who are close to graduation.

» A department store maintains customer records in ascending order by customer number, but at the end of a billing period, the credit manager wants to contact customers whose balances are 90 or more days overdue. The manager wants to list these overdue customers in descending order by the amount owed, so the customers maintaining the biggest debt can be contacted first.

» A sales manager keeps records for her salespeople in alphabetical order by last name, but needs to list the annual sales figure for each salesperson so she can determine the median annual sale amount. The **median** value in a list is the value of the middle item when the values are listed in order; it is not the same as the arithmetic average, or **mean**.

> **» NOTE** To help you understand the difference between median and mean, consider the following five values: 0, 7, 10, 11, 12. The median value is the middle position's value (when the values are listed in numerical order), or 10. The mean, however, is the sum (40) divided by the number of values (5), which evaluates to 8. The median is used as a statistic in many cases because it represents a more typical case—half the values are below it and half are above it. Unlike the median, the mean is skewed by a few very high or low values.

> **» NOTE** Sorting is usually reserved for a relatively small number of data items. If thousands of customer records are stored, and they frequently need to be accessed in order based on different fields (alphabetical order by customer name one day, zip code order the next), the records would probably not be sorted at all, but would be indexed or linked. You learn about indexing and linking later in this chapter.

When computers sort data, they always use numeric values when making comparisons between values. This is clear when you sort records by fields such as a numeric customer ID or balance due. However, even alphabetic sorts are numeric, because everything that is stored in a computer is stored as a number using a series of 0s and 1s. In every popular computer coding scheme, "B" is numerically one greater than "A", and "y" is numerically one less than "z". Unfortunately, whether "A" is represented by a number that is greater or smaller than the number representing "a" depends on your system. Therefore, to obtain the most useful and accurate list of alphabetically sorted records, either the data-entry personnel should be consistent in the use of capitalization, or the programmer should convert all the data to consistent capitalization.

>> **NOTE** Because "A" is always less than "B", alphabetic sorts are always considered ascending sorts. The most popular coding schemes include ASCII, Unicode, and EBCDIC. Each is a code in which a number represents every computer character. Appendix C contains additional information about these codes.

>> **NOTE** It's possible that as a professional programmer, you will never have to write a program that sorts records, because organizations can purchase prewritten, or "canned," sorting programs. Additionally, many popular language compilers come with built-in methods that can sort data for you. However, it is beneficial to understand the sorting process so that you can write a special-purpose sort when needed. Understanding sorting also improves your array-manipulating skills.

TWO TRUTHS AND A LIE:
UNDERSTANDING THE NEED FOR SORTING RECORDS

1. When you sort data in ascending order, you arrange records from lowest to highest based on the value in some field.

2. Alphabetical order is descending order.

3. When computers sort data, they always use numeric values when making comparisons between values.

The false statement is #2. Alphabetical order is ascending.

UNDERSTANDING HOW TO SWAP TWO VALUES

Computer professionals have developed many sorting techniques. **Swapping** two values is a concept that is central to most sorting techniques. When you swap the values stored in two variables, you reverse their positions; you set the first variable equal to the value of the second, and the second variable equal to the value of the first. However, there is a trick to reversing any two values. Assume you have declared two variables as follows:

```
num score1 = 90
num score2 = 85
```

You want to swap the values so that score1 is 85 and score2 is 90. If you first assign score1 to score2 using a statement such as score2 = score1, both score1 and score2 hold 90 and the value 85 is lost. Similarly, if you first assign score2 to score1 using a statement such as score1 = score2, both variables hold 85 and the value 90 is lost.

The solution to swapping the values lies in creating a temporary variable to hold one of the scores; then, you can accomplish the swap as shown in Figure 9-1. First, the value in score2, 85, is assigned to a temporary holding variable, named temp. Then, the score1 value, 90, is assigned to score2. At this point, both score1 and score2 hold 90. Then, the 85 in temp is assigned to score1. Therefore, after the swap process, score1 holds 85 and score2 holds 90.

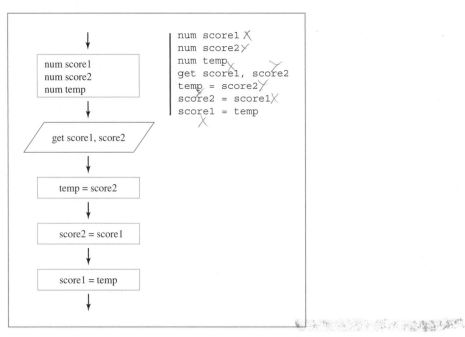

```
num score1
num score2
num temp

get score1, score2

temp = score2

score2 = score1

score1 = temp
```

```
num score1 X
num score2 Y
num temp X
get score1, score2 Y
temp = score2 Y
score2 = score1 X
score1 = temp X
```

» NOTE
In Figure 9-1, you can accomplish identical results by assigning score1 to temp, assigning score2 to score1, and finally assigning temp to score2.

Figure 9-1 Program segment that swaps two values

TWO TRUTHS AND A LIE: Cambiar valores
UNDERSTANDING HOW TO SWAP TWO VALUES

1. Swapping is a concept used in many types of sorts.

2. When you swap the values stored in two variables, you reverse their positions.

3. If you are careful, you can swap two values without creating any additional variables.

The false statement is #3. Swapping values requires a temporary variable so that you don't lose one of the values.

USING A BUBBLE SORT

Burbuja

One of the simplest sorting techniques to understand is a bubble sort. You can use a bubble sort to arrange records in either ascending or descending order. In a **bubble sort**, items in a list are compared with each other in pairs, and when an item is out of order, it swaps values with the item below it. With an ascending bubble sort, after each adjacent pair of items in a list has been compared once, the largest item in the list will have "sunk" to the bottom. After many passes through the list, the smallest items rise to the top like bubbles in a carbonated drink.

» NOTE A bubble sort is sometimes called a **sinking sort**.

>> **NOTE** When you learn a sort method, programmers say you are learning an algorithm. An **algorithm** is a list of instructions that accomplishes some task.

Assume that you want to sort five student test scores in ascending order. Figure 9-2 shows a program in which an array is declared to hold five scores. Three main procedures are called— one to get the five scores, one to sort them, and the final one, to display the sorted result.

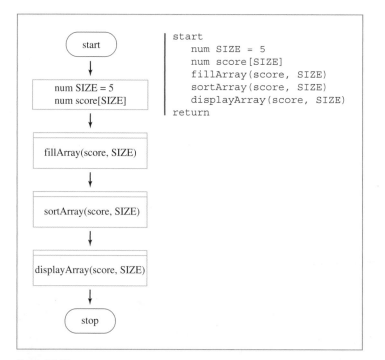

```
start
    num SIZE = 5
    num score[SIZE]
    fillArray(score, SIZE)
    sortArray(score, SIZE)
    displayArray(score, SIZE)
return
```

Figure 9-2 The SortScores program

>> **NOTE** In the program in Figure 9-2, each method receives the array and its size. Many programming languages provide a built-in constant that represents the size of each declared array. If the program in Figure 9-2 was implemented in one of those languages, there would be no need to pass the array size to the methods because it would automatically "come with" the array. The name that refers to the size differs among languages. For example, in C# or Visual Basic, it would be score.Length, and in Java, it would be score.length.

Figure 9-3 shows the `fillArray()` method. The method receives the array and its size. A subscript is initialized to 0 and each array element is filled in turn. After five scores have been entered, control returns to the main program. Recall from Chapter 7 that when an array is passed to a method, its address is passed, so there is no need to return anything from the method for the main method to have access to the newly entered array values.

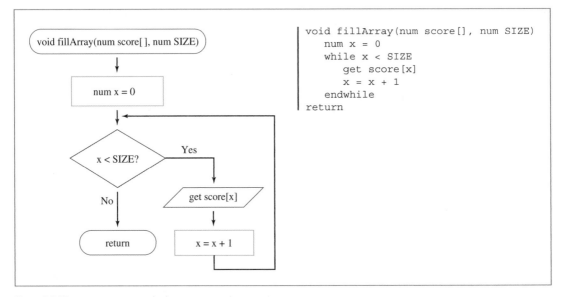

```
void fillArray(num score[], num SIZE)
    num x = 0
    while x < SIZE
        get score[x]
        x = x + 1
    endwhile
return
```

Figure 9-3 The `fillArray()` method

>> **NOTE** As with many other program examples you have seen in this book, the statement `get score[x]` might mean that each score is retrieved from any number of sources—perhaps from a file, or by a user typing at a keyboard or selecting options with a mouse. A user would probably need to see a few prompts directing the data entry, but the basic input process would be the same.

The `sortArray()` method in Figure 9-4 sorts the array elements by making a series of comparisons of adjacent element values and swapping them if they are out of order. For example, assume the five entered scores are:

```
score[0] = 90
score[1] = 85
score[2] = 65
score[3] = 95
score[4] = 75
```

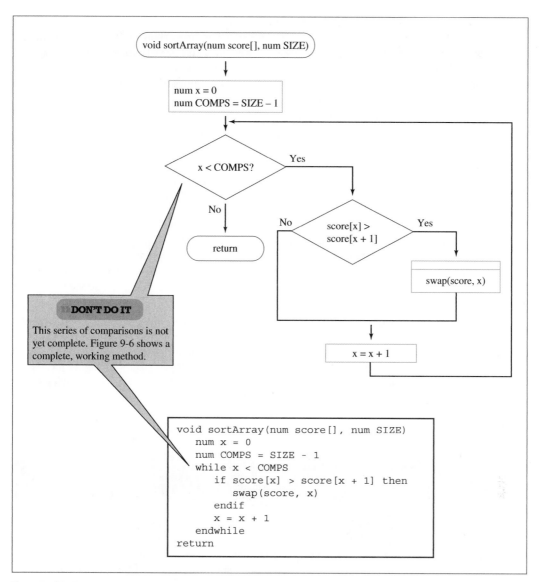

Figure 9-4 The incomplete `sortArray()` method

>> **NOTE** For a descending sort in which you want to end up with the highest value first, write the decision so that you perform the switch when `score[x]` is less than `score[x + 1]`.

To begin sorting this list of scores, you compare the first two scores, score[0] and score[1]. If they are out of order, that is, if score[0] is larger than score[1], you want to reverse their positions, or swap their values. For example, if score[0] is 90 and score[1] is 85, then you want score[0] to assume the value 85 and score[1] to take on the value 90. Therefore you call the swap() method that reverses the values of the two elements. After this swap, the scores are in slightly better order than they were originally.

In Figure 9-4, a constant named COMPS is declared and assigned the value of SIZE −1. That is, for an array of size 5, the COMPS constant will be 4. The while loop in the method continues as long as x is less than COMPS. The comparisons that are made, therefore, are as follows:

```
score[0] > score[1]?
score[1] > score[2]?
score[2] > score[3]?
score[3] > score[4]?
```

Each element in the array is compared to the one that follows it. When x becomes COMPS, the while loop ends. If it continued when x became equal to COMPS, then the next comparison would be score[4] > score[5]?. This would cause an error because the highest allowed subscript in a five-element array is 4. You must execute the decision score[x] > score[x + 1]? four times—when x is 0, 1, 2, and 3.

For an ascending sort, you need to perform the swap() method whenever any given element x of the score array has a value greater than the next element, x + 1, of the score array. For any x, if the xth element is not greater than the element at position x + 1, the swap should not take place. For example, when score[x] is 90 and score[x + 1] is 85, a swap should occur. On the other hand, when score[x] is 65 and score[x + 1] is 95, then no swap should occur.

> **NOTE** In the sort, you could use either greater than (>) or greater than or equal to (>=) to compare adjacent values. Using the greater than comparison to determine when to switch values in the sort is more efficient than using greater than or equal to, because if two compared values are equal, there is no need to swap them.

Figure 9-5 shows the swap() method. This module switches any two adjacent elements in the score array when the variable x represents the position of the first of the two elements, and the value x + 1 represents the subsequent position.

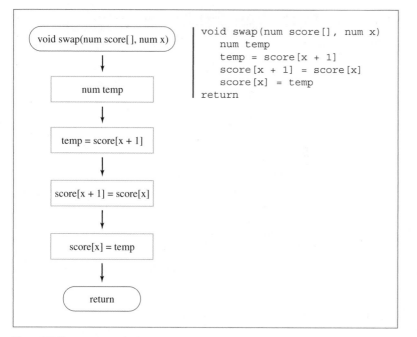

```
void swap(num score[], num x)
    num temp
    temp = score[x + 1]
    score[x + 1] = score[x]
    score[x] = temp
return
```

Figure 9-5 The swap() method

As an example of how this application works, suppose you have these original scores:

```
score[0] = 90
score[1] = 85
score[2] = 65
score[3] = 95
score[4] = 75
```

The logic of the sortArray() method proceeds like this:

1. Set x to 0.

2. The value of x is less than 4 (COMPS), so enter the loop.

3. Compare score[x], 90, to score[x + 1], 85. The two scores are out of order, so they are switched.

   The list is now:

```
score[0] = 85
score[1] = 90
score[2] = 65
score[3] = 95
score[4] = 75
```

4. After the swap, add 1 to x so x is 1.

5. Return to the top of the loop. The value of x is less than 4, so enter the loop a second time.

6. Compare `score[x]`, 90, to `score[x + 1]`, 65. These two values are out of order, so swap them.

   Now the result is:
   ```
   score[0] = 85
   score[1] = 65
   score[2] = 90
   score[3] = 95
   score[4] = 75
   ```

7. Add 1 to x, so x is now 2.

8. Return to the top of the loop. The value of x is less than 4, so enter the loop.

9. Compare `score[x]`, 90, to `score[x + 1]`, 95. These values are in order, so no switch is made.

10. Add 1 to x, making it 3.

11. Return to the top of the loop. The value of x is less than 4, so enter the loop.

12. Compare `score[x]`, 95, to `score[x + 1]`, 75. These two values are out of order, so switch them.

    Now the list is as follows:
    ```
    score[0] = 85
    score[1] = 65
    score[2] = 90
    score[3] = 75
    score[4] = 95
    ```

13. Add 1 to x, making it 4.

14. Return to the top of the loop. The value of x is 4, so do not enter the loop again.

When x reaches 4, every element in the list has been compared with the one adjacent to it. The highest score, 95, has "sunk" to the bottom of the list. However, the scores still are not in order. They are in slightly better ascending order than they were when the process began, because the largest value is at the bottom of the list, but they are still out of order. You need to repeat the entire procedure so that 85 and 65 (the current `score[0]` and `score[1]` values) can switch places, and 90 and 75 (the current `score[2]` and `score[3]` values) can switch places. Then, the scores will be 65, 85, 75, 90, and 95. You will have to go through the list yet again to swap 85 and 75.

As a matter of fact, if the scores had started out in the worst possible order (95, 90, 85, 75, 65), the comparison process would have to take place four times. In other words, you would have to pass through the list of values four times, making appropriate swaps, before the numbers would appear in perfect ascending order. You need to place the loop in Figure 9-4 within another loop that executes four times.

Figure 9-6 shows the complete logic for the `sortArray()` module. The module uses a loop control variable named y to cycle through the list of scores four times. (The initialization, comparison, and alteration of this loop control variable are shaded in the figure.) With an array of five elements, it takes four comparisons to work through the array once, comparing each pair, and it takes four sets of those comparisons to ensure that every element in the entire array is in sorted order.

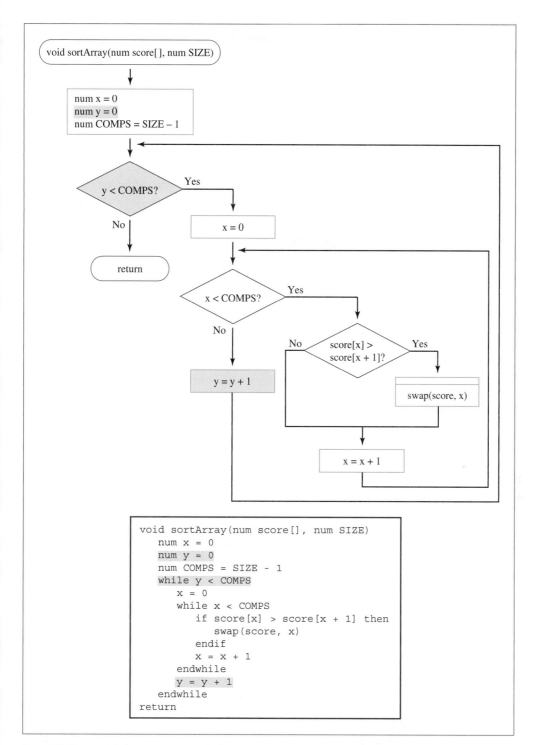

Figure 9-6 The completed sortArray() method

>> **NOTE** In the sortArray() method in Figure 9-6, it is important that x is reset to 0 for each new value of y so that the comparisons always start at the top of the list.

When you sort the elements in an array this way, you use nested loops—an inner loop within an outer loop. The general rule is that, whatever the number of elements in the array, the greatest number of pair comparisons you need to make during each loop is *one less* than the number of elements in the array. You use an inner loop to make the pair comparisons. In addition, the number of times you need to process the list of values is *one less* than the number of elements in the array. You use an outer loop to control the number of times you walk through the list. As an example, if you want to sort a 10-element array, you make nine pair comparisons on each of nine rotations through the loop, executing a total of 81 score comparison statements.

>> **NOTE** In many cases, you do not want to sort a single data item such as a score. Instead, you might want to sort data records that contain fields such as ID number, name, and score, placing the records in score order. The sorting procedure remains basically the same, but you need to store entire records in an array. Then, you make your comparisons based on a single field, but you make your swaps using entire records.

The last method called by the score-sorting program in Figure 9-2 is the one that displays the sorted array contents. Figure 9-7 shows this method.

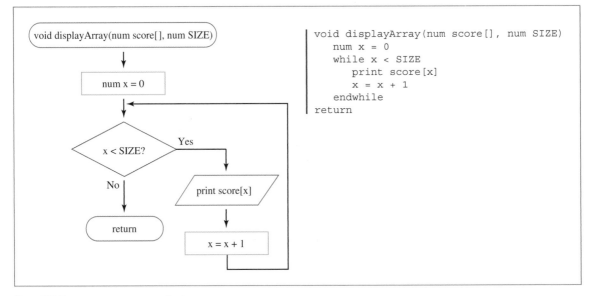

```
void displayArray(num score[], num SIZE)
    num x = 0
    while x < SIZE
        print score[x]
        x = x + 1
    endwhile
return
```

Figure 9-7 The displayArray() method

SORTING A LIST OF VARIABLE SIZE

In the score-sorting program in the previous section, a SIZE constant was initialized to the number of elements to be sorted at the start of the program. Sometimes, you don't want to create a value to represent the number of elements to be sorted at the start of the program because you might not know how many array elements will hold valid values. For example, sometimes when you run the program, you might want to sort only three or four scores, and sometimes you might want to sort 20. In other words, what if the size of the list to be sorted might vary? Rather than initializing a constant to a fixed value, you can count the input scores, and then give a variable the value of the number of array elements to use after you know how many scores exist.

To keep track of the number of elements stored in an array, you can create the application shown in Figure 9-8. As in the original version of the program, you pass the array and its size to the `fillArray()` method. Within the method, when you get each score, you increase x by 1 in order to place each new score into a successive element of the `score` array. The variable x is initialized to 0. After you read one `score` value and place it in the first element of the array, x is increased to 1. After a second score is read and placed in `score[1]`, x is increased to 2, and so on. After you reach the end of input (`eof`), x holds the number of scores that have been placed in the array, so you can return x to the main method where it is stored in `numberOfEls`. With this approach, it doesn't matter if there are not enough `score` values to fill the array. You simply pass `numberOfEls` to both `sortArray()` and `displayArray()` instead of passing `SIZE`. Using this technique, you avoid always making a larger fixed number of pair comparisons. For example, if there are 35 scores input, `numberOfEls` will be set to 35 in the `fillArray()` module, and when the program sorts, it will use 35 as a cutoff point for the number of pair comparisons to make. The sorting program will never make pair comparisons on array elements 36 through 100—those elements will just "sit there," never being involved in a comparison or swap.

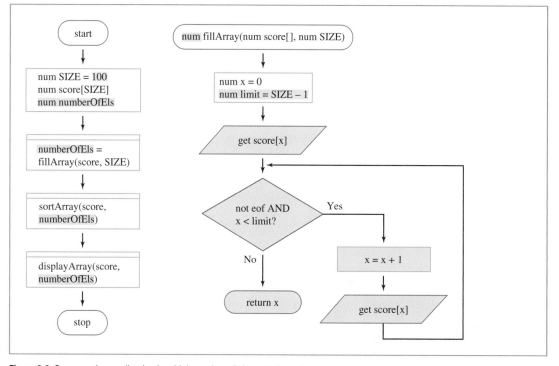

Figure 9-8 Score sorting application in which number of elements to sort can vary

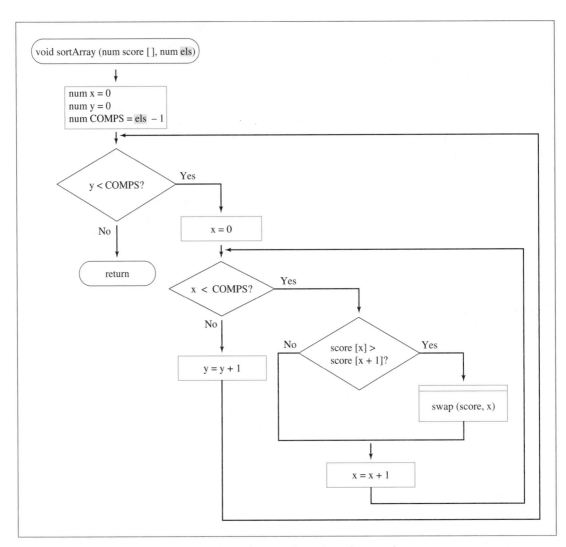

Figure 9-8 Score sorting application in which number of elements to sort can vary (*continued*)

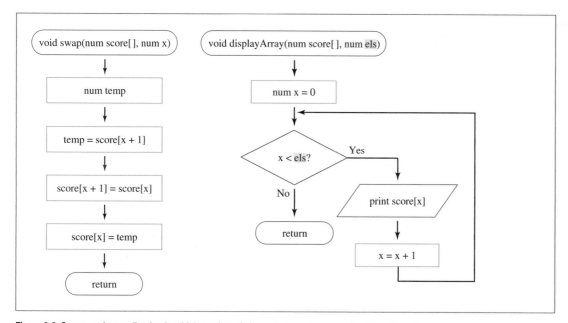

Figure 9-8 Score sorting application in which number of elements to sort can vary (*continued*)

```
start
   num SIZE = 100
   num score[SIZE]
   num numberOfEls
   numberOfEls = fillArray(score, SIZE)
   sortArray(score, numberOfEls)
   displayArray(score, numberOfEls)
stop

num fillArray(num score[], num SIZE)
   num x = 0
   num limit = SIZE - 1
   get score[x]
   while not eof AND x < limit
      x = x + 1
      get score[x]
   endwhile
return x

void sortArray(num score[], num els)
   num x = 0
   num y = 0
   num COMPS = els - 1
   while y < COMPS
      x = 0
      while x < COMPS
         if score[x] > score[x + 1] then
            swap(score, x)
         endif
         x = x + 1
      endwhile
      y = y + 1
   endwhile
return

void swap(num score[], num x)
   num temp
   temp = score[x + 1]
   score[x + 1] = score[x]
   score[x] = temp
return

void displayArray(num score[], num els)
   num x = 0
   while x < els
      print score[x]
      x = x + 1
   endwhile
return
```

Figure 9-8 Score sorting application in which number of elements to sort can vary (*continued*)

> **NOTE** In the `fillArray()` method in Figure 9-8, notice that a loop ending limit is calculated as `SIZE -1`. That's because 1 is added to `x` when the loop is entered, possibly increasing the value of `x` to equal `limit`, and that is the last legal array element in which you can store a value.

> **NOTE** In the `fillArray()` method in Figure 9-8, notice that a priming read has been added to the method. If `eof` is encountered when an attempt is made to read the first record, then the number of elements to be sorted will be 0. Within the loop, 1 is added to `x` before the next score is read. When `eof` finally is encountered, `x` represents the number of scores in the array.

> **NOTE** When you count the input records and use the `numberOfEls` variable, it does not matter if there are not enough scores to fill the array. However, it does matter if there are more scores than the array can hold. Every array must have a finite size, and it is an error to try to store data past the end of the array. When you don't know how many elements will be stored in an array, you must overestimate the number of elements you declare. If the number of scores in the score array can be 100 or fewer, then you can declare the score array to have a size of 100, and you can use 100 elements or fewer.

REFINING THE BUBBLE SORT BY REDUCING UNNECESSARY COMPARISONS

You can make additional improvements to the bubble sort created in the previous sections. As illustrated in Figure 9-8, when you perform the sorting module for a bubble sort, you pass through a list, making comparisons and swapping values if two adjacent values are out of order. If you are performing an ascending sort, then after you have made one pass through the list, the largest value is guaranteed to be in its correct final position at the bottom of the list. Similarly, the second-largest element is guaranteed to be in its correct second-to-last position after the second pass through the list, and so on. If you continue to compare every element pair in the list on every pass through the list, you are comparing elements that are already guaranteed to be in their final correct position. In other words, after the first pass through the list, there is no longer a need to check the bottom element; after the second pass, there is no need to check the two bottom elements.

On each pass through the array, you can afford to stop your pair comparisons one element sooner. You can avoid comparing the already-in-place values by creating a new variable, `pairsToCompare`, and setting it equal to the value of `numberOfEls - 1`. On the first pass through the list, every pair of elements is compared, so `pairsToCompare` *should* equal `numberOfEls - 1`. In other words, with five array elements to sort, there are four pairs to compare, and with 50 elements to sort, there are 49 pairs to compare. On each subsequent pass through the list, `pairsToCompare` should be reduced by 1, because after the first pass there's no need to check the bottom element anymore. See Figure 9-9 to examine the use of the `pairsToCompare` variable.

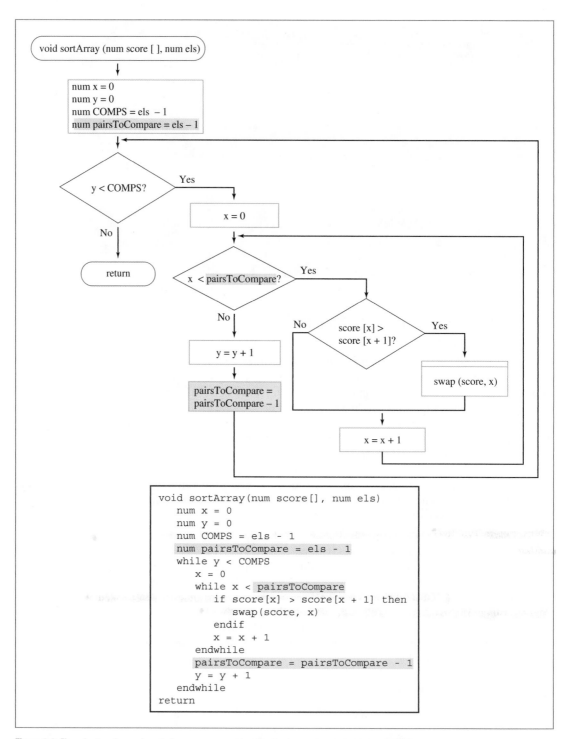

Figure 9-9 Flowchart and pseudocode for `sortArray()` method using `pairsToCompare` variable

REFINING THE BUBBLE SORT BY ELIMINATING UNNECESSARY PASSES

Another improvement that could be made to the bubble sort module in Figure 9-9 is one that reduces the number of passes through the array. If array elements are so badly out of order that they are in reverse order, then it takes many passes through the list to place it in order; it takes one fewer pass than the value in els to complete all the comparisons and swaps needed to get the list sorted. However, when the array elements are in order or nearly in order to start, all the elements might be correctly arranged after only a few passes through the list. All subsequent passes result in no swaps. For example, assume the original scores are as follows:

```
score[0]  =  65
score[1]  =  75
score[2]  =  85
score[3]  =  90
score[4]  =  95
```

The bubble sort module in Figure 9-9 would pass through the array list four times, making four sets of pair comparisons. It would always find that each score[x] is *not* greater than the corresponding score[x + 1], so no switches would ever be made. The scores would end up in the proper order, but they *were* in the proper order in the first place; therefore, a lot of time would be wasted.

A possible remedy is to add a flag variable that you set to a "continue" value on any pass through the list in which any pair of elements is swapped (even if just one pair), and that holds a different "finished" value when no swaps are made—that is, all elements in the list are already in the correct order. For example, you can create a variable named switchOccurred and set it to "No" at the start of each pass through the list. You can change its value to "Yes" each time the swap() module is performed (that is, each time a switch is necessary).

If you ever "make it through" the entire list of pairs without making a switch, the switchOccurred flag will *not* have been set to "Yes", meaning that no switch has occurred and that the array elements must already be in the correct order. This *might* be on the first or second pass through the array list, or it might not be until a much later pass. If the array elements are already in the correct order at any point, there is no need to make more passes through the list. You can stop making passes through the list when switchOccurred is "No" after a complete trip through the array.

Figure 9-10 illustrates a module that sorts scores and uses a switchOccurred flag. At the beginning of the sortScores() module, initialize switchOccurred to "Yes" before entering the comparison loop the first time. Then, immediately set switchOccurred to "No". When a switch occurs—that is, when the swap() module executes—set switchOccurred to "Yes".

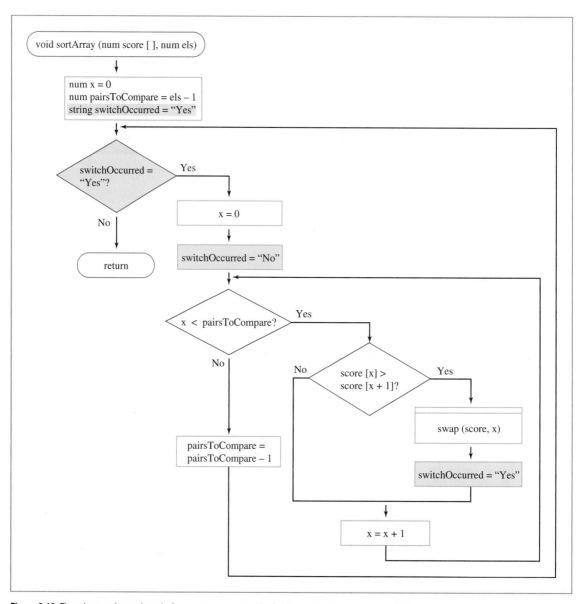

Figure 9-10 Flowchart and pseudocode for `sortArray()` method using `switchOccurred` variable

```
void sortArray(num score[], num els)
    num x = 0
    num pairsToCompare = els - 1
    string switchOccurred = "Yes"
    while switchOccurred = "Yes"
        x = 0
        switchOccurred = "No"
        while x < pairsToCompare
            if score[x] > score[x + 1] then
                swap(score, x)
                switchOccurred = "Yes"
            endif
            x = x + 1
        endwhile
        pairsToCompare = pairsToCompare - 1
    endwhile
return
```

Figure 9-10 Flowchart and pseudocode for `sortArray()` method using `switchOccurred` variable (*continued*)

»NOTE With the addition of the flag variable in Figure 9-10, you no longer need the variable `y`, which was keeping track of the number of passes through the list. You also no longer need the constant `COMPS`, which kept track of the number of comparisons to be made. Instead, you just keep going through the list until you can make a complete pass without any switches. For a list that starts in perfect order, you go through the loop only once. For a list that starts in the worst possible order, you will make a switch with every pair each time through the loop until `pairsToCompare` has been reduced to 0. In this case, on the last pass through the loop, `x` is set to 1, `switchOccurred` is set to "No", `x` is no longer less than or equal to `pairsToCompare`, and the loop is exited.

»NOTE If the programming language you use supports a Boolean-type variable (one that can be set to true or false), then you can define `switchOccurred` to be that type instead of a string.

TWO TRUTHS AND A LIE:
USING A BUBBLE SORT

1. You can use a bubble sort to arrange records in ascending or descending order.

2. In a bubble sort, items in a list are compared with each other in pairs, and when an item is out of order, it swaps values with the item below it.

3. With any bubble sort, after each adjacent pair of items in a list has been compared once, the largest item in the list will have "sunk" to the bottom.

The false statement is #3. With an ascending bubble sort, after each adjacent pair of items in a list has been compared once, the largest item in the list will have "sunk" to the bottom. However, with a descending bubble sort, after each adjacent pair of items in a list has been compared once, the smallest item in the list will have "sunk" to the bottom.

USING AN INSERTION SORT

The bubble sort works well and is relatively easy for novice array users to understand and manipulate, but even with all the improvements you added to the original bubble sort in previous sections, it is actually one of the least efficient sorting methods available. An insertion sort provides an alternate method for sorting data, and it usually requires fewer comparison operations.

> **▶▶NOTE** Although a sort (such as the bubble sort) might be inefficient, it is easy to understand. When programming, you frequently weigh the advantages of using simple solutions against writing more complicated ones that perform more efficiently.

As with the bubble sort, when using an **insertion sort**, you also look at each pair of elements in an array. When you find an element that is smaller than the one before it (for an ascending sort), this element is "out of order." As soon as you locate such an element, search the array backward from that point to see where an element smaller than the out-of-order element is located. At that point, you open a new position for the out-of-order element by moving each subsequent element down one position. Then, you insert the out-of-order element into the newly opened position.

For example, consider these scores:

```
score[0] = 65
score[1] = 80
score[2] = 95
score[3] = 75
score[4] = 90
```

If you want to rearrange the scores in ascending order using an insertion sort, you begin by comparing score[0] and score[1], which are 65 and 80, respectively. You determine that they are in order, and leave them alone. Then, you compare score[1] and score[2], which are 80 and 95, and leave them alone. When you compare score[2], 95, and score[3], 75, you determine that the 75 is "out of order." Next, you look backward from the score[3] of 75. The value of score[2] is not smaller than score[3], nor is score[1]; however, because score[0] is smaller than score[3], score[3] should follow score[0]. So you store score[3] in a temporary variable, then move score[1] and score[2] "down" the list to higher subscripted positions. You move score[2], 95, to the score[3] position. Then, you move score[1], 80, to the score[2] position. Finally, you assign the value of the temporary variable, 75, to the score[1] position. Figure 9-11 diagrams the movements as 75 moves up to the second position and 80 and 95 move down.

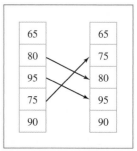

Figure 9-11 Movement of the value 75 to a "better" array position in an insertion sort

After the sort finds the first element that was out of order and inserts it in a "better" location, the results are:

```
score[0] = 65
score[1] = 75
score[2] = 80
score[3] = 95
score[4] = 90
```

You then continue down the list, comparing each pair of variables. A complete insertion sort module is shown in Figure 9-12.

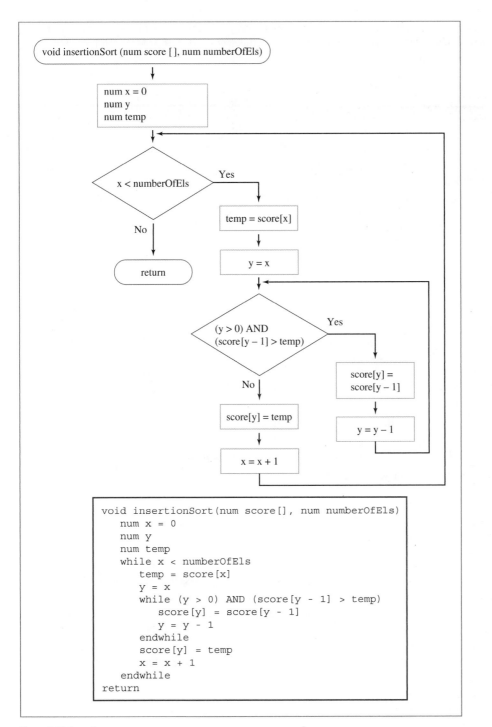

```
void insertionSort(num score[], num numberOfEls)
   num x = 0
   num y
   num temp
   while x < numberOfEls
      temp = score[x]
      y = x
      while (y > 0) AND (score[y - 1] > temp)
         score[y] = score[y - 1]
         y = y - 1
      endwhile
      score[y] = temp
      x = x + 1
   endwhile
return
```

Figure 9-12 Insertion sort

> **» NOTE**
> In Figure 9-12, parentheses enclose each half of the Boolean expression `(y > 0) AND (score[y - 1] > temp)` so you can more clearly discern the two parts of the question.

The logic for the insertion sort is slightly more complicated than that for the bubble sort, but the insertion sort is more efficient because, for the average out-of-order list, it takes fewer "switches" to put the list in order.

TWO TRUTHS AND A LIE:
USING AN INSERTION SORT

1. An insertion sort usually requires more comparison operations than a bubble sort.

2. As with the bubble sort, when using an insertion sort, the basis of the process is to compare array element pairs.

3. An insertion sort can be ascending or descending.

The false statement is #1. An insertion sort usually requires fewer comparison operations than a bubble sort.

USING A SELECTION SORT

A selection sort provides another sorting option. In an ascending **selection sort**, the first element in the array is assumed to be the smallest. Its value is stored in a variable—for example, smallest—and its position in the array, 0, is stored in another variable—for example, position. Then, every subsequent element in the array is tested. If one with a smaller value than smallest is found, smallest is set to the new value, and position is set to that element's position. After the entire array has been searched, smallest holds the smallest value and position holds its position.

The element originally in position[0]is then switched with the smallest value, so at the end of the first pass through the array, the lowest value ends up in the first position, and the value that was in the first position is where the smallest value used to be.

For example, assume you have the following list of scores:

```
score[0] = 95
score[1] = 80
score[2] = 75
score[3] = 65
score[4] = 90
```

First, you place 95 in smallest. Then check score[1]; it's less than 95, so place 1 in position and 80 in smallest. Then test score[2]; it's smaller than smallest, so place 2 in position and 75 in smallest. Then test score[3]; because it is smaller than smallest, place 3 in position and 65 in smallest. Finally, check score[4]; it *isn't* smaller than smallest.

So at the end of the first pass through the list, position is 3 and smallest is 65. You move the value 95 to score[position], or score[3], and the value of smallest, 65, to score[0]. The list becomes:

```
score[0] = 65
score[1] = 80
score[2] = 75
score[3] = 95
score[4] = 90
```

Now that the smallest value is in the first position, you repeat the whole procedure starting with the second array element, `score[1]`. After you have passed through the list `numberOfEls - 1` times, all elements will be in the correct order. Walk through the logic shown in Figure 9-13.

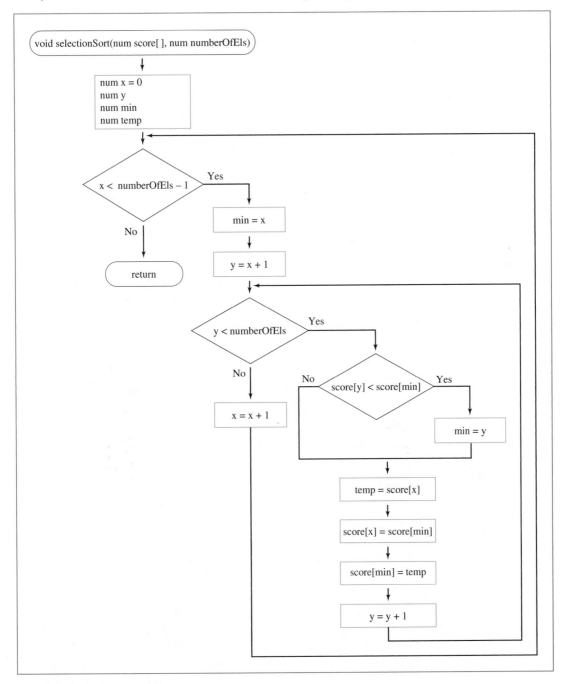

Figure 9-13 A selection sort method

```
void selectionSort(num score[], num numberOfEls)
   num x = 0
   num y
   num min
   num temp
   while x < numberOfEls - 1
      min = x
      y = x + 1
      while y < numberOfEls
         if score[y] < score[min] then
            min = y
         temp = score[x]
         score[x] = score[min]
         score[min] = temp
         y = y + 1
         endif
      endwhile
      x = x + 1
   endwhile
```

Figure 9-13 A selection sort method (*continued*)

Like the insertion sort, the selection sort almost always requires fewer switches than the bubble sort, but the variables might be a little harder to keep track of because the logic is a little more complex. Thoroughly understanding at least one of these sorting techniques provides you with a valuable tool for arranging data and increases your understanding of the capabilities of arrays.

>> **NOTE** Besides the bubble, insertion, and selection sorts, there are many other sorting algorithms with colorful names such as the cocktail sort, gnome sort, and quick sort.

>> **NOTE** Remember that you might never have to write your own sorting method. Many languages come with already created sorting methods that you use as black boxes. However, taking the time to understand some sorting procedures increases your ability to work with arrays.

TWO TRUTHS AND A LIE:
USING A SELECTION SORT

1. In an ascending selection sort, the first step is to swap the first element in an array with the smallest value.

2. In an ascending selection sort, at the end of the first pass through the array, the highest value ends up in the first position.

3. The selection sort almost always requires fewer switches than the bubble sort.

The false statement is #2. In an ascending selection sort, at the end of the first pass through the array, the smallest value ends up in the first position, and the value that was in the first position is where the smallest value used to be.

USING MULTIDIMENSIONAL ARRAYS

When you declare an array such as `numeric rent[5]`, you can envision the three declared numbers as a column of numbers in memory, as shown in Figure 9-14. In other words, you can picture the three declared numbers stacked one on top of the next. An array that you can picture as a column of values, and whose elements you can access using a single subscript, is a **one-dimensional** or **single-dimensional array**.

rent[0] = 350
rent[1] = 400
rent[2] = 475
rent[3] = 600
rent[4] = 1000

Figure 9-14 View of a single-dimensional array in memory

>> **NOTE**   You can think of the single dimension of a single-dimensional array as the height of the array.

The location of any `rent` value in Figure 9-14 depends on only a single variable—the floor of the building. Sometimes, however, locating a value in an array depends on more than one variable. If you must represent values in a table or grid that contains rows and columns instead of a single list, then you might want to use a **multidimensional array**. A multidimensional array contains more than one dimension. That is, the location of any element depends on more than one factor. For example, if an apartment's rent depends on both the floor of the building and the number of bedrooms, then you want to create a **two-dimensional array**.

As an example of how useful two-dimensional arrays can be, assume you own an apartment building with four floors—a basement, which you refer to as floor zero, and three other floors numbered one, two, and three. In addition, each of the floors has studios (with no bedroom) and one- and two-bedroom apartments. The monthly rent for each type of apartment is different—the higher the floor, the higher the rent (the view is better), and the rent is higher for apartments with more bedrooms. Table 9-1 shows the rental amounts.

Floor	Studio Apartment	1-bedroom Apartment	2-bedroom Apartment
0	350	390	435
1	400	440	480
2	475	530	575
3	600	650	700
4	1000	1075	1150

Table 9-1 Rent schedule based on floor and number of bedrooms

To determine a tenant's rent, you need to know two pieces of information: the floor on which the tenant rents an apartment and the number of bedrooms in the apartment. Each element in a two-dimensional array requires two subscripts to reference it—one subscript to determine the row and a second to determine the column. Thus, the 15 separate `rent` values for a two-dimensional array based on the rent table in Table 9-1 would be arranged in five rows and three columns and defined as shown in Figure 9-15. When you declare a one-dimensional array, you type a set of square brackets after the array type. To declare a two-dimensional array, many languages require you to type two sets of brackets after the array type. For each element in Figure 9-15, the first square bracket holds the row number, and the second one holds the column number.

```
rent[0][0] = 350
rent[0][1] = 390
rent[0][2] = 435
rent[1][0] = 400
rent[1][1] = 440
rent[1][2] = 480
•
•
•
rent[4][2] = 1150
```

Figure 9-15 Two-dimensional `rent` array based on rent schedule in Table 9-1

NOTE You can think of the two dimensions of a two-dimensional array as height and width.

NOTE Instead of two sets of brackets to indicate a position in a two-dimensional array, some languages use a single set of brackets but separate the subscripts with commas. Therefore, the elements in row 1, column 2 would be `rent[1, 2]`.

NOTE When mathematicians use a two-dimensional array, they often call it a **matrix** or a **table**; you might have used a two-dimensional array called a spreadsheet.

In many programming languages, if you do not provide initial values for a numeric array, then each element is 0 by default. Usually, you can initialize an array's values when you declare it. Therefore, a `RENT` array could be declared with a statement similar to the following:

```
num RENT[5][3] = {350, 390, 435},
                 {400, 440, 480},
                 {475, 530, 575},
                 {600, 650, 700},
                 {1000, 1075, 1150}
```

NOTE Just as within a one-dimensional array, each element in a multidimensional array must be the same data type.

In this example, the values that are assigned to each row are enclosed in braces to help you picture the placement of each number in the array. The first row of the array holds the three rent values 350, 390, and 435. The value of `rent[4][2]` is 1150. Also, in this example, the rents are assumed to be constant, so an all-uppercase identifier is used for the array. Assuming you declare two variables to hold the floor number and bedroom count as `num floor` and `num bedrooms`, any tenant's rent is `RENT[floor] [bedrooms]`.

Two-dimensional arrays are never actually *required* in order to achieve a useful program. The same 15 categories of rent information could be stored in three separate single-dimensional arrays of five elements each. Of course, don't forget that even one-dimensional arrays are never *required* for you to be able to solve a problem. You could also declare 15 separate rent variables and make 15 separate decisions to determine the rent.

Figure 9-16 shows a program that displays rents for apartments based on renter requests for bedrooms and floor. Notice that although significant setup is required to provide all the values for the rents, the basic program is extremely brief and easy to follow.

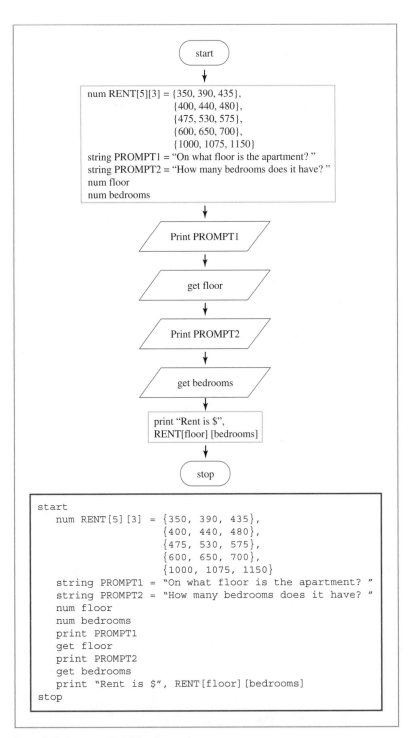

Figure 9-16 A program that determines rents

Besides one- and two-dimensional arrays, many programming languages also support **three-dimensional arrays**. For example, if you own an apartment building with a number of floors and different numbers of bedrooms available in apartments on each floor, you can use a two-dimensional array to store the rental fees, but if you own several apartment buildings, you might want to employ a third dimension to store the building number. An expression such as `rents[building][floor][bedrooms]` refers to a specific rent figure for a building whose building number is stored in the `building` variable, and whose floor and bedroom numbers are stored in the `floor` and `bedrooms` variables. Specifically, `rents[5][1][2]` refers to a two-bedroom apartment on the first floor of building 5 (which is the sixth building in an array where the first building is referenced with a 0 subscript).

Some languages allow even more dimensions. For example, in C# and Visual Basic, an array can have 32 dimensions. It's usually hard for people to keep track of more than three dimensions, but if five variables determine rent—for example, floor number, number of bedrooms, building number, city number, and state number—you might want to try using a five-dimensional array.

TWO TRUTHS AND A LIE:
USING MULTIDIMENSIONAL ARRAYS

1. In a multidimensional array, the location of any element depends on two factors.

2. For each element in a two-dimensional array, the first subscript represents the row number, and the second one represents the column.

3. Multidimensional arrays are never actually *required* in order to achieve a useful program.

The false statement is #1. In a two-dimensional array, the location of any element depends on two factors, but in a three-dimensional array, it depends on three factors, and so on.

USING A BUILT-IN ~~ARRAY~~ CLASS

Selection

When you fully understand the power of arrays, you will want to use them to store all kinds of objects. Frequently, you will want to perform similar tasks with different arrays—for example, filling them with values and sorting their elements. Many modern programming languages provide an **Array class**, which contains many useful methods for manipulating arrays. One of the advantages of using newer languages is the vast libraries of classes that contain useful built-in methods that are available to you. The `Array` class is just one of many examples.

»NOTE Many classes are built-in, but you can also create your own classes. You will learn more about classes in Chapter 11.

»NOTE If a language provides a class to help you work with arrays, it might have a name other than `Array`. For example, in C# and Visual Basic, the class is `Array` but in Java, the corresponding class is `Arrays`.

Table 9-2 shows some of the typically included, useful methods of the `Array` class. The most useful `Array` class would contain overloaded versions of each method for each appropriate data type. For example, you would want a version of the `sort()` method to sort numeric elements and another version to sort string elements.

Method	Purpose
`numeric binarySearch(type a[], type key)`	Searches the specified array (name `a` of type `type`) for the specified key value using the binary search algorithm
`boolean equals(type a[], type a2[])`	Returns true if the two specified arrays of the same type are equal to one another and false if they are not
`void fill (type a[], type val)`	Assigns the specified value `val` to each element of the specified array
`void sort (type a[])`	Sorts the specified array into ascending numerical order

Table 9-2 Typical useful methods of the `Array` class

If you are using a programming language that does not provide a built-in `Array` class to perform common array-based tasks, you could write one yourself. Doing so would require a lot of code-writing up front, but the future availability of useful methods to handle common array tasks would be well worth the effort.

TWO TRUTHS AND A LIE:
USING A BUILT-IN ARRAY **CLASS**

1. A typically included, useful method of an `Array` class is one that sorts array elements.

2. A typically included, useful method of an `Array` class is one that allows elements of diverse types to be stored in an array.

3. A typically included, useful method of an `Array` class is one that searches an array for a specified key.

The false statement is #2. Arrays are always composed of elements of the same type.

USING INDEXED FILES

Sorting a list of five or even 100 scores does not require significant computer resources. However, many data files contain thousands of records, and each record might contain dozens of data fields. Sorting large numbers of data records requires considerable time and computer memory. When a large data file needs to be processed in ascending or descending order based on some field, it is usually more efficient to store and access records based on their logical order than to sort and access them in their physical order. When records are stored, they are stored in some physical order. For example, if you write the names of 10 friends, each one on an index card, the stack of cards has a **physical order**—that is, a "real" order. You can arrange the cards alphabetically by the friends' last names, chronologically by age of the friendship, or randomly by throwing the cards in the air and picking them up as you find them. Whichever way you do it, the records still follow each other in *some* order. In addition to their current physical order, you can think of the cards as having a **logical order**; that is, a virtual order, based on any criterion you choose—from the tallest friend to the shortest, from the one who lives farthest away to the closest, and so on. Sorting the cards in a new physical order can take a lot of time; using the cards in their logical order without physically rearranging them is often more efficient.

A common method of accessing records in logical order is to use an index. Using an index involves identifying a key field for each record. A record's **key field** is the field whose contents make the record unique among all records in a file. For example, multiple employees can have the same last name, first name, salary, or street address, but each employee possesses a unique employee identification number, so an ID number field might make a good key field for a personnel file. Similarly, a product number makes a good key field on an inventory file.

When you **index** records, you store a list of key fields paired with the storage address for the corresponding data record. When you use an index, you can store records on a **random-access storage device**, such as a disk, from which records can be accessed in any logical order. Each record can be placed in any physical location on the disk, and you can use the index as you would use the index in the back of a book. If you pick up a 600-page American history text because you need some facts about Betsy Ross, you do not want to start on page one and work your way through the text. Instead, you turn to the index, discover that Betsy Ross is mentioned on page 418, and go directly to that page.

»NOTE
You do not need to determine a record's exact physical address in order to use it. A computer's operating system takes care of locating available storage for your records.

As pages in a book have numbers, computer memory and storage locations have **addresses**. In Chapter 1, you learned that every variable has a numeric address in computer memory; likewise, every data record on a disk has a numeric address where it is stored. You can store records in any physical order on the disk, but the index can find the records in order based on their addresses. For example, you might store a list of employees on a disk in the order in which they were hired. However, you often need to process the employees in identification number order. When adding a new employee to such a file, you can physically place the employee anywhere there is room available on the disk. Her ID number is inserted in proper order in the index, along with the physical address where her record is located.

You can picture an index based on ID numbers by looking at Table 9-3.

When you want to access the data for employee 333, you tell your computer to look through the ID numbers in the index, find a match, and then proceed to the memory location specified. Similarly, when you want to process records in order based on ID number, you tell

ID Number	Location
111	6400
222	4800
333	2400
444	5200

Table 9-3 Sample index

your system to retrieve records at the locations in the index in sequence. Thus, even though employee 111 may have been hired last and the record is stored at the highest physical address on the disk, if the employee record has the lowest ID number, it will be accessed first during any ordered processing.

When a record is removed from an indexed file, it does not have to be physically removed. Its reference can simply be deleted from the index, and then it will not be part of any further processing.

TWO TRUTHS AND A LIE:

USING INDEXED FILES

1. When a large data file needs to be processed in order based on some field, it is usually most efficient to sort the records.

2. A common method of accessing records in logical order is to use an index.

3. A record's key field is the field whose contents make the record unique among all records in a file.

The false statement is #1. It usually is most efficient to store and access records based on their logical order than to sort and access them in their physical order.

USING LINKED LISTS

Another way to access records in a desired order, even though they might not be physically stored in that order, is to create a linked list. In its simplest form, creating a **linked list** involves creating one extra field in every record of stored data. This extra field holds the physical address of the next logical record. For example, a record that holds a customer's ID, name, and phone number might contain the fields:

```
custId
custName
custPhoneNum
custNextCustAddress
```

Every time you use a record, you access the next record based on the address held in the `custNextCustAddress` field.

Every time you add a new record to a linked list, you search through the list for the correct logical location for the new record. For example, assume that customer records are stored at the addresses shown in Table 9-4 and that they are linked in customer ID order. Notice that the addresses of the records are not shown in sequential order. The records are shown in their logical order, with each one's `custNextCustAddress` field holding the address of the record shown in the following line.

Address of Record	custId	custName	custPhoneNum	custNextCustAddress
0000	111	Baker	234-5676	7200
7200	222	Vincent	456-2345	4400
4400	333	Silvers	543-0912	6000
6000	444	Donovan	329-8744	eof

Table 9-4 Sample linked customer list

You can see from Table 9-4 that each customer's record contains a custNextCustAddress field that stores the address of the next customer who follows in customer ID number order (and not necessarily in address order). For any individual customer, the next logical customer's address might be physically distant. Each customer record, besides containing data about that customer, contains a custNextCustAddress field that associates the customer with the next customer who follows in custId value order.

Examine the file shown in Table 9-4, and suppose a new customer with number 245 and the name Newberg is acquired. Also suppose the computer operating system finds an available storage location for Newberg's data at address 8400. In this case, the procedure to add Newberg to the list is:

1. Create a variable named currentAddress to hold the address of the record in the list you are currently examining. Store the address of the first record in the list, 0000, in this variable.

2. Compare the new customer Newberg's ID, 245, with the current (first) record's ID, 111 (in other words, the ID at address 0000). The value 245 is higher than 111, so you save the first customer's address (the address you are currently examining), 0000, in a variable you can name saveAddress. The saveAddress variable always holds the address you just finished examining. The first customer's record contains a link to the address of the next logical customer—7200. Store the 7200 in the currentAddress variable.

3. Examine the second customer record, the one that physically exists at the address 7200, which is currently held in the currentAddress variable.

4. Compare Newberg's ID, 245, with the ID stored in the record at currentAddress, 222. The value 245 is higher, so save the current address, 7200, in saveAddress and store its custNextCustAddress address field, 4400, in the currentAddress variable.

5. Compare Newberg's ID, 245, with 333, which is the ID at currentAddress (4400). Up to this point, 245 had been higher than each ID tested, but this time the value 245 is lower, so that means customer 245 should logically precede customer 333. Set the custNextCustAddress field in Newberg's record (customer 245) to 4400, which is the address of customer 333 and the address currently stored in currentAddress. This means that in any future processing, Newberg's record will logically be followed by the record containing 333. Also set the custNextCustAddress field of the record located at saveAddress (7200, Vincent, customer 222, the customer who logically preceded Newberg) to the new customer Newberg's address, 8400. The updated list appears in Table 9-5.

Address of Record	custId	custName	custPhoneNum	custNextCustAddress
0000	111	Baker	234-5676	7200
7200	222	Vincent	456-2345	8400
8400	245	Newberg	222-9876	4400
4400	333	Silvers	543-0912	6000
6000	444	Donovan	329-8744	eof

Table 9-5 Updated customer list

As with indexing, when removing records from a linked list, the records do not need to be physically deleted from the medium on which they are stored. If you need to remove customer 333 from the preceding list, all you need to do is change Newberg's custNextCustAddress field to the value in Silvers' custNextCustAddress field, which is Donovan's address: 6000. In other words, the value of 6000 is obtained not by knowing who Newberg should point to, but by knowing who Silvers used to point to. When Newberg's record points to Donovan, Silvers' record is then bypassed during any further processing that uses the links to travel from one record to the next.

More sophisticated linked lists store *two* additional fields with each record. One field stores the address of the next record, and the other field stores the address of the *previous* record so that the list can be accessed either forward or backward.

> **TWO TRUTHS AND A LIE:**
> **USING LINKED LISTS**
>
> 1. Creating a linked list requires you to create one extra field for every record; this extra field holds the physical address of the record.
>
> 2. Every time you add a new record to a linked list, you alter a field in an existing record to contain the address of the new record.
>
> 3. When removing records from a linked list, the records do not need to be physically deleted from the medium on which they are stored.
>
> The false statement is #1. In a linked list, the extra field in each record holds the physical address of the next logical record.

CHAPTER SUMMARY

» Frequently, data records need to be sorted, or placed in order, based on the contents of one or more fields. When you sort data, you can sort either in ascending order, arranging records from lowest to highest value, or descending order, arranging records from highest to lowest value.

» Swapping two values is a concept that is central to most sorting techniques. When you swap the values stored in two variables, you reverse their positions using a temporary variable to hold one of the values during the swap process.

» In a bubble sort, items in a list are compared with each other in pairs, and when an item is out of order, it swaps values with the item below it. With an ascending bubble sort, after each adjacent pair of items in a list has been compared once, the largest item in the list will have "sunk" to the bottom. After many passes through the list, the smallest items rise to the top like bubbles in a carbonated drink.

» Sometimes, the size of the list to be sorted might vary. Rather than initializing a constant to a fixed value, you can count the values to be sorted, and then give a variable the value of the number of array elements to use after you know how many scores exist.

» You can improve a bubble sort by stopping pair comparisons one element sooner on each pass through the array being sorted.

» You can improve a bubble sort by adding a flag variable that you set to a "continue" value on any pass through the sort in which any pair of elements is swapped (even if just one pair), and that holds a different "finished" value when no swaps are made—that is, all elements in the list are already in the correct order.

» An insertion sort provides an alternate method for sorting data, and it usually requires fewer comparison operations. As with the bubble sort, when using an insertion sort, you also look at each pair of elements in an array. When you find an element that is smaller than the one before it (for an ascending sort), this element is "out of order." As soon as you locate such an element, search the array backward from that point to see where an element smaller than the out-of-order element is located. At that point, you open a new position for the out-of-order element by moving each subsequent element down one position. Then, you insert the out-of-order element into the newly opened position.

» In an ascending selection sort, the first element in the array is assumed to be the smallest. Its value is stored in a variable—for example, `smallest`—and its position in the array, 0, is stored in another variable—for example, `position`. Then, every subsequent element in the array is tested. If one with a smaller value than `smallest` is found, `smallest` is set to the new value, and `position` is set to that element's position. After the entire array has been searched, `smallest` holds the smallest value and `position` holds its position. The element originally in `position[0]` is then switched with the `smallest` value, so at the end of the first pass through the array, the lowest value ends up in the first position, and the value that was in the first position is where the smallest value used to be.

» An array that you can picture as a column of values, and whose elements you can access using a single subscript, is a one-dimensional or single-dimensional array. Most object-oriented programming (OOP) languages also support two-dimensional arrays. Two-dimensional arrays have both rows and columns of values. You must use two subscripts when you access an element in a two-dimensional array.

» Many OOP languages provide an `Array` class, which contains many useful methods for manipulating arrays.

» You can use an index to access data records in a logical order that differs from their physical order. Using an index involves identifying a key field for each record.

» Creating a linked list involves creating an extra field within every record to hold the physical address of the next logical record.

KEY TERMS

When records are in **sequential order**, they are arranged one after another on the basis of the value in some field.

Sorted records are in order based on the contents of one or more fields.

Records in **ascending order** are arranged from lowest to highest, based on a value within a field.

Records in **descending order** are arranged from highest to lowest, based on a value within a field.

The **median** value in a list is the value in the middle position when the values are sorted.

The **mean** value in a list is the arithmetic average.

Swapping two values is the process of setting the first variable equal to the value of the second, and the second variable equal to the value of the first.

A **bubble sort** is a sort in which you arrange records in either ascending or descending order by comparing items in a list in pairs; when an item is out of order, it swaps values with the item below it. *Cambiar*

A **sinking sort** is another name for a bubble sort.

An **algorithm** is a list of instructions that accomplishes some task.

In an **insertion sort**, each pair of elements in an array is compared, and when an out-of-order element is found, a backward search is made for an element smaller than the out-of-order element located. At that point, a new position is opened for the out-of-order element and each subsequent element is moved down one position.

In an ascending **selection sort**, you search for the smallest list value, and then swap it with the value in the first position. You then repeat the process with each subsequent list position.

A **one-dimensional** or **single-dimensional array** is a list accessed using a single subscript.

Multidimensional arrays can have any number of dimensions.

Two-dimensional arrays have both rows and columns of values; you must use two subscripts when you access an element in a two-dimensional array.

When mathematicians use a two-dimensional array, they often call it a **matrix** or a **table**.

Three-dimensional arrays are arrays in which each element is accessed using three subscripts.

An `Array` **class** is a class provided with many OOP languages that contains useful methods for manipulating arrays.

A list's **physical order** is the order in which it is actually stored.

A list's **logical order** is the order in which you use it, even though it is not necessarily physically stored in that order.

A record's **key field** is the field whose contents make the record unique among all records in a file.

When you **index** records, you store a list of key fields paired with the storage address for the corresponding data record.

A **random-access storage device**, such as a disk, is one from which records can be accessed in any order.

Computer memory and storage locations have **addresses**.

Creating a **linked list** involves creating one extra field in every record of stored data. This extra field holds the physical address of the next logical record.

REVIEW QUESTIONS

1. **Employee records stored in order from highest-paid to lowest-paid have been sorted in _____ order.**

   a. ascending

   b. descending

   c. staggered

   d. recursive

2. **Student records stored in alphabetical order by last name have been sorted in _____ order.**

   a. ascending

   b. descending

   c. staggered

   d. recursive

3. **In the series of numbers 7, 5, 5, 5, 3, 2, and 1, what is the mean?**

   a. 3

   b. 4

   c. 5

   d. 6

4. **When computers sort data, they always _____.**

   a. place items in ascending order

   b. use a bubble sort

   c. use numeric values when making comparisons

   d. begin the process by locating the position of the lowest value

5. **Which of the following code segments correctly swaps the values of variables named x and y?**

   a.
   ```
   x = y
   y = temp
   x = temp
   ```

   b.
   ```
   temp = x
   x = y
   y = temp
   ```

   c.
   ```
   x = y
   temp = x
   y = temp
   ```

   d.
   ```
   temp = x
   y = x
   x = temp
   ```

6. **Which type of sort compares list items in pairs, swapping any two adjacent values that are out of order?**

   a. bubble sort   c. insertion sort

   b. indexed sort   d. selection sort

7. **Which type of sort compares pairs of values, looking for an out-of-order element, then searches the array backward from that point to see where an element smaller than the out-of-order element is located?**

   a. bubble sort   c. insertion sort

   b. indexed sort   d. selection sort

8. **Which type of sort tests each value in a list, looking for the smallest, then switches the element in the first list position with the smallest value?**

   a. bubble sort   c. insertion sort

   b. indexed sort   d. selection sort

9. **To sort a list of eight values using a bubble sort, the greatest number of times you would have to pass through the list making comparisons is _____ .**

   a. six   c. eight

   b. seven   d. nine

10. **To sort a list of eight values using a bubble sort, the greatest number of pair comparisons you would have to make before the sort is complete is _____ .**

    a. seven   c. 49

    b. eight   d. 64

11. **When you do not know how many items need to be sorted in a program, you create an array that has _____ .**

    a. variable-sized elements

    b. a variable number of elements

    c. at least one element less than the number you predict you will need

    d. at least as many elements as the number you predict you will need

12. **In a bubble sort, on each pass through the list that must be sorted, you can stop making pair comparisons _____ .**

    a. one comparison sooner

    b. two comparisons sooner

    c. one comparison later

    d. two comparisons later

13. When performing a bubble sort on a list of 10 values, you can stop making passes through the list of values as soon as _____ on a single pass through the list.

a. no swaps are made

b. exactly one swap is made

c. no more than nine swaps are made

d. no more than 10 swaps are made

14. Student records are stored in ID number order, but accessed by grade point average for a report. Grade point average order is a(n) _____ order.

a. imaginary

c. logical

b. physical

d. illogical

15. Data stored in a table that can be accessed using row and column numbers is stored as a _____ array.

a. single-dimensional

c. three-dimensional

b. two-dimensional

d. nondimensional

16. The Funland Amusement Park charges entrance fees, as shown in the following table. The table is stored as an array named `price` in a program that determines ticket price based on two factors: number of tickets purchased and month of the year. A clerk enters the month (5 through 9 for May through September), from which 5 is subtracted, so the month value becomes 0 through 4. A clerk also enters the number of tickets being purchased; if the number is over 6, it is forced to be 6. One is subtracted from the number of people, so the value is 0 through 5.

People in Party	Adjusted Month Number				
	0	1	2	3	4
0	29.00	34.00	36.00	36.00	29.00
1	28.00	32.00	34.00	34.00	28.00
2	26.00	30.00	32.00	32.00	26.00
3	24.00	26.00	27.00	28.00	25.00
4	23.00	25.00	26.00	27.00	23.00
5	20.00	23.00	24.00	25.00	21.00

What is the price of a ticket for any party purchasing tickets?

a. `price[tickets][month]`

b. `price[month][tickets]`

c. `month[tickets][price]`

d. `tickets[price][month]`

17. **Using the same table as in Question 16, where is the ticket price stored for a party of four purchasing tickets in September?**

    a. `price[4][9]`

    b. `price[3][4]`

    c. `price[4][3]`

    d. `price[9][4]`

18. **Many OOP languages provide an `Array` class, which _____ .**

    a. contains useful methods for manipulating arrays

    b. is used as the data type when you declare any array

    c. is used as the data type when you declare any array with more than one dimension

    d. is the child class of all declared arrays

19. **If you use a programming language that does not provide a built-in `Array` class, you _____ .**

    a. cannot declare arrays

    b. can declare arrays of simple data types, but not of objects

    c. can declare arrays of objects, but not of simple data types

    d. could write one yourself

20. **With a linked list, every record _____ .**

    a. is stored in sequential order

    b. contains a field that holds the address of another record

    c. contains a code that indicates the record's position in an imaginary list

    d. is stored in a physical location that corresponds to a key field

FIND THE BUGS

Each of the following pseudocode segments contains one or more bugs that you must find and correct.

1. **This application reads sales data for an automobile dealership. Up to 100 sale amounts can be entered. The entered sale amounts are sorted so the median sale can be displayed.**

```
start
   num SIZE = 100
   num saleAmount
   num sales[SIZE]
   num count = 0
   num middlePosition
   get saleAmount
   while not eof and count < SIZE
       sales[saleAmount] = saleAmount
       count = count + 1
   endwhile
   sort(sales, count)
   middlePosition = SIZE /2
   print "The median sale amount is ", count[saleAmount]
stop

void sort(num sales, num count)
   num x = 0
   num y = 0
   num COMPS = count - 1
   while y < COMPS
       while x < COMPS
           if sales[x] > sales[y] then
               swap(sales, x)
           endif
           x = x + 1
       endwhile
   endwhile
return

void swap(num sales[], num x)
   num temp
   temp = sales[x + 1]
   sales[x + 1] = sales[x]
   sales[x + 1] = temp
return
```

2. **This application reads student typing test data, including the number of errors on the test and the number of words typed per minute. Grades are assigned based on the following table:**

Errors			
Speed	0	1	2 or more
0–30	C	D	F
31–50	C	C	F
51–80	B	C	D
81–100	A	B	C
101 and up	A	A	B

```
start
    num MAX_ERRORS = 2
    num errors
    num wordsPerMinute
    num grades[5][3] = {"C", "D", "F"},
                       {"C", "C", "F"},
                       {"C", "C", "C"},
                       {"A", "B", "C"},
                       {"A", "A", "B"}
    num LIMITS = 5
    num speedLimits[LIMITS] = 0, 31, 51, 81, 101
    num row
    print "Enter number of errors on the test "
    get errors
    if errors > MAX_ERRORS then
        errors = 0
    endif
    print "Enter the speed in words per minute "
    get wordsPerMinute
    while row < LIMITS AND speed >= speedLimits[row]
        row = row + 1
    endwhile
    row = row - 1
    print "Your grade is ", grades[errors][row]
stop
```

EXERCISES

1. Design an application that allows you to enter 10 numbers and display them in descending order.

2. Design an application that allows you to enter eight friends' first names and display them in alphabetical order.

3. Professor Zak allows students to drop the two lowest scores on the 10 quizzes she gives during the semester. Each quiz is worth a maximum of 100 points.

   a. Design an application that allows the professor to enter a student name and 10 quiz scores for each of her 20 students. The output lists each student's name, and total points for each student's eight highest-scoring quizzes.

   b. Modify the application in Exercise 3a so that the students are displayed in alphabetical order by name.

   c. Modify the application in Exercise 3a so that the students are displayed in alphabetical order by total for the eight high-scoring quizzes.

   d. Modify the application in Exercise 3a so that at the end of the list of students the mean and median total points for the class are displayed.

4. The Hinner College Foundation holds an annual fundraiser for which the foundation director maintains records. Allow a user to enter donor names and contribution amounts until an appropriate end-of-data value is entered. Assume that there are never more than 300 donors. Develop the logic for a program that sorts the donation amounts in descending order and displays the highest five donors and their donation amounts (or fewer if at least five are not entered).

5. The Spread-a-Smile Greeting Card Store maintains customer records with data fields for first name, last name, address, and annual purchases in dollars. At the end of the year, the store manager invites the 100 customers with the highest annual purchases to an exclusive sales event. Develop the flowchart or pseudocode that allows the user to enter customer records (up to 1,000 of them) and sorts the customer records by annual purchase amount. The application prints the names and addresses for the top 100 customers (or fewer if less than 100 are entered).

6. The village of Ringwood has taken a special census. Every census record contains a household ID number, number of occupants, and income. Ringwood has exactly 75 households. Village statisticians are interested in the median household size and the median household income. Develop the logic for a program that determines these figures. (Remember, a list must be sorted before you can determine the median value.)

7. The village of Marengo has taken a special census and collected records that each contain a household ID number, number of occupants, and income. The exact number of household records has not yet been determined, but you know that there are fewer than 1,000 households in Marengo. Develop the logic for a program that determines the median household size and the median household income.

8. The MidAmerica Bus Company charges fares to passengers based on the number of travel zones they cross. Additionally, discounts are provided for multiple passengers traveling together. Ticket fares are shown in the following table:

Passengers	Zones Crossed			
	0	1	2	3
1	7.50	10.00	12.00	12.75
2	14.00	18.50	22.00	23.00
3	20.00	21.00	32.00	33.00
4	25.00	27.50	36.00	37.00

Develop the logic for a program that accepts the number of passengers and zones crossed as input. The output is the ticket charge.

9. In golf, par represents a standard number of strokes a player will need to complete a hole. Instead of using an absolute score, players can compare their scores on a hole to the par figure and determine whether they are above or below par. Families can play nine holes of miniature golf at the Family Fun Miniature Golf Park. So that family members can compete fairly, the course provides a different par for each hole based on the player's age. The par figures are shown in the following table:

Age	Holes								
	1	2	3	4	5	6	7	8	9
4 and under	8	8	9	7	5	7	8	5	8
5–7	7	7	8	6	5	6	7	5	6
8–11	6	5	6	5	4	5	5	4	5
12–15	5	4	4	4	3	4	3	3	4
16 and over	4	3	3	3	2	3	2	3	3

a. Develop the logic for a program that accepts a player's name, age, and nine-hole score as input. Display the player's name and score on each of the nine holes, with one of the phrases "Over par", "Par", or "Under par" next to each score.

b. Modify the program in Exercise 9a so that, at the end of the golfer's report, the total score is displayed. Include the figure indicating how many strokes over or under par the player is for the entire course.

10. **Parker's Consulting Services pays its employees an hourly rate based on two criteria—number of years of service and last year's performance rating, which is a whole number, 0 through 5. Employee records contain ID number, last and first names, year hired, and performance score. The salary schedule follows:**

	Performance Score					
Years of Service	0	1	2	3	4	5
0	8.50	9.00	9.75	10.30	12.00	13.00
1	9.50	10.25	10.95	11.30	13.50	15.25
2	10.50	11.00	12.00	13.00	15.00	17.60
3	11.50	12.25	14.00	14.25	15.70	18.90
4 or more	12.50	13.75	15.25	15.50	17.00	20.00

In addition to the pay rates shown in the table, an employee with more than 10 years of service receives an extra 5 percent per hour for each year over 10. Develop the logic for a program that continuously accepts employee data and prints each employee's ID number, name, and correct hourly salary for the current year.

11. **The Roadmaster Driving School allows students to sign up for any number of driving lessons. The school allows up to four attempts to pass the driver's license test; if all the attempts are unsuccessful, then the student's tuition is returned. The school maintains an archive containing student records for those who have successfully passed the licensing test over the last year. Each record contains a student ID number, name, number of driving lessons completed, and the number of the attempt on which the student passed the licensing test. Records are stored in alphabetical order by student name. The school administration is interested in examining the correlation between the number of lessons taken and the number of attempts required to pass the test. Develop the logic for a program that would produce a table for the school. Each row represents the number of lessons taken: 0–9, 10–19, 20–29, and 30 or more. Each column represents the number of test attempts in order to pass—1 through 4.**

12. **The Stevens College Testing Center creates a record each time a student takes a placement test. Students can take a test in any of 12 subject areas: Art, Biology, Chemistry, Computer Science, English, German, History, Math, Music, Psychology, Sociology, or Spanish. Each record contains the student's ID number, the test subject area, and a percent score on the test. Records are maintained in the order they are entered as the tests are taken. The college wants a report that lists each of the 12 tests along with a count of the number of students who have received scores in each of the following categories: at least 90 percent, 80 through 89 percent, 70 through 79 percent, and below 70 percent. Develop the logic that produces the report.**

GAME ZONE

1. In the Game Zone section of Chapter 7, you designed the logic for a quiz that contains questions about a topic of your choice. (Each question was a multiple-choice question with four answer options.) Now, modify the program so it allows the user to retake the quiz up to four additional times or until the user achieves a perfect score, whichever comes first. At the end of all the quiz attempts, display a recap of the user's scores.

2. In the Game Zone section of Chapter 5, you designed the logic for a guessing game in which the application generates a random number and the player tries to guess it. After each guess you displayed a message indicating whether the player's guess was correct, too high, or too low. When the player eventually guessed the correct number, you displayed a score that represented a count of the number of guesses that were required. Now, modify that program to allow a player to replay the game as many times as he likes, up to 20 times. When the player is done, display the scores from highest to lowest, and display the mean and median scores.

3. a. Create a TicTacToe game. In this game, two players alternate placing Xs and Os into a grid until one player has three matching symbols in a row, either horizontally, vertically, or diagonally. Create a game in which the user is presented with a three-by-three grid containing the digits 1 through 9, similar to the first window shown in Figure 9-17. When the user chooses a position by typing a number, place an X in the appropriate spot. For example, after the user chooses 3, the screen looks like the second window in Figure 9-17. Generate a random number for the position where the computer will place an O. Do not allow the player or the computer to place a symbol where one has already been placed. When either the player or computer has three symbols in a row, declare a winner; if all positions have been exhausted and no one has three symbols in a row, declare a tie.

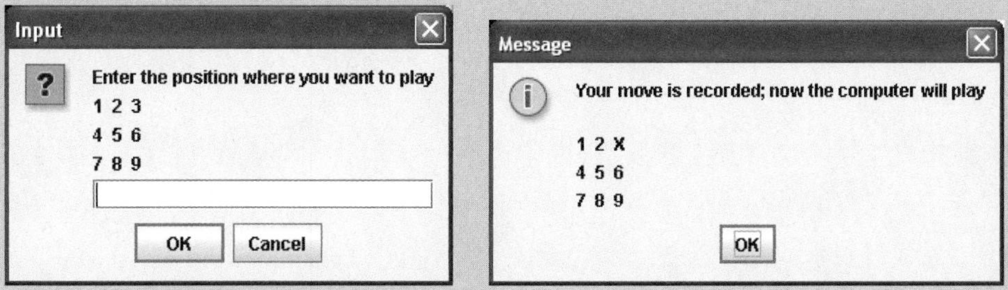

Figure 9-17 A TicTacToe game

b. In the TicTacToe game in Exercise 3a, the computer's selection is chosen randomly. Improve the game so that when the computer has two Os in any row, column, or diagonal, it selects the winning position for its next move rather than selecting a position randomly.

DETECTIVE WORK

1. Most personnel records include employees' Social Security numbers, and are frequently used to sort employee records. Is a Social Security number a unique key field?

2. This chapter examines the bubble, insertion, and selection sorting algorithms. What other named sort processes can you find?

UP FOR DISCUSSION

1. Now that you are becoming comfortable with arrays, you can see that programming is a complex subject. Should all literate people understand how to program? If so, how much programming should they understand?

2. What are language standards? At this point in your study of programming, what do they mean to you?

3. This chapter discusses sorting data. Suppose a large hospital hires you to write a program that displays lists of potential organ recipients. The hospital's doctors will consult this list if they have an organ that can be transplanted. The hospital administrators instruct you to sort potential recipients by last name and display them sequentially in alphabetical order. If more than 10 patients are waiting for a particular organ, the first 10 patients are displayed; a doctor can either select one of these or move on to view the next set of 10 patients. You worry that this system gives an unfair advantage to patients with last names that start with A, B, C, and D. Should you write and install the program? If you do not, many transplant opportunities will be missed while the hospital searches for another programmer to write the program. Are there different criteria you would want to use to sort the patients?

FILE HANDLING
AND APPLICATIONS

In this chapter you will:

Understand computer files and how they are stored

Understand sequential files and the need to merge them

Create the logic for a merge program

Understand master and transaction file processing

Match files to update master file fields

Allow multiple transactions for a single master file
   record

Update records in sequential files

UNDERSTANDING COMPUTER FILES AND HOW THEY ARE STORED

When data items are stored in a computer system, they can be stored for varying periods of time—temporarily or permanently.

Computer memory, or **random access memory (RAM)**, is temporary storage. When you write a program that stores a value in a variable, you are using temporary storage; the value you store is lost when the program ends or the computer loses power. This type of storage is **volatile**.

Permanent storage, on the other hand, is not lost when a computer loses power; it is **non-volatile**. When you write a program and save it to a disk, you are using permanent storage.

> **NOTE** When discussing computer storage, *temporary* and *permanent* refer to volatility, not length of time. For example, a *temporary* variable might exist for several hours in a large program or one that runs in an infinite loop, but a *permanent* piece of data might be saved and then deleted by a user within a few seconds.

A **computer file** is a collection of information stored on a nonvolatile device in a computer system. Files exist on **permanent storage devices** such as hard disks, floppy disks, Zip disks, USB drives, reels or cassettes of magnetic tape, and compact discs. Some files are **data files** that contain facts and figures, such as a payroll file that contains employee numbers, names, and salaries; some files are **program files** or **application files** that store software instructions. Other files can store graphics, text, or operating system instructions. Although their contents vary, files have many common characteristics—each file occupies space on a section of a storage device, and each has a name and a specific time of creation.

When you use data, you never directly use the copy that is stored in a file. Instead, you use a copy that is in memory. Especially when data items are stored on a hard disk, their location might not be clear to you—data just seems to be "in the computer." However, when you work with stored data, you must transfer a copy from the storage device into memory. When you store data in a computer file on a persistent storage device, you **write to the file**. This means you copy data from RAM to the file. When you copy data from a file on a storage device into RAM, you **read from the file**.

> **NOTE** Because you can erase data from files, some programmers prefer the term *persistent storage* to permanent storage. In other words, you can remove data from a file stored on a device such as a disk drive, so it is not technically permanent. However, the data remains in the file even when the computer loses power, so, unlike RAM, the data persists, or perseveres.

Computer files are the electronic equivalent of paper files stored in file cabinets. In a physical file cabinet, the easiest way to store a document is to toss it into a drawer without a folder. In storing computer files, this is the equivalent of placing a file in the main or root directory of your storage device. However, for better organization, most office clerks place documents in folders; most computer users also organize their files into folders or directories. Users can also place folders within folders to form a hierarchy. A path is the combination of the disk drive plus the complete hierarchy of directories in which a file resides. For example, in the Windows operating system, the following line would be the complete path for a file named Data.txt on the C drive in a folder named Chapter.10 within the Logic folder:

```
C:\Logic\Chapter.10\Data.txt
```

>> **NOTE** The terms *directory* and *folder* are used synonymously to mean an entity that is used to organize files. *Directory* is the more general term; the term *folder* came into use in graphical systems. For example, Microsoft began calling directories *folders* with the introduction of Windows 95.

>> **NOTE** In Chapter 1, you learned about the data hierarchy and that data items are stored in fields within records within files.

In most programming languages, before an application can use a data file, it must **open the file**. Opening a file locates it on a storage device and associates a variable name within your program with the file. Similarly, when you finish using a file, the program should **close the file**—that is, the file is no longer available to your application. If you fail to close an input file (a file from which you are reading data), there are usually no serious consequences; the data still exists in the file. However, if you fail to close an output file (a file to which you are writing data), the data might become inaccessible. You should always close every file you open, and you should close the file as soon as you no longer need it. When you leave a file open for no reason, you use computer resources, and your computer's performance suffers. Also, particularly within a network, another program might be waiting to use the file.

Figure 10-1 shows the generic steps in a program that opens two files, reads data for one employee from it, alters the employee's pay rate, writes the data to a new file, and closes the files. The statements that use the files are shaded.

>> **NOTE** In most programming languages, if you read data from a keyboard or write it to the display monitor, you do not need to open the device. The keyboard and monitor are the **default input and output devices**, respectively.

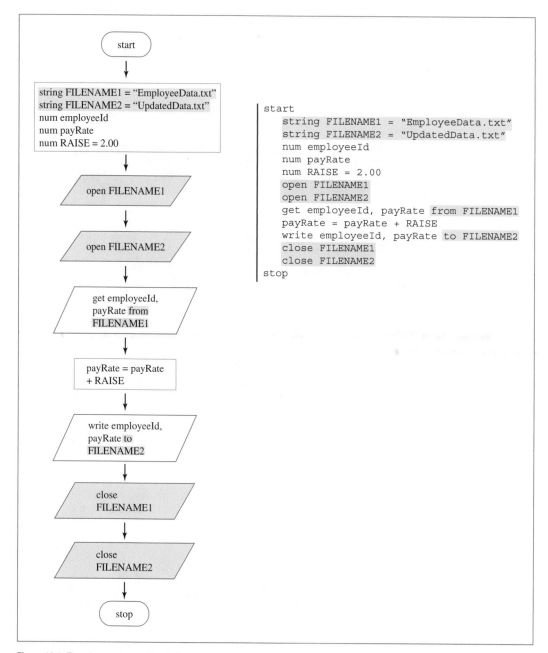

Figure 10-1 Flowchart and pseudocode for program that uses a file

»NOTE The convention in this book is to place file open and close statements in parallelograms in flowcharts, because they are operations closely related to input and output.

When you open a file, in many programming languages you must specify whether the file will be used for reading input or for writing output, and frequently, you must provide other details as well. The specific procedures for opening and closing files differ among programming languages. Figure 10-2 shows how opening a file for output is implemented in C# and Java, respectively. You can see from these examples that before you open a file in one of these languages you must understand quite a bit of confusing syntax and that the syntax is different in different languages. Therefore, this book follows the conventions used in Figure 10-1 as follows:

» open *filename* opens the file represented by *filename*; the same open statement is used whether the file is an input file or output file

» read data from *filename* accepts data as input from *filename*

» write data to *filename* sends data as output to *filename*

» close *filename* closes the file

> **NOTE** Logically, the verbs "print," "write," and "display" mean the same thing—all produce output. However, in conversations, programmers usually reserve the word "print" for situations in which they mean "produce hard copy output," and are more likely to use "write" when talking about sending records to a data file, and "display" when sending records to a monitor. In some programming languages, there is no difference in the verb you use for output, no matter what type of hardware you use; you simply assign different output devices (such as printers, monitors, and disk drives) as needed to programmer-named objects that represent them.

```
// Opening a file for output in C#
const string FILENAME1 = "EmployeeData.txt";
FileStream outFile = new FileStream(FILENAME,
    FileMode.Create, FileAccess.Write);
StreamWriter writer = new StreamWriter(outFile);
```

```
// Opening a file for output in Java
final string FILENAME1 = "EmployeeData.txt"
OutputStream ostream;
File outputFile = new File(FILENAME);
ostream = new FileOutputStream(outputFile);
```

Figure 10-2 Sample code that opens a file in C# and Java

> **NOTE** The two code samples in Figure 10-2 assume the EmployeeData.txt file is in the same folder as the executing program. You could indicate a path such as `FILENAME1 = "C:\CompanyFiles\EmployeeData.txt"` if the EmployeeData.txt file is in a different folder from the executing program.

Throughout this book you have been encouraged to think of input as basically the same process whether it comes from a user typing interactively at a keyboard, or from a stored file on a disk, or other media. That concept remains a valid one as you read this chapter. The rest of this chapter discusses applications that commonly use stored file data. It's not that applications such as these could not be executed by a data-entry operator from a keyboard; it's just that it is more common for the data used in these applications to have been entered, validated, and sorted earlier in another application, and then processed as input from files to achieve the results discussed in this chapter.

>> **NOTE** Logically, reading data from a keyboard and from a file are very similar—each involves getting data from an input device. The major difference is that when you get data from a user, you should provide prompts that tell the user what to enter.

>> **NOTE** Logically, writing to a file and writing a printed report are very similar—each involves sending data to an output device. The major difference is that when you write a data file, typically you do not include headings or other formatting for people to read, as you do when you create a printed report. A data file contains only data for another computer program to read.

>> **NOTE** In many organizations, both data files and printed report files are sent to disk storage devices when they are created. Later, as time becomes available on the organization's busy printers (often after business hours), the report disk files are copied to paper.

TWO TRUTHS AND A LIE:
UNDERSTANDING COMPUTER FILES AND HOW THEY ARE STORED

1. Temporary storage is usually volatile.

2. Computer files exist on permanent storage devices, such as RAM.

3. If you fail to close an input file, there are usually no serious consequences; the data still exists in the file.

The false statement is #2. Computer files exist on permanent storage devices, such as hard disks, floppy disks, Zip disks, USB drives, reels or cassettes of magnetic tape, and compact discs.

UNDERSTANDING SEQUENTIAL FILES AND THE NEED TO MERGE THEM

A **sequential file** is a file in which records are stored one after another in some order. One option is to store records in a sequential file in the order in which the records are created. For example, if you maintain records of your friends, you might store the records as you make the friends; you could say the records are stored in **temporal order**—that is, in order based on time. At any point in time, the records of your friends will be stored in sequential order based on how long you have known them—the data stored about your best friend from kindergarten is record 1, and the data about the friend you just made last week could be record 30.

Instead of temporal order, records in a sequential file are more frequently stored based on the contents of one or more fields within each record. Perhaps it is most useful for you to store your friends' records sequentially in alphabetical order by last name, or maybe in order by birthday.

Other examples of sequential files include:

>> A file of employees stored in order by ID number
>> A file of parts for a manufacturing company stored in order by part number
>> A file of customers for a business stored in alphabetical order by last name

> **» NOTE** Recall from Chapter 9 that the field that makes a record unique from all records in a file is the key field. Frequently, though not always, records are most conveniently stored in order by their key fields.

> **» NOTE** Files that are stored in order by some field have been sorted; they might have been sorted manually before they were saved, or a program might have sorted them. You learned about sorting in Chapter 9.

Businesses often need to merge two or more sequential files. **Merging files** involves combining two or more files while maintaining the sequential order. For example:

» Suppose you have a file of current employees in ID number order and a file of newly hired employees, also in ID number order. You need to merge these two files into one combined file before running this week's payroll program.

» Suppose you have a file of parts manufactured in the Northside factory in part-number order and a file of parts manufactured in the Southside factory, also in part-number order. You need to merge these two files into one combined file, creating a master list of available parts.

» Suppose you have a file that lists last year's customers in alphabetical order and another file that lists this year's customers in alphabetical order. You want to create a mailing list of all customers in order by last name.

Before you can easily merge files, two conditions must be met:

» Each file must contain the same record layout.

» Each file used in the merge must be sorted in the same order (ascending or descending) based on the same field.

For example, suppose your business has two locations, one on the East Coast and one on the West Coast, and each location maintains a customer file in alphabetical order by customer name. Each file contains fields for name and customer balance. You can call the fields in the East Coast file `eastName` and `eastBalance`, and the fields in the West Coast file `westName` and `westBalance`. You want to merge the two files, creating one master file containing records for all customers. Figure 10-3 shows some sample data for the files; you want to create a merged file like the one shown in Figure 10-4.

East Coast File

eastName	eastBalance
Able	100.00
Brown	50.00
Dougherty	25.00
Hanson	300.00
Ingram	400.00
Johnson	30.00

West Coast File

westName	westBalance
Chen	200.00
Edgar	125.00
Fell	75.00
Grand	100.00

Figure 10-3 Sample data contained in two customer files

mergedName	mergedBalance
Able	100.00
Brown	50.00
Chen	200.00
Dougherty	25.00
Edgar	125.00
Fell	75.00
Grand	100.00
Hanson	300.00
Ingram	400.00
Johnson	30.00

Figure 10-4 Merged customer file

CREATING THE LOGIC FOR A MERGE PROGRAM

The mainline logic for a program that merges two files is similar to the main logic you've used before in other programs: it contains preliminary, housekeeping tasks, a main loop that repeats until the end of the program, and some clean-up, end-of-job tasks. However, most programs you have studied processed records until an eof condition was met either because an input data file reached its end, or because a user entered a sentinel value in an interactive program. In a program that merges files, there are two input files, so checking for eof in one of them is insufficient. Instead, the program must check a flag variable with a name such as bothAtEof. For example, you might initialize bothAtEof to "N", but change its value to "Y" after you have encountered eof in both input files. Figure 10-5 shows the mainline logic. The program declares variables, opens the files, and reads one record from each of the two input files. Assuming there is at least one record available in each file, the logic enters the main loop of the program. (In Figure 10-5, the loop is shaded to show that more details will be provided shortly.) When both files are exhausted, all the files are closed and the program ends.

NOTE You used flag variables in Chapter 6 when searching for matches in an array. A flag is a variable that keeps track of whether an event has occurred.

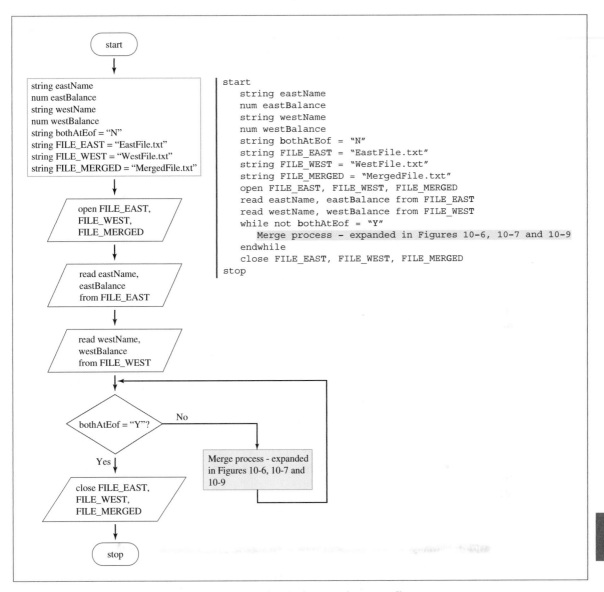

start

```
string eastName
num eastBalance
string westName
num westBalance
string bothAtEof = "N"
string FILE_EAST = "EastFile.txt"
string FILE_WEST = "WestFile.txt"
string FILE_MERGED = "MergedFile.txt"
```

open FILE_EAST,
FILE_WEST,
FILE_MERGED

read eastName,
eastBalance
from FILE_EAST

read westName,
westBalance
from FILE_WEST

bothAtEof = "Y"?

No

Yes

Merge process - expanded
in Figures 10-6, 10-7 and
10-9

close FILE_EAST,
FILE_WEST,
FILE_MERGED

stop

```
start
    string eastName
    num eastBalance
    string westName
    num westBalance
    string bothAtEof = "N"
    string FILE_EAST  = "EastFile.txt"
    string FILE_WEST  = "WestFile.txt"
    string FILE_MERGED = "MergedFile.txt"
    open FILE_EAST, FILE_WEST, FILE_MERGED
    read eastName, eastBalance from FILE_EAST
    read westName, westBalance from FILE_WEST
    while not bothAtEof = "Y"
        Merge process - expanded in Figures 10-6, 10-7 and 10-9
    endwhile
    close FILE_EAST, FILE_WEST, FILE_MERGED
stop
```

Figure 10-5 Beginning, but still incomplete, flowchart and pseudocode of program that merges files

When you begin the main loop in the program in Figure 10-5, two records—one from
FILE_EAST and one from FILE_WEST—are sitting in the memory of the computer. One of
these records needs to be written to the new output file first. Which one? Because the two
input files contain records stored in alphabetical order, and you want the new file to store
records in alphabetical order, you first output the input record that has the lower alphabetical
value in the name field. Therefore, the process begins as shown in Figure 10-6.

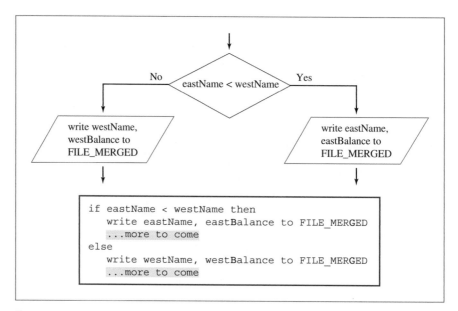

Figure 10-6 Start of merging process

Using the sample data from Figure 10-3, you can see that the record from the East Coast file containing "Able" should be written to the output file, while Chen's record from the West Coast file waits in memory because the eastName value "Able" is alphabetically lower than the westName value "Chen".

After you write Able's record, should Chen's record be written to the output file next? Not necessarily. It depends on the next eastName following Able's record in FILE_EAST. When data records are read into memory from a file, a program typically does not "look ahead" to determine the values stored in the next record. Instead, a program usually reads the record into memory before making decisions about its contents. In this program, you need to read the next FILE_EAST record into memory and compare it to "Chen". Because in this case the next record in FILE_EAST contains the name "Brown", and another FILE_EAST record is written; no FILE_WEST records are written yet.

After the first two FILE_EAST records, is it Chen's turn to be written now? You really don't know until you read another record from FILE_EAST and compare its name value to "Chen". Because this record contains the name "Dougherty", it is indeed time to write Chen's record. After Chen's record is written, should you now write Dougherty's record? Until you read the next record from FILE_WEST, you don't know whether that record should be placed before or after Dougherty's record.

Therefore, the merging method proceeds like this: compare two records, write the record with the lower alphabetical name, and read another record from the *same* input file. See Figure 10-7.

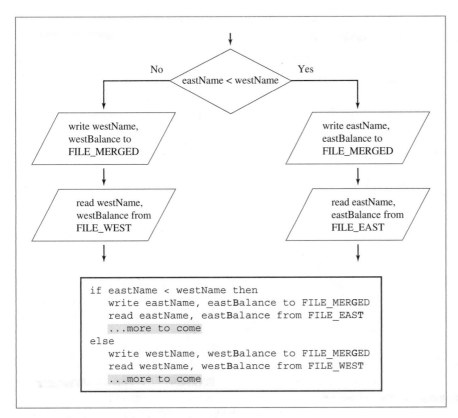

Figure 10-7 Continuation of development of merging process

Recall the names from the two original files (see Figure 10-8) and walk through the processing steps.

eastName	westName
Able	Chen
Brown	Edgar
Dougherty	Fell
Hanson	Grand
Ingram	
Johnson	

Figure 10-8 Names from two files to merge

1. Compare "Able" and "Chen". Write Able's record. Read Brown's record from FILE_EAST.

2. Compare "Brown" and "Chen". Write Brown's record. Read Dougherty's record from FILE_EAST.

3. Compare "Dougherty" and "Chen". Write Chen's record. Read Edgar's record from FILE_WEST.

4. Compare "Dougherty" and "Edgar". Write Dougherty's record. Read Hanson's record from FILE_EAST.

5. Compare "Hanson" and "Edgar". Write Edgar's record. Read Fell's record from FILE_WEST.

6. Compare "Hanson" and "Fell". Write Fell's record. Read Grand's record from FILE_WEST.

7. Compare "Hanson" and "Grand". Write Grand's record. Read from FILE_WEST, encountering eof.

What happens when you reach the end of the West Coast file? Is the program over? It shouldn't be because records for Hanson, Ingram, and Johnson all need to be included in the new output file, and none of them is written yet. You need to find a way to write the Hanson record as well as read and write all the remaining FILE_EAST records. And you can't just write statements to read and write from FILE_EAST; sometimes, when you run this program, records in FILE_EAST will finish first alphabetically, and in that case you need to continue reading from FILE_WEST.

An elegant solution to this problem involves setting the field on which the merge is based to a "high" value when the end of the file is encountered. A **high value** is one that is greater than any possible value in a field. Programmers often use all 9s in a numeric field and all Zs in a string field to indicate a high value. You can declare a constant such as END_NAME, assign "ZZZZZ" to it, and then every time you read from FILE_WEST you can check for eof, and when it occurs, set westName to END_NAME. Similarly, when reading FILE_EAST, set eastName to END_NAME when eof occurs. When both eastName and westName are END_NAME, then you set the bothAtEof variable to "Y". Figure 10-9 shows the complete logic for the program with the most recent additions shaded.

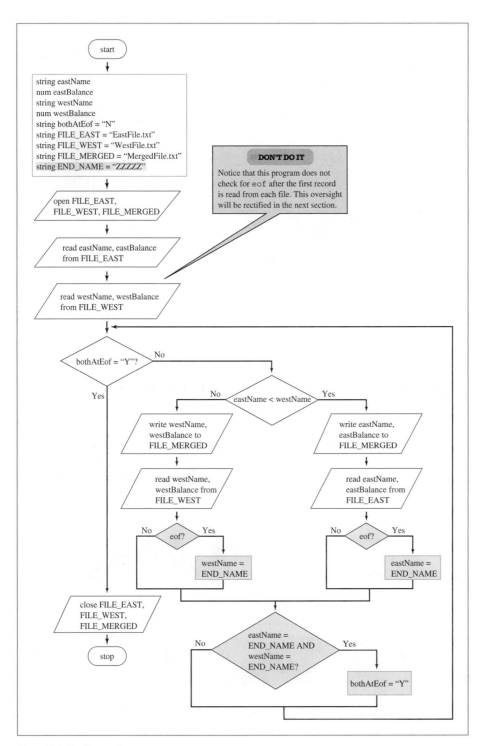

Figure 10-9 The file merging program

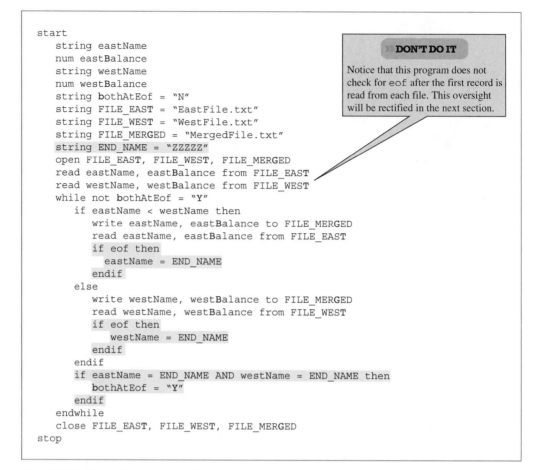

```
start
   string eastName
   num eastBalance
   string westName
   num westBalance
   string bothAtEof = "N"
   string FILE_EAST = "EastFile.txt"
   string FILE_WEST = "WestFile.txt"
   string FILE_MERGED = "MergedFile.txt"
   string END_NAME = "ZZZZZ"
   open FILE_EAST, FILE_WEST, FILE_MERGED
   read eastName, eastBalance from FILE_EAST
   read westName, westBalance from FILE_WEST
   while not bothAtEof = "Y"
      if eastName < westName then
         write eastName, eastBalance to FILE_MERGED
         read eastName, eastBalance from FILE_EAST
         if eof then
            eastName = END_NAME
         endif
      else
         write westName, westBalance to FILE_MERGED
         read westName, westBalance from FILE_WEST
         if eof then
            westName = END_NAME
         endif
      endif
      if eastName = END_NAME AND westName = END_NAME then
         bothAtEof = "Y"
      endif
   endwhile
   close FILE_EAST, FILE_WEST, FILE_MERGED
stop
```

DON'T DO IT

Notice that this program does not check for eof after the first record is read from each file. This oversight will be rectified in the next section.

Figure 10-9 The file merging program (*continued*)

> **»NOTE** At the end of the file, you might choose to use 10 or 20 Zs in the eastName and westName fields instead of using only five. Although it is unlikely that a person will have the last name ZZZZZ, you should make sure that the value you choose for a high value is actually a higher value than any legitimate value.

> **»NOTE** Several programming languages contain a name you can use for a value that occurs when every bit in a byte is an "on" bit, creating a value that is even higher than all Zs or all 9s. For example, in COBOL this value is called HIGH-VALUES, and in RPG it is called HIVAL.

Using the sample data in Figure 10-8, after Grand's record is processed, `FILE_WEST` is read and `eof` is encountered, so `westName` gets set to `END_NAME`. Now, when you enter the loop again, `eastName` and `westName` are compared, and `eastName` is still "Hanson". The `eastName` value (Hanson) is lower than the `westName` value (ZZZZZ), so the data for `eastName`'s record writes to the output file, and another `FILE_EAST` record (Ingram) is read.

The complete run of the file-merging program now executes the first six of the seven steps as listed previously, and then proceeds as shown in Figure 10-9 and as follows, starting with a modified Step 7:

7. Compare "Hanson" and "Grand". Write Grand's record. Read from `FILE_WEST`, encountering `eof` and setting `westName` to "ZZZZZ".

8. Compare "Hanson" and "ZZZZZ". Write Hanson's record. Read Ingram's record.

9. Compare "Ingram" and "ZZZZZ". Write Ingram's record. Read Johnson's record.

10. Compare "Johnson" and "ZZZZZ". Write Johnson's record. Read from the `FILE_EAST`, encountering `eof` and setting `eastName` to "ZZZZZ".

11. Now that both names are "ZZZZZ", set the flag `bothAtEof` equal to "Y".

When the `bothAtEof` flag variable equals "Y", the loop is finished, the files are closed, and the program ends.

> **NOTE** Notice that if two names are equal during the merge process—for example, when there is a "Hanson" record in each file—then both Hansons will be included in the final file. When `eastName` and `westName` match, `eastName` is not lower than `westName`, so you write the `FILE_WEST` "Hanson" record. After you read the next `FILE_WEST` record, `eastName` will be lower than the next `westName`, and the `FILE_EAST` "Hanson" record will be output. A more complicated merge program could check another field, such as first name, when last-name values match.

> **NOTE** You can merge any number of files. To merge more than two files, the logic is only slightly more complicated; you must compare the key fields from all the files before deciding which file is the next candidate for output.

AN IMPROVEMENT: CHECKING FOR EOF WHEN READING THE FIRST RECORD

The application in Figure 10-9 correctly merges two files that have been sorted alphabetically. However, to be complete, the program must provide for an additional condition. Any time you read a record from a file, it is possible that `eof` is encountered—even when reading the first record. Figure 10-10 provides for this unlikely, but possible occurrence by checking for `eof` every time a record is read, including the first time. When the first record is read from each file, if it is `eof`, the name is set to the `END_NAME` value. In the unlikely situation where both files are empty, the `bothAtEof` flag is set to "Y", the main loop of the program is never entered, and the program ends elegantly.

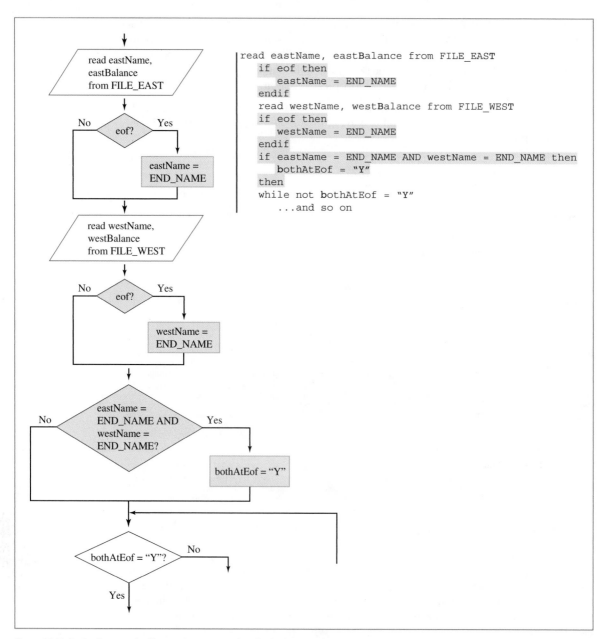

```
read eastName, eastBalance from FILE_EAST
    if eof then
        eastName = END_NAME
    endif
    read westName, westBalance from FILE_WEST
    if eof then
        westName = END_NAME
    endif
    if eastName = END_NAME AND westName = END_NAME then
        bothAtEof = "Y"
    then
    while not bothAtEof = "Y"
        ...and so on
```

Figure 10-10 Revised start to the file-merging program that checks for `eof` after the first record is read from each file

MASTER AND TRANSACTION FILE PROCESSING

When two related sequential files seem "equal," in that they hold the same *type* of information—for example, when one holds customers from the East Coast and another holds customers from the West Coast—you often need to merge the files to use them as a single unit. When you merge records from two or more files, the records (almost) always contain the same fields in the same order; in other words, every record in the merged file has the same format.

Some related sequential files, however, are unequal and you do not want to merge them. For example, you might have a file containing records for all your customers in which each record holds a customer ID number, name, address, and balance due. You might have another file that contains data for every purchase made, containing the customer ID number and other purchase information such as a dollar amount. Although both files contain a customer ID number, the file with the customer names and addresses is an example of a master file. You use a **master file** to hold relatively permanent data, such as customers' names. The file containing customer purchases is a **transaction file**, a file that holds more temporary data generated by the actions of the customers. You might maintain certain customers' names and addresses for years, but the transaction file will periodically contain new data—perhaps daily, weekly, or monthly, depending on your organization's billing cycle. Commonly, you periodically use a transaction file to find a **matching record** in a master file—one that contains data about the same customer. Sometimes, you match records so you can **update the master file** by making changes to the values in its fields. For example, the file containing transaction purchase data might be used to update each master file record's balance due field. At other times, you might match a transaction file's records to its master file counterpart, creating an entity that draws information from both files—an invoice, for example. This type of program requires matching, but no updating. Whether a program simply matches records in master and transaction files, or updates the master file, depending on the application, there might be none, one, or many transaction records corresponding to each master file record.

Here are a few other examples of files that have a master-transaction relationship:

» A library maintains a master file of all patrons and a transaction file with information about each book or other items checked out.

» A college maintains a master file of all students and a transaction file for each course registration.

» A telephone company maintains a master file for every telephone line (number) and a transaction file with information about every call.

When you update a master file, you can take two approaches:

» You can actually change the information in the master file. When you use this approach, the information that existed in the master file prior to the transaction processing is lost.

» You can create a copy of the master file, making the changes in the new version. Then, you can store the previous version of the master file for a period of time, in case there are questions or discrepancies regarding the update process. The saved version of a master file is the **parent file**; the updated version is the **child file**. This approach is used later in this chapter.

>> **NOTE** When a child file is updated, it becomes a parent, and its parent becomes a grandparent. Individual organizations create policies concerning the number of generations of backup files they will save before discarding them.

>> **NOTE** The terms "parent" and "child" refer to file backup generations, but they are used for a different purpose in object-oriented programming. When you base a class on another using inheritance, the original class is the parent and the derived class is the child. You will learn about these concepts in Chapter 11.

TWO TRUTHS AND A LIE:
MASTER AND TRANSACTION FILE PROCESSING

1. You use a master file to hold temporary data related to transaction file records.

2. You use a transaction file to hold data that is used to update a master file.

3. The saved version of a master file is the parent file; the updated version is the child file.

The false statement is #1. You use a master file to hold relatively permanent data.

MATCHING FILES TO UPDATE FIELDS IN MASTER FILE RECORDS

The logic you use to perform a match between master and transaction file records is similar to the logic you use to perform a merge. As with a merge, you must begin with both files sorted in the same order on the same field.

Assume you have a master file with the fields shown in Figure 10-11.

MASTER CUSTOMER FILE DESCRIPTION

File name: CUSTOMERS

FIELD DESCRIPTION	DATA TYPE	COMMENTS
Customer number	Numeric	3 digits
Name	String	
Address	String	
Phone number	String	10 characters
Total sales	Numeric	2 decimal places

Figure 10-11 Master customer file description

In the master customer file description, the total sales field holds the total dollar amount of all purchases the customer has previously made; in other words, it holds the total amount the customer has spent prior to the current week. Suppose that at the end of each week, you want to update this field with any new sales transaction that occurred during the week. Assume a transaction file contains one record for every transaction that has occurred and that each record holds a transaction number, the number of the customer who made the transaction, the transaction date, and the amount of the transaction. The fields in the transaction file are shown in Figure 10-12.

TRANSACTION FILE DESCRIPTION

File name: CUSTOMERS

FIELD DESCRIPTION	DATA TYPE	COMMENTS
Transaction number	Numeric	3 digits
Customer number	Numeric	3 digits
Transaction date	Numeric	8 digits - YYYYMMDD
Transaction amount	Numeric	2 decimal places

Figure 10-12 Transaction file description

You want to create a new master file in which almost all information is the same as in the original file, but the customer's total sales field increases to reflect the most recent transaction. The process involves going through the old master file, one record at a time, and determining whether there is a new transaction for that customer. If there is no transaction for a customer, the new customer record will contain exactly the same information as the old customer record. However, if there is a transaction for a customer, the transaction value is added to the customer's total sales field before you write the updated master file record.

Imagine you are going to update master file records by hand instead of using a computer program, and imagine each master and transaction record is stored on a separate piece of paper. The easiest way to accomplish the update is to sort all the master records by customer number and place them in a stack, and then sort all the transactions by customer number (not transaction number) and place them in another stack. You then would examine the first transaction, and look through the master records until you found a match. Any master records without transactions would be placed in a "completed" stack without changes. When a transaction matched a master record, you would correct the master record using the new transaction amount, and then go on to the next transaction. Of course, if there is no matching master record for a transaction, then you would realize an error had occurred, and you would probably set the transaction aside before continuing. The computer program you write to perform the update works exactly the same way.

The beginning part of the logic for this matching program looks similar to the beginning of the file-merging program discussed earlier in this chapter. Two records are read, one from the master file and one from the transaction file. When you encounter eof for either file, store a high value (in this case, 999) in the customer number field. See Figure 10-13.

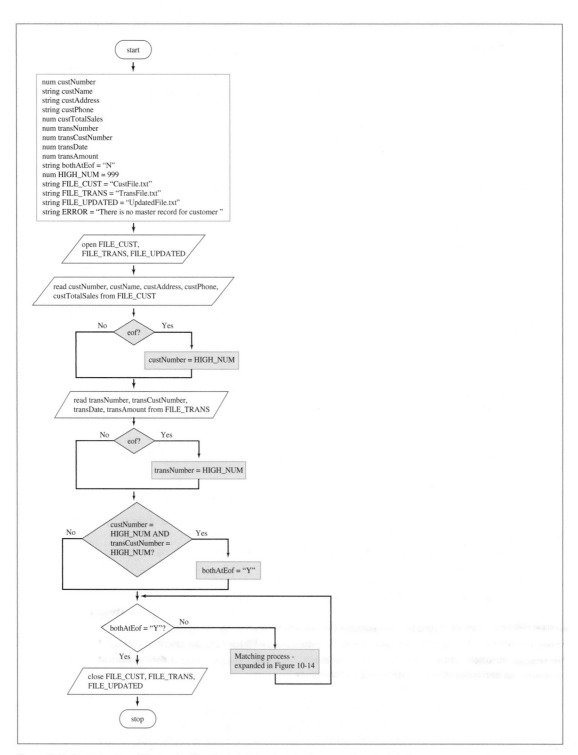

Figure 10-13 Beginning, but still incomplete flowchart and pseudocode of program that matches files

```
start
   num custNumber
   string custName
   string custAddress
   string custPhone
   num custTotalSales
   num transNumber
   num transCustNumber
   num transDate
   num transAmount
   string bothAtEof = "N"
   num HIGH_NUM = 999
   string FILE_CUST = "CustFile.txt"
   string FILE_TRANS = "TransFile.txt"
   string FILE_UPDATED = "UpdatedFile.txt"
   string ERROR = "There is no master record for customer "

   open FILE_CUST, FILE_TRANS, FILE_UPDATED
   read custNumber, custName, custAddress, custPhone, custTotalSales from FILE_CUST
   if eof then
      custNumber = HIGH_NUM
   endif
   read transNumber, transCustNumber, transDate, transAmount from FILE_TRANS
   if eof then
      transCustNumber = HIGH_NUM
   endif
   if custNumber = HIGH_NUM AND transCustNumber = HIGH_NUM then
      both at EOF = "Y"
   endif
   while bothAtEof not = "Y"
      Matching process - expanded in Figure 10-14
   endwhile
   close FILE_CUST, FILE_TRANS, FILE_UPDATED
stop
```

Figure 10-13 Beginning, but still incomplete flowchart and pseudocode of program that matches files (*continued*)

> **» NOTE** In the file-merging program presented earlier in this chapter, you placed "ZZZZZ" in the customer name field at the end of the file because string fields were being compared. In this example, because you are using numeric fields (customer numbers), you can store 999 in them at the end of the file. The value 999 is the highest possible numeric value for a three-digit number in the customer number field.

In the file-merging program presented earlier in this chapter, your first action in the main loop was to determine which file held the record with the lower value; then, you wrote that record. In a matching program, you need to determine more than whether one file's comparison field is larger than another's; it's also important to know if they are *equal*. In this example, you want to update the master file record's custTotalSales field only if the transaction record transCustNumber field contains an exact match for the customer number in the master file record. Therefore, you compare custNumber from the master file and transCustNumber from the transaction file. Three possibilities exist:

» The transCustNumber value equals custNumber. In this case, you add transAmount to custTotalSales, and then write the updated master record to the output file. Then, you read in both a new master record and a new transaction record.

» The `transCustNumber` value is higher than `custNumber`. This means there wasn't a sale for that customer. That's all right; not every customer makes a transaction every period, so you simply write the original customer record with exactly the same information it contained when input; then, you get the next customer record to see if this customer made the transaction currently under examination.

» The `transCustNumber` value is lower than `custNumber`. This means you are trying to record a transaction for which no master record exists, so there must be an error, because a transaction should always have a master record. You can handle this error in a variety of ways; here, you will write an error message to an output device before reading the next transaction record. A human operator can then read the message and take appropriate action.

> **NOTE** The logic used here assumes there can be only one transaction per customer. Later in this chapter, you will develop the logic for a program in which the customer can have multiple transactions.

Whether `transCustNumber` was higher than, lower than, or equal to `custNumber`, after reading the next transaction or master record (or both), you check whether both `custNumber` and `transCustNumber` have been set to 999. When both are 999, you set the `bothAtEof` flag to "Y".

Figure 10-14 shows the logic of the file-matching process. Figure 10-15 shows some sample data you can use to walk through the logic for this program.

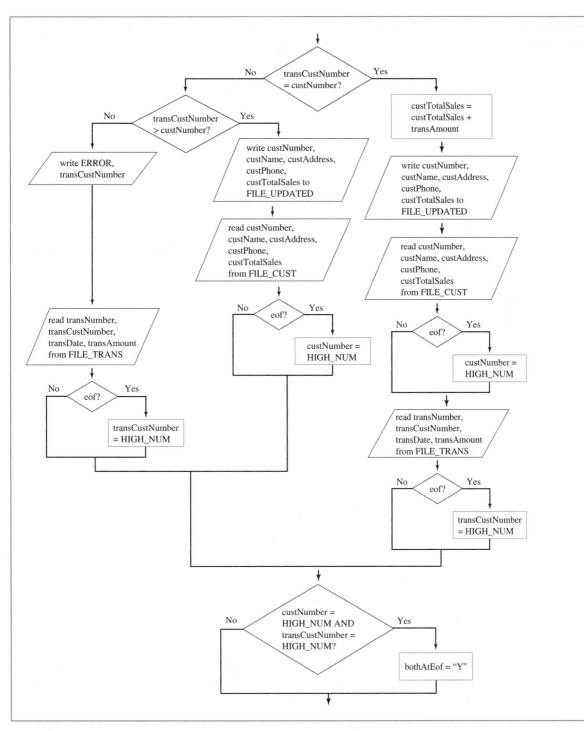

Figure 10-14 File-matching process

```
if transCustNumber = custNumber then
    custTotalSales = custTotalSales + transAmount
    write custNumber, custName, custAddress, custPhone, custTotalSales to FILE_UPDATED
    read custNumber, custName, custAddress, custPhone, custTotalSales from FILE_CUST
    if eof then
        custNumber = HIGH_NUM
    endif
    read transNumber, transCustNumber, transDate, transAmount from FILE_TRANS
    if eof then
        transCustNumber = HIGH_NUM
    endif
else
    if transCustNumber > custNumber then
        write custNumber, custName, custAddress, custPhone, custTotalSales to FILE_UPDATED
        read custNumber, custName, custAddress, custPhone, custTotalSales from FILE_CUST
        if eof then
            custNumber = HIGH_NUM
        endif
    else
        write ERROR, transCustNumber
        read transNumber, transCustNumber, transDate, transAmount from FILE_TRANS
        if eof then
            transCustNumber = HIGH_NUM
        endif
    endif
if custNumber = HIGH_NUM AND transCustNumber = HIGH_NUM then
    bothAtEof ="Y"
endif
```

Figure 10-14 File-matching process (*continued*)

Master File		Transaction File	
custNumber	custTotalSales	transCustNumber	transAmount
100	1000.00	100	400.00
102	50.00	105	700.00
103	500.00	108	100.00
105	75.00	110	400.00
106	5000.00		
109	4000.00		
110	500.00		

Figure 10-15 Sample data for the file-matching program

The program proceeds as follows:

1. Read customer 100 from the master file and customer 100 from the transaction file. Customer numbers are equal, so 400.00 from the transaction file is added to 1000.00 in the master file, and a new master file record is written with a 1400.00 total sales figure. Then, read a new record from each input file.

2. The customer number in the master file is 102 and the customer number in the transaction file is 105, so there are no transactions today for customer 102. Write the master record exactly the way it came in, and read a new master record.

3. Now, the master customer number is 103 and the transaction customer number is still 105. This means customer 103 has no transactions, so you write the master record as is and read a new one.

4. Now, the master customer number is 105 and the transaction number is 105. Because customer 105 had a 75.00 balance and now has a 700.00 transaction, the new total sales figure is 775.00, and a new master record is written. Read one record from each file.

5. Now, the master number is 106 and the transaction number is 108. Write customer record 106 as is, and read another master.

6. Now, the master number is 109 and the transaction number is 108. An error has occurred. The transaction record indicates that you made a sale to customer 108, but there is no master record for customer number 108. Either the transaction is incorrect (there is an error in the transaction's customer number) or the transaction is correct but you have failed to create a master record. Either way, write an error message so that a clerk is notified and can handle the problem. Then, get a new transaction record.

7. Now, the master number is 109 and the transaction number is 110. Write master record 109 with no changes and read a new one.

8. Now, the master number is 110 and the transaction number is 110. Add the 400.00 transaction to the previous 500.00 figure, and write a new record with a 900.00 value in the `custTotalSales` field. Read one record from each file.

9. Because both files are finished, end the job. The result is a new master file in which some records contain exactly the same data they contained going in, but others (for which a transaction has occurred) have been updated with a new total sales figure.

TWO TRUTHS AND A LIE:
MATCHING FILES TO UPDATE FIELDS IN MASTER FILE RECORDS

1. To update a master file with a transaction file, you begin with both files sorted in the same order on the same field.

2. The process of updating a master file involves going through the old master file, one record at a time, and determining whether there is a new transaction for each record.

3. If there is no transaction for a master file record, the master file record is deleted from the updated master file.

The false statement is #3. If there is no transaction for a master file record, the updated master file record will contain exactly the same information as the old record.

ALLOWING MULTIPLE TRANSACTIONS FOR A SINGLE MASTER FILE RECORD

In the last example, the logic provided for, at most, one transaction record per master customer record. You would use very similar logic if you wanted to allow multiple transactions for a single customer. Figure 10-16 shows the new logic for the file-matching process. Note a small but important difference between logic that allows multiple transactions and logic that allows only a single transaction per master file record. If a customer can have multiple transactions, whenever a transaction matches a customer, you add the transaction amount to the master total sales field. Then, instead of reading from both files, you read *only* from the transaction file. The next transaction might also pertain to the same master customer. (Compare the first "Yes" branch in Figure 10-16 with the one in Figure 10-14; the portion of the logic that reads the next customer record and checks for end of file is removed.) Only when a transaction number is greater than a master file customer number do you write the customer master record.

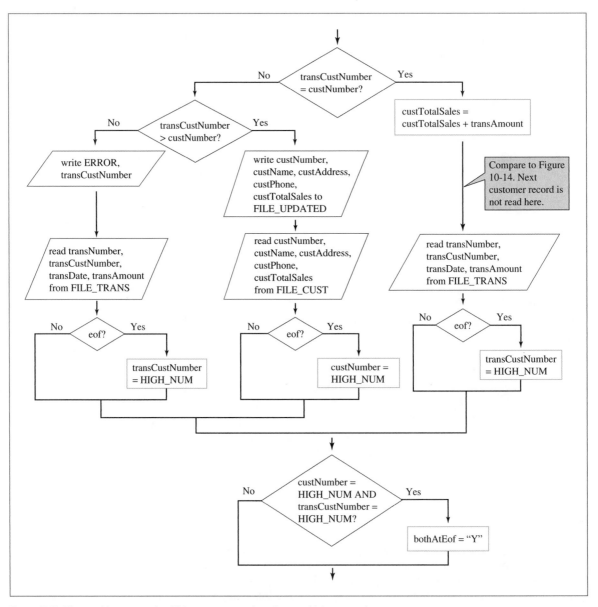

Figure 10-16 File-matching process in which a master record can have multiple transactions

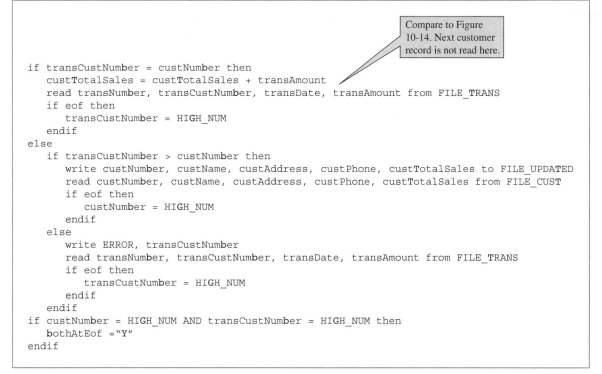

Figure 10-16 File-matching process in which a master record can have multiple transactions (*continued*)

UPDATING RECORDS IN SEQUENTIAL FILES

In the example in the preceding section, you needed to update a field in some of the records in a master file with new data. A more sophisticated update program allows you not only to make changes to data in a master file record, but also to update a master file either by adding new records or by eliminating the ones you no longer want.

Assume you have a master employee file, as shown on the left side of Figure 10-17, and a transaction file, as shown on the right side of the figure. The master file contains employee data, and the transaction file contains the same data with one additional field. The extra field holds a code that indicates whether the transaction is meant to be an addition to the master file (for example, when a new employee is hired), a deletion from the master file (for example, when an employee quits), or a change to the master file (for example, when an employee receives a raise).

MASTER AND TRANSACTION FILES FOR UPDATE PROGRAM

FILENAME: EMPLOYEES		FILENAME: TRANSACTIONS	
FIELD DESCRIPTION	DATA TYPE	FIELD DESCRIPTION	DATA TYPE
Employee number	Numeric	Employee number	Numeric
Name	String	Name	String
Salary	Numeric	Salary	Numeric
Department	Numeric	Department	Numeric
		Transaction code	String

The master file and transaction file formats are identical except for this code.

Figure 10-17 Formats of master and transaction files for an update program

The master file records contain data in each of the fields shown in Figure 10-17—an employee number, name, salary, and department number. The three types of transaction records stored in the transaction file would differ as follows:

» An **addition record** in a transaction file actually represents a new master file record. An addition record would contain data in each of the fields—the employee number, name, salary, and department; because an addition record represents a new employee, data for all the fields must be captured for the first time. Also, in this example, such a record contains an "A" for "Addition" in the transaction code field.

» A **deletion record** in a transaction file flags a master file record that should be removed from the file. In this example, a deletion record really needs data in only two fields—a "D" for "Deletion" in the transaction code field and a number in the employee number field. If a "D" transaction record's employee number matches an employee number on a master record, then you have identified a record you want to delete. You do not need data indicating the salary, department, or anything else for a record you are deleting.

» A **change record** indicates an alteration that should be made to a master file record. In this case, it contains a "C" code for "Change" and needs data only in the employee number field and any fields that are going to be changed. In other words, if an employee's salary is not changing, the salary field in the transaction record will be blank; but if the employee is transferring to Department 28, then the department field of the transaction record will hold 28.

The main logic for an update program is very similar to the merging and matching programs discussed earlier in this chapter. Both master and transaction files are opened, and a first record is read from each. As long as both files have not reached eof, a main loop continues. You test whether the employee numbers in a pair of master and transaction files are equal, or if not, then whether the master file employee number is larger or smaller than the current transaction file employee number. Figure 10-18 shows the format of the mainline logic.

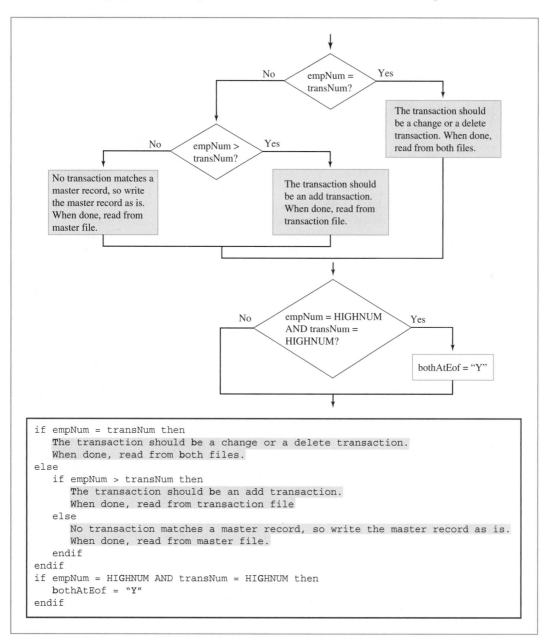

```
if empNum = transNum then
    The transaction should be a change or a delete transaction.
    When done, read from both files.
else
    if empNum > transNum then
        The transaction should be an add transaction.
        When done, read from transaction file
    else
        No transaction matches a master record, so write the master record as is.
        When done, read from master file.
    endif
endif
if empNum = HIGHNUM AND transNum = HIGHNUM then
    bothAtEof = "Y"
endif
```

Figure 10-18 Format for mainline logic for update program

The possibilities shown in Figure 10-18 are summarized as follows:

» If the employee numbers are equal, then the transaction should be an update record or a delete record. (If the master file and the transaction file record employee numbers are equal, but the transaction code is "A", then an error has occurred. You should not attempt to add a full employee record when the employee already exists in the master file.) After the equal records are processed, you read one new record from each of the two input files.

» If the master file record has a higher number than the transaction file record, this means you have read a transaction record for which there is no master file record. If the transaction record contains code "A", that's fine because an addition transaction shouldn't have a master record. However, if the transaction code is "C" or "D", an error has occurred. Either you are attempting to change a record that does not exist or you are attempting to delete a record that does not exist. Either way, a mistake has been made, and you must print an error message. Then, if the master file employee number is higher than the transaction file employee number, you should not read another master file record. After all, there could be several more transactions that represent new additions to the master file. You want to keep reading transactions until a transaction matches or is greater than a master record. Therefore, only a transaction record should be read.

» The final possibility is that a master file record's employee number is smaller than the transaction file record's number. If there is no transaction for a given master file record, it just means that the master file record has no changes or deletions; therefore, you simply write the new master record out exactly like the old master record and read another master record.

When the master file employee number and the transaction file employee number are equal, there are three possibilities:

» If the transaction code is an "A", you should print an error message. But what is the error? (Is the code wrong—was this meant to be a change or a deletion of an existing employee? Is the employee number wrong—was this meant to be the addition of some new employee?) Because you're not completely sure, you can only print an error message to let an employee know that an error has occurred; then, the employee can handle the error. You should also write the existing master record exactly the same way it came in, without making any changes.

» If the transaction code is a "C", you need to make changes. You must check each field in the transaction record. If any field is blank, the data in the new master record should come from the old master record. If, however, a field in the transaction record contains data, this data is intended to constitute a change, and the corresponding field in the new master record should be created from the transaction record. Then, for each changed field, you replace the contents of the old field in the master file with the new value in the corresponding field in the transaction file, and then write the master file record.

» If the code is not an "A" or a "C", it must be a "D" and the record should be deleted. How do you delete a record from a new master file? Just don't write it out to the new master file! In other words, as Figure 10-19 shows, no action is necessary when a record is deleted.

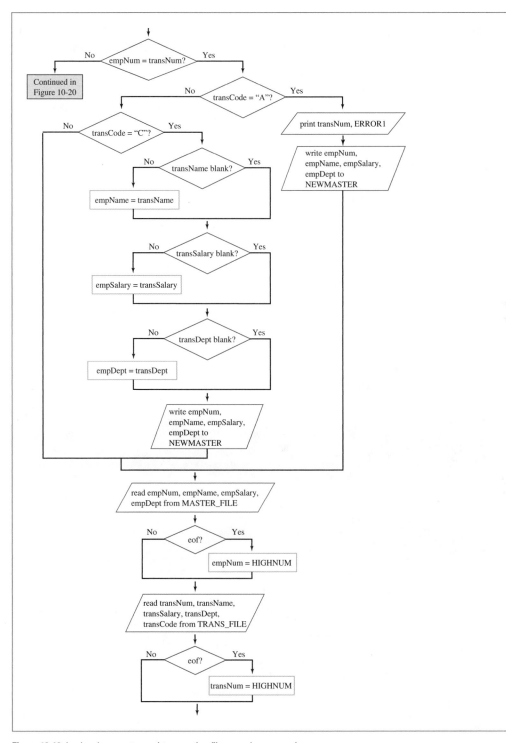

Figure 10-19 Logic when master and transaction file records are equal

```
if empNum = transNum then
    if transCode = "A" then
        print transNum, ERROR1
        write empNum, empName, empSalary, empDept to NEWMASTER
    else
        if transCode = "C" then
            if transName not blank then
                empName = transName
            endif
            if transSalary not blank then
                empSalary = transSalary
            endif
            if transDept not blank then
                empDept = transDept
            endif
            write empNum, empName, empSalary, empDept to NEWMASTER
        endif
    endif
    read empNum, empName, empSalary, empDept from MASTER_FILE
    if eof then
        empNum = HIGHNUM
    endif
    read transNum, transName, transSalary, transDept, transCode from TRANS_FILE
    if eof then
        transNum = HIGHNUM
    endif
```

Figure 10-19 Logic when master and transaction file records are equal (*continued*)

> » **NOTE** Various programming languages have different ways of checking a field to determine if it is blank. In some languages, you compare the field to an empty string, as in `transName = ""`. The quotation marks with nothing between them indicate an empty or null string. In some systems, you might need to compare the field to a space character, as in `transName = " "`, in which a literal space is inserted between the quotation marks. In other languages, you can use a predefined language-specific constant such as `BLANK`, as in `transName = BLANK`.

> » **NOTE** To keep the illustration simple here, you can assume that all the transaction records have been checked by a previous program, and all `transCode` values are "A", "C", or "D". If this were not the case, you could simply add one more decision to the `theyAreEqual()` module. If `transCode` is not "C", instead of assuming it is "D", ask if it is "D". If so, delete the record (by not writing it); if not, it must be something other than "A", "C", or "D", so print an error message.

When the master file employee number is higher than the transaction file employee number, there are two possibilities:

» If the transaction code is an "A", then the transaction record represents a new employee and the transaction record data items simply become the contents of a new master file record. Figure 10-20 shows that each transaction field is written to the new master file.

» If the transaction code is "C" or "D", then you must print an error message.

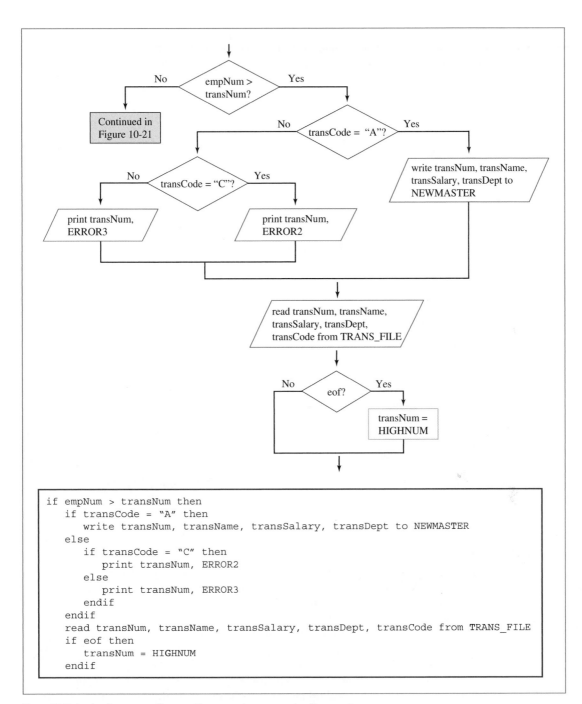

```
if empNum > transNum then
    if transCode = "A" then
        write transNum, transName, transSalary, transDept to NEWMASTER
    else
        if transCode = "C" then
            print transNum, ERROR2
        else
            print transNum, ERROR3
        endif
    endif
    read transNum, transName, transSalary, transDept, transCode from TRANS_FILE
    if eof then
        transNum = HIGHNUM
    endif
```

Figure 10-20 Logic when master file record is greater than transaction file record

Finally, when the master file employee number is not greater than or equal to the transaction file employee number, then the master file has no changes. Figure 10-21 shows the data is written without any changes.

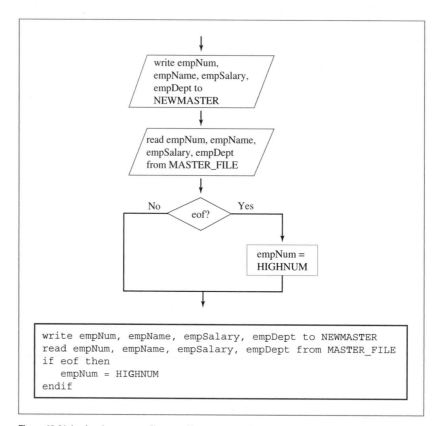

```
write empNum, empName, empSalary, empDept to NEWMASTER
read empNum, empName, empSalary, empDept from MASTER_FILE
if eof then
    empNum = HIGHNUM
endif
```

Figure 10-21 Logic when master file record is not greater than or equal to transaction file record

At some point in the master-transaction updating process, one of the files will reach eof.

» If the transaction file reaches the end first, transNum is set to 999. Then each time the program's main loop is entered, empNum will be lower than transNum and each remaining record on the master file will be written without alteration. (Obviously, there were no transactions for these final records in the master file, because all the records in the transaction file were used to apply to earlier master file records.)

» On the other hand, if the master file reaches its end first, empNum is set to 999. Now, each time the program enters the main loop, transNum will be lower than empNum. In turn, each remaining transaction will be compared to the possible code values. If any remaining transaction records are additions, they will be written to the new master file as new records. However, if any of the remaining transaction records represent changes or deletions, then a mistake has been made, because there are no corresponding master file records. In other words, error messages will then be printed for the remaining change and deletion transaction records as they are processed.

Whichever file reaches the end first, the other continues to be read and processed. When that file reaches `eof`, the `bothAtEof` flag will finally be set to "Y". Then, you can close all the files. Pseudocode for the entire program is shown in Figure 10-22.

```
start
    num empNum
    string empName
    num empSalary
    num empDept
    num transNum

    string transName
    num transSalary
    num transDept
    string transCode

    string bothAtEof = "N"
    num HIGHNUM = 999
    string MASTER_FILE = "Employees.txt"
    string TRANS_FILE = "Changes.txt"
    string NEWMASTER = "UpdatedFile.txt"
    string ERROR1 = "Trying to add record that already exists"
    string ERROR2 = "Trying to change record that does not exist"
    string ERROR3 = " Trying to delete record that does not exist"

    open MASTER_FILE, TRANS_FILE, NEWMASTER

    read empNum, empName, empSalary, empDept from MASTER_FILE
    if eof then
        empNum = HIGHNUM
    endif

    read transNum, transName, transSalary, transDept, transCode from TRANS_FILE
    if eof then
        transNum = HIGHNUM
    endif

    if empNum = HIGHNUM AND transNum = HIGHNUM then
        bothAtEof = "Y"
    endif

    while bothAtEof = "N"

        if empNum = transNum then
            if transCode = "A" then
                print transNum, ERROR1
                write empNum, empName, empSalary, empDept to NEWMASTER
            else
                if transCode = "C" then
                    if transName not blank then
                        empName = transName
                    endif
```

Figure 10-22 Pseudocode for master-transaction file program

```
                    if transSalary not blank then
                        empSalary = transSalary
                    endif
                    if transDept not blank then
                        empDept = transDept
                    endif
                    write empNum, empName, empSalary, empDept to NEWMASTER
                endif
            endif
            read empNum, empName, empSalary, empDept from MASTER_FILE
            if eof then
                empNum = HIGHNUM
            endif
            read transNum, transName, transSalary, transDept, transCode from TRANS_FILE
            if eof then
                transNum = HIGHNUM
            endif
        else
            if empNum > transNum then
                if transCode = "A" then
                    write transNum, transName, transSalary, transDept to NEWMASTER
                else
                    if transCode = "C" then
                        print transNum, ERROR2
                    else
                        print transNum, ERROR3
                    endif
                endif
                read transNum, transName, transSalary, transDept, transCode from
                    TRANS_FILE
                if eof then
                    transNum = HIGHNUM
                endif

            else
                write empNum, empName, empSalary, empDept to NEWMASTER
                read empNum, empName, empSalary, empDept from MASTER_FILE
                if eof then
                    empNum = HIGHNUM
                endif
            endif
        endif

        if empNum = HIGHNUM AND transNum = HIGHNUM then
            bothAtEof = "Y"
        endif

    endwhile
    close MASTER_FILE, TRANS_FILE, NEWMASTER
stop
```

Figure 10-22 Pseudocode for master-transaction file program (*continued*)

Merging files, matching files, and updating a master file from a transaction file require a significant number of steps, because as you read each new input record you must account for many possible scenarios. Planning the logic for programs like these takes a fair amount of time, but by planning the logic carefully, you can create programs that perform valuable work for years to come. Separating the various outcomes into manageable modules keeps the program organized and allows you to develop the logic one step at a time.

TWO TRUTHS AND A LIE:

UPDATING RECORDS IN SEQUENTIAL FILES

1. An addition record in a transaction file actually represents a new master file record.

2. If a master file record and an update record are equal, the update code should not represent an addition.

3. If a master file record has a higher key field than a transaction file record, the update code should not represent an addition.

The false statement is #3. If a master file record has a higher key field than a transaction file record, it means you have read a transaction record for which there is no master file record. If the transaction record contains an addition code, that's fine because an addition transaction shouldn't have a master record. However, if the transaction code is change or delete, an error has occurred. Either you are attempting to make a change to a record that does not exist or you are attempting to delete a record that does not exist.

CHAPTER SUMMARY

» A computer file is a collection of information stored on a nonvolatile device in a computer system. Although the contents of files differ (some files hold data, programs, graphics, text, operating system instructions, and so on), files have many common characteristics. Each file occupies space on a section of a storage device, and each has a name and a specific time of creation. When you store data in a computer file on a persistent storage device, you write to the file. This means you copy data from RAM to the file. When you copy data from a file on a storage device into RAM, you read from the file. In most programming languages, before an application can use a data file, it must open the file. Opening a file locates it on a storage device and associates a variable name within your program with the file. Similarly, when you finish using a file, the program should close the file so that the file is no longer available to your application.

» A sequential file is a file in which records are stored one after another in some order. Merging files involves combining two or more files while maintaining the sequential order.

» The mainline logic for a program that merges two files contains preliminary, housekeeping tasks, a main loop that repeats until the end of the program, and some clean-up, end-of-job tasks. In a program that merges files, there are two input files, so you must check for eof on both of them. The merging process involves comparing two records (one from each of two files), writing the record that should come first, and reading another record from the *same* input file. When either file reaches eof, you store a high value in the comparison field for that file.

» Some related sequential files are master files that hold relatively permanent data, and transaction files that hold more temporary data. Commonly, you periodically use a transaction file to find a matching record in a master file—one that contains data about the same customer. Sometimes, you match records so you can update the master file by making changes to the values in its fields. When you update a master file, you can take two approaches: You can actually change the information in the master file, or you can create a copy of the master file, making the changes in the new version.

» To match files, you must begin with both files sorted in the same order on the same field. The process involves going through the old master file, one record at a time, and determining whether there is a new transaction for that record. If not, the new master file record will contain exactly the same information as the old one. However, if there is a transaction for a master file record, the master file record is updated before you write the record.

» When you use the logic that allows multiple transactions per master file record, you apply the transaction to the master file record and then you read only from the transaction file. Only when a transaction number is greater than a master file customer number do you write the customer master record.

» An update program allows you not only to make changes to data in a master file record, but also to update a master file either by adding new records or by eliminating the ones you no longer want. An addition record in a transaction file actually represents a new master file record. A deletion record in a transaction file flags a master file record that should be removed from the file. A change record indicates an alteration that should be made to a master file record.

KEY TERMS

Random access memory (RAM) is temporary storage within the computer.

Volatile storage is lost when a program ends or the computer loses power.

Nonvolatile storage is permanent.

A **computer file** is a collection of information stored on a nonvolatile device in a computer system.

Files exist on **permanent storage devices**, such as hard disks, floppy disks, Zip disks, USB drives, reels or cassettes of magnetic tape, and compact discs.

Data files contain facts and figures.

Program files or **application files** store software instructions.

When you store data in a computer file on a persistent storage device, you **write to the file**.

When you copy data from a file on a storage device into RAM, you **read from the file**.

Opening a file locates it on a storage device and associates a variable name within your program with the file.

Closing a file makes it no longer available to an application.

Default input and output devices are those that do not require opening. Usually they are the keyboard and monitor, respectively.

A **sequential file** is a file in which records are stored one after another in some order.

Temporal order is order based on time.

Merging files involves combining two or more files while maintaining the sequential order.

A **high value** is one that is greater than any possible value in a field.

You use a **master file** to hold relatively permanent data.

A **transaction file** holds temporary data that you use to update a master file.

A **matching record** is one that contains data about the same entity as another.

To **update a master file** involves making changes to the values in its fields based on transactions.

A **parent file** is the saved version of a master file reflecting data before transactions were applied.

A **child file** is the new version of a master file after transactions have been applied.

An **addition record** in a transaction file represents a new master file record.

A **deletion record** in a transaction file flags a master file record that should be removed from the file.

A **change record** in a transaction file indicates an alteration that should be made to a master file record.

REVIEW QUESTIONS

1. Random access memory is _____ .

   a. permanent

   b. volatile

   c. persistent

   d. continual

2. The process of _____ a file locates it on a storage device and associates a variable name within your program with the file.

   a. opening

   b. closing

   c. declaring

   d. defining

3. A file in which records are stored one after another in some order is a(n) _____ file.

   a. temporal

   b. sequential

   c. random

   d. alphabetical

4. When you combine two or more sorted files while maintaining their sequential order based on a field, you are _____ the files.

   a. tracking

   b. collating

   c. merging

   d. absorbing

5. Unlike when you print a report, when a program's output is a data file, you do not _____ .

   a. include headings or other formatting

   b. open the files

   c. include all the fields represented as input

   d. all of the above

6. Assume you are writing a program to merge two files named FallStudents and SpringStudents. Each file contains a list of students enrolled in a programming logic course during the semester indicated, and each file is sorted in student ID number order. After the program compares two records and subsequently writes a Fall student to output, the next step is to _____ .

   a. read a SpringStudents record

   b. read a FallStudents record

   c. write a SpringStudents record

   d. write another FallStudents record

7. A value that is greater than any possible legal value in a field is called a(n) _____ value.

   a. great

   c. merging

   b. illegal

   d. high

8. When you merge records from two or more sequential files, the usual case is that the records in the files _____ .

   a. contain the same data

   b. have the same format

   c. are identical in number

   d. are sorted on different fields

9. A file that holds more permanent data than a transaction file is a _____ file.

   a. master

   c. key

   b. primary

   d. mega-

10. A transaction file is often used to _____ another file.

    a. augment

    c. verify

    b. remove

    d. update

11. The saved version of a file that does not contain the most recently applied transactions is known as a _____ file.

    a. master

    c. parent

    b. child

    d. relative

12. Ambrose Bierce High School maintains a master file containing records for each student in a class. Each record contains fields such as student ID, student name, home phone number, and grade on each exam. A transaction file is created after each exam. It contains records that each hold a test number, a student ID, and the student's grade on the exam. You would write a matching program to match the records in the _____ field.

    a. student ID

    b. student name

    c. test number

    d. grade on the exam

13. **Larry's Service Station maintains a master file containing records for each vehicle Larry services. Each record contains fields such as vehicle ID, owner name, date of last oil change, date of last tire rotation, and so on. A transaction file is created each day. It contains records that hold a vehicle ID and the name of the service performed. When Larry performs a match between these two files so that the most recent date can be inserted into the master file, which of the following should cause an error condition?**

    a. A specific vehicle is represented in each file.

    b. A specific vehicle is represented in the master file, but not in the transaction file.

    c. A specific vehicle is represented in the transaction file, but not in the master file.

    d. A specific vehicle is not represented in either file.

14. **Sally's Sandwich Shop maintains a master file containing records for each preferred customer. Each record contains a customer ID, name, e-mail address, and number of sandwiches purchased. A transaction file record is created each time a customer makes a purchase; the fields include customer ID and number of sandwiches purchased as part of the current transaction. After a customer surpasses 12 sandwiches, Sally e-mails the customer a coupon for a free sandwich. When Sally runs the match program with these two files so that the master file can be updated with the most recent purchases, which of the following should indicate an error condition?**

    a. master ID is greater than transaction ID

    b. master ID is equal to transaction ID

    c. master ID is less than transaction ID

    d. none of the above

15. **Which of the following is true of master-transaction file-matching processing?**

    a. A master file record must never match more than one transaction record.

    b. A transaction file record must never match any master records.

    c. When master and transaction file records match, you must always immediately read another record from each file.

    d. A transaction record must match, at most, one master file record.

16. **Which of the following is true of master-transaction file-matching processing?**

    a. A master file's records must be sorted in some sequential order.

    b. A transaction file's records must be sorted on a different field than the master file's records.

    c. A master file's records must contain more fields than a transaction file's records.

    d. A transaction file's records must contain more fields than a master file's records.

17. **In a program that updates a master file, a transaction file record might cause a master file record to be _____ .**

    a. modified

    b. deleted

    c. either of these

    d. neither a nor b

18. **In a program that updates a master file, if a transaction record indicates a change, then it is an error when the transaction record's matching field is _____ the field in a master file's record.**

    a. greater than

    b. less than

    c. both of these

    d. neither a nor b

19. **In a program that updates a master file, if a master and transaction file match, then it is an error if the transaction record is a(n) _____ record.**

    a. addition

    b. change

    c. deletion

    d. two of the above

20. **In a program that updates a master file, if a master file's comparison field is larger than a transaction file's comparison field, then it is an error if the transaction record is a(n) _____ record.**

    a. addition

    b. change

    c. deletion

    d. two of the above

FIND THE BUGS

The following pseudocode segment contains one or more bugs that you must find and correct.

1. **Each time a salesperson sells a car at the Pardeeville New and Used Auto Dealership, a record is created containing the salesperson's name and the amount of the sale. Sales of new and used cars are kept in separate files because several reports are created for one type of sale or the other. However, management has requested a merged file so that all of a salesperson's sales, whether the vehicle was new or used, are displayed together. The following code is intended to merge the files that have already been sorted by salesperson ID number.**

```
start
    string newSalesperson
    num newAmount
    string usedSalesperson
    num usedAmount

    string bothAtEof = "Y"
    num HIGHNAME = "ZZZZZ"
    string NEWSALES = "NewSales.txt"
    string USEDSALES = "UsedSales.txt"
    string ALLSALES = "AllSales.txt"

    open NEWSALES, USEDSALES, ALLSALES

    read newSalesperson, newAmount from NEWSALES
    if eof then
        newSalesperson = HIGHNAME
    endif

    read usedSalesperson, usedAmount from USEDSALES
    if eof then
        usedSalesperson = HIGHNAME
    endif

    if newSalesperson = HIGHNAME AND usedSalesperson = HIGHNAME then
        bothAtEof = "Y"
    endif
```

```
    while bothAtEof = "N"
        if newSalesPerson < usedSalesperson then
            write usedSalesperson, usedAmount to ALLSALES
            read newSalesperson, newAmount from NEWSALES
            if eof then
                usedSalesperson = HIGHNAME
            endif
        else
            write newSalesperson, usedAmount to ALLSALE
            read newSalesperson, newAmount from NEWSALE
            if eof then
                newSalesperson = usedSalesperson
            endif
        endif
        if newSalesperson = HIGHNAME AND usedSalesperson = HIGHNAME
then
            bothAtEof = "Y"
        endif
    endwhile
    close NEWSALES, USEDSALES, ALLSALES
stop
```

EXERCISES

> ⟩⟩ **NOTE** Your Student Disk contains one or more comma-delimited sample data files for each exercise in this section. You might want to use these files in any of several ways:
>
> ⟩ You can look at the file contents to gain a better understanding of the types of data each program uses.
>
> ⟩ You can use the files' contents as sample data when you desk check the logic of your flowcharts or pseudocode.
>
> ⟩ You can use the files as input files if you implement the solutions in a programming language and write programs that accept file input.
>
> ⟩ You can use the data as guides to appropriate values to enter if you implement the solutions in a programming language and write interactive programs.
>
> ⟩ When multiple files are included for an exercise, it is a reminder to you that the problem requires different procedures when the numbers of data records varies.

1. **The Springwater Township School District has two high schools—Jefferson and Audubon. Each school maintains a student file with fields containing student ID, last name, first name, and address. Each file is in student ID number order. Design the logic for a program that merges the two files into one file containing a list of all students in the district, maintaining student ID number order.**

2. **The Redgranite Library keeps a file of all books borrowed every month. Each file is in Library of Congress number order and contains additional fields for author and title.**

   a. Design the logic for a program that merges the files for January and February to create a list of all books borrowed in the two-month period.

   b. Modify the program from Exercise 2a so that if there is more than one record for a book number, you print the book information only once.

   c. Modify the program from Exercise 2b so that if there is more than one record for a book number, you not only print the book information only once, you also print a count of the total number of times the book was borrowed.

3. **Hearthside Realtors keeps a transaction file for each salesperson in the office. Each transaction record contains the salesperson's first name, date of the sale, and sale price. The records for the year are sorted in descending sale price order. Two salespeople, Diane and Mark, have formed a partnership. Design the logic that produces a merged list of their transactions (including name of salesperson, date, and price) in descending order by price.**

4. **Dartmoor Medical Associates maintains two patient files—one for the Lakewood office and one for the Hanover office. Each record contains the name, address, city, state, and zip code of a patient, with the file maintained in zip code order. Design the logic that merges the two files to produce one master name and address file that the Dartmoor office staff can use for addressing the practice's monthly Healthy Lifestyles newsletter mailing in zip code order.**

5. **The Willmington Walking Club maintains a master file that contains a record for each of its members. Fields in the master file include the walker's ID number, first name, last name, and total miles walked to the nearest one-tenth of a mile. Every week, a transaction file is produced. The transaction file contains a walker's ID number and the number of miles the walker has logged that week. Each file is sorted in walker ID number order.**

   a. Design the logic for a program that matches the master and transaction file records and updates the total miles walked for each club member by adding the current week's miles to the cumulative total for each walker. Not all walkers submit walking reports each week. The output is the updated master file and an error report listing any transaction records for which no master record exists.

   b. Modify the program in Exercise 5a to print a certificate of achievement each time a walker exceeds the 500-mile mark. That is, the certificate—containing the walker's name and an appropriate congratulatory message—is printed during the run of the update program when a walker's mile total changes from a value below 500 to one that is 500 or greater.

6. **The Timely Talent Temporary Help Agency maintains an employee master file that contains an employee ID number, last name, first name, address, and hourly rate for each of the temporary employees it sends out on assignments. The file has been sorted in employee ID number order.**

   Each week, a transaction file is created with a job number, address, customer name, employee ID, and hours worked for every job filled by Timely Talent workers. The transaction file is also sorted in employee ID order.

   a. Design the logic for a program that matches the master and transaction file records, and print one line for each transaction, indicating job number, employee ID number, hours worked, hourly rate, and gross pay. Assume each temporary worker works at most one job per week; print one line for each worker who has worked that week.

   b. Modify Exercise 6a so that any individual temporary worker can work any number of separate jobs in a week. Print one line for each job that week.

   c. Modify the program in Exercise 6b so that, although any worker can work any number of jobs in a week, you accumulate the worker's total pay for all jobs and print one line per worker.

7. **Claypool College maintains a student master file that contains a student ID number, last name, first name, address, total credit hours completed, and cumulative grade point average for each of the students who attend the college. The file has been sorted in student ID number order.**

   Each semester, a transaction file is created with the student's ID, number of credits completed during the new semester, and grade point average for the new semester. The transaction file is also sorted in student ID order.

   Design the logic for a program that matches the master and transaction file records, and updates the total credit hours completed and the cumulative grade point average on a new master record. Calculate the new grade point average as follows:

   » Multiply the credits in the master file by the grade point average in the master file, giving master honor points—that is, honor points earned prior to any transaction. The honor points value is useful because it is weighted—the value of the honor points is more for a student who has accumulated 100 credits with a 3.0 grade point average than it is for a student who has accumulated only 20 credits with a 3.0 grade point average.

   » Multiply the credits in the transaction file by the grade point average in the transaction file, giving transaction honor points.

   » Add the two honor point values, giving total honor points.

   » Add master and transaction credit hours, giving total credit hours.

   » Divide total honor points by total credit hours, giving the new grade point average.

8. The Amelia Earhart High School basketball team maintains a record for each team player, including player number, first and last name, minutes played during the season, baskets attempted, baskets made, free throws attempted, free throws made, shooting average from the floor, and shooting average from the free throw line. (Shooting average from the floor is calculated by dividing baskets made by baskets attempted; free throw average is calculated by dividing free throws made by free throws attempted.) The master records are maintained in player number order.

   After each game, a transaction record is produced for any player who logged playing time. Fields in each transaction record contain player number, minutes played during the game, baskets attempted, baskets made, free throws attempted, and free throws made.

   Design the logic for a program that updates the master file with the transaction file, including recalculating shooting averages, if necessary.

9. The Tip-Top Talent Agency books bands for social functions. The agency maintains a master file in which the records are stored in order by band code. The records have the following format:

```
TALENT FILE DESCRIPTION
File name: BANDS
FIELD DESCRIPTION      DATA TYPE      COMMENTS              EXAMPLE
Band Code              Numeric        3-digit number        176
Band Name              String                               The Polka Pals
Contact Person         String                               Jay Sakowicz
Phone                  Numeric        10 digits             5554556012
Musical Style          String                               Polka
Hourly Rate            Numeric        2 decimal places      75.00
```

The agency has asked you to write an update program, so that once a month the agency can make changes to the file, using transaction records with the same format as the master records, plus one additional field that holds a transaction code. The transaction code is "A" if the agency is adding a new band to the file, "C" if it is changing some of the data in an existing record, and "D" if it is deleting a band from the file.

An addition transaction record contains a band code, an "A" in the transaction code field, and the new band's data. During processing, an error can occur if you attempt to add a band code that already exists in the file. This is not allowed, and an error message is printed.

A change transaction record contains a band code, a "C" in the transaction code field, and data for only those fields that are changing. For example, a band that is raising its hourly rate from $75 to $100 would contain empty fields for the band name, contact person information, and style of music, but the hourly rate field would contain the new rate. During processing, an error can occur if you attempt to change data for a band number that doesn't exist in the master file; print an error message.

A deletion transaction record contains a band code, a "D" in the transaction code field, and no other data. During processing, an error can occur if you attempt to delete a band number that doesn't exist in the master file; print an error message.

Two forms of output are created. One is the updated master file with all changes, additions, and deletions. The other is a printed report of errors that occurred during processing. Rather than just a list of error messages, each line of the printed output should list the appropriate band code along with the corresponding message.

Design the logic for the program.

10. Cozy Cottage Realty maintains a master file in which records are stored in order by listing number, in the following format:

```
REALTY FILE DESCRIPTION
File name: HOUSES
FIELD DESCRIPTION    DATA TYPE    COMMENTS           EXAMPLE
Listing Number       Numeric      6-digit number     200719
Address              String                          348 Alpine Road
List Price           Numeric      0 decimals         139900
Bedrooms             Numeric      0 decimals         3
Baths                Numeric      1 decimal          1.5
```

The realty company has asked you to write an update program so that, every day, the company can make changes to the file, using transaction records with the same format as the master records, plus one additional field that holds a transaction code. The transaction code is "A" to add a new listing, "C" to change some of the data in an existing record, and "D" to delete a listing that is sold or no longer on the market.

An addition transaction record contains a listing number, an "A" in the transaction code field, and the new house listing's data. During processing, an error can occur if you attempt to add a listing number that already exists in the file. This is not allowed, and an error message is printed.

A change transaction record contains a listing number, a "C" in the transaction code field, and data for only those fields that are changing. For example, a listing that is dropping in price from $139,900 to $133,000 would contain empty fields for the address, bedrooms, and baths, but the price field would contain the new list price. During processing, an error can occur if you attempt to change data for a listing number that doesn't exist in the master file; print an error message.

A deletion transaction record contains a listing code number, a "D" in the transaction code field, and no other data. During processing, an error can occur if you attempt to delete a listing number that doesn't exist in the master file; print an error message.

Two forms of output are created. One is the updated master file with all changes, additions, and deletions. The other is a printed report of errors that occurred during processing. Rather than just a list of error messages, each line of the printed output should list the appropriate house listing number along with the corresponding message.

Design the logic for the program.

11. **Crown Greeting Cards maintains a master file of its customers stored in order by customer number, in the following format:**

```
CROWN CUSTOMER FILE DESCRIPTION
File name: CUSTS
FIELD DESCRIPTION        DATA TYPE   COMMENTS           EXAMPLE
Customer Number          Numeric     5 digits           34492
Name                     String                         Roberta Branch
Address                  String                         32 Pinetree Lane
Phone Number             Numeric     10 digits          5554448935
Value of Merchandise
   Purchased This Year   Numeric     2 decimal places   525.99
```

The card store has asked you to write an update program so that, every week, the store can make changes to the file, using transaction records with the same format as the master records, plus one additional field that holds a transaction code. The transaction code is "A" to add a new customer, "C" to change some of the data in an existing record, and "D" to delete a customer. In a transaction record, the amount field represents a new transaction instead of the total value of merchandise purchased.

An addition transaction record contains a customer number, an "A" in the transaction code field, and the new customer's name, address, phone number, and first purchase amount. During processing, an error can occur if you attempt to add a customer number that already exists in the file. This is not allowed, and an error message is printed.

A change transaction record contains a customer number, a "C" in the transaction code field, and data for only those fields that are changing. For example, a customer might have a new address or phone number. In a change record, if a value appears in the merchandise value field, it represents an amount that should be added to the total merchandise value in the master record. During processing, an error can occur if you attempt to change data for a customer number that doesn't exist in the master file; print an error message.

A deletion transaction record contains a customer number, a "D" in the transaction code field, and no other data. During processing, an error can occur if you attempt to delete a customer number that doesn't exist in the master file; print an error message.

a. Design the logic for a program in which three forms of output are created. One is the updated master file with all changes, additions, and deletions. The second output is a display of errors that occurred during processing; each line of the printed output should list the customer number along with an appropriate message. The third output is a report listing all customers who have currently met or exceeded the $1,000 purchase threshold for the year.

b. Modify the program in Exercise 11a so that the third output is not a report of all customers who have met or exceeded the $1,000 purchase threshold this year, but a report listing all customers who have just passed the $100 purchase threshold this week.

GAME ZONE

1. The International Rock Paper Scissors Society holds regional and national championships. Each region holds a semifinal competition in which competitors play 500 games of Rock Paper Scissors. The top 20 competitors in each region are invited to the national finals. Assume you are provided with files for the East, Midwest, and Western regions. Each file contains the following fields for the top 20 competitors: last name, first name, and number of games won. The records in each file are sorted in alphabetical order. Merge the three files to create a file of the top 60 competitors who will compete in the national championship.

2. In the Game Zone section of Chapter 9, you designed the logic for a guessing game in which the application generates a random number and the player tries to guess it. After each guess you displayed a message indicating whether the player's guess was correct, too high, or too low. When the player eventually guessed the correct number, you displayed a score that represented a count of the number of guesses that were required. Modify the game so that at the start of the game, the player enters his or her name. After a player plays the game exactly five times, save the best (lowest) score from the five games to a file. If the player's name already exists in the file, update the record with the new lowest score; if the player's name does not already exist in the file, create a new record for him or her. After the file is updated, display all the best scores stored in the file.

DETECTIVE WORK

1. **What is a random file and how does it differ from a sequential file? In what types of applications are sequential files most useful? In what types of applications are they least useful?**

2. **What is FIFO and how does it relate to file processing?**

UP FOR DISCUSSION

1. Suppose you are hired by a police department to write a program that matches arrest records with court records detailing the ultimate outcome or verdict for each case. You have been given access to current files so that you can test the program. Your friend works in the personnel department of a large company and must perform background checks on potential employees. (The job applicants sign a form authorizing the check.) Police records are open to the public and your friend could look up police records at the courthouse, but it takes many hours per week. As a convenience, should you provide your friend with outcomes of any arrest records of job applicants?

2. Suppose you are hired by a clinic to match a file of patient office visits with patient master records to print various reports. While working with the confidential data, you notice the name of the fiancé of one of your friends. Should you tell your friend that the fiancé is seeking medical treatment? Does the type of treatment affect your answer?

OBJECT-ORIENTED PROGRAMMING

In this chapter you will:

Understand some basic principles of object-oriented programming

Define classes and create class diagrams

Understand public and private access

Appreciate different ways to organize classes

Understand instance methods

Understand static, class methods

Understand constructors

Learn how to use objects

Understand destructors

Understand composition

Understand inheritance

Appreciate GUI objects

Summarize the advantages of object-oriented programming

AN OVERVIEW OF SOME PRINCIPLES OF OBJECT-ORIENTED PROGRAMMING

Object-oriented programming (OOP) is a style of programming that focuses on an application's data and the methods you need to manipulate that data. Object-oriented programming uses all of the concepts you are familiar with from modular procedural programming, such as variables, modules, and passing values to modules. Modules in object-oriented programs continue to use sequence, selection, and looping structures and make use of arrays. However, object-oriented programming adds several new concepts to programming and involves a different way of thinking. A considerable amount of new vocabulary is involved as well. First, you will read about object-oriented programming concepts in general; then you will learn the specific terminology.

> **»»NOTE** Throughout this book, the terms *module* and *method* have been used interchangeably. In Chapter 3 you learned that object-oriented programmers prefer the term *method*, so that's the term that will be used in this chapter.

Objects both in the real world and in object-oriented programming are made up of attributes and methods. **Attributes** are the characteristics that define an object as part of a class. For example, some of your automobile's attributes are its make, model, year, and purchase price. Other attributes include whether the automobile is currently running, its gear, its speed, and whether it is dirty. All automobiles possess the same attributes, but not, of course, the same values for those attributes. Similarly, your dog has the attributes of its breed, name, age, and whether its shots are current.

In object-oriented terminology, a **class** is a term that describes a group or collection of objects with common attributes. An **instance** of a class is an existing object of a class. Therefore, your red Chevrolet Automobile with the dent can be considered an instance of the class that is made up of all automobiles, and your Golden Retriever Dog named Ginger is an instance of the class that is made up of all dogs. Thinking of items as instances of a class allows you to apply your general knowledge of the class to individual members of the class. A particular instance of an object takes its attributes from the general category. If your friend purchases an Automobile, you know it has a model name, and if your friend gets a Dog, you know the dog has a breed. You might not know the current state of your friend's Automobile, such as its current speed, or the status of her Dog's shots, but you do know what attributes exist for the Automobile and Dog classes, and this allows you to imagine these objects reasonably well before you see them. When you visit your friend and see the Automobile or Dog for the first time, you probably will recognize it as the new acquisition. As another example, when you use a new application on your computer, you expect each component to have specific, consistent attributes, such as a button being clickable or a window being closeable, because each component gains these attributes as a member of the general class of GUI (graphical user interface) components.

> **»»NOTE** Most programmers who use more modern languages employ the format in which class names begin with an uppercase letter and in which multiple-word identifiers are run together. Each new word within the identifier starts with an uppercase letter. In Chapter 1, you learned that this format is known as *Pascal casing*.

Much of your understanding of the world comes from your ability to categorize objects and events into classes. As a young child, you learned the concept of "animal" long before you knew the word. Your first encounter with an animal might have been with the family dog, a neighbor's cat, or a goat at a petting zoo. As you developed speech, you might have used the same term for all of these creatures, gleefully shouting "Doggie!" as your parents pointed out cows, horses, and sheep in picture books or along the roadside on drives in the country. As you grew more sophisticated, you learned to distinguish dogs from cows; still later, you learned to distinguish breeds. Your understanding of the class "animal" helps you see the similarities between dogs and cows, and your understanding of the class "dog" helps you see the similarities between a Great Dane and a Chihuahua. Understanding classes gives you a framework for categorizing new experiences. You might not know the term "okapi," but when you learn it's an animal, you begin to develop a concept of what an okapi might be like.

When you think in an object-oriented manner, everything is an object, and every object is a member of a class. You can think of any inanimate physical item as an object—your desk, your computer, and your house are all called "objects" in everyday conversation. You can think of living things as objects, too—your houseplant, your pet fish, and your sister are objects. Events are also objects—the stock purchase you made, the mortgage closing you attended, and your graduation party are all objects.

Everything is an object, and every object is a member of a more general class. Your desk is a member of the class that includes all desks, and your pet fish is a member of the class that contains all fish. An object-oriented programmer would say that the desk in your office is an instance, or one tangible example, of the `Desk` class and your fish is an instance of the `Fish` class. These statements represent **is-a relationships** because you can say, "My oak desk with the scratch on top *is a* `Desk`, and my goldfish named Moby *is a* `Fish`." The difference between a class and an object parallels the difference between abstract and concrete. Your goldfish, my guppy, and the zoo's shark each constitute one instance of the `Fish` class.

》NOTE
Object-oriented programmers also use the term *is-a* when describing inheritance. You will learn about inheritance later in this chapter.

The concept of a class is useful because of its reusability. Objects receive their attributes from classes. For example, if you invite me to a graduation party, I automatically know many things about the object (the party). I assume there will be a starting time, a number of guests, some quantity of food, and some nature of gifts. I understand parties because of my previous knowledge of the `Party` class, of which all parties are members. I don't know the number of guests or the date or time of this particular party, but I understand that because all parties have a date and time, then this one must as well. Similarly, even though every stock purchase is unique, each must have a dollar amount and a number of shares. All objects have predictable attributes because they are members of certain classes.

》NOTE
Object-oriented programmers sometimes say an object is one **instantiation** of a class; this is just another form of *instance*.

The data components of a class that belong to every instantiated object are the class's **instance variables**. Also, object attributes are often called **fields** to help distinguish them from other variables you might use. The set of all the values or contents of a class object's instance variables is also known as its **state**. For example, the current state of a particular party is 8 p.m. and Friday; the state of a particular stock purchase is $10 and five shares.

In addition to their attributes, class objects have methods associated with them, and every object that is an instance of a class possesses the same methods. For example, at some point you might want to issue invitations for a party. You might name the method `issueInvitations()`, and it might display some text as well as the values of the party's date and time fields. Your graduation party, then, might possess the identifier `myGraduationParty`. As a member of the `Party` class, it might have data members for the date and time, like all parties, and it might have a method to issue invitations. When you use the method, you might want to be able to send an argument to `issueInvitations()` that indicates how many copies to print. When you think of an object and its methods, it's as though you can send a message to the object to direct it to accomplish some task—you can tell the party object named `myGraduationParty` to print the number of invitations you request. Even though `yourAnniversaryParty` is also a member of the `Party` class, and even though it also has an `issueInvitations()` method, you will send a different argument value to `yourAnniversaryParty`'s `issueInvitations()` method than I will send to `myGraduationParty`'s corresponding method. Within any object-oriented program, you continuously make requests to objects' methods, often including arguments as part of those requests.

>> **NOTE** In grammar, a noun is equivalent to an object and the values of a class's attributes are adjectives—they describe the characteristics of the objects. An object can also have methods, which are equivalent to verbs.

When you program in object-oriented languages, you frequently create classes from which objects will be instantiated. You also write applications to use the objects, along with their data and methods. Often, you will write programs that use classes created by others; other times, you might create a class that other programmers will use to instantiate objects within their own programs. A program or class that instantiates objects of another prewritten class is a **class client** or **class user**. For example, your organization might already have written a class named `Customer` that contains attributes such as `name`, `address`, and `phoneNumber`, and you might create clients that include arrays of thousands of `Customer`s. Similarly, in a GUI operating environment, you might write applications that include prewritten components that are members of classes with names like `Window` and `Button`. You expect each component on a GUI screen to have specific, consistent attributes, such as a button being clickable or a window being closeable, because each component gains these attributes as a member of its general class.

Besides classes and objects, three important features of object-oriented languages are:

» Polymorphism

» Inheritance

» Encapsulation

POLYMORPHISM

The real world is full of objects. Consider a door. A door needs to be opened and closed. You open a door with an easy-to-use interface known as a doorknob. Object-oriented programmers would say you are "passing a message" to the door when you "tell" it to open by turning its knob. The same message (turning a knob) has a different result when applied to your radio than when applied to a door. The procedure you use to open something—call it the "open" procedure—works differently on a door to a room than it does on a desk drawer, a bank account, a computer file, or your eyes. However, even though these procedures operate differently using the different objects, you can call all of these procedures "open." In object-oriented programming, procedures are called methods.

With object-oriented programming, you focus on the objects that will be manipulated by the program—for example, a customer invoice, a loan application, or a menu from which the user will select an option. You define the characteristics of those objects and the methods that each of the objects will use; you also define the information that must be passed to those methods.

You can create multiple methods with the same name, which will act differently and appropriately when used with different types of objects. In Chapter 7, you learned that this concept is *polymorphism* and you learned to overload methods. For example, you might use a method named `print()` to print a customer invoice, loan application, or envelope. Because you use the same method name, `print()`, to describe the different actions needed to print these diverse objects, you can write statements in object-oriented programming languages that are more like English; you can use the same method name to describe the same type of action, no matter what type of object is being acted upon. Using the method name `print()` is easier than remembering `printInvoice()`, `printLoanApplication()`, and so on. In English, you understand the difference between "running a race," "running a business," and "running a computer program." Object-oriented languages understand verbs in context, just as people do.

> **»»NOTE** Purists find a subtle difference between overloading and polymorphism. Some reserve the term "polymorphism" (or **pure polymorphism**) for situations in which one method body is used with a variety of arguments. For example, a single method that can be used with any type of object is polymorphic. The term "overloading" is applied to situations in which you define multiple functions with a single name (for example, three functions, all named `display()`, that display a number, an employee, and a student, respectively). Certainly, the two terms are related; both refer to the ability to use a single name to communicate multiple meanings. For now, think of overloading as a primitive type of polymorphism.

As another example of the advantages to using one name for a variety of objects, consider a screen you might design for a user to enter data into an application you are writing. Suppose the screen contains a variety of objects—some forms, buttons, scroll bars, dialog boxes, and so on. Suppose also that you decide to make all the objects blue. Instead of having to memorize the names that these objects use to change color—perhaps `changeFormColor()`, `changeButtonColor()`, and so on—your job would be easier if the creators of all those objects had developed a `setColor()` method that works appropriately with each type of object.

INHERITANCE

Another important concept in object-oriented programming is **inheritance**, which is the process of acquiring the traits of one's predecessors. In the real world, a new door with a stained glass window inherits most of its traits from a standard door. It has the same purpose, it opens and closes in the same way, and it has the same knob and hinges. The door with the stained glass window simply has one additional trait—its window. Even if you have never seen a door with a stained glass window, when you encounter one you know what it is and how to use it because you understand the characteristics of all doors. With object-oriented programming, once you create an object, you can develop new objects that possess all the traits of the original object plus any new traits you desire. If you develop a `CustomerBill` class of objects, there is no need to develop an `OverdueCustomerBill` class from scratch. You can create the new class to contain all the characteristics of the already developed one, and simply add necessary new characteristics. This not only reduces the work involved in creating new objects, it makes them easier to understand because they possess most of the characteristics of already developed objects.

ENCAPSULATION

Real-world objects often employ encapsulation and information hiding. In Chapter 3, you learned that encapsulation is the process of combining all of an object's attributes and methods into a single package. **Information hiding** is the concept that other classes should not alter an object's attributes—only the methods of an object's own class should have that privilege. Outside classes should only be allowed to make a request that an attribute be altered; then it is up to the class's methods to determine whether the request is appropriate. When using a door, you are usually unconcerned with the latch or hinge construction features, and you don't have access to the interior workings of the knob, or know what color of paint might have been used on the inside of the door panel. You care only about the functionality and the interface, the user-friendly boundary between the user and internal mechanisms of the device. Similarly, the detailed workings of objects you create within object-oriented programs can be hidden from outside programs and modules if you want them to be. When the details are hidden, programmers can focus on the functionality and the interface, as people do with real-life objects.

NOTE
Information hiding is also called **data hiding**.

In summary, understanding object-oriented programming means that you must consider five of its integral components: classes, objects, polymorphism, inheritance, and encapsulation.

TWO TRUTHS AND A LIE:

AN OVERVIEW OF SOME PRINCIPLES OF OBJECT-ORIENTED PROGRAMMING

1. Learning about object-oriented programming is difficult because it does not use the concepts you already know, such as declaring variables and using modules.

2. In object-oriented terminology, a class is a term that describes a group or collection of objects with common attributes, and an instance of a class is an existing object of a class.

3. A program or class that instantiates objects of another prewritten class is a class client or class user.

The false statement is #1. Object-oriented programming makes use of many of the features of procedural programming including declaring variables and using modules.

DEFINING CLASSES AND CREATING CLASS DIAGRAMS

A class is a category of things; an object is a specific instance of a class. A **class definition** is a set of program statements that tell you the characteristics of the class's objects and the methods that can be applied to its objects.

A class definition can contain three parts:

» Every class has a name.
» Most classes contain data, although this is not required.
» Most classes contain methods, although this is not required.

For example, you can create a class named Employee. Each Employee object will represent one employee who works for an organization. Data members, or attributes of the Employee class, include fields such as lastName, hourlyWage, and weeklyPay.

The methods of a class include all actions you want to perform with the class. Appropriate methods for an `Employee` class might include `setHourlyWage()`, `getHourlyWage()`, and `calculateWeeklyPay()`. The job of `setHourlyWage()` is to provide values for an `Employee`'s wage data field, the purpose of `getHourlyWage()` is to retrieve the wage value, and the purpose of `calculateWeeklyPay()` is to multiply the `Employee`'s `hourlyWage` by the number of hours in a workweek to calculate a weekly salary. With object-oriented languages, you think of the class name, data, and methods as a single encapsulated unit.

Declaring a class does not create any actual objects. A class is just an abstract description of what an object will be like if any objects are ever actually instantiated. Just as you might understand all the characteristics of an item you intend to manufacture long before the first item rolls off the assembly line, you can create a class with fields and methods long before you instantiate any objects that are members of that class. After an object has been instantiated, its methods can be accessed using the object's identifier, a dot, and a method call. When you declare a simple variable that is a built-in data type, you write a statement such as one of the following:

```
num money
string name
```

When you write a program that declares an object that is a class data type, you write a statement such as the following:

```
Employee myAssistant
```

> **NOTE** In some object-oriented programming languages, you need to add more to the declaration statement to actually create an `Employee` object. For example, in Java, you would write:
>
> ```
> Employee myAssistant = new Employee();
> ```
>
> You will understand more about the construction of this statement when you learn about constructors later in this chapter.

When you declare the `myAssistant` object, the object contains all the data fields and has access to all the methods contained within the class. In other words, a larger section of memory is set aside than when you declare a simple variable, because an `Employee` contains several fields. You can use any of an `Employee`'s methods with the `myAssistant` object. The usual syntax is to provide an object name, a dot (period), and a method name. For example, you can write a program that contains statements such as the ones shown in the pseudocode in Figure 11-1.

```
start
   Employee myAssistant
   myAssistant.setLastName("Reynolds")
   myAssistant.setHourlyWage(16.75)
   print "My assistant makes ",
      myAssistant.getHourlyWage(), " per hour"
stop
```

Figure 11-1 Application that declares and uses an `Employee` object

> **NOTE** Besides referring to `Employee` as a class, many programmers would refer to it as a **user-defined type**; a more accurate term is **programmer-defined type**. Object-oriented programmers typically refer to a class like `Employee` as an **abstract data type (ADT)**; this term implies that the type's data can be accessed only through methods.

When you write a statement such as `myAssistant.setHourlyWage(16.75)`, you are making a call to a method that is contained within the `Employee` class. Because `myAssistant` is an `Employee` object, it is allowed to use the `setHourlyWage()` method that is part of its class.

When you write the application in Figure 11-1, you do not need to know what statements are written within the `Employee` class methods, although you could make an educated guess based on the methods' names. Before you could execute the application in Figure 11-1, someone would have to write appropriate statements within the `Employee` class methods. If you wrote the methods, of course you would know their contents, but if another programmer has already written the methods, then you could use the application without knowing the details contained in the methods. In Chapter 7, you learned that the ability to use methods without knowing the details of their contents (called a "black box") is a feature of encapsulation. The real world is full of many black box devices. For example, you can use your television and microwave oven without knowing how they work internally—all you need to understand is the interface. Similarly, with well-written methods that belong to classes you use, you need not understand how they work internally to be able to use them; you need only understand what the ultimate result will be when you use them.

> **»NOTE** Some programmers write only client programs, never creating nonclient classes themselves, but using only classes that others have created.

In the client program segment in Figure 11-1, the focus is on the object—the `Employee` named `myAssistant`—and the methods you can use with that object. This is the essence of object-oriented programming.

> **»NOTE** Of course, the program segment in Figure 11-1 is very short. In a more useful real-life program, you might read employee data from a data file before assigning it to the object's fields, each `Employee` might contain dozens of fields, and your application might create hundreds or thousands of objects.

> **»NOTE** In older object-oriented programming languages, simple numbers and characters are said to be **primitive data types**; this distinguishes them from objects that are class types. In the newest programming languages, every item you name, even one that is a numeric or string type, really is an object that is a member of a class that contains both data and methods.

> **»NOTE** When you instantiate objects, the data fields of each are stored at separate memory locations. However, all members of the same class share one copy of the class's methods. You will learn more about this concept later in this chapter.

CREATING CLASS DIAGRAMS

Programmers often use a class diagram to illustrate class features or to help to plan them. A **class diagram** consists of a rectangle divided into three sections, as shown in Figure 11-2. The top section contains the name of the class, the middle section contains the names and data types of the attributes, and the bottom section contains the methods. This generic class diagram shows two attributes and three methods, but a given class might have any number of either, including none. Figure 11-3 shows the class diagram for the `Employee` class.

> **» NOTE** Class diagrams are a type of Unified Modeling Language (UML) diagram. Chapter 13 covers the UML.

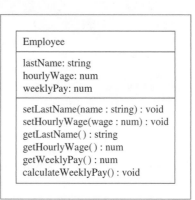

Class name
Attribute 1 : data type Attribute 2 : data type
Method 1( ) : data type Method 2( ) : data type Method 3( ) : data type

Figure 11-2 Generic class diagram

Figure 11-3 `Employee` class diagram

> **» NOTE** By convention, a class diagram lists the names of the data items first. Each name is followed by a colon and the data type. Similarly, method names are followed by their data types. Listing the names first emphasizes the purposes of the fields and methods more than their types.

Figures 11-2 and 11-3 both show that a class diagram is intended to be only an overview of class attributes and methods. A class diagram shows *what* data items and methods the class will use, not the details of the methods nor *when* they will be used. It is a design tool that helps you see the big picture in terms of class requirements. Figure 11-3 shows the `Employee` class that contains three data fields that represent an employee's name, hourly pay rate, and weekly pay amount. Every `Employee` object created in any program that uses this class will contain these three data fields. In other words, when you declare an `Employee` object, you declare three fields with one statement and reserve enough memory to hold all three fields.

> **» NOTE** You might design many programs for which you do not bother to create a class diagram, but instead simply start by writing the pseudocode or the actual code. Class diagrams are most useful for communicating about a class's contents with nonprogrammers.

Figure 11-3 also shows that the `Employee` class contains six methods. For example, the first method is defined as follows:

```
setLastName(name : string) : void
```

This notation means that the method name is `setLastName()`, that it takes a single `string` parameter named `name`, and that it returns nothing.

```
setLastName()
```

Some developers choose to list the method name and return type only, as in:

```
setLastName() : void
```

Some developers list the method name and return type as well as the parameter type, as in the following:

```
setLastName(string) : void
```

Still other developers list an appropriate identifier for the parameter, but not its type, as in the following:

```
setLastName(name) : void
```

This book will take the approach of being as complete as possible, so the class diagrams you see here will contain each method's identifier, parameter list with types, and return type. You should use the format your instructor prefers. When you are on the job, use the format your supervisor and coworkers understand.

The `Employee` class diagram shows that two of the six methods take parameters (`setLastName()` and `setHourlyWage()`). The diagram also shows the return type for each method—three void methods, two numeric methods, and one string method. The class diagram does not tell you what takes place inside the method (although you might be able to make an educated guess). Later, when you write the code that actually creates the `Employee` class, you include method implementation details. For example, Figure 11-4 shows some pseudocode you can use to show the details for the methods contained within the `Employee` class.

```
class Employee
    string lastName
    num hourlyWage
    num weeklyPay

    void setLastName(string name)
        lastName = name
    return

    void setHourlyWage(num wage)
        hourlyWage = wage
        calculateWeeklyPay()
    return

    string getLastName()
    return lastName

    num getHourlyWage()
    return hourlyWage

    num getWeeklyPay()
    return weeklyPay

    void calculateWeeklyPay()
        num WORK_WEEK_HOURS = 40
        weeklyPay = hourlyWage * WORK_WEEK_HOURS
    return
endClass
```

Figure 11-4 Pseudocode for `Employee` class described in the class diagram in Figure 11-3

In Figure 11-4, the `Employee` class attributes or fields are identified with a data type and a field name. In addition to listing the data fields required, Figure 11-4 shows the complete methods for the `Employee` class. The purposes of the methods can be divided into three categories:

» Two of the methods accept values from the outside world; these methods, by convention, start with the prefix *set*. These methods are used to set the data fields in the class.

» Three of the methods send data to the outside world; these methods, by convention, start with the prefix *get*. These methods return field values to a client program.

» One method performs work within the class; this method is named `calculateWeeklyPay()`. This method does not communicate with the outside; its purpose is to multiply `hourlyWage` by the number of hours in a week.

THE SET METHODS

In Figure 11-4, two of the methods begin with the word *set*; they are `setLastName()` and `setHourlyWage()`. They are known as **set methods** because their purpose is to set the values of data fields within the class. Each accepts data from the outside and assigns it to a field within the class. There is no requirement that such methods start with the prefix *set*; the prefix is merely conventional and makes the intention of the methods clear. The method `setLastName()` is implemented as follows:

```
void setLastName(string name)
    lastName = name
return
```

In this method, a string `name` is passed in as a parameter and assigned to the field `lastName`. Because `lastName` is contained in the same class as this method, the method has access to the field and can alter it.

Similarly, the method `setHourlyWage()` accepts a numeric parameter and assigns it to the class field `hourlyWage`. This method also calls the `calculateWeeklyPay()` method, which sets `weeklyPay` based on `hourlyWage`. By writing the `setHourlyWage()` method to call the `calculateWeeklyPay()` method automatically, you guarantee that the `weeklyPay` field is updated any time `hourlyWage` changes.

>> **NOTE** Methods that set values are called **mutator methods**.

When you create an `Employee` object with a statement such as `Employee mySecretary`, then you can use statements such as the following:

```
mySecretary.setLastName("Johnson")
mySecretary.setHourlyWage(15.00)
```

Similarly, you could pass variables or named constants to the methods as long as they were the correct data type. For example, if you write a program in which you make the following declarations, then the assignment in the next statement is valid.

```
num PAY_RATE_TO_START = 8.00
mySecretary.setHourlyWage(PAY_RATE_TO_START)
```

>> **NOTE** In some languages—for example, Visual Basic and C#—you can create a **property** instead of creating a set method. Using a property provides a way to set a field value using a simpler syntax. By convention, if a class field is `hourlyWage`, its property would be `HourlyWage`, and in a program you could make a statement similar to `mySecretary.HourlyWage = PAY_RATE_TO_START`. The implementation of the property `HourlyWage` (with an uppercase initial letter) would be written in a format very similar to that of the `setHourlyWage()` method.

Just like any other methods, the methods that manipulate fields within a class can contain any statements you need. For example, a more complicated setHourlyWage() method might be written as shown in Figure 11-5. In this version, the wage passed to the method is tested against minimum and maximum values, and is assigned to the class field hourlyWage only if it falls within the prescribed limits. If the wage is too low, the MINWAGE value is substituted, and if the wage is too high, the MAXWAGE value is substituted.

```
void setHourlyWage(num wage)
    num MINWAGE = 6.00
    num MAXWAGE = 70.00
    if wage < MINWAGE then
        hourlyWage = MINWAGE
    else
        if wage > MAXWAGE then
            hourlyWage = MAXWAGE
        else
            hourlyWage = wage
        endif
    endif
    calculateWeeklyPay()
return
```

Figure 11-5 More complex setHourlyWage() method

Similarly, if the set methods in a class required them, the methods could contain print statements, loops, array declarations, or any other legal programming statements. However, if the main purpose of a method is not to set a field value, then the method should not be named with the set prefix.

THE GET METHODS

In the Employee class in Figure 11-4, three of the methods begin with the prefix *get*: getLastName(), getHourlyWage(), and getWeeklyPay(). The purpose of a **get method** is to return a value to the world outside the class. The methods are implemented as follows:

```
string getLastName()
return lastName

num getHourlyWage()
return hourlyWage

num getWeeklyPay()
return weeklyPay
```

Each of these methods simply returns the value in the field implied by the method name. Like set methods, any of these get methods could also contain more complicated statements as needed. For example, in a more complicated class, you might want to return the hourly wage of an employee only if the user had also passed an appropriate access code to the method, or you might want to return the weekly pay value as a string with a dollar sign attached instead of as a numeric value.

>> NOTE
Methods that get values from class fields are known as **accessor methods**.

When you declare an `Employee` object such as `Employee mySecretary`, you can then make statements in a program similar to the following:

```
string employeeName
employeeName = mySecretary.getLastName()
print "Wage is ", mySecretary.getHourlyWage()
print "Pay for half a week is ", mySecretary.getWeeklyPay() * 0.5
```

In other words, the value returned from a get method can be used as any other variable of its type would be used. You can assign the value to another variable, print it, perform arithmetic with it, or make any other statement that works correctly with the returned data type.

>> **NOTE** In some languages—for example, Visual Basic and C#—instead of creating a get method, you can add statements to the property to return a value using simpler syntax. For example, if you create an `HourlyWage` property, you could write a program that makes the statement print `mySecretary.HourlyWage`.

OTHER METHODS

The `Employee` class in Figure 11-4 contains one method that is neither a get nor a set method. This method, `calculateWeeklyPay()`, is a **work method** within the class. It contains a locally named constant that represents the hours in a standard workweek and it computes the `weeklyPay` field value by multiplying `hourlyWage` by the named constant. The method is written as follows:

```
void calculateWeeklyPay()
    num WORK_WEEK_HOURS = 40
    weeklyPay = hourlyWage * WORK_WEEK_HOURS
return
```

>> **NOTE**
Some programmers call work methods **help methods** or **facilitators**.

No values need to be passed into this method, and no value is returned from it because this method does not communicate with the outside world. Instead, this method is called only from within another method in the same class (the `setHourlyWage()` method), and that method is called from the outside world. Any time a program uses the `setHourlyWage()` method to alter an `Employee`'s `hourlyWage` field, then `calculateWeeklyPay()` is called to recalculate the `weeklyPay` field.

>> **NOTE** No `setWeeklyPay()` method is included in this `Employee` class because the intention is that `weeklyPay` is set only each time the `setHourlyWage()` method is used. If you wanted programs to be able to set the `weeklyPay` field directly, you would have to write a method to allow it.

>> **NOTE** Programmers who are new to class creation often want to pass the `hourlyWage` value into the `setWeeklyPay()` method so it can use the value in its calculation. Although this technique would work, it is not required. The `setWeeklyPay()` method has direct access to the `hourlyWage` field by virtue of being a member of the same class.

For example, Figure 11-6 shows a program that declares an `Employee` object and sets the hourly wage value. The program prints the `weeklyPay` value. Then a new value is assigned to `hourlyWage` and `weeklyPay` is printed again. As you can see from the output in Figure 11-7, the `weeklyPay` value has been recalculated even though it was never set directly by the client program.

```
start
    num LOW = 9.00
    num HIGH = 14.65
    Employee myGardener
    myGardener.setLastName("Greene")
    myGardener.setHourlyWage(LOW)
    print "My gardener makes ",
       myGardener.getWeeklyPay(), " per week"
    myGardener.setHourlyWage(HIGH)
    print "My gardener makes ",
       myGardener.getWeeklyPay(), " per week"
stop
```

Figure 11-6 Program that sets and displays `Employee` data two times

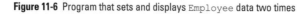

Figure 11-7 Execution of program in Figure 11-6

TWO TRUTHS AND A LIE:
DEFINING CLASSES AND CREATING CLASS DIAGRAMS

1. Every class has a name, data, and methods.

2. After an object has been instantiated, its methods can be accessed using the object's identifier, a dot, and a method call.

3. A class diagram consists of a rectangle divided into three sections; the top section contains the name of the class, the middle section contains the names and data types of the attributes, and the bottom section contains the methods.

The false statement is #1. Most classes contain data, and most classes contain methods, although this is not required.

UNDERSTANDING PUBLIC AND PRIVATE ACCESS

When you buy a product with a warranty, one of the conditions of the warranty is usually that the manufacturer must perform all repair work. For example, if your computer has a warranty and something goes wrong with its operation, you cannot open the system unit yourself, remove and replace parts, and then expect to get your money back for a device that does not work properly. Instead, when something goes wrong with your computer, you must take the device to a technician approved by the manufacturer. The manufacturer guarantees that your machine will work properly only if the manufacturer can control how the internal mechanisms of the machine are modified.

Similarly, in object-oriented design, usually you do not want any outside programs or methods to alter your class's data fields unless you have control over the process. For example, you might design a class that performs a complicated statistical analysis on some data and stores the result. You would not want others to be able to alter your carefully crafted result. As another example, you might design a class from which others can create an innovative and useful GUI screen object. In this case you would not want others altering the dimensions of your artistic design. To prevent outsiders from changing your data fields in ways you do not endorse, you force other programs and methods to use a method that is part of the class, such as setLastName() and setHourlyWage(), to alter data. (Earlier in this chapter, you learned that the principle of keeping data private and inaccessible to outside classes is called information hiding or data hiding.) Object-oriented programmers usually specify that their data fields will have **private access**; that is, the data cannot be accessed by any method that is not part of the class. The methods themselves, like setHourlyWage(), support **public access**—which means that other programs and methods may use the methods that control access to the private data. Figure 11-8 shows a complete Employee class to which the access specifier has been added to describe each attribute and method. An **access specifier** (or **access modifier**) is the adjective that defines the type of access that outside classes will have to the attribute or method (public or private). In the figure, each access specifier is shaded.

```
class Employee
    private string lastName
    private num hourlyWage
    private num weeklyPay

    public void setLastName(string name)
        lastName = name
    return

    public void setHourlyWage(num wage)
        hourlyWage = wage
        calculateWeeklyPay()
    return

    public string getLastName()
    return lastName

    public num getHourlyWage()
    return hourlyWage

    public num getWeeklyPay()
    return weeklyPay

    private void calculateWeeklyPay()
        num WORK_WEEK_HOURS = 40
        weeklyPay = hourlyWage * WORK_WEEK_HOURS
    return
endClass
```

Figure 11-8 Employee class including public and private access specifiers

>> **NOTE** In many object-oriented programming languages, if you do not declare an access specifier for a data field or method, then it is private by default. This book will follow the convention of explicitly specifying access for every class member.

In Figure 11-8, each of the data fields is private; that means each field is inaccessible to an object declared in a program. In other words, if a program declares an `Employee` object, such as `Employee myAssistant`, then the following statement is illegal:

`myAssistant.hourlyWage = 15.00`

DON'T DO IT
The `hourlyWage` field is not accessible outside the class.

Instead, `hourlyWage` can be assigned only through a public method as follows:

`myAssistant.setHourlyWage(15.00)`

If you made `hourlyWage` public instead of private, then a direct assignment statement would work, but you would violate an important principle of OOP—that of data hiding using encapsulation. Data fields should usually be private and a client application should be able to access them only through the public interfaces; that is, through the class's public methods. That way, if you have restrictions on the value of `hourlyWage`, those restrictions will be enforced by the public method that acts as an interface to the private data field. Similarly, a public get method might control how a private value is retrieved. Perhaps you do not want clients to have access to an `Employee`'s `hourlyWage` if it is more than a specific value, or perhaps you always want to return it to the client as a string with a dollar sign attached. Even when a field has no data value requirements or restrictions, making data private and providing public set and get methods establishes a framework that makes such modifications easier in the future.

In the `Employee` class in Figure 11-8, only one method is not public; the `calculateWeeklyPay()` method is private. That means if you write a program and declare an `Employee` object such as `Employee myAssistant`, then the following statement is not permitted:

`myAssistant.calculateWeeklyPay()`

DON'T DO IT
The `calculateWeeklyPay()` method is not accessible outside the class.

Because it is private, the only way to call the `calculateWeeklyPay()` method is from within another method that already belongs to the class. In this example, it is called from the `setHourlyWage()` method. This prevents any client program from setting `hourlyWage` to one value while setting `weeklyPay` to some incompatible value. By making the `calculateWeeklyPay()` method private, you ensure that the class retains full control over when and how it is used. Classes most often contain private data and public methods, but as you have just seen, they can contain private methods; they can contain public data items as well. For example, an `Employee` class might contain a public constant data field named `MINIMUM_WAGE`; outside programs then would be able to access that value without using a method. Public data fields are not required to be named constants, but they frequently are.

Many programmers like to specify in their class diagrams whether each component in a class is public or private. Figure 11-9 shows the conventions that are typically used. A minus sign (–) precedes the items that are private; a plus sign (+) precedes those that are public.

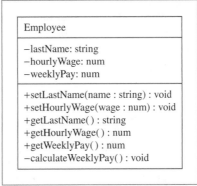

Figure 11-9 Employee class diagram with public and private access specifiers

TWO TRUTHS AND A LIE:
UNDERSTANDING PUBLIC AND PRIVATE ACCESS

1. Object-oriented programmers usually specify that their data fields will have private access.

2. Object-oriented programmers usually specify that their methods will have private access.

3. In a class diagram, a minus sign (–) precedes the items that are private; a plus sign (+) precedes those that are public.

The false statement is #2. Object-oriented programmers usually specify that their methods will have public access.

ORGANIZING CLASSES

The Employee class in Figure 11-9 contains just three data fields and six methods; most classes you create for professional applications will have many more. For example, in addition to requiring a last name and pay information, real employees require an employee number, a first name, address, phone number, hire date, and so on, as well as methods to set and get those fields. As classes grow in complexity, deciding how to organize them becomes increasingly important.

Although there is no requirement to do so, most programmers place data fields in some logical order at the beginning of a class. For example, an ID number is most likely used as a unique identifier for each employee (what database users often call a **primary key**), so it makes sense to list the employee ID number first in the class. An employee's last name and first name "go together," so it makes sense to store these two Employee components adjacently. Despite these common-sense rules, you have a lot of flexibility in how you position your data fields within any class. For example, depending on the class, you might choose to store the data fields alphabetically, or you might choose to group together all the fields that are the same data type. Alternatively, you might choose to store all public data items first, followed by private ones, or vice versa.

> **»NOTE** A unique identifier is one that should have no duplicates within an application. For example, an organization might have many employees with the last name Johnson or an hourly wage of $10.00, but only one employee will have employee number 12438.

In some languages you can organize a class's data fields and methods in any order within a class. For example, you could place all the methods first, followed by all the data fields, or you could organize the class so that several data fields are followed by methods that use them, and then several more data fields might be followed by the methods that use them. This book will follow the convention of placing all data fields first so that you can see their names and data types before reading the methods that use them. This format also echoes the way data and methods appear in standard class diagrams.

For ease in locating a class's methods, many programmers store them in alphabetical order. Other programmers arrange them in pairs of get and set methods, in the same order as the data fields are defined. Another option is to list all accessor (get) methods together and all mutator (set) methods together. Depending on the class, there might be other orders that result in logically functional groupings. Of course, if your company distributes guidelines for organizing class components, you must follow those rules.

TWO TRUTHS AND A LIE:
ORGANIZING CLASSES

1. As classes grow in complexity, deciding how to organize them becomes increasingly important.

2. You have a lot of flexibility in how you position your data fields within any class.

3. In a class, methods must be stored in the order in which they are used.

The false statement is #3. Methods can be stored in alphabetical order, in pairs of get and set methods, in the same order as the data fields are defined, or in any other logically functional groupings.

UNDERSTANDING INSTANCE METHODS

Class objects have data and methods associated with them, and every object that is an instance of a class is assumed to possess the same data and have access to the same methods. For example, Figure 11-10 shows a class diagram for a simple Student class that contains just one private data field that holds a student's grade point average. The class also contains get and set methods for the field. Figure 11-11 shows the pseudocode for the Student class. This class becomes the model for a new data type named Student; when Student objects eventually are created, each will have its own gradePointAverage field and have access to methods to get and set it.

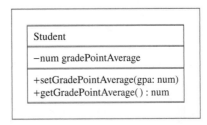

Figure 11-10 Class diagram for Student class

```
class Student
    private num gradePointAverage

    public num setGradePointAverage(num gpa)
        gradePointAverage = gpa
    return

    public num getGradePointAverage()
    return gradePointAverage
endClass
```

Figure 11-11 Pseudocode for the Student class

In the Student class in Figure 11-11, the method setGradePointAverage() takes one argument—a value for the Student's grade point average. The identifier gpa is local to the setGradePointAverage() method, and holds a value that will come into the method from the outside. Within the method, the value in gpa is assigned to gradePointAverage, which is a field within the class. The setGradePointAverage() method assigns a value to the gradePointAverage field for each separate Student object you ever create. Therefore, a method such as setGradePointAverage() is called an **instance method** because it operates correctly yet differently (using different values) for each separate instance of the Student class. In other words, if you create 100 Students and assign grade point averages to each of them, you need 100 storage locations in computer memory to store each unique grade point average.

Figure 11-12 shows a program that creates three Student objects and assigns values to their gradePointAverage fields. It also shows how the Student objects look in memory after the values have been assigned.

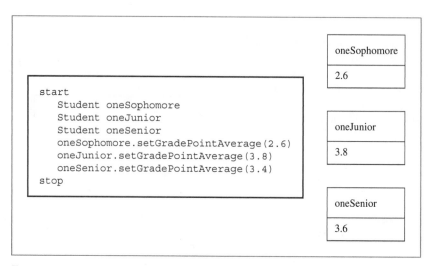

```
start
    Student oneSophomore
    Student oneJunior
    Student oneSenior
    oneSophomore.setGradePointAverage(2.6)
    oneJunior.setGradePointAverage(3.8)
    oneSenior.setGradePointAverage(3.4)
stop
```

oneSophomore

2.6

oneJunior

3.8

oneSenior

3.6

Figure 11-12 StudentDemo program and how Student objects look in memory

It makes sense for each Student object in Figure 11-12 to have its own gradePointAverage field, but it does not make sense for each Student to have its own copy of the methods that get and set gradePointAverage. Any method might have dozens of instructions in it, and to make 100 copies of identical methods would be inefficient. Instead, even though every Student has its own gradePointAverage field, only one copy of each of the methods getGradePointAverage() and setGradePointAverage() is stored in memory, but any instantiated object of the class can use the single copy.

Because only one copy of each instance method is stored, the computer needs a way to determine whose gradePointAverage is being set or retrieved when one of the methods is called. The mechanism that handles this problem is illustrated in Figure 11-13. When a method call such as oneSophomore.setGradePointAverage(2.6) is made, the true method call that is invisible and automatically constructed includes the memory address of the oneSophomore object. (These invisible and automatically constructed method calls are represented by the three narrow boxes in the center of Figure 11-13.)

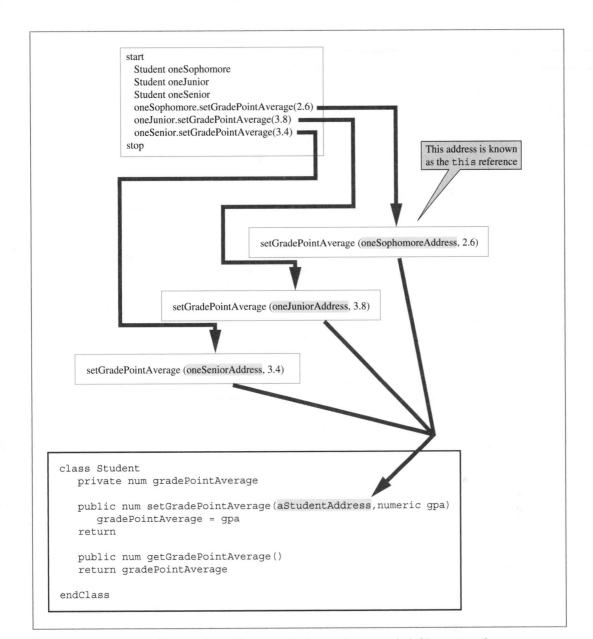

start
    Student oneSophomore
    Student oneJunior
    Student oneSenior
    oneSophomore.setGradePointAverage(2.6)
    oneJunior.setGradePointAverage(3.8)
    oneSenior.setGradePointAverage(3.4)
stop

This address is known as the this reference

setGradePointAverage (oneSophomoreAddress, 2.6)

setGradePointAverage (oneJuniorAddress, 3.8)

setGradePointAverage (oneSeniorAddress, 3.4)

```
class Student
    private num gradePointAverage

    public num setGradePointAverage(aStudentAddress,numeric gpa)
        gradePointAverage = gpa
    return

    public num getGradePointAverage()
    return gradePointAverage

endClass
```

Figure 11-13 How Student addresses are passed from an application to an instance method of the Student class

Within the setGradePointAverage() method in the Student class, an invisible and automatically created parameter is added to the list. (For illustration purposes, this parameter is named aStudentAddress and is shaded in the Student class definition in Figure 11-13. In fact, no parameter is created with that name.) This parameter accepts the address of a Student object because the instance method belongs to the Student class; if this method belonged to another class—Employee, for example—then the method would accept an address for that type of object. The shaded addresses in Figure 11-13 are not written as code in any program—they are "secretly" sent and received behind the scenes. The address variable in Figure 11-13 is called a this reference. A **this reference** is an automatically created variable that holds the address of an object and passes it to an instance method whenever the method is called. It is called a this reference because it refers to "this particular object" that is using the method at the moment. In the application in Figure 11-13, when oneSophomore uses the setGradePointAverage() method, the address of the oneSophomore object is contained in the this reference. Later in the program, when the oneJunior object uses the setGradePointAverage() method, the this reference will hold the address of that Student object.

Figure 11-13 shows each place the this reference is used in the Student class. It is implicitly passed as a parameter to each instance method. You never explicitly refer to the this reference when you write the method header for an instance method; Figure 11-13 just shows where it implicitly exists. Within each instance method, the this reference is implied any time you refer to one of the class data fields. For example, when you call setGradePointAverage() using a oneSophomore object, the gradePointAverage that is assigned within the method is the "*this* gradePointAverage", or the one that belongs to the oneSophomore object. The phrase "this gradePointAverage" is usually written as this, followed by a dot, followed by the field name—this.gradePointAverage.

The this reference exists throughout any instance method. You can explicitly use the this reference with data fields, as shown in the methods in the Student class in Figure 11-14, but you are not required to do so. Figure 11-14 shows you where the this reference can be used implicitly, but where you can (but do not have to) use it explicitly. When you write an instance method in a class, the following two identifiers within the method always mean exactly the same thing:

» any field name
» this, followed by a dot, followed by the same field name

For example, within the setGradePointAverage() method, gradePointAverage and this.gradePointAverage refer to exactly the same memory location.

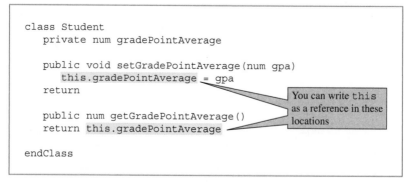

Figure 11-14 Explicitly using this in the Student class

Usually you neither want nor need to use the `this` reference explicitly within the methods you write, but the `this` reference is always there, working behind the scenes, so that the data field for the correct object can be accessed.

As an example of an occasion when you might use the `this` reference explicitly, consider the following `setGradePointAverage()` method and compare it to the version in the `Student` class in Figure 11-14.

```
public void setGradePointAverage(num gradePointAverage)
    this.gradePointAverage = gradePointAverage
return
```

In this version of the method, the programmer has chosen to use the variable name `gradePointAverage` as the parameter to the method as well as the instance field within the class. This means that `gradePointAverage` is the name of a local variable within the method whose value is received by passing, as well as the name of a class field. To differentiate the two, you explicitly use the `this` reference with the copy of `gradePointAverage` that is a member of the class. Omitting the `this` reference in this case would result in the local parameter `gradePointAverage` being assigned to itself. The class's instance variable would not be set.

TWO TRUTHS AND A LIE:
UNDERSTANDING INSTANCE METHODS

1. An instance method operates correctly yet differently for each separate instance of a class.

2. A `this` reference is a variable you can explicitly declare with each class you create.

3. When you write an instance method in a class, the following two identifiers within the method always mean exactly the same thing: any field name, `this`, followed by a dot, followed by the same field name.

The false statement is #2. A `this` reference is an automatically created variable that holds the address of an object and passes it to an instance method whenever the method is called. You do not declare it explicitly.

UNDERSTANDING STATIC, CLASS METHODS

Some methods do not require a `this` reference. For example, the `displayStudentMotto()` method in the `Student` class in Figure 11-15 does not use any data fields from the class, so it does not matter which `Student` object calls it. If you write a program in which you declare 100 `Student` objects, the `displayStudentMotto()` method executes in exactly the same way for each of them; it does not need to know whose motto is displayed and it does not need to access any specific object addresses. As a matter of fact, you might want to display the Student motto without instantiating any Student objects. Therefore, the displayStudentMotto() method can be written as a **class method** instead of an instance method.

```
public static void displayStudentMotto()
    print "Every student is an individual"
    print "in the pursuit of knowledge."
    print "Every student strives to be"
    print "a literate, responsible citizen."
return
```

Figure 11-15 Student class displayStudentMotto() method

When you write a class, you can indicate two types of methods:

» **Static methods** are those for which no object needs to exist, like the displayStudentMotto() method in Figure 11-15. Static methods do not receive a this reference as an implicit parameter. Typically, static methods include the word static in the method header, as shown shaded in Figure 11-15.

» **Nonstatic methods** are methods that exist to be used with an object created from a class. These instance methods receive a this reference to a specific object. In most programming languages, you use the word static when you want to declare a static class member, and do not use any special word when you want a class member to be nonstatic. In other words, methods in a class are nonstatic instance methods by default.

> **NOTE** In everyday language, the word *static* means "stationary"; it is the opposite of *dynamic*, which means changing. In other words, static methods are always the same for the class, whereas nonstatic methods act differently depending on the object used to call them.

In most programming languages, you use a static method with the class name, as in the following:

```
Student.displayStudentMotto()
```

In other words, no object is necessary with a static method.

> **NOTE** In some languages, notably C++, besides using a static method with the class name, you are also allowed to use a static method with any object of the class, as in oneSophomore.displayStudentMotto().

>> **NOTE** All the methods you have worked with in earlier chapters of this book, such as those that performed a calculation or printed some output, were static methods. That is, you did not create objects to call them.

TWO TRUTHS AND A LIE:
UNDERSTANDING STATIC, CLASS METHODS

1. Class methods do not receive a `this` reference.

2. Static methods do not receive a `this` reference.

3. Nonstatic methods do not receive a `this` reference.

The false statement is #3. Nonstatic methods receive a `this` reference automatically.

AN INTRODUCTION TO CONSTRUCTORS

When you use a class such as `Employee` to instantiate an object with a statement such as `Employee chauffeur`, you are actually calling a method named `Employee()` that is provided by default by the compiler of the object-oriented language in which you are working. A constructor method, or more simply, a **constructor**, is a method that establishes an object. A **default constructor** is one that requires no arguments; in object-oriented (OO) languages, a default constructor is created automatically by the compiler for every class you write.

When the prewritten, default constructor for the `Employee` class is called (the constructor is the method named `Employee()`), it establishes one `Employee` object with the identifier provided. Depending on the programming language, a default constructor might provide initial values for the object's data fields; for example, a language might set all numeric fields to zero by default. If you do not want an object's fields to hold these default values, or if you want to perform additional tasks when you create an instance of a class, you can write your own constructor. Any constructor you write must have the same name as the class it constructs, and constructor methods cannot have a return type. Normally, you declare constructors to be public so that other classes can instantiate objects that belong to the class.

>> **NOTE** When you create a class without writing a constructor, you get access to an automatically supplied one. However, if you write a constructor for any class, you lose the automatically created one.

For example, if you want every `Employee` object to have a starting hourly wage of $10.00 as well as the correct weekly pay for that wage, then you could write the constructor for the `Employee` class that appears in Figure 11-16. Any `Employee` object instantiated will have an `hourlyWage` field value equal to 10.00, a `weeklyPay` field equal to $400.00, and a `lastName` field equal to the default value for strings in the programming language in which this class is implemented.

```
class Employee
    private string lastName
    private num hourlyWage
    private num weeklyPay

    public Employee()
        hourlyWage = 10.00
        calculateWeeklyPay()
    return

    public void setLastName(string name)
        lastName = name
    return

    public void setHourlyWage(num wage)
        hourlyWage = wage
        calculateWeeklyPay()
    return

    public string getLastName()
    return lastName

    public num getHourlyWage()
    return hourlyWage

    public num getWeeklyPay()
    return weeklyPay

    private void calculateWeeklyPay()
        num WORK_WEEK_HOURS = 40
        weeklyPay = hourlyWage * WORK_WEEK_HOURS
    return
endClass
```

Figure 11-16 Employee class with a default constructor that sets hourlyWage and weeklyPay

The Employee constructor in Figure 11-16 calls the calculateWeeklyPay() method. You can write any statement in a constructor you like; it is just a method. Although you usually have no reason to do so, you could print a message from within a constructor, declare local variables, or perform any other task. You can place the constructor anywhere inside the class, outside of any other method. Typically, a constructor will be placed with the other methods. Often, programmers list the constructor first among the methods, because it is the first method used when an object is created.

Figure 11-17 shows a program in which two Employee objects are declared and their hourlyWage values are displayed. In the output in Figure 11-18, you can see that even though the setHourlyWage() method is never used in the program, the Employees possess valid hourly wages as set by their constructors.

```
start
   Employee myPersonalTrainer
   Employee myInteriorDecorator
   print "Trainer's wage: ",
      myPersonalTrainer.getHourlyWage()
   print "Decorator's wage: ",
      myInteriorDecorator.getHourlyWage()
stop
```

Figure 11-17 Program that declares Employee objects using class in Figure 11-16

Figure 11-18 Output of program in Figure 11-17

> **NOTE** If a class contained it, you could use its setHourlyWage() method to assign values to individual Employee objects after construction. A constructor assigns its values at the time an object is created.

A potentially superior way to write the Employee class constructor that initializes every Employee's hourlyWage field to 10.00 is shown in Figure 11-19. In this version of the constructor, a named constant containing 10.00 is passed to setHourlyWage(). Using this technique provides several advantages:

» The statement to call calculateWeeklyPay() is no longer required in the constructor because the constructor calls setHourlyWage(), which calls calculateWeeklyPay().

» In the future, if restrictions are imposed on hourlyWage, the code will need to be altered in only one location. For example, if setHourlyWage() is modified to disallow rates that are too high and too low, the code will change only in the setHourlyWage() method and will not have to be modified in the constructor. This reduces the amount of work required and reduces the possibility for error.

```
public Employee()
   num DEFAULT_WAGE = 10.00
   setHourlyWage(DEFAULT_WAGE)
return
```

Figure 11-19 Alternate and efficient version of the Employee class constructor

Of course, if different hourlyWage() requirements are needed at initialization than are required when the value is set after construction, then different code statements will be written in the constructor than those written in the setHourlyWage() method.

CONSTRUCTORS WITH PARAMETERS

Instead of forcing every Employee to be constructed with the same initial values, you might choose to create Employee objects with values that differ for each employee. For example, to initialize each Employee with a unique hourlyWage, you can pass a numeric value to the constructor; in other words, you can write constructors that receive arguments. Figure 11-20 shows an Employee class constructor that receives an argument. With this constructor, an argument is passed using a statement similar to one of the following:

```
Employee partTimeWorker(8.81)
Employee partTimeWorker(valueEnteredByUser)
```

When the constructor executes, the numeric value within the method call is passed to Employee() as the argument rate, which is assigned to the hourlyWage within the constructor.

```
public Employee(num rate)
    hourlyWage = rate
    calculateWeeklyPay()
return
```

Figure 11-20 Employee constructor that accepts a parameter

When you create an Employee class with a constructor such as the one shown in Figure 11-20, then every Employee object you create must use a numeric argument. In other words, with this new version of the class, the declaration statement Employee partTimeWorker no longer works. Once you write a constructor for a class, you no longer receive the automatically written default constructor. If a class's only constructor requires an argument, you must provide an argument for every object of that class you create.

OVERLOADING CLASS METHODS AND CONSTRUCTORS

In Chapter 7, you learned that you can overload methods by writing multiple versions of a method with the same name but different argument lists. In the same way, you can overload instance methods and constructors. For example, Figure 11-21 shows a version of the Employee class that contains two constructors. One version requires no argument and the other requires a numeric argument.

```
class Employee
   private string lastName
   private num hourlyWage
   private num weeklyPay

   public Employee()
      hourlyWage = 10.00
      calculateWeeklyPay()
   return

   public Employee(num rate)
      hourlyWage = rate
      calculateWeeklyPay()
   return

   public void setLastName(string name)
      lastName = name
   return

   public void setHourlyWage(num wage)
      hourlyWage = wage
      calculateWeeklyPay()
   return

   public string getLastName()
   return lastName

   public num getHourlyWage()
   return hourlyWage

   public num getWeeklyPay()
   return weeklyPay

   private void calculateWeeklyPay()
      num WORK_WEEK_HOURS = 40
      weeklyPay = hourlyWage * WORK_WEEK_HOURS
   return
endClass
```

Figure 11-21 Employee class with overloaded constructors

> **» NOTE**
> Recall from Chapter 7 that a method's name and parameter list together are its signature.

When you use Figure 11-21's version of the class, you can make statements like both of the following:

```
Employee deliveryPerson
Employee myButler(25.85)
```

When you declare an `Employee` using the first of these statements, an `hourlyWage` of 10.00 is automatically set because the statement uses the parameterless version of the constructor. When you declare an `Employee` using the second of these statements, the `hourlyWage` is set to the passed value. Any method or constructor in a class can be overloaded, and you can provide as many versions as you want. For example, you could add a third constructor to the `Employee` class, as shown in Figure 11-22. This version can coexist with the other two because the parameter list is different than either existing version. With this version you can specify the hourly rate for the `Employee` as well as a name. If an application makes a statement similar to the following, then this version would execute:

```
Employee myMaid(22.50, "Parker")
```

```
public Employee(num rate, string name)
    lastName = name
    hourlyWage = rate
    calculateWeeklyPay()
return
```

Figure 11-22 A third possible `Employee` class constructor

> **NOTE** You might create an `Employee` class with several constructor versions to provide flexibility for client programs. A particular client program might use only one version, and a different client might use another.

TWO TRUTHS AND A LIE:
AN INTRODUCTION TO CONSTRUCTORS

1. A constructor is a method that establishes an object.

2. A default constructor is one that is automatically created.

3. Depending on the programming language, a default constructor might provide initial values for the object's data fields.

The false statement is #2. A default constructor is one that takes no arguments. Although the automatically created constructor for a class is a default constructor, not all default constructors are automatically created.

USING OBJECTS

After you create a class from which you want to instantiate objects, you can use the objects in ways similar to how you would use any other simpler data type. For example, consider the `InventoryItem` class in Figure 11-23. The class represents items a company manufactures and holds in inventory. Each item has a number, description, and price. The class contains a single constructor that provides default values for `InventoryItem` objects. The class also contains a get and set method for each of the three fields.

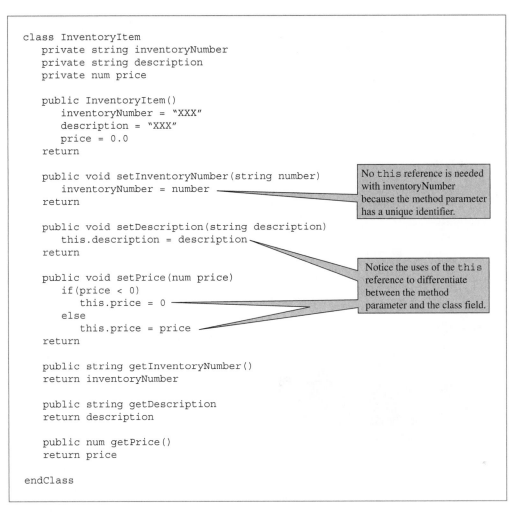

```
class InventoryItem
    private string inventoryNumber
    private string description
    private num price

    public InventoryItem()
        inventoryNumber = "XXX"
        description = "XXX"
        price = 0.0
    return

    public void setInventoryNumber(string number)
        inventoryNumber = number
    return

    public void setDescription(string description)
        this.description = description
    return

    public void setPrice(num price)
        if(price < 0)
            this.price = 0
        else
            this.price = price
    return

    public string getInventoryNumber()
    return inventoryNumber

    public string getDescription
    return description

    public num getPrice()
    return price

endClass
```

> No `this` reference is needed with inventoryNumber because the method parameter has a unique identifier.

> Notice the uses of the `this` reference to differentiate between the method parameter and the class field.

Figure 11-23 InventoryItem class

In Figure 11-23, Once you declare an InventoryItem object, you can use it in many of the ways you would use a simple numeric or string variable. For example, you could pass an InventoryItem object to a method or return one from a method. Figure 11-24 shows a program that declares an InventoryItem object and passes it to a method for printing. The InventoryItem is declared in the main program and assigned values. Then the completed item is passed to a method where it is displayed. Figure 11-25 shows the execution of the program.

```
start
   InventoryItem oneItem
   oneItem.setInventoryNumber("1276")
   oneItem.setDescription("Mahogany chest")
   oneItem.setPrice(450.00)
   displayItem(oneItem)
stop

public static void displayItem(InventoryItem item)
   num TAX_RATE = 0.06
   num tax
   num pr
   num total
   print "Item #", item.getInventoryNumber()
   print item.getDescription()
   pr = item.getPrice()
   tax = pr * TAX_RATE
   total = pr + tax
   print "Price is $", price, " plus $", tax, " tax"
   print "Total is $", total
return
```

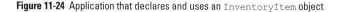

Figure 11-24 Application that declares and uses an `InventoryItem` object

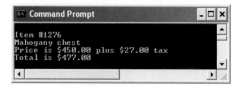

Figure 11-25 Execution of application in Figure 11-24

The `InventoryItem` declared in the main program in Figure 11-24 is passed to the `displayItem()` method in much the same way a numeric or string variable would be. The method receives a copy of the `InventoryItem` that is known locally by the identifier item. Within the method, the field values of the local item can be retrieved, displayed, and used in arithmetic statements in the same way they could have been in the main program where the `InventoryItem` was originally declared.

Figure 11-26 shows a more realistic application that uses `InventoryItem` objects. In the main program, an `InventoryItem` is declared and the user is prompted for a number. As long as the user does not enter the `QUIT` value, a loop is executed in which the entered inventory item number is passed to the `getItemValues()` method. Within that method, a local `InventoryItem` object is declared. This local object is used to gather and hold the user's input values. The user is prompted for a description and price; then the passed item number, as well as the newly obtained description and price, are assigned to the local `InventoryItem` object via its set methods. The completed object is returned to the program where it is assigned to the `InventoryItem` object. That item is then passed to the `displayItem()` method. As in the previous example, the method calculates tax and displays results. Figure 11-27 shows a typical execution.

```
start
    InventoryItem oneItem
    string itemNum
    string QUIT = "0"
    print "Enter item number or ", QUIT, " to quit… "
    get itemNum
    while itemNum not = "0"
        oneItem = getItemValues(itemNum)
        displayItem(oneItem)
        print "Enter next item number or ", QUIT, " to quit… "
        get itemNum
    endwhile
stop

public static InventoryItem getItemValues(string number)
    InventoryItem inItem
    string desc
    numeric price
    print "Enter description… "
    get desc
    print "Enter price… "
    get price
    inItem.setInventoryNumber(number)
    inItem.setDescription(desc)
    inItem.setPrice(price)
return inItem

public static void displayItem(InventoryItem item)
    num TAX_RATE = 0.06
    num tax
    num pr
    num total
    print "Item #", item.getInventoryNumber()
    print item.getDescription()
    pr = item.getPrice()
    tax = pr * TAX_RATE
    total = pr + tax
    print "Price is $", price, " plus $", tax, " tax"
    print "Total is $", total
return
```

Figure 11-26 Application that uses `InventoryItem` objects

> **»NOTE** In Figure 11-26, notice that the return type for the `getItemValues()` method is `InventoryItem`. A method can return only a single value. Therefore, it is convenient that the `getItemValues()` method can encapsulate two strings and a number in a single `InventoryItem` object that it returns to the main program.

Figure 11-27 Typical execution of program in Figure 11-26

TWO TRUTHS AND A LIE:
USING OBJECTS

1. You can pass an object to a method.

2. Because only one value can be returned from a method, you cannot return an object that holds more than one field.

3. You can declare an object locally within a method.

The false statement is #2. An object can be returned from a method.

UNDERSTANDING DESTRUCTORS

A **destructor** contains the actions you require when an instance of a class is destroyed. Most often, an instance of a class is destroyed when it goes out of scope. As with constructors, if you do not explicitly create a destructor for a class, one is automatically provided.

The most common way to explicitly declare a destructor is to use an identifier that consists of a tilde (~) followed by the class name. You cannot provide any parameters to a destructor; it must have an empty argument list. As a consequence, destructors cannot be overloaded; a class can have at most one destructor. Like a constructor, a destructor has no return type.

»NOTE The rules for creating and naming destructors vary among programming languages. For example, in Visual Basic.NET classes, the destructor is called `Finalize`.

Figure 11-28 shows an `Employee` class that contains only one field (`idNumber`), a constructor, and a shaded destructor. Although it is unusual for a constructor or destructor to print anything, these print messages so that you can see when the objects are created and destroyed. When you execute the program in Figure 11-29, you instantiate two `Employee` objects, each with its own `idNumber` value. When the program method ends, the two `Employee` objects go out of scope, and the destructor for each object is called automatically. Figure 11-30 shows the output.

```
class Employee
    private string idNumber
    public Employee(string empId)
        idNumber = empId
        print "Employee ", idNumber, " is created"
    return
    public ~Employee()
        print "Employee ", idNumber, " is destroyed"
    return
endClass
```

Figure 11-28 `Employee` class with destructor

```
start
    Employee aWorker("101")
    Employee anotherWorker("202")
stop
```

Figure 11-29 Program that declares two `Employee` objects

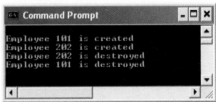

Figure 11-30 Output of program in Figure 11-29

The program in Figure 11-29 never explicitly calls the `Employee` class destructor, yet you can see from the output that the destructor executes twice. Destructors are invoked automatically; you cannot explicitly call one. Interestingly, the last object created is the first object destroyed; the same relationship would hold true no matter how many objects the program instantiated.

> **NOTE** An instance of a class becomes eligible for destruction when it is no longer possible for any code to use it—that is, when it goes out of scope. In many languages, the actual execution of an object's destructor might occur at any time after the object becomes eligible for destruction.

For now, you have little reason to create a destructor except to demonstrate how it is called automatically. Later, when you write more sophisticated programs that work with files, databases, or large quantities of computer memory, you might want to perform specific clean-up or close-down tasks when an object goes out of scope. Then you will place appropriate instructions within a destructor.

UNDERSTANDING COMPOSITION

A class can contain another class's objects as data members. For example, you might create a class named Date that contains a month, day, and year, and add two Date fields to an Employee class to hold the Employee's birth date and hire date. Then you might create a class named Department that represents every department in a company, and create each Department class member to contain an array of 50 Employee objects. Using a class object within another class object is known as **composition**. The relationship created is also called a **has-a relationship** because one class "has an" instance of another.

When your classes contain objects that are members of other classes, your programming job becomes increasingly complex. For example, you sometimes must refer to a method by a very long name. Suppose you create a Department class that contains a method named getHighestPaidEmployee(), a method that returns an Employee object. Suppose the Employee class contains a method that returns a Date object that is an Employee's hire date. Further suppose that the Date class contains a method that returns the year portion of the Date. Then an application might contain a statement such as the following:

```
salesDepartment.getHighestPaidEmployee().getHireDate().getYear()
```

Additionally, when classes contain objects that are members of other classes, all the corresponding constructors and destructors execute in a specific order. As you work with object-oriented programming languages, you will learn to manage these complex issues.

UNDERSTANDING INHERITANCE

Understanding classes helps you organize objects in real life. Understanding inheritance helps you organize them more precisely. Inheritance is the principle that you can apply your knowledge of a general category to more specific objects. You are familiar with the concept of inheritance from all sorts of situations. When you use the term *inheritance,* you might think of genetic inheritance. You know from biology that your blood type and eye color are the products of inherited genes.

You might choose to own plants and animals based on their inherited attributes. You plant the flower impatiens next to your house because they thrive in the shade; you adopt a poodle because you know poodles don't shed. Every plant and pet has slightly different characteristics, but within a species, you can count on many consistent inherited attributes and behaviors. In other words, you can reuse the knowledge you gain about general categories and apply it to more specific categories. Similarly, the classes you create in object-oriented programming languages can inherit data and methods from existing classes. When you create a class by making it inherit from another class, you are provided with data fields and methods automatically; you can reuse fields and methods that are already written and tested.

You already know how to create classes and how to instantiate objects that are members of those classes. For example, consider the Employee class in Figure 11-31. The class contains two data fields, empNum and weeklySalary, as well as methods that get and set each field.

```
class Employee
    private string empNum
    private num weeklySalary

    public void setEmpNum(string number)
        empNum = number
    return

    public string getEmpNum()
    return empNum

    public void setWeeklySalary(num salary)
        weeklySalary = salary
    return

    public num getWeeklySalary()
    return weeklySalary
endClass
```

Figure 11-31 An Employee class

Suppose you hire a new type of Employee who earns a commission as well as a weekly salary. You can create a class with a name such as CommissionEmployee, and provide this class with three fields (empNum, weeklySalary, and commissionRate) and six methods (to get and set each of the three fields). However, this work would duplicate much of the work that you have already done for the Employee class. The wise and efficient alternative is to create the class CommissionEmployee so it inherits all the attributes and methods of Employee. Then, you can add just the single field and two methods (the get and set methods for the new field) that are additions within the new class. Figure 11-32 depicts these relationships. The complete CommissionEmployee class is shown in Figure 11-33.

NOTE Recall from earlier in this chapter that a plus in a class diagram indicates public access and a minus indicates private access.

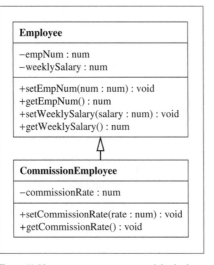

NOTE Figure 11-32 and several other figures in this chapter are examples of UML diagrams. Chapter 13 describes UML diagrams in more detail.

Figure 11-32 CommissionEmployee inherits from Employee

```
class CommissionEmployee inheritsFrom Employee
    private num commissionRate

    public void setCommissionRate(num rate)
        commissionRate = rate
    return

    public num getCommissionRate()
    return commissionRate
endClass
```

Figure 11-33 CommissionEmployee class

NOTE The class in Figure 11-33 uses the phrase "inheritsFrom Employee" (see shading) to indicate inheritance. Each programming language uses its own syntax. For example, using Java you would write "extends", in Visual Basic you would write "inherits", and in C++ and C# you would use a colon between the new class name and the one from which it inherits.

When you use inheritance to create the CommissionEmployee class, you acquire the following benefits:

» You save time, because you need not recreate the Employee fields and methods.

» You reduce the chance of errors, because the Employee methods have already been used and tested.

» You make it easier for anyone who has used the Employee class to understand the CommissionEmployee class because such users can concentrate on the new features only.

The ability to use inheritance makes programs easier to write, easier to understand, and less prone to errors. Imagine that besides CommissionEmployee, you want to create several other more specific Employee classes (perhaps PartTimeEmployee, including a field for hours worked, or DismissedEmployee, including a reason for dismissal). By using inheritance, you can develop each new class correctly and more quickly.

> **»NOTE** In part, the concept of class inheritance is useful because it makes class code reusable. However, you do not use inheritance simply to save work. When properly used, inheritance always involves a general-to-specific relationship.

UNDERSTANDING INHERITANCE TERMINOLOGY

A class that is used as a basis for inheritance, like Employee, is called a **base class**. When you create a class that inherits from a base class (such as CommissionEmployee), it is a **derived class** or **extended class**. When presented with two classes that have a base-derived relationship, you can tell which class is the base class and which is the derived class by using the two classes in a sentence with the phrase "is a." A derived class always "is a" case or instance of the more general base class. For example, a Tree class may be a base class to an Evergreen class. Every Evergreen "is a" Tree; however, it is not true that every Tree is an Evergreen. Thus, Tree is the base class and Evergreen is the derived class. Similarly, a CommissionEmployee "is an" Employee—not always the other way around—so Employee is the base class and CommissionEmployee is derived.

You can use the terms **superclass** and **subclass** as synonyms for base class and derived class, respectively. Thus, Evergreen can be called a subclass of the Tree superclass. You can also use the terms **parent class** and **child class**. A CommissionEmployee is a child to the Employee parent.

As an alternative way to discover which of two classes is the base class and which is the derived class, you can try saying the two class names together (although this technique might not work with every base-subclass pair). When people say their names together in the English language, they state the more specific name before the all-encompassing family name, such as "Mary Johnson." Similarly, with classes, the order that "makes more sense" is the child-parent order. Thus, because "Evergreen Tree" makes more sense than "Tree Evergreen," you can deduce that Evergreen is the child class.

> **»NOTE** It is also convenient to think of a derived class as building upon its base class by providing the "adjectives" or additional descriptive terms for the "noun." Frequently, the names of derived classes are formed in this way, as in CommissionEmployee or EvergreenTree.

Finally, you can usually distinguish base classes from their derived classes by size. Although it is not required, a derived class is generally larger than its base class, in the sense that it usually has additional fields and methods. A subclass description may look small, but any subclass contains all of its base class's fields and methods as well as its own more specific fields and methods.

A derived class can be further extended. In other words, a subclass can have a child of its own. For example, after you create a Tree class and derive Evergreen, you might derive a Spruce class from Evergreen. Similarly, a Poodle class might derive from Dog, Dog from DomesticPet, and DomesticPet from Animal. The entire list of parent classes from which a child class is derived constitutes the **ancestors** of the subclass.

> **»NOTE**
> Do not think of a subclass as a "subset" of another class—in other words, possessing only parts of its base class. In fact, a derived class usually contains more than its parent.

> **»NOTE** After you create the `Spruce` class, you might be ready to create `Spruce` objects. For example, you might create `theTreeInMyBackYard`, or you might create an array of 1000 `Spruce` objects for a tree farm.

Inheritance is **transitive**, which means a child inherits all the members of all its ancestors. In other words, when you declare a `Spruce` object, it contains all the attributes and methods of both an `Evergreen` and a `Tree`, and a `CommissionEmployee` contains all the attributes and methods of an `Employee`. In other words, the members of `Employee` and `CommissionEmployee` are as follows:

» `Employee` contains two fields and four methods, as shown in Figure 11-31.

» `CommissionEmployee` contains three fields and six methods, even though you do not see all of them in Figure 11-33.

Although a child class contains all the data fields and methods of its parent, a parent class does not gain any child class members. Therefore, when `Employee` and `CommissionEmployee` classes are defined as in Figures 11-31 and 11-33, the statements in Figure 11-34 are all valid in an application. The `salesperson` object can use all the methods of its parent, plus it can use its own `setCommissionRate()` and `getCommissionRate()` methods. Figure 11-35 shows the output of the program as it would appear in a command-line environment.

```
start
    Employee manager
    CommissionEmployee salesperson
    manager.setEmpNum("111")
    manager.setWeeklySalary(700.00)
    manager.getGreeting()
    salesperson.setEmpNum("222")
    salesperson.setWeeklySalary(300.00)
    salesperson.setCommissionRate(0.12)
    print "Manager ", manager.getEmpNum(), manager.getWeeklySalary()
    print "Salesperson ", salesperson.getEmpNum(),
        salesperson.getWeeklySalary(), salesperson.getCommissionRate()
stop
```

Figure 11-34 EmployeeDemo application that declares two `Employee` objects

Figure 11-35 Output of the program in Figure 11-34

The following statements would not be allowed in the EmployeeDemo application in Figure 11-34 because manager, as an Employee, does not have access to the methods of the CommissionEmployee child class.:

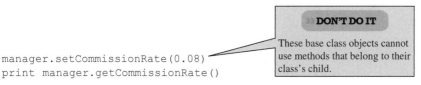

DON'T DO IT

These base class objects cannot use methods that belong to their class's child.

```
manager.setCommissionRate(0.08)
print manager.getCommissionRate()
```

>> **NOTE** When you create your own transitive inheritance chains, you want to place fields and methods at their most general level. In other words, a method named Grow() rightfully belongs in a Tree class, whereas LeavesTurnColor() does not, because the method applies to only some of the Tree child classes. Similarly, a LeavesTurnColor() method would be better located in a Deciduous class than separately within the Oak or Maple child class.

>> **NOTE** In math, a transitive relationship occurs when something that is true for a and b and for b and c is also true for a and c. For example, equality is transitive. If a = b and b = c, then a = c.

It makes sense that a parent class object does not have access to its child's data and methods. When you create the parent class, you do not know how many future child classes might be created, or what their data or methods might look like. In addition, derived classes are more specific. A HeartSurgeon class and an Obstetrician class are children of a Doctor class. You do not expect all members of the general parent class Doctor to have the HeartSurgeon's repairHeartValve() method or the Obstetrician's performCaesarianSection() method. However, HeartSurgeon and Obstetrician objects have access to the more general Doctor methods takeBloodPressure() and billPatients().

>> **NOTE** As with subclasses of doctors, it is convenient to think of derived classes as *specialists*. That is, their fields and methods are more specialized than those of the parent class.

>> **NOTE** In some programming languages, such as C#, Visual Basic, and Java, every class you create is a child of one ultimate base class, often called the Object class. The Object class usually provides you with some basic functionality that all the classes you create inherit, for example, the ability to show its memory location and name.

ACCESSING PRIVATE MEMBERS OF A PARENT CLASS

Earlier in this chapter you learned that when you create classes, the most common scenario is for methods to be public but for data to be private. Making data private is an important object-oriented programming concept. By making data fields private, and allowing access to them only through a class's methods, you protect the ways in which data can be altered and accessed.

When a data field within a class is private, no outside class can use it—including a child class. The principle of data hiding would be lost if all you had to do to access a class's private data was to create a child class. However, it can be inconvenient when a child class's methods cannot directly access its own inherited data.

For example, suppose you hire some employees who do not earn a weekly salary as defined in the Employee class but who are paid by the hour. You might create an HourlyEmployee class that descends from Employee, as shown in Figure 11-36. The class contains two new fields, hoursWorked and hourlyRate, and a get and set method for each.

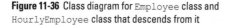

```
┌─────────────────────────────────────────────┐
│  ┌──────────────────────────────────────┐    │
│  │ Employee                             │    │
│  ├──────────────────────────────────────┤    │
│  │ −empNum : string                     │    │
│  │ −weeklySalary : num                  │    │
│  ├──────────────────────────────────────┤    │
│  │ +setEmpNum(number: string) : void    │    │
│  │ +getEmpNum( ) : string               │    │
│  │ +setWeeklySalary(salary : num) : void│    │
│  │ +getWeeklySalary( ) : num            │    │
│  └──────────────────────────────────────┘    │
│                    △                          │
│  ┌──────────────────────────────────────┐    │
│  │ HourlyEmployee                       │    │
│  ├──────────────────────────────────────┤    │
│  │ −hoursWorked : num                   │    │
│  │ −hourlyRate : num                    │    │
│  ├──────────────────────────────────────┤    │
│  │ +setHoursWorked(hours : num) : void  │    │
│  │ +getHoursWorked( ) : num             │    │
│  │ +setHourlyRate(rate : num) : void    │    │
│  │ +getHourlyRate( ) : num              │    │
│  └──────────────────────────────────────┘    │
└─────────────────────────────────────────────┘
```

Figure 11-36 Class diagram for Employee class and HourlyEmployee class that descends from it

Suppose you want to implement the new class as shown in Figure 11-37. Whenever you set either hoursWorked or hourlyRate you want to modify weeklySalary based on the product of the hours and rate. The logic makes sense, but the code does not compile. The two shaded statements show that the HourlyEmployee class is attempting to modify the weeklySalary field. Although every HourlyEmployee *has* a weeklySalary field by virtue of being a child of Employee, the HourlyEmployee class methods do not have access to the weeklySalary field, because weeklySalary is private within the Employee class. The weeklySalary field is **inaccessible** to any class other than the one in which it is defined.

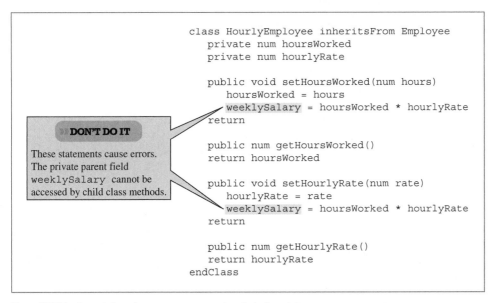

Figure 11-37 Implementation of HourlyEmployee class that attempts to access weeklySalary

One solution to this dilemma would be to make weeklySalary public in the parent Employee class. Then the child class could use it. However, that action would violate the important object-oriented principle of information hiding. When you use information hiding, you are assured that your data will be altered only by the properties and methods you choose and only in ways that you can control. If outside classes could alter an Employee's private fields, then the fields could be assigned values that the Employee class couldn't control. In such a case, the principle of information hiding would be destroyed, causing the behavior of the object to be unpredictable.

Therefore, object-oriented programming languages allow a medium-security access specifier that is more restrictive than public but less restrictive than private. The **protected access modifier** is used when you want no outside classes to be able to use a data field, except classes that are children of the original class. Figure 11-38 shows a rewritten Employee class that uses the protected access modifier on its data fields (see shading). When this modified class is used as a base class for another class such as HourlyEmployee, the child class's methods will be able to access any protected items (fields or methods) originally defined in the parent class.

```
class Employee
    private string empNum
    protected num weeklySalary

    public void setEmpNum(string number)
        empNum = number
    return

    public string getEmpNum()
    return empNum

    public void setWeeklySalary(num salary)
        weeklySalary = salary
    return

    public num getWeeklySalary()
    return weeklySalary
endClass
```

Figure 11-38 Employee class with a protected field

> **» NOTE** Although a child class's methods can access data fields originally defined in the parent class, a parent class's methods have no special privileges regarding any of its child's class's data fields. That is, unless the child class's data fields are public, a parent, just like any other unrelated class, cannot access them.

Figure 11-39 contains the class diagram for the version of the Employee class shown in Figure 11-38. Notice the weeklySalary field is preceded with an octothorpe (#)—the character that conventionally is used in class diagrams to indicate protected class members.

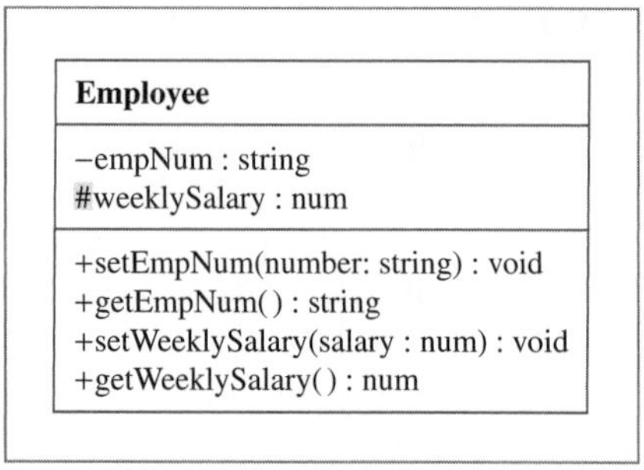

Employee
−empNum : string #weeklySalary : num
+setEmpNum(number: string) : void +getEmpNum( ) : string +setWeeklySalary(salary : num) : void +getWeeklySalary( ) : num

Figure 11-39 Employee class with protected member and HourlyEmployee which descends from it

Of course, if weeklySalary is defined as protected instead of private in the Employee class, then it means that either the creator of the Employee class knew that a child class would want to access the field, or the Employee class was revised after it became known the child class would need access to the field. If the Employee class's creator did not foresee that a field would need to be accessible, or if it is not preferable to revise the class, then weeklySalary will remain private. It is still possible to correctly set an HourlyEmployee's weekly pay—the HourlyEmployee is just required to use the same means as any other class would. That is, the HourlyEmployee class can use the public method setWeeklySalary() that already exists in the parent class. Any class, including a child, can use a public member of the base class. So, assuming weeklySalary remains private in Employee, Figure 11-40 shows how HourlyEmployee could be written to correctly set weeklySalary.

```
class HourlyEmployee inheritsFrom Employee
    private num hoursWorked
    private num hourlyRate

    public void setHoursWorked(num hours)
        hoursWorked = hours
        setWeeklySalary(hoursWorked * hourlyRate)
    return

    public num getHoursWorked()
    return hoursWorked

    public void setHourlyRate(num rate)
        hourlyRate = rate
        setWeeklySalary(hoursWorked * hourlyRate)
    return

    public num getHourlyRate()
    return hourlyRate
endClass
```

Figure 11-40 The `HourlyEmployee` class when `weeklySalary` remains private

In the version of `HourlyEmployee` in Figure 11-40, the shaded statements within `setHoursWorked()` and `setHourlyRate()` assign a value to the corresponding child class field (`hoursWorked` or `hourlyRate`, respectively). Each method then calls the public parent class method `setWeeklySalary()`. In this example, no protected access modifiers are needed for any fields in the parent class, and the creators of the parent class did not have to foresee that a child class would eventually need to access any of its fields. Instead, any child classes of `Employee` simply follow the same access rules as any other outside class would. As an added benefit, if the parent class method `setWeeklySalary()` contained additional code (for example, to require a minimum base weekly pay for all employees), then that code would be enforced even for `HourlyEmployees`.

So, in summary, when a child class must access a private field of its parent's class, you can take one of several approaches:

» You can modify the parent class to make the field public. Usually, this is not advised, because it violates the principle of information hiding.

» You can modify the parent class to make the field protected so that child classes have access to it, but other outside classes do not. This is necessary if no public methods to modify the field are desired within the parent class.

» The child class can use a public method within the parent class that modifies the field, just as any other outside class would. This is frequently, but not always, the best option.

Using the `protected` access modifier for a field can be convenient, and it also improves program performance a little by using a field directly instead of "going through" another method. Also, using the `protected` access modifier is occasionally necessary when no existing public method accesses a field in a way required by the specifications for the child class. However, `protected` data members should be used sparingly. Whenever possible, the principle of information hiding should be observed, and even child classes should have to go through methods to "get to" their parent's private data.

» NOTE
Classes that depend on field names from parent classes are said to be **fragile** because they are prone to errors—that is, they are easy to "break."

The likelihood of future errors increases when child classes are allowed direct access to a parent's fields. For example, if the child class is allowed direct access to the `Employee` field `weeklySalary` and a programmer changes the field name to `salaryPerWeek`, then the programmer will have to remember to change the field reference in the child class too. Worse, the programmer might not be aware of all the child classes that others have derived from the original class, and so might not be aware of all the changes that are required.

» NOTE Some OOP languages, such as C++, allow a subclass to inherit from more than one parent class. For example, you might create an `InsuredItem` class that contains data fields pertaining to each possession for which you have insurance (for example, value and purchase date), and an `Automobile` class that contains data fields pertaining to an automobile (for example, vehicle identification number, make, model, and year). When you create an `InsuredAutomobile` class for a car rental agency, you might want to include `InsuredItem` information and methods, as well as `Automobile` information and methods, so you might want to inherit from both. The capability to inherit from more than one class is called **multiple inheritance**.

» NOTE Sometimes, a parent class is so general that you never intend to create any specific instances of the class. For example, you might never create an object that is "just" an `Employee`; each `Employee` is more specifically a `SalariedEmployee`, `HourlyEmployee`, or `ContractEmployee`. A class such as `Employee` that you create only to extend from, but not to instantiate objects from, is an abstract class. An **abstract class** is one from which you cannot create any concrete objects, but from which you can inherit.

USING INHERITANCE TO ACHIEVE GOOD SOFTWARE DESIGN

When an automobile company designs a new car model, the company does not build every component of the new car from scratch. The company might design a new feature completely from scratch; for example, at some point someone designed the first air bag. However, many of a new car's features are simply modifications of existing features. The manufacturer might create a larger gas tank or more comfortable seats, but even these new features still possess many properties of their predecessors in the older models. Most features of new car models are not even modified; instead, existing components, such as air filters and windshield wipers, are included on the new model without any changes.

Similarly, you can create powerful computer programs more easily if many of their components are used either "as is" or with slight modifications. Inheritance does not give you the ability to write any programs that you could not write without it, because you could create every part of a program from scratch. Inheritance simply makes your job easier. Professional programmers constantly create new class libraries for use with OOP languages. Having these classes available to extend makes programming large systems more manageable. When you create a useful, extendable superclass, you and other future programmers gain several advantages:

» Subclass creators save development time because much of the code needed for the class has already been written.

» Subclass creators save testing time because the superclass code has already been tested and probably used in a variety of situations. In other words, the superclass code is **reliable**.

» Programmers who create or use new subclasses already understand how the superclass works, so the time it takes to learn the new class features is reduced.

» When you create a new subclass, neither the superclass source code nor the translated superclass code is changed. The superclass maintains its integrity.

When you consider classes, you must think about the commonalities between them, and then you can create superclasses from which to inherit. You might be rewarded professionally when you see your own superclasses extended by others in the future.

ONE EXAMPLE OF USING PREDEFINED CLASSES: CREATING GUI OBJECTS

When you purchase or download an object-oriented programming language compiler, it comes packaged with myriad predefined, built-in classes. The classes are stored in **libraries**— collections of classes that serve related purposes. Some of the most useful are the classes you can use to create GUI objects such as frames, buttons, labels, and text boxes. You place these GUI components within interactive programs so that users can manipulate them using input devices, most frequently a keyboard and a mouse. For example, if you want to place a clickable button on the screen using a language that supports GUI applications, you instantiate an object that belongs to the already created class named `Button`. In many object-oriented languages, a class with a name similar to `Button` is already created. It contains private data fields such as `text` and `height` and public methods such as `setText()` and `setHeight()` that allow you to place instructions on your `Button` object and to change its vertical size, respectively.

» NOTE
In some languages, such as Java, libraries are also called **packages**.

If no predefined GUI object classes existed, you could create your own. However, there would be several disadvantages:

» It would be a lot of work. Creating graphical objects requires a lot of code and at least a modicum of artistic talent.

» It would be repetitious work. Almost all GUI programs require standard components such as buttons and labels. If each programmer created the classes that represent these components from scratch, a lot of work would be unnecessarily repeated.

» The components would look different in various applications. If each programmer created his or her component classes, then objects like buttons would look and operate slightly differently in different applications. Users like standardization in their components—title bars on windows that are a uniform height, buttons that appear to be pressed when clicked, frames and windows that contain maximize and minimize buttons in predictable locations, and so on. By using standard component classes, programmers are assured that the GUI components in their programs have the same look and feel as those in other programs.

In programming languages that supply existing GUI classes, you are often provided with a **visual development environment** in which you can create programs by dragging components

»NOTE

In several languages, the visual development environment is known by the acronym **IDE**, which stands for Integrated Development Environment.

such as buttons and labels onto a screen and arranging them visually. Then you write programming statements to control the actions that take place when a user manipulates the controls by clicking them using a mouse, for example. Many programmers never create any classes of their own from which they will instantiate objects, but only write classes that are applications that use built-in GUI component classes. Some languages—for example, Visual Basic and C#—lend themselves very well to this type of programming.

In Chapter 12, you will learn more about creating programs that use GUI objects.

TWO TRUTHS AND A LIE:
ONE EXAMPLE OF USING PREDEFINED CLASSES:
CREATING GUI OBJECTS

1. Collections of classes that serve related purposes are called annals.

2. GUI components are placed within interactive programs so that users can manipulate them using input devices.

3. By using standard component classes, programmers are assured that the GUI components in their programs have the same look and feel as those in other programs.

The false statement is #1. Libraries are collections of classes that serve related purposes.

REVIEWING THE ADVANTAGES OF OBJECT-ORIENTED PROGRAMMING

Using the features of object-oriented programming languages provides you with many benefits as you develop your programs. Whether you use classes you have created or use those created by others, when you instantiate objects in programs, you save development time because each object automatically includes appropriate, reliable methods and attributes. When using inheritance, you can develop new classes more quickly by extending classes that already exist and work; you need to concentrate only on new features the new class adds. When using existing objects, you need to concentrate only on the interface to those objects, not on the internal instructions that make them work. By using polymorphism, you can use reasonable, easy-to-remember names for methods and concentrate on their purpose rather than on memorizing different method names.

TWO TRUTHS AND A LIE:
REVIEWING THE ADVANTAGES OF OBJECT-ORIENTED
PROGRAMMING

1. When you instantiate objects in programs, you save development time because each object automatically includes appropriate, reliable methods and attributes.

2. When using inheritance, you can develop new classes more quickly by extending classes that already exist and work.

3. By using polymorphism, you can avoid the strict rules of procedural programming and take advantage of more flexible object-oriented methods.

The false statement is #3. By using polymorphism, you can use reasonable, easy-to-remember names for methods and concentrate on their purpose rather than on memorizing different method names.

CHAPTER SUMMARY

» Classes are the basic building blocks of object-oriented programming. When you think in an object-oriented manner, everything is an object, and every object is an instance of a class. A class's fields, or instance variables, hold its data, and every object that is an instance of a class possesses the same methods. A program or class that instantiates objects of another prewritten class is a class client or class user. Besides classes and objects, three important features of object-oriented languages are polymorphism, inheritance, and encapsulation.

» A class definition is a set of program statements that tell you the characteristics of the class's objects and the methods that can be applied to its objects. A class definition can contain a name, data, and methods. Programmers often use a class diagram to illustrate class features. The purposes of many methods contained in a class can be divided into three categories: set methods, get methods, and work methods.

» Object-oriented programmers usually specify that their data fields will have private access—that is, the data cannot be accessed by any method that is not part of the class. The methods frequently support public access, which means that other programs and methods may use the methods that control access to the private data. In a class diagram, a minus sign (–) precedes the items that are private; a plus sign (+) precedes those that are public.

» As classes grow in complexity, deciding how to organize them becomes increasingly important. Depending on the class, you might choose to store the data fields by listing a key field first, listing fields alphabetically, by data type, or accessibility. Methods might be stored in alphabetical order or in pairs of get and set methods.

» An instance method operates correctly yet differently for every object instantiated from a class. When an instance method is called, a `this` reference that holds the object's memory address is automatically passed to the method.

» Some methods do not require a `this` reference. When you write a class you can indicate two types of methods: static methods, which are also known as class methods and do not receive a `this` reference as an implicit parameter; and nonstatic methods, which are instance methods and do receive a `this` reference.

» A constructor is a method that establishes an object. A default constructor is one that requires no arguments; in OO languages, a default constructor is created automatically by the compiler for every class you write. If you want to perform specific tasks when you create an instance of a class, then you can write your own constructor. Any constructor you write must have the same name as the class it constructs, and constructor methods cannot have a return type. Once you write a constructor for a class, you no longer receive the automatically written default constructor. If a class's only constructor requires an argument, then you must provide an argument for every object of that class that you create.

» You can overload instance methods and constructors.

» After you create a class from which you want to instantiate objects, you can use the objects in ways similar to the way you would use any other simpler data type.

» A destructor contains the actions you require when an instance of a class is destroyed. Most often, an instance of a class is destroyed when it goes out of scope. As with constructors, if you do not explicitly create a destructor for a class, one is automatically provided. The most common way to explicitly declare a destructor is to use an identifier that consists of a tilde (~) followed by the class name. You cannot provide any parameters to a destructor; it must have an empty argument list. As a consequence, destructors cannot be overloaded; a class can have at most one destructor. Like a constructor, a destructor has no return type.

» A class can contain another class's objects as data members. Using a class object within another class object is known as composition.

» Some of the most useful classes packaged in language libraries are the classes you can use to create graphical user interface (GUI) objects such as frames, buttons, labels, and text boxes. In programming languages that supply existing GUI classes, you are often provided with a visual development environment in which you can create programs by dragging components such as buttons and labels onto a screen and arranging them visually.

» When you instantiate objects in programs, you save development time because each object automatically includes appropriate, reliable methods and attributes. You can develop new classes more quickly by extending classes that already exist and work, and you can use reasonable, easy-to-remember names for methods.

KEY TERMS

Object-oriented programming (OOP) is a style of programming that focuses on an application's data and the methods you need to manipulate that data.

Attributes are the characteristics that define an object as part of a class.

A **class** is a term that describes a group or collection of objects with common attributes.

An **instance** is one tangible example of a class.

An **is-a relationship** exists between an object and its class.

An **instantiation** of a class is an instance.

A class's **instance variables** are the data components that belong to every instantiated object.

Fields are object attributes or data.

The **state** of an object is the set of all the values or contents of its instance variables.

A **class client** or **class user** is a program or class that instantiates objects of another prewritten class.

Pure polymorphism describes situations in which one method body is used with a variety of arguments.

Inheritance is the process of acquiring the traits of one's predecessors.

Information hiding (or **data hiding**) is the concept that other classes should not alter an object's attributes—only the methods of an object's own class should have that privilege.

A **class definition** is a set of program statements that tells you the characteristics of the class's objects and the methods that can be applied to its objects.

A **user-defined type**, or **programmer-defined type**, is a class.

An **abstract data type (ADT)** is a programmer-defined type; this term implies that the type's data can be accessed only through methods.

Primitive data types are simple numbers and characters that are not class types.

A **class diagram** consists of a rectangle divided into three sections that shows a class's name, data, and methods.

A **set method** sets the values of a data field within a class.

Mutator methods are ones that set values in a class.

A **property** provides methods that allow you to get and set a class field value using a simple syntax.

A **get method** returns a value from a class.

Accessor methods get values from class fields.

Work methods perform tasks within a class.

Help methods and **facilitators** are other names for work methods.

Private access, as applied to a class's data or methods, specifies that the data or method cannot be used by any method that is not part of the same class.

Public access, as applied to a class's data or methods, specifies that other programs and methods may use the specified data or methods.

An **access specifier** (or **access modifier**) is the adjective that defines the type of access that outside classes will have to the attribute or method.

A **primary key** is a unique identifier for each object in a database.

An **instance method** operates correctly yet differently for each class object. An instance method is nonstatic and receives a `this` reference.

A `this` **reference** is an automatically created variable that holds the address of an object and passes it to an instance method whenever the method is called.

A **class method** is a static method. Class methods are not instance methods and they do not receive a `this` reference.

Static methods are those for which no object needs to exist. Static methods are not instance methods and they do not receive a `this` reference.

Nonstatic methods are methods that exist to be used with an object created from a class; they are instance methods and they receive a `this` reference.

A **constructor** is an automatically called method that establishes an object.

A **default constructor** is one that requires no arguments.

A **destructor** is an automatically called method that contains the actions you require when an instance of a class is destroyed.

Using a class object within another class object is known as **composition**.

A **has-a relationship** is the type that exists when using composition.

A **base class** is one that is used as a basis for inheritance.

A **derived class** or **extended class** is one that is extended from a base class.

Superclass and **parent class** are synonyms for base class.

Subclass and **child class** are synonyms for derived class.

The **ancestors** of a derived class are the entire list of parent classes from which a class is derived.

Transitive describes the phenomena of inheriting all the traits of one's ancestors.

An **inaccessible** field is one that cannot be accessed by any class other than the one in which it is defined.

The **protected access modifier** is used when you want no outside classes to be able to use a data field, except classes that are children of the original class.

Fragile describes classes that depend on field names from parent classes. They are prone to errors—that is, they are easy to "break."

Multiple inheritance is the capability to inherit from more than one class.

An **abstract class** is one from which you cannot create any concrete objects, but from which you can inherit.

Code is **reliable** when it has already been tested and used in a variety of situations.

Libraries are stored collections of classes that serve related purposes.

Packages are another name for libraries in some languages.

A **visual development environment** is one in which you can create programs by dragging components such as buttons and labels onto a screen and arranging them visually.

In several languages, the visual development environment is known by the acronym **IDE**, which stands for Integrated Development Environment.

REVIEW QUESTIONS

1. **Which of the following means the same as *object*?**
   a. class
   b. field
   c. instance
   d. category

2. **Which of the following means the same as *instance variable*?**
   a. field
   b. instance
   c. category
   d. class

3. **A program that instantiates objects of another prewritten class is a(n) _____.**
   a. object
   b. client
   c. instance
   d. GUI

4. **The process of acquiring the traits of one's predecessors is _____.**
   a. inheritance
   b. encapsulation
   c. polymorphism
   d. orientation

5. **Every class definition must contain _____.**
   a. a name
   b. data
   c. methods
   d. all of the above

6. Assume a working program contains the following statement:

   `myDog.setName("Bowser")`

   Which of the following do you know?

   a. `setName()` is a public method

   b. `setName()` accepts a string parameter

   c. both of these

   d. none of these

7. **Which of the following is the most likely scenario for a specific class?**

   a. Its data is private and its methods are public.

   b. Its data is public and its methods are private.

   c. Its data and methods are both public.

   d. Its data and methods are both private.

8. **An instance method _____ .**

   a. is static   c. both of these

   b. receives a this reference   d. none of these

9. **Assume you have created a class named Dog that contains a data field named weight and an instance method named setWeight(). Further assume the setWeight() method accepts a numeric parameter named weight. Which of the following statements correctly sets a Dog's weight within the setWeight() method?**

   a. `weight = weight`

   b. `this.weight = this.weight`

   c. `weight = this.weight`

   d. `this.weight = weight`

10. **A static method is also known as a(n) _____ method.**

    a. instance   c. private

    b. public   d. class

11. **By default, methods contained in a class are _____ methods.**

    a. static   c. class

    b. nonstatic   d. public

12. **When you instantiate an object, the automatically created method that is called is a _____ .**

    a. creator   c. constructor

    b. initiator   d. architect

13. **Which of the following can be overloaded?**

    a. constructors   c. both of these

    b. destructors   d. none of these

14. **A default constructor is _____ .**

    a. another name for a class's automatically created constructor

    b. a constructor that requires no arguments

    c. a constructor that sets a value for every field in a class

    d. the only constructor that is explicitly written in a class

15. **When you write a constructor that receives an argument, _____ .**

    a. the argument must be numeric

    b. the argument must be used to set a data field

    c. the default constructor no longer exists

    d. the constructor body must be empty

16. **A class object can be _____ .**

    a. stored in an array   c. returned from a method

    b. passed to a method   d. all of the above

17. **Most often, a destructor is called when _____ .**

    a. an object is created

    b. an object goes out of scope

    c. you make an explicit call to it

    d. a value is returned from a class method

18. **Advantages of creating a class that inherits from another include all of the following except which?**

    a. You save time because subclasses are created automatically from those that come built-in as part of a programming language.

    b. You save time because you need not recreate the fields and methods in the original class.

    c. You reduce the chance of errors because the original class's methods have already been used and tested.

    d. You make it easier for anyone who has used the original class to understand the new class.

19. **Employing inheritance reduces errors because _____ .**

    a. the new classes have access to fewer data fields

    b. the new classes have access to fewer methods

    c. you can copy and paste methods that you already created

    d. many of the methods you need have already been used and tested

20. A class that is used as a basis for inheritance is called a _____.

a. derived class　　　　c. child class

b. subclass　　　　　　d. base class

FIND THE BUGS

The following pseudocode segment contains one or more bugs that you must find and correct.

1. **The Date class contains a month, day, and year, and methods to set and display the values. The month cannot be set to less than 1 or more than 12, and the day of the month cannot be set to less than 1 or more than the number of days in that month. The demonstration program instantiates four Dates and purposely assigns invalid values to some of the arguments; the class methods will correct the invalid values.**

```
class Date
    private num month
    private num day
    private num year
    public void setDate(num mo, num da, num yr)
        num HIGH_MONTH = 12
        num HIGHEST_DAYS[HIGH_MONTH] =
            31, 29, 31, 20, 31, 30, 31, 31, 30, 31, 30, 31
        if month > HIGH_MONTH then
            month = HIGH_MONTH
        else
            if mo < 1 then
                month = 1
            else
                mo = month
         endif
        endif
        if da > HIGHEST_DAYS[month] then
            day = HIGHEST_DAYS[month]
        else
            if da < 1 then
                da = 1
            else
                day = da
        endif
         yr = year
    return
    public void showDate()
        print "Date: ", month, "/", da, "/", year
    return
```

```
start
    Date birthday, anniversary, graduation, party
    birthday.setDate(6, 24, 1982)
    anniversary.setDate(10, 15, 2009)
    graduation.setDate(14, 19, 2011)
    party.setDate(7, 35, 2010)
    print "Birthday "
    birthday.showDate()
    print "Anniversary "
    anniversary.showDate()
    print "Graduation "
    graduation.showDate()
    print "Party "
    party.showDate()
stop
```

EXERCISES

1. **Identify three objects that might belong to each of the following classes:**

   a. `Automobile`

   b. `NovelAuthor`

   c. `CollegeCourse`

2. **Identify three different classes that might contain each of these objects:**

   a. Wolfgang Amadeus Mozart

   b. My pet cat named Socks

   c. Apartment 14 at 101 Main Street

3. **Design a class named `CustomerRecord` that holds a customer number, name, and address. Include methods to set the values for each data field and print the values for each data field. Create the class diagram and write the pseudocode that defines the class.**

4. **Design a class named `House` that holds the street address, price, number of bedrooms, and number of baths in a `House`. Include methods to set the values for each data field, and include a method that displays all the values for a `House`. Create the class diagram and write the pseudocode that defines the class.**

5. **Design a class named `Loan` that holds an account number, name of account holder, amount borrowed, term, and interest rate. Include methods to set values for each data field and a method that prints all the loan information. Create the class diagram and write the pseudocode that defines the class.**

6. **Complete the following tasks:**

   a. Design a class named Book that holds a stock number, author, title, price, and number of pages for a book. Include methods to set and get the values for each data field. Create the class diagram and write the pseudocode that defines the class.

   b. Design an application that declares two Book objects and sets and displays their values.

   c. Design an application that declares an array of 10 Books. Prompt the user for data for each of the Books, then display all the values.

7. **Complete the following tasks:**

   a. Design a class named Pizza. Data fields include a string field for toppings (such as pepperoni) and numeric fields for diameter in inches (such as 12) and price (such as 13.99). Include methods to get and set values for each of these fields. Create the class diagram and write the pseudocode that defines the class.

   b. Design an application that declares two Pizza objects and sets and displays their values.

   c. Design an application that declares an array of 10 Pizzas. Prompt the user for data for each of the Pizzas, then display all the values.

8. **Complete the following tasks:**

   a. Design a class named HousePlant. A HousePlant has fields for a name (for example, "Philodendron"), a price (for example, 29.99), and a field that indicates whether the plant has been fed in the last month (for example, "Yes"). Create the class diagram and write the pseudocode that defines the class.

   b. Design an application that declares two HousePlant objects and sets and displays their values.

   c. Design an application that declares an array of 10 HousePlants. Prompt the user for data for each of the HousePlants, then display all the values.

9. **Complete the following tasks:**

   a. Design a class named Circle with fields named radius, area, and diameter. Include a constructor that sets the radius to 1. Include get methods for each field, but include a set method only for the radius. When the radius is set, do not allow it to be zero or a negative number. When the radius is set, calculate the diameter (twice the radius) and the area (the radius squared times pi, which is approximately 3.14). Create the class diagram and write the pseudocode that defines the class.

   b. Design an application that declares two Circles. Set the radius of one manually, but allow the other to use the default value supplied by the constructor. Then, display each Circle's values.

10. **Complete the following tasks:**

   a. Design a class named Square with fields that hold the length of a side, the length of the perimeter, and the area. Include a constructor that sets the length of a side to 1. Include get methods for each field, but include a set method only for the length of a side, and do not allow a side to be zero or negative. When the side is set, calculate the perimeter length (four times the side length) and the area (a side squared). Create the class diagram and write the pseudocode that defines the class.

b. Design an application that declares two `Square`s. Set the side length of one manually, but allow the other to use the default value supplied by the constructor. Then, display each `Square`'s values.

c. Create a child class named `Cube`. `Cube` contains an additional data field named `depth`, and a `computeCubeSurfaceArea()` method that calculates surface area appropriately for a cube.

d. Create the logic for an application that instantiates a `Square` object and a `Cube` object and displays the surface areas of both objects.

11. **Complete the following tasks:**

a. Design a class named `GirlScout` with fields that hold a name, troop number, and dues owed. Include get and set methods for each field. Include a static method that displays the Girl Scout motto ("To obey the Girl Scout law"). Include three overloaded constructors as follows:

   » A default constructor that sets the name to "XXX" and the numeric fields to 0
   » A constructor that allows you to pass values for all three fields
   » A constructor that allows you to pass a name and troop number but sets dues owed to 0

   Create the class diagram and write the pseudocode that defines the class.

b. Design an application that declares three `GirlScout` objects using a different constructor version with each object. Display each `GirlScout`'s values. Then display the motto.

12. **Complete the following tasks:**

a. Create a class named `Commission` that includes two numeric variables: a sales figure and a commission rate. Also create two overloaded methods named `computeCommission()`. The first method takes two numeric arguments representing sales and rate, multiplies them, and then displays the results. The second method takes a single argument representing sales. When this method is called, the commission rate is assumed to be 7.5 percent and the results are displayed.

b. Create an application that demonstrates how both method versions can be called.

13. **Complete the following tasks:**

a. Create a class named `Pay` that includes five numeric variables: hours worked, rate of pay per hour, withholding rate, gross pay, and net pay. Also create three overloaded `computeNetPay()` methods. When `computeNetPay()` receives values for hours, pay rate, and withholding rate, it computes the gross pay and reduces it by the appropriate withholding amount to produce the net pay. (Gross pay is computed as hours worked, multiplied by pay per hour.) When `computeNetPay()` receives two arguments, they represent the hours and pay rate, and the withholding rate is assumed to be 15 percent. When `computeNetPay()` receives one argument, it represents the number of hours worked, the withholding rate is assumed to be 15 percent, and the hourly rate is assumed to be 6.50.

b. Create an application that demonstrates all the methods.

14. **Complete the following tasks:**

    a. Design a class named `Book` that holds a stock number, author, title, price, and number of pages for a book. Include methods to set and get the values for each data field. Also include a `displayInfo()` method that displays each of the `Book`'s data fields with explanation.

    b. Design a class named `TextBook` that is a child class of `Book`. Include a new data field for the grade level of the book. Create a `displayTextBookInfo()` method so that you accommodate the new grade-level field.

    c. Design an application that instantiates an object of each type and demonstrates all the methods.

15. **Complete the following tasks:**

    a. Design a class named `Player` that holds a player number and name for a sports team participant. Include methods to set the values for each data field and print the values for each data field.

    b. Design two classes named `BaseballPlayer` and `BasketballPlayer` that are child classes of `Player`. Include a new data field in each class for the player's position. Include an additional field in the `BaseballPlayer` class for batting average. Include a new field in the `BasketballPlayer` class for free-throw percentage. Create methods that set and print the data so that you accommodate the new fields.

    c. Design an application that instantiates an object of each type and demonstrates all the methods.

16. **Complete the following tasks:**

    a. Create a class named `Tape` that includes fields for length and width in inches and get and set methods for each field.

    b. Derive two subclasses—`VideoCassetteTape` and `AdhesiveTape`. The `VideoCassetteTape` class includes a numeric field to hold playing time in minutes and get and set methods for the field. The `AdhesiveTape` class includes a numeric field that holds a stickiness factor—a value from 1 to 10—and get and set methods for the field.

    c. Design a program that instantiates one object of each of the three classes, and that demonstrates each class's methods.

17. **Complete the following tasks:**

a. Create a class named `Order` that performs order processing of a single item. The class has four fields: customer name, customer number, quantity ordered, and unit price. Include set and get methods for each field. The set methods prompt the user for values for each field. This class also needs a method to compute the total price (quantity multiplied by unit price) and a method to display the field values.

b. Create a subclass named `ShippedOrder` that includes a `computeShippedPrice()` that adds shipping and handling charge of $4.00.

c. Create the logic for an application that instantiates an object of each of these classes. Prompt the user for data for the `Order` object, and display the results; then prompt the user for data for the `ShippedOrder` object, and display the results.

d. Create the logic for an application that continuously prompts a user for order information until the user enters "ZZZ" for the customer name or 10 orders have been taken, whichever comes first. Ask the user whether each order will be shipped, and create an `Order` or a `ShippedOrder` appropriately. Store each order in an array. When the user is done entering data, display all the order information taken as well as the total price that was computed for each order.

GAME ZONE

1. a. Playing cards are used in many computer games, including versions of such classics as Solitaire, Hearts, and Poker. Design a `Card` class that contains a string data field to hold a suit (spades, hearts, diamonds, or clubs) and an integer data field for a value from 1 to 13. Include `get` and `set` methods for each field. Write an application that randomly selects two playing cards and displays their values.

b. Using two `Card` objects, design an application that plays a very simple version of the card game War. Deal two `Cards`—one for the computer and one for the player—and determine the higher card, then display a message indicating whether the cards are equal, the computer won, or the player won. (Playing cards are considered equal when they have the same value, no matter what their suit is.) For this game, assume the Ace (value 1) is low. Make sure that the two cards dealt are not the same card. For example, a deck cannot contain more than one card representing the two of spades.

2. a. Computer games often contain different characters or creatures. For example, you might design a game in which alien beings possess specific characteristics such as color, number of eyes, or number of lives. Create an `Alien` class. Include at least three data members of your choice. Include a constructor that requires a value for each data field and a `toString()` method that returns a string that contains a complete description of the `Alien`.

b. Create two classes—`Martian` and `Jupiterian`—that descend from `Alien`. Supply each with a constructor that sets the `Alien` data fields with values you choose. For example, you can decide that a `Martian` object has four eyes but a `Jupiterian object` has only two.

c. Create an application that instantiates one object of each type (`Martian` and `Jupiterian`). Call the `toString()` method with each object and display the results.

DETECTIVE WORK

1. Many programmers think object-oriented programming is a superior approach to procedural programming. Others think it adds a level of complexity that is not needed in many scenarios. Find and summarize arguments on both sides.

2. When and why was the Java programming language created?

3. Many object-oriented programmers are opposed to using multiple inheritance. Find out why and decide whether you agree with this stance.

UP FOR DISCUSSION

1. In this chapter, you learned that instance data and methods belong to objects (which are class members), but that static data and methods belong to a class as a whole. Consider the real-life class named `StateInTheUnitedStates`. Name some real-life attributes of this class that are static attributes and instance attributes. Create another example of a real-life class and discuss what its static and instance members might be.

2. Some programmers use a system called Hungarian notation when naming their variables and class fields. What is Hungarian notation and why do many object-oriented programmers feel it is not a valuable style to use?

3. If you are completing all the programming exercises at the ends of the chapters in this book, you can see how much work goes into planning a full-blown professional program. How would you feel if someone copied your work without compensating you? Investigate the magnitude of software piracy in our society. What are the penalties for illegally copying software? Are there circumstances under which it is acceptable to copy a program? If a friend asked you to make a copy of a program for him, would you? What do you suggest we do about this problem, if anything?

EVENT-DRIVEN GUI PROGRAMMING, ANIMATION, AND EXCEPTION HANDLING

In this chapter you will:

Understand the principles of event-driven programming

Understand the actions that GUI components can initiate

Be able to design graphical user interfaces

Be able to modify the attributes of GUI components

Understand the steps to developing an event-driven application

Understand multithreading

Understand how to create animation

Understand the disadvantages of traditional error-handling techniques

Understand object-oriented exception handling

UNDERSTANDING EVENT-DRIVEN PROGRAMMING

From the 1950s, when businesses began to use computers to help them perform many jobs, right through the 1960s and 1970s, almost all interactive dialogues between people and computers took place at the command prompt (or on the command line). In Chapter 1 you learned that the command prompt is the location on your computer screen at which you type entries to communicate with the computer's **operating system**—the software that you use to run a computer and manage its resources. In the early days of computing, interacting with a computer operating system was difficult because the user had to know the exact syntax to use when typing commands, and had to spell and type those commands accurately. (Syntax is the correct sequence of words and symbols that form the operating system's command set.) Figure 12-1 shows a command in the Windows operating system.

Figure 12-1 Command prompt screen

»NOTE If you use the Windows operating system on a PC, you can locate the command prompt by clicking Start, and pointing to the command prompt window shortcut on the Start menu. Alternately, you can point to Start, click Run, type *CMD*, and press Enter. Still another option is to click Start, point to All Programs in Vista or Windows XP (or Programs in some earlier operating systems), then Accessories, and then click Command Prompt.

»NOTE Although you frequently use the command line to communicate with the operating system, you also sometimes communicate with software through the command line. For example, when you issue a command to execute some applications, you can include data values that the program uses.

Fortunately for today's computer users, operating system software allows them to use a mouse or other pointing device to select pictures, or **icons**, on the screen. As you learned in Chapter 1, this type of environment is a graphical user interface, or GUI. Computer users can expect to see a standard interface in the GUI programs they use. Rather than memorizing difficult commands that must be typed at a command line, GUI users can select options from menus and click buttons to make their preferences known to a program. Users can select objects that look like their real-world counterparts and get the expected results. For example, users may select an icon that looks like a pencil when they want to write a memo, or they may drag an icon shaped like a folder to another icon that resembles a recycling bin when they want to delete a file. Figure 12-2 shows a Windows program named Paint in which icons representing pencils, paint cans, and so on appear on clickable buttons. Performing an operation on an icon (for example, clicking or dragging it) causes an **event**—an occurrence that generates a message sent to an object.

Figure 12-2 A GUI application that contains buttons and icons

GUI programs are called **event-driven** or **event-based** because actions occur in response to user-initiated events such as clicking a mouse button. When you program with event-driven languages, the emphasis is on the objects that the user can manipulate, such as buttons and menus, and on the events that the user can initiate with those objects, such as clicking or double-clicking. The programmer writes instructions within modules that correspond to each type of event.

For the programmer, event-driven programs require unique considerations. The program logic you have developed within many of the methods of this book is procedural; each step occurs in the order the programmer determines. In a procedural application, if you issue a prompt and a statement to read the user's response, you have no control over how much time the user takes to enter a response, but you do control the sequence of events—the processing goes no further until the input is completed. In contrast, with event-driven programs, the user might initiate any number of events in any order. For example, if you use an event-driven word-processing program, you have dozens of choices at your disposal at any moment. You can type words, select text with the mouse, click a button to change text to bold or to italics, choose a menu item, and so on. With each word-processing document you create, you choose options in any order that seems appropriate at the time. The word-processing program must be ready to respond to any event you initiate.

NOTE
You first learned the term *procedural programming* in Chapter 1.

Within an event-driven program, a component from which an event is generated is the **source of the event**. A button that a user can click to cause some action is an example of a source; a text field that one can use to enter typed characters is another source. An object that is "interested in" an event you want it to respond to is a **listener**. It "listens for" events so it knows when to respond. Not all objects can receive all events—you probably have used programs in which clicking many areas of the screen has no effect at all. If you want an object, such as a button, to be a listener for an event such as a mouse click, you must write the appropriate program statements.

> **»NOTE** When an object should listen for events, you must write two types of statements. You write the statement or statements that define the object as a listener, and you write the statements that constitute the event.

Although event-driven programming is relatively new, the instructions that programmers write to correspond to events are still simply sequences, selections, and loops. Event-driven programs still declare variables, use arrays, and contain all the attributes of their procedural-program ancestors. An event-driven program might contain components with labels like "Sort Records," "Merge Files," or "Total Transactions." The programming logic you use when writing code for each of these processes is the same logic you have learned throughout this book. Writing event-driven programs simply involves thinking of possible events as the modules that constitute the program.

TWO TRUTHS AND A LIE:
UNDERSTANDING EVENT-DRIVEN PROGRAMMING

1. GUI programs are called event-driven or event-based because actions occur in response to user-initiated events such as clicking a mouse button.

2. With event-driven programs, the user might initiate any number of events in any order.

3. Within an event-driven program, a component from which an event is generated is a listener. An object that is "interested in" an event you want it to respond to is the source of the event.

The false answer is # 3. Within an event-driven program, a component from which an event is generated is the source of the event and an object that is "interested in" an event you want it to respond to is a listener.

USER-INITIATED ACTIONS AND GUI COMPONENTS

To understand GUI programming, you need to have a clear picture of the possible events a user can initiate. These include the events listed in Table 12-1.

Event	Description of user's action
Key press	Pressing a key on the keyboard
Mouse point or mouse over	Placing the mouse pointer over an area on the screen
Mouse click or left mouse click	Pressing the left mouse button
Right mouse click	Pressing the right mouse button
Mouse double-click	Pressing the left mouse button two times in rapid sequence
Mouse drag	Holding the left mouse button down while moving the mouse over the desk surface

Table 12-1 Common user-initiated events

You also need to be able to picture common GUI components. Some are listed in Table 12-2. Figure 12-3 shows a screen that contains several common GUI components.

Component	Description
Label	A rectangular area that displays text
Text field	A rectangular area into which the user can type text
Check box	A label placed beside a small square; you can click the square to display or remove a check mark; this component allows the user to select or deselect an option
Option buttons	A group of options that are similar to check boxes, but that are mutually exclusive. When the options are square, they are often called a check box group. When they are round, they are often called radio buttons.
List box	When the user clicks a list box, a menu of items appears. Depending on the options the programmer sets, you might be able to make only one selection, or you might be able to make multiple selections.
Button	A rectangular object you can click; when you do, it usually appears to be pressed

Table 12-2 Common GUI components

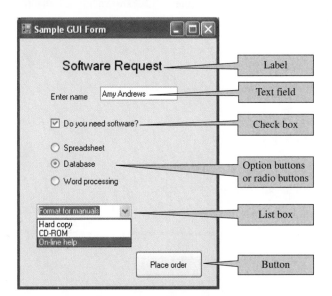

Figure 12-3 Illustration of common GUI components

» NOTE Although in many languages you can place square option buttons in a group and force them to be mutually exclusive, users conventionally expect a group of mutually exclusive buttons to appear as round radio buttons.

When you program in a language that supports event-driven logic, you do not create the GUI components you need from scratch. Instead, you call prewritten methods that draw the GUI components on the screen for you. The components themselves are constructed using existing classes complete with names, attributes, and methods. In some programming language environments, you write statements that call the methods that create the GUI objects; in others, you can drag GUI objects onto your screen from a toolbar and arrange them appropriately for your application. Either way, you do not worry about the details of constructing the components. Instead, you concentrate on the actions that you want to take place when a user initiates an event from one of the components. Thus, GUI components are excellent examples of the best principles of object-oriented programming (OOP)—they represent objects with attributes and methods that operate like black boxes, making them easy for you to use.

>> **NOTE** GUI components are often referred to as *widgets*, which some sources claim is a combination of the terms *window* and *gadgets*. Originally, "widget" comes from the 1924 play *Beggar on Horseback*, by George Kaufman and Marc Connelly. In the play, a young composer gets engaged to the daughter of a rich businessman, and foresees spending his life doing pointless work in a bureaucratic big business that manufactures widgets, which represent a useless item whose purpose is never explained.

When you use already created GUI components, you are instantiating objects, each of which belongs to a prewritten class. For example, you might use a `Button` class object when you want the user to be able to click a button to make a selection. Depending on the programming language you use, the `Button` class might contain attributes or properties such as the text written on the `Button` and the position of the `Button` on the screen. The class might also contain methods such as `setText()` and `setPosition()`. Figure 12-4 shows how a built-in `Button` class might have been written.

```
class Button
    private string text
    private num x_position
    private num y_position

    public void setText(string messageOnButton)
        text = messageOnButton
    return

    public void setPosition(num x, num y)
        x_position = x
        y_position = y
    return
endClass
```

Figure 12-4 `Button` class

>> **NOTE** The `x_position` and `y_position` of the `Button` object defined in Figure 12-4 refer to horizontal and vertical coordinates where the `Button` appears on an object, such as a window that appears on the screen during program execution. A **pixel** is one of the tiny dots of light that form a grid on your screen. The term *pixel* derives from combining the first syllables of *picture* and *element*. You will use x- and y-positions again when you learn about animation later in this chapter.

The Button class shown in Figure 12-4 is an abbreviated version so you can easily see its similarity to classes such as Student and Employee, which you read about in Chapter 11. A working Button class in most programming languages would contain many more fields and methods. For example, you might need to set a Button's font, color, size, and so on.

To create a Button object, you would write a statement similar to the following:

```
Button myProgramButton
```

In this statement, Button represents the type and myProgramButton represents the object you create. To use a Button's methods, you would write statements such as the following:

```
myProgramButton.setText("Click here")
myProgramButton.setPosition(10, 30)
```

Different GUI classes support different attributes and methods. For example, a CheckBox class might contain a method named getCheckedStatus() that returns true or false, indicating whether the CheckBox object has been checked. A Button, however, would have no need for such a method.

TWO TRUTHS AND A LIE:
USER-INITIATED ACTIONS AND GUI COMPONENTS

1. In a GUI program, a key press is a common user-initiated event and a check box is a typical GUI component.

2. When you program in a language that supports event-driven logic, you call prewritten methods that draw the GUI components on the screen for you.

3. An advantage of using GUI objects is that each class you use to create the objects supports identical methods and attributes.

The false statement is # 3. Different GUI classes support different attributes and methods.

DESIGNING GRAPHICAL USER INTERFACES

You should consider several general design principles when creating a program that will use a GUI:

» The interface should be natural and predictable.
» The interface should be attractive, easy to read, and nondistracting.
» To some extent, it's helpful if the user can customize your applications.
» The program should be forgiving. *Comprensivo*
» The GUI is only a means to an end.

THE INTERFACE SHOULD BE NATURAL AND PREDICTABLE

The GUI program interface should represent objects like their real-world counterparts. In other words, it makes sense to use an icon that looks like a recycling bin when you want to allow a user to drag files or other components to the bin to delete them. Using a recycling bin icon is "natural" in that people use one in real life when they want to discard real-life items; dragging files to the bin is also "natural" because that's what people do with real-life items they discard. Using a recycling bin for discarded items is also predictable, because users are already familiar with the icon in other programs. Some icons may be natural, but if they are not predictable as well, then they are not as effective. An icon that depicts a recycling truck is just as "natural" as far as corresponding to real-world recycling, but because other programs do not use a truck icon for this purpose, it is not as predictable.

GUIs should also be predictable in their layout. For example, when you use a menu bar, it is at the top of the screen in most GUI programs, and the first menu item is almost always *File*. If you design a program interface in which the menu runs vertically down the right side of the screen, or in which *File* is the last menu option instead of the first, you will confuse users. Either they will make mistakes when using your program, or they may give up using it entirely. It doesn't matter if you can prove that your layout plan is more efficient than the standard one—if you do not use a predictable layout, your program will meet rejection from users in the marketplace.

> **NOTE** Many studies have proven that the Dvorak keyboard layout is more efficient for typists than the QWERTY keyboard layout that most of us use. The QWERTY keyboard layout gets its name from the first six letter keys in the top row. With the Dvorak layout, which gets its name from its inventor, the most frequently used keys are in the home row, allowing typists to complete many more keystrokes per minute. However, the Dvorak keyboard has not caught on with the computer-buying public because it is not predictable.

> **NOTE** Stovetops in kitchens often have an unnatural interface, making unfamiliar stoves more difficult for you to use. Most stovetops have four burners arranged in two rows, but the knobs that control the burners frequently are placed in a single horizontal row. Because there is not a natural correlation between the placement of a burner and its control, you are more likely to select the wrong knob when adjusting the burner's flame or heating element.

THE INTERFACE SHOULD BE ATTRACTIVE, EASY TO READ, AND NONDISTRACTING

> **NOTE**
> An excellent way to learn about good GUI design is to pay attention to the design features used in popular applications and in Web sites you visit.

If your interface is attractive, people are more likely to use it. If it is easy to read, they are less likely to make mistakes and more likely to want to use it. And if the interface is easy to read, it will more likely be considered attractive. When it comes to GUI design, fancy fonts and weird color combinations are the signs of amateur designers. In addition, you should make sure that unavailable screen options are either sufficiently dimmed or removed, so the user does not waste time clicking components that aren't functional.

> **NOTE** Dimming a component is also called *graying* the component. Dimming a component provides another example of predictability—users with computer experience do not expect to be able to use a dimmed component.

Screen designs should not be distracting. When a screen has too many components, users can't find what they're looking for. When a text field or button is no longer needed, it should be removed from the interface. You also want to avoid distracting users with overly creative design elements. When users click a button to open a file, they might be amused the first time a filename dances across the screen or the speakers play a tune. But after one or two experiences with your creative additions, users find that intruding design elements simply hamper the actual work of the program.

>> **NOTE** GUI programmers sometimes refer to screen space as *real estate*. Just as a plot of real estate becomes unattractive when it supports no open space, your screen becomes unattractive when you fill the limited space with too many components.

TO SOME EXTENT, IT'S HELPFUL IF THE USER CAN CUSTOMIZE YOUR APPLICATIONS

Every user works in his or her own way. If you are designing an application that will use numerous menus and toolbars, it's helpful if users can position the components in the order that's easiest for them to work with. Users appreciate being able to change features like color schemes. Allowing a user to change the background color in your application may seem frivolous to you, but to users who are color-blind or visually impaired, it might make the difference in whether they use your application at all.

>> **NOTE** The screen design issues that make programs easier to use for people with physical limitations are known as **accessibility** issues.

>> **NOTE** Many programs are used internationally. If you can allow the user to work in a choice of languages, you might be able to market your program more successfully in other countries.

THE PROGRAM SHOULD BE FORGIVING

Perhaps you have had the inconvenience of accessing a voice mail system in which you selected several sequential options, only to find yourself at a dead end with no recourse but to hang up and redial the number. Good program design avoids equivalent problems. You should always provide an escape route to accommodate users who have made bad choices or changed their minds. By providing a Back button or functional Escape key, you provide more functionality to your users.

THE GUI IS ONLY A MEANS TO AN END

The most important principle of GUI design is to remember always that any GUI is only an interface. Using a mouse to click items and drag them around is not the point of any business programs except those that train people how to use a mouse. Instead, the point of a graphical interface is to help people be more productive. To that end, the design should help the user see what options are available, allow the use of components in the ordinary way, and not force the user to concentrate on how to interact with your application. The real work of any GUI program is done after the user clicks a button or makes a list box selection. Then actual program tasks take place.

TWO TRUTHS AND A LIE:
DESIGNING GRAPHICAL USER INTERFACES

1. To keep the user's attention, a well-designed GUI interface should contain unique and creative controls.

2. To be most useful to users, a GUI interface should be attractive, easy to read, and nondistracting.

3. To avoid frustrating users, a well-designed program should be forgiving.

The false statement is #1. A GUI interface should be natural and predictable.

MODIFYING THE ATTRIBUTES OF GUI COMPONENTS

When you design a program with premade or preprogrammed graphical components, you will want to change their appearance to customize them for the current application. Each programming language provides its own means of changing components' appearances, but all involve changing the values stored in the components' attribute fields. Some common changes include setting the following items:

» The size of the component
» The color of the component
» The screen location of the component
» The font for any text contained in or on the component
» The component to be visible or invisible
» The component to be dimmed or undimmed, sometimes called *enabled* or *disabled*

You must learn the exact names of the methods and what type of arguments you are allowed to use in each programming language you learn, but all languages that support creating event-driven applications allow you to set components' attributes and get the values for most of them.

When you use a graphical development environment in which you can drag a component such as a button onto a screen and type its text into a list of properties, program code statements are automatically generated for you. For example, when you drag a Button onto a screen, its setPosition() method is called automatically and passed the values of the coordinates where you drop it with your mouse. If you move the Button, the setPosition() method is called again and the new coordinates are passed to it. In graphical languages you always have the option of writing the code statements that set GUI objects' properties yourself instead of allowing them to be automatically generated. In other words, you always have the option of designing the screen "the hard way" by writing code. The drag-and-drop and property list features are available to you as a convenience.

TWO TRUTHS AND A LIE:
MODIFYING THE ATTRIBUTES OF GUI COMPONENTS

1. When you design a program with premade or preprogrammed graphical components, you will want to change their appearance to customize them for the current application.

2. In most programming languages, you change components' appearances by writing new specialized methods for their classes.

3. Some common changes include setting the size, color, and screen location of components, and the font of the text on components.

The false statement is #2. Each programming language provides its own means of changing components' appearances, but all involve changing the values stored in the components' attribute fields.

THE STEPS TO DEVELOPING AN EVENT-DRIVEN APPLICATION

In Chapter 1, you first learned the steps to developing a computer program. They are:

1. Understanding the problem.

2. Planning the logic.

3. Coding the program.

4. Translating the program into machine language.

5. Testing the program.

When you develop an event-driven application, you expand on the planning step, including three new substeps as follows:

2a. Creating storyboards.

2b. Defining the objects.

2c. Defining the connections between the screens the user will see.

For example, suppose you want to create a simple, interactive program that determines premiums for prospective insurance customers. Users should be able to use a graphical interface to select a policy type—health or auto. Next, the users answer pertinent questions, such as how old they are, whether they smoke, and what their driving records are like. Although most insurance premium amounts would be based on more characteristics than these, assume that policy rates are determined by using the factors shown in Table 12-3. The final output of the program is a second screen that shows the semiannual premium amount for the chosen policy.

Health policy premiums	Auto policy premiums
Base rate: $500	Base rate: $750
Add $100 if over age 50	Add $400 if more than 2 tickets
Add $250 if smoker	Subtract $200 if over age 50

Table 12-3 Insurance premiums based on customer characteristics

CREATING STORYBOARDS

A **storyboard** represents a picture or sketch of a screen the user will see when running a program. Filmmakers have long used storyboards to illustrate key moments in the plots they are developing; similarly, GUI storyboards represent "snapshot" views of the screens the user will encounter during the run of a program. If the user could view up to four screens during the insurance premium program, then you would draw four storyboard cells, or frames.

Figure 12-5 shows two storyboard sketches for the insurance program. They represent the introductory screen at which the user selects a premium type and answers questions, and the final screen that displays the semiannual premium.

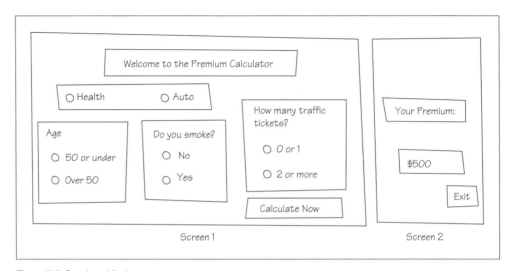

Figure 12-5 Storyboard for insurance program

DEFINING THE OBJECTS

An event-driven program may contain dozens or even hundreds of objects. To keep track of them, programmers often use an object dictionary. An **object dictionary** is a list of the objects used in a program, including which screens they are used on and whether any code, or script, is associated with them.

Figure 12-6 shows an object dictionary for the insurance premium program. The type and name of each object to be placed on a screen is listed in the left column. The second column shows the screen number on which the object appears. The next column names any variables that are affected by an action on the object. The right column indicates whether any code or script is associated with the object. For example, the label named `labelWelcome` appears on the first screen. It has no associated actions—it does not call any methods nor change any variables; it is just a label. The `calcButton`, however, does cause execution of a method named `calcRoutine()`. This method calculates the semiannual premium amount and stores it in the `premiumAmount` variable. Depending on the programming language you use, you might need to name `calcRoutine()` something similar to `calcButton.click()` to identify it as the module that executes when the user clicks the `calcButton`.

» **NOTE**
Some organizations also include the disk location where an object is stored as part of the object dictionary.

Object name	Screen number	Variables affected	Script?
Label labelWelcome	1	none	none
RadioButton radioButtonHealth	1	premiumAmount	none
RadioButton radioButtonAuto	1	premiumAmount	none
Label ageLabel	1	none	none
RadioButton radioButtonLowAge	1	premiumAmount	none
RadioButton radioButtonHighAge	1	premiumAmount	none
Label smokeLabel	1	none	none
RadioButton radioButtonSmokeNo	1	premiumAmount	none
RadioButton radioButtonSmokeYes	1	premiumAmount	none
Label ticketsLabel	1	none	none
RadioButton radioButtonLowTickets	1	premiumAmount	none
RadioButton radioButtonHighTickets	1	premiumAmount	none
Button calcButton	1	premiumAmount	calcRoutine()
Label labelPremium	2	none	none
Label premAmtLabel	2	none	none
Button exitButton	2	none	exitRoutine()

Figure 12-6 Object dictionary for insurance premium program

DEFINING THE CONNECTIONS BETWEEN THE SCREENS THE USER WILL SEE

The insurance premium program is a small one, but with larger programs you may need to draw the connections between the screens to show how they interact. Figure 12-7 shows an interactivity diagram for the screens used in the insurance premium program. An **interactivity diagram** shows the relationship between screens in an interactive GUI program. Figure 12-7 shows that the first screen calls the second screen, and the program ends.

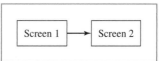

Figure 12-7 Diagram of interaction for insurance premium program

Figure 12-8 shows how a diagram might look for a more complicated program in which the user has several options available at Screens 1, 2, and 3. Notice how each of these three screens may lead to different screens, depending on the options the user selects at any one screen.

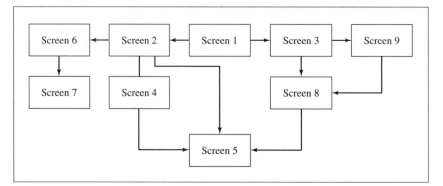

Figure 12-8 Diagram of interaction for a hypothetical complicated program

PLANNING THE LOGIC

In an event-driven program, you design the screens, define the objects, and define how the screens will connect. Then you can start to plan the insurance program class. For example, following the storyboard plan for the insurance program (see Figure 12-5), you need to create the first screen that contains a label, four sets of radio buttons, and a button. Figure 12-9 shows the pseudocode that creates these components.

```
Label labelWelcome
labelWelcome.setText("Welcome to the Premium Calculator")
labelWelcome.setPosition(30, 10)

RadioButton radioButtonHealth
radioButtonHealth.setText("Health")
radioButtonHealth.setPosition(15, 40)

RadioButton radioButtonAuto
radioButtonAuto.setText("Auto")
radioButtonAuto.setPosition(50, 40)

Label ageLabel
ageLabel.setText("Age")
ageLabel.setLocation(5, 60)

RadioButton radioButtonLowAge
radioButtonLowAge.setText("50 or under")
radioButtonLowAge.setPosition(5, 70)

RadioButton radioButtonHighAge
radioButtonHighAge.setText("Over 50")
radioButtonHighAge.setPosition(5, 80)

Label smokeLabel
smokeLabel.setText("Do you smoke?")
smokeLabel.setLocation(40, 60)

RadioButton radioButtonSmokeNo
radioButtonSmokeNo.setText("No")
radioButtonSmokeNo.setPosition(40, 70)

RadioButton radioButtonSmokeYes
radioButtonSmokeYes.setText("Yes")
radioButtonSmokeYes.setPosition(40, 80)

Label ticketsLabel
ticketsLabel.setText("How many traffic tickets?")
ticketsLabel.setLocation(60, 50)

RadioButton radioButtonLowTickets
radioButtonLowTickets.setText("0 or 1")
radioButtonLowTickets.setPosition(60, 70)

RadioButton radioButtonHighTickets
radioButtonHighTickets.setText("2 or more")
radioButtonHighTickets.setPosition(60, 90)

Button calcButton
calcButton.setText("Calculate Now")
calcButton.setLocation(60, 100)
calcButton.registerListener(calcRoutine())
```

Figure 12-9 Component definitions for first screen of insurance program

» NOTE Depending on the programming environment in which you are working, you might be able to drag the components in Figure 12-9 onto a screen without explicitly writing all the statements shown in the pseudocode. In that case, the coding statements will be generated for you.

» NOTE In Figure 12-9, the statement `calcButton.registerListener(calcRoutine())` specifies that `calcRoutine()` executes when a user clicks the `calcButton`. The syntax of this statement varies among programming languages.

» NOTE In reality, you might generate more code than that shown in Figure 12-9 when you create the insurance program components. For example, each component might require a color and font. You also might want to initialize some components with default values to indicate they are selected. For example, you might want one radio button in a group to be selected already, which allows the user to click a different option only if he does not want the default value.

You also need to create the component onto which all the GUI elements in Figure 12-9 are placed. Depending on the language you are using, you might use a class with a name such as `Screen`, `Form`, or `Window`. Each of these generically is a **container**, or a class of objects whose main purpose is to hold other elements. The container class contains methods that allow you to set physical properties such as height and width, as well as methods that allow you to add the appropriate components to a container. Figure 12-10 shows how you would define a `Screen` class, set its size, and add the components it needs.

```
Screen screen1
screen1.setSize(150, 150)
screen1.add(labelWelcome)
screen1.add(radioButtonHealth)
screen1.add(radioButtonAuto)
screen1.add(ageLabel)
screen1.add(radioButtonLowAge)
screen1.add(radioButtonHighAge)
screen1.add(smokeLabel)
screen1.add(radioButtonSmokeNo)
screen1.add(radioButtonSmokeYes)
screen1.add(ticketsLabel)
screen1.add(radioButtonLowTickets)
screen1.add(radioButtonHighTickets)
screen1.add(calcButton)
```

Figure 12-10 Statements that create `screen1`

Similarly, Figure 12-11 shows how you can create the components for the second screen in the insurance program, how to define its components, and how to add the components to the container. Notice the label that holds the user's insurance premium is not filled with text, because the amount is not known until the user makes all the selections on the first screen.

```
Screen screen2
screen2.setSize(100, 100)

Label labelPremium
labelPremium.setText("Your Premium")
labelPremium.setPosition(5, 30)

Label premAmtLabel
premAmtLabel.setPosition(20, 50)

Button exitButton
exitButton.setText("Exit")
exitButton.setLocation(60, 80)
exitButton.registerListener(exitRoutine())

screen2.add(labelPremium)
screen2.add(premAmtLabel)
screen2.add(exitButton)
```

Figure 12-11 Statements that define and create `screen2` and its components

After the GUI components are designed and arranged, you can plan the logic for each of the modules (or methods or scripts) that the program will use. For example, given the program requirements shown in Table 12-3, you can write the pseudocode for the `calcRoutine()` method of the insurance premium program, as shown in Figure 12-12. The `calcRoutine()` method does not execute until the user clicks the `calcButton`. At that point, the user's choices are sent to the method and used to calculate the premium amount.

```
public void calcRoutine()
   num HEALTH_AMT = 500
   num HIGH_AGE = 100
   num SMOKER = 250
   num AUTO_AMT = 750
   num HIGH_TICKETS = 400
   num HIGH_AGE_DRIVER_DISCOUNT = 200
   num premiumAmount
   if radioButtonHealth.getChecked() then
      premiumAmount = HEALTH_AMT
      if radioButtonHighAge.getChecked() then
         premiumAmount = premiumAmount + HIGH_AGE
      endif
      if radioButtonSmokeYes.getChecked() then
         premiumAmount = premiumAmount + SMOKER
      endif
   else
      premiumAmount = AUTO_AMT
      if radioButtonHighTickets.getChecked() then
         premiumAmount = premiumAmount + HIGH_TICKETS
      endif
      if radioButtonHighAge.getChecked() then
         premiumAmount = premiumAmount - HIGH_AGE_DRIVER_DISCOUNT
      endif
   endif
   premAmtLabel.setText(premiumAmount)
   screen1.remove()
   screen2.display()
return
```

Figure 12-12 Pseudocode for `calcRoutine()` method for insurance premium program

The pseudocode in Figure 12-12 should look very familiar to you—it declares numeric constants and a variable and uses decision-making logic you have used since the early chapters of this book. After the premium is calculated based on the user's choices, it is placed in the label that appears on the second screen. The basic structures of sequence, selection, and looping will continue to serve you well, whether you are programming in a procedural or event-driven environment.

The last two statements in the `calcRoutine()` method indicate that after the insurance premium is calculated and placed in its label, the first screen is removed and the second screen is displayed. Screen removal and display are accomplished differently in different languages; this example assumes that the appropriate methods are named `remove()` and `display()`.

Two more program segments are needed to complete the insurance premium program. These include the main program that executes when the program starts and the last method that executes when the program ends. In many GUI languages, the process is slightly more complicated, but the general logic appears in Figure 12-13. The final method in the program is the one that is associated with the `exitButton` on `screen2`. In Figure 12-13, this method is

```
start
   screen1.display()
stop

public void exitRoutine()
   screen2.remove()
return
```

Figure 12-13 The main program and `exitRoutine()` method for the insurance program

called `exitRoutine()`. In this program, the main program sets up the first screen and the last method removes the last screen.

TWO TRUTHS AND A LIE:
THE STEPS TO DEVELOPING AN EVENT-DRIVEN APPLICATION

1. A storyboard represents a diagram of the logic used in an interactive program.

2. An object dictionary is a list of the objects used in a program, including which screens they are used on and whether any code, or script, is associated with them.

3. An interactivity diagram shows the relationship between screens in an interactive GUI program.

The false statement is #1. A storyboard represents a picture or sketch of a screen the user will see when running a program.

UNDERSTANDING MULTITHREADING

A **thread** is the flow of execution of one set of program statements. When you execute a program statement by statement, from beginning to end, you are following a thread. Many applications follow a single thread; this means that at any one time the application executes only a single program statement. Every program you have studied so far in this book has contained a single thread.

Single-thread programs contain statements that execute in very rapid sequence, but only one statement executes at a time. When a computer contains a single central processing unit (CPU, or processor), it can execute only one computer instruction at a time, regardless of its processor speed. When you use a computer with multiple CPUs, the computer can execute multiple instructions simultaneously.

All major OOP languages allow you to launch, or start, multiple threads, no matter which type of processing system you use. Using multiple threads of execution is known as **multithreading**. As already noted, if you use a computer system that contains more than one CPU (such as a very large mainframe or supercomputer), multiple threads can execute simultaneously. Figure 12-14 illustrates how multithreading executes in a multiprocessor system.

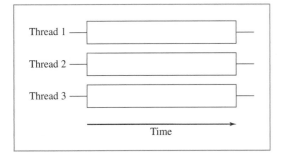

Figure 12-14 Executing multiple threads in a multiprocessor system

If you use a computer with a single processor, the multiple threads share the CPU's time, as shown in Figure 12-15. The CPU devotes a small amount of time to one task, and then devotes a small amount of time to another task. The CPU never actually performs two tasks at the same instant. Instead, it performs a piece of one task and then a piece of another task. The CPU performs so quickly that each task seems to execute without interruption.

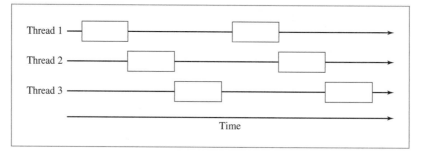

Figure 12-15 Executing multiple threads in a single-processor system

Perhaps you have seen an expert chess player participate in chess games with several opponents at once. The chess player makes a move on the first playing board, and then moves to the second board against a second opponent while the first opponent analyzes his next move. The master can move to the third board, make a move, and return to the first board before the first opponent is even ready to respond. To the first opponent, it might seem as though the expert player is devoting all of her time to him. Because the expert is so fast, she can play other opponents in the first opponent's "downtime." Executing multiple threads on a single CPU is a similar process. The CPU transfers its attention from thread to thread so quickly that the tasks don't even "miss" the CPU's attention.

You use multithreading to improve the performance of your programs. Multithreaded programs often run faster, but more importantly, they are more user-friendly. With a multithreaded program, your user can continue to click buttons while your program is reading a data file. With multithreading, an animated figure can appear on one part of the screen while the user makes menu selections on another part of the screen. When you use the Internet, multithreading increases in importance. For example, you can begin to read a long text file, watch a video, or listen to an audio file while the file is still downloading. Web users are likely to abandon a site if downloading a file takes too long. When you use multithreading to perform concurrent tasks, you are more likely to retain visitors to your Web site—this is particularly important if your site sells a product or service.

> **NOTE** Programmers sometimes use the terms *thread of execution* or *execution context* to describe a thread. They also describe a thread as a lightweight process because it is not a full-blown program. Rather, a thread must run within the context of a full, heavyweight program.

Object-oriented languages often contain a built-in `Thread` class that contains methods to help handle multiple threads. For example, one often-needed method is a `sleep()` method that can pause program execution for a specified amount of time. Computer instruction processing speed is so rapid that sometimes you have to slow processing down for human consumption. An application that frequently requires `sleep()` method calls is computer animation.

TWO TRUTHS AND A LIE:
UNDERSTANDING MULTITHREADING

1. In the last few years, hardly any programs are written that follow a single thread.

2. Single-thread programs contain statements that execute in very rapid sequence, but only one statement executes at a time.

3. When you use a computer with multiple CPUs, the computer can execute multiple instructions simultaneously.

The false statement is #1. Many applications follow a single thread; this means that at any one time the application executes only a single program statement.

CREATING ANIMATION

Many object-oriented languages offer built-in classes that contain methods you can use to draw geometric figures on the screen. The methods typically have names like `drawLine()`, `drawCircle()`, `drawRectangle()`, and so on. You place figures on the screen based on a graphing coordinate system. Typically, any component you place on the screen has a horizontal, or **x-axis**, position as well as a vertical, or **y-axis**, position in a screen window. The upper-left corner of any display is position 0, 0. The first, or **x-coordinate**, value increases as you travel from left to right across the window. The second, or **y-coordinate**, value increases as you travel from top to bottom. Figure 12-16 shows four screen coordinate positions. The more to the right a spot is, the higher its x-coordinate value, and the lower a spot is, the higher its y-coordinate value.

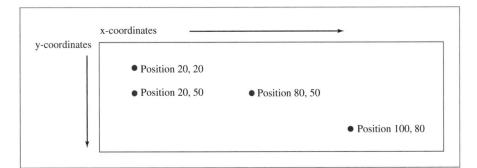

Figure 12-16 Selected screen coordinate positions

Cartoonists create animated films by drawing a sequence of frames or cells. These individual drawings are shown to the audience in rapid succession to give the illusion of natural movement. You create computer animation using the same techniques. If you display computer images as fast as your CPU can process them, you might not be able to see anything.

Most computer animation employs a `Thread` class `sleep()` method to pause for short periods of time between animation cells, so the human brain has time to absorb each image's content.

Artists often spend a great deal of time creating the exact images they want to use in an animation sequence. As a simple example, Figure 12-17 shows pseudocode for a `MovingCircle` class. As its name implies, the class moves a circle across the screen. The class contains data fields to hold x- and y-coordinates that identify the location at which a circle appears. The constants `SIZE` and `INCREASE`, respectively, define the size of the first circle drawn and the relative increase in size and position of each subsequent circle. The `MovingCircle` class assumes you are working with a language that provides a `drawCircle()` method, which takes care of the details of creating a circle when it is given parameters for horizontal and vertical positions and circle size. Assuming you are working with a language that provides a `sleep()` method that accepts a pause time in milliseconds, the `SLEEP_TIME` constant provides a 100-millisecond gap before the production of each new circle.

```
public class MovingCircle
    private num x = 20
    private num y = 20
    private num LIMIT = 300
    private num SIZE = 40
    private num INCREASE = SIZE / 10
    private num SLEEP_TIME = 100
    public void main()
        while(true)
            repaintScreen()
        endwhile
    return
    public void repaintScreen()
        drawCircle(x, y, x + SIZE)
        x = x + INCREASE
        y = y + INCREASE
        Thread.sleep(SLEEP_TIME)
    return
endClass
```

Figure 12-17 The `MovingCircle` class

In most object-oriented languages, a method named `main()` is one that executes automatically when a class object is created. The `main()` method in the `MovingCircle` class executes a continuous loop. A similar technique is used in many languages that support GUI interfaces. Program execution will cease only when the user quits the application by clicking a window's close button on the screen, for example. In the `repaintScreen()` method of the `MovingCircle` class, a circle is drawn at the x, y position, then x and y are both increased. The application sleeps for one-tenth of a second (the `SLEEP_TIME` value), and then the `repaintScreen()` method draws a new circle more to the right, further down, and a little larger. The effect is a moving circle that leaves a trail of smaller circles behind as it moves diagonally across the screen. Figure 12-18 shows the output as a Java version of the application executes.

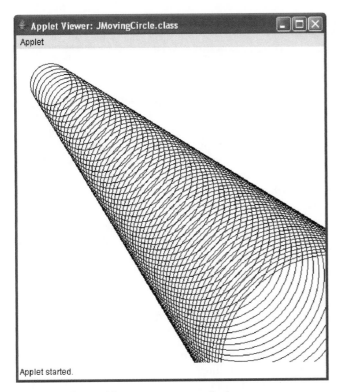

Figure 12-18 Output of the `MovingCircle` application

Although an object-oriented language might make it easy for you to draw geometric shapes, you can also substitute a variety of more sophisticated, predrawn animated images to achieve the graphic effects you want within your programs. An image is loaded in a separate thread of execution; this allows program execution to continue while the image loads. This is a great advantage because loading a large image can be time consuming.

> **» NOTE** Many animated images are available on the Web for you to use freely. Use your search engine to search for keywords such as *gif files*, *jpeg files*, and *animation* to find sources for shareware and freeware files.

TWO TRUTHS AND A LIE:
CREATING ANIMATION

1. Typically, any component you place on a screen has a horizontal, or x-axis, position as well as a vertical, or y-axis, position in a screen window.

2. The x-coordinate value increases as you travel from left to right across a window.

3. You almost always want to display animation cells as fast as your processor can handle.

The false answer is #3. If you display computer images as fast as your CPU can process them, you might not be able to see anything, so most computer animation employs a method to pause for short periods of time between animation cells.

UNDERSTANDING THE DISADVANTAGES OF TRADITIONAL ERROR-HANDLING TECHNIQUES

A great deal of the effort that goes into writing programs involves checking data items to make sure they are valid and reasonable. An important advantage of using GUI data-entry objects is that you often can control much of what a user enters by limiting the user's options. When you provide a user with a finite set of buttons to click, or a limited number of menu items from which to choose, the user does not have the opportunity to make unexpected, illegal, or bizarre choices. For example, if you provide a user with only two buttons, so that the only insurance policy types the user can select are *Health* or *Auto*, then you can eliminate checking for a valid policy type within your interactive program.

Not all user entries are limited to a finite number of possibilities, however; there are many occasions on which you must allow the user to enter data that you cannot validate—for example, names and addresses. Professional data-entry operators who create the files used in business computer applications (for example, typing data from phone or mail orders) spend their entire working day entering facts and figures that your applications use; operators can and do make typing errors. When programs depend on data entered by average users who are not trained typists, the chance of error is even more likely. Appendix E provides several useful techniques to check for valid and reasonable input data.

Programmers had to deal with error conditions long before object-oriented methods were conceived. Probably the most often used error-handling outcome was to terminate the program, or at least the module in which the offending statement occurred. For example, suppose a program prompts a user to enter an insurance premium type from the keyboard, and that the entered value should be "A" or "H" for *Auto* or *Health*. Figure 12-19 shows a segment of pseudocode that causes the insurance premium `calcRoutine()` module to end if `policyType` is invalid; in the shaded `if` statement, the module ends abruptly when `policyType` is not "A" or "H". Not only is this method of handling an error unforgiving, it isn't even structured. Recall that a structured module should have one entry and one exit point. The module in Figure 12-18 contains two exit points at the two `return` statements.

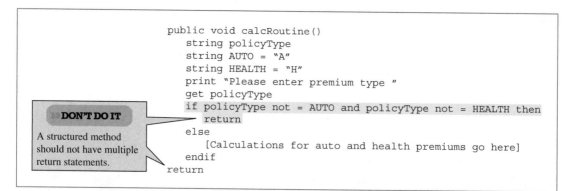

```
public void calcRoutine()
    string policyType
    string AUTO = "A"
    string HEALTH = "H"
    print "Please enter premium type "
    get policyType
    if policyType not = AUTO and policyType not = HEALTH then
        return
    else
        [Calculations for auto and health premiums go here]
    endif
return
```

»DON'T DO IT
A structured method should not have multiple return statements.

Figure 12-19 A method that handles an error in an unstructured manner

In the example in Figure 12-19, if `policyType` is an invalid value, the module in which the code appears is terminated. If the program that contains this module is part of a business program or a game, the user may be annoyed that the program has stopped working and that an early exit has been made. However, an early exit in a program that monitors a hospital patient's vital signs or navigates an airplane might cause results that are far more serious.

Rather than ending a method prematurely just because it encounters a piece of invalid data, a more elegant solution involves looping until the data item becomes valid, as shown in the highlighted portion of Figure 12-20. As long as the value of `policyType` is invalid, the user is continuously prompted to enter a new value. Only when `policyType` is "A" or "H", does the module continue.

```
public void calcRoutine()
    string policyType
    string AUTO = "A"
    string HEALTH = "H"
    print "Please enter premium type "
    get policyType
    while policyType not = AUTO and policyType not = HEALTH
        print "You must enter ", AUTO, " or ", HEALTH
        get policyType
    endwhile
    [Calculations for auto and health premiums go here]
return
```

Figure 12-20 Method that handles an error using a loop

There are at least two shortcomings to the error-handling logic shown in Figure 12-20. First, the module is not as reusable as it could be, and second, it is not as flexible as it might be.

One of the principles of modular and object-oriented programming is reusability. The module in Figure 12-20 is only reusable under limited conditions. The `calcRoutine()` module allows the user to reenter policy data any number of times, but other programs in the insurance system may need to limit the number of chances the user gets to enter correct data, or may allow no second chance at all. A more flexible `calcRoutine()` would simply calculate the premium amount without deciding what to do about data errors. The `calcRoutine()` method will be most flexible if it can detect an error and then notify the calling program or module that an error has occurred. Each program or module that uses the `calcRoutine()` module then can determine how it should best handle the mistake.

The other drawback to forcing the user to reenter data is that the technique works only with interactive programs. A more flexible program accepts any kind of input, including data stored on a disk. Program errors can occur as a result of many factors—for example, a disk drive might not be ready, a file might not exist on the disk, or stored data items might be invalid. You cannot continue to reprompt a disk file for valid data the way you can reprompt a user in an interactive program; if stored data is invalid, it remains invalid. Object-oriented exception-handling techniques overcome the limitations of simply repeating a request.

TWO TRUTHS AND A LIE:
UNDERSTANDING THE DISADVANTAGES OF TRADITIONAL ERROR-HANDLING TECHNIQUES

1. Programmers had to deal with error conditions long before object-oriented methods were conceived.
2. In traditional error handling, probably the most often used outcome was to call a module that explained the error to the user.
3. Traditional error-handling techniques are inflexible.

The false statement is #2. Probably the most often used error-handling outcome was to terminate the program, or at least the module in which the offending statement occurred.

UNDERSTANDING OBJECT-ORIENTED EXCEPTION HANDLING

Object-oriented and event-driven programs employ a more specific group of methods for handling errors called **exception-handling methods**. The methods check for and manage errors. The generic name used for errors in object-oriented languages is **exceptions** because, presumably, errors are not usual occurrences; they are the "exceptions" to the rule.

In object-oriented terminology, an exception is an object that represents an error. You **try** a module that might throw an exception. The module might **throw**, or pass, an exception out, and the original calling module can then **catch**, or receive, the exception and handle the problem. In some languages, the exception object that is thrown can be any data type—a numeric or string data item, or a programmer-created object such as a record complete with its own data fields and methods. Even when programmers use a language in which any data type can be thrown, most programmers throw an object of the built-in class `Exception`, or they derive a class from the built-in `Exception` class. For example, Figure 12-21 shows a `calcRoutine()` module that throws an exception only if `policyType` is neither "H" nor "A". If `policyType` is invalid, an object of type `Exception` named mistake is instantiated and thrown from the module by a `throw` statement. A **`throw` statement** is one that sends an `Exception` object out of a method so it can be handled elsewhere. If `policyType` is "H" or "A", the premium is calculated and the module ends naturally.

```
public void calcRoutine()
   string policyType
   string AUTO = "A"
   string HEALTH = "H"
   print "Please enter premium type "
   get policyType
   if policyType not = AUTO and policyType not = HEALTH
      Exception mistake
      throw mistake
   else
      [Calculations for auto and health premiums go here]
   endif
return
```

Figure 12-21 A method that creates and throws an `Exception` object

When you create a segment of code in which something might go wrong, you place the code in a **try block**, which is a block of code you attempt to execute while acknowledging that an exception might occur. A try block consists of the keyword try, followed by any number of statements, some that might cause an exception to be thrown. If a statement in the block causes an exception, the remaining statements in the try block do not execute and the try block is abandoned. For pseudocode purposes, you can end a try block with a sentinel such as endtry.

You almost always code at least one catch block immediately following a try block. A **catch block** is a segment of code that can handle an exception that might be thrown by the try block that precedes it. Each catch block "catches" one type of exception—in many languages the caught object must be of type Exception or one of its child classes. You create a catch block by typing the following elements:

» The keyword catch, followed by parentheses that contain an Exception type and an identifier

» Statements that take the action you want to use to handle the error condition

» For pseudocode purposes, an endcatch statement

Figure 12-22 shows a program that calls the calcRoutine() in Figure 12-21. Because calcRoutine() has the potential of throwing an exception, it is placed in a try block. If calcRoutine() throws an exception, the catch block in the program executes; if calcRoutine() does not throw an exception, the catch block is bypassed.

```
start
   try
      perform calcRoutine()
   endtry
   catch(Exception mistake)
      print "User entered invalid value"
   endcatch
      [Other statements that would execute
         whether or not the exception
         occurred could go here]
stop
```

Figure 12-22 A program that contains a try...catch pair

>> **NOTE** A catch block looks a lot like a method named catch() that takes an argument that is some type of Exception. However, it is not a method; it has no return type, and you can't call it directly.

>> **NOTE** Some programmers refer to a catch block as a catch clause.

In the program in Figure 12-22, a message is displayed when the exception is thrown. A different application might take different actions. For example, you might write an application in which the catch block calls a module that forces the policyType to "H" or to "A", or reprompts the user for a valid value. Various programs can use calcRoutine() and handle any error in a way most appropriate for that application.

>> **NOTE** In the method in Figure 12-22, the variable mistake in the catch block is an object of type Exception. The object is not used within the catch block, but it could be. For example, perhaps (depending on the language) the Exception class contains a method named getMessage() that returns a string that contains details about the cause of the error. In that case, you could place a statement such as print mistake.getMessage() in the catch block.

> **NOTE** When a program uses a module that throws an exception, the assumption is that usually there will be no need to throw the exception. In other words, exceptions are created and thrown only occasionally, when something goes wrong. Programmers sometimes refer to the situation where nothing goes wrong as the **sunny day case**.

The general principle of exception handling in object-oriented programming is that a module that uses data should be able to detect errors, but not be required to handle them. The handling should be left to the application that uses the object, so that each application can use each module appropriately.

USING BUILT-IN EXCEPTIONS AND CREATING YOUR OWN EXCEPTIONS

Many (but not all) OOP languages provide many built-in Exception types. For instance, Java, Visual Basic, and C# each provide dozens of categories of Exceptions that you can use in your programs. For example, in every object-oriented language there is an automatically created exception with a name similar to ArrayOutOfBoundsException that is thrown when you attempt to use an invalid subscript with an array. Similarly an exception with a name similar to DivideByZeroException might be generated automatically if your program attempts the invalid arithmetic action of dividing a number by zero.

Although some actions, such as dividing by zero, are errors in every programming situation, the programmers who create the built-in Exceptions that are part of a programming language cannot predict *every* condition that might be an Exception in your applications. For example, you might want to declare an Exception when your bank balance is negative or when an outside party attempts to access your e-mail account. Most organizations have specific rules for exceptional data; for example, an employee number must not exceed three digits, or an hourly salary must not be less than the legal minimum wage. Of course, you can handle these potential error situations with if statements, but you can also create your own Exceptions.

To create your own throwable Exception, you usually extend a built-in Exception class. For example, you might create a class named NegativeBankBalanceException or EmployeeNumberTooLargeException. Each would be a subclass of the more general, built-in Exception class. By inheriting from the Exception class, you gain access to methods contained in the parent class such as those that display a default message describing the Exception.

> **NOTE** Depending on the language you are using, you might be able to extend from other throwable classes as well as Exception.

> **NOTE** When you create an Exception, it's conventional to end its name with Exception, as in NegativeBankBalanceException.

Figure 12-23 shows a `HighBalanceException` class. This example assumes that the parent class contains a `setMessage()` method that assigns the passed string to a field in the parent class. Also assume that a parent class `getMessage()` method can retrieve the message. The `HighBalanceException` class constructor contains a single statement that sets the error message. This string would be retrieved if you called the `getMessage()` method using a `HighBalanceException` object.

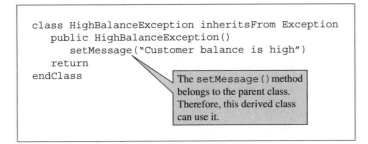

```
class HighBalanceException inheritsFrom Exception
    public HighBalanceException()
        setMessage("Customer balance is high")
    return
endClass
```

The `setMessage()` method belongs to the parent class. Therefore, this derived class can use it.

Figure 12-23 The `HighBalanceException` class

Figure 12-24 shows a `CustomerAccount` class that uses a `HighBalanceException`. The `CustomerAccount` class contains an account number, a balance, and a constant that stores a limit for customer credit. If the account balance exceeds the limit, an instance of the `HighBalanceException` class is created and thrown (see the shaded statements in the figure).

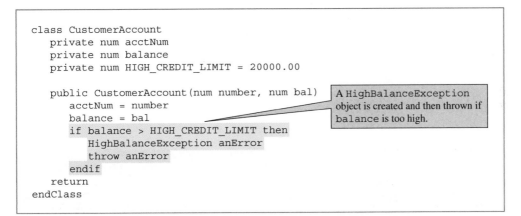

```
class CustomerAccount
    private num acctNum
    private num balance
    private num HIGH_CREDIT_LIMIT = 20000.00

    public CustomerAccount(num number, num bal)
        acctNum = number
        balance = bal
        if balance > HIGH_CREDIT_LIMIT then
            HighBalanceException anError
            throw anError
        endif
    return
endClass
```

A `HighBalanceException` object is created and then thrown if balance is too high.

Figure 12-24 The `CustomerAccount` class

Figure 12-25 shows an application that instantiates a `CustomerAccount`. In this application, a user is prompted for an account number and balance. After those values are entered, an attempt is made to construct a `CustomerAccount` in a `try` block (as shown in the first shaded section). If the attempt is successful—that is, if the CustomerAccount constructor does not throw an Exception—the CustomerAccount information is displayed. However, if the CustomerAccount constructor does throw a HighBalanceException, the catch block receives it (as shown in the second shaded section) and displays two messages. The catch block in this class demonstrates that you can decide to create your own message in the catch block, or use the message that is part of every HighBalanceException—the one that was set in the constructor in Figure 12-23. A different application could take any number of different actions in its catch block; for example, it could display only one of the messages or a different message, construct a new CustomerAccount object with a lower balance, or construct a different type of object—perhaps a child of CustomerAccount called PreferredCustomerAccount that allows a higher balance.

```
start
    num acctNum
    num balance

    print "Enter account number "
    get acctNum                          ┌─────────────────────────────────┐
    print "Enter balance "               │ In a full-blown application you might
    get balance                          │ want to perform other tasks at this point.
                                         │ For example, you might want to save
    try                                  │ CustomerAccount objects to a data file.
        CustomerAccount newAccount(acctNum, balance)
        print "Customer created"
    endtry

    catch(HighBalanceException hbe)
        print "Customer #", acctNum, "has a balance that is too high"
        print hbe.getMessage()
    endcatch
stop
```

Figure 12-25 An application that creates a CustomerAccount

> **NOTE** In Figure 12-25, balance is a local variable in the main program. When balance is passed to the CustomerAccount constructor, its value is assigned to the parameter bal as defined in the header of the CustomerAccount constructor class. Then, the parameter value is assigned to the balance field in the CustomerAccount class.

> **NOTE** In the `catch` block in the program in Figure 12-25, the `getMessage()` method is used with the `hbe` object. Because the `hbe` object is a `HighBalanceException`, which is an `Exception`, and because the `HighBalanceException` class defined in Figure 12-23 contains no method named `getMessage()`, you know that `HighBalanceException` must inherit the `getMessage()` method from the more general `Exception` class (or some other class from which `Exception` is derived).

You should not create an excessive number of special `Exception` types for your classes, especially if the language with which you are working already contains a built-in `Exception` that will catch the error. Extra `Exception` types add complexity for other programmers who use your classes. However, when appropriate, specialized `Exception` classes provide an elegant way for you to handle error situations. They enable you to separate your error code from the usual, nonexceptional sequence of events, and they allow clients of your classes to handle exceptional situations in the manner most suitable for their application.

> **NOTE** `Exception`s can be particularly useful when you throw them from constructors. Constructors do not have a return type, so they have no other way to send information back to the calling method.

> **NOTE** In most object-oriented programming languages, a module can throw any number of exceptions, with one restriction—there must be a `catch` block available for each type of exception. In other words, a module might throw a `HighBalanceException` under one error condition, a `NonNumericBalanceException` under another, and an `ArrayIndexOutOfBoundsException` under a third. When an exception is thrown, only the matching `catch` block executes. If all the `Exception` objects used are derived from a more general `Exception` class, then you can catch all the exceptions in a `catch` block that uses the parent class type.

TWO TRUTHS AND A LIE:
UNDERSTANDING OBJECT-ORIENTED EXCEPTION HANDLING

1. In object-oriented terminology, you try a module that might throw an exception; the module might throw, or pass, an exception out, and the original calling module can then catch, or receive, the exception and handle the problem.

2. A `catch` block is a segment of code that can handle an exception that might be thrown by the `try` block that precedes it.

3. The general principle of exception handling in object-oriented programming is that a module that uses data should be able to detect and handle most common errors.

The false statement is #3. The general principle of exception handling in object-oriented programming is that a module that uses data should be able to detect errors, but not be required to handle them.

CHAPTER SUMMARY

» Interacting with a computer operating system from the command line is difficult; it is easier to use an event-driven graphical user interface (GUI), in which users manipulate objects such as buttons and menus. Within an event-driven program, a component from which an event is generated is the source of the event. A listener is an object that is "interested in" an event to which you want it to respond.

» The possible events a user can initiate include a key press, mouse point, click, right-click, double-click, and drag. Common GUI components include labels, text fields, buttons, check boxes, check box groups, option buttons, lists, and toolbars. GUI components are excellent examples of the best principles of object-oriented programming (OOP)—they represent objects with attributes and methods that operate like black boxes.

» When you create a program that will use a GUI, the interface should be natural, predictable, attractive, easy to read, and nondistracting. It's helpful if the user can customize your applications. The program should be forgiving, and you should not forget that the GUI is only a means to an end.

» You can modify the attributes of GUI components. For example, you can set the size, color, screen location, font, visibility, and enabled status of the component.

» Developing an event-driven application is more complicated than developing a standard procedural program. You must understand the problem, create storyboards, define the objects, define the connections between the screens the user will see, plan the logic, code the program, translate the program into machine language, test the program, and put the program into production.

» A thread is the flow of execution of one set of program statements. Many applications follow a single thread; using multiple threads of execution is known as multithreading.

» Many object-oriented languages contain built-in classes that contain methods you can use to draw geometric figures on the screen. Typically, any component you place on the screen has a horizontal, or x-axis, position as well as a vertical, or y-axis, position in a screen window. You create computer animation by drawing a sequence of images that are shown in rapid succession.

» One common, traditional way to handle program errors was to terminate the program, or at least the module in which the offending statement occurred. However, this and other similar techniques made programs neither as reusable nor flexible as they might be.

» Exception-handling methods are those that handle errors in object-oriented and event-driven programs. When you try a statement or method, you attempt to use it while acknowledging that an exception might occur. If an exception does occur it is thrown. A catch block of the correct type can receive the exception and handle it. The general principle of exception handling in object-oriented programming is that a module that uses data should be able to detect errors, but not be required to handle them. The handling should be left to the application that uses the object, so that each application can use each module appropriately. Many OO languages provide built-in Exception types. You can also create your own by extending the Exception class.

KEY TERMS

An **operating system** is the software that you use to run a computer and manage its resources.

The **DOS prompt** is the command line in the DOS operating system.

Icons are small pictures on the screen that the user can select with a mouse.

An **event** is an occurrence that generates a message sent to an object.

GUI programs are called **event-driven** or **event-based** because actions occur in response to user-initiated events such as clicking a mouse button.

The **source of an event** is the component from which the event is generated.

A **listener** is an object that is "interested in" an event to which you want it to respond.

A **pixel** is a picture element, or one of the tiny dots of light that form a grid on your screen.

Accessibility issues are the screen design issues that make programs easier to use for people with physical limitations.

A **storyboard** represents a picture or sketch of a screen the user will see when running a program.

An **object dictionary** is a list of the objects used in a program, including which screens they are used on and whether any code, or script, is associated with them.

An **interactivity diagram** shows the relationship between screens in an interactive GUI program.

A **container** is a class of objects whose main purpose is to hold other elements—for example, a window.

In most object-oriented programming languages, you **register**, or sign up, components that will react to events initiated by other components.

A **thread** is the flow of execution of one set of program statements.

Multithreading is using multiple threads of execution.

The **x-axis** represents horizontal positions in a screen window.

The **y-axis** represents vertical positions in a screen window.

The **x-coordinate** value increases as you travel from left to right across a window.

The **y-coordinate** value increases as you travel from top to bottom in a window.

Exception-handling methods are techniques for handling errors employed by object-oriented and event-driven programs.

Exceptions is the generic term used for errors in object-oriented languages. This is because, presumably, errors are not usual occurrences; they are the "exceptions" to the rule.

In object-oriented terminology, you **try** a module that might throw an exception.

In object-oriented terminology, a module might **throw** out, or pass, an exception.

A module that tries a process that throws an exception can **catch**, or receive, the exception and handle the problem.

A **throw statement** is one that sends an `Exception` object out of a method so it can be handled elsewhere.

A **try block** is a block of code you attempt to execute while acknowledging that an exception might occur. A `try` block consists of the keyword `try`, followed by any number of statements, some that might cause an exception to be thrown.

A **catch block** is a segment of code that can handle an exception that might be thrown by the `try` block that precedes it.

The **sunny day case** is a case where nothing goes wrong.

REVIEW QUESTIONS

1. **As opposed to using a command line, an advantage to using an operating system that employs a GUI is _____.**

   a. you can interact directly with the operating system

   b. you do not have to deal with confusing icons

   c. you do not have to memorize complicated commands

   d. all of the above

2. **When users can initiate actions by clicking a mouse on an icon, the program is _____-driven.**

   a. event   c. command

   b. prompt   d. incident

3. **A component from which an event is generated is the _____ of the event.**

   a. base   c. listener

   b. icon   d. source

4. **An object that responds to an event is a _____.**

   a. source   c. transponder

   b. listener   d. snooper

5. **All of the following are user-initiated events except a _____.**

   a. key press   c. right mouse click

   b. key drag   d. mouse drag

6. **All of the following are typical GUI components except a _____.**

   a. label   c. list box

   b. text field   d. button box

7. **GUI components operate like _____ .**

    a. black boxes

    b. procedural functions

    c. looping structures

    d. command lines

8. **Which of the following is *not* a principle of good GUI design?**

    a. The interface should be predictable.

    b. The fancier the screen design, the better.

    c. The program should be forgiving.

    d. The user should be able to customize your applications.

9. **Which of the following aspects of a GUI layout is most predictable and natural for the user?**

    a. A menu bar runs down the right side of the screen.

    b. *Help* is the first option on a menu.

    c. A dollar sign icon represents saving a file.

    d. Pressing *Esc* allows the user to cancel a selection.

10. **In most GUI programming environments, you can change all of the following attributes of most components except their _____ .**

    a. color

    b. screen location

    c. size

    d. You can change all of these attributes.

11. **Depending on the programming language you use, you might _____ to change a screen component's attributes.**

    a. use an assignment statement

    b. call a module

    c. enter a value into a list of properties

    d. any of the above

12. **When you create an event-driven application, which of the following must be done before defining the objects you will use?**

    a. Plan the logic.

    b. Create storyboards.

    c. Test the program.

    d. Code the program.

13. **A _____ is a sketch of a screen the user will see when running a program.**

    a. flowchart

    b. hierarchy chart

    c. storyboard

    d. tale timber

14. **A list of objects used in a program is an object _____ .**

    a. thesaurus

    c. index

    b. glossary

    d. dictionary

15. **A(n) _____ diagram shows the connections between the various screens a user might see during a program's execution.**

    a. interactivity

    b. help

    c. cooperation

    d. communication

16. **The flow of execution of one set of program statements is a _____ .**

    a. thread

    c. path

    b. string

    d. route

17. **When a computer contains a single CPU, it can execute _____ computer instruction(s) at a time.**

    a. one

    b. several

    c. an unlimited number of

    d. from several to thousands (depending on the processor speed)

18. **You create computer animation by _____ .**

    a. drawing an image and setting its animation property to true

    b. drawing a single image and executing it on a multiprocessor system

    c. drawing a sequence of frames that are shown in rapid succession

    d. Animation is not used in computer applications.

19. **In object-oriented programs, errors are known as _____ .**

    a. faults

    c. exceptions

    b. gaffes

    d. omissions

20. **The general principle of exception handling in object-oriented programming is that a module that uses data should _____ .**

    a. be able to detect errors, but not be required to handle them

    b. be able to handle errors, but not detect them

    c. be able to handle and detect errors

    d. not be able to detect or handle errors

FIND THE BUGS

Each of the following pseudocode segments contains one or more bugs that you must find and correct.

1. **In the following code, the main program tries the `dataEntryRoutine()` module, which prompts the user for an item the user is ordering. If the item is valid, the price is returned from the function. Otherwise, an exception is thrown and the main program displays an error message and sets the price to 0. Finally, the main program calculates sales tax at a rate of 5%.**

```
start
   num price
   num TAXRATE = 0.05
   try
      dataEntryRoutine()
   endtry
   catch(error)
      price = 0
   endcatch
   print "Price is ", price
   print "Tax is ", price + TAXRATE
stop

num dataEntryRoutine()
   num NUM_ITEMS = 5
   num ITEMS[NUM_ITEMS] = 105, 108, 203, 211, 304
   num PRICES[NUM_ITEMS] = 0.99, 1.25, 3.59, 6.50, 7.99
   num itemNum
   num price
   string index
   string found = "N"
   print "Please enter item number "
   get itemNum
   index = 0
   while index <= NUM_ITEMS
      if itemNum = ITEMS[index] then
         price = PRICES[0]
         found = "Y"
      endif
   endwhile
   if found = "N" then
      Exception error
      throw error
   endif
   return price
```

2. The following main program represents a different application that can use the same `dataEntryRoutine()` module as in the previous exercise. Instead of forcing the user's price to 0 when an exception is thrown, this application requires the user to reenter the order until a valid item is ordered.

```
start
    num price
    num TAXRATE = 0.05
    string okFlag = "N"
    while okFlag not = "N"
        try
            price = dataEntryRoutine()
            okFlag = "Y"
        endtry
        catch(Exception)
            print "Please enter a valid item number "
        endcatch
    endwhile
    print "Price is ", price
    print "Tax is ", price * TAXRATE
stop
```

EXERCISES

1. Take a critical look at three GUI applications with which you are familiar—for example, a spreadsheet, a word-processing program, and a game. Describe how well each conforms to the GUI design guidelines listed in this chapter.

2. Select one element of poor GUI design in a program with which you are familiar. Describe how you would improve the design.

3. Select a GUI program that you have never used before. Describe how well it conforms to the GUI design guidelines listed in this chapter.

4. Design the storyboards, interactivity diagram, object dictionary, and any necessary scripts for an interactive program for customers of Sunflower Floral Designs.

   Allow customers the option of choosing a floral arrangement ($25 base price), cut flowers ($15 base price), or a corsage ($10 base price). Let the customer choose roses, daisies, chrysanthemums, or irises as the dominant flower. If the customer chooses roses, add $5 to the base price. After the customer clicks an `Order Now` button, display the price of the order.

5. Design the storyboards, interactivity diagram, object dictionary, and any necessary scripts for an interactive program for customers of Toby's Travels.

   Allow customers the option of at least five trip destinations and four means of transportation, each with a unique price. After the customer clicks the `Plan Trip Now` button, display the price of the trip.

6. **Design the storyboards, interactivity diagram, object dictionary, and any necessary scripts for an interactive program for customers of The Mane Event Hair Salon.**

   Allow customers the option of choosing a haircut ($15), coloring ($25), or perm ($45). After the customer clicks a button labeled `Select` button, display the price of the service.

7. **Complete the following tasks:**

   a. Design a method that calculates the cost of a painting job for College Student Painters. Variables include whether the job is location "I" for interior, which carries a base price of $100, or "E" for exterior, which carries a base price of $200. College Student Painters charges an additional $5 per square foot over the base price. The method should throw an exception if the location code is invalid.

   b. Write a module that calls the module designed in Exercise 7a. If the module throws an exception, force the price of the job to 0.

   c. Write a module that calls the module designed in Exercise 7a. If the module throws an exception, require the user to reenter the location code.

   d. Write a module that calls the module designed in Exercise 7a. If the module throws an exception, force the location code to "E" and the base price to $200.

8. **Complete the following tasks:**

   a. Design a method that calculates the cost of a semester's tuition for a college student at Mid-State University. Variables include whether the student is an in-state resident ("I" for in-state or "O" for out-of-state) and the number of credit hours for which the student is enrolling. The method should throw an exception if the residency code is invalid. Tuition is $75 per credit hour for in-state students and $125 per credit hour for out-of-state students. If a student enrolls in six hours or fewer, there is an additional $100 surcharge. Any student enrolled in 19 hours or more pays only the rate for 18 credit hours.

   b. Write a module that calls the module designed in Exercise 8a. If the module throws an exception, force the tuition to 0.

GAME ZONE

1. In Chapter 9, you created the logic for a Tic Tac Toe game. Design the storyboards, interactivity diagram, object dictionary, and any necessary scripts for an interactive program that allows users to play a Tic Tac Toe game by clicking a three-by-three grid of buttons.

2. Design the storyboards, interactivity diagram, object dictionary, and any necessary scripts for an interactive program that allows a user to play a card game named Lucky Seven. In real life, the game can be played with seven cards, each containing a number from 1 through 7, that are shuffled and dealt number-side down. To start the game, a player turns over any card. The exposed number on the card determines the position (reading from left to right) of the next card that must be turned over. For example, if the player turns over the first card and its number is 7, the next card turned must be the seventh card (counting from left to right). If the player turns over a card whose number denotes a position that was already turned, the player loses the game. If the player succeeds in turning over all seven cards, the player wins.

   Instead of cards, you will use seven buttons labeled 1 through 7 from left to right. Randomly associate one of the seven values 1 through 7 with each button. (In other words, the associated value might or might not be equivalent to the button's labeled value.) When the player clicks a button, reveal the associated hidden value. If the value represents the position of a button already clicked, the player loses. If the revealed number represents an available button, force the user to click it—that is, do not take any action until the user clicks the correct button. After a player clicks a button, remove the button from play.

   For example, a player might click Button 7, revealing a 4. Then the player clicks Button 4, revealing a 2. Then the player clicks Button 2, revealing a 7. The player loses because Button 7 is already "used."

3. In the Game Zone sections of Chapters 6 and 7, you designed and fine-tuned the logic for the game Hangman, in which the user guesses letters in a series of hidden words. Design the storyboards, interactivity diagram, object dictionary, and any necessary scripts for a version of the game in which the user clicks lettered buttons to fill in the secret words. This game is similar to the traditional letter-guessing game Hangman; draw a "hanged" person piece by piece with each missed letter. For example, when the user chooses a correct letter, place it in the appropriate position or positions in the word, but the first time the user chooses a letter that is not in the target word, draw a head for the "hanged" man. The second time the user makes an incorrect guess, add a torso. Continue with arms and legs. If the complete body is drawn before the user has guessed all the letters in the word, display a message indicating that the player has lost the game. If the user completes the word before all the body parts are drawn, display a message that the player has won. Assume you can use built-in methods named `drawCircle()` and `drawLine()`. The `drawCircle()` method requires three parameters—the x- and y-coordinates of the center, and a radius size. The `drawLine()` method requires four parameters—the x- and y-coordinates of the start of the line, and the x- and y-coordinates of the end of the line.

4. In Chapter 3, you learned that in many programming languages you can generate a random number between 1 and a limiting value named `LIMIT` by using a statement similar to `randomNumber = random(LIMIT)`. In Chapters 4 and 5, you created and fine-tuned the logic for a guessing game in which the application generates a random number and the player tries to guess it. As written, the game should work as long as the player enters numeric guesses. However, if the player enters a letter or other nonnumeric character, the game throws an exception. Improve the game by handling any exception so that the user is informed of the error and allowed to attempt correct data entry again.

DETECTIVE WORK

1. Find out what you can about the Visual Basic programming language. What are its origins? Describe the interface with which programmers work in this language. For what types of applications is Visual Basic most often used?

2. Is there a gender gap in programming? Is it different for traditional Web programming and GUI Web-based programming?

UP FOR DISCUSSION

1. Making exciting, entertaining, professional-looking GUI applications becomes easier once you learn to include graphics images. You can copy graphics images from many locations on the Web. Should there be any restrictions on what graphics you use? Does it make a difference if you are writing programs for your own enjoyment as opposed to putting them on the Web where others can see them? Is using photographs different from using drawings? Does it matter if the photographs contain recognizable people? Would you impose any restrictions on images posted to your organization's Web site?

2. Playing computer games has been shown to increase the level of dopamine in the human brain. High levels of this substance are associated with addiction to drugs. Suppose you work for a company that manufactures games and it decides to research how its games can produce more dopamine in the brains of players. Would you support the company's decision?

3. If you are completing all the programming exercises at the ends of the chapters in this book, you are beginning to understand that working programs require a lot of time to plan, write, and test. Professional programs require even more hours of work. In the workplace, programs frequently must be completed by strict deadlines—for example, a tax-calculating program must be completed by year's end, or an advertising Web site must be completed by the launch of the product. Programmers often find themselves working into the evenings or weekends to complete rush projects at work. How would you feel about having to do this? What types of compensation would make the extra hours worthwhile for you?

4. When people use interactive programs on the Web, when do you feel it is appropriate to track which buttons they select or to record the data they enter? When is it not appropriate? Does it matter how long the data is stored? Does it matter if a profit is made from using the data?

SYSTEM MODELING WITH THE UML

In this chapter you will:

Understand the need for system modeling

Be able to describe the UML

Understand use case diagrams

Understand class and object diagrams

Understand sequence and communication diagrams

Understand state machine diagrams

Understand activity diagrams

Understand component and deployment diagrams

Be able to diagram exception handling

Be able to decide when to use the UML and which
UML diagrams to use

UNDERSTANDING THE NEED FOR SYSTEM MODELING

Computer programs often stand alone to solve a user's specific problem. For example, a program might exist only to print paychecks for the current week. Most computer programs, however, are part of a larger system. Your company's payroll system might consist of dozens of programs, including programs that produce employee paychecks, apply raises to employee records, alter employee deduction options, and print federal and state tax forms at the end of the year. Each program you write as part of a system might be related to several others. Some programs depend on input from other programs in the system or produce output to be fed into other programs. Similarly, an organization's accounting, inventory, and customer ordering systems all consist of many interrelated programs. Producing a set of programs that operate together correctly requires careful planning. **System design** is the detailed specification of how all the parts of a system will be implemented and coordinated.

> **》》NOTE** Usually, system design refers to computer system design, but even a noncomputerized, manual system can benefit from good design techniques.

Many textbooks cover the theories and techniques of system design. If you continue to study in a Computer Information Systems program at a college or university, you probably will be required to take a semester-long course in system design. Explaining all the techniques of system design is beyond the scope of this book. However, some basic principles parallel those you have used throughout this book in designing individual programs:

- 》 Large systems are easier to understand when you break them down into subsystems.
- 》 Good modeling techniques are increasingly important as the size and complexity of systems increase.
- 》 Good models promote communication among technical and nontechnical workers while ensuring good business solutions.

In other words, developing a model for a single program or an entire business system requires organization and planning. In this chapter, you learn the basics of one popular design tool, the UML, which is based on these principles. The UML, or Unified Modeling Language, allows you to envision systems with an object-oriented perspective, breaking a system into subsystems, focusing on the big picture, and hiding the implementation details. In addition, the UML provides a means for programmers and businesspeople to communicate about system design. It also provides a way to plan to divide responsibilities for large systems. Understanding the UML's principles helps you design a variety of system types and talk about systems with the people who will use them.

> **》》NOTE** In addition to modeling a system before creating it, system analysts sometimes model an existing system to get a better picture of its operation. Creating a model for an existing system is called **reverse engineering**.

TWO TRUTHS AND A LIE:
UNDERSTANDING THE NEED FOR SYSTEM MODELING

1. Large systems are easier to understand when you break them down into subsystems.

2. Good modeling techniques are most important in small systems.

3. Good models promote communication among technical and nontechnical workers while ensuring good business solutions.

The false statement is #2. Good modeling techniques are increasingly important as the size and complexity of systems increase.

WHAT IS UML?

The **UML** is a standard way to specify, construct, and document systems that use object-oriented methods. (The UML is a modeling language, not a programming language. The systems you develop using the UML probably will be implemented later in object-oriented programming languages such as Java, C++, C#, or Visual Basic.) As with flowcharts, pseudocode, hierarchy charts, and class diagrams, the UML has its own notation that consists of a set of specialized shapes and conventions. You can use the UML's shapes to construct different kinds of software diagrams and model different kinds of systems. Just as you can use a flowchart or hierarchy chart to diagram real-life activities, organizational relationships, or computer programs, you can also use the UML for many purposes, including modeling business activities, organizational processes, or software systems.

> **NOTE** The UML was created at Rational Software by Grady Booch, Ivar Jacobson, and Jim Rumbaugh. The Object Management Group (OMG) adopted the UML as a standard for software modeling in 1997. The OMG includes more than 800 software vendors, developers, and users who seek a common architectural framework for object-oriented programming. The UML is in its second major version; the current version is UML 2.1.1. You can view or download the entire UML specification and usage guidelines from the OMG at *www.uml.org*.

> **NOTE** You can purchase compilers for most programming languages from a variety of manufacturers. Similarly, you can purchase a variety of tools to help you create UML diagrams, but the UML itself is vendor-independent.

When you draw a flowchart or write pseudocode, your purpose is to illustrate the individual steps in a process. When you draw a hierarchy chart, you use more of a "big picture" approach. As with a hierarchy chart, you use the UML to create top-view diagrams of business processes that let you hide details and focus on functionality. This approach lets you start with a generic view of an application and introduce details and complexity later. UML diagrams are useful as you begin designing business systems, when customers who are not technically oriented must accurately communicate with the technical staff members who will create the actual systems. The UML was intentionally designed to be nontechnical so that developers, customers, and implementers (programmers) could all "speak the same language." If business and technical people can agree on what a system should do, the chances improve that the final product will be useful.

The UML is very large; its documentation is more than 800 pages. The UML provides 13 diagram types that you can use to model systems. Each of the diagram types lets you see a business process from a different angle, and appeals to a different type of user. Just as an architect, interior designer, electrician, and plumber use different diagram types to describe the same building, different computer users appreciate different perspectives. For example, a business user most values a system's use case diagrams because they illustrate who is doing what. On the other hand, programmers find class and object diagrams more useful because they help explain details of how to build classes and objects into applications.

The UML superstructure defines six structure diagrams, three behavior diagrams, and four interaction diagrams. The 13 UML diagram types are:

» **Structure diagrams** emphasize the "things" in a system. These include:
  » Class diagrams
  » Object diagrams
  » Component diagrams
  » Composite structure diagrams
  » Package diagrams
  » Deployment diagrams
» **Behavior diagrams** emphasize what happens in a system. These include:
  » Use case diagrams
  » Activity diagrams
  » State machine diagrams
» **Interaction diagrams** emphasize the flow of control and data among the things in the system being modeled. These include:
  » Sequence diagrams
  » Communication diagrams
  » Timing diagrams
  » Interaction overview diagrams

> **»» NOTE** Interaction diagrams are considered to be a subset of behavior diagrams.

> **»» NOTE** You can categorize UML diagrams as those that illustrate the dynamic, or changing, aspects of a system and those that illustrate the static, or steady, aspects of a system. Dynamic diagrams include use case, sequence, communication, state machine, and activity diagrams. Static diagrams include class, object, component, and deployment diagrams.

> **»» NOTE** Diagram names have evolved. For example, in UML 1.5, communication diagrams were called collaboration diagrams, and state machine diagrams were called statechart diagrams.

> **»» NOTE**
> The UML Web site, at *www.uml.org*, provides links to several UML tutorials.

Each of the UML diagram types supports multiple variations, and explaining them all would require an entire textbook. This chapter presents an overview and simple examples of several diagram types, which provides a good foundation for further study of the UML.

USING USE CASE DIAGRAMS

The **use case diagram** shows how a business works from the perspective of those who approach it from the outside, or those who actually use the business. This category includes many types of users—for example, employees, customers, and suppliers. Although users can also be governments, private organizations, machines, or other systems, it is easiest to think of them as people, so users are called actors and are represented by stick figures in use case diagrams. The actual use cases are represented by ovals.

Use cases do not necessarily represent all the functions of a system; they are the system functions or services that are visible to the system's actors. In other words, they represent the cases by which an actor uses and presumably benefits from the system. Determining all the cases for which users interact with systems helps you divide a system logically into functional parts.

Establishing use cases usually follows from analyzing the main events in a system. For example, from a librarian's point of view, two main events are `acquireNewBook()` and `checkOutBook()`. Figure 13-1 shows a use case diagram for these two events.

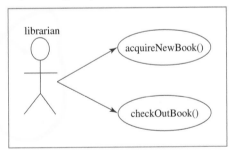

Figure 13-1 Use case diagram for librarian

> **NOTE** Many system developers would use the standard English form to describe activities in their UML diagrams—for example, `check out book` instead of `checkOutBook()`, which looks like a programming method call. Because you are used to seeing method names in camel casing and with trailing parentheses throughout this book, this discussion of the UML continues with the same format.

In many systems, there are variations in use cases. The three possible types of variations are:

» Extend

» Include

» Generalization

An **extend variation** is a use case variation that shows functions beyond those found in a base case. In other words, an extend variation is usually an optional activity. For example, checking out a book for a new library patron who doesn't have a library card is slightly more complicated than checking out a book for an existing patron. Each variation in the sequence of actions required in a use case is a **scenario**. Each use case has at least one main scenario, but might have several more that are extensions or variations of the main one. Figure 13-2 shows how you would diagram the relationship between the use case checkOutBook() and the more specific scenario checkOutBookForNewPatron(). Extended use cases are shown in an oval with a dashed arrow pointing to the more general base case.

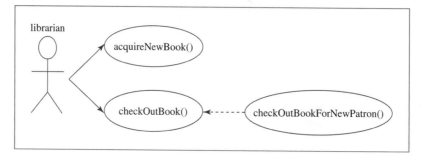

Figure 13-2 Use case diagram for librarian with scenario extension

For clarity, you can add "<<extend>>" near the line that shows a relationship extension. Such a feature, which adds to the UML vocabulary of shapes to make them more meaningful for the reader, is called a **stereotype**. Figure 13-3 includes a stereotype.

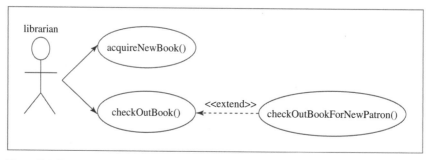

Figure 13-3 Use case diagram for librarian using stereotype

In addition to extend relationships, use case diagrams can also show include relationships. You use an **include variation** when a case can be part of multiple use cases. This concept is very much like that of a subroutine or submodule. You show an include use case in an oval with a dashed arrow pointing to the subroutine use case. For example, issueLibraryCard() might be a function of checkOutBook(), which is used when the patron checking out a book is new, but it might also be a function of registerNewPatron(), which occurs when a patron registers at the library but does not want to check out books yet. See Figure 13-4.

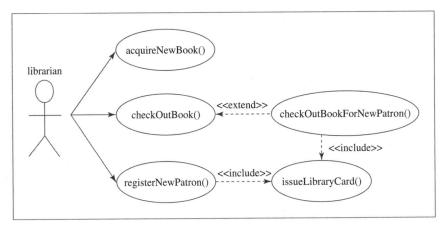

Figure 13-4 Use case diagram for librarian using include relationship

You use a **generalization variation** when a use case is less specific than others, and you want to be able to substitute the more specific case for a general one. For example, a library has certain procedures for acquiring new materials, whether they are videos, tapes, CDs, hardcover books, or paperbacks. However, the procedures might become more specific during a particular acquisition—perhaps the librarian must procure plastic cases for circulating videos or assign locked storage locations for CDs. Figure 13-5 shows the generalization `acquireNewItem()` with two more specific situations: acquiring videos and acquiring CDs. The more specific scenarios are attached to the general scenario with open-headed dashed arrows.

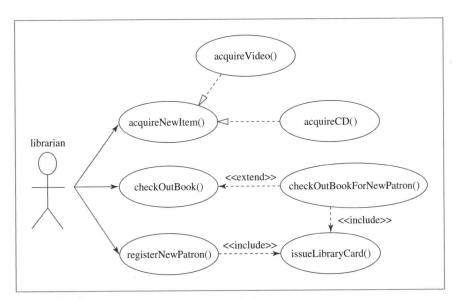

Figure 13-5 Use case diagram for librarian with generalizations

Many use case diagrams show multiple actors. For example, Figure 13-6 shows that a library clerk cannot perform as many functions as a librarian; the clerk can check out books and register new patrons but cannot acquire new materials.

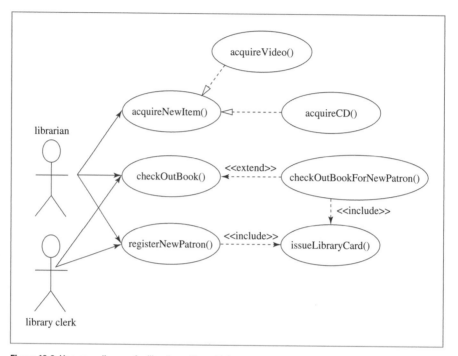

Figure 13-6 Use case diagram for librarian with multiple actors

While designing an actual library system, you could add many more use cases and actors to the use case diagram. The purpose of such a diagram is to encourage discussion between the system developer and the library staff. Library staff members do not need to know any of the technical details of the system that the analysts will eventually create, and they certainly do not need to understand computers or programming. However, by viewing the use cases, the library staff can visualize activities they perform while doing their jobs and correct the system developer if inaccuracies exist. The final software products developed for such a system are far more likely to satisfy users than those developed without this design step.

A use case diagram is only a tool to aid communication. No single "correct" use case diagram exists; you might correctly represent a system in several ways. For example, you might choose to emphasize the actors in the library system, as shown in Figure 13-7, or to emphasize system requirements, as shown in Figure 13-8. Diagrams that are too crowded are neither visually pleasing nor very useful. Therefore, the use case diagram in Figure 13-7 shows all the specific actors and their relationships, but purposely omits more specific system functions, whereas Figure 13-8 shows many actions that are often hidden from users but purposely omits more specific actors. For example, the activities carried out to manageNetworkOutage(), if done properly, should be invisible to library patrons checking out books.

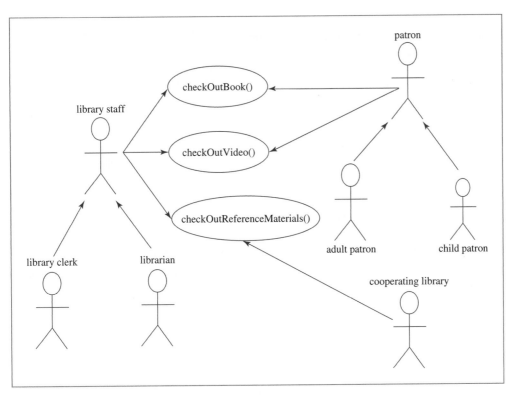

Figure 13-7 Use case diagram emphasizing actors

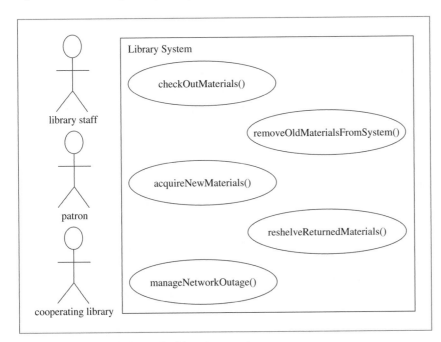

Figure 13-8 Use case diagram emphasizing system requirements

In Figure 13-8, the relationship lines between the actors and use cases have been removed because the emphasis is on the system requirements, and too many lines would make the diagram confusing. When system developers omit parts of diagrams for clarity, they refer to the missing parts as **elided**. For the sake of clarity, eliding extraneous information is perfectly acceptable. The main purpose of UML diagrams is to facilitate clear communication.

TWO TRUTHS AND A LIE:
USING USE CASE DIAGRAMS

1. A use case diagram shows how a business works from the perspective of those who approach it from the outside, or those who actually use the business.

2. Users are called actors and are represented by stick figures in use case diagrams. The actual use cases are represented by ovals.

3. Use cases are important because they describe all the functions of a system.

The false statement is #3. Use cases do not necessarily represent all the functions of a system; they are the system functions or services that are visible to the system's actors.

USING CLASS AND OBJECT DIAGRAMS

You use a class diagram to illustrate the names, attributes, and methods of a class or set of classes. Class diagrams are more useful to a system's programmers than to its users because they closely resemble code the programmers will write. A class diagram illustrating a single class contains a rectangle divided into three sections: the top section contains the name of the class, the middle section contains the names of the attributes, and the bottom section contains the names of the methods. Figure 13-9 shows the class diagram for a Book class. Each Book object contains an idNum, title, and author. Each Book object also contains methods to create a Book when it is acquired and to retrieve or get title and author information when the Book object's idNum is supplied.

Figure 13-9 Book class diagram

» NOTE
You first used class diagrams in Chapter 11.

In the preceding section, you learned how to use generalizations with use case diagrams to show general and more specific use cases. With use case diagrams, you drew an open-headed arrow from the more specific case to the more general one. Similarly, you can use generalizations with class diagrams to show more general (or parent) classes and more specific (or child) classes that inherit attributes from parents. For example, Figure 13-10 shows Book and Video classes that are more specific than the general LibraryItem class. All LibraryItem objects contain an idNum and title, but each Book item also contains an author, and each Video item also contains a runningTime. In addition, Video items contain a `rewind()` method not found in the more general `LibraryItem` class. Child classes contain all the attributes of their parents and usually contain additional attributes not found in the parent.

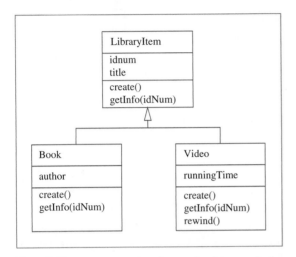

Figure 13-10 `LibraryItem` class diagram showing generalization

》NOTE When a child class contains a method with the same signature as one in the parent class, then the child class version **overrides** the version in the parent class. That is, by default, the child class version is used with any child class object. The `create()` and `getInfo()` methods in the `Book` and `Video` classes override the versions in the `LibraryItem` class.

Class diagrams can include symbols that show the relationships between objects. You can show two types of relationships:

» An association relationship

» A whole-part relationship

An **association relationship** describes the connection or link between objects. You represent an association relationship between classes with a straight line. Frequently, you include information about the arithmetical relationship or ratio (called **cardinality** or **multiplicity**) of the objects. For example, Figure 13-11 shows the association relationship between a `Library` and the `LibraryItems` it lends. Exactly one `Library` object exists, and it can be associated with any number of `LibraryItems` from 0 to infinity, which is represented by an asterisk. Figure 13-12 adds the `Patron` class to the diagram and shows how you indicate that any number of `Patrons` can be associated with the `Library`, but that each `Patron` can borrow only up to five `LibraryItems` at a time, or currently might not be borrowing any. In addition, each `LibraryItem` can be associated with at most one `Patron`, but at any given time might not be on loan.

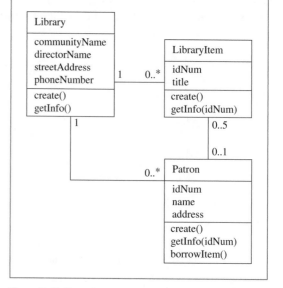

Figure 13-12 Class diagram with several association relationships

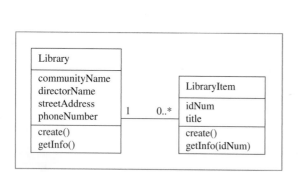

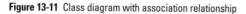

Figure 13-11 Class diagram with association relationship

A **whole-part relationship** describes an association in which one or more classes make up the parts of a larger whole class. For example, 50 states "make up" the United States, and 10 departments might "make up" a company. This type of relationship is also called an **aggregation** and is represented by an open diamond at the "whole part" end of the line that indicates the relationship. You can also call a whole-part relationship a **has-a relationship** because the phrase describes the association between the whole and one of its parts; for example, "The library has a Circulation Department." Figure 13-13 shows a whole-part relationship for a Library.

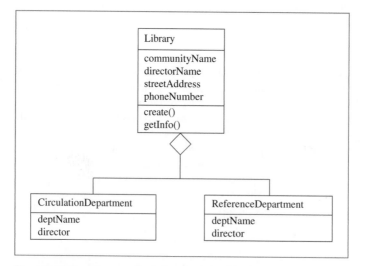

Figure 13-13 Class diagram with whole-part relationship

Object diagrams are similar to class diagrams, but they model specific instances of classes. You use an object diagram to show a snapshot of an object at one point in time, so you can more easily understand its relationship to other objects. Imagine looking at the travelers in a major airport. If you try to watch them all at once, you see a flurry of activity, but it is hard to understand all the tasks (buying a ticket, checking luggage, and so on) a traveler must accomplish to take a trip. However, if you concentrate on one traveler and follow his or her actions through the airport from arrival to takeoff, you get a clearer picture of the required activities. An object diagram serves the same purpose; you concentrate on a specific instance of a class to better understand how a class works.

Figure 13-14 contains an object diagram showing the relationship between one `Library`, `LibraryItem`, and `Patron`. Notice the similarities between Figures 13-12 and 13-14. If you need to describe the relationship between three classes, you can use either model—a class diagram or an object diagram—interchangeably. You simply use the model that seems clearer to you and your intended audience.

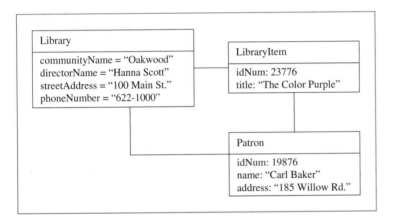

Figure 13-14 Object diagram for `Library`

USING SEQUENCE AND COMMUNICATION DIAGRAMS

You use a **sequence diagram** to show the timing of events in a single use case. A sequence diagram makes it easier to see the order in which activities occur. The horizontal axis (x-axis) of a sequence diagram represents objects, and the vertical axis (y-axis) represents time. You create a sequence diagram by placing objects that are part of an activity across the top of the diagram along the x-axis, starting at the left with the object or actor that begins the action. Beneath each object on the x-axis, you place a vertical dashed line that represents the period of time the object exists. Then, you use horizontal arrows to show how the objects communicate with each other over time.

For example, Figure 13-15 shows a sequence diagram for a scenario that a librarian can use to create a book check-out record. The librarian begins a `create()` method with `Patron idNum` and `Book idNum` information. The `BookCheckOutRecord` object requests additional `Patron` information (such as `name` and `address`) from the `Patron` object with the correct `Patron idNum`, and additional `Book` information (such as `title` and `author`) from the `Book` object with the correct `Book idNum`. When `BookCheckOutRecord` contains all the data it needs, a completed record is returned to the librarian.

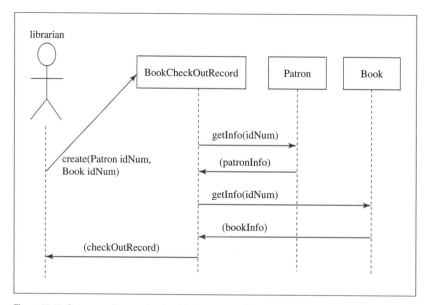

Figure 13-15 Sequence diagram for checking out a `Book` for a `Patron`

>> **NOTE** In Figures 13-15 and 13-16, `patronInfo` and `bookInfo` represent group items that contain all of a `Patron`'s and `Book`'s data. For example, `patronInfo` might contain `idNum`, `lastName`, `firstName`, `address`, and `phoneNumber`, all of which have been defined as attributes of that class.

A **communication diagram** emphasizes the organization of objects that participate in a system. It is similar to a sequence diagram, except that it contains sequence numbers to represent the precise order in which activities occur. Communication diagrams focus on object roles instead of the times that messages are sent. Figure 13-16 shows the same sequence of events as Figure 13-15, but the steps to creating a `BookCheckOutRecord` are clearly numbered (see the shaded sections of the figure). Decimal numbered steps (1.1, 1.2, and so on) represent substeps of the main steps. Checking out a library book is a fairly straightforward event, so a sequence diagram sufficiently illustrates the process. Communication diagrams become more useful with more complicated systems.

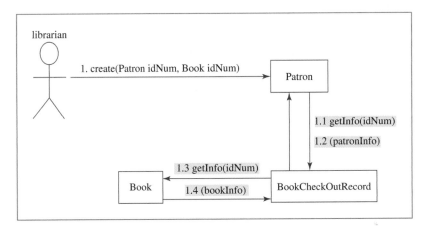

Figure 13-16 Communication diagram for `Book` class

TWO TRUTHS AND A LIE:

USING SEQUENCE AND COMMUNICATION DIAGRAMS

1. You use a sequence diagram to show the timing of events in a single use case.

2. A communication diagram emphasizes the timing of events in multiple use cases.

3. Communication diagrams focus on object roles instead of the times that messages are sent.

The false statement is #2. A communication diagram emphasizes the organization of objects that participate in a system.

USING STATE MACHINE DIAGRAMS

A **state machine diagram** shows the different statuses of a class or object at different points in time. You use a state machine diagram to illustrate aspects of a system that show interesting changes in behavior as time passes. Conventionally, you use rounded rectangles to represent each state and labeled arrows to show the sequence in which events affect the states. A solid dot indicates the start and stop states for the class or object. Figure 13-17 contains a state machine diagram you can use to describe the states of a Book.

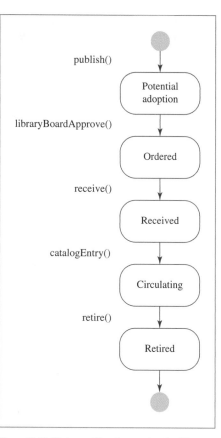

Figure 13-17 State machine diagram for checking out a Book for a Patron

> **NOTE** To make sure that your diagrams are clear, you should use the correct symbol in each UML diagram you create, just as you should use the correct symbol in each program flowchart. However, if you create a flowchart and use a rectangle for an input or output statement where a parallelogram is conventional, others will still understand your meaning. Similarly, with UML diagrams, the exact shape you use is not nearly as important as the sequence of events and relationships between objects.

TWO TRUTHS AND A LIE:
USING STATE MACHINE DIAGRAMS

1. A state machine diagram shows the permanent status of fixed data in a class.

2. You use a state machine diagram to illustrate aspects of a system that show interesting changes in behavior as time passes.

3. Conventionally, you use rounded rectangles to represent each state and labeled arrows to show the sequence in which events affect the states.

The false statement is #1. A state machine diagram shows the different statuses of a class or object at different points in time.

USING ACTIVITY DIAGRAMS

The UML diagram that most closely resembles a conventional flowchart is an activity diagram. In an **activity diagram**, you show the flow of actions of a system, including branches that occur when decisions affect the outcome. Conventionally, activity diagrams use flowchart start and stop symbols (called lozenges) to describe actions and solid dots to represent start and stop states. Like flowcharts, activity diagrams use diamonds to describe decisions. Unlike the diamonds in flowcharts, the diamonds in UML activity diagrams usually are empty; the possible outcomes are documented along the branches emerging from the decision symbol. As an example, Figure 13-18 shows a simple activity diagram with a single branch.

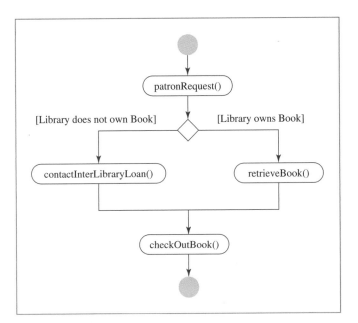

Figure 13-18 Activity diagram showing branch

>> **NOTE** In the first major version of the UML (UML 1.0), each lozenge was an activity. Starting with the second major version (UML 2.0), each lozenge is an action and a group of actions is an activity.

Many real-life systems contain actions that are meant to occur simultaneously. For example, when you apply for a home mortgage with a bank, a bank officer might perform a credit or background check while an appraiser determines the value of the house you are buying. When both actions are complete, the loan process continues. UML activity diagrams use forks and joins to show simultaneous activities. A **fork** is similar to a decision, but whereas the flow of control follows only one path after a decision, a fork defines a branch in which all paths are followed simultaneously. A **join**, as its name implies, reunites the flow of control after a fork. You indicate forks and joins with thick straight lines. Figure 13-19 shows how you might model the way an interlibrary loan system processes book requests. When a request is received, simultaneous searches begin at three local libraries that are part of the library system.

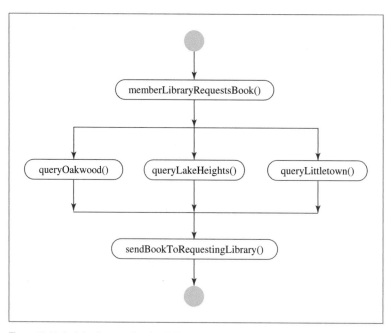

Figure 13-19 Activity diagram showing fork and join

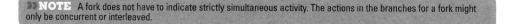

»NOTE A fork does not have to indicate strictly simultaneous activity. The actions in the branches for a fork might only be concurrent or interleaved.

An activity diagram can contain a time signal. A **time signal** indicates that a specific amount of time should pass before an action starts. The time signal looks like two stacked triangles (resembling the shape of an hourglass). Figure 13-20 shows a time signal indicating that if a patron requests a book, and the book is checked out to another patron, then only if the book's due date has passed should a request to return the book be issued. In activity diagrams for other systems, you might see explanations at time signals, such as "10 hours have passed" or "at least January 1st". If an action is time-dependent, whether by a fraction of a second or by years, using a time signal is appropriate.

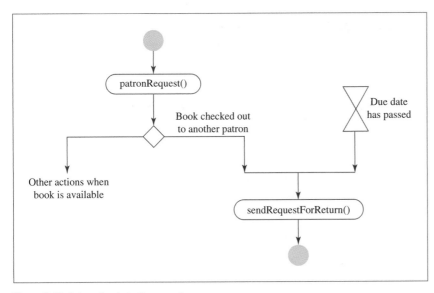

Figure 13-20 A time signal starting an action

»NOTE
The time signal
was a new feature
starting in UML 2.0.

»**NOTE** The connector is a fairly recently introduced symbol to the UML. It is a small circle used to connect diagrams that continue on a new page.

TWO TRUTHS AND A LIE:
USING ACTIVITY DIAGRAMS

1. The activity diagram is the UML diagram that most closely resembles a hierarchy chart.

2. Like flowcharts, activity diagrams use diamonds to describe decisions, but unlike the diamonds in flowcharts, the diamonds in UML activity diagrams are usually empty.

3. In an activity diagram, a fork is similar to a decision; a join, as its name implies, reunites the flow of control after a fork.

The false statement is #1. The activity diagram is the UML diagram that most closely resembles a conventional flowchart.

USING COMPONENT AND DEPLOYMENT DIAGRAMS

Component and deployment diagrams model the physical aspects of systems. You use a **component diagram** when you want to emphasize the files, database tables, documents, and other components that a system's software uses. You use a **deployment diagram** when you want to focus on a system's hardware. You can use a variety of icons in each type of diagram, but each icon must convey meaning to the reader. Figures 13-21 and 13-22 show component and deployment diagrams, respectively, that illustrate aspects of a library system. Figure 13-21 contains icons that symbolize paper and Internet requests for library items, the library database, and two tables that constitute the database. Figure 13-22 shows some commonly used icons that represent hardware components.

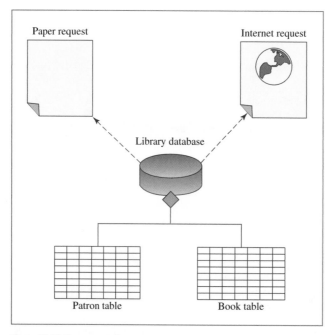

Figure 13-21 Component diagram

> **»NOTE** In Figure 13-21, notice the filled diamond connecting the two tables to the database. Just as it does in a class diagram, the diamond aggregation symbol shows the whole-part relationship of the tables to the database. You use an open diamond when a part might belong to several wholes (for example, `Door` and `Wall` objects belong to many `House` objects), but you use a filled diamond when a part can belong to only one whole at a time (the `Patron` table can belong only to the `Library` database). You can use most UML symbols in multiple types of diagrams.

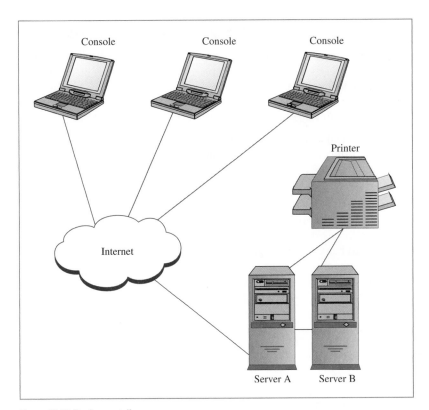

Console   Console   Console

Printer

Internet

Server A   Server B

Figure 13-22 Deployment diagram

TWO TRUTHS AND A LIE:
USING COMPONENT AND DEPLOYMENT DIAGRAMS

1. You use a component diagram when you want to emphasize the files, database tables, documents, and other components that a system's software uses.

2. You use a deployment diagram when you want to focus on a system's software components.

3. You can use a variety of icons in each type of UML diagram, but each icon must convey meaning to the reader.

The false statement is #2. You use a deployment diagram when you want to focus on a system's hardware.

DIAGRAMMING EXCEPTION HANDLING

Exception handling is a set of the object-oriented techniques used to handle program errors. When a segment of code might cause an error, you can place that code in a `try` block. If the error occurs, an object called an exception is thrown, or sent, to a `catch` block where appropriate action can be taken. For example, depending on the application, a `catch` block might display a message, assign a default value to a field, or prompt the user for direction.

In the UML, a `try` block is called a **protected node** and a `catch` block is a **handler body node**. In a UML diagram, a protected node is enclosed in a rounded rectangle and any exceptions that might be thrown are listed next to lightning-bolt-shaped arrows that extend to the appropriate handler body node.

Figure 13-23 shows an example of an activity that uses exception handling. When a library patron tries to check out a book, the patron's card is scanned and the book is scanned. These actions might cause three errors—the patron owes fines, and so cannot check out new books; the patron's card has expired, requiring a new card application; or the book might be on hold for another patron. If no exceptions occur, the activity proceeds to the `checkOutBook()` process.

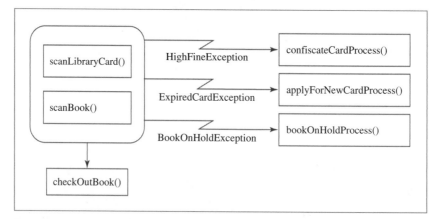

Figure 13-23 Exceptions in the Book check-out activity

DECIDING WHEN TO USE THE UML
AND WHICH UML DIAGRAMS TO USE

UML is widely recognized as a modeling standard, but it is also frequently criticized. The criticisms include:

» **Size**. The UML is often criticized as being too large and complex. Many of the diagrams are infrequently used, and some critics claim several are redundant.

» **Imprecision**. The UML is a combination of rules and English. In particular, problems occur when the diagrams are applied to tasks other than those implemented in object-oriented programming languages.

» **Complexity**. Because of its size and imprecision, the UML is relatively difficult to learn.

Still, under the right circumstances, the UML can increase communication between developers and users of a system. Each of the UML diagram types provides a different view of a system. Just as a portrait artist, psychologist, and neurosurgeon each prefer a different conceptual view of your head, the users, managers, designers, and technicians of computer and business systems each prefer specific system views. Very few systems require diagrams of all 13 types; you can illustrate the objects and activities of many systems by using a single diagram, or perhaps one that is a hybrid of two or more basic types. No view is superior to the others; you can achieve the most complete picture of any system by using several views. The most important reason you use any UML diagram is to communicate clearly and efficiently with the people for whom you are designing a system.

TWO TRUTHS AND A LIE:

DECIDING WHEN TO USE THE UML AND WHICH UML DIAGRAMS TO USE

1. The UML has been hailed as a practically perfect design tool because it is concise and easy to learn.

2. Very few systems require diagrams of all 13 UML types; you can illustrate the objects and activities of many systems by using a single diagram, or perhaps one that is a hybrid of two or more basic types.

3. The most important reason you use any UML diagram is to communicate clearly and efficiently with the people for whom you are designing a system.

The false statement is #1. The UML is often criticized as being too large and complex. Many of the diagrams are infrequently used, and some critics claim several are redundant. Because of its size and imprecision, the UML is relatively difficult to learn.

CHAPTER SUMMARY

» System design is the detailed specification of how all the parts of a system will be implemented and coordinated. Good designs make systems easier to understand. The UML (Unified Modeling Language) provides a means for programmers and businesspeople to communicate about system design.

» The UML is a standard way to specify, construct, and document systems that use object-oriented methods. The UML has its own notation, with which you can construct software diagrams that model different kinds of systems. The UML provides 13 diagram types that you use at the beginning of the design process.

» A use case diagram shows how a business works from the perspective of those who approach it from the outside, or those who actually use the business. The diagram often includes actors, represented by stick figures, and use cases, represented by ovals. Use cases can include variations such as extend relationships, include relationships, and generalizations.

» You use a class diagram to illustrate the names, attributes, and methods of a class or set of classes. A class diagram of a single class contains a rectangle divided into three sections: the name of the class, the names of the attributes, and the names of the methods. Class diagrams can show generalizations and the relationships between objects. Object diagrams are similar to class diagrams, but they model specific instances of classes at one point in time.

» You use a sequence diagram to show the timing of events in a single use case. The horizontal axis (x-axis) of a sequence diagram represents objects, and the vertical axis (y-axis) represents time. A communication diagram emphasizes the organization of objects that participate in a system. It is similar to a sequence diagram, except that it contains sequence numbers to represent the precise order in which activities occur.

» A state machine diagram shows the different statuses of a class or object at different points in time.

» In an activity diagram, you show the flow of actions of a system, including branches that occur when decisions affect the outcome. UML activity diagrams use forks and joins to show simultaneous activities.

» You use a component diagram when you want to emphasize the files, database tables, documents, and other components that a system's software uses. You use a deployment diagram when you want to focus on a system's hardware.

» Each of the UML diagram types provides a different view of a system. Very few systems require diagrams of all 13 types; the most important reason to use any UML diagram is to communicate clearly and efficiently with the people for whom you are designing a system.

KEY TERMS

System design is the detailed specification of how all the parts of a system will be implemented and coordinated.

Reverse engineering is the process of creating a model of an existing system.

The **UML** is a standard way to specify, construct, and document systems that use object-oriented methods. UML is an acronym for Unified Modeling Language.

Structure diagrams emphasize the "things" in a system.

Behavior diagrams emphasize what happens in a system.

Interaction diagrams emphasize the flow of control and data among the things in the system being modeled.

The **use case diagram** is a UML diagram that shows how a business works from the perspective of those who approach it from the outside, or those who actually use the business.

An **extend variation** is a use case variation that shows functions beyond those found in a base case.

Each variation in the sequence of actions required in a use case is a **scenario**.

A feature that adds to the UML vocabulary of shapes to make them more meaningful for the reader is called a **stereotype**.

An **include variation** is a use case variation that you use when a case can be part of multiple use cases in a UML diagram.

You use a **generalization variation** in a UML diagram when a use case is less specific than others, and you want to be able to substitute the more specific case for a general one.

When system developers omit parts of UML diagrams for clarity, they refer to the missing parts as **elided**.

When a method **overrides** another, it is used by default in place of one with the same signature.

An **association relationship** describes the connection or link between objects in a UML diagram.

Cardinality and **multiplicity** refer to the arithmetic relationships between objects.

A **whole-part relationship** describes an association in which one or more classes make up the parts of a larger whole class. This type of relationship is also called an **aggregation**.

You can also call a whole-part relationship a **has-a relationship** because the phrase describes the association between the whole and one of its parts.

Object diagrams are UML diagrams that are similar to class diagrams, but they model specific instances of classes.

A **sequence diagram** is a UML diagram that shows the timing of events in a single use case.

A **communication diagram** is a UML diagram that emphasizes the organization of objects that participate in a system.

A **state machine diagram** is a UML diagram that shows the different statuses of a class or object at different points in time.

An **activity diagram** is a UML diagram that shows the flow of actions of a system, including branches that occur when decisions affect the outcome.

A **fork** is a feature of a UML activity diagram; it is similar to a decision, but whereas the flow of control follows only one path after a decision, a fork defines a branch in which all paths are followed simultaneously.

A **join** is a feature of a UML activity diagram; it reunites the flow of control after a fork.

A **time signal** is a UML diagram symbol that indicates that a specific amount of time has passed before an action is started.

A **component diagram** is a UML diagram that emphasizes the files, database tables, documents, and other components that a system's software uses.

A **deployment diagram** is a UML diagram that focuses on a system's hardware.

A **protected node** is the UML diagram name for an exception-throwing `try` block.

A **handler body node** is the UML diagram name for an exception-handling `catch` block.

REVIEW QUESTIONS

1. **The detailed specification of how all the parts of a system will be implemented and coordinated is called _____ .**

   a. programming   c. system design

   b. paraphrasing   d. structuring

2. **The primary purpose of good modeling techniques is to _____ .**

   a. promote communication

   b. increase functional cohesion

   c. reduce the need for structure

   d. reduce dependency between modules

3. **The Unified Modeling Language provides standard ways to do all of the following to business systems except to _____ them.**

   a. construct   c. describe

   b. document   d. destroy

4. **The UML is commonly used to model all of the following except _____ .**

   a. computer programs   c. organizational processes

   b. business activities   d. software systems

5. **The UML was intentionally designed to be _____ .**

   a. low-level, detail-oriented

   b. used with Visual Basic

   c. nontechnical

   d. inexpensive

6. **The UML diagrams that show how a business works from the perspective of those who actually use the business, such as employees or customers, are _____ diagrams.**

   a. communication   c. state machine

   b. use case   d. class

7. **Which of the following is an example of a relationship that would be portrayed as an extend relationship in a use case diagram for a hospital?**

    a. the relationship between the head nurse and the floor nurses

    b. admitting a patient who has never been admitted before

    c. serving a meal

    d. scheduling the monitoring of patients' vital signs

8. **The people shown in use case diagrams are called _____ .**

    a. workers

    b. clowns

    c. actors

    d. relatives

9. **One aspect of use case diagrams that makes them difficult to learn about is that _____ .**

    a. they require programming experience to understand

    b. they use a technical vocabulary

    c. there is no single right answer for any case

    d. all of the above

10. **The arithmetic association relationship between a college student and college courses would be expressed as _____ .**

    a. 1   0

    b. 1   1

    c. 1   0..*

    d. 0..* 0..*

11. **In the UML, object diagrams are most similar to _____ diagrams.**

    a. use case

    b. activity

    c. class

    d. sequence

12. **In any given situation, you should choose the type of UML diagram that is _____ .**

    a. shorter than others

    b. clearer than others

    c. more detailed than others

    d. closest to the programming language you will use to implement the system

13. **A whole-part relationship can be described as a(n) _____ relationship.**

    a. parent-child

    b. has-a

    c. is-a

    d. creates-a

14. The timing of events is best portrayed in a(n) _____ diagram.

    a. sequence   c. communication

    b. use case   d. association

15. A communication diagram is closest to a(n) _____ diagram.

    a. activity   c. deployment

    b. use case   d. sequence

16. A(n) _____ diagram shows the different statuses of a class or object at different points in time.

    a. activity   c. sequence

    b. state machine   d. deployment

17. The UML diagram that most closely resembles a conventional flowchart is a(n) _____ diagram.

    a. activity   c. sequence

    b. state machine   d. deployment

18. You use a _____ diagram when you want to emphasize the files, database tables, documents, and other components that a system's software uses.

    a. state machine   c. deployment

    b. component   d. use case

19. The UML diagram that focuses on a system's hardware is a(n) _____ diagram.

    a. deployment   c. activity

    b. sequence   d. use case

20. When using the UML to describe a single system, most designers would use _____ .

    a. a single type of diagram

    b. at least three types of diagrams

    c. most of the available types of diagrams

    d. all 13 types of diagrams

FIND THE BUGS

The following use case diagram describes an elementary school classroom administered by a teacher with help from a teacher's aide. The diagram should show that the teacher can conduct parent meetings, teach a class, and assign grades. Both the teacher and the aide can help with desk work. While assigning grades or helping with desk work, the appropriate actor might deem it prudent to schedule a parent meeting. Correct any errors in the use case diagram in Figure 13-24.

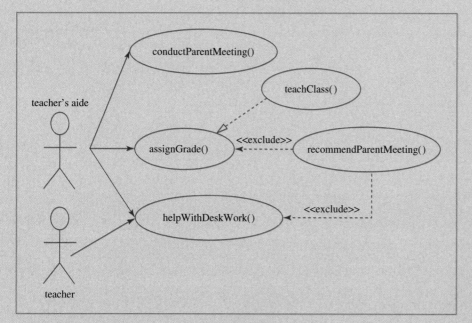

Figure 13-24 Incorrect use case diagram for elementary classroom

EXERCISES

1. **Complete the following tasks:**

   a. Develop a use case diagram for a convenience food store. Include an actor representing the store manager and use cases for `orderItem()`, `stockItem()`, and `sellItem()`.

   b. Add more use cases to the diagram you created in Exercise 1a. Include two generalizations for `stockItem()`: `stockPerishable()` and `stockNonPerishable()`. Also include an extension to `sellItem()` called `checkCredit()` for when a customer purchases items using a credit card.

   c. Add a customer actor to the use case diagram you created in Exercise 1b. Show that the customer participates in `sellItem()`, but not in `orderItem()` or `stockItem()`.

2. Develop a use case diagram for a department store credit card system. Include at least two actors and four use cases.

3. Develop a use case diagram for a college registration system. Include at least three actors and five use cases.

4. Develop a class diagram for a `Video` class that describes objects a video store customer can rent. Include at least four attributes and three methods.

5. Develop a class diagram for a `Shape` class. Include generalizations for child classes `Rectangle`, `Circle`, and `Triangle`.

6. Develop a class diagram for a `BankLoan` class. Include generalizations for child classes `Mortgage`, `CarLoan`, and `EducationLoan`.

7. Develop a class diagram for a college registration system. Include at least three classes that cooperate to achieve student registration.

8. Develop a sequence diagram that shows how a clerk at a mail-order company places a customer `Order`. The `Order` accesses `Inventory` to check availability. Then, the `Order` accesses `Invoice` to produce a customer invoice that returns to the clerk.

9. Develop a state machine diagram that shows the states of a `CollegeStudent` from `PotentialApplicant` to `Graduate`.

10. Develop a state machine diagram that shows the states of a `Book` from `Concept` to `Publication`.

11. Develop an activity diagram that illustrates how to build a house.

12. Develop an activity diagram that illustrates how to prepare dinner.

13. Develop the UML diagram of your choice that illustrates some aspect of your life.

14. Complete the following tasks:

   a. Develop the UML diagram of your choice that best illustrates some aspect of a place you have worked.

   b. Develop a different UML diagram type that illustrates the same functions as the diagram you created in Exercise 14a.

GAME ZONE

1. Develop a use case diagram for a baseball game. Include actors representing a player and an umpire. Create use cases for `hitBall()`, `runBases()`, and `makeCallAtBase()`. Include two generalizations for `makeCallAtBase()`: `callSafe()` and `callOut()`.

2. Develop a class diagram for a CardGame class. Include generalizations for child classes SolitaireCardGame and OpponentCardGame.

3. Choose a child's game such as Hide and Go Seek or Duck, Duck, Goose and describe it using UML diagrams of your choice.

DETECTIVE WORK

1. What are the education requirements for a career in system design? What are the job prospects and average salaries?

2. Find any discussion you can on the advantages and disadvantages of the UML as a system design tool. Summarize your findings.

UP FOR DISCUSSION

1. Which do you think you would enjoy doing more on the job—designing large systems that contain many programs, or writing the programs themselves? Why?

2. In Chapters 4 and 9, you considered ethical dilemmas in writing programs that select candidates for organ transplants. Are the ethical responsibilities of a system designer different from those of a programmer? If so, how?

USING RELATIONAL DATABASES

In this chapter you will:

Understand relational database fundamentals

Create databases and table descriptions

Be able to identify primary keys

Understand database structure notation

Understand the principles of adding, deleting, updating, and sorting records within a table

Create queries

Understand relationships between tables

Recognize poor table design

Understand anomalies, normal forms, and the normalization process

Understand database performance and security issues

UNDERSTANDING RELATIONAL DATABASE FUNDAMENTALS

When you store data items for use within computer systems, they are often stored in what is known as a data hierarchy, where the smallest usable unit of data is the character, often a letter or number. Characters are grouped together to form fields, such as `firstName`, `lastName`, and `socialSecurityNumber`. Related fields are often grouped together to form records—groups of fields that go together because they represent attributes of some entity, such as an employee, a customer, an inventory item, or a bank account. Files are composed of related records; for example, a file might contain a record for each employee in a company or each account at a bank.

> **NOTE** You first learned about the data hierarchy in Chapter 1 of this book. The terms *character, field, record*, and *file* were defined there, and you have been using these terms throughout this book.

Most organizations store many files that contain the data they need to operate their businesses; for example, businesses often need to maintain files containing data about employees, customers, inventory items, and orders. Many organizations use database software to organize the information in these files. A **database** holds a group of files that an organization needs to support its applications. In a database, the files are often called **tables** because you can arrange their contents in rows and columns. Real-life examples of database-like tables abound. For example, consider the listings in a telephone book. Each listing in a city directory might contain four columns—last name, first name, street address, and phone number—as shown in Figure 14-1. Although your local phone directory might not store its data in the rigid columnar format shown in the figure, it could. You can see that each column represents a field and that each row represents one record. You can picture a table within a database in the same way.

Last name	First name	Address	Phone
Abbott	William	123 Oak Lane	490-8920
Ackerman	Kimberly	467 Elm Drive	787-2781
Adams	Stanley	8120 Pine Street	787-0129
Adams	Violet	347 Oak Lane	490-8912
Adams	William	12 Second Street	490-3667

Figure 14-1 A telephone book table

> **NOTE** In Chapter 6, you learned that arrays are also sometimes referred to as tables. Arrays (stored in memory) and tables (stored in databases) are similar in that both contain rows and columns. When an array has multiple columns, all must have the same data type. The same is not true for tables stored in databases.

> **NOTE** Sometimes, one record or row is also called an **entity**; however, many definitions of "entity" exist in database texts. One column (field) can also be called an **attribute**.

Figure 14-1 includes five records, each representing a unique person. It is relatively easy to scan this short list of names to find a person's phone number; of course, telephone books contain many more records. Some telephone book users, such as telemarketers or even the phone company, might prefer to look up a number in a book in which the records are organized in telephone-number order. Others, such as door-to-door salespeople, might prefer a telephone book in which the records are organized in street-address order. Most people, however, prefer a telephone book in which the records are organized as shown, in alphabetical order by last name. It is most convenient for different users when computerized databases can sort records in various orders based on the contents of different columns.

Unless you are reading a telephone book for a very small town, a last name alone is often not sufficient to identify a person. In the example in Figure 14-1, three people have the last name of Adams. For these records, you need to examine the first name before you can determine the correct phone number. In a large city, many people might have the same first and last names; in that case, you might also need to examine the street address to identify a person. As with the telephone book, in most computerized database tables, it is important to have a way to identify each record uniquely, even if it means using multiple columns. A value that uniquely identifies a record is called a **primary key**, or a **key** for short. Key fields are often defined as a single table column, but as with the telephone book, keys can be constructed from multiple columns; a key constructed from multiple columns is a **compound key**, also known as a **composite key**.

NOTE
You learn more about key fields and compound keys later in this chapter.

Telephone books are republished periodically because changes have occurred—new people have moved into the city and become telephone customers, and others have left, canceled service, or changed phone numbers. With computerized database tables, you also need to add, delete, and modify records, although usually far more frequently than phone books are published.

Telephone books often contain thousands of records. Computerized database tables also frequently contain thousands of records, or rows, and each row might contain entries in dozens of columns. Handling and organizing all the data contained in an organization's tables requires sophisticated software. **Database management software** is a set of programs that allows users to:

» Create table descriptions.
» Identify keys.
» Add, delete, and update records within a table.
» Arrange records within a table so they are sorted by different fields.
» Write questions that select specific records from a table for viewing.
» Write questions that combine information from multiple tables. This is possible because the database management software establishes and maintains relationships between the columns in the tables. A group of database tables from which you can make these connections is a **relational database**.
» Create reports that allow users to easily interpret your data, and create forms that allow users to view and enter data using an easy-to-manage interactive screen.
» Keep data secure by employing sophisticated security measures.

If you have used different word-processing or spreadsheet programs, you know that each version works a little differently, although each carries out the same types of tasks. Like other computer programs, each database management software package operates differently; however, with each, you need to perform the same types of tasks.

CREATING DATABASES AND TABLE DESCRIPTIONS

Creating a useful database requires a lot of planning and analysis. You must decide what data will be stored, how that data will be divided between tables, and how the tables will interrelate. Before you create any tables, you must create the database itself. With most database software packages, creating the database that will hold the tables requires nothing more than providing a name for the database and indicating the physical location, perhaps a hard disk drive, where the database will be stored. When you save a table, it is conventional to provide it with a name that begins with the prefix "tbl"–for example, `tblCustomers`. Your databases often become filled with a variety of objects—tables, forms that users can use for data entry, reports that organize the data for viewing, queries that select subsets of data for viewing, and so on. Using naming conventions, such as beginning each table name with a prefix that identifies it as a table, helps you to keep track of the various objects in your system.

> **NOTE** When you save a table description, many database management programs suggest a default, generic table description name such as Table1. Usually, a more descriptive name is more useful to you as you continue to create objects.

Before you can enter any data into a database table, you must design the table. At minimum, this involves two tasks:

» You must decide what columns your table needs, and provide names for them.

» You must provide a data type for each column.

> **NOTE**
> A table description closely resembles the list of variables that you have used with every program throughout this book.

For example, assume you are designing a customer database table. Figure 14-2 shows some column names and data types you might use.

Column	Data type
customerID	text
lastName	text
firstName	text
streetAddress	text
balanceOwed	numeric

Figure 14-2 Customer table description

The table description in Figure 14-2 uses just two data types—text and numeric. Text columns can hold any type of characters—letters or digits. Numeric columns can hold numbers only. Depending on the database management software you use, you might have many more sophisticated data types at your disposal. For example, some database software divides the numeric data type into several subcategories such as integer (whole number only) values and double-precision numbers (numbers that contain decimals). Other options might include special categories for currency numbers (representing dollars and cents), dates, and Boolean columns (representing true or false). At the least, all database software recognizes the distinction between text and numeric data.

The table description in Figure 14-2 uses one-word column names and camel casing, in the same way that variable names have been defined throughout this book. Many database software packages do not require that data column names be single words without embedded spaces, but many database table designers prefer single-word names because they resemble variable names in programs. In addition, when you write programs that access a database table, the single-word field names can be used "as is," without special syntax to indicate the names that represent a single field. As a further advantage, when you use a single word to label each database column, it is easier to understand whether just one column is being referenced, or several.

The customerID column in Figure 14-2 is defined as a text field or text column. If customerID numbers are composed entirely of digits, this column could also be defined as numeric. However, many database designers feel that columns should be defined as numeric only if they need to be—that is, only if they might be used in arithmetic calculations. The description in Figure 14-2 follows this convention by declaring customerID to be a text column.

Many database management software packages allow you to add a narrative description of each data column to a table. This allows you to make comments that become part of the table. These comments do not affect the way the table operates; they simply serve as documentation for those who are reading a table description. For example, you might want to make a note that customerID should consist of five digits, or that balanceOwed should not exceed a given limit. Some software allows you to specify that values for a certain column are required—the user cannot create a record without providing data for these columns. In addition, you might be able to indicate value limits for a column—high and low numbers between which the column contents must fall.

IDENTIFYING PRIMARY KEYS

In most tables you create for a database, you want to identify a column, or possibly a combination of columns, as the table's key column or field, also called the primary key. The primary key in a table is the column that makes each record different from all others. For example, in the customer table in Figure 14-2, the logical choice for a primary key is the `customerID` column—each customer record that is entered into the customer table has a unique value in this column. Many customers might have the same first name or last name (or both), and multiple customers might also have the same street address or balance due. However, each customer possesses a unique ID number.

Other typical examples of primary keys include:

» A student ID number in a table that contains college student information
» A part number in a table that contains inventory items
» A Social Security number in a table that contains employee information

In each of these examples, the primary key uniquely identifies the row. For example, each student has a unique ID number assigned by the college. Other columns in a student table would not be adequate keys—many students have the same last name, first name, hometown, or major.

> **NOTE** It is no coincidence that each of the preceding examples of a key is a number, such as a student ID number or item number. Usually, assigning a number to each row in a table is the simplest and most efficient method of obtaining a useful key. However, it is possible that a table's key could be a text field.

The primary key is important for several reasons:

» You can configure your database software to prevent multiple records from containing the same value in this column, thus avoiding data-entry errors.
» You can sort your records in this order before displaying or printing them.
» You use this column when setting up relationships between this table and others that will become part of the same database.
» In addition, you need to understand the concept of the primary key when you normalize a database—a concept you will learn more about later in this chapter.

> **NOTE** In some database software packages, such as Microsoft Access, you indicate a primary key simply by selecting a column name and clicking a button that is labeled with a key icon.

In some tables, when no identifying number has been assigned to the rows, more than one column is required to construct a primary key. A multicolumn key is a compound key. For example, consider Figure 14-3, which might be used by a residence hall administrator to store data about students living on a university campus. Each room in a building has a number and two students, each assigned to either bed A or bed B.

hall	room	bed	lastName	firstName	major
Adams	101	A	Fredricks	Madison	Chemistry
Adams	101	B	Garza	Lupe	Psychology
Adams	102	A	Liu	Jennifer	CIS
Adams	102	B	Smith	Crystal	CIS
Browning	101	A	Patel	Sarita	CIS
Browning	101	B	Smith	Margaret	Biology
Browning	102	A	Jefferson	Martha	Psychology
Browning	102	B	Bartlett	Donna	Spanish
Churchill	101	A	Wong	Cheryl	CIS
Churchill	101	B	Smith	Madison	Chemistry
Churchill	102	A	Patel	Jennifer	Psychology
Churchill	102	B	Jones	Elizabeth	CIS

Figure 14-3 Table containing residence hall student records

In Figure 14-3, no single column can serve as a primary key. Many students live in the same residence hall, and the same room numbers exist in the different residence halls. In addition, some students have the same last name, first name, or major. It is even possible that two students with the same first name, last name, or major are assigned to the same room. In this case, the best primary key is a multicolumn key that combines residence hall, room number, and bed number (`hall`, `room`, and `bed`). "Adams 101 A" identifies a single room and student, as does "Churchill 102 B".

>> **NOTE** A primary key should be **immutable**, meaning that a value does not change during normal operation. In other words, in Figure 14-3, "Adams 102 A" will always pertain to a fixed location, even though the resident or her major might change. Of course, the school might choose to change the name of a residence hall–for example, to honor a benefactor— but that action would fall outside the range of "normal operation." (In object-oriented programming, a class is immutable if it contains no methods that allow changes to its attributes after construction.)

>> **NOTE** Sometimes, there are several columns that could serve as the key. For example, if an employee record contains both a company-assigned employee ID and a Social Security number, then both columns are **candidate keys**. After you choose a primary key from among candidate keys, the remaining candidate keys become **alternate keys**.

>> **NOTE** Even if there were only one student named Smith, for example, or only one Psychology major in the table in Figure 14-3, those fields still would not be good primary key candidates because of the potential for future Smiths and Psychology majors within the database. Analyzing existing data is not a foolproof way to select a good key; you must also consider likely future data.

>> **NOTE** As an alternative to selecting three columns to create the compound key for the table in Figure 14-3, many database designers prefer to simply add a new column containing a bed location ID number that would uniquely identify each row. Many database designers feel that a primary key should be short to minimize the amount of storage required for it in all the tables that refer to it.

Usually, after you have identified the necessary fields and their data types, and identified the primary key, you are ready to save your table description and begin to enter data.

UNDERSTANDING DATABASE STRUCTURE NOTATION

A shorthand way to describe a table is to use the table name followed by parentheses containing all the field names, with the primary key underlined. Thus, when a table is named `tblStudents` and contains columns named `idNumber`, `lastName`, `firstName`, and `gradePointAverage`, and `idNumber` is the key, you can reference the table using the following notation:

```
tblStudents(idNumber, lastName, firstName, gradePointAverage)
```

Although this shorthand notation does not provide you with information about data types or range limits on values, it does provide you with a quick overview of the structure of a table.

》NOTE
The key does not have to be the first attribute listed in a table reference, but frequently it is.

》NOTE Some database designers insert an asterisk after the key instead of underlining it.

ADDING, DELETING, UPDATING, AND SORTING RECORDS WITHIN TABLES

Entering data into an already created table is not difficult, but it requires a good deal of time and accurate typing. Depending on the application, the contents of the tables might be entered over the course of many months or years by any number of data-entry personnel. Entering data of the wrong type is not allowed by most database software. In addition, you might have set up your table to prevent duplicate data in specific fields, or to prevent data entry outside of specified bounds in other fields. With some database software, you type data into rows representing each record, and columns representing each field in each record, much as you would enter data into a spreadsheet. With other software, you can create on-screen forms to make data entry more user-friendly. Some software does not allow you to enter a partial record; that is, you might not be allowed to leave any fields blank.

>>**NOTE** In Chapter 12, you learned that computer professionals use the acronym GIGO, which stands for "Garbage in; garbage out." It means that if you enter invalid input data into an application, the output results will be worthless.

Deleting records from and modifying records within a database table are also relatively easy tasks. In most organizations, most of the important data is in a constant state of change. Maintaining the data records so they are up to date is a vital part of any database management system.

>>**NOTE** In many database systems, some "deleted" records are not physically removed. Instead, they are just marked as deleted so they will not be used to process active records. For example, a company might want to retain data about former employees, but not process them with current personnel reports. On the other hand, an employee record that was entered by mistake would be permanently removed from the database.

SORTING THE RECORDS IN A TABLE

Database management software generally allows you to sort a table based on any column, letting you view your data in the way that is most useful to you. For example, you might want to view inventory items in alphabetical order, or from the most to the least expensive. You can also sort by multiple columns—for example, you might sort employees by first name within last name (so that Aaron Black is listed before Andrea Black), or by department within first name within last name (so that Aaron Black in Department 1 is listed before another Aaron Black in Department 6).

>>**NOTE** When performing sorts on multiple fields, the software sorts first by a primary sort—for example, last name. After all those with the same primary sort key are grouped, the software sorts by the secondary key—for example, first name.

After rows are sorted, they usually can be grouped. For example, you might want to sort customers by their zip code, or employees by the department in which they work; in addition, you might want counts or subtotals at the end of each group. Database software provides the means to create displays in the formats that suit your present information needs.

>>**NOTE** When a database program includes counts or totals at the end of each sorted group, it is creating a control break report. You learned about control break reports in Chapter 8.

CREATING QUERIES

Data tables often contain hundreds or thousands of rows; making sense out of that much information is a daunting task. Frequently, you want to cull subsets of data from a table you have created. For example, you might want to view only those customers with an address in a specific state, only those inventory items whose quantity in stock has fallen below the normal reorder point, or only those employees who participate in an insurance plan. Besides limiting records, you might also want to limit the columns that you view. For example, student records might contain dozens of fields, but a school administrator might only be interested in looking at names and grade point averages. The questions that cause the database software to extract the appropriate records from a table and specify the fields to be viewed are called queries; a **query** is simply a question asked using the syntax that the database software can understand.

Depending on the software you use, you might create a query by filling in blanks (a process called **query by example**) or by writing statements similar to those in many programming languages. The most common language that database administrators use to access data in their tables is **Structured Query Language**, or **SQL**. The basic form of the SQL command that retrieves selected records from a table is **SELECT-FROM-WHERE**. The SELECT-FROM-WHERE SQL statement:

» *Selects* the columns you want to view
» *From* a specific table
» *Where* one or more conditions are met

> **»NOTE** "SQL" frequently is pronounced "sequel"; however, several SQL product Web sites insist that the official pronunciation is "S-Q-L." Similarly, some people pronounce GUI as "gooey" and others insist that it should be "G-U-I." In general, a preferred pronunciation evolves in an organization. The TLA, or three-letter abbreviation, is the most popular type of abbreviation in technical terminology.

For example, suppose a customer table named tblCustomer contains data about your business customers and that the structure of the table is tblCustomer(custId, lastName, state). Then, a statement such as:

```
SELECT custId, lastName FROM tblCustomer WHERE state = "WI"
```

would display a new table containing two columns—custId and lastName—and only as many rows as needed to hold those customers whose state column contains "WI". Besides using = to mean "equal to," you can use the comparison conditions > (greater than), < (less than), >= (greater than or equal to), and <= (less than or equal to). As you have already learned from working with programming variables throughout this book, text field values are always contained within quotes, whereas numeric values are not.

NOTE Conventionally, SQL keywords such as SELECT appear in all uppercase; this book follows that convention.

> **NOTE** In database management systems, a particular way of looking at a database is sometimes called a **view**. Typically, a view arranges records in some order and makes only certain fields visible. The different views provided by database software are virtual; that is, they do not affect the physical organization of the database.

To select all fields for each record in a table, you can use the asterisk as a wildcard; a **wildcard** is a symbol that means "any" or "all." For example, SELECT * from tblCustomer WHERE state = "WI" would select all columns for every customer whose state is "WI", not just specifically named columns. To select all customers from a table, you can omit the WHERE clause in a SELECT-FROM-WHERE statement. In other words, SELECT * FROM tblCustomer selects all columns for all customers.

You learned about making selections in computer programs much earlier in this book, and you have probably noticed that SELECT-FROM-WHERE statements serve the same purpose as programming decisions. As with decision statements in programs, when using SQL, you can create compound conditions using AND or OR operators. In addition, you can precede any condition with a NOT operator to achieve a negative result. In summary, Figure 14-4 shows a database table named tblInventory with the following structure: tblInventory(<u>itemNumber</u>, description, quantityInStock, price). The table contains five records. Figure 14-5 lists several typical SQL SELECT statements you might use with tblInventory, and explains each.

itemNumber	description	quantityInStock	price
144	Pkg 12 party plates	250	$14.99
231	Helium balloons	180	$2.50
267	Paper streamers	68	$1.89
312	Disposable tablecloth	20	$6.99
383	Pkg 20 napkins	315	$2.39

Figure 14-4 The tblInventory table

SQL statement	Explanation
SELECT itemNumber, price FROM tblInventory	Shows only the item number and price for all five records.
SELECT * FROM tblInventory WHERE price > 5.00	Shows all fields from only those records where price is over $5.00—items 144 and 312.
SELECT itemNumber FROM tblInventory WHERE quantityInStock > 200 AND price > 10.00	Shows item number 144—the only record that has a quantity greater than 200 as well as a price greater than $10.00.
SELECT description, price FROM tblInventory WHERE description = "Pkg 20 napkins" OR itemNumber < 200	Shows the description and price fields for the package of 12 party plates and the package of 20 napkins. Each selected record must satisfy only one of the two criteria.
SELECT itemNumber FROM tblInventory WHERE NOT price < 14.00	Shows the item number for the only record where the price is not less than $14.00—item 144.

Figure 14-5 Sample SQL statements and explanations

TWO TRUTHS AND A LIE:
CREATING QUERIES

1. A query is a question that causes database software to extract appropriate fields and records from a table.

2. The most common language that database administrators use to access data in their tables is Structured Query Language, or SQL.

3. The basic form of the SQL command that retrieves selected records from a table is RETRIEVE-FROM-SELECTION.

The false statement is # 3. The basic form of the SQL command that retrieves selected records from a table is SELECT-FROM-WHERE.

UNDERSTANDING RELATIONSHIPS BETWEEN TABLES

Most database applications require many tables, and these applications also require that the tables be related. The connection between two tables is a **relationship**, and the database containing the relationships is called a relational database. Connecting two tables based on the values in a common column is called a **join operation**, or more simply, a **join**; the column on which they are connected is the **join column**. A virtual, or imaginary, table that is displayed as the result of the query takes some of its data from each joined table. For example, in Figure 14-6, the `customerNumber` column is the join column that could produce a virtual image when a user makes a query. When a user asks to see the name of a customer associated with a specific order number, or a list of all the names of customers who have ordered a specific item, then a joined table is produced. The three types of relationships that can exist between tables are:

» One-to-many

» Many-to-many

» One-to-one

tblCustomers

customerNumber	customerName
214	Kowalski
215	Jackson
216	Lopez
217	Thompson
218	Vitale

tblOrders

orderNumber	customerNumber	orderQuantity	orderItem	orderDate
10467	215	2	HP203	10/15/2009
10468	218	1	JK109	10/15/2009
10469	215	4	HP203	10/16/2009
10470	216	12	ML318	10/16/2009
10471	214	4	JK109	10/16/2009
10472	215	1	HP203	10/16/2009
10473	217	10	JK109	10/17/2009

Figure 14-6 Sample customers and orders

UNDERSTANDING ONE-TO-MANY RELATIONSHIPS

A **one-to-many relationship** is one in which one row in a table can be related to many rows in another table. It is the most common type of relationship between tables. Consider the following tables:

```
tblCustomers(customerNumber, customerName)
tblOrders(orderNumber, customerNumber, orderQuantity, orderItem,
   orderDate)
```

The `tblCustomers` table contains one row for each customer, and `customerNumber` is the primary key. The `tblOrders` table contains one row for each order, and each order is assigned an `orderNumber`, which is the primary key in this table.

In most businesses, a single customer can place many orders. For example, in the sample data in Figure 14-6, customer 215 has placed three orders. One row in the `tblCustomers` table can correspond to, and can be related to, many rows in the `tblOrders` table. This means there is a one-to-many relationship between the two tables `tblCustomers` and `tblOrders`. The "one" table (`tblCustomers`) is the **base table** in this relationship, and the "many" table (`tblOrders`) is the **related table**.

When two tables are related in a one-to-many relationship, the relationship occurs based on the values in one or more columns in the tables. In this example, the column, or attribute, that links the two tables together is the `customerNumber` attribute. In the `tblCustomers` table, `customerNumber` is the primary key, but in the `tblOrders` table, `customerNumber` is not a key—it is a **nonkey attribute**. When a column that is not a key in a table contains an attribute that is a key in a related table, the column is called a **foreign key**. When a base table is linked to a related table in a one-to-many relationship, it is always the primary key of the base table that is related to the foreign key in the related table. In the example in Figure 14-6, `customerNumber` in the `tblOrders` table is a foreign key.

> **NOTE** A key in a base table and the foreign key in the related table do not need to have the same name; they only need to contain the same type of data. Some database management software programs automatically create a relationship for you if the columns in two tables you select have the same name and data type. However, if this is not the case (for example, if the column is named `customerNumber` in one table and `custID` in another), you can explicitly instruct the software to create the relationship.

UNDERSTANDING MANY-TO-MANY RELATIONSHIPS

Another example of a one-to-many relationship is depicted with the following tables:

```
tblItems(itemNumber, itemName, itemPurchaseDate, itemPurchasePrice,
   itemCategoryId)
tblCategories(categoryId, categoryName, categoryInsuredAmount)
```

Assume you are creating these tables to keep track of all the items in your household for insurance purposes. You want to store data about items such as your sofa, stereo, refrigerator, and so on. The `tblItems` table contains the name, purchase date, and purchase price of each item. In addition, this table contains the ID number of the item category (Appliance, Jewelry, Antique, and so on) to which the item belongs. You need the category of each item because your insurance policy has specific coverage limits for different types of property. For example, with many insurance policies, antiques might have a different coverage limit than appliances, or jewelry might have a different limit than furniture. Sample data for these tables is shown in Figure 14-7.

tblItems

itemNumber	itemName	itemPurchaseDate	itemPurchasePrice	itemcategoryId
1	Sofa	1/13/2003	$6,500	5
2	Stereo	2/10/2005	$1,200	6
3	Refrigerator	5/12/2005	$750	1
4	Diamond ring	2/12/2006	$42,000	2
5	TV	7/11/2006	$285	6
6	Rectangular pine coffee table	4/21/2007	$300	5
7	Round pine end table	4/21/2007	$200	5

tblCategories

categoryId	categoryName	categoryInsuredAmount
1	Appliance	$30,000
2	Jewelry	$15,000
3	Antique	$10,000
4	Clothing	$25,000
5	Furniture	$5,000
6	Electronics	$2,500
7	Miscellaneous	$5,000

Figure 14-7 Sample items and categories: a one-to-many relationship

The primary key of the tblItems table is itemNumber, a unique identifying number that you have assigned to each item that you own. (You might even prepare labels with these numbers and stick a label on each item in an inconspicuous place.) The tblCategories table contains the category names and the maximum insured amounts for the specific categories. For example, one row in this table may have a categoryName of "Jewelry" and a categoryInsuredAmount of $15,000. The primary key for the tblCategories table is categoryId, which is simply a uniquely assigned value for each property category.

The two tables in Figure 14-7 have a one-to-many relationship. Which is the "one" table and which is the "many" table? Or, asked in another way, which is the base table and which is the related table? You have probably determined that the tblCategories table is the base table (the "one" table), because one category can describe many items that you own. Therefore, the tblItems table is the related table (the "many" table); that is, there are many items that fall into each category. The two tables are linked with the category ID attribute, which is the primary key in the base table (tblCategories) and a foreign key in the related table (tblItems).

In the tables in Figure 14-7, one row in the tblCategories table relates to multiple items you own. The opposite is not true—that is, one item in the tblItems table cannot relate to multiple categories in the tblCategories table. The row in the tblItems table that describes the "rectangular pine coffee table" relates to one specific category in the `tblCategories` table—the Furniture category. However, what if you own a rectangular pine coffee table that has a built-in DVD player, or a diamond ring that is an antique, or a stereo that could also be worn as a hat on a rainy day? Even though this last example is humorous, it does bring up an important consideration.

The structure of the tables shown in Figure 14-7 and the relationship between those tables are designed to support a particular application—keeping track of possessions for insurance purposes. If you acquired a sofa with a built-in CD player and speakers, what would you do? For guidance, you would probably call your insurance agent. If the agent said, "Well, for insurance purposes that item is considered a piece of furniture," then the existing table structures and relationships are adequate.

However, if the insurance agent said, "Well, actually a sofa with a CD player is considered a special type of hybrid item, and that category of property has a specific maximum insured amount," then you could simply create a new row in the `tblCategories` table to describe this special hybrid category—perhaps Electronic Furniture. This new category would acquire a category number, and then you could associate the CD-sofa to the new category using the foreign key in the `tblItems` table.

However, what if your insurance agent said, "You know, that's a good question. We've never had that come up before—a sofa with a CD player. What we would probably do if you filed a claim because the sofa was damaged is to take a look at it to try to determine whether the sofa is mostly a piece of furniture or mostly a piece of electronics." This answer presents a problem to your database. You may want to categorize your new sofa as both a furniture item *and* an electronic item. The existing table structures, with their one-to-many relationship, would not support this because the current design limits any specific item to one and only one category. When you insert a row into the `tblItems` table to describe the new CD-sofa, you can assign the Furniture code to the foreign key `itemCategoryId`, or you can assign the Electronics code, but not both.

If you want to assign the new CD-sofa to both categories (Furniture and Electronics), you have to change the design of the table structures and relationships, because there is no longer a one-to-many relationship between the two tables. Now, there is a **many-to-many relationship**—one in which multiple rows in each table can correspond to multiple rows in the other. That is, in this example, one row in the `tblCategories` table (for example, Furniture) can relate to many rows in the `tblItems` table (for example, sofa and coffee table), *and* one row in the `tblItems` table (for example, the sofa with the built-in CD player) can relate to multiple rows in the `tblCategories` table.

The `tblItems` table contains a foreign key named `itemCategoryId`. If you want to change the application so that one specific row in the `tblItems` table can link to many rows (and, therefore, many `categoryIds`) in the `tblCategories` table, you cannot continue to maintain the foreign key `itemCategoryId` in the `tblItems` table, because one item may be assigned to many categories. You could change the structure of the `tblItems` table so that you can assign multiple `itemCategoryIds` to one specific row in that table, but as you will learn later in this chapter, that approach leads to many problems using the data. Therefore, it is not an option.

The simplest way to support a many-to-many relationship between the `tblItems` and `tblCategories` tables is to remove the `itemCategoryId` attribute (what was once the foreign key) from the `tblItems` table, producing:

```
tblItems(itemNumber, itemName, itemPurchaseDate, itemPurchasePrice)
```

The `tblCategories` table structure remains the same:

```
tblCategories(categoryId, categoryName, categoryInsuredAmount)
```

With just the preceding two tables, there is no way to know that any specific row(s) in the `tblItems` table link(s) to any specific row(s) in the `tblCategories` table, so you create a new table called `tblItemsCategories` that contains the primary keys from the two tables that you want to link in a many-to-many relationship. This table is depicted as:

```
tblItemsCategories(itemNumber, categoryId)
```

Notice that this new table contains a compound primary key—both `itemNumber` and `categoryId` are underlined. The `itemNumber` value of 1 might be associated with many `categoryId`s. Therefore, `itemNumber` alone cannot be the primary key because the same value may occur in many rows. Similarly, a `categoryId` might relate to many different `itemNumber`s; this would disallow using just the `categoryId` as the primary key. However, a combination of the two attributes `itemNumber` and `categoryId` results in a unique primary key value for each row of the `tblItemsCategories` table.

The purpose of all this is to create a many-to-many relationship between the `tblItems` and `tblCategories` tables. The `tblItemsCategories` table contains two attributes; together, these attributes are the primary key. In addition, each of these attributes separately is a foreign key to one of the two original tables. The `itemNumber` attribute in the `tblItemsCategories` table is a foreign key that links to the primary key of the `tblItems` table. The `categoryId` attribute in the `tblItemsCategories` table links to the primary key of the `tblCategories` table. Now, there is a one-to-many relationship between the `tblItems` table (the "one," or base table) and the `tblItemsCategories` table (the "many," or related table) and a one-to-many relationship between the `tblCategories` table (the "one," or base table) and the `tblItemsCategories` table (the "many," or related table). This, in effect, implies a many-to-many relationship between the two base tables (`tblItems` and `tblCategories`).

Figure 14-8 shows the new tables holding a few items. The sofa (`itemNumber` 1) in the `tblItems` table is associated with the Furniture category (`categoryId` 5) in the `tblCategories` table because the first row of the `tblItemsCategories` table contains a 1 and a 5. Similarly, the stereo (`itemNumber` 2) in the `tblItems` table is associated with the Electronics category (`categoryId` 6) in the `tblCategories` table because in the `tblItemsCategories` table there is a row containing the values 2, 6.

tblItems

itemNumber	itemName	itemPurchaseDate	itemPurchasePrice
1	Sofa	1/13/2003	$6,500
2	Stereo	2/10/2005	$1,200
3	Sofa with CD player	5/24/2007	$8,500
4	Table with DVD player	6/24/2007	$12,000
5	Grandpa's pocket watch	12/24/1929	$100

tblItemsCategories

itemNumber	categoryId
1	5
2	6
3	5
3	6
4	5
4	6
5	2
5	3

tblCategories

categoryId	categoryName	categoryInsuredAmount
1	Appliance	$30,000
2	Jewelry	$15,000
3	Antique	$10,000
4	Clothing	$25,000
5	Furniture	$5,000
6	Electronics	$2,500
7	Miscellaneous	$5,000

Figure 14-8 Sample items, categories, and item categories: a many-to-many relationship

The fancy sofa with the built-in CD player (itemNumber 3 in the tblItems table) occurs in two rows in the tblItemsCategories table, once with a categoryId of 5 (Furniture) and once with a categoryId of 6 (Electronics). Similarly, the table with the DVD player and Grandpa's pocket watch both belong to multiple categories. It is the tblItemsCategories table, then, that allows the establishment of a many-to-many relationship between the two base tables, tblItems and tblCategories.

UNDERSTANDING ONE-TO-ONE RELATIONSHIPS

In a **one-to-one relationship**, a row in one table corresponds to exactly one row in another table. This type of relationship is easy to understand, but is the least frequently encountered. When one row in a table corresponds to a row in another table, the columns could be combined into a single table. A common reason you create a one-to-one relationship is security. For example, Figure 14-9 shows two tables, tblEmployees and tblSalaries. Each employee in the tblEmployees table has exactly one salary in the tblSalaries table. The salaries could have been added to the tblEmployees table as an additional column; the salaries are separate only because you want some clerical workers to be allowed to view only names, addresses, and other nonsensitive data, so you give them permission to access only the tblEmployees table. Others who work in payroll or administration can create queries that allow them to view joined tables that include the salary information.

tblEmployees						tblSalaries	
empId	empLast	empFirst	empDept	empHireDate		empId	empSalary
101	Parker	Laura	3	4/07/2000		101	$42,500
102	Walters	David	4	1/19/2001		102	$28,800
103	Shannon	Ewa	3	2/28/2005		103	$36,000

Figure 14-9 Employees and salaries tables: a one-to-one relationship

»NOTE You learn more about security issues later in this chapter.

»NOTE Another reason to create tables with one-to-one relationships is to avoid lots of empty columns, or **nulls**, if a certain subset of columns is applicable only to specific types of rows in the main table.

TWO TRUTHS AND A LIE:
UNDERSTANDING RELATIONSHIPS BETWEEN TABLES

1. A one-to-many relationship is one in which one row in a table can be related to many rows in another table; it is the most common type of relationship between tables.

2. A many-to-many relationship is one in which multiple rows in a table each correspond to a single row in many different tables.

3. In a one-to-one relationship, a row in one table corresponds to exactly one row in another table; this type of relationship is easy to understand, but is the least frequently encountered.

The false statement is #2. A many-to-many relationship is one in which multiple rows in each table can correspond to multiple rows in the other.

RECOGNIZING POOR TABLE DESIGN

As you create database tables that will hold the data that an organization needs, you will encounter many occasions when the table design, or structure, is inadequate to support the needs of the application. In other words, even if a table contains all the attributes required by a specific application, the structural design of the table may make the application cumbersome to use (you will see examples of this later) and prone to data errors.

For example, assume that you have been hired by an Internet-based college to design a database to keep track of its students. After meeting with the college administrators, you determine that you need to know the following information:

» Students' names
» Students' addresses
» Students' cities
» Students' states
» Students' zip codes
» ID numbers for classes in which students are enrolled
» Titles for classes in which students are enrolled

> **NOTE** Of course, in a real-life example you could probably think of many other data requirements for the college, in addition to those listed here. The number of attributes is small here for simplicity.

Figure 14-10 contains the `Students` table. Assume that because the Internet-based college is new, only three students have already enrolled. Besides the columns you identified as being necessary, notice the addition of the `studentId` attribute. Given the earlier discussions, you probably recognize that this is the best choice to use as a primary key, because many students can have the same names and even the same addresses. Although the table in Figure 14-10 contains a column for each of the data requirements decided upon with the college administration, the table is poorly designed and will create many problems for the users of the database.

studentId	name	address	city	state	zip	class	classTitle
1	Rodriguez	123 Oak	Schaumburg	IL	60193	CIS101 PHI150 BIO200	Computer Literacy Ethics Genetics
2	Jones	234 Elm	Wild Rose	WI	54984	CHM100 MTH200	Chemistry Calculus
3	Mason	456 Pine	Dubuque	IA	52004	HIS202	World History

Figure 14-10 `Students` table before normalization process

What if a college administrator wanted to view a list of courses offered by the Internet-based college? Can you answer that question by reviewing the table? Well, you can see six courses listed for the three students, so you can assume that at least six courses are offered. But, is it possible that there is also a Psychology course, or a class whose code is CIS102? You can't determine this from the table because no students have enrolled in those classes. Wouldn't it be nice to know all the classes that are offered by your institution, regardless of whether any students have enrolled in them?

Consider another potential problem: What if student Mason withdraws from the school, and, therefore, his row is deleted from the table? You would lose some valuable information that really has nothing to do specifically with student Mason, but that is very important for running the college. For instance, if Mason's row is deleted from the table, you no longer know, from the remaining data in the table, whether the college offers any History classes, because Mason was the only student enrolled in a class with the HIS prefix (the HIS202 class).

Why is it so important to discuss the deficiencies of the existing table structure? You have probably heard the saying, "Pay me now or pay me later." This is especially true as it relates to table design. If you do not take the time to ensure well-designed table structures when you are initially designing your database, then you (or the users of your database) will surely spend lots of time later fixing data errors, typing the same information multiple times, and being frustrated by the inability to cull important subsets of information from the database. If you were really hired to create this database and this table structure was your solution to the college's needs, then it is unlikely you would be hired for future database projects.

UNDERSTANDING ANOMALIES, NORMAL FORMS, AND THE NORMALIZATION PROCESS

Database management programs can maintain all the relationships you need. As you add records to, delete records from, and modify records within your database tables, the software keeps track of all the relationships you have established, so that you can view any needed joins any time you want. The software, however, can only maintain useful relationships if you have planned ahead to create a set of tables that supports all the applications you will need. The process of designing and creating a set of database tables that satisfies the users' needs and avoids many potential problems is called **normalization**.

The normalization process helps you reduce data redundancies and anomalies. **Data redundancy** is the unnecessary repetition of data. An **anomaly** is an irregularity in a database's design that causes problems and inconveniences. Three common types of anomalies are:

» Update anomalies
» Delete anomalies
» Insert anomalies

If you look ahead to the college database table in Figure 14-11, you will see an example of an **update anomaly**, which is a problem that occurs when the data in a table needs to be altered. Because the table contains redundant data, if student Rodriguez moves to a new residence, you have to change the values stored as address, city, state, and zip in more than one location. Of course, this table example is small; imagine if additional data were stored about Rodriguez, such as birth date, e-mail address, major field of study, and previous schools attended.

The database table in Figure 14-10 contains a **delete anomaly**, which is a problem that occurs when a row is deleted. If student Jones withdraws from the college, and his entries are deleted from the table, important data regarding the classes CHM100 and MTH200 are lost.

With an **insert anomaly**, problems occur when new rows are added to a table. In the table in Figure 14-10, if a new student named Ramone has enrolled in the college, but has not yet registered for any specific classes, then you can't insert a complete row for student Ramone;

» NOTE
In some databases, you might be able to enter an incomplete row for a student.

the only way to do so would be to "invent" at least one phony class for him. It would certainly be valuable to the college to be able to maintain data on all enrolled students, regardless of whether those students have registered for specific classes—for example, the college might want to send catalogs and registration information to these students.

When you normalize a database table, you walk through a series of steps that allows you to remove redundancies and anomalies. The normalization process involves altering a table so that it satisfies one or more of three **normal forms**, which are sets of rules for constructing a well-designed database. The three normal forms are:

- » **First normal form**, also known as **1NF**, in which you eliminate repeating groups
- » **Second normal form**, also known as **2NF**, in which you eliminate partial key dependencies
- » **Third normal form**, also known as **3NF**, in which you eliminate transitive dependencies

Each normal form is structurally better than the one preceding it. In any well-designed database, you almost always want to convert all tables to 3NF.

> » NOTE In a 1970 paper titled "A Relational Model of Data for Large Shared Data Banks," Dr. E. F. Codd listed seven normal forms. For business applications, 3NF is usually sufficient, and so only 1NF through 3NF are discussed in this chapter.

FIRST NORMAL FORM

A table that contains repeating groups is **unnormalized**. A **repeating group** is a subset of rows in a database table that all depend on the same key. A table in 1NF contains no repeating groups of data.

The table in Figure 14-10 violates this 1NF rule. The `class` and `classTitle` attributes repeat multiple times for some of the students. For example, student Rodriguez is taking three classes; her `class` attribute contains a repeating group. To remedy this situation, and to transform the table to 1NF, you simply repeat the rows for each repeating group of data. Figure 14-11 contains the revised table.

studentId	name	address	city	state	zip	class	classTitle
1	Rodriguez	123 Oak	Schaumburg	IL	60193	CIS101	Computer Literacy
1	Rodriguez	123 Oak	Schaumburg	IL	60193	PHI150	Ethics
1	Rodriguez	123 Oak	Schaumburg	IL	60193	BIO200	Genetics
2	Jones	234 Elm	Wild Rose	WI	54984	CHM100	Chemistry
2	Jones	234 Elm	Wild Rose	WI	54984	MTH200	Calculus
3	Mason	456 Pine	Dubuque	IA	52004	HIS202	World History

Figure 14-11  Students table in 1NF

The repeating groups have been eliminated from the table in Figure 14-11. However, as you look at the table, you will notice a problem—the primary key, `studentId`, is no longer unique for each row in the table. For example, the table in Figure 14-11 now contains three rows in which `studentId` equals 1. You can fix this problem, and create a primary key, by simply adding the `class` attribute to the primary key, creating a compound key. (Other problems still exist, as you will see later in this chapter.) The table's key then becomes a combination of `studentId` and `class`. By knowing the `studentId` *and* `class`, you can identify one, and only one, row in the table—for example, a combination of `studentId` 1 and `class` BIO200 identifies a single row. Using the notation discussed earlier in this chapter, the table in Figure 14-11 can be described as:

```
tblStudents(studentId, name, address, city, state, zip, class,
    classTitle)
```

»NOTE
When you combine two columns to create a compound key, you are **concatenating the columns**.

Both the `studentId` and `class` attributes are underlined, showing that they are both part of the key.

The table in Figure 14-11 is now in 1NF because there are no repeating groups and the primary key attributes are defined. Satisfying the "no repeating groups" condition is also called making the columns **atomic attributes**; that is, making them as small as possible, containing an undividable piece of data. In 1NF, all values for an intersection of a row and column must be atomic. Recall the table in Figure 14-10 in which the class attribute for `studentId` 1 (Rodriguez) contained three entries: CIS101, PHI150, and BIO200. This violated the 1NF atomicity rule because these three classes represented a set of values rather than one specific value. The table in Figure 14-11 does not repeat this problem because, for each row in the table, the class attribute contains one and only one value. The same is true for the other attributes that were part of the repeating group.

»NOTE Database developers also refer to operations or transactions as **atomic transactions** when they appear to execute completely or not at all.

Now, think back to the earlier discussion about why we want to normalize tables in the first place. Look at Figure 14-11. Are there still redundancies? Are there still anomalies? Yes to both questions. Recall that you want to have your tables in 3NF before actually defining them to the database. Currently, the table in Figure 14-11 is only in 1NF.

In Figure 14-11, notice that Student 1, Rodriguez, is taking three classes. If you were the college employee who was responsible for typing the data into this table, would you want to type this student's name, address, city, state, and zip code for each of the three classes Rodriguez is taking? It is very probable that you may, for one of her classes, type her name as "Rodrigues" instead of "Rodriguez." Or, you might misspell the city of "Schaumburg" as "Schamburg" for one of Rodriguez's classes. A college administrator looking at the table might not know whether Rodriguez's correct city of residence is Schaumburg or Schamburg. If you queried the database to select or count the number of classes being taken by students residing in "Schaumburg," one of Rodriguez's classes would be missed.

»NOTE Misspelling the student name "Rodriguez" is an example of a data integrity error. You learn more about this type of error later in this chapter.

Consider the student Jones, who is taking two classes. If Jones changes his residence, how many times will you need to retype his new address, state, city, and zip code? What if Jones is taking six classes?

SECOND NORMAL FORM

To improve the design of the table and bring the table in Figure 14-11 to 2NF, you need to eliminate all **partial key dependencies**; that is, no column should depend on only part of the key. Restated, this means that for a table to be in 2NF, it must be in 1NF and all nonkey attributes must be dependent on the entire primary key.

In the table in Figure 14-11, the key is a combination of `studentId` and `class`. Consider the `name` attribute. Does the `name` "Rodriguez" depend on the entire primary key? In other words, do you need to know that the `studentId` is 1 *and* that the `class` is CIS101 to determine that the `name` is "Rodriguez"? No, it is sufficient to know that the `studentId` is 1 to know that the `name` is "Rodriguez." Therefore, the `name` attribute is only partially dependent on the primary key, and so the table violates 2NF. The same is true for the other attributes of `address`, `city`, `state`, and `zip`. If you know, for example, that `studentId` is 3, then you also know that the student's `city` is "Dubuque"; you do not need to know any class codes.

Similarly, examine the `classTitle` attribute in the first row in the table in Figure 14-11. This attribute has a value of "Computer Literacy". In this case, you do not need to know both the `studentId` and the `class` to predict the `classTitle` "Computer Literacy". Rather, just the `class` attribute, which is only part of the compound key, is required. Looked at in another way, class "PHI150" will always have the associated `classTitle` "Ethics", regardless of the particular students who are taking that class. So, `classTitle` represents a partial key dependency.

You bring a table into 2NF by eliminating the partial key dependencies. To accomplish this, you create multiple tables so that each nonkey attribute of each table is dependent on the *entire* primary key for the specific table within which the attribute occurs. If the resulting tables are still in 1NF and there are no partial key dependencies, then those tables will also be in 2NF.

Figure 14-12 contains three tables: `tblStudents`, `tblClasses`, and `tblStudentClasses`. To create the `tblStudents` table, you simply take those attributes from the original table that depend on the `studentId` attribute, and group them into a new table; name, address, city, state, and zip code all can be determined by the `studentId` alone. The primary key to the `tblStudents` table is `studentId`. Similarly, you can create the `tblClasses` table by simply grouping the attributes from the 1NF table that depend on the `class` attribute. In this application, only one attribute from the original table, the `classTitle` attribute, depends on the `class` attribute. The first two Figure 14-12 tables can be notated as:

```
tblStudents(studentId, name, address, city, state, zip)
tblClasses(class, classTitle)
```

tblStudents

studentId	name	address	city	state	zip
1	Rodriguez	123 Oak	Schaumburg	IL	60193
2	Jones	234 Elm	Wild Rose	WI	54984
3	Mason	456 Pine	Dubuque	IA	52004

tblClasses

class	classTitle
CIS101	Computer Literacy
PHI150	Ethics
BIO200	Genetics
CHM100	Chemistry
MTH200	Calculus
HIS202	World History

tblStudentClasses

studentId	class
1	CIS101
1	PHI150
1	BIO200
2	CHM100
2	MTH200
3	HIS202

Figure 14-12 Students table in 2NF

The tblStudents and tblClasses tables contain all the attributes from the original table. Remember the prior redundancies and anomalies. Several improvements have occurred:

» You have eliminated the update anomalies. The name "Rodriguez" occurs just once in the tblStudents table. The same is true for Rodriguez's address, city, state, and zip code. The original table contained three rows for student Rodriguez. By eliminating the redundancies, you have fewer anomalies. If Rodriguez changes her residence, you only need to update one row in the tblStudents table.

» You have eliminated the insert anomalies. With the new configuration, you can insert a complete row into the tblStudents table even if the student has not yet enrolled in any classes. Similarly, you can add a complete row for a new class offering to the tblClasses table even though no students are currently taking the class.

» You have eliminated the delete anomalies. Recall from the original table that student Mason was the only student taking HIS202. This caused a delete anomaly because the HIS202 class would disappear if student Mason was removed. Now, if you delete Mason from the tblStudents table in Figure 14-12, the HIS202 class remains in the tblClasses list.

If you create the first two tables shown in Figure 14-12, you have eliminated many of the problems associated with the original version. However, if you have those two tables alone, you have lost some important information that you originally had while at 1NF—specifically, which students are taking which classes or which classes are being taken by which students. When breaking up a table into multiple tables, you need to consider the type of relationship among the resulting tables—you are designing a *relational* database, after all.

You know that the Internet-based college application requires that you keep track of which students are taking which classes. This implies a relationship between the `tblStudents` and `tblClasses` tables. Your job is to determine what type of relationship exists between the two tables. Recall from earlier in the chapter that the two most common types of relationships are one-to-many and many-to-many. This specific application requires that one specific student can enroll in many different classes, and that one specific class can be taken by many different students. Therefore, there is a many-to-many relationship between the tables `tblStudents` and `tblClasses`.

As you learned in the earlier example of categorizing insured items, you create a many-to-many relationship between two tables by creating a third table that contains the primary keys from the two tables that you want to relate. In this case, you create the `tblStudentClasses` table in Figure 14-12 as:

    tblStudentClasses(<u>studentId</u>, <u>class</u>)

If you examine the rows in the `tblStudentClasses` table, you can see that the student with `studentId` 1, Rodriguez, is enrolled in three classes; `studentId` 2, Jones, is taking two classes; and `studentId` 3, Mason, is enrolled in only one class. Finally, the table requirements for the Internet-based college have been fulfilled.

Or have they? Earlier, you saw the many redundancies and anomalies that were eliminated by structuring the tables into 2NF, and it is certainly true that the 2NF table structures result in a much "better" database than the 1NF structures. But look again at the `tblStudents` table in Figure 14-12. What if, as the college expands, you need to add 50 new students to this table, and all of the new students reside in Schaumburg, IL? If you were the data-entry person, would you want to type the city of "Schaumburg", the state of "IL", and the zip code of "60193" 50 times? This data is redundant, and you can improve the design of the tables to eliminate this redundancy.

THIRD NORMAL FORM

3NF requires that a table be in 2NF and that it have no transitive dependencies. A **transitive dependency** occurs when the value of a nonkey attribute determines, or predicts, the value of another nonkey attribute. Clearly, the `studentId` attribute of the `tblStudents` table in Figure 14-12 is a determinant—if you know a particular `studentId` value, you can also know that student's `name`, `address`, `city`, `state`, and `zip`. But this is not considered a transitive dependency because the `studentId` attribute is the primary key for the `tblStudents` table, and, after all, the primary key's job is to determine the values of the other attributes in the row.

There is a problem, however, if a nonkey attribute determines another nonkey attribute. In the Figure 14-12 `tblStudents` table, there are five nonkey attributes: `name`, `address`, `city`, `state`, and `zip`.

The name is a nonkey attribute. If you know the value of `name` is "Rodriguez", do you also know the one specific address where Rodriguez resides? In other words, is this a transitive dependency? No, it isn't. Even though only one student is named "Rodriguez" now, there may be many more in the future. So, though it may be tempting to consider that the `name` attribute is a determinant of `address`, it isn't. Looked at another way, if your boss said, "Look at the `tblStudents` table and tell me Jones' address," you wouldn't be able to do so if you had 10 students named "Jones".

The `address` attribute is a nonkey attribute. Does it predict anything? If you know the value of `address` is "20 N. Main Street", can you, for instance, determine the name of the student who is associated with that address? No, because in the future, you might have many students who live at "20 N. Main Street," but they might live in different cities, or you might have two students who live at the same address in the same city. Therefore, `address` does not cause a transitive dependency.

Similarly, the `city` and `state` attributes are not keys, but they are also not determinants because knowing their values alone is not sufficient to predict another nonkey attribute value. You might argue that if you know a city's name, you know the state, but many states contain cities named, for example, Union or Springfield.

But what about the nonkey attribute `zip`? If you know, for example, that the zip code is 60193, can you determine the value of any other nonkey attributes? Yes, a zip code of 60193 indicates that the `city` is Schaumburg and the `state` is IL. This is the "culprit" that is causing the redundancies with regard to the `city` and `state` attributes. The attribute `zip` is a determinant because it determines `city` and `state`; therefore, the `tblStudents` table contains a transitive dependency and is not in 3NF.

To convert the `tblStudents` table to 3NF, simply remove the attributes that depend on, or are **functionally dependent** on, the `zip` attribute. For example, if attribute `zip` determines attribute `city`, then attribute `city` is considered to be functionally dependent on attribute `zip`. So, as Figure 14-13 shows, the new `tblStudents` table is defined as:

```
tblStudents(studentId, name, address, zip)
```

tblStudents

studentId	name	address	zip
1	Rodriguez	123 Oak	60193
2	Jones	234 Elm	54984
3	Mason	456 Pine	52004

tblZips

zip	city	state
60193	Schaumburg	IL
54984	Wild Rose	WI
52004	Dubuque	IA

tblClasses

class	classTitle
CIS101	Computer Literacy
PHI150	Ethics
BIO200	Genetics
CHM100	Chemistry
MTH200	Calculus
HIS202	World History

tblStudentClasses

studentId	class
1	CIS101
1	PHI150
1	BIO200
2	CHM100
2	MTH200
3	HIS202

Figure 14-13 The complete `Students` database

>> **NOTE** A functionally dependent relationship is sometimes written using an arrow that extends from the depended-upon attribute to the dependent attribute—for example, `zip → city`.

Figure 14-13 also shows the `tblZips` table, which is defined as:

```
tblZips(zip, city, state)
```

The new `tblZips` table is related to the `tblStudents` table by the `zip` attribute. Using the two tables together, you can determine, for example, that `studentId` 3, Mason, in the `tblStudents` table resides in the `city` of Dubuque and the `state` of IA, attributes stored in the `tblZips` table. When you encounter a table with a functional dependence, you almost always can reduce data redundancy by creating two tables, as in Figure 14-13. With the new configuration, a data-entry operator must still type a zip code for each student, but the drudgery of typing and the possibility of introducing data-entry errors in city and state names for each student is eliminated.

Is the students-to-zip-codes relationship a one-to-many relationship, a many-to-many relationship, or a one-to-one relationship? You know that one row in the `tblZips` table can relate to many rows in the `tblStudents` table—that is, many students can reside in zip code 60193. However, the opposite is not true—one row in the `tblStudents` table (a particular student) cannot relate to many rows in the `tblZips` table, because a particular student can only reside in one zip code. Therefore, there is a one-to-many relationship between the base table, `tblZips`, and the related table `tblStudents`. The link to the relationship is the `zip` attribute, which is a primary key in the `tblZips` table and a foreign key in the `tblStudents` table.

This was a lot of work, but it was worth it. The tables are in 3NF, and the redundancies and anomalies that would have contributed to an unwieldy, error-prone, inefficient database design have been eliminated.

Recall that the definition of 3NF is 2NF plus no transitive dependencies. What if you were considering changing the structure of the `tblStudents` table by adding an attribute to hold the students' Social Security numbers (`ssn`)? If you know a specific `ssn` value, you also know a particular student `name`, `address`, and so on; in other words, a specific value for `ssn` determines one and only one row in the `tblStudents` table. No two students have the same Social Security number (ruling out identity theft, of course). However, `studentId` is the primary key; `ssn` is a nonkey determinant, which, by definition, seems to violate the requirements of 3NF. However, if you add `ssn` to the `tblStudents` table, the table is still in 3NF because a determinant is allowed in 3NF if the determinant is also a candidate key. Recall that a candidate key is an attribute that could qualify as the primary key but has not been used as the primary key. In the example concerning the `zip` attribute of the `tblStudents` table (Figure 14-11), `zip` was a determinant of the `city` and `state` attributes. Therefore, the `tblStudents` table was not in 3NF because many rows in the `tblStudents` table can have the same value for `zip`, meaning `zip` is not a candidate key. The situation with the `ssn` column is different because `ssn` could be used as a primary key for the `tblStudents` table.

> **NOTE** In general, you try to create a database in the highest normal form. However, when data items are stored in multiple tables, it takes longer to access related information than when it is all stored in a single table. So, sometimes, for performance, you might **denormalize** a table, or reduce it to a lower normal form, by placing some repeated information back into the table. Deciding on the best form in which to store a body of data is a sophisticated art.

In summary:

» A table is in first normal form when there are no repeating groups.

» A table is in second normal form if it is in first normal form and no nonkey column depends on just part of the primary key.

» A table is in third normal form if it is in second normal form and the only determinants are candidate keys.

>> **NOTE** Not every table starts out denormalized. For example, a table might already be in third normal form when you first encounter it. On the other hand, a table might not be normalized, but after you put it in 1NF, you may find that it also satisfies the requirements for 2NF and 3NF.

TWO TRUTHS AND A LIE:
UNDERSTANDING ANOMALIES, NORMAL FORMS,
AND THE NORMALIZATION PROCESS

1. The normalization process helps you reduce data redundancies and anomalies.

2. Data redundancy is the unnecessary repetition of data.

3. First normal form is structurally better than third normal form.

The false statement is #3. Third normal form is structurally better than both first and second normal form. In any well-designed database, you almost always want to convert all tables to 3NF.

DATABASE PERFORMANCE AND SECURITY ISSUES

Frequently, a company's database is its most valuable resource. If buildings, equipment, or inventory items are damaged or destroyed, they can be rebuilt or re-created. However, the information contained in a database is often irreplaceable. A company that has spent years building valuable customer profiles cannot re-create them at the drop of a hat; a company that loses billing or shipment information might not simply lose the current orders—it might also lose the affected customers forever as they defect to competitors who can serve them better. Keeping an organization's data secure is often the most economically valuable responsibility in the company.

You can study entire books to learn all the details involved in data security. The major issues include:

» Providing data integrity

» Recovering lost data

» Avoiding concurrent update problems

» Providing authentication and permissions

» Providing encryption

PROVIDING DATA INTEGRITY

Database software provides the means to ensure that data integrity is enforced; a database has **data integrity** when it follows a set of rules that makes the data accurate and consistent. For example, you might indicate that a quantity in an inventory record can never be negative, or that a price can never be higher than a predetermined value. In addition, you can enforce integrity between tables; for example, you might prohibit entering an insurance plan code for an employee if the insurance plan code is not one of the types offered by the organization.

RECOVERING LOST DATA

An organization's data can be destroyed in many ways—legitimate users can make mistakes, hackers or other malicious users can enter invalid data, and hardware problems can wipe out records or entire databases. **Recovery** is the process of returning the database to a correct form that existed before an error occurred.

Periodically making a backup copy of a database and keeping a record of every transaction together provide one of the simplest approaches to recovery. When an error occurs, you can replace the database with an error-free version that was saved at the last backup. Usually, there have also been changes to the database, called transactions, since the last backup; if so, you must then reapply those transactions.

> **»NOTE** Many organizations keep a copy of their data off-site (sometimes hundreds or thousands of miles away) so that if a disaster such as a fire or flood destroys data, the remotely stored copy can serve as a backup.

AVOIDING CONCURRENT UPDATE PROBLEMS

Large databases are accessible by many users at a time. The database is stored on a central computer, and users work at terminals in diverse locations. For example, several order takers might be able to update customer and inventory tables concurrently. A **concurrent update problem** occurs when two database users need to make changes to the same record at the same time. Suppose two order processors take a phone order for item number 101 in an inventory file. Each gets a copy of the quantity in stock—for example, 25—loaded into the memory of her terminal. Each accepts her customer's order and subtracts 1 from inventory. Now, in each local terminal, the quantity is 24. One order gets written to the central database, then the other, and the final inventory is 24, not 23 as it should be.

Several approaches can be used to avoid this problem. With one approach, a lock can be placed on one record the moment it is accessed. A **lock** is a mechanism that prevents changes to a database for a period of time. While one order taker makes a change, the other cannot access the record. Potentially, a customer on the phone with the second order taker could be inconvenienced while the first order taker maintains the lock, but the data in the inventory table would remain accurate.

> **»NOTE** A **persistent lock** is a long-term database lock required when users want to maintain a consistent view of their data while making modifications over a long transaction.

Another approach to preventing the concurrent update problem is to not allow the users to update the original database at all, but to have them store transactions, which then can be applied to the database all at once, or in a **batch**, at a later time—perhaps once or twice a day or after business hours. The problem with this approach is that as soon as the first transaction occurs and until the batch processing takes place, the original database is out of date. For example, if several order takers place orders for the same item, the item might actually be out of stock. However, none of the order takers will realize the item is unavailable because the database will not reflect the orders until it is updated with the current batch of transactions.

PROVIDING AUTHENTICATION AND PERMISSIONS

Most database software can authenticate that those who are attempting to access an organization's data are legitimate users. **Authentication techniques** include storing and verifying passwords or even using physical characteristics, such as fingerprints or voice recognition, before users can view data. When a user is authenticated, the user typically receives authorization to all or part of the database. The **permissions** assigned to a user indicate which parts of the database the user can view, and which parts he or she can change or delete. For example, an order taker might not be allowed to view or update personnel data, whereas a clerk in the personnel office might not be allowed to alter inventory data.

PROVIDING ENCRYPTION

Database software can be used to encrypt data. **Encryption** is the process of coding data into a format that human beings cannot read. If unauthorized users gain access to database files, the data will be in a coded format that is useless to them. Only authorized users see the data in a readable format.

TWO TRUTHS AND A LIE:
DATABASE PERFORMANCE AND SECURITY ISSUES

1. A database has data integrity when it follows a set of rules that makes the data accurate and consistent.

2. Encryption is the process of returning the database to a correct form that existed before an error occurred.

3. A concurrent update problem occurs when two database users need to make changes to the same record at the same time.

The false statement is #2. Encryption is the process of coding data into a format that human beings cannot read Recovery is the process of returning the database to a correct form that existed before an error occurred.

CHAPTER SUMMARY

» A database holds a group of files that an organization needs to support its applications. In a database, the files are often called tables because you can arrange their contents in rows and columns. A value that uniquely identifies a record is called a primary key, a key field, or a key for short. Database management software is a set of programs that allows users to create table descriptions; identify keys; add records to, delete records from, and update records within a table; arrange records so they are sorted by different fields; write questions that select specific records from a table for viewing; write questions that combine information from multiple tables; create reports and forms; and keep data secure by employing sophisticated security measures.

» Creating a useful database requires a lot of planning and analysis. You must decide what data will be stored, how that data will be divided between tables, and how the tables will interrelate.

» In most tables you create for a database, you want to identify a column, or possibly a combination of columns, as the table's key column or field, also called the primary key. The primary key is important because you can configure your software to prevent multiple records from containing the same value in this column, thus avoiding data-entry errors. In addition, you can sort your records in primary key order before displaying or printing them, and you need to use this column when setting up relationships between the table and others that will become part of the same database.

» A shorthand way to describe a table is to use the table name followed by parentheses containing all the field names, with the primary key underlined.

» Entering data into an already created table requires a good deal of time and accurate typing. Depending on the application, the contents of the tables might be entered over the course of many months or years by any number of data-entry personnel. Deleting records from and modifying records within a database table are relatively easy tasks. In most organizations, most of the important data is in a constant state of change.

» Database management software generally allows you to sort a table based on any column, letting you view your data in the way that is most useful to you. After rows are sorted, they usually can be grouped.

» Frequently, you want to cull subsets of data from a table you have created. The questions that cause the database software to extract the appropriate records from a table and specify the fields to be viewed are called queries. Depending on the software you use, you might create a query by filling in blanks, a process called query by example, or by writing statements similar to those in many programming languages. The most common language that database administrators use to access data in their tables is Structured Query Language, or SQL.

» Most database applications require many tables, and these applications also require that the tables be related. The three types of relationships are one-to-many, many-to-many, and one-to-one.

» As you create database tables that will hold the data an organization needs, you will encounter many situations in which the table design, or structure, is inadequate to support the needs of the application.

» Normalization is the process of designing and creating a set of database tables that satisfies the users' needs and avoids many potential problems. The normalization process helps you reduce data redundancies, update anomalies, delete anomalies, and insert anomalies. The normalization process involves altering a table so that it satisfies one or more of three normal forms, or rules, for constructing a well-designed database. The three normal forms are: first normal form, also known as 1NF, in which you eliminate repeating groups; second normal form, also known as 2NF, in which you eliminate partial key dependencies; and third normal form, also known as 3NF, in which you eliminate transitive dependencies.

» Frequently, a company's database is its most valuable resource. Major security issues include providing data integrity, recovering lost data, avoiding concurrent update problems, providing authentication and permissions, and providing encryption.

KEY TERMS

A **database** holds a group of files, or tables, that an organization needs to support its applications.

A database **table** contains data in rows and columns.

An **entity** is one record or row in a database table.

An **attribute** is one field or column in a database table.

A **primary key**, or **key** for short, is a field or column that uniquely identifies a record.

A **compound key**, also known as a **composite key**, is a key constructed from multiple columns.

Database management software is a set of programs that allows users to create table descriptions; identify key fields; add records to, delete records from, and update records within a table; arrange records so they are sorted by different fields; write questions that select specific records from a table for viewing; write questions that combine information from multiple tables; create reports and forms; and keep data secure by employing sophisticated security measures.

A **relational database** contains a group of tables from which you can make connections to produce virtual tables.

Immutable means not changing during normal operation.

Candidate keys are columns or attributes that could serve as a primary key in a table.

Alternate keys are the remaining candidate keys after you choose a primary key from among candidate keys.

A **query** is a question asked using syntax that the database software can understand. Its purpose is often to display a subset of data.

Query by example is the process of creating a query by filling in blanks.

Structured Query Language, or **SQL**, is a commonly used language for accessing data in database tables.

The **SELECT-FROM-WHERE** SQL statement is the command that selects the fields you want to view from a specific table where one or more conditions are met.

A **view** is a particular way of looking at a database.

A **wildcard** is a symbol that means "any" or "all."

A **relationship** is a connection between two tables.

A **join operation**, or a **join**, connects two tables based on the values in a common column.

A **join column** is the column on which two tables are connected.

A **one-to-many relationship** is one in which one row in a table can be related to many rows in another table. It is the most common type of relationship among tables.

The **base table** in a one-to-many relationship is the "one" table.

The **related table** in a one-to-many relationship is the "many" table.

A **nonkey attribute** is any column in a table that is not a key.

A **foreign key** is a column that is not a key in a table, but contains an attribute that is a key in a related table.

A **many-to-many relationship** is one in which multiple rows in each of two tables can correspond to multiple rows in the other.

In a **one-to-one relationship**, a row in one table corresponds to exactly one row in another table.

In a database, empty columns are **nulls**.

Normalization is the process of designing and creating a set of database tables that satisfies the users' needs and avoids redundancies and anomalies.

Data redundancy is the unnecessary repetition of data.

An **anomaly** is an irregularity in a database's design that causes problems and inconveniences.

An **update anomaly** is a problem that occurs when the data in a table needs to be altered; the result is repeated data.

A **delete anomaly** is a problem that occurs when a row in a table is deleted; the result is loss of related data.

An **insert anomaly** is a problem that occurs when new rows are added to a table; the result is incomplete rows.

Normal forms are rules for constructing a well-designed database.

First normal form, also known as **1NF**, is the normalization form in which you eliminate repeating groups.

Second normal form, also known as **2NF**, is the normalization form in which you eliminate partial key dependencies.

Third normal form, also known as **3NF**, is the normalization form in which you eliminate transitive dependencies.

An **unnormalized** table contains repeating groups.

A **repeating group** is a subset of rows in a database table that all depend on the same key.

To **concatenate columns** is to combine columns to produce a compound key.

Atomic attributes or columns are as small as possible so as to contain an undividable piece of data.

Atomic transactions appear to execute completely or not at all.

A **partial key dependency** occurs when a column in a table depends on only part of the table's key.

A **transitive dependency** occurs when the value of a nonkey attribute determines, or predicts, the value of another nonkey attribute.

An attribute is **functionally dependent** on another if it can be determined by the other attribute.

You might **denormalize** a table, or place it in a lower normal form, by placing some repeated information back into it.

A database has **data integrity** when it follows a set of rules that makes the data accurate and consistent.

Recovery is the process of returning the database to a correct form that existed before an error occurred.

A **concurrent update problem** occurs when two database users need to make changes to the same record at the same time.

A **lock** is a mechanism that prevents changes to a database for a period of time.

A **persistent lock** is a long-term database lock required when users want to maintain a consistent view of their data while making modifications over a long transaction.

A **batch** is a group of transactions applied all at once.

Authentication techniques include storing and verifying passwords or even using physical characteristics, such as fingerprints or voice recognition, before users can view data.

The **permissions** assigned to a user indicate which parts of the database the user can view, and which parts he or she can change or delete.

Encryption is the process of coding data into a format that human beings cannot read.

REVIEW QUESTIONS

1. **A field or column that uniquely identifies a row in a database table is a(n) _____.**

   a. variable   c. principal

   b. identifier   d. key

2. **Which of the following is *not* a feature of most database management software?**

   a. sorting records in a table

   b. creating reports

   c. preventing poorly designed tables

   d. relating tables

3. **Before you can enter any data into a database table, you must do all of the following except _____.**

   a. determine the attributes the table will hold

   b. provide names for each attribute

   c. provide data types for each attribute

   d. determine maximum and minimum values for each attribute

4. **Which of the following is the best key for a table containing a landlord's rental properties?**

   a. `numberOfBedrooms`

   b. `amountOfMonthlyRent`

   c. `streetAddress`

   d. `tenantLastName`

5. **A table's notation is: `tblClients(socialSecNum, lastName, firstName, clientNumber, balanceDue)`. You know that _____.**

   a. the primary key is `socialSecNum`

   b. the primary key is `clientNumber`

   c. there are four candidate keys

   d. there is at least one numeric attribute

6. **You can extract subsets of data from database tables using a(n) _____.**

   a. query   c. investigation

   b. sort   d. subroutine

7. **A database table has the structure `tblPhoneOrders(orderNum, custName, custPhoneNum, itemOrdered, quantity)`. Which SQL statement could be used to extract all attributes for orders for item AB3333?**

   a. `SELECT * FROM tblPhoneOrders WHERE itemOrdered = "AB3333"`

   b. `SELECT tblPhoneOrders WHERE itemOrdered = "AB3333"`

   c. `SELECT itemOrdered FROM tblPhoneOrders WHERE = "AB3333"`

   d. Two of these are correct.

8. **Connecting two database tables based on the value of a column (producing a virtual view of a new table) is a _____ operation.**

   a. merge   c. join

   b. concatenate   d. met

9. Heartland Medical Clinic maintains a database to keep track of patients. One table can be described as: `tblPatients` (`patientId`, `name`, `address`, `primaryPhysicianCode`). Another table contains physician codes along with other physician data; it is described as `tblPhysicians` (`physicianCode`, `name`, `officeNumber`, `phoneNumber`, `daysOfWeekInOffice`). In this example, the relationship is _____ .

    a. one-to-one

    b. one-to-many

    c. many-to-many

    d. impossible to determine

10. Edgerton Insurance Agency sells life, home, health, and auto insurance policies. The agency maintains a database containing a table that holds customer data—each customer's name, address, and types of policies purchased. For example, customer Michael Robertson holds life and auto policies. Another table contains information on each type of policy the agency sells—coverage limits, term, and so on. In this example, the relationship is _____ .

    a. one-to-one

    b. one-to-many

    c. many-to-many

    d. impossible to determine

11. Kratz Computer Repair maintains a database that contains a table that holds job information about each repair job the company agrees to perform. The jobs table is described as: `tblJobs` (`jobId`, `dateStarted`, `customerId`, `technicianId`, `feeCharged`). Each job has a unique ID number that serves as a key to this table. The `customerId` and `technicianId` columns in the table each link to other tables where customer information, such as name, address, and phone number, and technician information, such as name, office extension, and hourly rate, are stored. When the `tblJobs` and `tblCustomers` tables are joined, which is the base table?

    a. `tblJobs`

    b. `tblCustomers`

    c. `tblTechnicians`

    d. a combination of two tables

12. When a column that is not a key in a table contains an attribute that is a key in a related table, the column is called a(n) _____ .

    a. foreign key

    b. merge column

    c. internal key

    d. primary column

13. The most common reason to construct a one-to-one relationship between two tables is _____ .

    a. to save money

    b. to save time

    c. for security purposes

    d. so that neither table is considered "inferior"

14. The process of designing and creating a set of database tables that satisfies the users' needs and avoids many potential problems is _____ .

   a. purification

   b. normalization

   c. standardization

   d. structuring

15. The unnecessary repetition of data is called data _____ .

   a. amplification

   b. echoing

   c. redundancy

   d. mining

16. Problems with database design are caused by irregularities known as _____ .

   a. glitches

   b. anomalies

   c. bugs

   d. abnormalities

17. When you place a table into first normal form, you have eliminated _____ .

   a. transitive dependencies

   b. partial key dependencies

   c. repeating groups

   d. all of the above

18. When you place a table into third normal form, you have eliminated _____ .

   a. transitive dependencies

   b. partial key dependencies

   c. repeating groups

   d. all of the above

19. If a table contains no repeating groups, but a column depends on part of the table's key, the table is in _____ normal form.

   a. first

   b. second

   c. third

   d. fourth

20. Which of the following is not a database security issue?

   a. providing data integrity

   b. recovering lost data

   c. providing normalization

   d. providing encryption

FIND THE BUGS

1. **The following employee table is not in 3NF. Create tables as needed so it is.**

empId	lastName	firstName	dept	floor	supervisor	payRate
123	Henderson	Robert	HR	1	Rollings	11.00
124	Barker	Anne	MKTG	2	Jenkins	23.50
145	Lee	Benjamin	MFG	3	Liu	15.00
157	Davis	Robert	MFG	3	Liu	14.75
178	Nance	Cody	MKTG	2	Jenkins	24.00
184	Rice	Paula	HR	1	Rollings	12.45
189	Lee	Anne	MFG	3	Liu	15.55
243	Saunders	Marcie	MKTG	2	Jenkins	25.75
256	Freize	Michael	MFG	3	Liu	15.00

2. **Suppose you have started a collection of old records. You want to store them in a database so you can select records by title, artist, or condition of the recording. The following table is not in 3NF. Create tables as needed so it is.**

idNum	title	artists	condition
11	Ebony and Ivory	Paul McCartney Stevie Wonders	Good
12	Yesterday	Paul McCartney John Lennon	Excellent
13	Just a Gigolo	Louis Prima	Fair
14	I've Got You Under My Skin	Peggy Lee	Fair
15	I've Got You Under My Skin	Louis Prima Keely Smith	Excellent

EXERCISES

1. **The Lucky Dog Grooming Parlor maintains data about each of its clients in a table named `tblClients`. Attributes include each dog's name, breed, and owner's name, all of which are text attributes. The only numeric attributes are an ID number assigned to each dog and the balance due on services. The table structure is `tblClients(dogId, name, breed, owner, balanceDue)`. Write the SQL statement that would select each of the following:**

   a. names and owners of all Great Danes

   b. owners of all dogs with balance due over $100

   c. all attributes of dogs named "Fluffy"

   d. all attributes of poodles whose balance is no greater than $50

2. Consider the following table with the structure `tblRecipes(recipeName, timeToPrepare, ingredients)`. If necessary, redesign the table so it satisfies each of the following:

a. 1NF

b. 2NF

c. 3NF

recipeName	timeToPrepare	ingredients
Baked lasagna	1 hour	1 pound lasagna noodles ½ pound ground beef 16 ounces tomato sauce ½ pound ricotta cheese ½ pound parmesan cheese 1 onion
Fruit salad	10 minutes	1 apple 1 banana 1 bunch grapes 1 pint blueberries
Marinara sauce	30 minutes	16 ounces tomato sauce ¼ pound parmesan cheese 1 onion

3. Consider the following table with the structure `tblFriends(lastName, firstName, address, birthday, phoneNumbers, emailAddresses)`. If necessary, redesign the table so it satisfies each of the following:

a. 1NF

b. 2NF

c. 3NF

lastName	firstName	address	birthday	phoneNumbers	emailAddresses
Gordon	Alicia	34 Second St.	3/16	222-4343 349-0012	agordon@mail.com
Washington	Edward	12 Main St.	12/12	222-7121	ewash@mail.com coolguy@earth.com
Davis	Olivia	55 Birch Ave.	10/3	222-9012 333-8788 834-0112	olivia@abc.com

4. You have created the following table to keep track of your DVD collection. The structure is tblDVDs(<u>movie</u>, year, stars). If necessary, redesign the table so it satisfies each of the following:

   a. 1NF

   b. 2NF

   c. 3NF

movie	year	stars
The Departed	2006	Leonardo DiCaprio
		Matt Damon
Hairspray	2007	John Travolta
		Michelle Pfeiffer
		Christopher Walken
Catch Me If You Can	2002	Leonardo DiCaprio
		Tom Hanks
		Christopher Walken

5. The Midtown Ladies Auxiliary is sponsoring a scholarship for local high-school students. They have constructed a table with the structure tblScholarshipApplicants(<u>appId</u>, lastName, hsAttended, hsAddress, gpa, honors, clubsActivities). The hsAttended and hsAddress attributes represent high school attended and its street address, respectively. The gpa attribute is a grade point average. The honors attribute holds awards received, and the clubsActivities attribute holds the names of clubs and activities in which the student participated. If necessary, redesign the table so it satisfies each of the following:

   a. 1NF

   b. 2NF

   c. 3NF

appId	lastName	hsAttended	hsAddress	gpa	honors	clubsActivities
1	Wong	Central	1500 Main	3.8	Citizenship award	Future teachers
						Class officer
						Model airplane
						Soccer MVP
						Newspaper
2	Jefferson	Central	1500 Main	4.0	Valedictorian	Pep
					Citizenship award	Yearbook
						Homecoming court
						Football MVP
3	Mitchell	Highland	200 Airport	3.6	Class officer	Pep
						Homecoming court
						Future teachers
4	O'Malley	St. Joseph	300 Fourth	4.0	Valedictorian	Pep
						Chess
5	Abel	Central	1500 Main	3.7	Citizenship award	Yearbook
						Class officer

6. **Assume you want to create a database to store information about your music collection. You want to be able to query the database for each of the following attributes:**

   » A particular title (for example, Tapestry or Beethoven's Fifth Symphony)
   » Artist (for example, Carole King or the Chicago Symphony Orchestra)
   » Format of the recording (for example, CD or tape)
   » Style of music (for example, rock or classical)
   » Year recorded
   » Year acquired as part of your collection
   » Recording company
   » Address of the recording company

   Design the tables you would need so they are all in third normal form. Create at least five sample data records for each table you create.

7. **Design a group of database tables for the St. Charles Riding Academy. The academy teaches students to ride by starting them on horses that have been ranked as to their manageability, using a numeric score from 1 to 4. The data you need to store includes the following attributes:**

   » Student's last name
   » Student's first name
   » Student's address
   » Student's age
   » Student's emergency contact information—name and phone number
   » Student's riding level—1, 2, 3, or 4
   » Horse's name
   » Horse's age
   » Horse's color
   » Horse's manageability level—1, 2, 3, or 4
   » Horse's veterinarian's name
   » Horse's veterinarian's phone number

   Design the tables you would need so they are all in third normal form. Create at least five sample data records for each table you create.

GAME ZONE

1. Massively Multiplayer Online Role-Playing Games (MMORPG) are online computer role-playing games (RPGs) in which a large number of players interact with one another in a virtual world. Players assume the role of a fictional character and control that character's actions. MMORPGs are distinguished from single-player or small multiplayer RPGs by the number of players, and by the game's persistent world, usually hosted by the game's publisher, which continues to exist and evolve while the player is away from the game. Design the database you would use to host an MMORPG including at least three tables.

DETECTIVE WORK

1. What is data mining? Is it a good or bad thing?

2. How many free databases can you locate on the Web? What types of data do they offer?

3. What organization uses the world's most heavily used database system?

UP FOR DISCUSSION

1. In this chapter, a phone book was mentioned as an example of a database you use frequently. Name some other examples.

2. Suppose you have authority to browse your company's database. The company keeps information on each employee's past jobs, health insurance claims, and any criminal record. Also suppose that there is an employee at the company whom you want to ask out on a date. Should you use the database to obtain information about the person? If so, are there any limits on the data you should use? If not, should you be allowed to pay a private detective to discover similar data?

3. The FBI's National Crime Information Center (NCIC) is a computerized database of criminal justice information (for example, data on criminal histories, fugitives, stolen property, and missing persons). It is available to federal, state, and local law enforcement and other criminal justice agencies 24 hours a day, 365 days a year. It is almost inevitable that such large systems will contain some inaccuracies. Various studies have indicated that perhaps less than half the records in this database are complete, accurate, and unambiguous. Do you approve of this system or object to it? Would you change your mind if there were no inaccuracies? Is there a level of inaccuracy you would find acceptable to realize the benefits such a system provides?

4. What type of data might be useful to a community in the wake of a natural disaster? Who should pay for the expense of gathering, storing, and maintaining this data?

SOLVING DIFFICULT STRUCTURING PROBLEMS

In Chapter 2, you learned that you can solve any logical problem using only the three standard structures—sequence, selection, and loop. Often it is a simple matter to modify an unstructured program to make it adhere to structured rules. Sometimes, however, it is a challenge to structure a more complicated program. Still, no matter how complicated, large, or poorly structured a problem is, the same tasks can *always* be accomplished in a structured manner.

Consider the flowchart segment in Figure A-1. Is it structured?

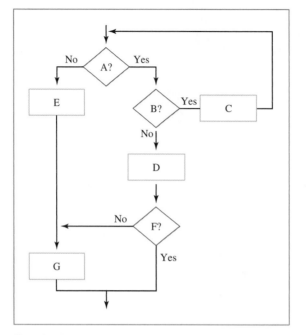

Figure A-1 Unstructured flowchart segment

No, it's not. To straighten out the flowchart segment, making it structured, you can use the "spaghetti" method. Using this method, you untangle each path of the flowchart as if you were attempting to untangle strands of spaghetti in a bowl. The objective is to create a new flowchart segment that performs exactly the same tasks as the first, but using only the three structures—sequence, selection, and loop.

To begin to untangle the unstructured flowchart segment, you start at the beginning with the decision labeled A, shown in Figure A-2. This step must represent the beginning of either a selection or a loop, because a sequence would not contain a decision.

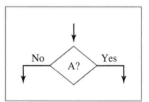

Figure A-2 Structuring, Step 1

If you follow the logic on the No, or left, side of the question in the original flowchart, you can pull up on the left branch of the decision. You encounter process E, followed by G, followed by the end, as shown in Figure A-3. Compare the "No" actions after Decision A in the first flowchart (Figure A-1) with the actions after Decision A in Figure A-3; they are identical.

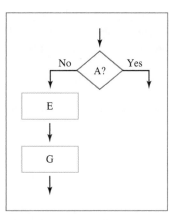

Figure A-3 Structuring, Step 2

Now continue on the right, or Yes, side of Decision A in Figure A-1. When you follow the flowline, you encounter a decision symbol, labeled B. Pull on B's left side, and a process, D, comes up next. See Figure A-4.

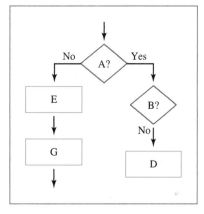

Figure A-4 Structuring, Step 3

After Step D in the original diagram, a decision labeled F comes up. Pull on its left, or No, side and you get a process, G, and then the end. When you pull on F's right, or Yes, side in the original flowchart, you simply reach the end, as shown in Figure A-5. Notice in Figure A-5 that the G process now appears in two locations. When you improve unstructured flowcharts so that they become structured, you often must repeat steps. This eliminates crossed lines and difficult-to-follow spaghetti logic.

The biggest problem in structuring the original flowchart segment from Figure A-1 follows the right, or Yes, side of the B decision. When the answer to B is Yes, you encounter process C, as shown in both Figures A-1 and A-6. The structure that begins with Decision C looks like a loop because it doubles back, up to Decision A. However, the rules of a structured loop say that it must have the appearance shown in Figure A-7: a question, followed by a structure, returning right back to the question. In Figure A-1, if the

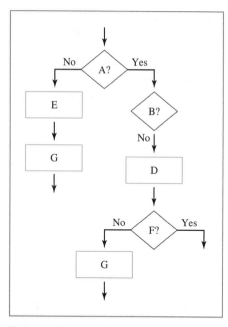

Figure A-5 Structuring, Step 4

path coming out of C returned right to B, there would be no problem; it would be a simple, structured loop. However, as it is, Question A must be repeated. The spaghetti technique says if things are tangled up, start repeating them. So repeat an A decision after C, as Figure A-6 shows.

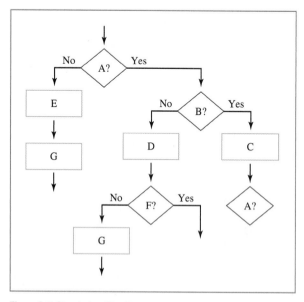

Figure A-6 Structuring, Step 5

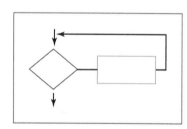

Figure A-7 A structured loop

In the original flowchart segment in Figure A-1, when A is Yes, Question B always follows. So, in Figure A-8, after A is Yes, B is Yes, Step C executes, and A is asked again; when A is Yes, B repeats. In the original, when B is Yes, C executes, so in Figure A-8, on the right side of B, C repeats. After C, A occurs. On the right side of A, B occurs. On the right side of B, C occurs. After C, A should occur again, and so on. Soon you should realize that, to follow the steps in the same order as in the original flowchart segment, you will repeat these same steps forever. See Figure A-8.

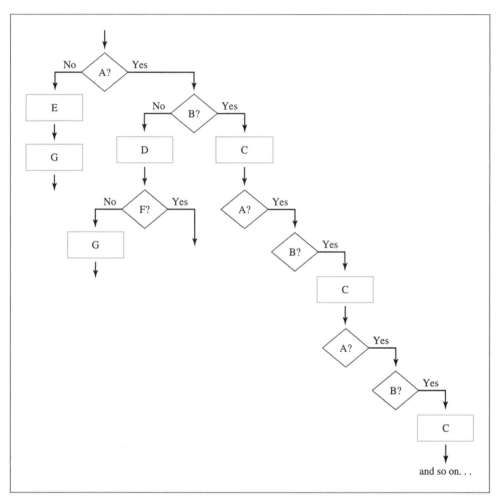

Figure A-8 Structuring, Step 6

If you continue with Figure A-8, you will never be able to end; every C is always followed by another A, B, and C. Sometimes, to make a program segment structured, you have to add an extra flag variable to get out of an infinite mess. A flag is a variable that you set to indicate a true or false state. Typically, a variable is called a flag when its only purpose is to tell you whether some event has occurred. You can create a flag variable named shouldRepeat and set the value of shouldRepeat to "Yes" or "No," depending on whether it is appropriate to repeat Decision A. When A is No, the shouldRepeat flag should be set to "No" because, in this situation, you never want to repeat Question A again. See Figure A-9.

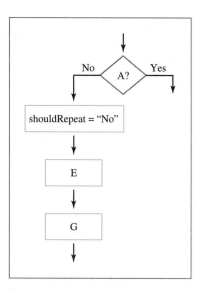

Figure A-9 Adding a flag to the flowchart

Similarly, after A is Yes, but when B is No, you never want to repeat Question A again, either. Figure A-10 shows that you set shouldRepeat to "No" when the answer to B is No. Then you continue with D and the F decision that executes G when F is No.

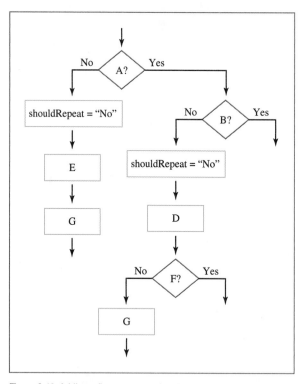

Figure A-10 Adding a flag to a second path in the flowchart

However, in the original flowchart segment in Figure A-1, when the B decision result is Yes, you *do* want to repeat A. So when B is Yes, perform the process for C and set the shouldRepeat flag equal to "Yes", as shown in Figure A-11.

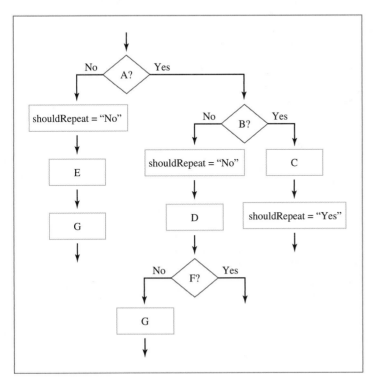

Figure A-11 Adding a flag to a third path in the flowchart

Now all paths of the flowchart can join together at the bottom with one final question: Is shouldRepeat equal to "Yes"? If it isn't, exit; but if it is, extend the flowline to go back to repeat Question A. See Figure A-12. Take a moment to verify that the steps that would execute following Figure A-12 are the same steps that would execute following Figure A-1.

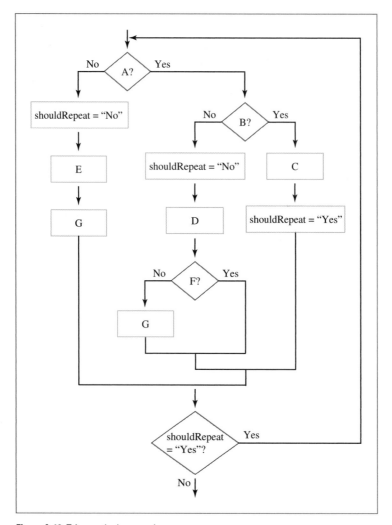

Figure A-12 Tying up the loose ends

» When A is No, E and G always execute.
» When A is Yes and B is No, D and decision F always execute.
» When A is Yes and B is Yes, C always executes and A repeats.

The flowchart segment in Figure A-12 performs identically to the original spaghetti version in Figure A-1. However, is this new flowchart segment structured? There are so many steps in the diagram, it is hard to tell. You may be able to see the structure more clearly if you create a module named aThroughG(). If you create the module shown in Figure A-13, then the original flowchart segment can be drawn as in Figure A-14.

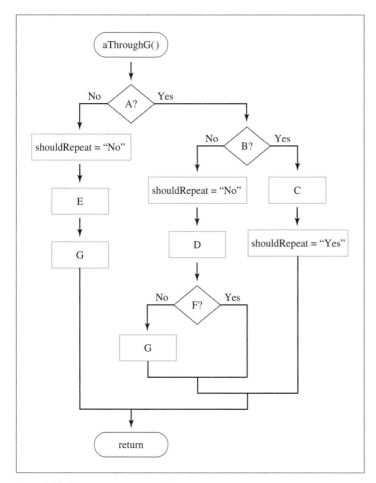

Figure A-13 The aThroughG() module

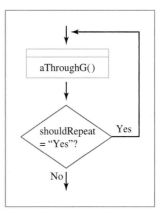

Figure A-14 Logic in Figure A-12, substituting a module for Steps A through G

Now you can see that the completed flowchart segment in Figure A-14 is a do-until loop. If you prefer to use a while loop, you can redraw Figure A-14 to perform a sequence followed by a while loop, as shown in Figure A-15.

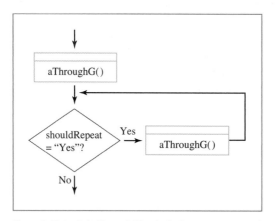

Figure A-15 Logic in Figure A-15, substituting a sequence and while loop for the do-until loop

It has taken some effort, but any logical problem can be made to conform to structured rules. It may take extra steps, including repeating specific steps and using some flag variables, but every logical problem can be solved using the three structures: sequence, selection, and loop.

CREATING PRINT CHARTS

A very common type of output is a printed report. In Chapter 3, you learned that you can design a printed report on a printer spacing chart, which also is called a print chart or a print layout. Many modern-day programmers use various software tools to design their output, but you can also create a print chart by hand. This appendix provides some of the details of creating a traditional handwritten print chart. Even if you never design output on your own, you might see print charts similar to the one described in the appendix in the documentation of existing programs.

Figure B-1 shows a printer spacing chart, which basically looks like graph paper. The chart has many boxes, and in each box the designer places one character that will be printed. The rows and columns in the chart usually are numbered for reference.

	1	2	3	4	5	6	7	8	9	1 0	1 1	1 2	1 3	1 4	1 5	1 6	1 7	1 8	1 9	2 0	2 1	2 2	2 3	2 4	2 5	2 6	2 7	2 8	2 9	3 0	3 1	3 2	3 3	3 4	3 5	3 6	3 7	3 8	3 9	4 0	4 1	4 2	4 3	4 4	4 5	4 6	4 7	4 8	4 9	5 0	5 1	5 2	5 3	5 4	5 5	5 6	5 7
1																																																											
2											I N V E N T O R Y								R E P O R T																																									
3																																																											
4		I T E M N A M E																	P R I C E										Q U A N T I T Y I N S T O C K																														
5																																																											
6		X X X X X X X X X X X X X X X X X X X X																	9 9 9 . 9 9									9 9 9 9																										
7		X X X X X X X X X X X X X X X X X X X X																	9 9 9 . 9 9									9 9 9 9																										
8																																																											

Figure B-1 A printer spacing chart

For example, suppose you want to create a printed report with the following features:

» A printed title, INVENTORY REPORT, that begins 11 spaces over from the left of the page and one line down

» Column headings for ITEM NAME, PRICE, and QUANTITY IN STOCK two lines below the title and placed over the actual data items that display

» Variable data appearing below each of the column headings

With these features, the print chart you create would resemble the one in Figure B-1.

The exact spacing and the use of uppercase or lowercase characters in the print chart make a difference. Notice that the constant data in the output, the items that do not vary but remain the same in every execution of the report, do not need to follow the same rules as variable names in the program. Within a report, constants like INVENTORY REPORT and ITEM NAME can contain spaces. These headings exist to help readers understand the information presented in the report—not for a computer to interpret; there is no need to run the names together, as you do when choosing identifiers for variables.

A print layout typically shows how the variable data will appear on the report. Of course, the data will probably be different every time the program is executed. Thus, instead of writing in actual item names and prices, the users and programmers usually use Xs to represent generic variable character data and 9s to represent generic variable numeric data. (Some program-mers use Xs for both character and numeric data.) Each line containing Xs and 9s represent-ing data is a detail line, or a line that displays the data details. Detail lines typically appear many times per page, as opposed to heading lines, which contain the title and any column headings, and usually appear only once per page.

Even though an actual inventory report might eventually go on for hundreds or thousands of detail lines, writing two or three rows of Xs and 9s is sufficient to show how the data will appear. For example, if a report contains employee names and salaries, those data items will occupy the same print positions on output for line after line, whether the output eventually contains 10 employees or 10,000. A few rows of identically positioned Xs and 9s are sufficient to establish the pattern.

In any report layout, then, you write in constant data (such as headings) that will be the same on every run of the report. You write Xs and 9s to represent the variable data (such as the items, their prices, and their quantities) that will change from run to run.

UNDERSTANDING NUMBERING SYSTEMS AND COMPUTER CODES

The numbering system with which you are most familiar is the decimal system—the system based on ten digits, 0 through 9. When you use the decimal system, there are no other symbols available; if you want to express a value larger than 9, you must resort to using multiple digits from the same pool of ten, placing them in columns.

When you use the decimal system, you analyze a multicolumn number by mentally assigning place values to each column. The value of the rightmost column is 1, the value of the next column to the left is 10, the next column is 100, and so on, multiplying the column value by 10 as you move to the left. There is no limit to the number of columns you can use; you simply keep adding columns to the left as you need to express higher values. For example, Figure C-1 shows how the value 305 is represented in the decimal system. You simply sum the value of the digit in each column after it has been multiplied by the value of its column.

Column value:	100	10	1
Number:	30	0	5
Evaluation:	3*100	+0*10	+5*1

Figure C-1 Representing 305 in the decimal system

The binary numbering system works in the same way as the decimal numbering system, except that it uses only two digits, 0 and 1. When you use the binary system, if you want to express a value greater than 1, you must resort to using multiple columns, because no single symbol is available that represents any value other than 0 or 1. However, instead of each new column to the left being 10 times greater than the previous column, when you use the binary system, each new column is only two times the value of the previous column. For example, Figure C-2 shows how the number 9 is represented in the binary system, and Figure C-3 shows how the value 305 is represented. Notice that in both figures that show binary numbers, as well as in the decimal system, it is perfectly acceptable—and often necessary—to write a number containing 0 as some of the digits. As with the decimal system, when you use the binary system, there is no limit to the number of columns you can use—you use as many as it takes to express a value.

Column value:	8	4	2	1
Number:	1	0	0	1

Conversion to decimal:
$$
\begin{aligned}
1*8 &= 8 \\
+\ 0*4 &= 0 \\
+\ 0*2 &= 0 \\
+\ 1*1 &= 1 \\
\hline
\text{Total:} &\quad 9
\end{aligned}
$$

Figure C-2 Representing 9 in the binary system

Column value:	256	128	64	32	16	8	4	2	1
Number:	1	0	0	1	1	0	0	0	1

Conversion to decimal:
$$
\begin{aligned}
1 * 256 &= 256 \\
+\ 0 * 128 &= 0 \\
+\ 0 * 64 &= 0 \\
+\ 1 * 32 &= 32 \\
+\ 1 * 16 &= 16 \\
+\ 0 * 8 &= 0 \\
+\ 0 * 4 &= 0 \\
+\ 0 * 2 &= 0 \\
+\ 1 * 1 &= 1 \\
\hline
\text{Total:} &\quad 305
\end{aligned}
$$

Figure C-3 Representing 305 in the binary system

Every computer stores every piece of data it ever uses as a set of 0s and 1s. Each 0 or 1 is known as a bit, which is short for binary digit. Every computer uses 0s and 1s because all values in a computer are stored as electronic signals that are either on or off. This two-state system is most easily represented using just two digits.

Every computer uses a set of binary digits to represent every character it can store. If computers used only one binary digit to represent characters, then only two different characters could be represented, because the single bit could be only 0 or 1. If they used only two digits, then only four characters could be represented—one that used each of the four codes 00, 01, 10, and 11, which in decimal values are 0, 1, 2, and 3, respectively. Many computers use sets of eight binary digits to represent each character they store, because using eight binary digits provides 256 different combinations. One combination can represent an "A", another a "B", still others "a" and "b", and so on. Two hundred fifty-six combinations are enough so that each capital letter, small letter, digit, and punctuation mark used in English has its own code; even a space has a code. For example, in some computers 01000001 represents the character "A". The binary number 01000001 has a decimal value of 65, but this numeric value is not important to ordinary computer users; it is simply a code that stands for "A". The code that uses 01000001 to mean "A" is the American Standard Code for Information Interchange, or ASCII.

The ASCII code is not the only computer code; it is typical, and is the one used in most personal computers. The Extended Binary Coded Decimal Interchange Code, or EBCDIC, is an 8-bit code that is used in IBM mainframe computers. In these computers, the principle is the same—every character is stored as a series of binary digits. The only difference is that the actual values used are different. For example, in EBCDIC, an "A" is 11000001, or 193. Another code used by languages such as Java and C# is Unicode; with this code, 16 bits are used to represent each character. The character "A" in Unicode has the same decimal value as the ASCII "A", 65, but it is stored as 0000000001000001. Using 16 bits provides many more possible combinations than using only 8—65,536 to be exact. With Unicode, not only are there enough available codes for all English letters and digits, but also for characters from many international alphabets.

Ordinary computer users seldom think about the numeric codes behind the letters, numbers, and punctuation marks they enter from their keyboards or see displayed on a monitor. However, they see the consequence of the values behind letters when they see data sorted in alphabetical order. When you sort a list of names, "Andrea" comes before "Brian," and "Caroline" comes after "Brian" because the numeric code for "A" is lower than the code for "B", and the numeric code for "C" is higher than the code for "B" no matter whether you are using ASCII, EBCDIC, or Unicode.

Table C-1 shows the decimal and binary values behind the most commonly used characters in the ASCII character set—the letters, numbers, and punctuation marks you can enter from your keyboard using a single key press.

> **》 NOTE** Mathematicians call decimal numbers **base 10 numbers** and binary numbers **base 2 numbers**.

> **》 NOTE** A set of 8 bits is called a **byte**. Half a byte, or 4 bits, is a **nibble**.

> **》 NOTE** Most of the values not included in Table C-1 have a purpose. For example, the decimal value 7 represents a bell—a dinging sound your computer can make, often used to notify you of an error or some other unusual condition.

> **》 NOTE** Each binary number in Table C-1 is shown containing two sets of four digits; this convention makes the long eight-digit numbers easier to read.

Decimal Number	Binary Number	ASCII Character
32	0010 0000	Space
33	0010 0001	! Exclamation point
34	0010 0010	" Quotation mark, or double quote
35	0010 0011	# Number sign, also called an octothorpe or a pound sign
36	0010 0100	$ Dollar sign
37	0010 0101	% Percent
38	0010 0110	& Ampersand
39	0010 0111	' Apostrophe, single quote
40	0010 1000	(Left parenthesis
41	0010 1001	) Right parenthesis
42	0010 1010	* Asterisk
43	0010 1011	+ Plus sign
44	0010 1100	, Comma
45	0010 1101	- Hyphen or minus sign
46	0010 1110	. Period or decimal point
47	0010 1111	/ Slash or front slash
48	0011 0000	0
49	0011 0001	1
50	0011 0010	2
51	0011 0011	3
52	0011 0100	4
53	0011 0101	5
54	0011 0110	6
55	0011 0111	7
56	0011 1000	8
57	0011 1001	9
58	0011 1010	: Colon
59	0011 1011	; Semicolon
60	0011 1100	< Less-than sign
61	0011 1101	= Equal sign
62	0011 1110	> Greater-than sign
63	0011 1111	? Question mark
64	0100 0000	@ At sign

Table C-1 Decimal and binary values for common ASCII characters

Decimal Number	Binary Number	ASCII Character
65	0100 0001	A
66	0100 0010	B
67	0100 0011	C
68	0100 0100	D
69	0100 0101	E
70	0100 0110	F
71	0100 0111	G
72	0100 1000	H
73	0100 1001	I
74	0100 1010	J
75	0100 1011	K
76	0100 1100	L
77	0100 1101	M
78	0100 1110	N
79	0100 1111	O
80	0101 0000	P
81	0101 0001	Q
82	0101 0010	R
83	0101 0011	S
84	0101 0100	T
85	0101 0101	U
86	0101 0110	V
87	0101 0111	W
88	0101 1000	X
89	0101 1001	Y
90	0101 1010	Z
91	0101 1011	[Opening or left bracket
92	0101 1100	\ Backslash
93	0101 1101	] Closing or right bracket
94	0101 1110	^ Caret
95	0101 1111	_ Underline or underscore
96	0110 0000	` Grave accent
97	0110 0001	a
98	0110 0010	b

Table C-1 Decimal and binary values for common ASCII characters (*continued*)

Decimal Number	Binary Number	ASCII Character
99	0110 0011	c
100	0110 0100	d
101	0110 0101	e
102	0110 0110	f
103	0110 0111	g
104	0110 1000	h
105	0110 1001	i
106	0110 1010	j
107	0110 1011	k
108	0110 1100	l
109	0110 1101	m
110	0110 1110	n
111	0110 1111	o
112	0111 0000	p
113	0111 0001	q
114	0111 0010	r
115	0111 0011	s
116	0111 0100	t
117	0111 0101	u
118	0111 0110	v
119	0111 0111	w
120	0111 1000	x
121	0111 1001	y
122	0111 1010	z
123	0111 1011	{ Opening or left brace
124	0111 1100	| Vertical line or pipe
125	0111 1101	} Closing or right brace
126	0111 1110	~ Tilde

Table C-1 Decimal and binary values for common ASCII characters (*continued*)

KEY TERMS

Base 10 numbers are decimal numbers—those that are represented by the digits 0 through 9.

Base 2 numbers are binary numbers—those that are represented by the digits 0 and 1.

A **byte** is a set of 8 bits.

A **nibble** is half a byte, or 4 bits.

USING A LARGE
DECISION TABLE

In Chapter 4, you learned to use a simple decision table, but real-life problems often require many decisions. A complicated decision process is represented in the following situation. Suppose your employer sends you a memo outlining a year-end bonus plan with complicated rules. This appendix walks you through the process of solving this problem by using a large decision table.

> To: Programming staff
> From: The boss
> I need a report listing every employee and the bonus I plan to give him or her. Everybody gets at least $100. All the employees in Department 2 get $200, unless they have more than 5 dependents. Anybody with more than 5 dependents gets $1000 unless they're in Department 2. Nobody with an ID number greater than 800 gets more than $100 even if they're in Department 2 or have more than 5 dependents.
> P.S. I need this by 5 o'clock.

Drawing the flowchart or writing the pseudocode for this task may seem daunting. You can use a decision table to help you manage all the decisions, and you can begin to create one by listing all the possible decisions you need to make to determine an employee's bonus. They are:

» `empDept = 2?`

» `empDepend > 5?`

» `empIdNum > 800?`

Next, determine how many possible Boolean value combinations exist for the conditions. In this case, there are eight possible combinations, shown in Figure D-1. An employee can be in Department 2, have more than five dependents, and have an ID number greater than 800. Another employee can be in Department 2, have more than five dependents, but have an ID number that is 800 or less. Because each condition has two outcomes and there are three conditions, there are 2 * 2 * 2, or eight possibilities. Four conditions would produce 16 possible outcome combinations, five would produce 32, and so on.

Condition	Outcome							
empDept = 2	T	T	T	T	F	F	F	F
empDepend > 5	T	T	F	F	T	T	F	F
empIdNum > 800	T	F	T	F	T	F	T	F

Figure D-1 Possible outcomes of bonus decisions

» **NOTE** In Figure D-1, notice how the pattern of Ts and Fs varies in each row. The bottom row contains one T and F, repeating four times, the second row contains two of each, repeating twice, and the top row contains four of each without repeating. If a fourth decision was required, you would place an identical grid of Ts and Fs to the right of this one, then add a new top row containing eight Ts (covering all eight columns you see currently) followed by eight Fs (covering the new copy of the grid to the right).

Next, list the possible outcome values for the bonus amounts. If you declare a numeric variable named bonus by placing the statement num bonus in your list of variables at the beginning of the program, then the possible outcomes can be expressed as:

» `bonus = 100`

» `bonus = 200`

» `bonus = 1000`

Finally, choose one required outcome for each possible combination of conditions. For example, the first possible outcome is a $100 bonus. As Figure D-2 shows, you place Xs in the bonus = 100 row each time empIdNum > 800 is true, no matter what other conditions exist, because the memo from the boss said, "Nobody with an ID number greater than 800 gets more than $100, even if they're in Department 2 or have more than 5 dependents."

Condition	Outcome							
empDept = 2	T	T	T	T	F	F	F	F
empDepend > 5	T	T	F	F	T	T	F	F
empIdNum > 800	T	F	T	F	T	F	T	F
bonus = 100	X		X		X		X	
bonus = 200								
bonus = 1000								

Figure D-2 Decision table for bonus, part 1

Next, place an X in the `bonus = 1000` row under all remaining columns (that is, those without a selected outcome) in which `empDepend > 5` is true *unless* the `empDept = 2` condition is true, because the memo stated, "Anybody with more than 5 dependents gets $1000 unless they're in Department 2." The first four columns of the decision table do not qualify, because the `empDept` value is 2; only the sixth column in Figure D-3 meets the criteria for the $1000 bonus.

Condition	Outcome							
empDept = 2	T	T	T	T	F	F	F	F
empDepend > 5	T	T	F	F	T	T	F	F
empIdNum > 800	T	F	T	F	T	F	T	F
bonus = 100	X		X		X		X	
bonus = 200								
bonus = 1000						X		

Figure D-3 Decision table for bonus, part 2

Place Xs in the `bonus = 200` row for any remaining columns in which `empDept = 2` is true and `empDepend > 5` is false, because "All the employees in Department 2 get $200, unless they have more than 5 dependents." Column 4 in Figure D-4 satisfies these criteria.

Condition	Outcome							
empDept = 2	T	T	T	T	F	F	F	F
empDepend > 5	T	T	F	F	T	T	F	F
empIdNum > 800	T	F	T	F	T	F	T	F
bonus = 100	X		X		X		X	
bonus = 200				X				
bonus = 1000						X		

Figure D-4 Decision table for bonus, part 3

Finally, fill any unmarked columns with an X in the `bonus = 100` row because, according to the memo, "Everybody gets at least $100." The only columns remaining are the second column and the last column on the right. See Figure D-5.

Condition	Outcome							
empDept = 2	T	T	T	T	F	F	F	F
empDepend > 5	T	T	F	F	T	T	F	F
empIdNum > 800	T	F	T	F	T	F	T	F
bonus = 100	X	X	X		X		X	X
bonus = 200				X				
bonus = 1000						X		

Figure D-5 Decision table for bonus, part 4

The decision table is complete. When you count the Xs, you'll find there are eight possible outcomes. Take a moment and confirm that each bonus is the appropriate value based on the specifications in the original memo from the boss. Now you can start to plan the logic. If you choose to use a flowchart, you start by drawing the path to the first outcome, which occurs when `empDept = 2`, `empDepend > 5`, and `empIdNum > 800` are all true, and which corresponds to the first column in the decision table. See Figure D-6.

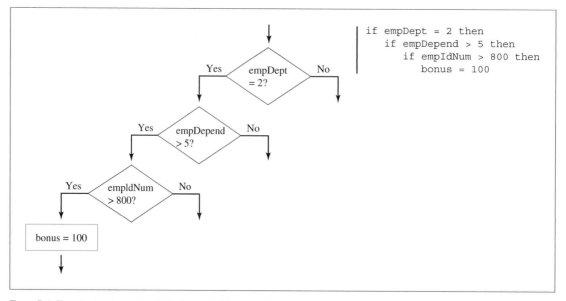

Figure D-6 Flowchart and pseudocode for bonus decision, part 1

To continue creating the diagram started in Figure D-6, add the "false" outcome to the `empIdNum > 800` decision; this corresponds to the second column in the decision table. When an employee's department is 2, dependents greater than 5, and ID number not greater than 800, the employee's bonus should be $100. See Figure D-7.

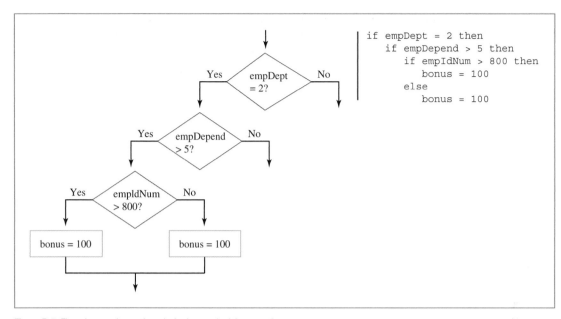

Figure D-7 Flowchart and pseudocode for bonus decision, part 2

Continue the diagram in Figure D-7 by adding the "false" outcome when the empDepend > 5 decision is No and the empIdNum > 800 decision is Yes, which is represented by the third column in the decision table. In this case, the bonus is again $100. See Figure D-8.

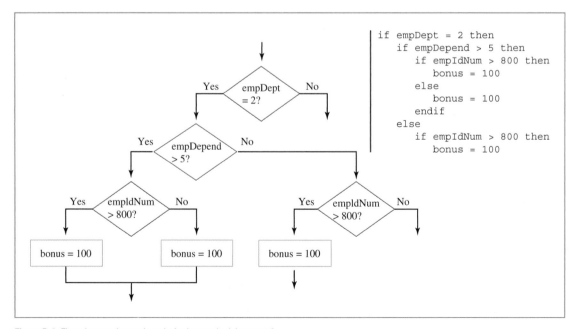

Figure D-8 Flowchart and pseudocode for bonus decision, part 3

Continue adding decisions until you have drawn all eight possible outcomes, as shown in Figure D-9.

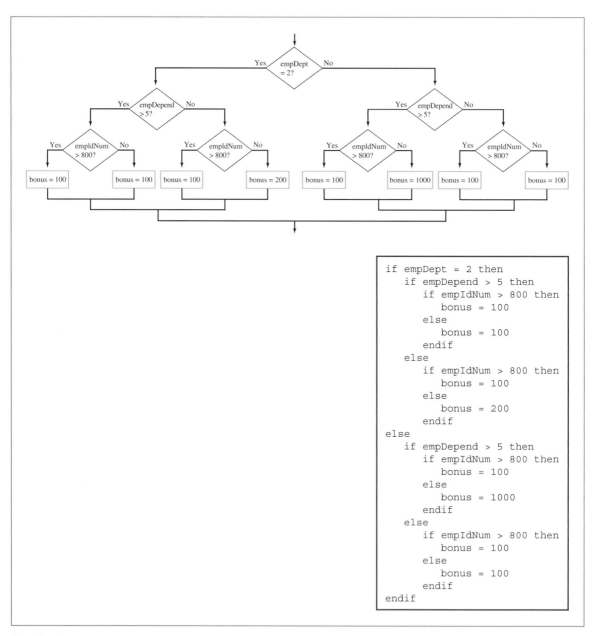

```
if empDept = 2 then
    if empDepend > 5 then
        if empIdNum > 800 then
            bonus = 100
        else
            bonus = 100
        endif
    else
        if empIdNum > 800 then
            bonus = 100
        else
            bonus = 200
        endif
else
    if empDepend > 5 then
        if empIdNum > 800 then
            bonus = 100
        else
            bonus = 1000
        endif
    else
        if empIdNum > 800 then
            bonus = 100
        else
            bonus = 100
        endif
endif
```

Figure D-9 Flowchart and pseudocode for bonus decision, part 1

The logic shown in Figure D-9 correctly assigns a bonus to any employee, no matter what combination of characteristics the employee's record holds. However, you can eliminate many of the decisions shown in Figure D-9; you can eliminate any decision that doesn't make a difference. For example, if you look at the far left side of Figure D-9, you see that when empDept is 2 and empDepend is greater than 5, the outcome of empIdNum > 800 does not matter; the bonus value is 100 either way. You might as well eliminate the selection. Similarly, on the far right, the empIdNum question makes no difference. Finally, many programmers prefer the True, or Yes, side of a flowchart decision to always appear on the right side. The result is Figure D-10.

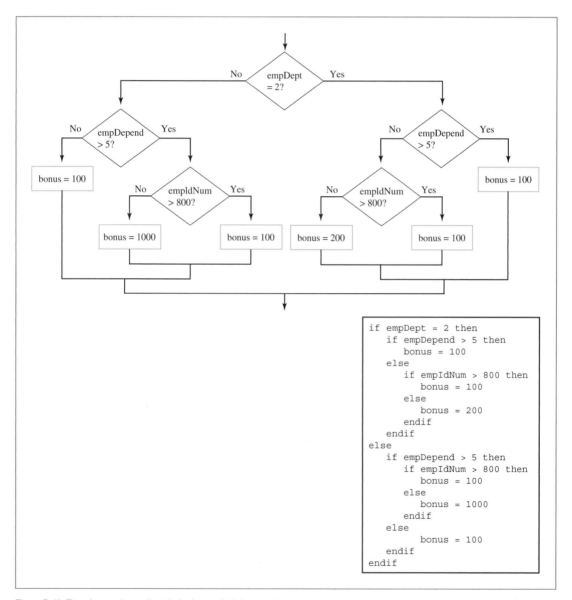

```
if empDept = 2 then
    if empDepend > 5 then
        bonus = 100
    else
        if empIdNum > 800 then
            bonus = 100
        else
            bonus = 200
        endif
    endif
else
    if empDepend > 5 then
        if empIdNum > 800 then
            bonus = 100
        else
            bonus = 1000
        endif
    else
        bonus = 100
    endif
endif
```

Figure D-10 Flowchart and pseudocode for bonus decision, part 1

SOFTWARE TESTING AND DATA VALIDATION

Computer programming is an error-prone task. When you start to write computer programs, it is likely that even your first, small programs that require no more than 10 or 20 statements will contain some small error when you first write them. Fortunately, if your mistakes are simply typographical errors, such as misspelling a programming language keyword, the language translator will identify the errors and list them for you. For example, Figure E-1 shows a program written in C# that contains two mistakes, and Figure E-2 shows an attempt to compile it.

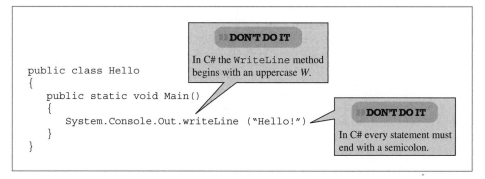

Figure E-1 A C# program that contains two mistakes

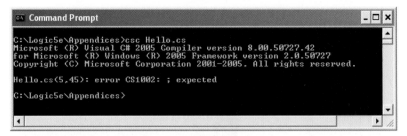

Figure E-2 Attempt to compile the program in Figure E-1

After some copyright information, Figure E-2 shows an error message that explains that in the program named Hello.cs there is a mistake in line 5 (of the seven lines in the file), position 45 (counting from left to right). The error number is CS1002 (which you could look up in the language documentation if necessary), and the brief explanation of it is "; expected". If you were a C# programmer, you would immediately realize that this message meant the semicolon was missing at the end of line 5 of the program; therefore, you would insert it, save the program, and attempt to compile it again. Figure E-3 shows the results.

Figure E-3 Attempt to recompile the program in Figure E-1 after adding a semicolon to the end of the fifth line

The error message in Figure E-3 states that the compiler does not recognize 'writeLine'. If you were a C# programmer, you would immediately recognize that the correct method name begins with an uppercase letter, and you would fix the problem. At your next attempt to compile the program, there finally would be no error messages.

Although *WriteLine* was typed incorrectly when the program was first compiled in Figure E-2, that error was masked by the more serious error of omitting the end-of-statement semicolon. When you write computer programs you will often find that you think you have fixed all the mistakes, only to find that after you did so, new errors that were not apparent at first have been uncovered.

After all the syntax errors in a program are fixed, you do not necessarily have a working program. As a very simple example, if the C# program in Figure E-1 was supposed to print "Goodbye" instead of "Hello", then the users of your program will be dissatisfied or perhaps confused. In this case, although you have included no syntax errors in your program, you have committed a logical error. To fix all the logical errors in a program you have two additional responsibilities:

» Debugging

» Software testing

Debugging and software testing are closely related terms, and many years ago they actually meant the same thing. However, in modern programming terminology, debugging is performed by the programmer or programmers who wrote the application, and **software testing** is performed by users (or test users) who do not know or care what the program code includes—but care only that the program performs as expected.

> **»NOTE** The testing that programmers perform is called **white box testing**, because programmers can "see inside the box" to understand how the code works. The testing that users perform is called **black box testing**, because they do not know how the program works; they simply test whether the program *does* work.

Both debugging and testing are important phases of software development. Although you might be annoyed if a program prints "Hellloo" when you wanted it to print "Hello", computers and software are used in even more critical applications such as navigating airplanes and monitoring surgery patients' vital signs. In these applications, the result of an error in the software is literally a matter of life or death.

As a simple example, suppose you write a program in which the user should enter a value no greater than 5. You might write pseudocode for this part of the program as shown in Figure E-4. This program contains a loop that continuously accepts a user's number until it does not exceed 5.

```
num inputValue
num MAX = 5
print "Enter a number no bigger than ", MAX
get inputValue
while inputValue > MAX
    print "Number too large - please reenter "
    get inputValue
endwhile
```

Figure E-4 Pseudocode that forces user to reenter a number if it is more than MAX

A programmer who understands the code might test the program by executing it several times. A good testing process would be to run the program at least three times, entering a number under 5 (such as 4), a number over 5 (such as 7), and 5. (Testing at the exact limit of the value of MAX is very important because the programmer might have inadvertently used >= in the comparison that controls the loop instead of =.) The programmer might conclude that the code works correctly and add it to a complete application.

What the programmer might not foresee is that a user might enter a negative value (which might or might not be okay according to the program specifications) or a nonnumeric value (which is definitely not okay as the program is written). A good software tester, however, would enter all kinds of values, including letters, punctuation marks, function key presses, and so on, because a user might inadvertently take any of those actions.

> **»NOTE** Software testing can be **alpha testing**, which is testing by potential users at the developers' site. Beta testing occurs after alpha testing. With **beta testing**, software is tested by a limited group of trial customers, or sometimes by the public in general.

Because user data entry is such an error-prone activity, programmers can eliminate a lot of potential trouble by including several standard tests in their code. Many of these techniques are discussed in the next section. However, software testing involves many additional issues such as:

» Is the software easy to understand and use?

» Is there a way to back up or escape? Are there other ways to recover from user errors?

» Are the results consistent with what was expected?

Software testing is not a mature science; it is an art, because each new application that is written might present new problems never before encountered. Software testing can be very expensive, but not testing software is even more expensive, especially in applications that involve high-priced equipment or human lives. Most programmers agree that we never can be sure that a piece of software is completely correct; we simply must try to come as close as possible.

VALIDATING INPUT

Menu programs rely on a user's input to select one of several paths of action. Other types of programs also require a user to enter data. Unfortunately, you cannot count on users to enter valid data, whether they are using a menu or supplying information to a program. Users will make incorrect choices because they don't understand the valid choices, or simply because they make typographical errors. Therefore, the programs you write will be improved if you employ **defensive programming**, which means trying to prepare for all possible errors before they occur. Incorrect user entries are by far the most common source of computer errors.

You can circumvent potential problems caused by a user's invalid data entries by validating the user's input. **Validating input** involves checking the user's responses to ensure they fall within acceptable bounds. Validating input does not eliminate all program errors. For example, if a user can choose option *1* or option *2* from a menu, validating the input means you check to make sure the user response is *1* or *2*. If the user enters a *3*, you can issue an error message. However, if the user enters a *2* when she really wants a *1*, there is no way you can validate the response. Similarly, if a user must enter his birth date, you can validate that the month falls between 1 and 12; you usually cannot verify that the user has typed his true birth date.

The correct action to take when you find invalid data depends on the application. Within an interactive program, you might require the user to reenter the data. If your program uses a data file, you might print a message so someone can correct the invalid data. Alternatively, you can force the invalid data to a default value. **Forcing** a field to a value means you override incorrect data by setting the field to a specific value. For example, you might decide that if a month value does not fall between 1 and 12, you will force the field to 0 or 99. This indicates to those who use the data that no valid value exists.

The data you use within computer programs is varied. It stands to reason that validating data requires a variety of methods. Some of the techniques you want to master include validating:

» Data type

» Range

» Reasonableness and consistency of data

» Presence of data

VALIDATING A DATA TYPE

Some programming languages allow you to check data items to make sure they are the correct data type. Although this technique varies from language to language, you can often make a statement like the one shown in Figure E-5. In this program segment, isNumeric() represents a method call; it is used to check whether the entered employeeSalary falls within the category of numeric data. A method such as isNumeric() is most often provided with the language translator you use to write your programs. Such a method operates as a black box; you can use its results without understanding its internal statements.

```
num salary
print "Enter salary "
get salary
while not isNumeric(salary)
    print "Invalid entry – try again "
    get salary
endwhile
```

Figure E-5 Method for checking data for correct type

》NOTE
Some languages require you to check data against the actual machine codes used to store the data, to determine if the data is the appropriate type.

Besides allowing you to check whether a value is numeric, some languages contain methods with names like isChar() (for "is the value a character data type?"), isWhitespace() (meaning "is the value a nonprinting character such as a space, a tab, or the Enter key?"), isUpper() (meaning "is the value a capital letter?"), and isLower() (meaning "is the value a lowercase letter?").

In many languages, you accept all user data as a string of characters, and then use built-in methods to attempt to convert the characters to the correct data type for your application. When the conversion methods succeed, you have useful data; when the conversion methods fail because the user has entered the wrong data type, you can take appropriate action, such as issuing an error message, reprompting the user, or forcing the data to a default value.

VALIDATING A DATA RANGE

Sometimes, a user response or other data must fall within a range of values. For example, when the user enters a month, you typically require it to fall between 1 and 12, inclusive.

》NOTE
Chapter 4 describes range-checking in detail.

VALIDATING REASONABLENESS AND CONSISTENCY OF DATA

Data items can be the correct type and within range, but still be incorrect. You have experienced this phenomenon yourself if anyone has ever misspelled your name or overbilled you. The data might have been the correct type—that is, alphabetic letters were used in your name—but the name itself was incorrect. There are many data items that you cannot check for reasonableness; it is just as reasonable that your name is Catherine as it is that your name is Katherine or Kathryn.

However, there are many data items that you can check for reasonableness. If you make a purchase on May 3, 2010, then the payment cannot possibly be due prior to that date. Perhaps within your organization, if you work in Department 12, you cannot possibly make more than $20.00 per hour. If your zip code is 90201, your state of residence cannot be New York. If your pet's breed is stored as "Great Dane," then its species cannot be "bird." Each of these examples involves comparing two data fields for reasonableness and consistency. You should consider making as many such comparisons as possible when writing your own programs.

Frequently, testing for reasonableness and consistency involves using additional data files. For example, to check that a user has entered a valid county of residence for a state, you might use a file that contains every county name within every state in the United States, and check the user's county against those contained in the file.

VALIDATING PRESENCE OF DATA

Sometimes, data is missing from a file, either for a reason or by accident. A job applicant might fail to submit an entry for the `salaryAtPreviousJob` field, or a client might have no entry for the `emailAddress` field. A data-entry clerk might accidentally skip a field when typing records. Many programming languages allow you to check for missing data and take appropriate action with a statement similar to `if emailAddress is blank perform noEmailModule()`. You can place any instructions you like within `noEmailModule()`, including forcing the field to a default value or issuing an error message.

Good defensive programs try to foresee all possible inconsistencies and errors. The more accurate your data, the more useful information you will produce as output from your programs.

KEY TERMS

Software testing is testing performed by users (or test users) who do not know or care what the program code includes, but care only that the program performs as expected.

White box testing is the type of testing programmers perform; they can "see inside the box" to understand how the code works.

Black box testing is the type of testing users perform; they do not know how the program works; they simply test whether the program does work.

Alpha testing is software testing by potential users at the developers' site.

Beta testing is software testing by a limited group of trial customers, or sometimes by the public in general.

Defensive programming is a technique in which the programmer tries to prepare for all possible errors before they occur.

Validating input involves checking the user's responses to ensure they fall within acceptable bounds.

Forcing a field to a value means you override incorrect data by setting the field to a specific value.

GLOSSARY

A

abstract class—In object-oriented programming, a class from which you cannot create any concrete objects, but from which you can inherit.

abstract data type (ADT)—A programmer-defined type.

abstraction—The process of paying attention to important properties while ignoring nonessential details.

access specifier (or **access modifier**)—In object-oriented programming, the adjective that defines the type of access that outside classes will have to the attribute or method. Typical access specifiers include `public`, `private`, and `protected`.

accessibility—Describes the screen design issues that make programs easier to use for people with physical limitations.

accessor methods—In object-oriented programming, methods get values from class fields. *See also* get method. Contrast with set method.

accumulator—A variable that you use to gather or accumulate values.

activity diagram—A UML diagram that shows the flow of actions of a system, including branches that occur when decisions affect the outcome.

actual parameter—An argument in a method call.

addition record—A record in a transaction file that represents a new master file record. Contrast with deletion record and change record.

addresses—Numbered locations in storage where data or instructions can be stored.

aggregation—Describes an association in which one or more classes make up the parts of a larger whole class. *See also* whole-part relationship.

algorithm—The sequence of steps necessary to solve any problem.

alpha testing—Software testing by potential users at the developers' site.

alternate keys—In a database, the remaining candidate keys after you choose a primary key from among candidate keys.

ambiguous method—A method that the compiler cannot distinguish from another because it has the same name and parameter types.

ancestors—In object-oriented programming, the entire list of parent classes from which a class is derived.

AND decision—A decision in which two conditions must both be true for an action to take place.

anomaly—An irregularity in a database's design that causes problems and inconveniences.

application files—Computer files that store software instructions. *See also* program files. Contrast with data files.

argument—A data item that is sent to a method.

arithmetic expression—A statement, or part of a statement, that performs arithmetic and has a value.

array—A series or list of variables in computer memory, all of which have the same name but are differentiated with subscripts.

Array class—A class provided with many OOP languages that contains useful methods for manipulating arrays.

ascending order—Describes values arranged from lowest to highest. Contrast with descending order.

assignment operator—The equal sign; it always requires the name of a memory location on its left side.

assignment statement—A statement that stores the result of any calculation performed on its right side to the named location on its left side.

association relationship—Describes the connection or link between objects in a UML diagram.

atomic attributes—Columns in a database table that are as small as possible so as to contain an undividable piece of data.

atomic transactions—In a database, transactions that appear to execute completely or not at all.

attributes—In object-oriented programming, the characteristics that define an object as part of a class. In a database, an attribute is one field or column in a table.

authentication techniques—Database techniques that include storing and verifying passwords or even using physical characteristics, such as fingerprints or voice recognition, before users can view data.

B

base 10 numbers—Decimal numbers; numbers represented by the digits 0 through 9.

base 2 numbers—Binary numbers; numbers represented by the digits 0 and 1.

base class—In object-oriented programming, a class that is used as a basis for inheritance. *See also* parent class and superclass. Contrast with extended class, derived class, child class, and subclass.

base table—The "one" table in a one-to-many relationship in a database.

batch—A group of transactions applied all at once.

behavior diagram—A type of UML diagram that emphasizes what happens in a system.

beta testing—Software testing by a limited group of trial customers, or sometimes by the public in general.

binary—A numbering system that uses two values, 0s and 1s.

binary decision—A yes-or-no decision; so called because there are two possible outcomes.

black box—A device or program you can use without understanding its internal processes; its module statements are "invisible" to the rest of the program.

black box testing—The type of testing users perform; they do not know how the program works; they simply test whether the program does work.

block—A group of statements that execute as a single unit.

body—The part of a method that contains all the statements in the method. Contrast with header.

Boolean expression—An expression that represents only one of two states, usually expressed as true or false.

bubble sort—A sort in which you arrange records in either ascending or descending order by comparing items in a list in pairs; when an item is out of order, it swaps values with the item below it. *See also* sinking sort.

byte—A unit of computer storage. It can contain any of 256 combinations of 0s and 1s that often represent a character.

C

called method—A method invoked by a program or another module.

calling—To execute a method from another method.

calling module—A module that calls another module.

calling program—A program that calls a module.

camel casing—The format for naming variables in which the initial letter is lowercase, multiple-word variable names are run together, and each new word within the variable name begins with an uppercase letter.

candidate keys—In a database, columns or attributes that could serve as a primary key in a table; those that are not chosen as the primary key become alternate keys.

cardinality—Refers to the arithmetic relationships between objects.

cascading if statement—A series of nested if statements.

case structure—A structure that provides a convenient alternative to using a series of decisions when you must make choices based on the value stored in a single variable.

catch—In object-oriented programming exception handling, to receive a thrown exception in a block of code that can handle the problem.

catch block—In object-oriented programming exception handling, a segment of code that can handle an exception that might be thrown by the `try` block that precedes it.

central processing unit (CPU)—The piece of hardware that processes data.

change record—A record in a transaction file that indicates an alteration that should be made to a master file record. Contrast with addition record and deletion record.

character—A letter, number, or special symbol such as "A", "7", or "$".

child class—In object-oriented programming, a class is extended from a base class. *See also* derived class, extended class, and subclass. Contrast with base class, parent class, and superclass.

child file—The new version of a master file after transactions have been applied. Contrast with parent file.

class—A group or collection of objects with common attributes.

class client or **class user**—A program or class that instantiates objects of another prewritten class.

class definition—A set of program statements that contains the characteristics of the class's objects and the methods that can be applied to its objects.

class diagram—A UML diagram that consists of a rectangle divided into three sections that shows a class's name, data, and methods.

class method—In object-oriented programming, a static method. Class methods are not instance methods and they do not receive a `this` reference. Contrast with instance method and nonstatic methods.

client—A program or other method that uses a method.

closing a file—To make a file no longer available to an application. Contrast with opening a file.

coding—To write the statements of a program in a programming language.

cohesion—A measure of how the internal statements of a module serve to accomplish the module's purposes. *See also* functional cohesion and logical cohesion.

command prompt—The location on your computer screen at which you type entries to communicate with the computer's operating system using text.

communication diagram—A UML diagram that emphasizes the organization of objects that participate in a system.

compiler—Software that translates a high-level language into machine language and tells you if you have used a programming language incorrectly. Similar to an interpreter. However, a compiler translates all the statements in a program prior to executing them.

component diagram—A UML diagram that emphasizes the files, database tables, documents, and other components that a system's software uses.

composite key—A key constructed from multiple columns. *See also* compound key.

composition—In object-oriented programming, the act of using a class object within another class object. *See also* has-a relationship.

compound condition—A condition in which multiple questions are needed before determining an outcome.

compound key—A key constructed from multiple columns. *See also* composite key.

computer file—A collection of information stored on a nonvolatile device in a computer system.

concatenate columns—To combine columns in a database table to produce a compound key.

concurrent update problem—A database flaw that occurs when two database users need to make changes to the same record at the same time.

conditional AND operator—A symbol that you use to combine decisions so that two (or more) conditions must be true for an action to occur. Also called an AND operator.

conditional OR operator—A symbol that you use to combine decisions when any one condition can be true for an action to occur. Also called an OR operator.

connector symbol—A flowchart symbol used when limited page size forces you to continue the flowchart elsewhere on the same page or on another page.

constant array—An array whose values are assigned permanently when you write the program code. Contrast with variable array.

constructor—In object-oriented programming, an automatically called method that establishes an object.

container—In object-oriented programming and in GUI programming, a class of objects whose main purpose is to hold other elements—for example, a window.

control break—A temporary detour in the logic of a program based on a change in the value of some field.

control break field—A variable that holds the value that signals a temporary break in the logic of a program.

control break program—A program in which a change in the value of a variable initiates special actions or causes special or unusual processing to occur.

control break report—A report that lists items in groups. Frequently, each group is followed by a subtotal.

conversion—The entire set of actions an organization must take to switch over to using a new program or set of programs.

counted loop—A loop for which the number of repetitions is a predetermined value.

counter—A numeric variable you use to count the number of times an event has occurred.

coupling—A measure of the strength of the connection between two program modules.

D

data—All the text, numbers, and other information that are processed by a computer.

data dictionary—A list of every variable name used in a program, along with its type, size, and description.

data files—Computer files that contain facts and figures. Contrast with program files and application files.

data hiding—The concept that other classes should not alter an object's attributes—only the methods of an object's own class should have that privilege. *See also* information hiding.

data hierarchy—Represents the relationship of databases, files, records, fields, and characters.

data integrity—Feature of a database when it follows a set of rules that makes the data accurate and consistent.

data redundancy—The unnecessary repetition of data in a database.

data type—The characteristic of a variable that describes the kind of values the variable can hold, the amount of memory it occupies, and the types of operations that can be performed with it.

database—A logical container that holds a group of files, often called tables, that together serve the information needs of an organization.

database management software—A set of programs that allows users to create table descriptions; identify key fields; add records to, delete records from, and update records within a table; arrange records so they are sorted by different fields; write questions that select specific records from a table for viewing; write questions that combine information from multiple tables; create reports and forms; and keep data secure by employing sophisticated security measures.

dead path—A logical path that can never be traveled. Also called an unreachable path.

decision structure—A program structure in which you ask a question, and, depending on the answer, you take one of two courses of action. Then, no matter which path you follow, you continue with the next task. *See also* selection structure, `if-then`, and `if-then-else`.

decision symbol—A symbol that represents a decision in a flowchart, and is shaped like a diamond.

decision table—A problem-analysis tool that lists conditions, Boolean combinations of outcomes when those conditions are tested, and possible actions based on the outcomes.

declaration—A statement that names a variable and tells the computer which type of data to expect.

declaring variables—The process of naming program variables and assigning a type to them.

decrementing—To change a variable by decreasing it by a constant value, frequently 1. Contrast with incrementing.

default constructor—In object-oriented programming, a constructor that requires no arguments.

default input and output devices—Hardware devices that do not require opening to accept input or produce output; usually they are the keyboard and monitor, respectively.

default value—A value assigned after all test conditions are found to be false.

defensive programming—A technique in which the programmer tries to prepare for all possible errors before they occur.

definite loop—A loop for which the number of repetitions is a predetermined value.

delete anomaly—A problem that occurs when a row in a table in a database is deleted; the result is loss of related data.

deletion record—A record in a transaction file that indicates that a master file record should be removed from the file. Contrast with addition record and change record.

delimiter—A character used to separate fields in a file.

denormalize—To place a database table in a lower normal form by placing some repeated information back into it.

deployment diagram—A UML diagram that focuses on a system's hardware.

derived class—In object-oriented programming, a class is extended from a base class. *See also* extended class, child class, and subclass. Contrast with base class, parent class, and superclass.

descending order—Describes values arranged from highest to lowest. Contrast with ascending order.

desk-checking—The process of walking through a program solution on paper.

destructor—In object-oriented programming, an automatically called method that contains the actions required when an instance of a class is destroyed.

detail line—A line that contains data details. Most reports contain many detail lines.

dispatcher module—A module that calls other modules in which diverse tasks take place.

do-until loop—A loop in which a procedure executes at least once; then, as long as a test condition remains false, the loop executes additional times.

do-while loop—A loop in which a procedure executes at least once; then, as long as a test condition remains true, the loop executes additional times.

documentation—All of the supporting material that goes with a program.

DOS prompt—The command line in the DOS operating system.

dual-alternative if—A selection structure that defines one action to be taken when the tested condition is true, and another action to be taken when it is false.

dual-alternative selection—A selection structure that defines one action to be taken when the tested condition is true, and another action to be taken when it is false.

dummy value—A preselected value that stops the execution of a program.

dynamic array—An array whose size can be altered. Also called a dynamically allocated array.

E

early exit—Leaving a loop before its last potential repetition.

element—A separate item in an array.

elided—Describes parts of UML diagrams that have been omitted for clarity.

else clause—A part of a decision that holds the action or actions that execute only when the Boolean expression in the decision is false. Contrast with `if` clause.

encapsulation—The act of containing a task's instructions and data in the same method.

encryption—The process of coding data into a format that human beings cannot read.

end-of-job task—A step you take at the end of the program to finish the application.

end user—A person who uses completed computer programs. Also called a user.

entity—One record or row in a database table.

eof—An end-of-data file marker, short for "end of file."

event—In object-oriented programming and in GUI programming, an occurrence that generates a message sent to an object.

event-driven (or **event-based**)—Describes GUI programs in which actions occur in response to user-initiated events such as clicking a mouse button.

exception-handling methods—In object-oriented programming and event-driven programs, techniques for handling errors.

exceptions—The generic term used for errors in object-oriented languages. This is because, presumably, errors are not usual occurrences; they are the "exceptions" to the rule.

executing—To have a computer use a written and compiled program. Also called running.

extend variation—A UML use case variation that shows functions beyond those found in a base case.

extended class—In object-oriented programming, a class is extended from a base class. *See also* derived class, child class, and subclass. Contrast with base class, parent class, and superclass.

external program documentation—All the external material that programmers develop to support a program. Contrast with program comments, which are internal program documentation.

external storage—Persistent, relatively permanent storage outside the main memory of the machine, on a device such as a floppy disk, hard disk, or flash media.

F

facilitators—Work methods. *See also* work methods and help methods.

field—A single data item, such as `lastName`, `streetAddress`, or `annualSalary`. In object-oriented programming, a field is also called an attribute of an object.

file—A group of records that go together for some logical reason.

file description—A document that describes the data contained in a file.

first normal form (1NF)—In database design, the normalization form in which you eliminate repeating groups.

flag—A variable that you set to indicate whether some event has occurred.

flat file—A data file that can only be written or read sequentially and is not part of a relational database.

floating-point value—A fractional, numeric value that contains a decimal point.

flowchart—A type of pictorial representation of the logical steps it takes to solve a problem.

flowline—An arrow that connects the steps in a flowchart.

footer lines—End-of-report message lines. Also called footers.

`for` statement—A statement that can be used to code definite loops. It contains a loop control variable that it automatically initializes, evaluates, and increments. Also called a `for` loop.

forcing—To assign a value to a field, overriding incorrect data by setting the field to a specific value.

foreign key—In a database, a column that is not a key in a table, but contains an attribute that is a key in a related table.

fork—A feature of a UML activity diagram; it is similar to a decision, but whereas the flow of control follows only one path after a decision, a fork defines a branch in which all paths are followed simultaneously.

formal parameter—A variable in a method declaration that accepts the values from an actual parameter.

fragile—In object-oriented programming, describes classes that depend on field names from parent classes; they are prone to errors—that is, they are easy to "break."

functional cohesion—A measure of the degree to which all the statements in a module contribute to the same task.

functional decomposition—The act of reducing a large program into more manageable modules.

functionally dependent—Describes an attribute of a database table if it can be determined by another attribute.

G

generalization variation—Feature in a UML diagram used when a use case is less specific than others, and you want to be able to substitute the more specific case for a general one.

get method—In object-oriented programming, a method that returns a value from a class. *See also* accessor methods.

global variable—A variable declared outside any modules, and that can be used in all modules of the program. Contrast with local variable.

graphical user interface (GUI)—A program interface that uses screens to display program output and allows users to interact with a program in a graphical environment.

H

handler body node—The UML diagram name for an exception-handling `catch` block.

hard-coded value—A value that is explicitly assigned.

hard copy—A printed output.

hardware—The equipment of a computer system.

has-a relationship—In object-oriented programming, the type of relationship that exists when using composition; it describes the relationship between a whole and one of its parts.

header—The part of a method that includes the method identifier and possibly other necessary identifying information. Contrast with body.

heading line—A line on a report containing the title and any column headings, and usually appears only once per page or group of data.

help methods—Work methods. *See also* work methods and facilitators.

hierarchy chart—A diagram that illustrates modules' relationships to each other.

high-level programming language—A programming language that is English-like, as opposed to a low-level programming language.

high value—A value that is greater than any possible value in a field.

housekeeping—The characteristic of tasks that includes steps you must perform at the beginning of a program to get ready for the rest of the program.

Hungarian notation—A variable-naming convention in which a variable's data type or other information is stored as part of its name.

I

icons—Small pictures on the screen that the user can select with a mouse.

IDE—Integrated Development Environment; the visual development environment used by several programming languages.

identifier—A variable name.

if clause—A part of a decision that holds the action that results when a Boolean expression in a decision is true. Contrast with else clause.

if-then—A structure similar to an if-then-else, but no alternative or "else" action is necessary.

if-then-else—Another name for a selection structure.

immutable—Not changing during normal operation.

implementation hiding—A programming principle that describes the encapsulation of method details.

implicitly sized array—An array that is automatically given a size based on a list of provided values.

in scope—The state of variables and constants when they can be used by a method. Compare with local and visible.

inaccessible—In object-oriented programming, describes a field that cannot be accessed by any class other than the one in which it is defined.

include variation—In the UML, a use case variation that you use when a case can be part of multiple use cases in a diagram.

incrementing—To change a variable by adding a constant value to it, frequently 1. Contrast with decrementing.

indefinite loop—A loop for which you cannot predetermine the number of executions.

index—In an array, a number that indicates the position of a particular item within an array. Also called a subscript. In data storage, to store a list of record key fields so each key field is paired with the storage address for the corresponding data record.

infinite loop—A repeating flow of logic without an end.

information hiding—The concept that other classes should not alter an object's attributes—only the methods of an object's own class should have that privilege. *See also* data hiding.

inheritance—The process of acquiring the traits of one's predecessors.

initialization loop—A loop structure that provides initial values for every element in any array.

inner loop—A loop that contains a nested, outer loop.

input device—Hardware such as keyboards and mice; through these devices, data items enter the computer system. Data can also enter a system from storage devices such as magnetic disks and CDs.

input symbol—A symbol that indicates input operations, and is represented as parallelograms in flowcharts.

insert anomaly—A problem that occurs when new rows are added to a table in a database; the result is incomplete rows.

insertion sort—Sort in which each pair of elements in an array is compared and when an out-of-order element is found, a backward search is made for an element smaller than the out-of-order element located. At that point, a new position is opened for the out-of-order element and each subsequent element is moved down one position.

instance—One tangible example of a class; an object.

instance method—In object-oriented programming, a nonstatic method in a class that operates correctly yet differently for each instantiated object. An instance method is nonstatic and receives a `this` reference. Contrast with class method and static methods.

instance variables—The data components of a class that belong to, and might hold different values for, every instantiated object.

instantiation—An instance of a class, an object.

integer value—A whole-number, numeric value.

interaction diagram—A type of UML diagram that emphasizes the flow of control and data among the things in the system being modeled.

interactivity diagram—Diagram that shows the relationship between screens in an interactive GUI program.

interface to a method—Includes the method's return type, name, and parameter list. It is the part that a client sees and uses. Contrast with signature.

internal program documentation—Documentation within a program. *See also* program comments.

internal storage—Temporary storage within the computer; also called memory, main memory, primary memory, or random access memory (RAM).

interpreter—Software that translates a high-level language into machine language and tells you if you have used a programming language incorrectly. Similar to a compiler. However, an interpreter translates one statement at a time, executing each statement as soon as it is translated.

invoking—To execute a method from another method.

IPO chart—A program development tool that delineates input, processing, and output tasks.

is-a relationship—In object-oriented programming, the relationship that exists between an object and its class.

iteration—Another name for repetition or a loop structure.

J

join column—In a database, the column on which two tables are connected.

join operation or **join**—In a database, operation that connects two tables based on the values in a common column. Also a feature of a UML activity diagram that reunites the flow of control after a fork.

K

key field—The field in a record whose contents make the record unique among all records in a file or database table. *See also* primary key.

L

libraries—In object-oriented programming, stored collections of classes that serve related purposes. *See also* packages.

linked list—A structure in which an extra field is created in every record of stored data; this extra field holds the physical address of the next logical record.

listener—In object-oriented programming and in GUI programming, an object that is "interested in" an event to which you want it to respond.

literal numeric constant—A specific numeric value. Also called a numeric constant.

literal string constant—A text constant. In most modern languages, a literal string is enclosed within quotation marks.

local variable—A variable declared within a module and known only to that module. Compare to in scope and visible. Contrast with global.

lock—A mechanism that prevents changes to a database for a period of time.

logic—Instructions given to the computer in a specific sequence, without leaving any instructions out or adding extraneous instructions.

logical cohesion—Cohesion that takes place when a member module performs one or more tasks depending on a decision.

logical error—An error that occurs when incorrect instructions are performed, or when instructions are performed in the wrong order. Contrast with syntax error.

logical NOT operator—A symbol that reverses the meaning of a Boolean expression.

logical order—Describes the order in which you use a list, even though it is not necessarily physically stored in that order.

loop—A structure that repeats actions while a condition continues.

loop control variable—A variable that determines whether a loop will continue.

loop structure—A structure that repeats actions based on the answer to a question.

loose coupling—Coupling that occurs when modules do not depend on others. Contrast with tight coupling.

low-level detail—A small, nonabstract step in a program.

low-level language—A programming language not far removed from machine language, as opposed to a high-level programming language.

M

machine language—A computer's on/off circuitry language; the low-level language made up of 1s and 0s that the computer understands.

magic number—An unnamed numeric constant.

main loop task—A step that is repeated for every record.

main program—A program that runs from start to stop and calls other modules. Also called a main program method.

mainline logic—The overall logic of the main program from beginning to end.

maintenance—All the improvements and corrections made to a program after it is in production.

major-level break—A break in the flow of logic that is caused by a change in the value of a higher-level field.

making a decision—To test a value resulting in a true or false outcome.

making declarations—The process of naming program variables and assigning a type to them.

many-to-many relationship—In a database, a relationship in which multiple rows in each of two tables can correspond to multiple rows in the other.

master file—A data file that holds relatively permanent data. Contrast with transaction file.

matching record—A record that contains data about the same entity as another.

matrix—When used by mathematicians, a two-dimensional array. *See also* table.

mean—Arithmetic average.

median—The value in the middle position of a sorted list.

merging files—To combine two or more files while maintaining the sequential order.

method—A program module that contains a series of statements that carry out a task.

method's body—The part of a method that contains all the statements in the method. Contrast with method's header.

method's header—The part of a method that includes the method identifier and possibly other necessary identifying information such as a return type and a parameter list. Contrast with method's body.

method's type—Another name for a method's return type—the part of a method that defines the data type for any value the method returns.

minor-level break—A break in the flow of logic that is caused by a change in the value of a lower-level field.

mnemonic—A memory device; variable identifiers act as mnemonics for hard-to-remember memory addresses.

modularization—The process of breaking down a program into modules.

module—A relatively small program unit that you can use with other modules to make a program. Programmers also refer to modules as subroutines, procedures, functions, and methods.

multidimensional arrays—Arrays with multiple dimensions; arrays that must be accessed using multiple subscripts. Contrast with one-dimensional array or single-dimensional array.

multiple inheritance—In object-oriented programming, the capability to inherit from more than one class.

multiple-level control break—A break in which the normal flow of control breaks away for special processing in response to a change in more than one field.

multiplicity—Refers to the arithmetic relationships between objects.

multithreading—To use multiple threads of execution.

mutator methods—In object-oriented programming, methods that set values in a class. *See also* set method.

N

named constant—A named memory location, similar to a variable, except its value never can change during the execution of a program. Conventionally, constants are named using all capital letters.

nested decision—A decision "inside of" another decision. Also called a nested if.

nested loop—A loop structure within another loop structure; nesting loops are loops within loops. *See also* inner loop and outer loop.

nesting—To place a structure within another structure.

nibble—Half a byte, or 4 bits.

nonkey attribute—Any column in a table in a database that is not a key.

nonstatic methods—In object-oriented programming, instance methods that exist to be used with an object created from a class; they receive a this reference.

nonvolatile—Describes storage that is permanent. Contrast with volatile.

normal forms—Rules for constructing a well-designed database.

normalization—The process of designing and creating a set of database tables that satisfies the users' needs and avoids redundancies and anomalies.

null case—The branch of a decision in which no action is taken.

nulls—Empty columns in a database table.

numeric constant—A specific numeric value. Also called a literal numeric constant.

numeric variable—A variable that holds numeric values.

O

object diagrams—UML diagrams that are similar to class diagrams, except they model specific instances of classes.

object dictionary—In object-oriented programming and in GUI programming, a list of the objects used in a program, including which screens they are used on and whether any code, or script, is associated with them.

object-oriented programming—A programming technique that focuses on objects, or "things," and describes their features, or attributes, and their behaviors. Contrast with procedural programming.

one-dimensional array—A list accessed using a single subscript. *See also* single-dimensional array. Contrast with multi-dimensional array.

one-to-many relationship—In a database, a relationship in which one row in a table can be related to many rows in another table. It is the most common type of relationship among tables.

one-to-one relationship—In a database, a relationship in which a row in one table corresponds to exactly one row in another table.

opening a data file—The process of locating a file on a storage device, physically preparing it for reading, and associating it with an identifier inside a program. Contrast with closing a file.

operating system—the software that you use to run a computer and manage its resources.

OR decision—A decision that contains two (or more) decisions; if at least one condition is met, the resulting action takes place.

out of bounds—State of an array subscript when it is not within the range of acceptable subscripts.

outer loop—A loop that contains a nested, inner loop.

output device—A computer device such as a printer or monitor that lets people view, interpret, and work with information processed by the computer.

output documentation—Supporting documents that describe the results the user will be able to see when a program is complete.

output symbol—A symbol that indicates output operations, and is represented as a parallelogram in flowcharts.

overhead—All the resources and time required by an operation.

overloading—To supply diverse meanings for a single identifier.

overloading a method—To create multiple method versions with the same name but different parameter lists.

P

packages—In some object-oriented programming languages, stored collections of classes that serve related purposes. *See also* libraries.

padding a field—To add extra characters, such as spaces, to the end of a data field to force it to be a specific size.

parallel arrays—Two or more arrays in which each element in one array is associated with the element in the same relative position in the other array or arrays.

parameter list—All the data types and parameter names that appear in a method header.

parameters—The data items received by methods.

parent class—In object-oriented programming, a class that is used as a basis for inheritance. *See also* base class and superclass. Contrast with extended class, derived class, child class, and subclass.

parent file—The saved version of a master file reflecting data before transactions were applied. Contrast with child file.

partial key dependency—In a database, occurs when a column in a table depends on only part of the table's key.

Pascal casing—The format for naming variables in which the initial letter is uppercase, multiple-word variable names are run together, and each new word within the variable name begins with an uppercase letter.

passed by reference to a method—Action that occurs when a method receives an actual memory address as a parameter. For example, arrays are passed by reference. Contrast with passed by value.

passed by value—Action that occurs when a method receives a copy of a value as a parameter; the value is stored in a new memory location accessible to the method. Contrast with passed by reference.

passing data—To exchange local data between one method and another.

permanent storage devices—Nonvolatile storage hardware, such as hard disks, floppy disks, Zip disks, USB drives, reels or cassettes of magnetic tape, and compact discs.

permissions—Authorizations assigned to a user indicate which parts of the database the user can view, and which parts he or she can change or delete.

persistent lock—A long-term database lock required when users want to maintain a consistent view of their data while making modifications over a long transaction.

physical order—Describes the order in which a list is actually stored. Contrast with logical order.

pixel—A picture element, or one of the tiny dots of light that form a grid on your screen.

polymorphism—The ability of a method to act appropriately depending on the context.

populating an array—To assign values to array elements.

portable method—A method that can relatively easily be reused in multiple programs.

posttest loop—A loop in which a condition is tested after the loop body has executed, such as do-while and do-until loops. Contrast with pretest loop.

precedence—The quality of an operation that determines its order of operation or evaluation with others.

prefix—A set of characters used at the beginning of related variable names.

pretest loop—A loop in which a condition is tested before entering the loop even once. Contrast with posttest loop.

primary key—A unique identifier for each object in a database. *See also* key.

priming input—The statement that reads the first input data record prior to starting a structured loop.

priming read—The statement that reads the first input data record prior to starting a structured loop.

primitive data types—The data types that describe simple numbers and characters that are not class types.

printer spacing chart—A tool for planning program output; also called a print chart or a print layout.

private access—In object-oriented programming, as applied to a class's data or methods, specifies that the data or method cannot be used by any method that is not part of the same class. Contrast with public access.

procedural programming—A programming technique that focuses on the procedures or modules that programmers create. Contrast with object-oriented programming.

processing—To organize data items, check them for accuracy, or perform mathematical operations on them.

processing symbol—A symbol that contains program processes, such as arithmetic statements, and is represented as a rectangle in flowcharts.

program comment—A nonexecuting statement that programmers place within their code to explain program statements in English. *See also* internal program documentation.

program documentation—The set of instructions and other supporting documents that programmers use when they begin to plan the logic of a program.

program files—Computer files that store software instructions. *See also* application files. Contrast with data files.

program level—The level at which global variables are declared.

programmer-defined type—A class. *See also* user-defined type and abstract data type.

programming language—A language such as Visual Basic, C#, C++, Java, or COBOL, used to write programs.

prompt—A message that is displayed on a monitor, asking the user for a response.

property—In many object-oriented programming languages, an entity that provides methods that allows you to get and set a class field value using a simple syntax.

protected access modifier—In object-oriented programming, an access modifier that is used when you want no outside classes to be able to use a data field, except classes that are children of the original class.

protected node—The UML diagram name for an exception-throwing `try` block.

pseudocode—An English-like representation of the logical steps it takes to solve a problem.

public access—In object-oriented programming, as applied to a class's data or methods, specifies that other programs and methods may use the specified data or methods. Contrast with private access.

pure polymorphism—Describes situations in which one method body is used with a variety of arguments.

Q

query—A question that pulls related data items together from a database in a format that enhances efficient management decision making.

query by example—In a database, the process of creating a query by filling in blanks.

R

random access memory (RAM)—Memory; temporary storage within the computer.

random-access storage device—A hardware component from which records can be accessed in any order; for example, a disk.

range check—Comparing a variable to a series of values that mark the limiting ends of ranges.

range of values—A set of contiguous values.

read from the file—To copy data from a file on a persistent storage device into memory (RAM).

record—A group of fields that go together for some logical reason.

recovery—The process of returning a database to a correct form that existed before an error occurred.

register—In object-oriented programming, to sign up components that will react to events initiated by other components.

related table—The "many" table in a database with a one-to-many relationship.

relational comparison operator—A symbol that expresses Boolean comparisons. Examples include =, >, <, >=, <=, and <>. These operators are also called relational operators or comparison operators.

relational database—Database that contains a group of tables from which you can make connections to produce virtual tables.

relationship—A connection between two tables in a database.

reliability—The feature of modular programs that assures you that a module has been tested and proven to function correctly.

reliable—The quality of code that has already been tested and used in a variety of situations.

repeating group—In a database table, a subset of rows that all depend on the same key.

repetition—Another name for a loop structure or iteration.

return statement—The statement in a method that marks the end of the method and identifies the point at which control returns to the calling method or program.

return type—The part of a method that defines the data type for any value it returns. Also called the method's type.

returning a value—The process whereby a called module sends a value to its calling module.

reusability—The feature of modular programs that allows individual modules to be used in a variety of applications.

reverse engineering—The process of creating a model of an existing system.

rolling up the totals—To add a total to a higher-level total.

rules of precedence—Rules that dictate the order the operations in the same statement are carried out.

running—To have a computer use a written and compiled program. Also called executing.

S

saving—To store a program on some nonvolatile medium.

scenario—In the UML, each variation in the sequence of actions required in a use case.

scripting language—A language such as Python, Lua, Perl, or PHP used to write programs that are typed directly from a keyboard and are stored as text rather than as binary executable files. Also called scripting programming languages or script languages.

second normal form (2NF)—In database design, the normalization form in which you eliminate partial key dependencies.

SELECT-FROM-WHERE—The SQL statement is the command that selects the fields you want to view from a specific table where one or more conditions are met.

selection sort—Sort in which you search for the smallest list value (in the ascending version of the sort), and then swap it with the value in the first position. You then repeat the process with each subsequent list position.

selection structure—A program structure in which you ask a question, and, depending on the answer, you take one of two courses of action. Then, no matter which path you follow, you continue with the next task. *See also* decision structure, if-then and if-then else.

self-documenting—Description of a program that contains meaningful data and module names that describe the program's purpose.

semantic error—An error that occurs when a correct word is used in an incorrect context.

sentinel value—A value that represents an entry or exit point.

sequence diagram—A UML diagram that shows the timing of events in a single use case.

sequence structure—A program structure in which you perform an action or task, and then you perform the next action, in order. A sequence can contain any number of tasks, but there is no chance to branch off and skip any of the tasks.

sequential file—A file in which records are stored one after another in some order.

sequential order—Describes the order of records when they are arranged one after another on the basis of the value in some field.

set method—In object-oriented programming, a method that sets the values of a data field within a class. *See also* mutator methods. Contrast with get method.

short-circuit evaluation—A logical feature in which expressions in each part of a larger expression are evaluated only as far as necessary to determine the final outcome.

signature—The part of a method that includes its name and argument list. Contrast with interface.

single-alternative if—A selection structure where action is required for only one branch of the decision. You call this form of the selection structure an if-then, because no "else" action is necessary. Also called a single-alternative selection.

single-dimensional array—A list accessed using a single subscript. *See also* one-dimensional array. Contrast with multi-dimensional array.

single-level control break—A break in the logic of a program based on the value of a single variable.

sinking sort—A bubble sort.

size of the array—The number of elements the array can hold.

soft copy—Screen output.

software—The programs used by a computer.

software testing—Testing performed by users (or test users) who do not know or care what the program code includes, but care only that the program performs as expected.

sorted—Describes records that are in order based on the contents of one or more fields.

sorting records—To take records that are not in order and rearrange them to be in order based on some field.

source code—The readable statements of a program, written in a programming language.

source of an event—In object-oriented programming and in GUI programming, the component from which the event is generated.

spaghetti code—Snarled, unstructured program logic.

stack—A memory location in which the computer keeps track of the correct memory address to which it should return after executing a module.

stacking—To attach program structures end-to-end.

standard input device—The default device from which input comes, most often the keyboard.

standard output device—The default device to which output is sent, usually the monitor.

state—Condition of an object that is the set of all the values or contents of its instance variables.

state machine diagram—A UML diagram that shows the different statuses of a class or object at different points in time.

static methods—In object-oriented programming, methods for which no object needs to exist. Static methods are not instance methods and they do not receive a `this` reference. Contrast with nonstatic methods.

step value—A number you use to increase a loop control variable on each pass through a loop.

stereotype—A feature that adds to the UML vocabulary of shapes to make them more meaningful for the reader.

storage device—A hardware apparatus that holds information for later retrieval.

storyboard—A picture or sketch of a screen the user will see when running a program.

string variable—A variable that holds character or text values.

structure—A basic unit of programming logic; each structure is a sequence, selection, or loop.

structure diagram—A type of UML diagram that emphasizes the "things" in a system.

Structured Query Language (SQL)—A commonly used language for accessing data in database tables.

subclass—In object-oriented programming, a class is extended from a base class. *See also* derived class, child class, and extended class. Contrast with base class, parent class, and superclass.

submodule—A module called by another module.

subscript—A number that indicates the position of a particular item within an array. Also called an index.

summary line—A line that contains end-of-report information.

summary report—A report that does not include any information about individual records, but instead includes only group totals.

sunny day case—Describes a case where nothing goes wrong.

superclass—In object-oriented programming, a class that is used as a basis for inheritance. *See also* base class and parent class. Contrast with extended class, derived class, child class and subclass.

swapping—The process of reversing the values of two variables, setting the first variable equal to the value of the second, and the second variable equal to the value of the first.

syntax—The rules of a language.

syntax error—An error in language or grammar. Contrast with logical error.

system design—The detailed specification of how all the parts of a system will be implemented and coordinated.

T

table—In a database, a structure that contains data in rows and columns. When used by mathematicians, a two-dimensional array. *See also* matrix.

temporal order—Order based on time.

temporary variable—A variable that you use to hold intermediate results during a program's execution. *See also* work variable.

terminal symbol—A symbol used at each end of a flowchart. Its shape is that of a lozenge. Also called a start/stop symbol.

text constant—A constant enclosed within quotation marks. A literal string.

text variable—A variable that holds character values. A string variable.

third normal form (3NF)—In database design, the normalization form in which you eliminate transitive dependencies.

this reference—In object-oriented programming, an automatically created variable that holds the address of an object and passes it to an instance method whenever the method is called.

thread—In object-oriented programming, the flow of execution of one set of program statements.

three-dimensional arrays—Arrays in which each element is accessed using three subscripts. An example of a multi-dimensional array.

throw—In object-oriented programming exception handling, to pass an exception out of a method.

throw statement—In object-oriented programming exception handling, a statement that sends an exception out of a method so it can be handled elsewhere.

tight coupling—Coupling that occurs when modules excessively depend on each other; it makes programs more prone to errors. Contrast with loose coupling.

time signal—A UML diagram symbol that indicates that a specific amount of time has passed before an action is started.

TOE chart—A program development tool that lists tasks, objects, and events.

total line—A line that contains end-of-report information. A form of footer.

transaction file—A data file that holds temporary data that you use to update a master file.

transitive—In object-oriented programming, describes the phenomena of inheriting all the traits of one's ancestors.

transitive dependency—In a database, occurs when the value of a nonkey attribute determines, or predicts, the value of another nonkey attribute.

trivial—Description of a Boolean expression that always evaluates to the same result.

truth table—A diagram used in mathematics and logic to help describe the truth of an entire expression based on the truth of its parts.

try—In object-oriented programming exception handling, to attempt a method or block of code that might throw an exception.

try block—In object-oriented programming exception handling, a block of code you attempt to execute while acknowledging that an exception might occur. A `try` block consists of the keyword `try`, followed by any number of statements, some that might cause an exception to be thrown.

two-dimensional arrays—Arrays with both rows and columns of values; you must use two subscripts when you access an element in a two-dimensional array. An example of a multi-dimensional array.

U

UML—Acronym for Unified Modeling Language; a standard way to specify, construct, and document systems that use object-oriented methods.

unnormalized—Describes a database table that contains repeating groups.

unreachable path—A logical path that can never be traveled. Also called a dead path.

update a master file—To make changes to the values in a master file's fields based on transactions.

update anomaly—A problem that occurs when the data in a table in a database needs to be altered; the result is repeated data.

use case diagram—A UML diagram that shows how a business works from the perspective of those who approach it from the outside, or those who actually use the business.

user-defined type—A class. *See also* programmer-defined type and abstract data type.

user documentation—All the manuals or other instructional materials that nontechnical people use, as well as the operating instructions that computer operators and data-entry personnel need.

V

validating data—To make sure data falls within acceptable ranges.

validating input—The process of checking a user's responses to ensure they fall within acceptable bounds.

variable—A named memory location of a specific data type, whose contents can vary or differ over time.

variable array—An array whose values change during program execution. Contrast with constant array.

view—A particular way of looking at a database.

visible—The state of variables and constants that describes when they can be used by a method. Compare to in scope and local variable.

visual development environment—Program development environment in which you can create programs by dragging components such as buttons and labels onto a screen and arranging them visually.

void method—A method that returns no value.

volatile—The characteristic of internal memory, which loses its contents every time the computer loses power. Contrast with nonvolatile.

W

while loop—A loop in which a condition is tested before entering the loop even once, and in which the body continues to execute while some condition continues to be true.

while...do—A loop in which a process continues while some condition continues to be true. More commonly called a `while` loop.

white box testing—The type of testing programmers perform; they can "see inside the box" to understand how the code works.

whole-part relationship—Describes an association in which one or more classes make up the parts of a larger whole class. *See also* aggregation.

wildcard—A symbol that means "any" or "all."

work methods—Methods that perform tasks within a class but typically do not set or get field values. *See also* help methods and facilitators.

work variable—A variable that you use to hold intermediate results during a program's execution. *See also* temporary variable.

write to the file—To store data from memory (RAM) in a computer file on a persistent storage device.

X

x-axis—Imaginary horizontal line that describes positions in a screen window. Contrast with y-axis.

x-coordinate—A value on an x-axis; it increases as you travel from left to right across a window.

Y

y-axis—Imaginary vertical line that describes positions in a screen window. Contrast with x-axis.

y-coordinate—A value on a y-axis; it increases as you travel from top to bottom across a window.

INDEX

Note: Page numbers in **bold** reflect key words in text.

A

abstract classes, **530**, **536**
abstract data types (ADTs), **491**, **535**
abstraction
  described, **124**
  and modularization, **93–94**
access, private and public, 498–501, **535**
access modifiers, **499**
access specifiers, **499**, **535**
accessibility issues, **555**, **579**
accessing private members of parent class, 526–530
accessor methods, **535**
accumulating totals using loop, 222–224
accumulators described, **222**, **228**
activity diagrams, **605–607**, **613**
actual parameters, **297**, **325**
adding records to tables, 629
addition records, **460**, **471**
addresses, memory locations, **416**, **422**
aggregations, **600**, 608, **613**
algorithms described, 7, **31**, **389**, **421**
alpha testing, **695**, **698**
alternate keys, **627**, **653**
ambiguous methods, **314–317**, **326**
ampersands (&), and conditional AND operator, 149
ancestors and derived classes, **523**, **536**
AND decisions
  conditional, described, **180**
  described, **180**
  making, 144–145
  nesting for efficiency, 146–147
AND operator
  combining decisions using, **148–149**
  nested, described, **180**
AND selections
  avoiding errors in, 150–151
  operator precedence in, **168–170**

animation, creating, 567–569
anomalies
  database, and normalization, **641–649**
  described, **654**
application files, **434**, **471**
application software, 2
applications, common loop, 222–226
arguments described, **102**, **125**, **286**, **325**
arithmetic expressions, **126**
Array class, using, 414–415, **421**
array subscripts, out of bounds, 272
arrays
  constant, described, **272**
  and database tables, 622
  declaring and initializing, 247–250
  described, **238–239**, **271**
  dynamic, **249**, **271**
  manipulating to replace nested decisions,
    239–246
  multidimensional, using, **411–414**, **421**
  one- and two-dimensional, **411**, **421**
  parallel, using, **257–262**, **272**
  passing by reference, **306**
  passing to methods, 304–310
  populating, **249**, **271**
  processing using for loops, 217, 269–270
  remaining within bounds, 265–269
  searching for exact matches, 253–256
  searching for range matches, 262–265
  subscripts. See subscripts
  three-dimensional, **414**
  using named constant to refer to size of,
    246–247
  using variable and constant, **250–253**
ascending order of records, **386**, 387, **421**
ASCII codes, characters, 682–684
assigning values to variables, 25–26
assignment operators, statements, **25**, **33**
association relationships, **599**, **613**